GERMANY

METHUEN'S COMPANIONS TO
MODERN STUDIES

SPAIN: A COMPANION TO SPANISH STUDIES. Edited by E. ALLISON PEERS.

GERMANY: A COMPANION TO GERMAN STUDIES. Edited by J. BITHELL.

FRANCE: A COMPANION TO FRENCH STUDIES. Edited by R. L. GRAEME
RITCHIE.

GERMANY

A COMPANION TO GERMAN STUDIES

EDITED BY

JETHRO BITHELL, M.A.

SOMETIME READER IN GERMAN, UNIVERSITY OF LONDON, AND HEAD OF THE
DEPARTMENT OF GERMAN, BIRKBECK COLLEGE

METHUEN & CO. LTD, LONDON
11 New Fetter Lane, EC4

First published 15th September 1932
Second Edition, revised and enlarged March 1937
Third Edition April 1942
Fourth Edition February 1948
Fifth Edition, revised, enlarged and reset 1955
Reprinted three times
Reprinted 1968

SBN 416 33090 8

5.5

PRINTED IN GREAT BRITAIN
BY ROBERT CUNNINGHAM AND SONS LTD
LONGBANK WORKS, ALVA, SCOTLAND
AND BOUND BY JAMES BURN AND CO. LTD, ESHER

PREFACE

THE plan of the present volume is modelled – though with the freedom required by certain differences between the two countries – on that followed by Professor Allison Peers in *Spain* (1929), the immediate success of which proved the need for a series of books dealing comprehensively with the physical and intellectual landscapes of the countries of the world.

The essentials of the plan are: (*a*) that the chapters should be written by specialists; (*b*) that these specialists should be British-born; (*c*) that the information provided should be what is required for examinational and other purposes by serious students, academic or otherwise, and by travellers in the country concerned who take an intelligent interest in what they hear and see.

Since we are anxious to give a picture of British scholarship as a whole in the field of German, we have been at pains to recruit our specialists from the various Universities of the Kingdom; we come from Cam and Isis and Thames, Avon and Clyde, Mersey and even Irwell.

Care has been taken, too, to assure the support of German-born specialists in England; they will be the last to think they have been slighted by old students of their own who are bound to them by ties of affection as well as of respect; as a matter of fact, German professors here have been consulted at all stages, and we have their assurance that none more than they realize how vital it is that their students should have a chance of expressing the British view of German subjects. It is indeed only by self-expression of native-born scholars that we can hope to build up an English school of German studies at all comparable, if not with that of the Germans themselves – though why should we aim at less? – at least with that of industrious and self-assertive France. A glance at the Bibliography to the Literature chapters of this volume will show how far we lag behind France in the mass of our original work on sections of German literature: we know that there is at least one authoritative French book on nearly every German author, while English books on German authors are few and far between, and none of them are authoritative out of England, with the exception perhaps of C. H. Herford's *Studies in the Literary Relations of England and Germany in the Sixteenth Century*. (And one should remember that golden fragments of W. P. Ker are quoted with marked appreciation by German authorities.) In the field of history, of course, we present a more imposing front; and if we adopted the bold handling which comes natural to our English historians, it would no doubt be a wiser plan than if we followed the meticulously analytical and often unimaginative fashion of the French in their spate of monographs on German literature.

Actually, German studies in England set in with a splash of glory. Apart from Coleridge, whose most telling matter has sometimes an air of being brilliantly lifted from familiar German texts, Carlyle's essays on Goethe stand out to us still as a marvel of insight and loving interpretation never again to be attained; and H. G. Lewes's *Life of Goethe* and Matthew Arnold's essay on Heine are still unrivalled in their kind. But the actual knowledge of German literature of these brilliant critics was, judged by the standards of today, fragmentary; Carlyle's review of Grillparzer's *Ottokar* – to give one example – betrayed his limited vision and the impenetrability to sensuous softness of verse of his hard nature. Even in fairly recent years there has been a survey of German literature in which Hebbel is barely mentioned and Otto Ludwig not at all, while Maria Stona (of whom few Germans have ever heard) gets half a page of appreciation, but Richard Dehmel not a word, and Nietzsche is alleged to have preached the *Umwerthung aller Werthen* [*sic*]. Such dreadful things would not happen if surveys of German literature were written by specialists in German literature and not, as the custom has been, by specialists of acknowledged brilliance in the criticism of English literature. It may be, of course, that mere *Germanisten* cannot be expected to rise to the 'higher form of criticism', or 'appreciation', because their brains are dulled by constant contact with the literature of a people who, we are pontifically told, are 'intellectual but not intelligent' (p. 22). The literal truth is that our writers on German literature have in criticism shown insular narrowness and in scholarship mimetic timidity: our critics have not been scholars, our scholars have not been critics.

There is, however, a changing orientation of interest which may ere long bring us into more productive fields. The tradition of German studies here has hitherto duplicated that of Germany; of necessity so, for our various schools of German have been directed by Germans (Germans, let us agree, who have enriched English life and whose children have rendered, and are rendering, sterling service to the realm as the most British of the British). But now by the incidence of the war it seems likely that the teachers of German at our Universities will in future be native-born scholars, who may – if they have sufficient originality – establish a native tradition.

There is, moreover, a marked change coming over the scope of German studies themselves. The intensive study of medieval texts as a philological discipline is yielding to a more practical concern with the *Realien* of the modern period. We cling to Gothic; it is slipping from us. We older men are being forced to realize that by training we are – or were – impractical Romanticists, with the outlook still of those who founded our science and generously over-estimated the Middle Ages because they discovered them. '*Wir sind vielleicht zu antik gewesen*', said Goethe in his old age, '*nun wollen wir es moderner lesen.*' The *Nibelungenlied* is packed with interest; but side by side with the *Iliad* it is not literature. Chaucer is more modern than Tennyson; but students told impressively in the bitter light of a post-war class-room that Wolfram is the German Dante – '*schlagen solche Augen auf | wie kleine Kinder unter Kirschenbäumen.*' We who love to dream *wo die Brunnen verschlafen rauschen* now run the risk of being shocked by a demand for strange knowledge: Which is the best way to take a yacht overland from Hamburg to the Black Sea? What canals does Father Rhine feed? Why does the blue Danube flow east? Does Kiel butter come from Kiel, and if not, why not? Where is Dessau, where the Junkers come from? The very spirit of our studies has changed: we interpret a poem now by its genesis in brain and body. All pre-Freudian biography is obsolete; we must begin again; and then start once more. Geography was not long ago sister to commercial correspondence; it is now as much an interpretation of the universe as philosophy. The study of economics spreads ramifications like tentacular cities, and is the very base of statesmanship. The hoary past we reverenced we are now asked to regard only as interesting in so far as it explains the present. We know now that we must study Germany, not merely German; we must follow the Germans themselves and busy ourselves with *Deutschkunde*; fortunately this is, racially considered, part and parcel of *Englischkunde*, so that we may harmonize our study of Germany with the conviction we should all have that the first of all studies for us is the study of our own race.

J. BITHELL

BIRKBECK COLLEGE
UNIVERSITY OF LONDON
April 1932

PREFACE TO FIFTH EDITION

IT can hardly be necessary to point out that a radically revised edition is needed if only because there is a new Germany. The extensions required have been made, and in particular there has been added a chapter on philosophy, which today, apart from its value for itself, is indispensable for the comprehension of the new literature.

It has been a sad task of mine to revise Chapters written by old friends who have passed away. Here and there I have made additions and added notes for clarification. Mrs Hannah Closs had revised and expanded her Chapter before her tragic death in 1953.

A glance at the new Bibliographies will make it clear that the editor's reference in his first Preface to the dearth of authoritative books by British scholars no longer holds good; indeed for a considerable period now the tendency has rather been for standard books by our own scholars to be acclaimed in Germany.

There has been no attempt in Chapter I to adapt the geographical and political picture to that of today; this cannot last: the Germany that will be again is the Germany of our first edition, and this is the Germany our students need to know.

J. BITHELL

September 1954

BIBLIOGRAPHICAL NOTE

THE Bibliographies at the end of the chapters have been compiled separately by each contributor, except in the case of Literature, the list for which is the joint work of the four writers and is placed at the end of the section for Literature.

A select list of current periodicals may be helpful. *German Life and Letters* (Oxford) is a quarterly review which concerns itself with all phases and aspects of literature and of life in Germany. *The Modern Language Review*, the quarterly organ of the Modern Humanities Research Association (Cambridge University Press), deals with modern language studies generally. *Germanisch-Romanische Monatsschrift* (Heidelberg), *Archiv für das Studium der neueren Sprachen und Literaturen* (Brunswick), and *Zeitschrift für deutsches Altertum und deutsche Literatur* (Wiesbaden) combine philological and literary research, while *Euphorion* (Cologne) is specifically devoted to literature.

Of the reviews which deal with current literature the most serviceable are *Neue literarische Welt* (Heidelberg), *Die Literatur der Gegenwart* (Recklinghausen), and *Welt und Wort* (Tübingen). The title of *Rufer und Hörer* (Stuttgart) indicates its close concern with broadcasting.

CONTENTS

MAP

CHAPTER I

THE COUNTRY: ITS PEOPLES AND ITS LANGUAGE

THE COUNTRY

GERMANY today occupies pretty much the territory ascribed to it by Tacitus, between Rhine and Vistula, and by later Roman writers between the Alps and the North Sea. A glance at the map shows that Germany is in the very centre of Europe. 'O heilig Herz der Völker, O Vaterland!' sang Hölderlin. It is 'das Reich der Mitte'; in the First World War we were fighting 'the Central Powers'. This central position means inevitably, through all history, concentric pressure; and the Germans, it is obvious, can only subsist in measure as they resist this pressure; 'by the place we occupy, crushed in between our neighbours,' Bismarck told the Reichstag in 1888, 'God has made it impossible for us to sink into degenerate sloth.' The German tribes have repeatedly broken through their present frontiers; to west and south, however, they have always been assimilated with the races they have overrun. There are golden-haired[1] Spanish nobles, descendants of the Goths, who took possession of Spain as well as of Aquitaine; there are blond Italians in the Lombard plain, where once Langobardi had a Germanic kingdom. The very name of the hereditary foe, the French, recalls the kingdom of the West Franks; that is, of Germany west of the Rhine. In one region only have the German tribes absorbed subjected races: in 'Ostelbien', the lands east of the Elbe. The process of extinction can be followed: as at Berlin, which as a village of Frisian and Low Saxon colonists existed side by side with the original Wendish population at Kölln till the German settlement, spreading over broad fields, by sheer weight of wealth and numbers hemmed in and effaced the once more favoured village on the dumpy hill. But the Germans who in the Middle Ages colonized East Prussia were only recovering territory which was Germanic at the dawn of history; there is plenty of evidence that Germanic tribes migrated south from the region round the Vistula. In modern times, however, German

---

[1] 'Caerulei oculi, rutilae comae.' Tacitus, Germania, IV.

1

efforts at absorption have failed even in the east; the Germans preserved
language and *Deutschtum* in the Baltic Provinces of Russia till recently,
but the University of Dorpat was made Russian in 1895;[1] and not all the
statecraft of Prussia could germanize Poland, where the boot is now on
the other leg. In Brazil[2] there was a possibility – or a plan – of germani-
zation by peaceful penetration; it was a dream.[3]

Pre-war Germany was hemmed in by more nations than any other
European State; post-war Germany is hemmed in by still more. Germany's crowd of neighbours, if they were at war, frequently found it
convenient to fight their battles on German soil; Germany has been the
cockpit of Europe. In times of peace, however, this central position has
the advantages the middleman enjoys in trade; goods from east and west,
north and south are exchanged where trade routes meet; or they pass
through the central region. This explains the wealth of old-time cities
such as Augsburg, 'the gate of Italy', where the Fuggers were the bankers
of Europe long before the Rothschilds rose to power in Frankfurt-am-
Main, the centre of traffic between France and Bohemia. The Hanse ports
were mighty, not because they were good natural ports (comparatively
speaking they are poor ones), but because they were necessary centres.
The same advantages of the central position are telling today in the growth
of another means of traffic: there is some prospect of air-routes being
controlled by or centred in Germany.

The frontiers of a country are natural or artificial. In the north and
south Germany has strong natural frontiers – the North Sea, the Baltic
(die Ostsee), the Lake of Constance, and the Alps. In the west the Rhine
runs close to the frontier, but only forms it for a length of 150 kilometres
between Alsace and Baden; beyond the Rhine the actual frontier is
artificial, and affords little natural protection. It was an obsession of the

---

[1] Dorpat was founded by Gustavus Adolphus as a Swedish-German University in
1632, was a German University 1802-95, and after 1919 was a German-Esthonian
University.

[2] The life of German colonists in Brazil and South America is described in Hans
Friedrich Blunck's novels *Die Weibsmühle* (1927) and *Land der Vulkane* (1929).

[3] Actually 'Germany' – and for the matter of that 'Deutschland' – never existed
as a country proper – except, perhaps, from 1933 to 1945, when the German-speaking
nations were united by force in Hitler's new Reich. The Kaiser as head of the
Second Reich (1871-1918) was 'the German Emperor', 'der deutsche Kaiser', not
'the Emperor of Germany'; and this was so because the Reich was a union of Free
States (Länder): the four kingdoms of Prussia, Saxony, Württemberg, and Bavaria;
the five Grand Duchies of Hesse, Mecklenburg-Schwerin, Mecklenburg-Strelitz,
Saxe-Weimar, and Baden; the three Free Towns of Hamburg, Bremen and Lübeck
(the latter united with Schleswig-Holstein in 1937); seven Principalities; and the
Reichsland of Alsace-Lorraine, taken from France in 1871 and restored in 1919 by
the Treaty of Versailles.

Germans before the war that Luxemburg, Belgium, and Holland – in Ratzel's picturesque phrase, lands lying like fallen débris at the base of the German Empire – were geographically and ethnologically German, and that the natural German frontier was the North Sea as far south as Flemish is spoken, i.e. to Dunkirk. Holland, they claimed, was German; for, as Napoleon pointed out, it is nothing but German soil washed down by the Rhine. The name of Burgundy lies at the tragic heart of German saga; but 'die burgundische Pforte', the gap between Switzerland and the Vosges – 'the bolt of Germany' and the exit to the Mediterranean – is in the hands of France. France holds the Vosges, which are hard to pass except by the gap at Zabern. Another lost hope is the Brenner Pass, which, if Austria had joined the Empire, would have brought the latter by the shortest route to the Adriatic. To Germans today it must seem that a hostile fate has shut them off from their natural and nearest exits to the ocean.

The great danger is the open eastern frontier, still more so now that German territory is split by the Polish corridor: Poland west of the Vistula takes the form of a curve ('der polnische Bogen') pushing on to Berlin. Here perhaps lies the problem of the future for the old world: the antagonism of Europe and Asia; time alone will show whether Poland and Russia are European or Asiatic. In the German mind as reflected in literature the Poles and the Russians are a peril ever luring to sin and sloth.[1] A still more ugly Slavonic wedge is that shown by Czecho-slovakia, which (taking Deutsch-Österreich as German) is almost sur-rounded by German states; but here there are natural frontiers of mountains, only the Danube plain lying open.[2]

Germany was once covered with Alps; of one range not more than traces remain in the ridges of hills along the northern plain; the substructure of another range still dominates central Germany. Where depressions (Senken) were formed by the sinking of the soil (as in the valley of the Upper Rhine) alluvial soil washed down by the rivers made fertile plains which are now the corn-growing lands of Germany. There were many volcanoes; hills long famous in song and story – der Meissner near Cassel, der Hohentwiel near Singen (the scene of Scheffel's Ekkehard) – once belched fire; the little lakes called Maare in the Eifel district hide old craters, the lovely Laacher See here was formed by an eruption, and the hot springs belong to the volcanic landscape. Twenty thousand years ago Germany was all ice and glaciers; Germany was then as Greenland is

[1] See pp. 339-41, and (e.g.) Sudermann's Der Katzensteg.
[2] The frontiers as fixed by the Peace Treaty of 1947 are: N, Denmark to Poland, the Baltic; E, the river Oder and its tributary the Neisse; S, Czechoslovakia, Austria, Switzerland; W, the Rhine, Luxemburg, Belgium, Holland, the North Sea from Holland to Denmark.

today and the whole configuration of Germany is in the main the result of glacial action. In the sand and loam of north Germany granite boulders are found (*Findlingsblöcke*, 'erratic blocks'); even Mephistopheles, who knew a great deal, admitted he could not tell where these *Zentnermassen* came from;[1] when it was proved that they were of the same formation as the rocks of Scandinavia our own geologist Lyell said they must have drifted on icebergs; but in 1875 the Swedish geologist Torell found in the shell-lime rocks at Rüdersdorf near Berlin abrasions that could only have been scratched by glaciers, and it is now known that glaciers moving south from Norway had brought not only these erratic blocks, but also the sand and loam and alluvial soil that cover the northern plain, from which the rocks that form the central range of mountains only emerge at a few places (the island of Rügen, Heligoland, and the chalk hills of Rüdersdorf). Other glaciers moved to the Danube plain from the Alps. Skeletons have been discovered of mammals and human beings who occupied the land when the glaciers melted; those of the human beings have been found in the erratic blocks, and since such huge masses could not have been moved by the race of today there was a popular belief that the land was once inhabited by giants, and the places where the bones were found were called *Hünengräber*.[2]

At a cursory glance at the map Germany is seen to be divided into plains (*Tiefland*) and mountains (*Hochland*); the plains are Low Germany (*Niederdeutschland*), the mountains are Upper Germany (*Oberdeutschland*). As seen from south to north Germany is a gradual slope (*Stufenland*) of four zones: (1) the Bavarian Alps; (2) the plateau or tableland of the Prealps (*Voralpen*), which drain into the Danube; (3) the Central Range (*Mittelgebirge*), whose rivers flow to the Danube from their south slope but to the North Sea and the Baltic on the north side; (4) the North German Plain (*Tiefebene*). A closer survey shows three parallel belts running from east to west: (1) the Alps with their tableland, to the north of which runs (2) a central range (*das Mitteldeutsche Gebirge*), beginning where the Oder rises in the west of the Carpathians, and consisting of the Sudetic Range, the Riesengebirge, the Erzgebirge (from which the Böhmerwald and the Bayrischer Wald strike off to the south-east to the Danube plain to shut in Bohemia), das Fichtelgebirge, Thüringer Wald, Harz Mountains, Weser Bergland, Teutoburger Wald where the Ems begins, and more to the south das Rheinische Schiefergebirge (Westerwald

---

[1] *Faust*, line 10,111. Goethe indicated the correct explanation (*Geologische Probleme und Versuch ihrer Auflösung*, 1829).

[2] *Hüne* (*Heune*) is not the same word as *Hunne*, 'Hun'; its meaning of 'giant' is disguised in compounds such as 'Humboldt'.

and Taunus on the right bank of the Rhine, Eifel, and Hunsrück on the left); and (3) the north German plain which stretches from the Ural Mountains to the North Sea, forming a bay in Saxony but otherwise gradually narrowing till it ends like a wedge on the North Sea. The northern plain is flat where it approaches the North Sea, but along the Baltic it is ridged by undulating hills, and its rivers flow between cliffs which rise as high as 100 metres; the highest elevation is the Turmberg (330 m.) near Danzig. The pivot or central knot of the Central Range is the desolate Fichtelgebirge, from which all the other ranges radiate. There are two directions (*Streichrichtungen*) of the mountains: one from south-west to north-east (called *die erzgebirgische* or *rheinische Richtung*) and the other (called *die herzynische* or *sudetische Richtung*) from south-east to north-west. The rivers of course flow in the same directions: mostly north-west, but the Rhine north-east in the Upper Rhine valley, the Vistula and the Oder in their final courses. The Danube flows north-east to Regensburg, then east-south.

Rivers and mountains are more than geography: this is a school discipline, and may fade from the memory; but song and saga roll on for ever. Of the mountains the Brocken – capped with mist on 241 days of the year – is, because of *Faust* and Heine's *Harzreise*, the best-known name out of Germany. The Rhine is the darling among the rivers of the world; so much so that, like Yarrow, it should perhaps only be visited in the light of fond imagination. The Rhine steamers make it ideal for an idle holiday; but for scenery it cannot be compared with the Clyde, which is also wrapped in romance. The Alpine rivers – Rhine, Lech, Isar, Inn – are never low because they flow from permanent glaciers; they have the colours of glaciers – green or greenish-blue, but grey in spate. They are rapid; every Englishman when he first sees the Isar instantaneously remembers 'the flow | Of Isar rolling rapidly'. In the Baltic ridge the Oder is brown, the Vistula yellow. The 'blue Danube' we hear so much of is by virtue of its chief tributaries an Alpine river, though it rises in the Black Forest; Ratzel describes it as 'muddy and yellowish' at Passau.

On and near the Rhine and the Danube the Romans built their cities: Basel, Strassburg, Speyer, Worms, Mainz, Cologne; Augsburg, Regensburg, Passau, Vienna. Between the Danube and the Rhine they built a wall to ward off the 'barbarians'. Through the Roman city of Treves, where their mighty gate, the Porta Nigra, still stands at the entrance to the main street, Roman culture passed into Germany from Gaul by the side valley of the Moselle.

The Rhine from its sources to Basel is called Hochrhein; from Basel to Mainz, Oberrhein; from Mainz to Bonn, Mittelrhein; from Bonn to the sea, Niederrhein. From south to north the plain of the Rhine lies between ranges of mountains on either side: Jura, Vosges, Hunsrück, and Eifel on the left, Black Forest, Odenwald, Taunus, and Westerwald on the right bank. Black Forest and Vosges are geographically one range and there is the same formation of rocks below the river: in the centre the crust of the earth cracked and sank and thus formed the river bed (*Grabenversenkung*). Between Odenwald and Taunus is the plain of the Main, with the Spessart range north of the river. The range called die Rhön lies between the Spessart and the Thüringer Wald; south to west from the Thüringer Wald run the Fränkischer Jura and the Schwäbischer Jura (also called Rauhe Alb). Two hills famous in history, der Hohenstaufen and der Hohenzollern, lie isolated by valleys from the bulk of the ridge. The territory of Hohenzollern, the original home of the Prussian dynasty, still belongs to Prussia. The triangle closed in by these ranges and falling gradually to the valley of the Neckar and the Main is called *das Schwäbisch-Fränkische Stufenland*.

The Main is peculiar for its snake-like windings and its westward direction. It is, roughly, the dividing line between North and South Germany. It joins the Rhine at Mainz. Between Mainz and Bonn the Rhine is the river of song and legend; from Cologne it serves the industrial districts.

The German North Sea has the salt and the tides of the Atlantic. Hamburg and Bremen depend as ports on the tide, which brings vessels in and takes them out. Heine's *Nordsee* (1827) first made the Germans conscious of the grandeur and beauty of the North Sea, which had figured in popular language as '*der blanke Hans*', fiercely coming with the north-west wind to break through the dikes which are built all along the coast. The smaller rivers are emptied through the dikes by sluices; hence the names of villages ending in -*siel* on the Hanover coast. The care of the dikes, both by the sea and along the rivers where the banks are low, is enforced in the earliest compilation of laws in the vernacular, the thirteenth century *Sachsenspiegel*; the dike-law was compressed into a rhyming formula: *Wer nicht will deichen, muss weichen*, i.e. he who neglected his duty lost his land. Detlev von Liliencron (see p. 315) was in charge of the dikes (*Deichhauptmann*) on the island of Pellworm near Husum on the coast of Schleswig-Holstein. The dikes enclose stretches of mud deposited by the rivers; these have settled into flat marshland, excellent for grazing. Out to sea lies a chain of islands which were obviously once connected. The East Frisian Islands off the coast of Hanover continue the chain of the West Frisian Islands, which belong to Holland. The first of the East Frisian Islands is Borkum, the most westerly point of Germany. Borkum and Norderney are fashionable wateiing-places. North of the estuary of the Elbe, along the west coast of Schleswig-Holstein, are the North Frisian Islands; Sylt, Föhr, and Amrum are popular watering-places. To the North Frisian Islands belong *die Halligen*, low islands overgrown with grass, a few inhabited by fishermen who augment their living by cattle grazing; they live in houses built on mounds (*Wurten, Bühel*). Between the East Frisian Islands and the shore are the *Watten*. A *Watte* is a shoal of sand and mud covered by the tide but passable at low water by carts and on foot. Winding channels or tidal swatchways (called by various names – *Balje, Diep, Gat, Loch, Rinne*) run through the *Watten* and make navigation so difficult that the coast is protected automatically.[1]

Thirty miles out between the North and the East Frisian Islands lies Heligoland, exchanged by England in 1890 for Zanzibar; it consists of a steep sandstone rock, the Oberland, and a shelf of sand, the Unterland. The whole island is only one mile long and three-quarters of a square mile in superficial area; it is a fashionable watering-place.

This north-west corner of the Empire belongs to Prussia (Schleswig-Holstein and Hanover) and the Free States of Oldenburg, Hamburg, and Bremen. It is vital to Germany, and in importance to trade and defence is now what the west corner of the Baltic with Lübeck was in the palmy days of the Hanseatic League. Into the Heligoland Bight flows the Elbe, with Cuxhaven, the outport of Hamburg, at its mouth; farther west is the mouth of the Weser with Bremen and its outport Bremerhafen, the seat of the North German Lloyd as Hamburg is that of the '*Hapag*' (Hamburg-Amerikanische Paketfahrtaktiengesellschaft), the Jadebusen with Wilhelmshafen, and the Dollart, into which flows the Ems. The Ems and the Weser are the only two main German rivers which have their sources in Germany. The port of Emden, at the mouth of the Ems, is connected by the Dortmund-Ems Canal (built 1892-1901 at a cost of £25,000 a mile) with the industrial districts of the Rhine, which are thus not absolutely dependent on Rotterdam and Antwerp. There is a short cut to the Baltic by one of the greatest waterways of the world, the Kaiser Wilhelm Canal, from Brunsbüttel at the mouth of the Elbe to Holtenau above Kiel; small ships can reach the middle of the canal by way of the river Eider from Tönning.

In the western part of the northern plain (*das Westdeutsche Tiefland*) there is (1) a rim of marshland, (2) the sandy Geest or dry heathland interspersed with boggy moors, and (3) a stretch of rich corn-growing

---

[1] There is a description of this coast and its ramifications in Erskine Childers's novel, *The Riddle of the Sands* (1903).

land at the foot of the most northerly hills of the Central Range. *Die Marschen* are really marshes of alluvial mud diked in from the sea; the first stage is that of the *Polder* or *Koog*. The marshland, the best grazing-land in Germany, is pictured in a descriptive flash of the school geographies as 'the golden hem on the ragged purple mantle of the heathland'. In the marshes of the Ems the farmers live on the mounds or *Wurten*, as they do on the *Halligen*; in the marshes by the sea they usually build their farms on the dry Geest. Frenssen's *Jörn Uhl* (see p. 332) gives an idea of the district.[1] Between the Elbe and the Weser, with its tributary the Aller, lies the vast sandy tract of the Lüneburger Heide, one of the most romantic districts of Germany, where the Low Saxon types of German speech and of architecture are preserved much as they were (it is claimed) at the time of the Thirty Years' War. The most eastern part of the cornland is the Magdeburger Börde (*Börde = Ebene*), formed of glacial loam and alluvial soil; it is connected by the Mittellandkanal, which joins Weser and Elbe with the industrial districts of Westphalia. This district is rich in potash and salts, the remains of an ancient sea, and in lignite (*Braunkohle*).

The Baltic is tideless. Into it flow more than 200 streams, bringing fresh water; and since it is connected with the North Sea merely by a narrow channel it has only 0·7 per cent of salt compared with 3½ per cent in the North Sea. The feature of the Schleswig-Holstein coast is that it is indented by long fjords (*Förden*) with the town from which they have their name at the head of them, e.g. Flensburg at the head of the Flensburger Förde. The narrowest fjord (thirty miles long) is the Schlei, with Schleswig, the capital of the province, at the head of it; the entrance is only eighty yards wide. The chief port of Schleswig-Holstein is Kiel, famous for smoked sprats (*Kieler Sprotten*) and men-of-war. The rounder indentations along the Baltic coast are called *Bodden* (e.g. Wismar Bodden, Greifswalder Bodden); these are parted from the sea by islands, peninsulas, or dunes. Rügen is lovely with its towering chalk cliffs crowned with beechwoods; the train ferry for Sweden crosses from Stralsund and leaves the island at Sassnitz. To the west is another long island, hardly more than a range of dunes, Hiddensee or Hiddensoe.

The Baltic provides protection from its own encroachments by a range of dunes along the coast. Whole villages have in former times been buried by *wandernde Dünen*; they are now stabilized by planting them with grasses such as *elymus arenarius*, which send up fresh shoots every time the sand covers them; in due course loam is worked in to make a

---

[1] The first book to bring out the poetry of *Geest* and *Marschen* was Hermann Allmers's *Marschenbuch* (1857); the second edition (1874) found the public ready.

soil in which pines and dwarf pines (*pinus Mughus*) will grow; thus are sandy wastes turned into woodlands. This fierce sand – minute particles ground by the old glaciers, or the detritus of rivers – has formed another distinguishing feature of the Baltic, its Haffs and Nehrungs. Originally these Haffs (Kurisches Haff, Frisches Haff, Stettiner Haff) were open bays which have been almost closed off by a *Nehrung*; this is a spit of land formed by the sinking of heavy matter washed down by the rivers with further accretions of sand; in some places the topping of sand drifts across the *Nehrung* and is filling the *Haffe*.

South of the dunes a low range of hills (called *der Nördliche Landrücken* or *der Baltische Höhenrücken*) runs along the Baltic. It is cut into four Lake Districts (*Seenplatten*) by the Vistula, the Oder, and the Elbe-Trave Canal. These hills are accumulations of boulders and represent the terminal moraines (*Endmoränen*) of the old glaciers; the débris at the bottom of the glaciers has remained at the north of the hills as fertile land; on the south of the range rivers have washed away the heavy soil and left plains of sand now covered by pine forests and heather. Where the torrents have washed deep, or where there are banks of glacier-drift, lakes have formed. To the east of the Vistula, i.e. in East Prussia, we have *die Preussische Seenplatte*; it is the district of the Masurian Lakes, where Hindenburg won the victories of Tannenberg in 1914 and of Masuria in 1915. In the Rominter Heide elks are still bred, and wolves and lynxes cross over from Poland to the Johannisburger Heide. East Prussia (with Lithuania) is a great horse-breeding district. Between the Kurisches Haff and the Frisches Haff lies the peninsula of Samland, famous since the days of the Romans for amber.

The valley of the Vistula is very fertile alluvial soil. South of Marienburg, where the beautiful castle of the Teutonic Knights who colonized this district still stands, the Nogat branches off from the Vistula; between the two rivers lies a fertile delta with the Free State of Danzig, created by the Treaty of Versailles at the head of the Polish Corridor which gives Poland access to the sea. Danzig, it is true, was the ward of Poland once before, when the power of the Teutonic Knights dwindled; but Danzig is so German that it can only be natural if every German thinks it is merely a political wheeze that it is at present not German; before the war it was the capital of West Prussia, which no longer exists, as most of it was ceded to Poland by the Treaty of Versailles.

South of the Baltic ridge of hills is a depression stretching from the Elbe to the Vistula; in this depression between Elbe and Oder lies Brandenburg, mostly lakes, sand, and pines. The sand was left by the rivers that rushed west to the Elbe as the old glaciers melted, taking the loam with them. The old joke was that Brandenburg was the sandbox of the Holy Roman Empire. Few people out of Germany realize that this sand with its pine forests, its chains of lakes, its sleepy reed-rimmed rivers, make Berlin a delightful holiday centre. The most characteristic district is the Spreewald; here the Spree is so sluggish that it spreads in a network of canal-like arms, which are the streets of the district; the haystacks are raised on poles, and the houses too are raised above the ground. The Spree, on which stands Berlin, flows into the Havel, the chief tributary of the Elbe. There are more canals in Brandenburg than anywhere else in Germany; they join river to river, and make Berlin one of the busiest inland ports of Europe. Berlin, which covers the area of the Island of Rügen, is famous for electrical appliances, furniture, pianos, clothing.

Below Brandenburg, the Northern Plain reaches south-east to form the Silesian depression (*die Schlesische Mulde*). Through it flow the Oder and its tributaries. Silesia is separated from Czechoslovakia by the Sudetic Mountains, which at their northern end include the Riesengebirge, after the Bavarian Alps the highest mountains in Germany (the Schnee-koppe is 1600 metres high). Upper Silesia is a densely populated industrial region. Breslau, on the Oder, in Lower Silesia, is the third city of Prussia (the second is Cologne). West of Silesia are the Free States of Saxony and Thuringia; the Saale forms the boundary between them. In the north Saxony is a flat plain; in the south are the Lausitzergebirge and the Erzgebirge with the Elbsandgebirge between them. The region among the foothills of the Erzgebirge is a hive of industry; there are mines and mills at Plauen and Zwickau; Chemnitz is known as 'the Manchester of Germany'. The district where the Elbe pierces the Elbsandgebirge at the Bohemian frontier is known as *die Sächsische Schweiz*; the sandstone rocks have been worn by the weather into quaint shapes with flattened tops. This is a favourite place for picnics from Dresden, a little to the north. In the art galleries of Dresden, the capital of Saxony ('Elb-Florenz'), are priceless pictures, including Raphael's 'Sistine Madonna'. Farther down the Elbe we come to Meissen, where the oldest porcelain in Europe was made. In the Saxon plain lies Leipzig, which has the biggest railway station in Germany.

West of Saxony is Thuringia, 'the green heart of Germany'. It is bounded on the south-west by the Thüringer Wald; here lies the lovely village of Ilmenau; and near Eisenach is the Wartburg, in the Middle Ages the residence of the Landgraves of Thuringia; here in 1206 that legendary contest of minstrels took place with which we are familiar from Wagner's *Tannhäuser*. Here, too, lived Saint Elizabeth; and here Luther threw his ink-pot at the devil. To the north of the Thüringer Wald are the Kyffhäusergebirge, where, according to legend, Barbarossa is slumbering with his red beard growing through the marble table till time shall restore the Empire to its olden glory. The present Free State of Thuringia was made up in 1920 of eight smaller states; Weimar, once the home of Goethe and Schiller, is the capital; here after the Revolution of 1919 the new constitution was framed. North of Thuringia is the Prussian province of Saxony, and embedded in this is the *Freistaat* of Anhalt, the capital of which, Dessau, is famous for its aeroplanes. Erfurt, the centre of the flower and seed trade, is in Prussian Saxony, though Thuringia is all round it. South of Thuringia is Bavaria. To the south, between the Danube and the Alps, the capital, Munich, lies on the Schwäbisch-Bayrische Hochebene; famous as an art city, it is still more renowned for its beer. The plateau rises from Munich to the Bavarian Alps, the highest peaks of which are Zugspitze (2963 m.) and Watzmann (2714 m.); at the foot of Watzmann dreams the deep-set Königssee; other famous Bavarian lakes are the Starnberger See, where King Ludwig II drowned himself, and Chiemsee, where he left one of his fairy palaces unfinished. Nuremberg, famous for toys and Hans Sachs, is in Bavaria, but is geographically to the north in the Fränkisches Stufenland; the old part (*Altstadt*) is preserved as it was in medieval times, but the most medieval town in Europe is Rothenburg ob der Tauber near the Württemberg frontier.

West of Thuringia are the Free State of Hesse (capital, Darmstadt), the Prussian province of Hesse-Nassau, and the Prussian Rhine Province. This (with the Black Forest) is the best-known region of Germany. The holiday resorts are household names; in the side valleys are spas with medicinal springs, e.g. Ems in the Lahn Valley; in the Taunus are Wiesbaden and Homburg vor der Höhe.[1] At the south-west of the Hunsrück lies the *Saarbrücker Kohlengebiet*, which by a provision of the Treaty of Versailles was administered for fifteen years by the League of Nations. The most densely populated regions of Germany are the industrial districts to the north and east of Duisburg;[2] silk is woven at Elberfeld and Barmen; steel wares are made at Solingen, 'the German Sheffield', and tools at Remscheid. Duisburg with Ruhrort is the greatest inland port of Europe. Essen, like Doctor Johnson's Charles XII, has 'a name at which the world grew pale'. North of Bonn a fertile plain (*die Niederrheinische Tiefebene*) stretches to Holland and away to the sea. Aix-la-Chapelle, where in the Cathedral Charlemagne lies buried, is still a spa with hot sulphurous springs. Krefeld is the centre of the silk industry.

[1] Höhe = the hills as seen from Frankfurt.
[2] Pronounce *Düsburg*.

Cologne, at the southernmost point of the plain, where it makes a bay (Kölner Bucht) east of the Hohes Venn range of hills, is important as a crossing-point of the main routes of the European railways. Düsseldorf, also on the Rhine and in the Kölner Bucht, keeps its pride of place as an art city in spite of its industries.

The climate differs between East and West Germany more than it does between North and South – the south is higher and therefore cooler, while the north gets something of the warmth of the Gulf Stream, not directly, but by way of west winds from the Shetlands. Swabia (that is Württemberg and Baden) and Bavaria are actually cooler than Holstein and the Frisian Islands. The warmest climate is that of the Rhine Valley; here the vine grows farther north than in any other part of Europe. In East Prussia the beech tree, which only grows where the temperature is moderated by ocean winds, does not occur north of Königsberg. Extremes of temperature are most marked in central Germany, where, moreover, the changes come suddenly. The climate of the Fichtelgebirge at the heart of Germany, though the highest peak is only 1053 m., is notoriously inclement; snow often lingers till June. The Rauhe Alb, which dominates the Neckar Valley, is swept by piercing winds; hence its name. Prussia is cold because there is no protection from the east. In South and East Germany the winter is severe for from three to four months; snow is expected, and therefore German Christmas cards are not, like ours, a fairy tale. Rain is brought in plenty by the prevailing west and south-west winds, which have great velocity on the northern plain, less on the southern plateau. The mountains are famous for their persistent mists; but sometimes it is not rain vapour but *Haarrauch*,[1] smoke from the vast moors which are set on fire in the autumn to fertilize the poor soil.

THE PEOPLE

If mere names went for anything, the Germans would be *the* people. The name we give the race, 'Germans' (Latin, *Germani*) is the name of *one* of their tribes generalized, transferred to the other tribes, and taken over by the Romans. The adjective *deutsch* comes from Old High German *diutisc*, which is the adjective corresponding to *deota*, 'people' or 'nation'; '*deutsch*' thus originally means 'national', 'belonging to the people', '*volkstümlich*'. (The Gothic form of the noun is familiar in the name Theoderich = 'people + rex', 'king of the people'.) We use the term for the inhabitants of Holland; but till the seventeenth century 'Dutch' might mean 'German'. Strange to say, where it is first used of the language by a German author, Otfried, he only gives it when he is writing Latin

---

[1] Also *Herauch* (and in Austria *Heerrauch*), *Höhenrauch*; peat-smoke.

('*theodisce*');[1] when he is writing German he calls the language *frenkisc*, a word which in its present form is written '*fränkisch*' but also 'French'! (The French, of course, have kept the name of the old Frank or Franconian invaders; see p. 28.) If the ancient Germans regarded themselves as *the* people, it is clear that they regarded all other peoples as barbarians; one of their neighbours was the Celtic tribe of the Volcae; now, since Indo-European *o* and *c* (= *k*) appear in Germanic as *a* and *ch*, it is evident that the Germanic form of *Volca* is *Walha* (*h* = *ch*); and *Walha* with its derivatives occurs in the Germanic languages in place-names[2] and otherwise wherever Germans came into contact with Celts. We have the old plural in our 'Wales', the adjective to which is 'Welsh', corresponding to Old High German *walhisc*. What happened was that the Teutonic tribes called all the Celts by the name of *one* Celtic tribe, just as the French lumped all Germans together as Alemanni (*Allemands*). The German form of the adjective is *welsch*, and this now means 'romance', 'Italian', 'French'. The disrespect associated with the idea of 'non-German' is seen in *Kauderwelsch*, 'gibberish', and in the verb *verwelschen*, 'to frenchify'. A 'walnut' or *eine Walnuss* is *eine welsche Nuss*, a foreign (Italian or French) nut. A Dutch proverb runs: '*Wat walsch is, valsch is*,' all that is French is false; we on the other hand talk of 'Dutch courage' for false courage. The etymology of 'welsher' and 'to welsh', one hopes, is unrelated.

'*Deutsch*' is a general name for a number of tribes (*Stämme*) which have to a large extent retained their special characteristics to this day. The chief of these *Stämme* are: the Alemanni in Switzerland, Württemberg, Baden, and Alsace; the Bavarians in Bavaria and Austria; the Franconians (*die Franken*) in West Germany from Nuremberg (*Ostfranken*) to Amsterdam (*Niederfranken*); the Thuringians in Thuringia, Upper Saxony, and parts of Brunswick; the Low Saxons north of Thuringia to the Baltic and from the Zuider Zee to the East frontier of Mecklenburg; the Frisians along the coast of the North Sea and on the islands from Denmark to the Zuider Zee.

To a German the differences between tribe and tribe are obvious and familiar; a foreigner misses the finer characteristics, but cannot miss the features which distinguish South Germans from North Germans. The usual statement is that the South Germans are *gemütlich* (good-natured,

---

[1] It is possible that since the Gothic plural *thiudōs* stands for *gentes*, 'heathen', the adjective = *gentilis*, 'heathen'; *theodisca lingua* would thus mean the 'vulgar' tongue in contradistinction to the priest's language, Latin. The first recorded use of *theodisce*, in 786, refers to Anglo-Saxon; it was only used of the German people at the end of the tenth century.

[2] Those beginning with Wahlen-, Wal(l)en-, Walch(en)-, Waal-. Wallis (Valais) in Switzerland has the same origin as our 'Wales'.

genial, sociable) and the North Germans *ungemütlich*. This is, however, too general. The Bavarians are notoriously *gemütlich*; but there is a marked difference between the *Gemütlichkeit* of the Bavarians and that of their more refined next of kin, the Austrian Germans; the Bavarians have zest and go, the Austrians are melancholy and delicately listless. It would be too paradoxical to say that in Bavaria the way out of trouble is to get drunk, while in Austria it is to commit suicide, but the truth inclines in that direction. The Swiss is a South German, but who shall say that he is jolly? The Rhinelander is a North German, but who will say that he is not jolly? As a matter of fact the Swiss Germans have marked affinities, seen even in the style of their farm-houses, with the taciturn Westphalians; both – if they are to be represented by the farmers, who best preserve the traditional features – live in isolated dwellings in close communion with elemental nature. Climate and landscape un-doubtedly have their effect on character. The character of the South Germans responds to the warmer tones of their scenery; in Swabia and Bavaria they are apt to be imperturbably contented. The North Germans are hard and stern like their skies; they have the silence that fits the melancholy monotony of their heathlands, and a clear vision of mind that sweeps far horizons like those of their plains. They have the ruthless will-power which we associate with Prussia. South Germany cradles musicians, North Germany rears scientists, philosophers, and clear-headed politicians. Poets are evenly distributed, and this is to be expected, for German poets are thinkers; but the poets with the least fund of thought (the Swabian school) are of the south. Poets of the south who have the deep philosophical groundwork of the north are Alemanni (Keller, Spitteler). On the other hand, though Romantic poetry – the most fanciful of all poetry – is associated with Heidelberg and Swabia, its guiding lights were North Germans, and some of its most productive writers (Achim von Arnim, Fouqué, Eichendorff) were actually *Junker* from the lands east of the Elbe; Gustav Roethe[1] explains this by the rule of contraries, as a reaction against the rigid drill and the flat prose of the life of Prussia. The pessimists belong mostly to the north (Schopenhauer, Eduard von Hartmann, Hebbel).

A little acquaintance with German literature makes one familiar with the popular picture of the various tribes. The most familiar figure is that of the Bavarian, partly because, with his blunt outspokenness, his self-assertiveness, his mastery of picturesque swear-words, his (generally speaking) obtrusive rotundity, and his inbred detestation of Prussians, he is and ever has been a stock comic figure in the *Witzblätter* (these being

[1] *Deutsche Reden* (1927).

traditionally Bavarian because obscene) and in the serious literature of the other States.[1] Above all the Bavarian loves comfort – with beer. Thomas Mann in *Buddenbrooks* (see p. 338) has drawn a classical portrait of the easy-going Bavarian and brought it into stark contrast with the Northern zest in business; before the daughter of the Lübeck merchant house is allowed to marry the Bavarian merchant Permaneder the greatest care is taken to verify his commercial prospects; once safely married, however, he retires from business; since he has his wife's dowry and his own savings there is no need to work; *'jetzt will i mei Rua'*, he says (*meine Ruhe will ich haben*). The Swiss Alemanni, on the other hand, are keen business men; their satirical bent comes out in Gottfried Keller's short stories. The Swabians one associates with domestic idylls and flowers, and with a certain guilelessness which is certainly foreign to their kindred in Switzerland; the Swabians (*'plumpe Schwaben'*) are popularly supposed to remain childish till they are forty years old (hence forty is *das Schwabenalter*); *Schwabenstreiche*[2] are tomfoolery. The qualities of the Franconian are still those indicated by his name: he is frank in his manner and free or independent in his attitude; he loves town life, and his sociability is shown by the form of his villages – whereas the Alemanni and the Low Saxons have the *Langhaus* or *Einzelhof* or *Einödhof* in the centre of its fields, the Franconians have the *Haufendorf* or farms clustered sociably round church and village pond. The men of the Palatinate (*die Pfälzer*), who belong politically partly to Bavaria and partly to Baden, have the reputation of being quarrelsome. The Rhinelanders to the north of them are too obliging to their visitors to be quarrelsome; they are as sparkling as their wines, but they are (shall one say?) a trifle keen on gain (they are nearest to France . . .). Equally capable in business are the Upper Saxons; they are often credited with those grasping proclivities which visitors to Scotland look for and never find. They and the Thuringians are famous for their love of music: Bach was a Thuringian; Handel, Wagner, and Schumann were Saxons; the mention of these names is enough to indicate that modern music derives from Thuringia and Saxony. Moreover, Tannhäuser is still the minion of Frau Venus in the Hörselberg near Eisenach. German chivalry radiated from the Wartburg, as did the Reformation; and Thuringia and Saxony are the cradle of German socialism (Bebel was member for Leipzig, and a programme that the party long swore to was hatched at Eisenach). The other *Stämme* think the Saxons funny because of the soft drawl of their dialect; and the fact

---

[1] There is a delightful picture of Bavarians and Bavarian life in Friedrich Michael's novel *Silvia und die Freier* (3rd ed., 1947).
[2] See Uhland's ballad *Schwäbische Kunde*.

that they have driven out or absorbed a former Slav population of their districts (there is still an enclave of Wends in the East of Saxony) may explain some of their peculiarities. A Slav admixture is often given as the explanation of Prussian amenability to discipline[1] and devotion to the monarchy, and it seems true that east of the Elbe that stubborn independence and reliance on self which is the stuff of the Swiss, the Dutchmen, and the Westphalians, yielded to a willing subservience to authority; 'verboten' as a fetish would thus be Prussian in origin and in the undiluted tribes an infection. It is possible, in any case, to envy the clockwork precision of the Prussian machine, seen best at Berlin, where the rush of the strenuous life is the nearest possible to America. The Pomeranians are reckoned the Boeotians among the tribes. The Mecklenburgers (except for a Slav admixture) and the Hanoverians are the same race as the Westphalians; there are shades of difference – the Hanoverians (with their British connections) have a cosmopolitan outlook, and, frequently, the scholarship of Göttingen; in Mecklenburg, where serfdom was not abolished till 1820, Slav features persist. That there is humour – of a sort – in these septentrional spaces can be proved by a few names: Baron von Münchhausen, whose adventures were first told in English in 1785 by a German (Rudolph Erich Raspe) and translated into German in 1786 by August Wilhelm Bürger, was a Hanoverian; Josef Winckler's *Der tolle Bomberg* (1923) tells similar tales of a Westphalian baron; and the classical German humorist, Fritz Reuter (1810-74) was a Mecklenburger.[2] But the classical qualities of the Low Saxons, particularly of the Westphalians, are miles away from humour. At their very best these qualities are seen in Moltke, a Mecklenburger; the name that is given to him, *der grosse Schweiger*, is eloquent of the taciturnity which is natural to this pristine race. Typical Mecklenburgers, too, were Johann Heinrich Voss, the gaunt bucolic poet, and Blücher, stolid and steadfast and grotesquely illiterate, who could not spell German, but swore it magnificently. The *Stamm* is equally famous for its obstinacy: it took Charlemagne forty years to induce the Low Saxons – with the sword – to accept Christianity; and even then there is news of a sacrifice made to Wodan at Rostock in the sixteenth century. The Low Saxons were even too obstinate to adopt the second sound-shifting; they stopped it between the Harz and the Thüringer Wald, and thus put a dividing line for evermore between them and their more pliable brethren. With all their faults, the Westphalians[3]

---

[1] Nietzsche, a Saxon born but of Polish descent, was an intellectual rebel, but his doctrines fitted in with Prussian policy.

[2] '*Westphalus est sine pietate, sine pudore, conscientia, veritate*' is an old saying.

[3] Immermann's *Oberhofschulze* in *Der Oberhof* is the classical picture of a Westphalian.

preserve the primitive German type with the least suspicion of admixture; we have only to compare them with their neighbours, the (Low Franconian) Dutch and the Flemings, to see the difference: owing no doubt to an admixture of Celtic or Romance blood the Netherlanders are less rigid, while the Flemings have something of the artistic softness and adaptability of the Austrian Germans. Tribal characteristics are largely effaced in the colonized provinces of the East; Flemish and Frisian features are still prominent; Danzig, called 'the Naples of the North', is a sister city of Amsterdam. The Frisians are linguistically 'Teutonic' rather than 'German'; that is, Frisian is West Germanic but not Low German; but the mass of the Frisians have given up Frisian for Low and High German; Gustav Frenssen, for instance, was a Frisian writer in High German in whose work the Frisian traits would be hard to distinguish from Low German characteristics.

One characteristic is common to all German tribes: unmitigated honesty. All who have travelled over Europe know that one's purse is safer where German is spoken than anywhere else. Cleanliness is another ubiquitous quality.

Our music-hall or caricature picture of the German – the pot-bellied, bushy-bearded, blob-nosed, rubicund German of the brass-band type – exists about as much as the long-toothed, elongated, flat-footed, pipe-sucking Englishman in a check suit of German caricature. The noisy, self-assertive, aggressive German of our pre-war nightmares was a somewhat overdrawn picture of the Prussian – preferably the non-commissioned officer whom one met before the war as a post-office or railway official; he is now, probably, an extinct type – officials all over Germany are now impossibly courteous and positively low-voiced. The physical type most seen in Germany is that of Stresemann (the new edition of Bismarck) – the bull neck with the rolls of fat, the clean-shaven pasty face, the colourless hair clipped to one millimetre, i.e. apparently bald – the 'pow', as they call it in Lancashire, is said to be more hygienic; the fashion fits in with *die Neue Sachlichkeit* (see p. 354) – why hair when it has no purpose? The German as he sees himself in his own mind is true in the ideal sense of truth. *Der deutsche Michel*, however, could never stand up to John Bull in a straight fight. *Der deutsche Michel* and Eichendorff's *Taugenichts* are one and the same: the dreamer with his head in the clouds and old songs singing through his soul. The most modern version of him is Michel Hellriegel in Gerhart Hauptmann's Märchendrama *Und Pippa tanzt* (see p. 297); he 'does not know where he is'; he is wandering through the wastes of the world looking for *die blaue Blume*, or for beauty that brute hands snatch from him and that breaks in his grasp if in one supreme

moment of dream it comes to him. He is incorporeal; but German critics
have tried to give us his chemical composition. He is compounded, they
say, of *Gemüt* (no translation!), mysticism, *Innerlichkeit* (translation = ?)
introspectiveness (*Selbstbetrachtung*), childlikeness (*Kindlichkeit*), and
Schweigsamkeit (not 'taciturnity', but love of silence). This is perhaps the
German one dreams of when listening to Mendelssohn's *Frühlingslied*; or,
he is young Strauss in *Waltzes from Vienna*. That is German idealism; to
German realism belongs, not only the old war-machine, but the almost
fabulous thoroughness of the German scientist; a German takes his time
with a thing, but he exhausts it.

THE LANGUAGE

The ideal qualities of the race are reflected in the language rather than
their (perhaps acquired) practical propensities. English and Danish have
shorn grammar to a minimum; German has complicated it. French has
fixed it beyond appeal; no German authority can explain why *Zimmer mit
warmem fliessenden Wasser* is not incorrect, or state a definite rule for the
use of the weak or strong form in adjectives following indefinite numeral
adjectives. There are seven different renderings of English 'the'; and
some of these have different meanings according to case. But precisely
because of these alluring difficulties and labyrinthine endings our Ministry
of Education are no doubt wise in recommending German to schools as
a mental discipline equal to that of ancient Greek. So much for the
trappings of the language, its externals; the richness of it is in its inner
convolutions, its folded depth, its sudden coruscations and discreet shades,
its intimate clasping of word with word in intensification or transformation
of meaning. All the soul of a nation is in its language. The German
language is like Rembrandt's painting: it is dark and difficult to unimaginative minds; to those who love the light of dreams its chiaroscuro
is full of mystic and glowing beauty. The crowded consonants[1] sound
harsh to those who have grown fond of the liquid flow and the idle
elisions of the Romance languages; they who live with it know that it is
a man's language, inexhaustible in its sonorous strength, hiding a heart of
the deepest tenderness.

German, like English, retains the old device of alliteration, particularly
in compounds; but whereas in English such an adjective as 'grass-green'
is poetical, *grasgrün* is prose diction. *Aalglatt* (with its cold slippery
assonance quickening as it escapes in the second syllable) is more vivid
than 'smooth as an eel'. German abstract philosophy flees reality; the

---

[1] E.g. *Jetztzeit* (i.e. *jetsttseit*), a neologism for *Gegenwart*, which has established itself,
though it made Schopenhauer, Wagner, and Nietzsche grind their teeth with rage.

language, on the other hand, seizes on essential concrete features, and clasps them together often in vigorous compounds: *rabenschwarz*, and if that is not enough *kohlpechrabenschwarz*; 'stark naked' is the language of the *Police Gazette*, *splitterfasernackt* shows the delinquent shivering, or flaunting the *Nacktkultus* of post-war athleticism; 'clean as a new pin' is dainty, but *funkelnagelneu* makes the pin sparkle. Rhyme, assonance, or alliteration kiss in multitudinous linked words such as *Ach und Krach, Mann und Maus, Gift und Galle, Wind und Wetter, dick und dünn, klipp und klar, kurz und gut, toll und voll, biegen oder brechen, zittern und zagen.* These intensifications sometimes give a delightful twist to the meaning, as in the *scheiden und meiden* of the *Volkslieder*: 'to part and to meet no more'. 'In these double forms,' says Oskar Weise,[1] 'the idea is variously reflected with shades of meaning, like a ray of light broken in a prism.' There is an effect of quaint tautology when preposition is heightened by adverb in such expressions as *durch den Wald hindurch, auf den Berg hinauf*. Child-like and tender is the fondness for diminutives which makes grown-ups neuter: *das Mütterchen, das Väterchen*. Lifeless things are made personal: *Frau Sorge* (familiar to all from Goethe's *Faust* and Sudermann's novel) is as real and certainly more pathetic than our 'wolf at the door'; there is a ghostlike tread in *wenn die Not an den Mann geht* ('when the worst comes to the worst'), and in *ein schleichendes Fieber*. The little pronoun *es* ('provisional subject') serves for a ghostlike doubling of the subject (event, and shadow cast before): *Es zogen drei Burschen wohl über den Rhein.* Onomatopoeia (*Klangmalerei*) is one of the main elements of word-formation; sound paints things in verbs such as *säuseln, lispeln, knarren, dröhnen*. Poets like Stefan George produce the effects of colour by vowel arrangement (see p. 319), but the veriest journalese commands such magic: *das Boot gleitet totenstill* I find in the first newspaper I look at. How white and cold is *Silbernacht!* Other effects come to the help of the poet; that of rapidity for instance; for all its panoply of consonants the language leaps in Goethe's: *Es schlug mein Herz! Geschwind zu Pferde . . .*; or in Platen's: *Wie raffi' ich mich auf in der Nacht, in der Nacht. . . .* The language even of strict prose is richly imaged: *steinreich, blutarm* express more than *sehr reich, sehr arm*; and age-old poetry lives in common expressions such as the euphemisms which veil the sadness of death: *erbleichen* or *verblassen*, to grow very pale; *das Zeitliche segnen*, to give one's blessing to time. An Englishman talks of his 'late' or 'deceased' father; 'late' has the melancholy of mutability; 'deceased' is horribly close to 'diseased' and suggests decomposition; a German assumes that his mother is in Paradise and says *selig*. But if he is speaking sardonically of the death of a mere friend,

---

[1] *Das geistige Gepräge der deutschen Sprache.*

he can say: *er hat ins Gras beissen müssen*. Fossils of old kennings – the poetic device by which the Germanic scop or skald christened the sea 'the whale's path' – exist in such terms as *Fingerhut* for 'thimble' or *Handschuh* for 'glove'. The German child learning his language has an advantage over his English cousin in that the names of things say what they are or do: a 'vessel' may be anything, but a *Fahrzeug* is a thing that goes or that one goes with; 'telephone' and 'nitrogen' are all very well when the child knows Greek, but *Fernsprecher* is a 'far-speaker' and *Stickstoff* is 'stifling stuff.' This germanizing of technical expressions may of course go too far; as when a pedant of the seventeenth century, believing he recognized the vile Latinism *nasus* in the word *Nase*, is said to have suggested as a substitute: *Löschhorn*. Interesting is popular interference with etymology (*Volksetymologie*) as old meanings disappear: *Maulwurf*, 'mole', has been made to sound like 'mouth-thrower', but originally the first part of the compound was our word 'mould'; *Dienstag* sounds to the weary workman who, it may be, has devoted Monday to recovering from Sunday (cf. *blauen Montag feiern!*) like *Diensttag*, but actually it is the day of the god Mars Thingsus (see p. 212), *dingstag*, court-day; *Schlafrock* is not the coat a German sleeps in, but the one he 'slips into' (*slouprock*); *Fastnacht*, originally *vasenacht*, is not the time for fasting, but for making a fool of oneself (*faseln*).

Humour conscious and unconscious enlivens the language: *das passt wie die Faust aufs Auge* is a drastic way of saying a thing won't do. Much of this rollicking humour is *burschikos* (*Bursche*, student + -κῶς), i.e. it comes from the *Studentensprache*; an example is the word for 'flapper', *Backfisch*, taken from the jargon of fishermen who separate the little fish for frying from the big fish for boiling.[1] *Katzenjammer* and *Kater* for 'the morning after' are *burschikos*.

The musical effect of English and German vowels is quite different, and this is largely due to the drawl of the English glide vowel: 'boat' is pronounced *bo^ut*, whereas German *Boot* is *bōt*. That is, the German consonant closely clasps the vowel. The energetic ring of German speech is partly due to the 'glottal stop': every syllable beginning with a vowel, if it has chief or subsidiary accent, begins with a kind of bark; it is owing to the glottal stop that liaison, which is so common a feature of other languages, is impossible in German[2] ('an apple' may be sounded 'a napple', but *ein Apfel* cannot be *ei napfel*). The commonest taunt flung at German

---

[1] In the fables of Martin Luther's friend Erasmus Alberus *Backfisch* is a term for '*baccalaureus*'.

[2] There is no possibility of confusing (e.g.) *vereist* and *verreist*, because in the first word *-eist* is accented and begins with the glottal stop.

is that it is 'guttural'; this is sheer ignorance (there are no 'gutturals'), but the velar *ch* is referred to (the hard *ch* sound in Scotch 'loch'); this is, it is true, the sound one makes in snoring, but snoring is another matter. It seems more to the point to quarrel with the soft *ch* which an Englishman finds hard to distinguish from *sch*, so that he is apt to make no difference, when speaking German, between a church and a cherry. Another not very lovable sound is the uvular *r* which is displacing the trilled one, so that when a German says *warten* it sounds like *wachten*.

The taunt of taunts is that, since German verbs in dependent clauses, and some of them in main clauses, come at the end of the sentence, one has to hang on to the words till the bitter end to grasp (in a state of exhaustion) the meaning. This is a great joke to jokers. Mark Twain took his German sentences to the long bridge over the Danube at Vienna, hung each individual word on a pillar, and then paced to and fro till they were disentangled. The Swedish poet Esaias Tegnér apostrophized the German language with the distich: 'Lay by thy phlegma and quicken the pace of thy sentences, lest one | Should the beginning forget, ere one has got to the end.' In sober truth this peculiarity of construction is a source of strength to an orator, who gathers the verbs at the end like chains running home, or hammers in the sense they convey like blows rained on a nail. There is the same bracing tension of expectation when the substance of an adjectival clause, or it may be of several adjectival clauses, is crushed between defining word (*der*, *kein*, etc.) and the noun qualified; e.g. *der aus den Kordilleren in den Atlantischen Ozean fliessende und wegen seiner schwarzen Farbe so genannte Rio Negro* – one hears *der* and holds it poised in the sounding-chamber of one's mind till the long roll of the other words bridges the gap to sense.

Contempt for the German language is a matter of history in Germany itself. Generations of Germans have been ashamed of their own tongue. In the seventeenth century societies were founded (*Sprachgesellschaften*) whose members were pledged to respect their native language; one such union, *der Deutsche Sprachverein*, still exists and is still fighting *Verwelschung* and Anglophilia. But not the little linguists and fops only have scorned German. Frederick the Magnificent,[1] the greatest of the Hohenstaufen emperors, a humanist before humanism, was never at home in Germany, and wrote Arabic, Italian, and Provençal poetry; the Emperor Charles V only spoke German to his dogs. Frederick the Great (it is said) only spoke German to his horse; he wrote it atrociously. But Frederick the Great not only forced Europe to respect Germany, he forced the Germans to respect themselves. A French wit, le père Bouhours, had amused Europe

---

[1] He, and not Barbarossa, was the original Emperor of the *Kyffhäusersage*.

B

by proving that no German could be a *bel esprit*:[1] Lessing demolished the strongholds of French conceit as thoroughly as Frederick smashed the French armies. The language, however, was still scorned; even Goethe could still say (in his twenty-ninth Venetian Epigram) that he was wasting his life and his art by writing in a poor medium (*in dem schlechtesten Stoff*); Schiller in 1792 complained that German was 'an inflexible, sprawling, dissonant language' to turn Virgil into; and Wieland in 1784 said German was the worst language in Europe.[2] There was no real appreciation of the language till the Romanticists came; *they* loved it. The classical writers and the Neo-Hellenists could not rid their mind of the classical idea that German was spoken by descendants of the barbarians; it was not even a bastard of Latin. The Romanticists, whose greatest achievement after their lyric verse was the new discipline of comparative philology, knew that German had a pedigree as noble as that of Greek or Sanscrit, and that the Goths who sacked Rome spoke a language as sonorous and richly moulded as Latin. They made the *Volkslied* live again. The classical writers had given the language dignity, the Romanticists gave it tenderness. A Jew, Heine, who infuriated all Germans who were then and ever will be by his gibes at Germany, proved wherever songs are sung that German can be as soft as Italian.[3] And in England not our German dynasty but the praise of Carlyle made German a necessary part of our culture.

The language we learn in England is *Schriftdeutsch*. But *Schriftdeutsch* is the official language, and it is superimposed on the dialects. Just as Germany is divided geographically into three parallel belts (see p. 4), so it is linguistically. (The central geographical and linguistic belts interlock.) In German Switzerland, Swabia, Bavaria, and Austria, Upper German (*Oberdeutsch*) is spoken. Upper German is subdivided into *Alemannisch* (in Switzerland), *Schwäbisch* (in Swabia), and *Elsässisch* (in Alsace) in the west, and *Bayrisch-Österreichisch* in the east. In the central belt *Mitteldeutsch* is spoken, consisting of *Fränkisch* (Franconian) in the west, and farther in the east the dialects grouped as *Ostmitteldeutsch*: *Thüringisch*, *Obersächsisch*, and *Schlesisch*. The north belt runs today approximately from Aix-la-

---

[1] This picture of the Germans as thick-skinned blockheads has persisted; Nietzsche, in *Vom Nutzen und Nachteil der Historie für das Leben*, quotes '*ein wackerer Engländer*' (it was Matthew Arnold!) who denies the Germans 'delicacy of perception', and says: 'in the German mind there does seem to be something splay, something blunt-edged, unhandy and infelicitous'; even Professor Saintsbury, in his queer account of modern German literature in his *The Later Nineteenth Century*, says the Germans are intellectual, but not intelligent.

[2] See Oskar Weise, *Æsthetik der deutschen Sprache*, p. 17.

[3] Hitler had to authenticate *Die Lorelei* by saying that it was by an anonymous writer.

Chapelle over Cologne, Cassel, Wittenberg, and Frankfurt-on-the-Oder. Formerly it was more to the south. In the northern belt various dialects of *Niederdeutsch* are spoken, and all are grouped as *Plattdeutsch*. *Niedersächsisch*, the eastern form of *Niederdeutsch*, is the descendant of *Altsächsisch*; Dutch and Flemish in the west are the descendants of *Niederfränkisch*. There is little difference between Dutch and Flemish and Plattdeutsch, so that much the same language is spoken along the northern plain beginning with the coast between Dunkirk and Amsterdam and ending at Lithuania. All these dialects, together with Old English or Anglo-Saxon, are grouped as Low German or *Niederdeutsch*. *Mitteldeutsch* and *Oberdeutsch* are grouped as *Hochdeutsch*.

The difference between Low German and Upper German is chiefly in certain consonants (see pp. 209-10).

Schriftdeutsch (*die Schriftsprache*) is the compromise language propagated by Martin Luther, a Low German – for Eisleben, where he was born, and Wittenberg, where he lived, were in his day Low German territory –, who thus made a blend of Middle German and Upper German intelligible all over Germany. He took the dry bones of the official language (*Kanzleisprache*) which had already been evolved in the Chanceries of the Empire – the form used in the Saxon Chancery was the nearest to him – and breathed into it the breath of life (see p. 233). It was an irony of fate that this language, composed for the Protestant Bible, had to be accepted as the official language by the Catholic states. Luther's *Schriftsprache* is one of the wonders of the world: his translation of the Bible is as beautiful as our own authorized version; and yet it was the work of a scholar who fashioned it by instinctive selection of whatever best suited his purpose; fortunately for him he was of peasant stock, and, as he himself tells us, he used the vivid words he heard spoken in the market-places; moreover ('out of the fulness of the heart the mouth speaketh', he quoted) all he wrote flows with the rhythm of his warm heart and passionate personality.

Schriftdeutsch is the literary language, i.e. German as she is written. But what of the spoken language? Where Germans speak as they write we get *papierner Stil*. Spoken *Hochdeutsch* is the *Umgangssprache*, and this is everywhere coloured by the native dialect of the speaker.[1] The *Umgangssprache* again may be subdivided into the *Vortragssprache* (the language of oratory), the *Verkehrssprache* (the language of official intercourse), and the *Familiensprache* (the language of easy conversation). The *Familiensprache* is nearest to dialect. *Hochdeutsch* is said to be spoken best where it

---

[1] Goethe, reproached for sticking to his Frankfurt dialect, replied: *Man soll sich sein Recht nicht nehmen lassen, der Bär brummt nach der Höhle, in der er geboren ist.*

differs most widely from the dialect, say in Hanover; but even here there are dialectal peculiarities of pronunciation (e.g. *ng* at the end of a word pronounced as *nk*). In Hamburg and Hanover *st* and *sp* are pronounced as in English, not as *scht* and *schp*. Notorious is the popular language of Berlin (*Berliner Jargon*), which is a mixture of *Platt* and *Hochdeutsch*. The standard pronunciation is that used on the stage in classical plays; this, known as *Bühnendeutsch*, corresponds to 'broadcasting English' here.

In England the tendency will probably be for dialects to die out in favour of the centralized language: broadcasting alone has an insidious levelling effect. In Germany the tendency is for dialects to be cultivated and preserved; from them the *Schriftsprache* is constantly drawing new words and idioms.[1] The *Schriftsprache* is fixed; the dialects evolve; and the evolution of the dialects in time affects the artificial language. The dialects have a proud place in the public esteem, for there is a classical dialect literature: Johann Peter Hebel (1760-1826) for Alemannic, Klaus Groth (1819-99) for the Platt of Holstein, and Fritz Reuter (see p. 272) for that of Mecklenburg, the dramatist Fritz Stavenhagen (1876-1906) for Hamburg Platt. The naturalistic school made the use of dialect a part of their programme (see p. 293); and the movement was continued by *Heimatkunst*, which registers all that is racial, including dialect, in a given district.

The modern study of dialects (*Mundartgeographie*) has proved that these cannot safely be classed as spoken by the *Stämme* from which they were originally derived. Thus today *Sächsisch*, as spoken by the Saxons of (Upper) Saxony, is philologically the language of the Thuringians; ethnologically *Sächsisch* is represented by the Lower Saxon dialects; in other words, the Saxons are a stock of Thuringian and East Franconian colonists who keep a Middle German dialect. East of the Elbe generally the dialects are mixed, as these districts, Slav till the twelfth century, were colonized by settlers from various districts of the west.

The determined practice of the dialects goes with the local patriotism of the separate states. *Lokalpatriotismus* and that *Kleinstaaterei* which, historically, has been Germany's tragedy, explain the decentralization which is peculiar to the German Empire. Paris is the brain of France, but Berlin is not the brain of Germany. Berlin has developed as the capital of the Hohenzollerns, but Munich has developed as the capital of the Wittelsbachs, and that means quite as much. People who wish to study music are more likely to go to Leipzig or to Dresden than to Berlin; and

---

[1] The eighteenth century Swiss writers (Haller, Gessner, Bodmer) introduced new words; *entsprechen, Staunen, Heimweh, anheimeln, au wiegeln, Putsch, Töchterschule* were imported from Switzerland.

the art-capital is generally understood to be Munich, where, too, many authors have preferred to live. Again, the centre of the bookselling trade as of the fur trade is Leipzig. Liverpool and Glasgow are 'provincial' cities; Hamburg, Bremen, and Lübeck are independent states. Similarly, English university life has been centralized at Oxford and Cambridge, whereas in Germany one university is as good as another; it is indeed the custom for an undergraduate to take so many terms of his course at one university and so many at another.

GERMAN THOUGHT

On the recurring traits of German character depends the nature of German thought. Germany is the 'nation of poets and thinkers'; and though the term refers to the great creative minds it is true of the mass of the people – rhyming of verses for family and local festivities ('*Gelegenheitsgedichte*') is a common custom, and every German has a *Weltanschauung*. In the realm of ideas there are two parallel phases which represent the two tendencies of the German mind: one to truth and the application of truth, that is, to logic and practical science; and the other to an imaginative and emotional illumination of truth. The one is *terra firma*, the other is the ever-changing, mysterious ocean. No one will dispute that the thinking which is congenial to the German soul is that which soars above fixed limits. Famous is Lessing's saying that if God were to offer him in one hand truth and in the other the quest of truth he would take the latter.[1] One might perhaps take a hint from Nietzsche[2] and define *Deutschtum* as *im Werden*: whereas Classical and Romance art is fixed by rigid rules and finished to perfection, German art is never finished but always forming; the classical example might be Goethe's *Faust*, a master piece billowing vastly in the void; but the conflict between Germanic tragedy (including Shakespeare) and the tragedy of the three unities also illuminates he statement. The parallel movement towards accuracy and fixity of style as it appears mainly in literature is perhaps nothing more than an attraction to the contrary from which there is always a violent reaction (e.g. *Sturm und Drang*, Expressionism, free rhythms in verse). These

---

[1] Cf. Graf Hermann Keyserling (1880–1946) in *Das Spektrum Europas* (1928): '*Dem Deutschen bedeuten Vorstellung und Ideen mehr als Realität. Ein Brite prägte einmal ein Witzwort: Gäbe es einmal zwei Tore, auf deren erstem stände: Eingang ins Himmelreich, und auf deren zweitem: Eingang zu Vorträgen über das Himmelreich alle Deutschen drängten sich durch das zweite.*'

[2] '*Ist es wahr, dass es zum Wesen des Deutschen gehört, stillos zu sein? Oder ist es ein Zeichen seiner Unfertigkeit? Es ist wohl so: das, was deutsch ist, hat sich noch nicht völlig klar herausgestellt. Das deutsche Wesen ist noch gar nicht da, es muss erst werden.*' Cf. F. Schlegel, *Fragmente*, and Paul Bourget, *Essais de psychologie contemporaine* (chapter on Renan).

interchanging currents of thought have been fully discussed in the
chapters which follow on Literature and Philosophy.

BIBLIOGRAPHY TO CHAPTER I

Baier, C. *Deutschland und die Deutschen.* London, 1952
Bithell, Jethro. *Germany.* In *Hutchinson's Pictorial Encyclopedia.* London, 1943
Briggs, Martin S. *Freiburg and the Black Forest.* London, 1936
Dickinson, Robert E. *The Regions of Germany.* London, 1945
Dickinson, Robert E. *The German Lebensraum.* A Penguin Special, 1943
Diesel, Eugen. *Germany and the Germans.* Translated by W. D. Robson-Scott.
    London, 1931
Hawgood, John A. *The Evolution of Germany.* (Methuen's Home Study Books.)
    London, 1955.
Ludwig, Emil. *The Germans.* London, 1942
Ratzel, Friedrich. *Deutschland.* Berlin, 6th ed., 1931
Remme, Karl. *Deutschland.* Berlin, 3rd ed., 1929
Riehl, W. H. *Von deutscher Landes- und Volkskunde.* (Hirts deutsche Sammlung.)
    Breslau
Schuster, George Naumann. *The Germans: An Enquiry and an Estimate.* New
    York, 1932
Barraclough, G. *Factors in German History.* Oxford, 1946
Deutsche Stammeskunde (a series of monographs: *Westfälische Stammeskunde,
    Rheinische St.k., Schwäbische St.k.,* etc.). Eugen Dieterichs, Jena
Much, Rudolf. *Deutsche Stammeskunde.* Sammlung Göschen. Leipzig, 1900
Zaunert, Paul. *Die Stämme im neuen Reich.* Jena, 1933
Hofstaetter, W., and Panzer, F. *Grundzüge der Deutschkunde.* Bd. 1. Bd. 2 von W.
    Hofstaetter und F. Schnabel. Teubner, Leipzig, 1925-29
Hofstaetter, W., and Peters, Th. *Sachwörterbuch der Deutschkunde.* Leipzig, 1929-30

CHAPTER II

GERMAN HISTORY TO 1618

GERMAN medieval history is dominated by an ideal: *Omnium Christianorum una respublica est.* From the time of Charlemagne the destiny of the German people was inextricably interwoven with the conception of a united Christendom under the dual headship of Pope and Emperor. To the end of the Hohenstaufen period the attempt to create a political reality approximating to this ideal is the guiding thread through the maze of German history: even when the logic of events taught the more prosaic Luxemburg and Habsburg rulers that it was not practical politics, its influence was still strong enough to make Germany's development markedly different from that of her neighbours. The imperial ideal gave to Germany intellectual and spiritual inspiration, but it was her political damnation. The German kings hitched their waggon to a star while other rulers elected to progress by less exalted methods; these achieved unity, nationhood, and power for their people, while Germany remained divided and leaderless, a prey to the ambition of her neighbours and the turbulence of her princes. Medieval history closes, broadly speaking, with the advent of the despotically ruled, sovereign nation-state, of which France in the seventeenth century is the supreme example. At the opening of the Thirty Years' War, Germany presented a very different spectacle. She had not pressed forward along the path of political development as her neighbour had done. Dissipation rather than concentration of effort had marked the policy of her rulers; preoccupation with grandiose schemes of empire had distracted them from their immediate task of strengthening their authority within their own dominions; the constantly recurring struggles with the Papacy, which arose in consequence of their intervention in Italy, had exhausted their resources and lessened their prestige. Inspiring as German medieval history is, it is yet disappointing: it is a record of political frustration, misfortune, and ultimate failure. The greatness of Germany was to come in a later age.

German medieval history may well begin after the fall of the Roman Empire in the West. Space does not permit of a discussion of the tribal communities which occupied the plains of Central Europe beyond the

27

confines of the Empire in the first four centuries A.D. Nor is such a discussion necessary, for many of the tribes so vividly described in the *Germania*, though Teutonic, were not specifically German; their characteristics, their activities, and their migrations lie outside the scope of German history. It is only after the fall of the Western Empire, when Goths, Vandals, and Burgundians had poured into the territories of the Empire, leaving their old haunts to others, that the specifically German peoples emerge to form something of a coherent whole in the basins of the Rhine, the Elbe, and the upper Danube. Of these people, the Franks were easily the most virile; spreading westward from the lands around the lower Rhine and the Meuse, they formed the kingdom of the Franks; and it was under the ægis of the Merovingian kings that the union of the principal stocks constituting the German people began. Clovis[1] conquered the Alemanni early in the sixth century, his son and grandson the Thuringians and Bavarians. In the seventh century these peoples regained their independence; the subjection of the Alemanni and the Thuringians was reaccomplished by Charles Martel, in fact, if not in name, the first Carolingian ruler of the Franks. He also subdued the Frisians, while his grandson, Charlemagne, finally reconquered the Bavarians, and, after thirty years of incessant fighting, added to his Empire the territory of the Saxons. At the opening of the ninth century the lands between the Rhine and the Elbe, from the North Sea to the Alps, were united under a single rule and subjected to a common administration. Medieval Germany was in being, though it had yet to be extricated from the Frankish Empire in order to emerge as a separate political entity with a history of its own.

Charlemagne – Karl der Grosse in German history – is as much a hero to the German as to the French people. The story of his reign has been recounted not only by Einhard, his secretary, but also by the unnamed monk of the German abbey of St. Gall. He was a commanding figure even in his own day, before men had had time to judge of his achievements. His massive frame, his love of physical exercise, his sensuality and his indulgence in the pleasures of the table all gave the impression of inexhaustible vitality. Remorseless and sometimes cruel as he was, his courage and skill as a warrior excited the admiration even of the conquered, while as a ruler men respected his ability and were impressed by

[1] Clovis (481-511) is the French form of Chlodwig, the earlier form of Ludwig and Lewis or Louis; he became king of the Salian or Salic Franks (*Salier*) in Belgium in 481. The territory of the Salian Franks lay to the north of that of the Ripuarian Franks (*Ripuarier = Uferbewohner*) along the Middle Rhine. Clovis became an orthodox Roman Catholic after his victory over the Alemanni near Zülpich in 496.

his dignity. The simplicity of his dress and habits, his gaiety and approachability, his piety, fervent and profound in spite of a moral standard in some respects utterly at variance with the teachings of the Church, all endeared him to his people. A great admirer of St. Augustine, he took for his pattern the prince mirrored in *De Civitate Dei*:

> Happy are they if they reign justly ... and if they do all things not for glory, but for charity, and with all and before all give God the due sacrifice of prayer for their imperfections.

He gave his vast realms peace, prosperity, and justice; though his work did not endure, because it was too dependent upon his own resolute will and untiring energy, he left to the German people one great institution, a powerfully organized Church, and one great idea, the tradition of Empire.

To defend his eastern frontiers from the onslaughts of the Slavs and the Avars, Charlemagne created a line of marches, studded with fortresses and governed by margraves with armed forces permanently at their disposal. It was from these marches that there began the steady eastward expansion which is one of the outstanding features of German medieval history. To enforce his authority in his unwieldy Empire, he built up an administrative system unknown since the days of the Roman Empire. The counts or local governors were kept in touch with the king's court by the *missi dominici*, royal officials who travelled regularly throughout the Empire and supervised the local administration. General assemblies of the great men of the land were summoned to advise the king, who enforced his will by means of edicts or capitularies binding upon all his subjects. But the strongest unifying force within the Empire was the Church. Paganism had given place to Christianity among the Franks when Clovis was baptized in 496, and as the boundaries of the Frankish kingdom were extended conversion followed upon conquest. It was not, however, till the time of the Carolingians that the Church in Germany was placed on a firm basis. All the Carolingian rulers maintained a close accord with the Papacy, and one of their first objects was to give the Church within their realm the benefit of complete union with Rome. St. Boniface, founder of the abbey of Fulda, and first Archbishop of Mainz, worked to this end in the time of Charles Martel, and did for the German Church what Theodore of Tarsus had done in England a century earlier. But his work was incomplete because the Saxons, outside the Frankish kingdom, remained also outside the influence of the Church. It was not until Charlemagne enforced Christianity upon these hardy pagans at the point of the sword that it reigned supreme in Germany. Charlemagne, however, was not content merely to extend the Church: he endowed it with lands, he fostered its influence and supported its authority in every way. Moreover, he exercised a dominant influence upon the appointment of bishops, whom he used as counsellors and administrators in secular affairs. As a result the German Church became a wealthy and powerfully organized corporation, a bulwark of the royal authority against the disintegrating influences which grew rapidly after the break-up of the Carolingian Empire.

The coronation of Charlemagne by the Pope, on Christmas Day, 800, as 'Emperor ever august of the Romans', is generally accepted as the culminating point of his reign. Its significance has, however, been much over-estimated. It made a great impression upon Christendom, but it added little to the substance of his power. It was as King of the Franks and Lombards that he exercised authority in Germany, France, and Italy; it was before he became Emperor that he did his great work of organization both in Church and State. If Einhard is to be believed, Charlemagne himself was displeased at the Pope's action, for he was shrewd enough to see that the papal conferment of the imperial dignity might easily lead to a papal claim to suzerainty in temporal as well as in spiritual affairs. If, then, the revival of the Empire was of no real benefit, why did it impress contemporary opinion so deeply, why did it exercise a fatal attraction over so many able rulers, why did its prestige last, even though diminished and distorted, until the opening of the nineteenth century? The answer is to be found in the tradition of Roman imperialism which had survived through the centuries of barbarism which had followed its overthrow. Men believed that if Roman unity, Roman law, and Roman order could be revived in the secular sphere and yoked with the divine ordering of the Holy Catholic Church in the spiritual, then peace would come to a distracted world. At first it seemed as if the ideal was to be realized, for Pope and Emperor worked together to maintain the order which Charlemagne, as Frankish king, had imposed on Christendom. But how insecure were the foundations of the structure, how much depended on the king's own personality was revealed after his death. The glamour of Rome remained, however, and the fascination of the great idea blinded men to the practical impossibility of realizing it. So it continued through medieval times to draw the finest spirits into renewed efforts to make it a reality, to their own ultimate undoing and to the detriment of the people with whose destiny it was to be associated. Conferred upon a Frankish ruler, the imperial dignity became the accompaniment of German kingship, and by the consequent entanglement of German with Italian affairs, it altered the whole course of Germany's political development.

The separation of the German stocks from the heterogeneous empire of Charlemagne took place in the century following his death in 814. Degeneration set in during the reign of his successor, Louis the Pious: when the latter divided his dominions among his sons, disintegration followed. By the treaties of Verdun and Mersen the lands between the Elbe and the Rhine, together with a good stretch of territory west of the Rhine, became the kingdom of Lewis the German. But though now separated from the West Franks, the German people did not attain unity. The sceptre slipped from the hands of Lewis's incompetent successors into those of the territorial lords. The ravages of the Northmen in the ninth century helped to increase the power of the local magnate: men turned from the king who could not protect them to the duke who would. At the opening of the tenth century, four great principalities had arisen in Germany – the stem duchies of Saxony, Swabia, Franconia, and Bavaria. At the death of Lewis the Child, the last of the East Frankish Carolingian kings, it seemed as if nascent Germany was to give place to a collection of independent states. This disaster was, however, averted by the election of Duke Conrad of Franconia as king in 911. With his election there comes to an end the long process by which the German people had emerged from the stage of tribal particularism, had been subjected to the formative influences of a great empire, and had dissociated themselves from it to follow their own destiny under their own ruler. Conquest and inclusion, separation and independence, each plays its part in bringing into being the Germany of the Middle Ages; until the last is attained, its full stature is not reached.

The two great tasks facing the German king were the assertion of his authority over the dukes and the defence of his eastern boundaries against the Wends and the Magyars. Conrad I failed in both; he left them as a legacy to his rival, Henry of Saxony. With the accession of Henry I in 918 begins the line of Saxon kings which in Otto I produced a ruler outstanding in German history. Henry was more successful than Conrad in defending his kingdom against invasion. He kept the Wends and Magyars at bay, subdued the Bohemians, and established the frontier march of Schleswig against the Danes. On the extinction of the West Frankish Carolingian monarchy, he added to his kingdom the duchy of Lotharingia, of outstanding importance on account of its agricultural wealth and general advance in civilization. On the other hand, he was unable to make much headway against the dukes; except in Saxony and Thuringia his authority was merely nominal, and internal consolidation was still the most urgent problem that faced his son Otto, when he became king in 936.

Not without reason did Otto I win the title of 'Great' from his contemporaries. His noble bearing, his gaiety and generosity made him
admired and beloved by his people; his energy and military skill, inherited
from his father, won him the respect of the nobles; and his shrewd
judgment enabled him to draw to his service the most capable men of his
time. Hermann Billung, the ablest of the margraves who ruled the line
of marches that he established beyond the Elbe, was his most trusted
friend and adviser. By a skilful policy of intermarriage, he gained the
duchies of Bavaria, Swabia, and Lotharingia for his brother, his son, and
his son-in-law, and by the appointment of royal officials, the Counts
Palatine, he sought still further to safeguard his authority in the duchies.
But neither family ties nor royal supervision prevented the dukes from
rebelling in their own interests, and Otto turned to find an ally in the
Church. Through his control over the appointment of bishops, he secured
the loyalty and co-operation of a body of men whose training made them
able administrators and whose dues and services as feudal landholders
were a source of wealth and military strength on which he could rely at
need. It was his close alliance with the bishops, who saw that their interests
lay in supporting monarchical unity rather than ducal disruption, that
enabled Otto to entrench his authority sufficiently in Germany to start
on his Italian policy.

The events which took Otto the Great into Italy were very similar to
those which had caused the intervention of Charlemagne. Since the
break-up of the Frankish Empire, Italy had become a prey to increasing
faction and disorder. In the north the nobles struggled among themselves
for the crown of Lombardy, the south was menaced by the Saracens,
already established in Sicily, while the Papacy, which through simony
and corruption had sunk to the lowest ebb, was the sport of factions
within Rome itself. It was partly zeal for the Church, partly the disorder
of northern Italy that caused Otto to cross the Alps in 951. By this
expedition he restored order in Lombardy, and established Berengar,
Marquis of Ivrea, as king on condition that he acknowledged German
overlordship. After an interval of eleven years, spent in quelling insur-
rection at home and crushing an invading Hungarian force at the battle
of the Lechfeld, he returned to Italy to receive the imperial crown from
the hands of the Pope as a reward for his protection against the unruly
Berengar. Thus for a second time the imperial dignity was revived, and
from 962 dates the 'Holy Roman Empire of the German Nation',
though it did not receive its full title till the twelfth century. But the
relationship between Pope and Emperor was very different on this
occasion. In 800 the Pope had claimed equality with the Emperor in the

rule of Christendom, now he had to swear fealty to his protector, who made it clear that he regarded the Empire as supreme over the Papacy. Such a position could not be maintained once the Papacy had emerged from the slough of corruption into which it had fallen, and the claim to supremacy instituted by Otto was at the root of the suicidal struggle between Empire and Papacy in the Middle Ages.

What were the motives that led Otto I to assume the imperial crown? The generally accepted view is that it was the irresistible attraction of the Carolingian ideal, a vision of a *pax Romana* combined with a *pax Christiana*. A recent German historian has controverted this view.[1] He points out that Saxons, Salians, and Staufens all carried on Otto's policy, and that they were most of them capable, some of them even brilliant rulers. For a policy to persist for nearly three hundred years there must have been more than a visionary ideal behind it. He sees the interference in Italy as prompted by practical considerations; the danger to Germany's growing trade if Italy were united under an unfriendly ruler, the additional wealth and power which an Italy restored to peace and prosperity could give to the German king, the value of controlling the Papacy in view of the close union between Church and Crown in Germany and northern Italy. There is truth in both views. Idealism and practical advantage, altruism and self-interest, it may well be, joined hands when Otto I accepted the imperial dignity for himself and his heirs, and laid upon the German people the burden of maintaining it. That it would lead to humiliation and disaster instead of a glorious world pre-eminence could hardly be foreseen.

Otto I died in 973; his son, Otto II, struggled fairly successfully during his short reign with the insubordinate German dukes and with the faction and disorder endemic in Rome and northern Italy. His plans for extending the imperial power in southern Italy were cut short by his death in 983 at the age of twenty-eight. His three-year-old son, Otto III, had already been elected German king, and so there began the first of the long minority rules which it was the fate of Germany to undergo at the most critical moments of her history. Quarrels within and invasion from without taxed to the full the powers of the council of regency that ruled in his name. At fifteen he was declared of age, but his assumption of responsibility brought no good to Germany. Son of a Greek princess, and trained by ecclesiastics, he was brilliant, gifted, and sincerely religious, but he was the least practical of all the Saxon house. He neglected Germany in order to co-operate with Pope Sylvester II in the establishment of a Christian Roman Empire. He preferred Italy to Germany; he sought

[1] J. Haller, *Epochs of German History*, 1930.

to restore order and dignity to Rome, which he planned to make his capital. The fickle Romans repaid his benefactions with rebellion; in Germany the work of consolidation which his grandfather had begun was rapidly being undermined when he died in 1002. He left behind him the memory of a personality of singular charm, a record of disappointed hopes and unfulfilled promise – and no heir.

After the reign of Henry of Bavaria, a man of action who did much to repair the ruin wrought by Otto, the throne passed to Conrad, Duke of Franconia, in 1024. But the change of dynasty did not involve any change of policy. The Salian kings had as high a conception of the royal and imperial office as had any of their predecessors. Both Conrad II and Henry III were crowned at Rome, and both of them succeeded in maintaining the royal authority in Germany in spite of repeated intrigue and rebellion. German overlordship was enforced on Hungary and Poland, and German territory was extended by the incorporation of the kingdom of Burgundy. The contest between Empire and Papacy is, however, the outstanding factor in the history of Germany in the eleventh century. It was already casting its ominous shadow in the reign of Henry III; it reached its climax in the reign of his luckless son. Henry III, who succeeded Conrad II in 1039, was a man of sincere piety, and it was as much to secure reform in the Church as to further his own political interests that he revived the Ottonian claim to depose an unworthy Pope, and appointed a German bishop to the papal chair in 1046. Clement II was the first of a line of German Popes, following one another steadily until it appeared almost a *sine qua non* that the vicegerent of God should be a nominee of the Roman Emperor. Henry's action rescued the Papacy from the degradation into which it had fallen. The German Popes led the movement for reform, and they were vigorously supported by the Cluniac monks[1] who, by the middle of the eleventh century, had attained widespread influence. But the very zeal with which the Emperor aided the movement proved the undoing of the imperial control over the Church. The more eager advocates of reform soon began a violent attack on the system of lay control, both as regards the investiture of bishops by the secular ruler and the imperial claim to control the papal election. The leader of the movement was the Cluniac monk Hildebrand, whose opportunity came with the Emperor's premature death in 1056. The minority of Henry IV allowed the Hildebrandine party to mature its plans for vindicating the independence of the Church. During the

[1] The Benedictine abbey of Clugny near Mâcon (founded 910) sent out colonies of monks to found new monasteries and spread the reform.

pontificate of Nicholas II, a Lateran Council passed a decree vesting the right of electing the Pope in the College of Cardinals, who were chiefly Italian priests, and restricting the imperial right to confirmation only. Moreover, guided by the statesmanship of Hildebrand, the Pope, already secure in the friendship of the Tuscan counts, gained the alliance of the Lombard towns in the north and of the Normans in the south of Italy. With a firm basis of temporal support the Papacy could press its claim to spiritual independence, and the issue was joined in 1073 when Hildebrand became Pope as Gregory VII.

The scales were weighted against the Emperor from the start. The handsome young ruler was no match for the little pale priest. Gregory was an experienced man of affairs. Henry had passed his boyhood under the tutelage of men whose main object was to keep the reins of government in their own hands. Gregory had behind him wealthy and loyal supporters, Henry a kingdom riddled with faction, where even the bishops were now divided in their allegiance. Finally Gregory had all the fiery enthusiasm of a fanatic, who conceived it to be his mission not only to purify the Church and free it from secular control, but to make it supreme in temporal as well as spiritual affairs. The Pope, as vicegerent of God, disposed of all earthly dominion, therefore kings and princes must be confirmed in their authority by him. Such a claim struck at the root of all secular sovereignty, and particularly at that of the Emperor. When, therefore, Gregory VII opened his campaign in 1076 by demanding the universal renunciation of the practice of lay investiture, Henry IV stood forward as the champion of the secular rulers. For him, moreover, the investiture question was a crucial one: it was through his appointment of the bishops that he controlled the German Church and maintained his influence in Italy. Without the support of the Church he could not hope to succeed in his efforts to control his great feudatories. Henry, therefore, ignored the papal fiat; and when taken to task by Gregory he summoned a synod of German bishops and declared him deposed. Gregory retorted by a counter-deposition and excommunication, and a bitter struggle ensued in which the German dukes saw their opportunity to advance their own interests against the king, while the German bishops, even if loyal at heart, dared not fight openly against their ecclesiastical suzerain. Deprived of support within his own kingdom, Henry had to submit. At Canossa the Pope gained a signal but short-lived triumph. The humiliation of the Emperor rallied the German nobility to his defence, and many of the bishops supported him, now he had put himself right with the Church. Henry reopened the struggle: in 1084, in spite of renewed deposition and excommunication and of renewed faction among the nobles, who set up a rival king, he captured Rome, and was crowned Emperor. Gregory fled southwards and died the following year. But if he had failed, Henry had not succeeded; the papal allies leagued with the princes of South Germany against him, and though, after the lapse of years, the coalition was broken up and the Emperor was able to return to Germany, he never recovered his power. In 1106 he died, one of the most tragic figures in German history. He was the victim of forces beyond his control which he was not small enough to ignore nor great enough to direct. He fought indomitably for the Empire, yet he left it hopelessly weakened. Well might he say with Gil Vicente's dying emperor:

> O blind and strange the ills that in thy narrow range
> Thou yieldest, bitter life and gloomy.

The investiture contest lingered on till 1122 when Henry V made a compromise which in form rendered unto Caesar the things that were Caesar's, but in reality seriously impaired the imperial power. By the Concordat of Worms it was agreed that in Germany the bishops were to be elected in the royal presence, investiture with the temporalities of the see and homage to the Emperor as temporal overlord were to follow, and then consecration. In Italy, on the other hand, there was to be free election, followed at once by consecration. Thus, while the Emperor could influence the choice of the German bishops and claim their allegiance as feudal landholders, he was rendered practically powerless as regards the Italian bishops, who, once consecrated to their spiritual office, could deny the right of a temporal ruler to claim their homage. In this inconclusive fashion ended a struggle spread over fifty years in which the prestige of the Crown was greatly diminished and Germany lost what little of unity and consolidation she possessed.

The death of Henry V in 1125 without an heir left the German throne at the mercy of the princes. It was one of Germany's misfortunes that never for any length of time had she an uninterrupted hereditary succession. As the Saxon house had died out, so did the Salian; and the old German right of election, which tended, when there was an hereditary successor, to become a formality, became an actuality. The new king was Lothar of Supplinburg; he also died without a male heir, and the crown passed to Conrad of Franconia, brother of Frederick, Duke of Swabia. His election in 1138 ushered in the rule of the Hohenstaufen, the most brilliant period in medieval history, and began the great feud between Welf and Waiblingen (Guelph and Ghibelline). The cause of the quarrel was the electors' rejection of Henry the Proud, Welf Duke of

Bavaria, who by his marriage with Gertrude, Lothar's heiress, had united Bavaria and Saxony and become the most powerful territorial lord in Germany. Not unnaturally he hoped to succeed his father-in-law as German king, but the electors saw in Conrad of Hohenstaufen a man more amenable to pressure. Conrad's election meant, however, an antagonism between the Bavarian-Saxon and the Franconian-Swabian houses which was to have a decisive effect on the fortunes of Germany and on the imperial power in Italy.

The reign of Conrad III gave little presage of the renewed greatness which the Hohenstaufen rule was to bring to Germany. It was a time 'of much sadness and the tumult of many wars', a constant struggle with the Welfs, broken only by a short period when Conrad was absent on the Second Crusade and Henry the Lion, successor of Henry the Proud, was crusading nearer home among the heathens of Pomerania. Conrad's preoccupation in Germany allowed Italy to slip from the imperial control. The middle of the twelfth century saw southern Italy and Sicily united under the Norman Roger II, who held his kingdom as a fief of the Papacy. In the north the communes were growing rapidly and becoming yet another menace to the imperial power, while the decline of the Papacy from the position achieved for it by Gregory VII had made it once more the prey of Roman factions and rival claimants. A strong emperor might have taken advantage of this to re-enforce the imperial suzerainty. Not so Conrad; he did not once appear in Italy, and when he died the effective power of the Emperor beyond the Alps had dwindled almost to nothingness.

'A magnificent magnanimous man.' Carlyle's estimate of Frederick Barbarossa has in it more of truth than many of his high-sounding phrases. The nephew of Conrad III (who passed over his own six-year-old son in his favour) and the son of Judith, sister of Henry the Proud, he reconciled the conflicting claims of Welf and Waiblingen, and men saw in him the harbinger of domestic peace in Germany. Dignified and attractive in appearance, combining charm of manner with strength of purpose and force of character, a proved warrior and an able administrator, he was marked out to put an end to the feuds that distracted Germany and to reassert the imperial power in Italy. Even though he did not achieve all that was expected of him in Italy, his work in Germany was so successful that he stands out as the greatest of all German kings, the embodiment of the German spirit and of all that was best in the German character.

Immediately on his accession in 1152 Frederick announced the purpose he had set before himself – to restore the glorious Roman Empire to its

old power and dignity. But his ardent imperialism did not lead him to
neglect Germany. He was a German prince; with far-reaching ambition
he united an intense devotion to his own land. Moreover, his political
acumen showed him that a restored Empire must be firmly rooted in
German peace and prosperity. In a bare recital of events, the Italian
expeditions of Barbarossa occupy a prominent position, but behind them
there is a record of steady work for Germany's welfare to which insufficient attention is often given. Frederick's first object was to restore order
in Germany. To put an end to the lawlessness of the nobility, which was
devastating Germany and bringing famine and misery in its train, he
promulgated a general land peace, intended to be permanent, which was
a marked advance on the local and temporary *Landfrieden*, hitherto the
only means of keeping private warfare in check. To signalize the reconciliation with the Welfs, he restored Bavaria, which since 1143 had
been in the hands of Henry, Margrave of Austria, to Henry the Lion,
who thus became the greatest prince in the land, rivalling the Emperor
in power. If, by his concessions, Frederick hoped to convert a determined
adversary into an enthusiastic supporter, he was disappointed. Henry
followed him in the first two Italian expeditions: then he retired to
Saxony and occupied himself with the administration of his duchies, the
development of trade in the Baltic, and the extension of his power by
conquest in the Slav lands to the east of Saxony. In spite of his intransi-
geance with regard to imperial affairs, the Emperor supported him at first
because the strong Saxon duchy secured the eastern frontiers and helped
to maintain peace in Germany. But Henry's pride, his severity, and his
almost royal power alienated the Saxon nobles, who conspired against
him, were subdued, and finally appealed to the Emperor. Summoned to
answer his accusers before the Diet, Henry refused to appear; then began
the struggle between the two men, embittered still further by Henry's
refusal to aid his suzerain in the Italian expedition of 1174, which finally
ended in the exile of the Welf and the break-up of his duchies. The might
of Henry stood Frederick in good stead in one respect; the nobles supported the Emperor in the struggle because they preferred his rule to the
domination of one of their own order. Frederick did not, however, rely
on their loyalty alone to maintain himself in Germany; he allied himself
with the Church, the ancient supporter of the monarchy, and with the
towns, already a growing political force. The weakness of the Papacy
enabled Frederick, when he became king, to resume the old control exercised by the Crown over the Church. He regained its influence in the
appointment of bishops, and he used men like Rainald of Dassel, Archbishop of Cologne, and Christian of Mainz, politicians first and churchmen

afterwards, to carry on his administration. His ecclesiastical policy is open to the charge of being too purely traditional and of taking insufficient account of changed conditions. But for his own time it was successful; the men he appointed administered their great dioceses successfully, and were the mainstay of the imperial authority in Germany against the feuds and private warfare that broke out again directly the Emperor departed for Italy. In respect of his economic policy, no such criticism can be offered. There is no better proof of Frederick's foresight and shrewd judgment than his steady encouragement of town life. The twelfth century was a great period of communal growth; in Germany, as elsewhere, old towns were gaining independence from feudal seigneurs and ecclesiastical overlords, and new towns were springing up on the trade routes and along the Baltic coast as commerce and industry increased. These towns sought privileges from the Emperor who, alive to their political as well as their economic importance, was always ready to consider their petitions. So there grew up in Germany the imperial free cities, protected by their stout walls from the welter of warfare around them, and a burgher class that was ultimately to outweigh both Church and nobility in strength and importance and to be the preponderating influence in German national life.

Frederick's Italian policy, though more spectacular, was less successful in its outcome than his German policy. At first it seemed as if his determination to restore the Empire would be easy of achievement. For the Pope, threatened from the south by the powerful kingdom of Sicily, opposed within Rome itself by the Senate and People – the medieval imitation of the ancient Roman Republic – and fearing the ambitious communes of the north, turned naturally to the Emperor for support. The first fruit of the alliance was the coronation of Frederick in Rome in 1155. But the open antagonism of the Romans and the veiled hostility of the Lombard cities, who saw that the vigorous Emperor would brook neither their quarrels among themselves nor their open assumption of independence, caused him to retire to Germany; and when he returned to Italy in 1158 the situation had entirely altered. Hadrian IV, the English Pope, had claimed to 'confer' the imperial crown as if it were a feudal benefice; Frederick had retorted by issuing a manifesto in which he claimed that he held the Empire from God alone, 'by the election of the princes'. It was the beginning of the papal-imperial controversy that was to contribute to the ruin of both powers in the fourteenth century; its immediate result was that the Pope began to look for allies in Italy rather than in Germany. Frederick was faced with the prospect of an Italy united under the leadership of the Papacy to resist his schemes for the resurrection of the Empire. He resolved to make his authority effective in north Italy, where Milan's oppression of her smaller neighbours gave him an excuse for interference. At the assembly of Roncaglia jurists from the University of Bologna drew up an exhaustive list of the royal privileges, and Frederick appointed *podestàs*, alien royal officers, in the towns to keep peace among the warring factions and to see that the imperial rights were maintained. Frederick's claims were met with sullen resistance, and the position was complicated by the schism in the Papacy at the death of Hadrian IV. Anti-imperialism found a leader in Alexander III, a man every whit as obstinate and sagacious as Frederick himself. Alexander gained the support of most of the other princes of Europe, and so the succession of anti-Popes put forward by the Emperor was practically of no account. The enmity of the Papacy hampered the Emperor in Italy; though he was able, after a hard struggle, to crush the towns, he maintained his hold on them with difficulty. In 1166 he determined to strike directly at Rome; he besieged and captured it, and Alexander fled to Sicilian territory. Then, as it appeared to his enemies, the judgment of God fell upon the Emperor; a pestilence ravaged the city, the imperial army was decimated, and Frederick had to withdraw to Germany. The Lombard cities, thus encouraged, raised their heads again. They formed the Lombard League, and Frederick, returning to Italy for the fifth time, was utterly defeated at Legnano in 1176. Realizing that he could no longer carry on the struggle, he came to terms with the cities, which, in return for the recognition of the imperial suzerainty, were granted the enjoyment of those regalian rights which had been withdrawn at Roncaglia, the right of fortification of their cities, and the right to maintain the League. It was a triumph for the cities; henceforward they, and neither Emperors, bishops, nor feudal lords, were to be the arbiters of northern Italy. At the same time Frederick saw the necessity of a reconciliation with the Pope. At Venice he met Alexander, prostrated himself, and was given the kiss of peace. Once more only he went to Italy; this time it was to witness the consummation of a diplomatic success which promised to counterbalance his military failure. At Milan, in 1186, his eldest son Henry was married to Constance, heiress of Roger of Sicily. With the kingdom of Sicily in their hands, the Emperors could dominate the Papacy from the south: its seaports and its connection with the east would open up new avenues of trade and new sources of wealth. It was a great conception; it was the last political achievement of the Emperor. The Third Crusade began in 1189; Frederick, a mirror of knightly chivalry, took the cross with all the enthusiasm of his younger contemporaries, but he was fated never to reach the Holy Land. The story of his death by drowning in 1190 is too well known to need repetition. His

people monrned him as *pater patriae*; an anonymous contemporary poet
sang of him:

> Tu foves et protegis magnos et minores,
> magnis et minoribus tue patent fores.
> Omnes ergo Cesari sumus debitores,
> qui pro nostra requie sustinet labores.

Later generations saw in him the embodiment of their national aspirations,
and the Kyffhäuser legend, transferred to him from his grandson little
more than a century ago, reflects the continued affection of the German
people for the noblest figure among their rulers.

Henry VI, his son, reigned only seven years. In that time he raised
himself to a pinnacle of greatness beyond that attained by any previous
German king. He was crowned Emperor at Rome. In Sicily, which had
fallen to the Empress Constance on the death of William the Good, he
crushed a revolt engineered by the national party and enforced his
authority as king. In Germany he had to face the disaffection of the
nobility, of which the centre was the Welf-Waiblingen feud. The Welfs
were now led by Henry of Brunswick, son of Henry the Lion, and the
danger to the Emperor lay in the possibility of joint action between the
German and Sicilian rebels and in the support which the Saxon duke
might receive from England, the old-time ally of the Welf house. Henry's
success in Sicily deprived the German party of assistance from that quarter,
while the capture of Richard Cœur de Lion in imperial territory on his
way back from the Crusade enabled Henry to extort from him an oath
of homage. Richard's capture served a further purpose in enhancing the
Emperor's European position: as feudal suzerain of the English king as
well as undisputed master of Germany and Italy and heir of the Caesars
he was the outstanding ruler of his time. Lacking all his father's nobler
qualities, cruel and relentless, he yet approached greatness through his
intellectual power and constructive genius. He planned to make the
Empire hereditary in his own house, to make Italy the centre of his rule,
and to extend his sovereignty over the Byzantine Empire. It was the
ambition of Otto III, envisaged by a far more capable man. How far
he would have achieved it is an interesting question. A hereditary
empire would have united the princes in determined opposition, while
the advent of Innocent III to the Papacy would have given him an opponent in whom even he might have met his match. His death in 1197,
at the early age of thirty-two, put an end to his dreams: for the Hohenstaufen line it spelt utter disaster. He left a baby son, Frederick, heir to
too much greatness. The rule of Germany and Sicily, together with the
imperial dignity, would have taxed the powers of the greatest statesman;

a child king was impotent against the forces marshalling themselves in opposition to his authority. Frederick II's life was a tragedy – he was the sport of fate and the victim of his predecessor's ambition.

Dissension with regard to the succession at once broke out in Germany. Frederick's election, procured by Henry in 1196, was set aside, but the princes quarrelled as to who should be his supplanter. The Waiblingen party put forward Philip of Swabia, Henry's brother; the Welfs chose Otto of Brunswick, son of Henry the Lion. A ten years' struggle ensued, brought to an end by the death of Philip and the general acceptance of Otto as German king, a triumph which was followed by his coronation as Emperor in 1209. Otto was a man of considerable capacity; having vindicated his title against the Hohenstaufen line, he assumed the mantle of Barbarossa and prepared to make good the imperial rights in Italy, which had suffered considerable diminution owing to the internecine warfare in Germany. This policy brought him into bitter conflict with Pope Innocent III, who had hitherto supported him because a Welf triumph in Germany meant the end of the alliance between the German and Sicilian crowns. Innocent was the outstanding figure of his age. A second Hildebrand in his ideals, he was possessed of far more political capacity than Gregory VII. Boldly he claimed universal sovereignty for the Church. 'God', he wrote, 'has instituted two high dignities: the Papacy, which reigns over the souls of men; and Monarchy, which reigns over their bodies. But the first is far above the second.' Italy was to be ruled from Rome, the apostolic and imperial city; Christendom was to be united under the leadership of an Italian spiritual-secular power. Innocent's schemes, involving as they did temporal as well as spiritual domination in Europe, required for their realization a complaisant Emperor: when, therefore, Otto revived the Hohenstaufen policy in Italy, Innocent became his most tenacious opponent. He directed all his restless energy and his diplomatic talent towards engineering an opposition party to Otto in Germany; this party put forward Frederick of Sicily as rival Emperor. Innocent viewed the renewed possibility of the union of German and Sicilian kingship with misgiving, but he counted on Frederick's youth, his own influence over his former ward, and the turbulence of the Sicilian nobles to render him less of an immediate danger than Otto. The next step was to gain allies. Innocent drew in France to his support, while Otto turned to John of England and the Saxon nobles. The battle of Bouvines sealed Otto's fate; in 1215 Frederick was crowned at Aachen. In return for his support Innocent exacted from Frederick a profession of humble obedience and territorial concessions which made the Papacy supreme in central Italy. But he did not live long to enjoy his triumph, and with his death in 1216 begins the struggle between Frederick II and the Papacy which resulted in the downfall of the Hohenstaufen line.

As a personality Frederick II is one of the most interesting of German rulers; as a king he must be counted among his country's worst enemies. Far more the son of his Sicilian-Norman mother than of his German father and educated in the semi-oriental atmosphere of southern Italy, his whole interests were centred in Italy. That he was a capable ruler his administration in Sicily shows; that he was an intriguer and a fighter his relations with the successors of Innocent III proclaim. On the other hand, he had little of the religious enthusiasm or the knightly spirit of the age: the Crusades gave him no inspiration, and the only one he undertook was in bold defiance of the Pope who had excommunicated him. He had little sympathy with Germany and the Germans; his love of luxury and spectacular display found no outlet; his subtle, sceptical mind evoked no response among the German people. Of the thirty-eight years of his reign he spent less than eight in Germany; his policy was to rule through the princes. He bought their support by concessions which gave them practically absolute authority in their own domains; in their interests he reversed the policy of his grandfather and restricted the liberties of the cities. He gained the support of the Church by a similar policy: the Golden Bull of Eger, which had surrendered the imperial control over the German Church, was supplemented by the *constitutio in favorem principum ecclesiasticorum*, which provided a legal foundation for their territorial sovereignty. It was to placate the Church also that Frederick sanctioned the violent persecution of heretics, so apparently at variance with the natural instincts of a man whose breadth and audacity of thought aroused the admiration or the abhorrence of his contemporaries. It is true that by his policy Frederick contrived to maintain himself in Germany; during his reign there was little open revolt, and it was only as part of the papal-imperial struggle, which was waged with renewed violence during the last ten years of his reign, that the anti-kings, Henry Raspe and William of Holland, were elected by the papalists. When, however, Frederick died in 1250, still pertinaciously carrying on the struggle against Pope Innocent IV and the rebellious Lombard cities, Germany was in a sorry plight. The authority of the king, re-established by Frederick Barbarossa, had reached its nadir: the authority of the territorial prince, henceforth the dominant feature of German political life, was firmly established. The dream of a reconstituted Holy Roman Empire was utterly dispelled. In the anarchy of Germany there could be no solid substructure for the edifice of imperialism.

Lastly, Frederick brought about the downfall of the Hohenstaufen line.

Conrad IV and his little son, Conradin, carried on the dynasty, but their authority in Germany was superseded by that of William of Holland. His death in 1256 was followed by the Great Interregnum, in which an English prince, Richard of Cornwall, and the Castilian king, Alfonso X, were rival Emperors and substantiated their claims by hardly setting foot in Germany. Anarchy and disorder reached such a pitch that it seemed as if the dissolution of the kingdom was imminent. To this the rule of the brilliant Hohenstaufens had reduced Germany. With remarkable gifts of character and political ability, they had yet failed to achieve their ambitions as signally as the Ottos and the Henrys. It is usual to see in this a proof that the Holy Roman Empire was an ideal impossible of fulfilment, and to blame the German kings for sacrificing their country's interests in order to follow a visionary project. Professor Haller denies the impossibility of maintaining permanently an Italian-German Empire; he puts the blame of failure on the princes, whose particularism caused them to fail the Emperor at crucial moments and to play into the hands of the Papacy. Whatever the cause, the failure of the Hohenstaufen emperors convinced nearly all the later rulers of Germany of the unwisdom of attempting to revive their policy, and thus there arose at the end of the century a new conception of Empire which gave a new trend to German history.

None the less, the Hohenstaufen period is universally accounted the greatest age in German medieval history. To explain this, we must turn from rulers and politics to the life and spirit of Germany itself. The princes were not universally turbulent and self-seeking; among them were many able men and wise administrators who, by the order and prosperity they created within their own borders, contributed to the welfare of Germany as a whole. In spite of Frederick II's reactionary policy, the towns on the whole maintained their privileges; there was a steady growth of the middle classes and a rapid expansion of trade and industry. The free cities of the south linked Germany with the Italian trading communities and so with the commerce of the East; in the north the cities of the rising Hanseatic League drew the trade of the Baltic more and more into German hands. This German domination of the Baltic was aided by the steady progress of German expansion eastward. The border marches which had been established by Saxon and Salian kings were consolidated in the hands of strong princes. The Babenberg line in Austria (made into a duchy by Frederick Barbarossa), Albert the Bear and his sons in Brandenburg, Henry the Lion in Mecklenburg and Pomerania, by sound administration, colonization, and conversion, furthered the interests of Church and State alike. At the beginning of the thirteenth century the Teutonic Order conquered Prussia and entered Livonia, creating thus a semi-ecclesiastical semi-secular state which spread German civilization and German material progress among the still barbarous northern Slavs. Prince and burgher alike contributed to the extension of German territory and the increase of German wealth and prosperity; though the Emperors were too occupied with imperial affairs to take an active part in the movement, they aided it by steady support and by a far-sighted encouragement of the progressive elements in economic and political life.

But it is in the realm of mind and spirit that the Hohenstaufen age is supreme. It is no mere coincidence that the great age of German medieval history is also the great period of German medieval literature. The vitalizing influence of the Crusades, the ideals of chivalry and knightly honour that were their spiritual gift to Europe were as potent in Germany as elsewhere; associated with the vigorous national life of the time they gained a singular depth and intensity. It is true there is little actual reflection of contemporary history in the poetry of the period (that was left for chroniclers like Otto of Freising and the writer of the rhymed *Kaiserchronik*), but in Wolfram's *Parzival* there is mirrored the perfect knight, in Gottfried's *Tristan* the passion of love beside which worldly honour and power, even faith and loyalty, weighed little. In the *Nibelungenlied*, with its strength, its barbarism, its imaginative grasp of the eternal tragedy of things, is to be seen another aspect of the many-sided genius of the age. And beside the epics there is the wealth of lyric poetry which is the glory of the thirteenth century. Walther von der Vogelweide, the greatest of the minnesingers, is the great exponent of the lyric of his day. Master of the courtly lyric as well as of the lyric of the simple life, the veritable folk-song, he is one of the few poets who also take cognizance of the political events of his time. In the poetry, epic and lyric alike, of the Hohenstaufen age are reflected those currents of thought and feeling, of aspiration and endeavour which contributed to the hold which it gained on men's imagination in after days. It was not only what men did, it was what they thought and felt and said that made the era of the Hohenstaufen greater than any that had preceded it, and immeasurably greater than that which was to follow it. It was not a golden age, but it was at least a time when men aspired to something beyond the mere business of living: it was because they personified these aspirations that the Hohenstaufen emperors hold their place securely in German history.

The election of Rudolf of Habsburg as German king in 1273 brought the Great Interregnum to an end. It also ushered in a new era. The high ideals, the great conceptions, the heroic figures of the earlier period disappear: the fourteenth and fifteenth centuries are a period of small personalities and limited ambitions. The imperial dignity survives, but its prestige in Europe diminishes steadily in the hands of men who, for the most part, made family aggrandisement the first object of their policy. In so far as they thought of the Empire, they thought of it as a German rather than a European power. Had they succeeded in erecting a new national Empire out of the ruins of the old cosmopolitan one, their achievement would have rendered the epoch a decisive one; their failure to do so, some through circumstances, others through their own self-seeking ambition, gives the imperial rule an aspect of futility all the more marked by contrast with the steady growth of national unity in France and England in the same period. But though there is little progress at the centre, the same cannot be said of Germany as a whole. Individual states flourished under the rule of princes who were now their effective sovereigns, and the towns continued their growth, leaguing themselves together for the extension of commerce and forming a third estate of growing importance in political life. German universities were founded, German architecture reached its height in the great churches and the dignified civic buildings of the fourteenth century. It is in movements such as these, rather than in the personality and achievements of the rulers, that the progress of Germany is to be looked for.

The election of Rudolf I was due to the comparative unimportance of the house of Habsburg;[1] the nobles hoped that he was neither strong enough nor rich enough to interfere with their schemes for their own advancement. But Rudolf had character and political acumen; he saw that to make his authority effective the Emperor must beat the princes at their own game. In a struggle with Ottokar II of Bohemia he wrested from him Austria and its dependent territories, which he added to the family possessions in Swabia and Alsace. With these resources at his command he proceeded to restore some measure of peace to Germany. Italy he left severely alone; 'the lion's cave', as he called it, where 'one sees traces of the steps of those who go thither, but never of those who return'. Rudolf died in 1291; after an interval of seven years, his work was continued by his son, Albert I, an even stronger, more ruthless man than his father. His schemes for the further enrichment of the Habsburg house were defeated by nationalist opposition in Bohemia and noble opposition in Thuringia and Meissen; his plans for making the Empire hereditary in his own house were cut short by his murder in 1308. The electors, determined not to permit a powerful hereditary Empire to be established, rejected his son, Frederick, and chose Henry, Count of Luxemburg, as German king. Thus comes to the fore another house of

[1] Habsburg is a little castle near Königsfelden in Switzerland.

secondary rank among the nobility, yet possessed of a prince, in the person of Charles IV, who, in astuteness, unscrupulousness, and political capacity, was the equal of the Habsburg dukes. A struggle between the two houses was bound to come.

The Emperor Henry VII, who combined intellectual power and visionary idealism with military skill, followed the policy of his predecessors in one respect: he obtained the election of his son, John, as King of Bohemia, seeking thus to buttress the territorial power of the Luxemburgs in western Germany with a royal authority in the east. In other ways he reversed it completely. He looked back to the glories of the Hohenstaufen and determined to revive the imperial claims in Italy. He heard the call of Dante who, in *De Monarchia*, voiced the growing opinion that in matters temporal the Emperor ruled by as divine a right as the Pope in the spiritual world, and descended into Italy, where he was crowned Holy Roman Emperor in 1312. But his political capacity was not equal to his idealism. The favour he showed to Ghibelline nobles roused the hostility of the communes, which had welcomed him at first, and Pope Clement V, in his 'Babylonish Captivity' at Avignon, fanned the flames of discontent. Only his death in 1313 prevented Henry's failure from being more apparent than it was. In Germany it meant another disputed election. Frederick of Austria and Lewis of Bavaria struggled for the crown; fear of the Habsburg power gave the victory to the latter. Lewis had possibilities as a king; he was popular on account of his courage and good temper, and had he possessed enough political insight to turn the growing national feeling in Germany to his own advantage, his fate might have been very different. But the cynical unscrupulousness with which he pursued the acquisition of wealth for his own house raised up enemies for him on all sides, and the interference of the Pope added to his difficulties. After his victory over Frederick at Mühldorf John XXII declared that he was merely king *de facto*, since no election was valid until it had received papal sanction. Such a claim, coming from a Pope well known to be a tool of the French king, roused the German nobility to the support of Lewis, and drew from the electors the indignant proclamation that 'since the Empire depends on God alone, he who is elected by the majority of votes can take the title of king and exercise all sovereign rights without need of the consent or confirmation of the Pope'. But Lewis threw away his advantage by his vacillating and self-seeking policy. A strong party grew up demanding his deposition; its influence secured the election of Charles of Luxemburg, who had long been working in subterranean fashion to obtain the imperial crown. At Rense, in 1346, five out of the seven electors gave him their votes, his father's death shortly

afterwards made him King of Bohemia, and his triumph in Germany was
secured by the death of Lewis in 1347.

The reputation of Charles IV has suffered in the hands of English
historians; with one or two notable exceptions they have accepted too
uncritically the verdict of German writers who have no love for him.
He is accused of neglecting the Empire in order to concentrate on the
interests of Bohemia and the aggrandisement of the house of Luxemburg.
Such a judgment puts Charles on a level with the princes who surrounded
him, whereas he towered far above them. That he laboured whole-
heartedly to restore the royal authority in Bohemia and to bring order
and prosperity to his native land is undoubted; it is equally true that
he lost no opportunity to increase the wealth and influence of his own
house. But these were also means to a greater end. He inherited something of his grandfather's idealism, limited, however, by the inexorable
logic of facts. He, too, dreamed of restoring the Empire, but it was to
be a German Empire, resting upon Bohemian power and an hereditary
Luxemburg succession. For such an edifice to stand, the foundations
must be firmly laid; Charles concentrated on the foundations, hoping
that his successors would raise the superstructure. Had they done so, he
would have been lauded as the statesman he was; because they failed him,
he has met with unmerited obloquy.

Charles's neglect of Italy was the natural corollary of his policy. Though
he was ceremoniously crowned Emperor at Rome, he formally abandoned
any claim to overlordship in the Papal States, and contented himself with
a nominal suzerainty in Lombardy. With the Papacy he cultivated
friendly relations, led thereto by his natural piety as well as his political
insight. The support of the Pope and of the German Church was of
incalculable value in his imperial schemes; he heaped favours upon the
latter and paid every mark of outward deference to the former. But, in
spite of the accusations made against him, he did not betray German
interests or surrender German independence. The derisive epithet of
Pfaffenkaiser is as little merited as the adverse judgment upon his aims and
ambitions.

In Germany Charles's first object was to extend the boundaries of
Bohemia as widely as possible. By diplomacy, by purchase, by marriage
alliances he added to the lands of the Bohemian crown Brandenburg,
Lower Lusatia, and a large slice of the Upper Palatinate, thus creating a
compact and wealthy state, buttressed on the east by alliances with Poland
and Hungary and linked to the Luxemburg lands in the west by a chain
of small territories, procured by similar means. From this position of
superiority he sought to impose some measure of order in Germany. His

policy was to accept the *status quo* and to render the Emperor's task easier by granting imperial recognition to powers exercised in practice but denied in theory. This is Bryce's 'legalization of anarchy'. The Golden Bull of 1356 dealt with the powers and precedence of the electors. Originally all the great nobles had a vote at the election of the king, but the breaking up of the great duchies and the creation of new principalities during the twelfth and thirteenth centuries had made the princes such an unwieldy body that in practice the electoral college had come to consist of seven great princes, the King of Bohemia, the Duke of Saxony, the Count Palatine, the Margrave of Brandenburg, and the Archbishops of Mainz, Cologne, and Treves. The manner in which the imperial election was to be conducted, the rights and duties of the individual electors, the lineal descent of the electoral dignity (a frequent cause of strife where sub-division of family estates was the usual practice), the powers of the electors within their own territories were all explicitly laid down. Charles showed his political good sense by not attempting to take from the princes privileges which were of far too long standing to be given up lightly; instead he sought to govern Germany through the princes, and by personal influence and the possession of two electoral votes, Bohemia and Brandenburg, to ensure the pre-eminence of the Emperor and the succession of the Luxemburg house. In the latter respect at least he triumphed; in 1376, two years before his death, he secured the election of his son, Wenceslaus, as German king. His last advice to him is an epitome of his own policy as well as a guiding maxim for his successor: 'Have the Pope, priests, and Germans as friends; thus wilt thou live and die in peace.'

The statesmanship of Charles IV was not confined within narrow bounds; it embraced economic and intellectual progress as well as political power. The German cities flourished in his reign, and the leagues, which had been in their infancy in the days of the Hohenstaufen, became powerful in the political as well as in the economic sphere. Many of them, like the Swabian League, were temporary, especially if their ends were predominantly political, for they incurred the enmity of Emperor and princes alike, and could not resist for long a combined attack. Others, whose ends were primarily economic, had a more enduring life. Most widespread was the Hanseatic League, at its zenith in the time of Charles IV. Its cities were scattered all over northern Germany; it had courts or self-governing factories in foreign cities; it monopolized the lucrative herring fishery. To further its economic interests it interfered in Scandinavian politics, and became for a time the arbiter of the Baltic.

In intellectual life also Charles's reign was a period of growth. The desire to vindicate the secular sovereignty against the claims of the Papacy gave an impetus to political theory, and Marsilius of Padua and William of Ockham had many supporters in Germany. Mysticism and humanism, the two forces which in the realm of mind and spirit prepared the way for the Reformation, both have their beginnings in the fourteenth century. Johannes Tauler and the disciples of Meister Eckhart preached the necessity of a personal relation between the soul and God; in the next century Geiler of Kaisersberg inveighed also against the ecclesiastical abuses of the time. The beginnings of German humanism date from the foundation of Prague University by Charles IV, followed within half a century by those of Vienna, Erfurt, Heidelberg, and Cologne. With the thought of the mystics Charles had little sympathy; he was too unaffectedly pious along orthodox lines for it to gain any hold on him; on the other hand, the humanistic movement in Germany owed a great deal to his Italian sympathies, his patronage of learning, and his own considerable intellectual attainments.

The year 1378 saw the beginning of the Great Schism which brought the Papacy into complete disrepute and led to the era of the Church Councils. In Germany it saw the rule of a statesman replaced by that of a youth who, with considerable natural gifts, had also a fundamental weakness of character which eventually brought about his ruin. Wenceslaus started his reign well, but growing steadily more indolent, dissipated, and self-indulgent, he let the imperial power go completely to pieces. In 1400 the electors deposed him and put Rupert of the Palatinate in his place. The struggle to maintain his authority proved too much for Rupert; after his death in 1410 the electors reverted to the house of Luxemburg and chose Sigismund, the younger son of Charles IV. Wenceslaus retired to Bohemia, and Sigismund, already King of Hungary through his marriage with Mary, heiress of Lewis the Great, essayed the task of governing the Empire. Fussy and conceited, with lofty ideals of universal peace, but too impatient to carry through any concerted plan, he proved little better than his brother. For him Germany was too small a stage, nothing less than Christendom contented him. He presided at the Council of Constance (1414-18), where, though he succeeded in putting an end to the Great Schism, he covered himself with ignominy by allowing John Huss[1] to be burned as a heretic after he had granted him an imperial safe-conduct. It was when he was attending the Council of Constance that Sigismund, in April 1415, to provide himself with money to pay his debts, invested Count Friedrich VI of Hohenzollern, Burgrave of Nuremberg, with the Electorate (Kurfürstentum) of Brandenburg, which

[1] Johann Hus (1369-1415), a Bohemian Czech, was rector of the University of Prague; he had come under the influence of John Wyclif.

had devolved on him by inheritance. The Hohenzollerns had been powerful as Swabian princelings; henceforth their dynasty developed as rulers (Kurfürsten) of the March of Brandenburg, until in 1701 this became the kingdom of Prussia (p. 69). He interfered in Spanish affairs; he roused French indignation by his overbearing conduct in Paris; he paid a six months' visit to England. As King of Hungary he had to defend the line of the Danube against the Turks; as King of Bohemia, after the death of Wenceslaus, he was involved in a bitter struggle with the Hussites. Finally he considered it essential that the 'lord of all the world' should be crowned at Rome. He accomplished his ambition. Indeed as a show figure Sigismund was successful, but as German king he failed as signally as Wenceslaus. During the rule of the two brothers Germany went steadily downhill. Private warfare remained unchecked; the knights pillaged the land; except where a strong prince enforced law and order, life and property were insecure. In the north the Hanseatic League, weakened by its political activity and by the disappearance of the herring shoals from the Baltic, was losing ground to the Dutch. Most significant of all, the Empire was losing territory. The Teutonic Knights, who had ruled Prussia with signal success in the fourteenth century, lost the day to the Poles at Tannenberg, and then set in the decline which was ultimately to make Prussia the vassal state of Poland. In Germany itself the successful struggle of the Swiss peasant communes against the Habsburgs brought about the virtual independence of the Confederate Cantons. On the west the rising Burgundian state was enriching itself with German as well as with French territory. In Italy the imperial power was dead, for the Visconti in Milan now dominated the Lombardy plain. To such a pass had the sons of Charles IV brought the Empire. The glory had indeed departed from the house of Luxemburg: with the death of Sigismund without a male heir the sceptre departed also, to go to its most pertinacious rival, the house of Habsburg.

Albert II survived his election less than two years; he was succeeded in 1440 by his cousin Frederick, whose main claim to attention is the length of his reign. Fifty-three years enabled him to consolidate the Habsburg territories and establish the imperial office firmly in Habsburg hands. On the European stage he played no part; to German interests he was frankly indifferent. It has been said of him that he was always thinking and could never make up his mind. His inactivity was often, however, definite policy: easy-going by nature, doing nothing was the best way out of a difficulty. The wily Aeneas Sylvius[1] easily persuaded him to give

[1] The Italian humanist Enea Silvio de' Piccolomini, afterwards Pope Pius II. His

up his lukewarm support of the Council of Basel; his desertion was rewarded by the imperial coronation, but it was the death-blow to the conciliar movement and to all hopes of reform within the Church. In Germany he pursued a narrowly territorial policy; to secure the interests of the Habsburg house was his only care. He allowed Charles the Bold to increase the Burgundian state by further additions of German territory; it mattered little to him since the marriage of his son, Maximilian, to Charles's heiress, Mary (1477), would secure the devolution of Burgundy to the Habsburgs. In the east the union of Bohemia and Hungary under Ladislas of Poland menaced German interests; Frederick was satisfied when he had negotiated a treaty whereby the Habsburgs were to become the heirs of Ladislas when the male line of his house failed. So Germany suffered but the Habsburgs throve. The Burgundian marriage in 1477 brought them such an increase of power that they were lifted far above Wittelsbachs, Wettins,[1] and Hohenzollerns. The imperial dignity was henceforth unquestionably the prerogative of the Habsburgs: the remaining princes concentrated on increasing their own territories and making the seat of the Emperor as uncomfortable as possible. Albert of Hohenzollern, Margrave of Brandenburg, is a typical figure, endlessly active in pursuit of his own advantage and using his not inconsiderable talents to further petty ends. Emperor and princes alike thought only of themselves; for German unity nobody cared. Meanwhile the modern world, with its new learning, its new geography, its new nation-states, was coming into being. 'Le nouveau Messie est le roi.' It was Germany's tragedy that she had no new Messiah to save her from herself.

Maximilian I (1493-1519) stands on the border-line between medieval and modern times; in him can be traced the characteristics of both. Chivalrous and brave, skilled in arms and devoted to sport, he has been called the last of the knights. Yet he had all the cosmopolitanism, the versatility and the eager joy in life that characterized the Renaissance. Maximilian was a munificent patron of learning and the arts; his example was followed by many of the German princes and by the wealthy burghers of towns like Augsburg and Nuremberg. Yet, except on the side of

experiences on diplomatic missions and as private secretary at the court of the Emperor Frederick III provided him with the matter of his important historical works. His memoirs written as Pope reach to 1458. He lived a loose life in his early years and wrote a novel, *Lucretia and Euryalus*.

[1] The Electors of Saxony. On the extinction of the Ascanian line the Emperor Sigismund invested Frederick the Quarrelsome (Friedrich der Streitbare), Margrave of Meissen and Landgrave of Thuringia, of the House of Wettin, with the Electorate of Saxony. The history of the Wettins is complicated; they split into two main branches, the Ernestine and the Albertine, from the name of the two brothers, Ernest and Albert, who divided the territories between them.

humanism, Germany was remarkably little affected by the Renaissance. Though she had great artists like Holbein and Dürer, sculptors like Adam Krafft and Peter Vischer, and wood-carvers of outstanding eminence like Tilman Riemenschneider, she had not the widespread love of beauty and the wealth of creative genius that marked Italy. The literature of the time was classical neither in form nor spirit; it had its roots in the *bürgerlich* literature of the fourteenth and fifteenth centuries. The poetry and the *Fastnachtsspiele* of Hans Sachs are German to the core; the natural humour of *Reynke de Vos* and the biting satire of *Das Narrenschyff* are far removed from the polished suavity of the classical tradition. Even humanism was confined to a comparatively small class, centred in the universities. Wimpheling and Pirckheimer, Crotus Rubianus, Reuchlin and Melanchthon were scholars of outstanding achievement, but they were men of the study rather than of the world. Ulrich von Hutten is an exception: his best writings are in Latin, but he also wrote German verse in a style reminiscent of the *Volkslied*. In the practical art of printing Germany contributed to the spread of knowledge and the freedom of thought; she herself had as great a share of that freedom as any people in Europe. But it ran virtually in one channel, that of religion. Because Germany was the home of the Reformation, she had little share in the wider movement of the Renaissance; her quest for freedom was deeply earnest, full of the sense of the spiritual issues involved; there was in it little of Renaissance catholicity, tolerance, and instinctive response to beauty in all its aspects.

To the question of German government, Maximilian was not as completely indifferent as his father. He co-operated with a reforming party among the princes in a scheme for an Imperial Chamber, which was to be both a court of justice and a means of raising an imperial revenue through a general system of taxation. As, however, his main motive in assenting to the scheme was his need of money, he lost interest in it when the revenue side broke down, and devoted his administrative abilities to carrying through reforms in Austria. But the greater part of his energy was expended on European politics, where his real interests lay. A pressing problem was that of the Turks, who were sweeping over the Hungarian plains and threatening the frontiers of the Empire; in Austrian, even if not in German interests, they must be kept at bay. In the west the Burgundian inheritance of the Habsburgs involved the Emperor in hostility to France and began the quarrel concerning frontiers which has ever since been the crucial question in Franco-German relations. Hostility to France involved war in Italy, for in 1494 the French king crossed the Alps and began the struggle with Spain for the hegemony of Italy which the folly of her own princes had invited. Maximilian embarked upon a

c

series of Italian expeditions, in which he allied sometimes with one party, sometimes with another, his guiding motive being to prevent the French becoming masters of Italy. For once entrenched there, they could threaten his Austrian possessions as well as the Flemish and Burgundian lands. But want of money, together with the unwillingness of the princes to fight in a quarrel provoked by Austrian interests, brought all Maximilian's schemes to nought: in spite of his restless intriguing, the French became masters of north Italy and the Spaniards gained possession of Naples and Sicily. It appeared as if the Habsburg influence in Italy was entirely lost: it was not through military activity, but by a marriage alliance and the chances of death that it was regained and ultimately became dominant.

Maximilian was as active as his father in furthering family interests by dynastic schemes. To strengthen the Habsburg claim to Hungary and Bohemia he married his daughter, Mary, to Lewis, the heir to the throne, and his son Ferdinand to Ladislas's daughter, Anna. His foresight was rewarded; when in 1526 Lewis was killed at Mohacz, Hungary and Bohemia fell to Ferdinand. Of even greater significance was the marriage he arranged between his son, Philip, Duke of Burgundy, and Juana, the eldest daughter of Ferdinand and Isabella of Spain. Their son was Charles, who inherited his father's duchy in 1506, his maternal grandfather's kingdom in 1516, and the Habsburg lands in Germany on the death of Maximilian in 1519. In the imperial election he was victorious over his rival, the French king. Thus in extent of territory as well as in dignity Charles of Habsburg was the first prince in Europe. Austria, Styria, Carinthia, and Carniola formed a solid block in south-eastern Germany, and the scattered possessions on the upper Rhine formed a bridge to Franche-Comté and the Netherlands. With the Spanish kingdom he inherited the South American possessions, those legendary lands of gold on the fringe of which Columbus had stumbled in his search for a western route to Cathay. Belonging to Spain also were the Italian possessions, Naples, Sicily, and Sardinia. Well might the other European rulers look askance at an Emperor who had a foothold in almost every corner of Europe and a potential source of revenue such as none of them could boast. But Charles's position was not as unassailable as it appeared. His possessions were scattered, and communication was difficult. His subjects were so heterogeneous that the problem of getting them to work together defied all solution. Each country had its own internal difficulties, demanding constant attention. Moreover, Charles inherited his grandfather's European commitments, the defence of Europe against the Turks, rendered doubly onerous since he had now to guard the shores of the

Mediterranean as well as the Empire from their attacks, and the struggle with France, both in Italy and on the western frontier of the Empire. It is small wonder that Charles, though a man of considerable political ability, conscientious and industrious, failed in his task, and after an unequal struggle of thirty-six years divided his unwieldy dominions between his son and his brother in 1555, and retired to a monastery.

Two factors combined to determine the course of German history in the reign of Charles V: the Habsburg-Valois conflict, which was waged with but little respite during the whole of his reign, and the Reformation. The former belongs rather to Franco-Spanish than to German history, but its reaction on the course of events in Germany was so great that it cannot be entirely neglected. Its most fatal effect was that it distracted the Emperor's attention from German affairs at a critical period and allowed the Reformation movement to grow virtually unchecked. It provided the princes with an opportunity for continuing their policy of opposition to any centralization of government and strengthened their hands by giving them a foreign ally. It rendered German support in men and money so indispensable that the Emperor was forced to temporize when he should have acted, and it prevented him from tackling the social evils that were eating like a canker into the body of the land and showing themselves in peasant risings and knights' wars. Had Charles V been able to live at peace with his powerful neighbour, Germany might have been saved from religious as well as political disruption. *Une loi, un roi, une foi*, the maxim of the sixteenth century nation-states, had no meaning for Germany as a whole. Instead there were many kings and two opposed faiths, and German national unity was farther off than ever.

Though social discontent, political intrigue and intellectual ferment all played their part in the Reformation movement, its dominant impulse was religious. Ignorance and immorality, pluralism, simony, and preoccupation with worldly ends were widespread, both among the higher and the lower clergy, while the exactions of the Papacy drained the land of money and ranked the Church with the feudal aristocracy in popular opinion as the oppressor of the poor. The literature of the period witnesses to the widespread contempt for the Church; Erasmus in *Encomium Moriae* was the most brilliant but by no means the only satirist of the clergy, regular and secular alike. The state of Rome and the papal court under Popes like the Borgias and the Medici, worldly, loose-living, and openly irreligious, provoked the condemnation of all honest men. Martin Luther's visit to Rome in 1511 brought the two streams of criticism together; not only the abuses in Germany, but also the authority of the Pope and the principles of the Church were called in question. The sale of indulgences

which provoked Luther's ninety-five theses was the match which set fire
to the mass of inflammable material in Germany; his controversy with
Eck and his burning of the papal bull of excommunication made him the
great protagonist of the movement for reform, just as Charles V, a sincere
Catholic, became inevitably, through the imperial election, the champion
of the Church.

The condemnation of Luther at the Diet of Worms was inevitable;
Charles, though anxious to reform abuses, was rigidly orthodox, and the
tactics of Eck had pushed Luther into the expression of opinions which
were undoubtedly heretical. The Edict of Worms, which decreed the
suppression of Lutheran teaching, was practically the beginning of the
Protestant movement. Luther's *Appeal to the Christian Nobility of the
German Nation* had already rallied to his cause those of the princes who
sincerely believed in its justice; his fervent defence of his beliefs at Worms
gained him the support of the mass of the people, who saw in his teaching
regarding the paramount authority of the Bible hope for a social as well
as a religious reform. Luther's strong condemnation of the Peasants'
Revolt of 1525 dispelled this illusion; the peasantry slipped back into the
lethargy of despair, and Lutheranism became more and more an urban
and a princely movement. Its original religious purity became sullied with
worldly motives, until finally Protestantism came to mean not only a
religious faith but also a political movement.

The history of the thirty-five years between the Diet of Worms and
the Peace of Augsburg is full of cross currents, but the growth of the
Protestant faith was steady. While Luther in the Wartburg began his
translation of the Bible, the greatest monument of German literature in
the sixteenth century, his followers spread his teaching far and wide.
Charles's attempt to enforce the Edict of Worms, then practically in
abeyance, provoked the Protest of 1529, signed by a large number of
princes and towns; this was followed by the Confession of Augsburg, a
vigorous exposition of the leading tenets of the reformers. Charles's
external difficulties, together with the obstinate refusal of the Pope to
call a General Council to set on foot a reform of the Church on Catholic
lines, forced him to temporize; in 1540 he returned to the charge and
sought in the Conference of Regensburg to reach a settlement by agreement. In spite of goodwill and moderation on both sides, the conference
broke down. On essential points of doctrine Catholics and Protestants
were now irretrievably divided. Its failure determined Charles to resort
to warfare, a decision in which religious conviction was supported by
political necessity, since the growth of the Schmalkaldic League of the
princes, formed in 1531, was becoming a menace to the imperial authority.

Charles, at first successful, was able to force on Germany the *Interim* of 1548, 'a masterpiece of ambiguity', inconsistent in doctrine and indefinite in practice. Hostilities broke out again four years later; through the aid of Henry II of France and the adhesion of the powerful Maurice of Saxony, the Leaguers were victorious, and Charles was forced to assent to the Peace of Augsburg (1555). The root principle of the peace was that each prince should settle the religion of his own state. The 'seamless robe of Christ' was admittedly rent in Germany: the unity of Christendom slipped into the limbo of a past from which men were divided not so much by time as by a radical difference of outlook. As in England and Sweden, the secular sovereign became the arbiter of men's souls as well as of their bodies, and a State Church was established to support the authority of the ruler. It was a political triumph for the princes, even more than a religious revolution, for it was not individual freedom of belief that was permitted. The battle for toleration had yet to be fought out.

The years between the Peace of Augsburg and the Thirty Years' War saw the gathering of forces for a fresh struggle. In 1555 Pope Paul IV initiated a vigorous policy of Catholic reform, and his successors continued his work. The papal court was purged of its worst evils. The Tridentine Decrees, the outcome of the third and most successful session of the Council of Trent, vindicated the papal authority and restated in clear and unambiguous terms the Catholic doctrine. The machinery of Church government was thoroughly reorganized. The Counter Reformation took the field against heresy; its forces were the Society of Jesus, the reformed monastic orders, and the great saints and mystics; its weapons were the Inquisition and the Index. From the first the centre of its activity was Germany, where circumstances made rapid success most likely. The imperial authority could be counted on to support the Catholic cause. Ferdinand I, Charles V's successor in the Habsburg lands and the Empire, pursued a moderate policy, both from conviction and necessity; but his successors, Maximilian II, Rudolf II and Matthias, were Catholic zealots who worked steadily and with increasing fervour to eradicate Protestantism in their ancestral lands, and who threw all their influence on the side of Catholicism in the Empire. Protestantism, moreover, was suffering from the lassitude which follows the successful emergence from a great struggle. It was rent with faction within itself. Even in the time of its struggle, this had been a source of weakness. Extremists of the Protestant movement, like the Anabaptists at Münster, had brought it into disrepute and associated it with lawlessness and defiance of authority; Calvinism, spreading rapidly from Switzerland, had attracted many from the Lutheran ranks by the greater clarity of its doctrine and the greater cohesion of its organization. Now, when the struggle was over, Protestantism was divided within itself. Calvinist States lay mingled with Lutheran principalities, and their rulers occupied themselves with making leagues to extend their own particular shade of thought rather than in uniting against the common foe. Finally, the Peace of Augsburg contained within itself the seeds of fresh warfare. The term Protestantism was considered to include only those who had signed the Confession of Augsburg; toleration for adherents of the Lutheran faith in Catholic lands was refused; and no satisfactory settlement was made of the crucial question of the secularized territories, the lands of the bishoprics which had been converted to Protestantism.

In all these circumstances Protestantism was bound to suffer when a vigorous attack was launched upon it. Between 1555 and 1618 there was widespread reversion to Catholicism, especially in the ecclesiastical territories; it was the fear that the forces of the Church would soon be everywhere triumphant that at last drew the Protestant princes together in some sort of unity. With Protestantism once more in fighting mood, war in Germany was inevitable. Progress towards an internal struggle was eagerly watched by France, which, under the leadership of Henry IV, was rapidly regaining her internal prosperity and beginning to envisage a European hegemony. The power of the Habsburgs in Spain and Austria was an obstacle to this; the weakening of the imperial power by an internecine struggle in Germany was to France's advantage. Sweden, too, would profit by German weakness in her plans for the domination of the Baltic. The actual cause of the outbreak of the Thirty Years' War, the Bohemian succession, was but a minor matter; the effective causes must be looked for in the Counter Reformation, the determination of the princes to render impotent the imperial power in Germany, and the ambitions of European rulers.

BIBLIOGRAPHY TO CHAPTER II

The bibliographical material for such a long period is too extensive for any ade quate bibliography to be given. The following list is only intended to suggest some German authorities which cover the whole period, and a few outstanding English works.

Deutsche Geschichte im Überblick, ed. Peter Rassow. Stuttgart, 1952–53

Haller, Johannes. *Epochs of German History*. London, 1930

Monumenta Germaniae historica, ed. Pertz. 1826

   (The standard collection of chronicles, laws, letters, and miscellaneous documents between 500 and 1500 A.D. Includes such writings as Einhard's *Vita Karoli Magni*, and Otto of Freising's *Gesta* [*Frederici imperatoris*].)

Prutz, H. *Staatengeschichte des Abendlandes von Karl dem Grossen bis Maximilian*
    1885-87

Giesebrecht, W. von. *Geschichte der deutschen Kaiserzeit.* 1855-95

Hampe, K. *Deutsche Kaisergeschichte in der Zeit der Salier und Staufer*

Jastrow, J., u. Winter, G. *Deutsche Geschichte im Zeitalter der Hohenstaufen.* 1893-1901

Haller, J. *Das altdeutsche Kaisertum,* 1926

Lindner, T. *Deutsche Geschichte unter den Hapsburgern und Luxemburgern.* 1888-93

Ranke, L. von. *Deutsche Geschichte im Zeitalter der Reformation.* 1881

Ranke, L. von. *Vom Religionsfrieden bis zum dreissigjährigen Kriege.* 1888

Janssen, J. *Geschichte des deutschen Volkes seit dem Ausgang des Mittelalters.* 1913
    [Trans.: M. A. Mitchell and A. M. Christie]

Bryce, J. *The Holy Roman Empire.* 1904

Fisher, H. A. L. *The Mediæval Empire.* 1898

Boehmer, Heinrich. *Luther and the Reformation in the Light of Modern Research.*
    London. 1930

Mackinnon, J. *Luther and the Reformation.* 1928

Cambridge Mediæval History. 1911-34

Cambridge Modern History. 1902-11

CHAPTER III

GERMAN HISTORY FROM 1618 TO 1900

I. THE THIRTY YEARS' WAR

FAR from healing the divisions which the Reformation had caused in Germany, the Peace of Augsburg (1555) did little more than register an armistice between the contending factions. A compromise had been accepted upon the religious issue, but like most half-measures it did not prove final, and long before the century had ended it broke down. Under the weak Emperor Rudolf II (1576-1612), who had been brought up under Spanish and Jesuit influences, the Counter Reformation began, and therewith the struggle between the confessions and their defenders among the rulers was resumed. In 1608 the Protestant princes, under the leadership of the Elector Palatine, Frederick IV, concluded an alliance known as the Union, while the Catholic princes promptly responded with the League, at the head of which was Duke Maximilian of Bavaria. As before, the main strength of the reformed faith lay in the north and centre of the country, while Bavaria was the seat of the reaction. The temper which inspired this fresh attempt to undo the Reformation was well shown by the saying of one of its bitterest enemies, Archduke Ferdinand of Styria, who later became Emperor, that he would rather rule over a desert than over a land of heretics. No sooner did this prince come to the ducal throne than he annulled the religious liberty of his Protestant subjects, expelled their clergy and teachers, and gave to nobles and commonalty alike the choice between returning to the forsaken faith or accepting it under compulsion.

The still harsher action of this ruler in Bohemia, of which he became king in 1617, mainly furnished the occasion, if not the cause, of the Thirty Years' War. More truly it was a sequence of four wars, fought for the most part in different fields – the Bohemian and Palatinate war (1618-23), the Lower Saxon and Danish war (1624-29), the Swedish war (1630-35), and the Franco-Swedish war (1635-48). As the result of a collision between the two confessions in Prague the Protestants, who formed the majority of the population both there and in the rural districts, set up a government of their own; and when, on the death of the Emperor Matthias,

Ferdinand II (1619-37) succeeded him, they chose the young Elector Palatine, Frederick V, the son-in-law of James I of England, as a rival king.
Reinforced by the troops of Duke Maximilian and of the League, a strong
imperial army descended into Bohemia and soon restored order, whereupon the fanatical Emperor visited terrible vengeance upon the insurgents.
Twenty-seven of their most prominent leaders were summarily beheaded
in the market-place of Prague; thousands of families were exiled and
dispossessed of their houses and chattels; the Protestant churches and
schools were appropriated by Catholic priests and Jesuit teachers; and to
outward appearance the reformed faith seemed to be stamped out in the
kingdom.

How little some of the Protestant princes of Germany were concerned
for the religious aspect of the Reformation was illustrated by the apathy
with which they stood by when the reduction of Bohemia was followed
by the harrying of the Palatinate by Spanish troops under Tilly.[1] It was
only when the Emperor outlawed the ruler of that territory and proposed
to install the Bavarian duke in his place, so increasing the number of the
Catholic Electors at the expense of the Protestant, that these half-hearted
defenders of the Evangelical cause began to be alarmed. Of the two
German princes who should have taken the lead in resisting the challenge
to their faith and their independence, John George of electoral Saxony
went over to the Emperor, while George William, Elector of Brandenburg, lay low and said nothing. Maximilian duly received at the Emperor's hand the Upper Palatinate together with the Elector's hat.

In the long struggle so begun Austria and Spain, with Bavaria as a
useful auxiliary, stood for the Emperor and Catholicism, while at one
time or another, singly or in combinations, Denmark, Sweden, Holland,
France, and England espoused the cause of the Protestant princes and
peoples, though with less unity and elevation of motive. For the confessional questions over which contention first raged were soon overshadowed by those of purely political moment, and eventually the war
developed into a general European *mêlée*, with territorial rewards for the
successful contestants. King Christian of Denmark, Duke of Holstein,
entered the struggle at an early stage, bent on acquiring Bremen and
other North German districts. France, who subsidized all the Emperor's
enemies in turn and attacked his armies in Spain, was primarily concerned for the downfall of a southern neighbour not less ambitious than
herself, but she likewise sought territorial enrichment at Germany's
expense. Gustavus Adolphus of Sweden, who in 1630 landed in Pomerania

---

[1] Johann Tserklaes Count of Tilly, a general from the Netherlands, who was
given command of the army of the League at the outbreak of the war.

with an army of 15,000 men, mostly Swedes, Germans, and Scots, looked also for compensation in kind. He fell at the battle of Lützen two years later, but his country continued in the war till the end. The King of England sent money but few men, yet gave important naval assistance to the Protestant cause at different times.

The war lasted until 1648, and was concluded by the Peace of Westphalia (27th October), which partitioned a large part of Germany. Sweden, renouncing her original claim to Silesia and Mecklenburg, wanted the whole of the Duchy of Pomerania, which had suffered terribly from Wallenstein's soldiers. That territory, however, adjoined Brandenburg, and contained seaports important for the future development of the Electorate, whose ruler, the strong-willed Frederick William, known as the Great Elector (1640-88), also advanced hereditary claims. Accordingly the Swedish share was reduced to West Pomerania (*Vorpommern*) as far as the Oder, with Stettin, Stralsund, and the island of Rügen, and also Wismar in Mecklenburg-Schwerin, while Brandenburg obtained the eastern half of the duchy, and towns which gave Frederick William a footing in Westphalia and Saxony. It was part of the arrangement as to Pomerania that the duchy should remain in the Empire, and in consequence Sweden was henceforth represented in the Diet.

France was still less easy to satisfy. During the war she had occupied German Alsace as the friendly act of an ally, but when the fighting was over Louis XIV, who was now on the throne, refused to withdraw. Eventually his claim to the whole of the territory was reduced to portions of Upper and Lower Alsace and the administration of the 'ten cities', which he hoped to annex at a more convenient season. Strasburg and the properties of the episcopal Sees and the religious houses remained to the Empire. France further attained formal title to Metz, Toul, and Verdun, which she had occupied irregularly for over a century. At last she had reached the upper Rhine, and the cherished ambition of many of her rulers and statesmen had to that extent been realized. Bavaria, which at a late stage of the war was twice ravaged by French troops under Turenne, kept the Upper Palatinate, while the Rhenish Palatinate went back to the family of the dispossessed ruler. The treaty also made the Netherlands and Switzerland legally independent of the Empire, as they were already in fact. So far as the warring confessions were concerned the treaty practically confirmed the Augsburg pact, with its stipulation of equal religious liberties and rights for both parties, whether rulers or subjects, the Calvinists, hitherto ostracized, being now recognized as belonging to the Protestant fold.

The war and the peace left the Empire more than ever weakened, while the Emperor became increasingly a shadow sovereign, decked with the outward trappings of state, but deprived of real power. From that time dated the progressive decline of the house of Habsburg, which had played so large a part in the history not only of Germany but of all Western Europe. On the other hand the German princes had gained further independence, one token of which was the right to conclude treaties with foreign rulers, so long as their liabilities did not conflict with their duty to the Empire and its head. Henceforth the Hohenzollerns, whose subjects had embraced the Protestant faith wholly and heartily, ranked unmistakably as the second most powerful reigning house in the Empire.

To the nation at large, however, had come not gain but loss, for its cultural no less than its material life had suffered serious check. The Reformation had carried further and deeper the intellectual ferment to which the Renaissance had given rise. Luther, with all his narrowness, saw that the new faith, if it were to hold its own against the unchanging challenge of ignorance, superstition, and inertia, must find auxiliaries in reason and knowledge, and to that end he gave powerful impetus to the founding of schools, both popular and higher, a movement which Saxony and North Germany warmly embraced. A new and wider interest was awakened in the things of the spirit; the revival of religion gave increased importance to Bible and prayer-book; and the printing press poured out a steady stream of literature of a didactic and edifying character.

The wars had brought all such progress to a standstill. When towns and villages never knew from day to day whether hordes of hungry and undisciplined troops would descend upon them, plundering and burning, and when neither sex nor age proved a defence against brutal violence, people had little time or inclination for study and culture. Even the printed language was denationalized by a grotesque admixture of foreign words, incomprehensible to the unlettered.

The material and economic condition of the country had likewise been left disordered and ruined. Whole regions had been laid waste by rude and ruthless soldieries, the houses of the peasants burnt to the ground, and the land left uncultivated and given over to wild animals, so that often where before inhabitants were plentiful and prosperity prevailed, human beings now lived a day's march apart. During the later years of the war a Swedish general refused to take his army from North to South Germany on the plea that in traversing the intervening desert he would be sure to lose more men than in the worst of defeats. It is estimated that famine, disease, slaughter, and emigration together had reduced the population of the Empire from over sixteen to less than six millions; in

Württemberg only one-sixth and in the Lower Palatinate only one-tenth of the population remained.

Home and foreign commerce had decayed, manufacturer, craftsman, and merchant alike sharing in the general misfortune. It was as impossible to get merchandise out of the country as into it, for the trade routes, where not unsafe, were wrecked. Moreover, Germany's extremity had been the opportunity of rival maritime countries. Even the powerful Hanseatic League, which for centuries had poured German goods into foreign ports, and had been accustomed to make and unmake sovereigns, lost and never regained its old influence and fame. The great hope of the nation lay in the fact that the spirit of the Reformation, which a century before had done so much for the renewal of its life, still survived.

The prestige which Austria lost in Europe during the first half of that century was gained for France in the reigns of Louis XIII (1610-43) and his greater son, Louis XIV (1643-1715), by the two most brilliant statesmen of whom her annals contain record, and the end of the war left her the paramount continental Power. The aim of French policy, directed by Cardinal Richelieu until the end of 1642 and thereafter for nearly twenty years by Cardinal Mazarin, was plainly shown in the demands for territory made and sustained in the peace negotiations. What France gained at that time, however, was only another instalment of an ambitious scheme of aggrandisement which was to be completed by the extension of her eastern frontiers to the Rhine and the absorption of the Spanish possessions in the Low Countries. The weakened condition in which the war had left Austria, Spain, and the German principalities alike seemed propitious to this bold design, provided only that Sweden and England, the latter chiefly dangerous on sea, might be persuaded or cajoled into neutrality. That it would be thwarted by any resistance possible in Germany was scarcely contemplated, though the Great Elector of Brandenburg had come out of the war with a military reputation which had raised him head and shoulders above the ruck of his princely neighbours.

For a time dynastic and territorial disputes within the Empire which had been left undecided by the Peace of Westphalia kept alive the spirit of unrest and rivalry in Germany, and led to the formation of a fresh series of alliances and counter-alliances between the princes concerned and their foreign sympathizers. Sweden, too, under an ambitious king, Charles X, advanced new claims to German lands, so challenging Brandenburg, now the ally of Austria. From all such complications France was not slow to seek advantage. Bent on compassing the permanent enfeeblement of Austria, Louis XIV pursued that aim by taking some of the German princes of the meaner sort into his pay and by joining others in the Rhenish League, formed for the purpose of keeping the Emperor in his rightful place. On the death of Ferdinand III (1637-57) he also tried to secure the choice of the Elector of Bavaria as Emperor. Foiled in that design, however, he unwillingly accepted the Habsburg candidate, Leopold I (1658-1705), and turned his attention to more profitable projects.

His invasion of the Spanish Netherlands in 1667 brought him up against a forbidding alliance, consisting of Holland, Sweden, and England, and he gained little by the adventure. Five years later, having made sure of the neutrality of his principal earlier opponents – Charles II of England betraying his allies and selling his country's honour for French gold –, he attacked the Dutch Republic and might have subjugated it but for the manly resistance of its Stadtholder, William III, Prince of Orange, and of the Great Elector.

Subsequently the Empire and Spain completed an alliance so strong that France was compelled to draw back. Angered by failure Louis illegally annexed the ten imperial towns of Alsace and caused the Palatinate to be devastated by Marshal Turenne. By the succeeding Peace of Nymwegen (1678-79) he obtained from Spain the Franche-Comté in Upper Burgundy and a number of places on the frontier of Flanders, and from the German Empire the fortified Swabian town of Freiburg im Breisgau. These treaty acquisitions he supplemented by others obtained by violent seizure. On the left bank of the Rhine he occupied Saarlouis, Saarbrücken, Luxemburg and other districts, and in Alsace he annexed outright the old German city of Strassburg.

At last the German princes, after years of paltering and disunion, were stirred to resolute action. Convinced that common danger called for common effort, most of them joined the Augsburg League, formed by William of Orange, embracing also the Emperor and the Kings of Spain and Sweden. Knowing that the French king was determined to have the Palatinate by foul means if not by fair, the allies mounted ward upon the historical boundaries between the Empire and France, and this plain warning, 'Thus far and no farther', stung Louis to the quick. Foiled again as he had been by the triple alliance of 1668, he vented his spleen in characteristic fashion. If he could not possess that province he could at least diminish its attraction and value for others. With incredible barbarity he caused an army to be marched into the country with the deliberate object of spreading desolation, ruin, and misery. No military episode in modern history is comparable in unreasoning brutality with the invasion of the Palatinate in the winter of 1688-89. Wherever the troops went the

country passed under the hideous dominion of fire and sword; from the
frontier onward the land was laid waste; Heidelberg, which had suffered
badly when besieged by Tilly in 1622, was now half burnt down, and a
large part of its noble castle blown up in sheer lust of destruction. Mannheim, Worms, Spires and other towns were similarly wrecked, cathedral
and mansion, burgher's house and labourer's cot sharing indifferently the
same fate. Hundreds of people of all classes and all ages were turned out
of their homes and driven into the open country, there to seek shelter
under cover of the forest or in hospitable huts, though many succumbed
to the bitter cold. It was a repetition, on a small but more intensive scale,
of the worst horrors of the Thirty Years' War.

The entire Protestant world, whose indignation had already been
aroused by Louis's revocation of the Edict of Nantes (1685), by which the
religious liberties of the Huguenots of France were annulled, was horrified
by this greater and coarser crime. The Augsburg League was converted
into the Grand Alliance by the adhesion of England, Holland, and
Denmark. William of Orange was now King of England, with stronger
military and naval arguments at his command than those which he had
been able to employ as Stadtholder of the Netherlands, and he was the
guiding mind and supporting arm of the combination to which his
enthusiasm, resource, and daring gave added power. Hostilities continued
both on land and sea for eight years, fortune favouring each side in turn,
but at least a period was now put to Louis's will to further mischief.
The war was wound up in 1697 by the Treaty of Ryswick (30th September). Germany's allies negotiated conditions which were probably
more favourable to her than any that she could have hoped to attain
alone. France gave back most of the territory which she had occupied
since the Peace of Nymwegen (1678), but retained Saarlouis and the
Alsatian imperial towns, and obtained the formal cession of Strasburg in
full sovereignty.

II. THE RISE OF BRANDENBURG-PRUSSIA

The rise of Brandenburg and its expansion into modern Prussia was
substantially the work of three members of the Hohenzollern family –
Frederick William, the Great Elector, Frederick William I (the second
king), and Frederick the Great. In tracing this notable achievement in
state-building it is necessary to go back some years. If during the reign
of Louis XIV France rose to a dizzy height of power, Brandenburg
simultaneously gained pre-eminence in Germany under the Elector
Frederick William. His first concern on his accession in 1640 was to
provide himself with a serviceable army. The force of a few thousand

mercenaries which his predecessor had recruited with difficulty, and paid as funds allowed, had ultimately deserted its Protestant war-lord and gone over to the Emperor and the Catholic cause. In its place he organized a small standing army of chosen men, and the change at once brought great relief to the civil population, for there was no more thieving and plundering. Whereas the mercenaries, when their pay was overdue, were allowed to pay themselves in kind by the simple device of pillaging, the Elector made the commissariat from first to last his business, remembering that discipline and loyalty depended in the last resort upon the due performance of their reciprocal obligations by lord and liege alike. He further strengthened his position by marrying the daughter of Frederick Henry, the hereditary Stadtholder of the Netherlands.

After the Peace of Westphalia the relations between Brandenburg and Sweden became increasingly strained. Pomerania was the cause of disagreement; for though the Elector had been compelled to agree to the division of the duchy with Sweden, he had not waived his legal claim to the whole. It has been placed to his account by some historians as a cardinal sin, by others as a positive virtue, that in political dealings he was apt to resort to somewhat shifty methods. He certainly showed great adroitness in changing his loyalties and forsaking his allies when the interests of his country made that course advantageous. He used his opportunities very craftily when in 1655 Sweden and Poland went to war over the question of the Swedish succession. He had then at his disposal an army of 26,000 men. First actively allying himself with the northern kingdom, whose ruler had rapidly subdued Poland, he took part in the victorious battle of Warsaw, in reward for which he was to be allowed to assert formal sovereignty over the Duchy of Prussia (East Prussia), hitherto held as a feud of Poland. When later, however, the Polish king made him the same offer, he promptly joined him for the remainder of the war, and by the final Peace of Oliva (1660) he gained that desirable territory with a full and clear title. On the other hand, it was creditable to the Elector that when a new Emperor was elected in 1658, he rejected the bribe offered for his support by Louis XIV, who wanted the title himself, and gave to the Austrian candidate, Leopold I, the decisive vote which turned the scale.

Now for a time the Elector had peace, and was able to carry forward the work of consolidating his power, developing his territories, and improving the system of administration both in national and local affairs. At times his passion for efficiency led him to commit acts of great harshness and even cruelty. When opposition was offered to his attempt to introduce in East Prussia more systematic methods of government than had prevailed under Polish rule, he caused one of the malcontent leaders to be thrown into prison, where he died, while another, who had resorted to open sedition, was by his orders kidnapped in Warsaw, conveyed to Memel, and there promptly beheaded.

When Louis XIV, resuming his policy of aggression, attacked Holland in 1672, the Elector was the first to take up arms against the threatened republic, Spain and Denmark coming in later, while most of the German princes who took sides at all followed the line of apparent safety and profit, and accepted paid service with France. In a year's time, his Rhenish and Westphalian territories being in the enemy's occupation and his treasury empty, the Elector was compelled to cease fighting, but he regained his lost lands in return for an undertaking not to support the enemies of the French king unless he attacked the Empire. France soon did the latter, the result being a new alliance against her, embracing now the Emperor, Spain, Holland, and Brandenburg. Louis thereupon won Sweden to his side, and while the Elector and his army were in winter quarters on the Main, Swedish troops invaded the Mark from East Pomerania and wrought terrible havoc. This disaster he amply avenged in the battle of Fehrbellin (June 1675), inflicting a crushing defeat upon a force twice as strong as his own. That success brought him allies in the Danes, who had old scores to settle with Sweden, and in the course of the following two years the Swedes were temporarily driven out of Germany. When subsequently Brandenburg's other allies concluded with the common enemy the Peace of Nymwegen, already mentioned, the Great Elector was left to face the power of France single-handed, with the result that he had to accept the Peace of St. Germain (June 1679), by which he renounced all the territory of which he had deprived Sweden.

That time when, at the height of his success and fame, he was suddenly overwhelmed by misfortune and humiliation, was the saddest in his life; for to the crushing disappointment of foiled hopes and futile exertions came resentment at what he regarded as the treachery of his friends. Human to the core he showed his pique against Spain, whose defection had especially annoyed him, by attacking her at sea with his newly-built little fleet, and for a time he brooded over the thought of making a firm peace with Louis at any price. He did, in fact, conclude an incongruous treaty of friendship with his country's enemy at the end of the same year. Later, when Leopold I sought his help in his war against Turkey for the recovery of Hungary (1686) he hastened to his side. His last notable political act was the signing in March 1688 of a secret treaty with his nephew, Prince William of Orange, pledging himself to despatch 6000 Brandenburg troops under Marshal von Schomberg to Holland, whence they were to accompany the Prince to England, there to consummate the 'glorious revolution'.

Crowded with military exploits though his life was, the Great Elector nevertheless accomplished a great work of development at home which continued to bear fruit for generations. He found his country impoverished and disordered, its towns misgoverned, its villages neglected and largely deserted, the peasantry for the most part reduced to beggary, and the land so ill tilled for want of labour, implements, and capital that it yielded little food for man or beast, while much of it was given over to game. All this he changed. By reforms in the system of tenure, and by introducing improved methods of cultivation, he helped the peasants to make agriculture again profitable. He encouraged trade and industry in many ways, facilitating intercourse and traffic in merchandise by building roads and canals and introducing the post; and he not only founded companies for the promotion of trade with the Indies, but he established on the west coast of Africa the first of German oversea colonies. He had also a firm faith in education and took care that schools were available in sufficiency both in town and country. To this truly great ruler, who was enlightened far beyond the measure of his times, Prussia owed much of the strength, capacity, and ambition which enabled her at a later date to lead Germany into new paths of endeavour and achievement. More than any other German sovereign he may claim to have originated the patriarchal state.

It was the good fortune of the succeeding Elector of Brandenburg, Frederick III (1688-1713), that he lived on the whole in quieter times, for his gifts were more artistic and æsthetic than practical. Though inconsiderable as a soldier or statesman, he at least stood up manfully for Germany and the Protestant cause. In 1701 he, with the consent of the Emperor, assumed the title of King of Prussia, crowning himself at Königsberg as Frederick I. His electoral title was still derived from Brandenburg; Prussia lay outside the Empire. Probably his love of ostentation had as much to do with his wish for the regal status as the fact that high titular dignities had of late fallen to his friends. Brandenburg soldiers had helped to settle William of Orange upon the English throne; the Emperor had made the Duke of Hanover the ninth Elector in 1692; and he had himself had a hand in winning for the Elector Frederick Augustus of Saxony, known as Augustus the Strong, the crown of Poland. For the Elector of Hanover a greater prize was in store, for on the death of Queen Anne in 1714 the succession passed to his house, and the first of four Georges reigned in England.

To the same reign fell the War of the Spanish Succession (1701-13), following the death of Charles II, in which struggle Prussia, like most of the other German states, together with England and Holland, fought with the Emperor Leopold I in support of the claim of his son Charles to the throne, while Bavaria sided with France and the Bourbon claimant, Philip of Anjou. The battles of Blenheim, Ramillies, Oudenarde, and Malplaquet recall the brilliant feats of Marlborough and Prince Eugene of Savoy – loyal comrades throughout – in a war which dispelled for a century the menace of French domination in Europe. The treaties of Utrecht (1713) and Rastatt (1714) awarded Spain and her colonial possessions to Philip, but to Charles – since 1711 German Emperor as Charles VI – the Spanish territories in Italy and the Netherlands. England gained by the war Gibraltar and French colonies in North America, while to Prussia fell Upper Gelderland, on her Dutch frontier, and Neuchâtel, which incongruous Swiss enclave she retained until 1848. Germany in general benefited immediately by the European 'balance of power' which now held France in check; but the cost had been great, for her settlement and material recovery had once more been thrown back by the long war, which was fought in part within her frontiers, though more in the Low Countries.

In Frederick William I (1713-40) there followed a man made of sterner stuff. The father had been an easy-going, spendthrift dilettante: the son was a hard, miserly, military martinet. Prussia had not of late made any marked growth in strength, influence, or territory, and he was determined to quicken the pace. To that end he saw that a larger and more efficient army, a more self-conscious nation, and a more purposeful national policy were needed, and to bring these to effect was the absorbing aim of his life. For his regiments only the best material was good enough, and he took as much pleasure in his 'long fellows' as a child in its dolls, sending his recruiting agents far and wide with *carte blanche* to catch monsters for him wherever they might be found. So it was that he was able to hand forward to his greater successor the nucleus of a fighting force which was able to hold its own with the strongest in Europe.

Following the example of the Great Elector he carried out important constructive works in various parts of the country, and he did much for commerce and agriculture, rigorously protecting home industries against foreign competition. A fierce worker himself, he made his daughters engage in house and farm work like any serving-maids; idleness was to him one of the worst of crimes, and when on one of his periodical rounds of visits to the provinces he heard that a certain labour leader was giving trouble in Berlin, he sent word post-haste, 'Off with his head.' To high and low, however, he meted equal justice, though often of a merciless kind. He also enforced on all classes, and most of all on himself, the practice of thrift, and he covered the country with schools. He subjected his people to a hard, and as it proved a hardening discipline, and it was not surprising that it had, together with many valuable effects, others that were little to be desired. He may be said to have personified what the world later came to regard as the characteristic virtues and vices of the typical Prussian – amongst the former, energy, order, discipline, application, frugality; amongst the latter, bellicosity, self-assertiveness, and an intellectual myopia which sees only one side of a question, and that its own.

In 1720 the Treaty of Stockholm, following a series of wars with Poland, Russia, and Denmark, registered the overthrow of Sweden's greatness as a military Power. Prussia came in only at the end of the struggle, but gained as a reward a large part of Western Pomerania, the residue remaining Swedish until 1814. The last of this king's military expeditions was the despatch of troops to the assistance of Austria in a dispute with France over the succession to the Polish crown on the death in 1733 of the Saxon King Augustus II. The French favourite was Stanislaus Leszcynski, father-in-law of the young Louis XV, who had also the support of the Electors of Bavaria, Mayence, Cologne, and the Palatinate; while Austria and Russia put forward the late ruler's son, the Elector Frederick Augustus. Russian troops quelled Polish resistance, but before a collision occurred in the west France sacrificed her candidate as part of a bargain by which the Duchy of Lorraine, which she had already occupied, was to be nominally ceded to Stanislaus as puppet ruler for life, with reversion to the French crown at his death, an arrangement which duly took effect. Another quarrel was thus settled, as so many before, at the expense of the Empire, which in those days was treated like the joint on the hostelry sideboard at which guests might cut and come again at will. France, Sweden, Brandenburg, Poland, and Denmark had all enlarged their frontiers at its expense, and still more excisions were to follow.

The marriage of this rough Hohenzollern afforded an interesting illustration of sexual polarity, since his character was diametrically opposite to that of his intellectually gifted and exceptionally refined wife, Sophie, daughter of the Elector of Hanover, who never really tamed her bear.

III. The Age of Frederick the Great

Reared under the stern eye and ever-threatening hand of perhaps the grimmest caricature of fatherhood known to political biography, the only son of Frederick William II of Prussia should, by all the accepted laws of modern psychiatry, have been a nervous wreck at fifteen and a confirmed hypochondriac, if not an outright lunatic, after thirty. Instead he became the most brilliant soldier and statesman of his age, and won by the accord, not only of posterity, but of his contemporaries, the name 'Frederick the Great'. The unhappy story of his youth and adolescence is too long to be told in these pages. Only towards the end of his life did the father condescend to hold towards his son a decently natural relationship. Perhaps it was in memory – or even in condemnation – of the harsh treatment which he had experienced that Frederick said in later life, 'No man has the right to assume unlimited mastery over his fellows, in virtue of which he may be in a position, if he so wills, to dispose of their lives and goods, and to make them unhappy.'

For over twenty years this ruler was engaged in an almost unbroken succession of wars. It was his engrossing ambition to round off and consolidate the young kingdom, still a concatenation of disjointed territories, with enclaves here and exclaves there, making defence difficult and security uncertain. The legacy into which he entered of a well-trained army of 83,000 men and a healthy State treasury made him ready to seize at any opportunity of advantage.

While his father lay on his deathbed in the simple *château* at Rheinsberg in late October of 1740 the Emperor, Charles VI, passed away – a momentous event which was to entail another war of succession. By the 'Pragmatic Sanction' of 1713 Charles had secured the Habsburg possessions to his daughter, Maria Theresa. Her title, however, was challenged, on hereditary grounds, by the Elector Charles Albert of Bavaria and the Elector Frederick Augustus II of Saxony, both of whom had married daughters of the Emperor Joseph I. Spain and Sardinia also put in less serious claims. With two powerful rulers vexing and harassing the young queen,[1] Frederick grasped at the chance of entering the dispute as the 'laughing third'. His house had long advanced claims to certain Silesian lands which Austria, not as yet accustomed to take her ambitious neighbour seriously, had refused to entertain. Now the time seemed ripe for the argument of deeds. Without warning of any kind he led a large army into Lower Silesia in the middle of December, justifying his act to the inhabitants by his alleged legal rights and the less convincing plea that the possession of their land was necessary to the greater security of his own. He simultaneously offered the queen an alliance provided she agreed to recognize his claims; but the overture was rejected, and the first Silesian war and the war of the Austrian succession ran concurrently. Russia, Holland, and England sided with Maria Theresa and hence against Prussia, while

[1] Her titles to begin with on the death of her father were: Queen of Hungary and Bohemia and Archduchess of Austria.

France, Spain, Bavaria, and also Saxony, whose ruler claimed lands both in Silesia and Bohemia, were in the opposite camp. Fortune favoured Frederick, who gained by the Treaty of Breslau (July 1742) Upper and Lower Silesia with Maria Theresa's unwilling assent, since English advisers had persuaded her to agree with her adversary quickly lest worse should befall. Having procured the election of the Bavarian claimant as Charles VII, Frederick now undertook to remain neutral in the undecided quarrel over the question of title.

A little later Prussia made a further small but useful acquisition of territory in the north-west of Germany. This was the coastal region of East Friesland, adjacent to the Ems, which belonged to the Empire and had for centuries been under the rule of petty princes. When the last of these died in 1744 Frederick claimed succession and planted a garrison in the land. There was no resistance, and while Prussia gained the port of Emden on the North Sea, the Frisians had henceforth good government.

A second Silesian war began in the same year, Frederick now taking sides openly with the Emperor, France, and Bavaria, an alliance opposed by Austria, England, and Sardinia. This campaign was less successful for him than the first, but the Treaty of Dresden with which it ended (25th December 1745) confirmed his gains under that of Breslau. In the meantime death had made necessary the election of another Emperor, and as Bavaria stood aside on this occasion, Maria Theresa's husband succeeded as Francis I (1745-65). The continental war – no longer one of succession but of prestige – continued for three years longer, France and Spain being opposed by Austria, England, the Netherlands, and Sardinia, and ended with the Peace of Aix-la-Chapelle (18th October 1748), which gave back to Maria Theresa all the territories that France had occupied, though the loss of Silesia remained.

New complications soon led to a further reshuffling of the allies, and England, engaged in war with France in North America, withdrew for a time from active participation in European operations. Alarmed for the safety of his Electorate, since France had been offered the adjacent Spanish Netherlands, George II of Hanover threw himself into the arms of Prussia, and Maria Theresa replied with an alliance with Russia and France. Now began the Seven Years' War (1756-63) which finally settled the Silesian question. Several of the minor German princes joined Frederick, but otherwise he stood practically alone, opposed by the armies of three Powers of the first rank, besides Swedes and troops of Bavarian, Württemberg, and Saxon mercenaries, bought with French money. The war was fought mainly in Saxony and Bohemia. After six years of fighting Russia fell out of the struggle with the death of the Empress Elizabeth

(January 1762), which brought to the throne a warm admirer of Frederick in the person of Peter III, and Sweden followed suit. France, weakened and disheartened by the colonial war with England, was glad to conclude the Peace of Fontainebleau a year later, so that of Prussia's antagonists only Austria and her German allies stood out at the end of 1762. The last hopes of the brave but ill-fortuned Empress-Queen were shattered, and all that now remained was to accept an unalterable situation. The Treaty of Hubertusburg (15th February 1763), which wound up the war, simply confirmed the *status quo ante bellum*, implying the definitive recognition of Prussia's claim to Silesia with the town of Gratz. The war is said to have cost a million men, while it laid desolate for years large regions of North and Central Germany and Bohemia.

But the acquisition of Silesia did not still Frederick's craving for terri-tory. Nine years later he made a further addition without resort to arms by the tripartite division of Poland, instigated by Catherine II of Russia. West Prussia, the lower reaches of the Vistula and the Netze district, but not Thorn and Danzig, fell to Prussia, and Galicia to Austria.

This greatest of the Hohenzollerns interests the world at large as a soldier more than as a statesman, yet it would be a mistake to suppose that because of his long preoccupation with wars and foreign affairs the domestic welfare of his people was neglected. Far from that, he had it at heart at all times, and supremely so during the last twenty-three years of his reign, during which came seasons of peace and tranquility. True to the example of his father and the Great Elector, he now devoted himself more than ever to the development of his country's resources – its agri-culture, trade, and industries, the ordering of its administration and finance, and its intellectual life and interests. Towards the end of his life he caused a code of common law to be drawn up which, with amend-ments and additions, has lasted to the present day in the greater part of Prussia and in some other German states.

He, too, was a despot, though a benevolent one, keeping all authority in his own hands, yet using it on the whole wisely and mildly. Tolerant beyond the rule of his age, he relaxed the restraints which had narrowed the life of the people during the preceding reign; now men breathed a freer atmosphere, could talk of liberty and enjoy it. He bade every man follow the religion of his choice and be happy in it; when clumsy critics plastered rude pasquinades high on the street hoardings he ordered them to be put lower so that they might be the better read; when courtiers flattered he snubbed and shamed them; and he claimed to be the first servant of the State.

Prussia had now been established as a sound going concern, yet with all its merits some things were wrong with a system of government which had not been evolved by the genius of the nation, but imposed upon the nation by the arbitrary will of its rulers. The three makers of Prussia had created a powerful military state, but they had also made a people lacking in the essentials of a vigorous, independent nationhood. The ideas of discipline, authority, and subordination had been hammered into the Prussians, as into no other German stock, until with most of them passive, unthinking obedience had become a second nature. That was not good for them or their country, nor yet, on a long calculation of probabilities, for the rulers themselves.

There was a certain irony in the fact that Frederick's immediate successors were out of sympathy with his military obsessions. The first of them was his nephew, Frederick William II, fat, sensuous, good-natured, and well-meaning, but weak and easily led and duped by clever men and voluptuous women. Slackness became apparent everywhere; the army was neglected, finance fell again into disorder, and the public debt increased; business of state was allowed to wait while the ruler attended spiritistic *séances* or listened to fantastic stories of alchemic processes which were able to produce gold but never did; in foreign affairs in particular he systematically bungled when not following the advice of shrewder men; while the frivolous life of the court and the laxity of his personal habits exercised a demoralizing influence which spread far and deep in the population.

It was one of his greatest political mistakes that he went out of his way to strengthen Austria's position in Germany. To the later years of his reign (1793 and 1795) fell the second and third partitions of Poland. By the earlier Prussia received, in addition to Thorn and Danzig, a large part of the Grand Duchy, including the Posen and Gnesen districts, and the later one added to her share Masuria and the Warsaw and other districts; while Austria received West Galicia, with the Cracow district, and Russia all that remained. For Prussia this was the worst of the three partitions, not because she received too little, but because she received too much, for with the new territory came into the monarchy a large and compact population of Poles, of whose assimilation there could be no possibility. (There was, in fact, a variation of this partition in 1807 and again in 1815.) When in 1797 Prussia's fourth king died at the early age of fifty-three, after a short reign of eleven years, the country had gained in extent but lost in strength and cohesion, as well as in prestige abroad. That short time had witnessed the deaths of two Emperors, Joseph II and Leopold II, and since 1792 Francis II, the last of the long Habsburg line of German Emperors, had occupied an already tottering throne.

IV. The Napoleonic Wars

The next King of Prussia was Frederick William III (1797-1840). It was the misfortune of this high-minded but unpractical and irresolute ruler that there fell to him problems of State which would have severely tasked the genius of the famous Frederick. Long before he came to the throne the dull rumblings of a coming political storm had been wafted across Germany's western frontier. Between 1773 and 1783 had been fought the American War of Independence, and out of the old British colonies a republic had been formed, with a constitution embodying conceptions of human rights which, though the commonplaces of political philosophy, were but little understood by the Sovereigns and statesmen of Europe.

In France, weary of the absolutist state, and crushed by public debts and an iniquitous system of taxation, the *tiers état*, comprising the mass of the population outside the privileged nobility and clergy, had at once welcomed these new ideas enthusiastically as a message of hope. Popular leaders arose, public opinion was organized, the monarchy was overthrown, and there, too, a republic arose on the ruins of the old régime. Then, with the transference of power to unaccustomed custodians, restraints were thrown aside, intolerance, excess, and violence broke out, and a reign of terror followed. Convinced that the success of the doctrines which France was propagating would mean the general overthrow of political stability, the Sovereigns and ruling classes of Europe, and earliest those of Germany, made common cause against the common enemy. In the late summer of 1792 small Austrian and Prussian forces marched through Luxemburg into Champagne with no very definite military plan or political policy in view, and after one or two slight skirmishes ingloriously marched back again, followed by the republican army of the Rhine as far as Frankfort.

The execution in the following January of the unhappy Louis XVI, who deserved a better fate, quickened the Powers to action, and the First Coalition, consisting of the two German Great Powers, the Empire as represented by the other German States, Great Britain, Holland, Spain, Sardinia, and Naples, was the answer to the republican challenge, 'Death to all princes, and destruction to all monarchies!' There was fighting on both banks of the Rhine, and the French occupied Holland, but a two years' campaign led to no positive result. Petty jealousies and division of counsels broke up the alliance, and the King of Prussia so far forgot himself as to conclude a separate peace with France (5th April 1795). It was the first of a long series of blunders and miscalculations which eventually proved his country's undoing.

From the beginning of 1796 Napoleon Bonaparte, now at the age of twenty-seven, commander-in-chief of the republican forces, dominated the French, indeed the European scene. Five French armies were in the field, opposed by Great Britain, Austria, and Sardinia, and two years of fighting ended with the Treaty of Campo Formio (17th October 1797), by which Austria was forced to cede to France the Netherlands, and to Napoleon's Cisalpine Republic the Duchy of Milan, receiving in compensation Venice, Istria, and Dalmatia. How little the German Sovereigns trusted each other was shown by a secret article by which France was to have the left bank of the Rhine, to the exclusion of Prussian territory, and Austria to have a piece of Bavaria. Forsaken by the powerful rulers who should have been its defenders, the Empire was already doomed. In 1799 the Second Coalition was formed, Russia joining England, Austria, Naples, and Turkey, while Prussia stood aside. In a new campaign Napoleon, now First Consul, beat the Austrians at Marengo and Moreau was victor at Hohenlinden; by the ensuing Peace of Lunéville (9th February 1801) Germany lost a large tract of territory and a population of over three millions. The partition of Germany begun by Napoleon was continued by the German princes, who at the Diet of Ratisbon (February 1803) secularized the ecclesiastical territories, and therewith compensated themselves for their own losses. The Prussian king still sought safety for his country in neutrality, and by so doing sank yet deeper in the morass of difficulty and misfortune. On the other hand England, inspired by Pitt, though as ever slow at first to take the situation tragically, was now throwing herself with increasing vigour and sacrifice into the struggle.

In May 1804 Napoleon was crowned Emperor of the French, and a little later, probably with premonition of events, Francis II constituted his Austrian territories a hereditary empire, while retaining for the present the title of Holy Roman Emperor. In the following year Russia formed with England and Austria the Third Coalition. Against the pressure of his wife, the patriotic and resolute Queen Louise, the Prussian king again remained outside, even refusing to allow a Russian army to cross his territory. Neither neutrality nor subservience helped him long, however, for in December Austria and Russia were defeated in the battle of Austerlitz, and in the peace which followed Prussia was compelled to drink from the same cup of humiliation as her deserted allies. The victor rewarded his active vassals, the rulers of Bavaria, Württemberg, and Baden, with German territory and made the first two of them kings. Of the Prussian court Napoleon spoke at this time as 'no less false than stupid', and it was with the intention of luring him into irretrievable disaster that he compelled Frederick William to enter into a formal treaty of alliance (February 1806). This he followed with the formation of the Rhenish Confederation, consisting of sixteen German princes who accepted him as liege lord. The dissolution of the Empire and the formal abdication of Francis II followed (6th August).

By this time the King of Prussia was convinced that his only hope lay in throwing himself into the war with the whole strength of his forces and resources. He did it, but it was then too late. In not trying to save the other German states he failed to save his own. The crushing defeats of Jena and Auerstädt on 14th October 1806 marked the beginning of the end. Elated by his success Napoleon led his troops to Berlin, where he was received at the gate by fawning City Fathers and treacherous servants of the Crown – so far had the example of poltroonery spread from high to lower places. The Fourth Coalition of 1807, between Russia and Prussia, was a last feeble struggle, and it failed to avert the further disaster of Friedland and the subsequent Peace of Tilsit, by which Prussia was compelled to cede half of her territory.

Napoleon's treatment of the other German states, whether friendly or hostile in the past, was governed by the one consideration, how best might his own position be assured. Several of them were extinguished or added to the Rhenish Confederation, while others either lost or gained territory according to circumstances. Most of the spoils of victory went to the formation of a kingdom of Westphalia for his brother Jerome to rule, and a Duchy of Warsaw, which he put under the Elector of Saxony, first promoting him to kingship over an augmented territory. Two years later (1809) Austria made alone one more desperate attempt to withstand the all-conquering Corsican, but failed, and, having occupied Vienna, Napoleon imposed on the Emperor the Peace of Schönbrunn, which deprived him of much territory. France now ruled over Holland and North-western Germany as far as Hamburg and Lübeck.

The six years from 1807 to 1813 were for Prussia a period of profound humiliation, but also of vigorous effort at recovery. The imposing state of Frederick the Great had collapsed because it had been built on purely military foundations. Far-seeing statesmen like Stein, Hardenberg, and Wilhelm von Humboldt saw that renewal would come only by enlisting in the service of the country the energies and devotion of a united people, by departing from the old systems of absolutism and centralization, by liberating the nation's latent intellectual and moral forces, and mobilizing these for the common service of the fatherland. In their view political and civic freedom would give unity, and that same unity would be a pledge of freedom's security.

The bold laws of Stein and Hardenberg abolished serfdom and all kinds of forced service, gave liberty in the choice of trades and occupations, and conferred upon the towns wide powers of self-government, so converting dependent subjects into free citizens. Under the influence of Humboldt the educational system was reformed and extended; while the eloquent 'Addresses to the German Nation' of Fichte and the inspiring songs of poets like Arndt, Körner, and Rückert braced the flagging will of a people at heart more patriotic than its king. Simultaneously the reform of the army and the removal from it of the many defects and abuses which defeat had brought to light proceeded vigorously beneath the strong hand of soldiers of genius like Gneisenau, Scharnhorst, von York, and Blücher. The nobility was no longer allowed to monopolize all the posts of honour and profit; the principle of universal service was introduced, and provision was made for a reserve of trained troops in the form of a *Landwehr* or militia.

In the meantime Napoleon (1812), concerned to complete the confusion of his continental enemies, made his historical invasion of Russia at the head of an army more than half a million strong, composed in large part of forced or mercenary aliens. His last act before leaving German soil was to compel Prussia and Austria to enter into an alliance and to furnish him with troops. The expedition was a ghastly failure. Hunger and above all the rigour of a Russian winter fought against the invaders, barely one in ten of whom lived to trudge and crawl, often in rags and bare-footed, back to the frontier.

The disaster, which seemed to them like the visitation of an avenging Providence, heartened both Prussia and Austria. In 1813 they were joined by Russia, Sweden, and also Great Britain, who, fighting in another part of the war zone, and defying all Napoleon's attempts to weaken her by his continental blockades, had done fine service against France both on land (in Spain) and sea. Now began the great concerted effort known in Prussian history as the 'War of Liberation'. Each of the three eastern Powers had at command about a quarter of a million men, who were organized in a northern (mainly Prussian), a Silesian (Russian), and a Bohemian (Austrian) army. Minor engagements, with honours divided, led up to a converging movement on Saxony, where was fought the three-days' battle of Leipzig, which ended in the complete victory of the allies (16th-18th October). Napoleon headed the slow retreat of his decimated army to the Rhine and France, followed by that of the exultant victors. From the frontier forward every mile of the way was contested and in several collisions the allied forces suffered reverse, but on the last day of March they entered Paris in triumph. Then followed closely the rejection of Napoleon's offer to abdicate in favour of his young son, his banishment to the island of Elba, and the restoration of the Bourbon line in the person of Louis XVIII.

The allied governments treated France with great magnanimity, not only allowing her to take part in the negotiations which led to the First Peace of Paris (30th May 1814), but also depriving her of no territory to which she had a right. All they required was that she should renounce the fruits of conquest and withdraw within the frontiers of 1st November 1792. The working out of the details of the general settlement was the task of the Congress of Vienna, which met at the end of October, but its deliberations were interrupted by the ex-Emperor's flight from Elba and his landing at Cannes (8th March 1815). At once the army and the greater part of the population rallied to the returned exile and acclaimed him as still their Emperor. In the Prussian military councils there were men who, embittered by what they regarded as the scurvy treatment of their country in the territorial readjustments proposed, favoured either neutrality or an open alliance with Napoleon. Gneisenau, a good soldier but emotional and untrustworthy as a statesman, proposed the latter course in a formal memorandum which he asked Hardenberg to communicate to the king. The Minister rejected the proposal as a 'moral enormity' and refused its author's request.

All the allied Powers, therefore, renewed the old allegiance, and remobilized the dispersed armies. Fortune had forsaken once for all the victor of a hundred fights. On 18th June Napoleon's power was finally shattered on the field of Waterloo, called by the Prussians 'La Belle Alliance', and he was doomed to spend his remaining years on the lonely mid-Atlantic island of St. Helena.

The Second Peace of Paris was concluded on 20th November 1815 between the allies and Louis XVIII, who had been again recalled. France was now restricted within the less favourable frontiers of 1790, subject to certain modifications, and was required to pay reparations to the amount of 700 million francs, and to maintain 150,000 allied troops on her territory for five years as a surety of peace.

The reorganization of Germany after the long period of French domination involved many changes in the boundaries of the States which Napoleon had either amalgamated or abolished, enlarged or curtailed, but neither the hopes nor the fears of any one of the princes were quite realized. The King of Prussia wished to annex the whole of Saxony as a penalty for its treason to the Empire, and the British plenipotentiary, Lord Castlereagh, at first supported this claim; but the opposition of Russia and France prevailed, and Prussia obtained only the northern part of the kingdom, which became later the province of Saxony. The territory east of the Elbe, including Great Poland, which Napoleon had wrested from her, was returned, and in addition she received part of Westphalia, Swedish Pomerania, and some Rhenish districts, while she ceded East Friesland, Goslar, and Hildesheim to Hanover, and Ansbach and Bayreuth to Bavaria, which also received Würzburg and Aschaffenburg, in turn ceding the Tyrol and Salzburg to Austria. Subject to some of the foregoing and other exchanges the dispossessed princes re-entered into their old territories. A united German demand for the restitution of Alsace was refused by the other Powers, but Austria was reinstated in her Italian possessions, disadvantageously for both sides, while Belgium was united with Holland. Of the foreign territories occupied by Great Britain during the war some were returned, but most were retained – of the latter Heligoland (ceded by Denmark), Malta, Ceylon, Cape Colony, Demerara, Mauritius, and Trinidad.

V. From Bund to Empire

Part of the work of the Congress of Vienna[1] was the determination of Germany's future political organization. The old Empire had been dissolved, and though the wish for its resuscitation was widespread and loudly expressed in Germany while the Congress was sitting, it was not revived because of the objection of Austria. Instead, the Congress devised a new and looser federal union bearing the name *Deutscher Bund* (Germanic Confederation), and its form, functions, and powers were duly set forth in the *Bundesakte* or Federal Statute of 8th June 1815. The federation was to comprise all the reigning princes and free cities of the old Empire, with Austria as its hereditary president; the King of Denmark joined in respect of the duchies of Holstein and Lauenburg, and the King of the Netherlands in respect of the grand duchy of Luxemburg. Its purpose was described as 'to protect the independence and integrity of the States contained in the Bund and to maintain the internal and external security of Germany'. The powers and duties assigned to the Bund were vested in the Federal Diet, a legislative council consisting of the plenipotentiaries of the State-members, with Frankfort as its meeting-place.

From first to last there was no suggestion of even the faintest form of popular representation: the nation at large might never have existed at all. Nevertheless, for half a century this cumbrous institution maintained a far from glorious existence, functioning with ever-increasing inefficiency and inutility, acting as a heavy drag upon German progress, a continual menace to political liberty, an obstacle to every movement in the direction

[1] *Der Wiener Kongress*, opened 1st October 1814.

of national unity, and a source of friction between the two major States, Austria and Prussia, which was eventually to develop into open rupture and war.

A Bund formed on such narrowly oligarchic principles was not the gift which the peoples of Germany had expected as a reward for their patient endurance through the long years of struggle and sacrifice and suffering. From Austria, whose Chancellor, Metternich, represented in political life intransigent reaction in every form, nothing was to be hoped; but the King of Prussia had repeatedly promised his people a direct participation in State affairs, and for such a measure several of the liberal-minded princes of the south were ready. The Federal Act, indeed, stipulated that each State should receive an assembly or representation of the estates, yet even that mild obligation was cancelled. Re-established in their old powers, most of the rulers forgot all they had said about popular legislatures in the time of their extremity, and it became a crime to remind them publicly of their promises. In a few States – Baden, Bavaria, Hanover, Nassau, Weimar, Württemberg – princes more enlightened than their fellows introduced constitutions, but the rulers of Austria and Prussia refused, and so held back the rest. Under the Carlsbad Decrees of 1819 democratic ideas were systematically repressed throughout the greater part of Germany, in some States with extreme rigour, even the advocacy of national unity being regarded as a form of sedition and punished accordingly. In the execution of the Decrees Austria was the leader, though Prussia made a zealous second. At that time and for long afterwards Metternich was in effect Minister not only in Vienna but in Berlin, for he dictated the policy of both countries. The Paris *révolution à demi* of 1830 for a moment roused hopes in liberal breasts, but the reaction was too firmly established to be either disturbed or alarmed; and when in 1837 Hanover became detached from the British Crown its Sovereign signalized his independence by repealing the very moderate constitution of 1819.

It was only when the French revolution of 1848 provoked similar violent outbursts in Germany that the autocrats who had sat so long upon the safety-valve recognized their danger, and, panic-stricken, conceded in hours reforms which they had refused for years. In the meantime a new ruler had come to the Prussian throne in the person of Frederick William IV (1840), an idealist and dreamer, given to wordy rhetoric, whose head was filled with extravagant notions about the 'divine right' of kings. He, too, had stood out against political concessions as long as he dared, but fear for his crown and dynasty led to a quick conversion. There was an irony no less fitting than unique in a situation which led to a

Prussian king receiving orders instead of giving them and made the Prince of Prussia,[1] and even the grim die-hard Metternich, fugitives to England's more democratic and also more hospitable shores. Constitutions were granted in both of the major States, and this example the smaller retrograde States were obliged to follow. In December of the same eventful year (1848) Ferdinand I of Austria, who had succeeded Francis I in 1835, abdicated and Francis Joseph I came to the throne to retain it until the eve of the break-up of the Habsburg Empire seventy years later.

Nevertheless, the greater cause of national unity made for the time but little progress. The Frankfort National Assembly of 1848, after months of professorial debate, produced a constitution for a new German Empire, which would have transferred power from the princes to the people; but the King of Prussia's refusal of the imperial crown wrecked the scheme, and the Assembly ended its career in unmerited ignominy. Thereupon reaction re-enthroned itself and the realization of the dream of a united Germany seemed to have been indefinitely postponed.

The later history of the Germanic Confederation is little more than a record of the events which brought to a head the growing rivalry between the two larger German Powers and gave to Prussia and the Hohenzollern family the primacy which had been enjoyed for centuries by Austria and the Habsburgs.

Austria had entered the Bund with the fixed determination to maintain in a new union the dominant position which she had held in the old Empire, and so long as Metternich continued in power she succeeded. With the revolution of 1848 that Minister's career ended, and it was not until 1851 that he ventured to visit Vienna again. While thus Austria had lost her most powerful statesman since Kaunitz,[2] Prussia had just found her most powerful since Stein. In 1847 there had entered into the political life of that country Otto von Bismarck, a Prussian junker then of only local repute and apparently of no great promise, yet in fact destined to stand out as the representative and the protagonist of a new and fateful conception of German nationalism. He saw how for centuries his country had been the sport of more powerful European States and nations, how again and again they had embroiled it in quarrels in which it had no interest, and had made it the cockpit of their wars. It was his burning ambition to change all this, and to win for Germans, if possible, the right to be masters in their own house and to live their own life; and intuition

---

[1] Prinz von Preussen was the title of the king's brother and heir; he was regent during the king's insanity from 1858 to 1861, when he came to the throne as William I.

[2] Fürst Kaunitz, as Maria Theresa's Chancellor, signed the Treaty of Aix-la-Chapelle in 1748 (p. 73).

no less than the warnings of history told him that the first and most necessary step towards that goal must be the expulsion of Austria from the Bund which now she dominated.

Appointed in 1851 Prussian envoy in the Federal Diet, of which from the first he formed a very unfavourable opinion, he challenged Austria's arrogant pretensions with great decision. He also resisted every proposal which seemed to subordinate the interests of his country to those of Europe. It was largely due to his influence that Prussia kept out of the Crimean War when British statesmen assumed that she would join the allies as a matter of course. Becoming Prussian Minister President in 1862 he engaged in a bitter dispute with the Lower House of the Diet over the constitutional question whether he was entitled without its assent to raise money wherewith to pay for a large scheme of military reorganization upon which the king, William I, had set his heart. Untroubled by the hair-splittings of lawyers and professors he settled the matter to his own satisfaction by allowing the Diet to do the debating while he levied the taxes and went on with the army reforms.

No sooner was he convinced that Prussia was able to speak to Austria on equal terms than he sought and gained her co-operation in a war against Denmark over the Elbe duchies of Schleswig and Holstein, the latter part of the old German Empire and both bound by personal union to the Danish Crown, though enjoying a wide measure of autonomy, with separate constitutions, legislatures, and administrations. The status of the duchies, which had been affirmed but not secured by the London Protocol of 1852, was violated when, in 1864, contrary to repeated pledges, Denmark annexed Schleswig with its German population, a proceeding which she was required to defend with the sword. The issue of a struggle so unequal was never doubtful, and as a penalty of defeat Denmark was deprived of both of the duchies. The territories remained for a time in the hands of the victors as common property, but Bismarck had no intention of a division, though he opened negotiations to that end. Shrewdly he drew the Austrian Foreign Minister, Mensdorff, into toils from which he could only free himself by the sword, and in 1866 the question not merely of the reversion of the duchies but of primacy in Germany was fought out in the short but decisive Bohemian War, from which Austria emerged beaten, though not humiliated beyond need – since for that Bismarck was far too discreet – and pledged to accept the dissolution of the Bund and her exclusion from the new German union which was already planned.

Prussia annexed the two duchies outright, together with four of the States which had fought on Austria's side, viz. Hanover, electoral Hesse,

Nassau, and Frankfort; while Hesse-Darmstadt was required to cede Mayence and the adjoining district. The other hostile States escaped with moderate reparations and a promise to join the new union, or, as in the case of the South German States, to enter into a military alliance with Prussia.

The North German Confederation (*Norddeutscher Bund*) was now formed, comprising all the States north of the river Main, to the number of twenty-two, with a President, or more accurately, a Presidency (*Präsidium*), vested in the King of Prussia; a Federal Council (*Bundesrat*) consisting of the plenipotentiaries of the sovereign states; a Diet to be elected on manhood suffrage; and a single Minister, the Federal Chancellor. The States of the south were given permission to join voluntarily, but they did this only to the extent of sending representatives to a Customs Parliament for Germany, which introduced, in place of many separate tariff treaties between individual States and groups of States, a *Zollverein*, with a uniform fiscal system for the whole country.

Across Germany's western frontier the course of events had been watched with increasing alarm. Louis Napoleon, elected Emperor of the French in 1852, had pretended to favour German unity, yet in fact he had done his best to obstruct it, his last device being a proposal to form a South German Federation, to include Austria, as a counterpoise to Bismarck's creation. His political hostility to Prussia, which no professions of personal friendship made to her king and Minister could veil, combined with repeated attempts to obtain on his eastern frontier 'compensations' – a word he greatly loved – first in Rhenish territory, and later in the buffer states of Belgium and Luxemburg – convinced Bismarck that there could be no peace for Germany and no hope of a larger unification until an end had been made to French interferences in German affairs, and he saw that this could only result from a successful war.

For a war with France the candidature for the Spanish throne of Prince Leopold of Hohenzollern-Sigmaringen, a young member of a Roman Catholic branch of the Hohenzollern line, furnished the occasion, though it was neither its purpose nor its cause. There had been rumours of the candidature for some time, but it came to light only at the beginning of July 1870. Bismarck had certainly promoted it by secret methods, but, while it would be unjust to attribute to him sinister motives, his action in the matter was undoubtedly governed by the wish that the Spanish throne might be occupied by a friendly ruler when the inevitable clash between Germany and France came. France at once protested in due diplomatic form, on which the Prussian king not only disavowed his distant relative's action but promised to advise (which meant to command)

D

his withdrawal from an unwise position. That was all that had so far been asked of him, and had Napoleon been satisfied there would have been no further trouble. No sooner had his first demands been met, however, than he instructed his Foreign Minister, the Duc de Gramont, to require through Mons. Benedetti, the French ambassador in Berlin, a formal and written prohibition of the candidature which should hold good for all time and in all circumstances. Compliance with such a demand, 'pressed' as it was, according to the king's story of the interview, in a manner 'almost impertinent', was declared to be impossible. It was none the lessn ufortunate that the refusal, as published to the world, was so worded by Bismarck the statesman and Moltke the soldier as to wound French pride, which presumably was their intention.

War was declared by France, and Mons. Ollivier, the Minister President, who had been satisfied with the formal withdrawal of the candidature and King William's disapproval, declared in the House of Deputies that he entered on it *'avec cœur léger'*. Napoleon wrote a few days later that he had been 'forced into war by public opinion'. The truth is that both nations wanted and welcomed it.

The struggle was a desperate one, but to France it brought a continuous series of disasters, since Prussia, with now at her side a united and militarized nation, was prepared for war, and she was not. All the fighting took place on French soil, and the successive battles of Weissenburg, Wörth, Spicheren, Mars-la-Tour, Gravelotte, and St. Privat prepared the way for Sedan and the capitulation of the invested strongholds of Toul and Strasburg, Bazaine's disastrous surrender of Metz and 170,000 men. On 4th September, two days after Napoleon was taken prisoner at Sedan with Marshal MacMahon and his army of 100,000, revolution broke out in Paris; weary of being fed with false news, the third republic was proclaimed, and the Empress fled to England. Before the end of the month Paris was besieged, yet in spite of hunger and epidemic disease its defenders and citizens held out bravely until the end of January, when the investment was raised in consequence of an armistice preparatory to the negotiations for peace. In the meantime fighting had continued in the east and west, in the north and south, for the more desperate the situation became, the more resolute grew the spirit of the nation, and new armies seemed to spring up as by magic. Peace preliminaries were signed on 26th February, and were embodied in the Treaty of Frankfort of 10th May, under which France ceded to Germany Alsace with Strasburg and the German-speaking part of Lorraine with Metz, and undertook to pay within three years an indemnity of 200 million pounds.

The war brought home to the German tribes, as nothing in their history had done before, the two inspiring facts of a common nationality and a common fatherland. Of that fatherland Arndt, the statesman-poet, had sung in the dark and evil days of the tribulation, 'All Germany it shall be', and such after the long process of time it had now become. The union *de facto* consecrated by struggle and sacrifice was made a union *de jure* when the new German Empire was proclaimed in the Hall of Mirrors in Versailles on 18th January 1871, the anniversary of the creation of the Kingdom of Prussia 170 years before. As later constituted the Empire comprised twenty-five sovereign States, besides the imperial province of Alsace-Lorraine; the imperial office and title were restored in the person of the King of Prussia; the Federal Council and Diet of the North German Confederation were continued in enlarged form, and the Federal Chancellor became Imperial Chancellor; but the status, powers, and functions of the earlier organs of government remained substantially unchanged as did the democratic basis of the legislature.

Inasmuch as Prussia was the predominant partner in the Empire, her king being the Emperor and her Minister President the Imperial Chancellor, while Prussian votes virtually controlled the Federal Council, it followed that she would be able to direct national policy henceforth just as completely as Austria had done in the Bund and the earlier Empire, and that is what happened.

VI. THE BISMARCK RÉGIME – (i) DOMESTIC AFFAIRS

The thirty years following were for Germany a time of marked advance in many directions. During nearly twenty of those years Bismarck was at the helm of State, guiding its destinies with a firm hand, and on the whole with a sure and safe judgment. In foreign affairs his success was almost unqualified, and it was only in some aspects of his domestic policy that his masterful will led him astray. With his fondness for homely metaphor he had once said, 'Let Germany be put in the saddle and she will ride of herself'. It was his one thought and aim to keep her way clear of obstacles. He regarded the reorganized Empire as a 'saturated State', for which any further extension of frontiers could only be harmful. All he wanted, all he asked, was that it should have peace at home and abroad, and be allowed henceforth to develop its capacities to the full, free from outside meddling, and to make its own history in its own way.

It was an irony that the first difficulties with which he had to contend were of a purely domestic kind. Before the Empire was a year old he allowed himself to be drawn into a dispute with the Papacy. It seemed an ominous beginning for a State built on the ruins of the Holy Roman Empire of the German Nation, whose history had been for centuries full of quarrels between the Church and the secular power, in which the former had invariably won in the end. The trouble was caused by the promulgation of the papal dogma of infallibility, on 13th July 1871, the day after the French declaration of war. Suspicious of the political implications of the dogma, and fearing the formation in the Imperial and Prussian Diets of special Roman Catholic groups, Bismarck awaited developments with anxiety. When before the close of the year Roman Catholic professors and teachers were being coerced by their bishops into accepting the dogma, he took up the challenge, and the ten-years' struggle known from that time to this as the *Kulturkampf* opened. In that struggle, which was mainly confined to Prussia, the entire nation was divided on the old Reformation lines; and, while intense bitterness prevailed on both sides, the suffering was almost wholly on the side of the Roman clergy, from the prelacy downwards, and their flocks. Drastic laws were passed, most of them associated with the name of Dr Falk, then Prussian Minister of Public Worship, making it clear that in secular, including educational, matters, the State would not admit of interference by the spiritual arm; and the defiance of these laws led to the closing of hundreds of churches and schools, the wholesale imprisonment of archbishops, bishops, and priests, the sequestration of their goods, and the dissolution of the religious orders. From that time dates the institution of civil marriage, adopted as a weapon against Roman Catholic contumacy but made applicable to the entire Empire.

When the struggle had lasted eight years without any weakening of opposition, and further repressive measures seemed impracticable, voices everywhere began to call for peace, and no sooner was the will for compromise shown on both sides than ways for its exercise were found. One by one the exceptional laws were either repealed or put into cold storage, and before long people began to wonder why they had ever been passed. The time came when Bismarck complained that if repression had gone too far it had not been his intention, and that the fault lay with his adjutants and their subordinates.

Simultaneously with the fight with the Roman Catholic hierarchy the combative Chancellor challenged conclusions with the powerful movement known as Social Democracy. Since 1848, when the French Revolution gave a new stimulus to democratic endeavours, there had steadily grown amongst the working classes of Germany a parallel movement which combined economic with political aims. Early in the 'sixties more definite form was given to this movement by the brilliant Hebrew social agitator and reformer, Ferdinand Lassalle, whose most scholarly work, *The System of Acquired Rights*, appeared six years before the *Capital* of

Karl Marx, some of whose basic ideas it anticipated. The amelioration of the existing social conditions by far-going transformations was the ultimate object in view, and it was to be attained by the replacement of the oligarchic by the democratic State, many classes being in effect replaced by one, consisting of the manual workers.

Here was a clear challenge to the entire social order, and Bismarck was not the man to take lightly the disturbance of existing institutions. He began to follow the movement closely in 1871, when the single Socialist in the first Diet of the new Empire avowed sympathy with the Paris Commune, but it was only when the voting power of the party in the country had reached half a million, and the workers of the towns were being more and more won over by a skilful and highly developed system of agitation, that he began to contemplate legal measures of restraint.

Action was precipitated by two foul attempts upon the old Emperor's life in 1878. Bismarck's first Bill was rejected by 281 votes against 57 as a panic measure, but a new Diet passed a second by 222 votes against 149. It introduced drastic police measures for the regulation of associations, public meetings, and festivities, and the printing, sale, and circulation of books and newspapers, with heavy penalties for offenders; while Socialist agitators might be imprisoned, refused domicile in given areas, or deported from the country. The law was rigorously enforced, with the result of a repression of public opinion worthy of the Carlsbad Decrees (p. 82) of sixty years before. Few Socialist leaders escaped imprisonment or banishment or both. Bismarck wished to restrict free speech in the Diet itself, but so far few even of his friends were prepared to go. This coercive legislation lasted until 1890; but, far from being checked, the Socialist Party increased its voting power in the interval to nearly a million and a half, and its representation in the Diet to thirty-five, and the movement was still in flood.

He was equally unsuccessful in his endeavour to stamp out disaffection in the annexed Danish portion of Schleswig, the old German territory taken from France after the war, and the Polish districts of Eastern Prussia. In all cases harsh methods of administration were applied, and the only effect was to exasperate still more populations which refused to render a forced loyalty. Millions of pounds were expended in expropriating Polish landowners and replacing their tenants by German settlers, but the remedy proved worse than the disease, for the Poles promptly combined to form land banks and began to acquire German-owned properties in turn. Strong as was his belief in force as a bulwark of order, however, Bismarck was not blind to the existence of social evils which contributed to the spread of Socialism, and to the abatement of these he turned his attention. Here he had his Sovereign's cordial support. In 1871 he passed an Employers' Liability Act applying to factories, mines, and quarries, and factory inspection was introduced in Prussia in 1874, Saxony following suit. As soon as the anti-Socialist Law had been put in operation he embarked on a novel scheme of social insurance, the first instalment of which was to have been a measure of accident insurance. A bill was introduced in 1881, but as it was received unsympathetically he withdrew it and dissolved the Diet. The new Diet was opened on 17th November 1881, with a memorable Imperial Message on the social question, ever since regarded as the German charter of social reform, in which measures for insuring the working classes against sickness, accident, invalidity, and old age were promised, and these were passed between 1883 and 1889, since which time they have been repeatedly amended. When social reform legislation was promised in 1880 the Socialist leader and deputy August Bebel told the Government: 'To your positive measures for their benefit the workers reply with ringing laughter.' While that was incorrect it is no doubt true that the welcome given to the early social insurance laws was greatly tempered by the fact that benevolence and repression went hand in hand. In later years the value of these reforms was increasingly recognized, and they have been imitated in one way or another in most European countries.

Greater and more immediate success attended the Government's fiscal and economic reforms. From 1876 forward the railways of Prussia and other States were nationalized, and in 1879 the system of free trade gave place to a customs tariff, moderate at first but gradually extended both in scope and the scale of duties, and proving the precursor of a general resurgence of protection on the Continent. Throughout these years army bills rained incessantly upon the Diet, all justified by suspicion of the efforts of France to overtake and even pass her rival in warlike resources.

VII. THE BISMARCK RÉGIME – (ii) FOREIGN POLICY

The problem of foreign relations presented Bismarck with equally arduous tasks, and the first of them was the maintenance of the newly established political status. His immediate concern was to avert danger from France, which the war had left wounded more in spirit than in substance, and already cherishing thoughts of revenge. He sought to do this by isolating her, to which end he endeavoured to draw her possible friends into the orbit of Germany's influence. By the autumn of 1872 he had succeeded in bringing about a cordial *rapport* or *entente* between the three Emperors (of Germany, Austro-Hungary, and Russia), which Italy joined in the following year, so preparing the ground for the formal alliances which later became the foundation of his foreign policy.

Did Bismarck overreach himself by this adroit move? One result certainly was to throw France for the time wholly upon her own resources, but another was to spur her to redoubled efforts to overtake her rival in military strength and efficiency. It was possible to do this with the greater success and secrecy, since before the end of 1873, a year before the due time, the last instalment of the indemnity had been paid and the last German soldier had left French soil. In 1875 a war scare was engineered in Berlin, by way of warning France that if she wanted to fight, her old adversary was prepared, but its only effect was to alarm Russia and cause her to doubt the wisdom of exclusive friendships.

Directly Bismarck saw that the policy of isolation had failed he performed a *volte-face* and tried conciliation, encouraging France in colonial enterprises, and inviting her to take territory wherever it was to be had, so long as Strassburg and Metz were left alone. Bismarck was now approaching the zenith of his fame and influence, and was everywhere regarded as the pivot upon which European politics turned, yet while ready at all times to advise other Powers when asked, and occasionally when not asked, he resolutely refused to allow Germany to be entangled in their disputes. When in 1876 the revolts in Turkey's Balkan provinces led to the reopening of the Eastern question he would not interfere. After the Russo-Turkish War, however, he played a prominent and benevolent part as President of the Berlin Congress (1878) in adjusting rival claims and so making possible a fairly equitable settlement.

It was ominous, however, that Russia and Austria, who entered the congress as friendly neighbours, left it committed to rivalry in the Balkans. When in the following year, during the execution of the treaty, the Czar vigorously reproached the German Emperor for the failure of his Chancellor to give Russia the support she had a right to expect, Bismarck promptly concluded an alliance with Austria, with a view to providing against unseen yet possible dangers. Lord Salisbury, still distrustful of Russia, welcomed news of this stroke as 'good tidings of great joy', but if he believed that Bismarck intended to alienate that Power he was mistaken. In 1884, with his traditional preference for *coalitions à trois*, Bismarck drew Italy into the alliance. Then, fearing that he might have gone too far, he concluded in the same year a separate and secret treaty with Russia by which each Power undertook to maintain an attitude of 'benevolent neutrality' in the event of the other being attacked. This reinsurance policy only became known to the world in 1896, after Bismarck had ceased to be Chancellor. To the end of his career, while his fidelity to Austria never visibly weakened, he had the satisfaction of knowing that the wire between Berlin and St. Petersburg continued 'uncut'.

German policy in the Egyptian imbroglio, dating from Ismail Pasha's *coup d'état* of 1879, followed the same principal of non-intervention. When the spendthrift Khedive wished to repudiate his debts Bismarck was the first European Minister to protest; but as soon as Great Britain and France showed readiness to take the matter in hand he willingly withdrew into the background, declaring that Germany had no wish to 'throw any stones into the Egyptian garden'. Throughout the succeeding developments – the rebellion of Arabi and the soldiers, the bombardment of Alexandria and the British occupation – he continued to hold an observant, advisory, yet detached attitude, wishful that the two Powers which had begun the good work of establishing order in Egyptian affairs should continue it, and also fall out if they so pleased.

In spite of his qualified denial he certainly advised the British Government to 'take Egypt', just as he had advised France in 1874 and again in 1878 to take Tunis, which she did in 1881. How far his wish to see England in control of Egypt was dictated by the hope that she might be involved in interminable disputes with France is a question as impossible of proof as of disproof. Nevertheless, one may recall the fact that when in 1889 Bismarck urged Crispi[1] to join with him in favouring Russia's occupation of Constantinople a sinister tactical motive was admitted. 'Situated as she (Russia) is,' he said, 'it is impossible to attack her. On the Bosphorus she would be weakened and might easily be overpowered.'

Before long Great Britain fell out not only with France over the question of Egypt, but also with Germany over that of colonial rivalry. Interest in colonial enterprise, first aroused by the Great Elector two centuries before, was revived in the first half of last century by the band of gallant explorers and travellers which Germany then gave to the cause of science and civilization. In his *Memoirs*, Charles Greville relates how, when visiting Germany in 1843, he was surprised to hear people talking of the need for 'colonies and a navy'. Frederick William IV of Prussia was, in fact, willing at that time to buy California from Mexico as a home for the Germans who were emigrating to America in legions. As early as 1865 Bismarck himself was convinced that 'without colonies Prussia could never become a great maritime nation', though later he appears to have disavowed any wish to possess them; and he received unfavourably several projects of the kind which were pressed upon him by German oversea traders and others.

[1] The Italian statesman who had been drawn into the *Dreibund*.

The movement took more practical shape with the establishment of several propagandist associations from 1880 forward; and in 1884, acting at first hesitantly, the Chancellor yielded to the request of a Bremen merchant that he would give the Empire's protection to territories lying between Cape Colony and the Portuguese colony of Angola, over which he had obtained control. As protracted correspondence with the British Government on the question of title failed to elicit a definite statement, he proclaimed a protectorate over the territories, fortified by the knowledge that the Colonial Office had never claimed them, but, on the contrary, had down to the end of 1880 expressly refused to extend British jurisdiction to them. Only when possession had thus been taken was objection offered, though not even then on a plea of prior rights, and the resulting dispute temporarily disturbed the harmonious relations of the two Governments and nations. Other acquisitions followed, adding to the existing friction – in 1884 the Cameroons and Togoland in West Africa, and the north-eastern part of New Guinea; in 1885 territory in East Africa and some small island groups in the Pacific; and in 1889 the Caroline and Pelew Islands (bought from Spain), and other Pacific islands, with a hand in the *condominium* of Samoa.

Simultaneously with the bold pledge thus offered to commerce the Imperial Diet was persuaded to vote large subsidies to mail steamship services to various parts of Africa and America. Already Germany had a penny post to Australia, but twenty years were to pass before Great Britain similarly encouraged commercial dealings with her own colony.

For a long time the administration of some of the colonies was far from satisfactory, and many excesses of a deplorable kind occurred, due to the choice of men who deserved more to experience in their own persons the heavy hand of authority than the power to apply it to others. It was in the territories which had the misfortune to be misgoverned in those early years that native risings, of the kind which have so often resulted from the first contact of uncivilized populations with white men who came to them not as missionaries but as masters, chiefly occurred. The new century had opened before the colonial empire, comprising territories with an aggregate area of over a million square miles, and a coloured population of twelve millions, became completely pacified.

Until the colonial era opened, Bismarck's attitude to Great Britain had been consistently friendly, and, though the misunderstandings of that time tempted him to occasional petulant outbursts, he never wished for, and never would have tolerated, open rupture, even of a diplomatic kind, with a country and a nation which he counted amongst the strongest pillars of European stability, and whose success in the world evoked at once his admiration and his envy. In November 1887 he delicately sounded Lord Salisbury as to the possibility of Great Britain joining the Triple Alliance, though without response; and as late as 1889, when his Ministerial career was about to close, he said that if ever there seemed danger of losing the traditional friendly *rapport* with England he would 'be cautious and seek to prevent its loss'.

When the year 1888 opened, Bismarck was still at the height of his power, still the true ruler of Germany and the foremost of European statesmen. In that year William I died full of years and revered in a way that no German Emperor of the earlier order had ever been (9th March). Little as he had figured publicly in affairs of State, particularly in his later years, he had a large portion of the sagacity, judgment, and insight of the true statesman, and though he generally deferred to Bismarck, it seldom happened that he had not first been 'persuaded in his own mind'. He was a man of rare probity of character, and the example which he set of a pure court and of a blameless private life was not the least valuable of his legacies to his people.

There followed the short reign – in effect an *interregnum* – of Frederick III, who knew while still uncrowned that the common doom of humanity would not be long spared to him. Hitherto he had not been allowed to take an active part in public life except during the short regency which was occasioned by a madman's attempted assassination of his father, but enough was known of him to justify the Liberals in hoping, and the Conservatives in fearing, that he would introduce a more progressive and tolerant spirit into political life and legislation. For any such change his hundred days of little more than titular sovereignty (9th March to 15th June) offered no opportunity; during the tragic time no incidents of importance disturbed the tranquil current of domestic life, and foreign relations and policy continued as before.

VIII. The Third Emperor and the 'New Course'

About the character of the Emperor Frederick's son and successor, William II, far less uncertainty prevailed, though as events proved many of the current opinions and speculations concerning him were singularly wide of the mark. The speech with which he opened the Imperial Diet ten days after his accession, with its promise in domestic policy to 'care for the weak and crushed in the struggle for existence', and in foreign policy to 'live in peace with every man so far as in me lies', made an excellent impression, and it was observed with satisfaction that his old intimate, and almost filial, relations with the Chancellor were maintained.

Nevertheless, the young ruler soon gave signs that he had a mind of his own and that he did not intend his high office to be a sinecure.

The first serious friction between the Sovereign and his chief Minister occurred at the end of 1889 over a proposal to prolong the anti-Socialist Law. This course the former disapproved, and Bismarck unwillingly yielded. In the following February the Emperor, again contrary to the Chancellor's advice, convened an international conference on the subject of labour law reform. The critical strain came, however, when he summarily cancelled the right which Bismarck had hitherto enjoyed, both as Prussian Minister President and Imperial Chancellor, of being present at audiences given by the Sovereign to other Ministers. The clash of temperaments and wills which these and several minor episodes occasioned gave little promise of future amicable co-operation, and when Bismarck sent in his resignation (18th March 1890), firmly believing that it would at once bring his 'young master' to his senses, just as the mere threat of resignation had often overborne the opposition of his grandfather, it was accepted, as much to his astonishment as to his chagrin. Within ten days he had left Berlin and retired into the seclusion of his rural seat, Friedrichsruh, in the Sachsenwald. Count Herbert, his eldest son, for some time past Foreign Minister, was invited to remain, but he declined. Four years later anxious patriots patched up a reconciliation, in sign of which Bismarck visited the Court in Berlin, while the Emperor in turn made pilgrimage to Friedrichsruh, but the healing of the rupture was superficial; beneath the scar remained an incurable wound.

With the appointment to the Chancellorship of Count von Caprivi, a man of irreproachable character, a 'very perfect knight', but as yet, on his own admission, 'strange to political affairs', the epical era of modern German history may be said to have closed; but a period rich in domestic developments of a practical kind opened. It fell to Caprivi to carry out in 1890 a bargain already concluded with Great Britain, whereby Germany secured possession of the long-coveted island of Heligoland, lying in the estuary of the Elbe, in return for territory in East Africa and the recognition of a British protectorate in Zanzibar. Bismarck had tried to obtain this cession in 1884 and again in 1885, Lord Granville declining where now Lord Salisbury complied. In the same year the Labour Conference bore fruit in the form of legislation restricting the work hours of children, juveniles, and women, the levelling up of factory inspection, and the formation of tribunals for the settlement of disputes between work-people and their employers. A more liberal spirit was shown in the administration of Alsace-Lorraine and the Polish districts of Prussia, though in the latter case without response, with the result that the policy of expropriation and resettlement by German families was later resumed and extended.

The policy of high tariffs for agricultural produce was modified, on proof of the hardship to which dear food had exposed labour and industry since Germany had become more than before a manufacturing and exporting country. A number of commercial treaties were now concluded on the principle of 'conventional' tariffs, resulting from special bargaining with the States concerned, and in consequence several tariff wars were either ended or avoided. In compensation the agriculturists, now organized in a powerful Agrarian League, obtained ameliorations of different kinds, such as relief in taxation, State loans, subsidies towards the construction of light railways, drainage and irrigation schemes, and works of reclamation, a stricter law against usury, and the abolition of the sugar convention.

In foreign affairs the first Chancellor's cautious policy was reversed, with untoward results. It had been a leading object of Bismarck's diplomatic manœuvring to maintain friendly relations with Russia at all costs. That was why he immediately followed the formal alliance with Austria with a supplementary reinsurance treaty with Russia, so making it as certain as was humanly possible that while in the event of war Germany would be able to rely upon a pledged friend on one frontier she would be secure against a potential enemy on the other. Both the new Emperor and the new Chancellor were convinced that this arrangement was unfair to Austria and morally untenable, and the semi-alliance with Russia was allowed to lapse. From his retreat in the Sachsenwald Bismarck, smarting from the slings and arrows of outrageous fortune, uttered a sharply worded criticism of this step as likely to prove disastrous, and the warning was soon justified. On the Russian side coolness set in, and the French Government, which had long hankered for closer friendship, was not slow to notice and profit by it. In the summer of 1891 the Czar welcomed a French fleet at Cronstadt, and the festivities begun there were continued in St. Petersburg. Two years later a Russian fleet called at Toulon, and the conclusion of a military convention followed. In 1895 Mons. Ribot, then the French Premier, publicly claimed Russia as 'our ally', and when in 1897 President Faure made a ceremonial visit to the Russian capital the Czar spoke of *'les deux nations amies et alliées'* – an open attestation of a firm alliance.

A departure from the spirit of Bismarck's principles of foreign policy even more fundamental was the Emperor's disposition, shown from the earliest months of what came to be known as the 'new course', to plunge into international disputes without need and sometimes without evident purpose. No contemporary statesman played so prominent a part in foreign affairs as Bismarck, yet he never intervened except with the object of protecting vital national interests, or preserving peace in Europe, or, if that were impossible, of narrowing the area of conflict. Some of the third Emperor's excursions in what came to be known as *Weltpolitik* were dictated quite openly by the wish for prestige, a species of policy which Bismarck severely condemned. Challenging phrases, loosely strung and lightly flung, like 'Henceforth nothing in the world must be settled without the intervention of Germany and the German Emperor', were ominous of the direction in which events were tending. In January 1896 occurred the incident of the Kruger telegram, intimating that he would have been prepared to send assistance against the Transvaal raiders had it been necessary – an impetuous interference unexcused by the crime which provoked it, since it was diplomatically irregular in view of the known fact that under the London Convention of 1884 the foreign relations of the Transvaal State were controlled by Great Britain. Episodes of that kind shocked sober statesmen, and created everywhere feelings of uneasiness and apprehension.

An instability of character which led the Emperor to be the friend of every one in turn but of no one long, while it made any calculation of political probabilities as difficult for foreign Governments as for his own nominal advisers, was bound to produce curious consequences, occasionally making for discomfort one day and convenience the next, both in the same quarter. Thus directly he saw the harm which had been done by the Kruger manifesto his love for the Boers waxed cold as he hastened to make amends. He also did Great Britain valuable service when France was again making trouble in Egypt, a service which probably influenced Lord Salisbury in concluding with Germany the treaty of 1898 for the partition of the Portuguese colonies in the event of their coming into the market and in agreeing in the following year to the cession to her of the British islands in the Samoan group. The reconciliation thus effected seemed likely at one time to lead to a more or less formal alliance, to which end Mr Chamberlain, then Colonial Secretary, made overtures on the occasion of the Emperor's visit to Windsor in November 1899; but the idea did not pass beyond the stage of polite discussion. The Emperor's influence was still more helpful when, on the outbreak of the Boer War, France and Russia were eager to intervene, and were only prevented because Germany declined to join them.

It would be unjustifiable to suggest that the Emperor ever wanted war: his fault was that so many of his actions seemed to create the impression that he would not have minded it. A speech intended to prove to the

world that it had no stronger and sincerer friend of peace would be followed soon after by sword-rattling and minatory utterances more suited
to the after-dinner rhetoric of the officers' mess-room. It was simply a
question of mood: all his emotions, good and bad, were evanescent, and
his preferences and sympathies veered from one extreme to the other like
the weather-vane in a gale. If during his reign military preparations
never ceased, almost every session of the Diet producing new army
schemes and demands for additional votes, large or small, the cause was
as much the unrest and suspicion caused abroad by the ruler himself as
the growing menace of France.

In his relations with the Chancellor and other Ministers his special
weakness was an exaggerated egoism. Under the obsession of extravagant
notions about the rights and duties of monarchs he reintroduced what
was virtually the old system of personal government, and his constitutional advisers became for the time mere ciphers. He had publicly
declared at Düsseldorf in 1891: 'One only is master in the Empire and it
is I – I will tolerate no other'; and to this provocative sentiment he
constantly gave effect. He claimed the right to control and, if so minded,
to veto both domestic and foreign policy; not only did he insist on approving or disapproving all acts of State at will, but he initiated measures
of the most delicate and contentious character, and publicly discussed
them not as a judge but as an advocate; occasionally he formed important
decisions and acted upon them without informing his principal Minister.

The position of Chancellor becoming at last intolerable, Caprivi resigned in October 1894, and was succeeded by Prince Hohenlohe, a
practised diplomatist who added to the wide education and generous
outlook which the modern statesman should possess but rarely does the
calm judgment of the philosopher, and the practical knowledge of the
man of affairs. For a time the current of domestic legislation ran more
sluggishly. One of the most important measures which matured during
his tenure of office was the Civil Code of the Empire (1896), upon which
jurisconsults had worked for twenty years, and it came into operation in
1900. At the instigation of the reactionary parties which, stronger or
weaker, have always been able to influence legislation and policy in the
German Imperial and Prussian parliaments, two attempts were made to
stem the growth of Socialism by restrictive measures recalling the defunct
and discredited Bismarckian law; but they were frustrated, and Hohenlohe
never fell into that trap again.

During his Chancellorship, man of peace though he was, the question
of naval expansion became prominent, the Emperor providing the stimulus.
When Heligoland came to Germany in 1890 he had welcomed the

acquisition as 'a bulwark by sea, a protection for German fishermen, a base for my ships of war, and a shield and shelter for the German Ocean and against every enemy who may venture to show himself upon it'. Five years later the great Kiel ship canal, connecting two seas, was opened; and in the meantime the expenditure on the navy had increased from two and a half to five million pounds. In 1897 the Emperor publicly stated that he would not rest until the navy had been 'brought to the same standard as the army'. That meant a large increase in quantity as well as in quality, and after first reorganizing the Admiralty and putting Admiral Tirpitz in charge, he caused the Navy Bill of 1898 to be introduced. It made financial provision for the first instalment of a grandiose programme of shipbuilding, to be executed within a period of seven years.

Before this time the Navy League had been formed, and its vehement agitation, carried on throughout the length and breadth of the land, greatly strengthened the hands of the Government. Other events which helped to create a universal eagerness for a powerful and mobile fleet were the murder of German missionaries and the wrecking of German mission stations in China in 1897; the Boer War which broke out in 1899, and divided German opinion very unequally, the nation siding as one man with the Boers, and the Emperor standing alone with the British; and arising out of that war the outburst of indignation caused at the close of 1899 by the seizure of German mail steamers on the high seas, on suspicion – in the event unjustified – of carrying contraband. Henceforth it was as easy to pass a fresh Navy Bill as it had been aforetime to obtain larger votes for the army, with the result of increasing anxiety in Great Britain and eventually of a tension in the political relationship of the two countries which from the end of the century steadily grew more acute.

Meanwhile, the material life of the nation had made rapid progress. Here the Emperor's energetic initiative and his personal influence generally were altogether helpful. In encouraging industrial, mercantile, and maritime enterprise he emulated the example of his great ancestors, the three 'makers of Prussia'. He had no false pride on the subject of honest trading, and was as ready to act as propagandist in friendly foreign courts for a patent spirit lamp as to open a canal or launch an ocean-going steamship at home. He was also an educational enthusiast; and, though as *Gymnasiast* he had himself passed through the usual classical mill, he had the courage to preach the importance of imparting to the German youth of his day an adequate knowledge of history, especially the history of its own country, and of relating the work of the schools generally to the conditions and needs of modern life.

During his reign, and in part owing to his encouragement, a strong

impulse was given to the extension and reconditioning of towns, many
of which doubled and trebled in population during the last three decades
of the century. The old seaports began a new and more vigorous life,
and on the great rivers – the Rhine, the Elbe, the Oder, and the Vistula –
and their larger tributaries, extensive harbours and quays were built and
equipped by the municipalities at an expense beyond the power of private
corporations. Agriculture likewise throve under the shelter of the tariff
walls and the assistance given in many other ways by the Imperial and
State Governments.

So great was the economic expansion that the earlier loss of population
by emigration, which even in 1880 amounted to 200,000 a year, gradually
fell to one-tenth of that figure, and in normal times it was only possible
to meet the needs of industry and agriculture by a large importation of
labour, mainly Polish, Russian, Italian, and Austrian, according to locality.
In the fruits of this progress the working classes shared liberally. Work
was abundant, wages increased, and the large amount of town-building
led to extensive slum clearances and a general improvement in housing
conditions, though the evil system of huge tenement blocks continued,
except where the single family house had been traditional.

Hohenlohe resigned in October 1900, tired of office and still more tired
of the humiliation of feeling that he was in the way. His experience had
been that of Caprivi: he was the Minister of a Sovereign who would
rather have governed without Ministers, the chief counsellor of a man
who himself possessed all counsel. Directly he felt sure that the Emperor
had no more need of him and wanted him to go, he went.

His successor was Count (later Prince) Bernhard von Bülow, another
ex-diplomatist, but one of the more professional type, a man of brilliant
if somewhat showy talents, unrivalled as a political strategist, singularly
eloquent and persuasive as an advocate, yet, though a statesman of conspicuous parts, lacking somewhat in the essential solidity of the true
German character. Nevertheless, it stood to him as a supreme merit, his
rightful claim to which alone proved his exceptional strength, that he
was the only Chancellor of the last reign who possessed the ability to
control the Emperor and dared to use it, yet was himself immovable
against his will and better knowledge.

BIBLIOGRAPHY TO CHAPTER III

Bismarck, Prince. *Gedanken und Erinnerungen.* 2 vols. 1898. Eng. trans. 1898

Darmstaedter, F. *Bismarck and the Creation of the Second Reich.* 1948

Dawson, W. H. *The Evolution of Modern Germany.* 2nd ed. 1919

Dawson, W. H. *The German Empire, 1867-1914.* 2 vols. 1919

Dawson, W. H. *Bismarck and State Socialism.* 1890

Eyck, Erich. *Bismarck: Leben und Werk.* 3 vols. Zürich, 1941-44

Gooch, G. P. *Germany.* Modern World Series. 1925

Henderson, E. F. *A Short History of Germany.* 2 vols. 1902

Lamprecht, K. *Deutsche Geschichte.* 1891-1909

Marriott, J. A. R., and Robertson, C. G. *The Evolution of Prussia.* 1915

Meyer, A. O. *Bismarck. Der Mensch und der Staatsmann.* Stuttgart, 1950

Robertson, C. G. *Prince Bismarck.* 1918

Rose, J. H., and others. *Germany in the 19th Century.* 1915

Treitschke, H. von. *Deutsche Geschichte im 19ten Jahrhundert.* 5 vols. 1879-94

Ward, A. W. *Germany.* 3 vols. 1916-18

Cambridge Modern History. 1902-9, passim

CHAPTER IV

GERMAN HISTORY FROM 1900 TO 1931

POLITICAL DEVELOPMENT

DURING the period of economic and political expansion the foreign policy of Germany was of greater importance than developments at home, and the reason for this can be seen quite clearly in the rapid growth of international trade in the latter decades of the nineteenth century, the enormously complicated ramifications of international finance, generally allied with industry, and in the new conception of economic power which was rapidly coming into prominence – the conception of power based on world rather than purely national frontiers. One must, in order to obtain a just perspective, examine German foreign policy from the double point of view of colonization and of international trade.

From 1878 onwards, one could see emerging three great colonizing powers, Great Britain which was already firmly established, Russia and France; and many of the political changes of the period were dictated by adjustments in the colonizing sphere. Thus, Russia aimed at expanding its sphere of influence eastwards into Manchuria and Korea, south into Persia, Afghanistan and India, and south-west into the Balkans. To render such penetration possible, in the Balkans for example, it was necessary to solve the problem of communications between the Black Sea, the Sea of Marmora and the Mediterranean, so that any Slav confederacy which would be built up in the Balkans could be joined to Russia by sea as well as by land. France extended its control over Northern Africa, aimed at cutting across Central Africa through the Sudan into Arabia, with possibly some idea of establishing a French zone in the Middle East. Great Britain found itself forced to defend its position against Russia in India, Afghanistan and Persia, while it had to check the ambitions of France in North-East Africa and render impossible the penetration of France into the Middle East. Britain was concerned, therefore, to maintain the integrity of Turkey and strengthen the hands of Japan, while its paramount interest, as far as France was concerned, was to develop closer Anglo-Italian relations. The theory was – the neutralization of the colonizing ambitions of Russia and France by the use of powers in active or potential opposition to them.

To this series of intrigues and adjustments should be added the rivalry between Austria and Russia in the Balkans – a rivalry which threatened on several occasions to cause a European war. From the Congress of Berlin onwards this threat of war was never entirely absent from European calculations. It was the distinction of Bismarck that he understood exactly the international political situation as it became defined through negotiations between the principal colonizing powers, while he had a very clear understanding of European cross-currents which, if led into the wrong channels, would cause international difficulties. He made Germany an enormously powerful European power, with very high prestige both at home and abroad, by his capacity to act as a balancing element between diverging forces and to draw to himself any strength that the play of those forces generated, while avoiding at the same time responsibility. His ambition was to maintain the *status quo* in European politics, and to keep France and Russia isolated from each other, while damping down the ambitions and the intransigence of Austria. His principle was to affirm the position of Germany by isolating the great European powers which, united, could overcome him. Thus he was able, for example, to keep Russia and France quiet, while he defeated Austria in 1866 and broke the domination of Austria as a German-speaking power. Four years later he was able to keep Russia again at bay and maintain friendly relations with Austria and Great Britain and defeat France. In 1876, when the ambitions of Austria and Russia in the Balkans threatened to precipitate a European war, he aimed at creating an Anglo-Franco-Russian concert to deal with the Balkan problems, while restraining Austria.

In the 'eighties his negotiations were aimed at strengthening Germany in the centre of Europe, flanked on one side by the Three Emperors' Alliance (Austria, Russia, and Germany) and on the other side by an entente between Germany, Italy, Austria, and Great Britain. By bringing these forces into balance through direct negotiation he expected to maintain the *status quo*, avoid war, and bring favourable conditions to bear on the consolidation and economic expansion of the German Empire. The balance of power, according to his conception, would be obtained through the smoothing out of Russian and Austrian interests in the Balkans and the Near East, the adoption by Russia of a defensive position which could only be maintained with the assistance of a German alliance, the detachment of Great Britain from France through skilful utilization of the Mediterranean and the Egyptian questions, and, finally, the creation of closer relations with Austria and Russia, which would render impossible the combination of both of these Powers against Germany. The position would then be reached where the leading Powers in Europe, with the exception of France, would require German assistance or mediation, and in this way strengthen the prestige of the new Empire.

At this time Bismarck was able to carry out much of his programme, owing to the fact that he had no desire to carry out ambitious colonization schemes. It was evident, however, that Russian and Austrian differences could not be neutralized in this fashion for more than a few years, and difficulties in Bulgaria followed on the Revolution of September 1885. The union of Ostrumelia with Bulgaria was held by all the Powers, with the exception of Great Britain, as a breach of the Berlin Peace of 1878, and Serbia demanded the cession of Old Serbia as some balance against the expansion of Bulgaria itself. In the war which intervened the Serbians were completely defeated; and only through the intervention of Austria did Serbia avoid complete disaster. The Peace that was arranged confirmed the occupation of Ostrumelia, while it saved Serbia. Russia, finding itself outmanœuvred, forced ultimately Prince Alexander to abdicate in Bulgaria, and the Czar attempted to dominate matters by sheer force. To this procedure both Great Britain and Austria took exception, and Germany found itself in the position of having to decide between supporting Russia or approving the attitude adopted by Austria. In this case Bismarck placed himself on the Russian side and in this way encouraged Great Britain and Italy to link up with Austria in defending Bulgaria against Russian claims.

The Bulgarian crisis was solved by the defeat of the Russian plans, and the Three Emperors' Pact, which had been renewed in 1884, ceased to have any effect. To avoid war again, Bismarck made a Reinsurance Treaty with Russia in 1887 which determined the limits within which the neutrality of both Russia and Germany should be maintained against a third power. Bulgaria was recognized, for example, as being within the range of Russian influence. This Reinsurance Pact showed apparently that Germany had abandoned Austria. We know now that Bismarck's intention was purely to allay the suspicions of Russia, while he actively pursued the idea of closer alliance with Great Britain. He seconded the efforts made by Austria, Italy, and Great Britain to form a triple alliance to maintain largely the *status quo* in the Mediterranean and the Near East, while nominally Germany stood aside; and at the end of his reign as Chancellor he had reached the stage where an alliance with Great Britain was no longer a matter of somewhat doubtful discussion but of actual negotiation.

Both Beaconsfield and Salisbury, although they were influenced by the desire to maintain British isolation, recognized that the peace of Europe would be guaranteed most completely by some form of agreement or joint working with Germany where German aims could be identified with the will to preserve peace. On two occasions at least Bismarck attempted to bring Great Britain into the Triple Alliance of Germany, Italy, and Austria: once in 1887 when he raised the matter in a private letter; and again in 1889 when a formal proposal was definitely made to Salisbury. It was generally agreed at that time that a European war would be precipitated, not by any attack made by France against Germany or by Russia against Germany, but by Russia against Austria, when Germany, through its alliance with Austria, would be involved even against the agreement made in the Reinsurance Pact. Under these conditions alliance with Great Britain would be a possibility; but if Germany pursued an active colonial policy, or aimed definitely at political control of the whole eastern section of Europe, the opposition of Great Britain would almost automatically take place, and so the motive for closer relations of Great Britain with France and Russia would be created. We know that from 1890 onwards attempts had been made to create conditions favourable to an Anglo-Franco-Russian entente, but the Fashoda incident and the sympathy shown by practically all the continental powers to the Boers in the Boer War confirmed Great Britain in her policy of isolation.

The advent to power of Wilhelm II and the dismissal of Bismarck brought to an end any possibility of *rapprochement* between Germany and Great Britain in the future, and from 1890 onwards the cleavage between these two countries became wider and wider – a cleavage the responsibility for which must be attributed to Wilhelm and to his advisor Bülow. At this distance of time we can see that the German foreign policy, interfused as it was by the imperialistic desire to become a great colonial power like France and Great Britain, and to affirm a predominant position both on land and sea, was peculiar stupidity, since it transgressed one of the great principles on which Bismarck had realized his great achievement of German political unity and prestige in foreign affairs, namely, that of balance and moderation.

Economic conditions at no time justified Germany in aiming at an extensive colonial policy. From 1895 onwards the industrial development of Germany had reached such a stage that there was no pressure of population outside of the frontiers. The balance of migration which, up to 1895, had been in favour of emigration and had shown that the growth of population in Germany was greater than its resources could bear, changed to one in favour of immigration from 1896 onwards. In other words, Germany had no need of outlets for her surplus population during the period of greatest stress in foreign affairs, and was actually able to absorb additional workers from other countries, especially Poland. There was little economic justification, therefore, for the widely advertised and somewhat theatrically-posed colonial expansion policy, and it served merely to antagonize Great Britain, while the useless parade of the German fleet and the proclamation of determination to make this fleet second to none in the world only served to engender deeper suspicion of German plans and motives. Under the triumvirate Wilhelm, Tirpitz, and Bülow, the policy of Germany seemed to aim at consolidating the Anglo-Franco-Russian entente, while it gave little real basis for direct hostility between Germany and Great Britain. Examination of the Bülow Memoirs shows that the element of uncertainty and theatrical display is never entirely absent, and one has a feeling at times that if European statesmen had had a sense of humour and been capable of appreciating performance at its real and not at its propagandist value, the war of 1914 might have been avoided. The German politicians took themselves and were in turn taken too seriously. There is a very pertinent observation of King Edward: 'If only I knew who really rules in Berlin' (1901).

There was, however, some justification for German distrust of British intentions. At the time when Great Britain was most anxious to cultivate German friendship, at the beginning of 1898, France was threatening the Upper Nile and Russia was developing imperialistic aims in the Far East. Again, at the end of the following year, the Boer War, which created a definite reaction against Great Britain and made real for once the gesture of splendid isolation which was characteristic of British diplomacy during the nineteenth century, showed that a certain danger to Britain might arise from continental intervention. Again, in 1901, when the Boxer movement took place in China and Russia marched into Manchuria, and, through the occupation of Port Arthur, was assured of an additional outlet on the Yellow Sea, Great Britain became alarmed and discussed with Germany the possibility of a general defensive alliance and a special agreement regarding Morocco. Germany's attitude in 1901 was definitely unfavourable to such an alliance, and so Great Britain was forced to the conclusion that it would be better to develop friendly relations both with Russia and France, and through agreement solve the colonial problem. On the 8th April 1903 an arrangement was made with France whereby Morocco, with certain limitations, should be recognized as within the sphere of influence of the French, and Egypt as within the British sphere.

In 1905 France occupied Morocco and, in the resulting Morocco crisis, precipitated by the attitude of Germany, who demanded a conference before Morocco should become definitely French, Great Britain took the part of France, with the result that Germany was forced to give way. In the case of Russia, British policy aimed at close alliance with Japan; so much so, that in the Russo-Japanese War of 1904-5 Japan received very considerable assistance from Great Britain, above all in the supply of munitions. In the peace which ensued, Great Britain used its influence in favour of conciliation, and, in this way, prepared Russia for a change of attitude towards British plans in the Far East. The settlement of Algeciras, which concluded the Morocco difficulties, consolidated the Franco-English alliance against Germany, and French and British military conversations were begun, the object of these conversations being the preparation of a joint defence against a German attack on France through Belgium.

At the end of 1905 the encirclement of Germany was all but complete, and much of this must be attributed to the clumsiness of German diplomacy. From the time when the Kaiser sent a telegram to Kruger in 1896 to the Dogger Bank Affair, when Germany showed her sympathy with Russia, and Britain expressed her objection to the coaling of Russian ships by Germany, a whole series of incidents testified to a growing psychological strain. The German naval programme of 1898 was followed by the much more extensive plans of 1900, the concessions obtained by Germany to extend the Bagdad Railway from Konia to Basra, the change in tone of the German Press, which began to be anti-British in the extreme, and gave expression to extreme views of military and naval experts on the necessity for an enormously powerful German army and navy. The effect of these incidents was to create a situation in 1906 where Britain was prepared to form an alliance both with Russia and with France.

In 1907 an Anglo-Russian Treaty was signed which stabilized conditions in the Far East, recognized Tibet to be a buffer state between British India and Siberia, Afghanistan to be outside the Russian sphere of interests, Northern Persia to be recognized as within the Russian, and Southern Persia within the British range of interests, with a neutral section between. In the Balkans the general effect of such a Treaty was to substitute for Austro-Russian co-operation Anglo-Russian. In this way difficulties outside of Europe, as far as France and Russia were concerned, were cleared away. Russia, weakened in its desire to extend to the East, became more directly interested in Europe and the Balkans, while France could devote its attention purely to the German menace. The encirclement of Germany was not only far advanced, but its opponents had cleared up the international situation so completely that Europe alone could enter into discussion.

In 1907 the conditions were ripe for a European war, and we are justified in regarding the period which intervened between 1907 and 1914 merely as an interval before the final trial of strength. At that time it should have been apparent to the German politicians that their whole policy since 1890 had been mistaken. In international affairs German prestige was lower than it had ever been. Germany had ceased to be the centre of balance and was regarded with suspicion by the majority of European countries. Its attempts to form treaties with Great Britain in 1901 and Russia in 1904 had been a failure, owing to the attitude adopted by German politicians, and it had been quite unsuccessful as a colonizing power at a time when both France and Britain were extending their possessions and their spheres of influence.

If attention is devoted purely to the period 1890 to 1907, we find Great Britain in 1890 consolidating, through agreement with Germany, the possession of South-West Africa and, through agreement with France, the possession of Lake Chad; while, in that year, Germany's acquisitions were represented by Heligoland, East Africa, the coast of German East Africa and Zambesiland.[1] Between 1891 and 1900 we find Great Britain consolidating still more her position in Africa on the Niger coast and Nyassaland, Central Africa, Matabeleland, Swaziland, Tongaland, Ashanti, Somaliland, Southern Rhodesia and Gold Coast, while it made agreement with Portugal and France regarding the delimitation of territories. In the East the position on the North-West Frontier of India was cleared up; British Baluchistan was extended; while a whole series of islands in the Malay Archipelago and in the vicinity of Australia was recognized as British territory, and the Sudan reoccupied. During this period German acquisitions were represented by a small additional section of Togoland and the occupation of the Caroline, Palos, and Marianne islands. At the time that Britain occupied Wei-hai-wei in China, Germany occupied Kiao-chow. From 1901 to 1908, while Britain was creating the Commonwealth of Australia, moving northwards in Ashanti and making agreements with Turkey bearing on the hinterland of Aden and the island of Perim, with Persia on the frontiers of Baluchistan, with Abyssinia on the frontiers of East Africa, with Russia on Persia, Afghanistan and Tibet, with Italy on Somaliland, and with France on the government of the New Hebrides, Germany could only point to occupation of several areas in the vicinity of Lake Chad and an agreement with France on the Cameroons. From 1908 to 1913, which was a comparatively inactive

[1] German East Africa, between what was then British East Africa and Portuguese East Africa, after the war the Tanganyika territory. Zanzibar and other islands remained British.

period in colonization, when Britain acquired a number of States in Malaya, the Sandwich, South Shetland and Graham islands, Germany had no developments of any importance to record other than extension of the Cameroons.

On balance, therefore, the colonizing efforts of Germany were confined to gestures mostly of an irritating type, and this whole period from 1892 to 1913 was characterized by a lack of achievement compared with which the work of Bismarck in acquiring through agreement German centres of influence in Africa and in Oceania must be regarded as impressive, even if Bismarck attached no importance to colonial development.

German policy had, in 1907, reached the position where it could point to no positive achievement in any sphere, while there was a fairly clear impression that, in the event of a European war, Russia and France at least were so strongly linked together that they alone could thwart any attempt made by Germany to dominate Europe. At the end of 1907 the Kaiser visited London and delivered a wholly conciliatory speech at the Guildhall; and the speech was followed by an attempted agreement over the Bagdad Railway, where the Emperor offered the control of a section in Persia to Great Britain in accordance with the request made previously by Haldane. This attempt at conciliation failed, largely owing to the indecision of Sir Edward Grey and his insistence that France and Russia should be consulted. In 1908 again Lloyd George raised the question of more friendly relations with Germany: 'Why should there not be an Anglo-German Entente? We have done it with France, we have done it with Russia, we have done it with the United States.' But two acts of indiscretion by the German Emperor: the letter to Lord Tweedmouth on naval policy and the *Daily Telegraph* interview which, while affirming the Kaiser's personal goodwill towards Great Britain, stated that the German people were unfriendly, made a further *rapprochement* difficult. On the other side, mention must be made of the visit of Clemenceau to King Edward at Marienbad in 1908 and the motion of Lord Roberts which was carried in the House of Lords: 'That the defence of these islands necessitates the immediate provision of an army so strong ... that the most formidable nation would hesitate to attempt a landing on these shores.'

The visit of King Edward to the Czar at Reval in June 1908, and proposals for Anglo-Russian co-operation in carrying out reforms in Macedonia, were causes of some anxiety, but the first crisis of any significance after 1907 was that resulting from the Revolution in Turkey and the annexation of Bosnia by Austria. It was suggested in 1908 that Austria and Russia should negotiate an agreement whereby Austria, in return for

Russian recognition of the annexation of Bosnia and Herzegovina and the Sanjak, would raise no objection to the opening of the Straits to Russian warships. It was decided, however, to consult other countries before such an agreement could be put in force, but meantime Austria proposed to proclaim the independence of Bulgaria on 6th October 1908 and to annex Bosnia on 7th October. These proposals were adversely criticized by Britain and Russia on the grounds that they were a violation of the Treaty of Berlin, and could not be implemented without an international conference, while Serbia demanded, as a price for recognizing the annexation, compensation from Austria. Austria made her peace with Turkey on the basis of compensation for the loss of crown lands and railway rights, and, in view of this arrangement, Russia, Italy, and France agreed to accept the German proposal that the Berlin Treaty be modified to cover the annexation. On 27th March of the following year the crisis came to an end. The solution of the Bosnian crisis was, in many ways, a victory for Russia, and in the hands of a skilful German foreign minister an opportunity might have been taken to drive a wedge between British and Russian relations, but such a development was rendered impossible by the intensification of Anglo-German naval rivalry.

In 1906 two important changes took place in the naval sphere, namely, the concentration of the greater part of the British fleet in the North Sea and the appearance of the large capital ship, the Dreadnought. The Dreadnought rendered necessary the reconstruction of the Kiel Canal and justified in a sense the extensions which were proposed in German naval budgets at that time.

In 1908 it was calculated that the programmes as they stood would give Britain a bare twelve vessels of modern type compared with nine of German, but by 1920 Germany would have attained equality. The claim was made by McKenna in the British Parliament that Britain should build at once four extra Dreadnoughts. He foretold in his speech that Germany would have thirteen and possibly seventeen Dreadnoughts by April 1912, when, as a matter of fact, there were only nine. As the result of this largely artificial agitation an increased British programme of eight ships for 1909 received the approval of Parliament and condemned to ineffectiveness in advance the proposals of the new German Chancellor, Theobald von Bethmann-Hollweg, for a closer *rapprochement* with Great Britain. The negotiations for a naval holiday between Germany and Great Britain failed, and were brought abruptly to an end by the Agadir crisis of 1911.

This event was almost as artificial in origin as the speech by McKenna in favour of an increased British navy. Owing to the inability of the

Sultan of Morocco to maintain order in the interior and protect foreign interests, the French decided to occupy Fez, even against the claim made by Germany and Spain that such an occupation constituted a breach of the Algeciras Settlement (p. 107) and the Hague Court Agreement of 1909. The German attitude in this matter was purely commercial. It was believed that, if Germany opposed the occupation of Fez and claimed in turn that the interests of German firms at Agadir were threatened by the Moorish disturbances, such a threat necessitating occupation, the French would buy off the Germans by the grant of part of their African colonial Empire. Germany forgot that the Power most immediately concerned in the occupation of Agadir was not France, but Great Britain, and that any arrangement made with Germany would require to have British agreement. The crisis was transferred, therefore, from France and Germany to Germany and Great Britain. The reaction by Great Britain was so definite that German claims were very considerably modified, and the crisis ended with the withdrawal of the *Panther*, the warship sent by Germany to Agadir, and the modification of French borders in the Congo to allow Germany to occupy a part of it.

A very significant statement at that time was made by the Russian Ambassador to Sir Edward Grey: 'If there is war between Germany and France England will have to take part. If Russia is involved it would be ... a universal war. I do not think the Kaiser desired war when this began. I do not think he wants war today.'

Arising partly out of the Agadir crisis and the Moroccan disturbances came the proposal by Italy to annex Tripoli. The Treaty of Lausanne, on the 18th October 1912, brought the Italo-Turkish War to an end and confirmed the Italian occupation.

At the beginning of 1912 an attempt was made to smooth out British and German differences regarding naval construction, at the suggestion of Albert Ballin, the Chairman of the Hamburg-Amerika Line. The proposal was made that 'friendly, cordial and confidential negotiations' covering a naval understanding preliminary to examination of the German and British colonial position should take place between both countries, and Sir Ernest Cassel was instructed to go to Berlin and get into direct touch with the Emperor. In June he presented at Berlin a short memorandum outlining the position. The three points of the memorandum were: that naval superiority should be recognized as essential to Great Britain and, consequent on such recognition, that the German naval programme should not be increased, but, if possible, be reduced; that, in return for this, Britain was prepared to discuss with Germany the possibility of satisfying German aspirations in colonial expansion; and, in the third place, that reciprocal assertions should be given debarring either Power from joining in aggressive designs or combines against each other. With these proposals the German Government was in substantial agreement, with the proviso, however, that the German naval programme of 1912 should be allowed to be carried out, since the necessary arrangements had already been made. Following on this preliminary step, Lord Haldane was sent to Berlin to carry out in detail the proposals sketched in Sir Edward Cassel's memorandum; but it was unfortunate that just before he arrived the Emperor should have announced in the Reichstag the introduction of Bills for the increase both of the army and navy, while Mr Churchill made a declaration of Britain's naval policy to the effect that 'the British navy is to us a necessity and from some points of view the German navy is to them more in the nature of a luxury; it is existence to us; it is extension to them'.

The essence of Haldane's offer was an agreement of neutrality, elaboration of the Treaty about Portuguese colonies to meet German wishes, cession of Zanzibar and Pemba (this denied later by Lord Haldane), and a share in the railway construction in Southern Persia. In return for this, he asked for accommodation in naval supplementary bills and the construction of the Bagdad Railway. He suggested a three years' holiday from naval construction. The agreement broke down over the neutrality formula, the definition of a war whereby Germany would be the victim of aggression and the co-operation which would be afforded by Britain in such an event. The task of reconciling neutrality towards Germany with an Anglo-Franco-Russian entente appeared to be insuperable. The suggestion also for the naval holiday was rejected by Germany and was followed by the recall of the German Ambassador in London. The effect of this collapse was to consolidate the Entente and bring more closely into the discussion the possibility of Anglo-French co-operation both on land and sea.

In the middle of these developments the first Balkan War of 1912 broke out, and it is very significant that England, France, and Germany should have combined at that time to localize hostilities and prevent the war from spreading in Europe. Sir Edward Grey and Prince Lichnowsky, the German Ambassador in London, made strong efforts to ensure more cordial relations between Germany and Great Britain through their combined action in the Balkan question, but the danger lay outside these two countries and was rather to be found in the antagonism of Austria and Russia. Intrigues carried out by Serbia were also a factor making for intensification of Austrian suspicion, while the Russians mobilized but hesitated, not definitely entering the field in support of Slav aspirations.

In December 1912 a peace was patched together and the whole matter referred to a conference of ambassadors.

This conference was notable for the close co-operation between Great Britain and Germany against the intransigence of Austria and Russia, both of whose armies were mobilized, the mutual hatred of Austria and Serbia, and the determination of Russia to consolidate the Slav element in the Balkans. The result of this conference was the cession of a large part of Turkey to Bulgaria, but the refusal of Turkey to recognize the cession caused war to break out again in February 1913. The war was ended by the Treaty of London on 30th May, whereby Albania was declared to be an autonomous State; but no sooner had this been done than Austria began to intrigue among the Balkan States with a view to inciting a third war. The third war was brought to a conclusion in August 1913, when the peace was dictated by Serbia, Greece and Roumania, and Bulgaria was forced to give up most of the territory it had conquered in the first Balkan War. The effect of Serbia's victory was to increase Germany's alarm at the growth of Russian influence and to relax her pressure on Austria, whose desire was to join Bulgaria against Serbia. The appointment of Liman von Sanders as reorganizer of the Turkish army excited the suspicion of Russia, since such reorganization would tend to strengthen Turkey against Russian aspirations and reduce the sphere of influence of that country. The position at the end of 1913 was more difficult in the Balkans and in the Near East than before hostilities began, but a definite improvement in Anglo-German relations, resulting from the Haldane mission, the naval negotiations and agreement over the Bagdad Railway, clarified the international political situation and postponed the risk of a European war.

The Bagdad Railway negotiations, which began in March 1911 with the proposal of the Sublime Porte to internationalize the operation of the railway, came to an end on 15th June 1914 with a definite agreement made between Prince Lichnowsky and Sir Edward Grey. The text of the Treaty was finally signed on 27th July, a week before the war broke out between Great Britain and Germany. The Treaty provided for the nomination of two British directors on the Board of the Bagdad Company, while Germany should entrust the section from Basra to the Persian Gulf to a British Company and should not construct a competing line. Germany should have 20 per cent of the shares of the Company for navigating the river, a guarantee being given that there should be no discrimination against German goods, while the Bagdad Railway Company made the same concessions in connection with British goods.

These developments alarmed France and led to a question being posed by President Poincaré regarding the British attitude towards the Entente. The answer given by Sir Edward Grey to this question was to the effect that nothing had transpired which had brought into existence new relations with other Powers or weakened the close Entente with France. Cambon viewed suspiciously the proposals by Great Britain for a naval holiday with Germany, since savings made on the construction of warships by the latter might be used to strengthen the army against France.

On 28th June the Archduke Francis Ferdinand and his wife were murdered at Sarajevo, the murder being attributed by the Austrians to the activities of the Narodna Obrana, a nationalist patriotic secret society of a pan-Serbian type; but it was maintained that the Serbian Government had not only prior knowledge of the murder, but actively supported this organization.

On 5th July the German Emperor sent a letter to Francis Joseph promising support to Austria within the terms of the Treaties, while Lichnowsky suggested that Sir Edward Grey should use his influence with Russia to make Serbia agree to the Austrian demands. The position in the Balkans was exactly the same as that which Bismarck had to face in 1878 when he had to decide between supporting Austria against Russia or maintaining neutrality with an exact understanding of conflicting forces in Austria and Russia. At that time Bismarck used his intelligence to maintain and consolidate peace; but in July 1914 there was no statesman of the ability of Bismarck in control in any of the countries concerned. Germany, dominated by Wilhelm II, was unable, or unwilling, to intervene in the cause of peace between Austria and Russia. It exercised little pressure on Austria to modify its demands on Serbia and made intervention dependent on a direct request by Austria itself.

The effect of this was the maintenance of extremism, the refusal of Serbia to accept all the Austrian demands, the mobilization of Russian troops, the war against Serbia followed by the proclamation of war between Germany and France, the German ultimatum to Belgium on 1st August, requesting a passage through that country to France, the violation of the neutrality of Belgium, the British ultimatum and the beginning of the European War.

It is almost certain that if Great Britain had adopted the role of mediator between conflicting forces, if it had affirmed its decision, in the event of war, to support France and Russia, if it had insisted on the Austro-Russian differences being submitted to an international tribunal, if it had co-operated more closely with Germany in maintaining a balance of power between Eastern and Western Europe, the conflagration of 1914 might not have occurred. But against that one must take into account the extremism of Austria, the preponderating rule of militaristic factions in Russia which were determined to divert attention from the unrest which was overtaking the country, and the irredentism of Poincaré.

It is unnecessary to describe in any detail the European War of 1914-18, since such a description would require a very long thesis, and our concern is more to trace the political evolution of the German State than to examine tactical manœuvres. It is only necessary, therefore, to outline the effect of the war during its various phases on the German political mentality.

The German public as a whole had no great desire for hostilities, but the German Chancellor had explained that the extremism of Russia had forced the war on Germany and that the struggle was now between everything that Germany stood for in every sphere of life and the bardarism and inefficiency of a Slav régime. On this basis it was easy to arouse a crusading enthusiasm, while Germany had never forgotten the work of Bismarck and the early years of the consolidation of the Empire. The German people were unwilling to sacrifice political prestige arising from the period of expansion after 1870; they enjoyed a high measure of prosperity and knew that their standard of living and of enjoyment of the arts of life was higher than in any other European State. The war was regarded as a test of the strength and endurance of German civilization, and the early successes of the German armies in the field confirmed the people in the belief that they were entering on a new stage of expansion similar to that which had occurred after the Franco-Prussian War. Skilful propaganda kept hidden as far as possible the real difficulties of the German armies. Even the triumphant invasion of Belgium was successful largely owing to the military worthlessness of the Belgian troops, and one German officer, the novelist Walter Bloem, has described how, at the encounter of the British army at Mons, the morale of the German troops suffered a severe setback. The check of the German advance at the Marne was neutralized by the remarkable victories in East Prussia and the elimination of the Russian menace which, to Germany, was a much more dangerous obsession than anything that could come through France. The consistent failure of the Austrian army to maintain its position against Russia and the Russian invasion of Galicia, although they were a source of anxiety to the German General staff, had little immediate bearing on the internal political situation in Germany.

The test of the imperial régime, which at the beginning of the war stood at its highest point, was that of its capacity not merely to hold the German people together, but also to carry it through a successful war. It was shown early after the beginning of hostilities that German democracy in the Reichstag virtually abdicated its functions and that Socialist leaders acted as agents for the old régime. Karl Liebknecht failed to protest effectively against the war. In addition to that, propaganda to maintain the German crusading spirit was wrongly conceived inasmuch as it held out the hope of a powerful central European confederation which would be the achievement of Germany and would place the crown on the work carried out by Bismarck. The obsession of this central European confederation is one of the most remarkable characteristics of German discussions during the early years of the war and especially in 1915. That should be attributed to the enormous influence which was exerted by the book on *Mitteleuropa*, written by Friedrich Naumann in the spring of 1915.

In 1916, however, when events in the battlefields showed that the victory of Germany was at least in doubt and the blockade began to exert its pressure on food-stuffs and raw material supplies in Germany, this theory of German imperialistic advance received a severe shock; and coupled to it was the failure of Imperial diplomacy not only in the United States and Italy, but also in Roumania. The beginning of hardship and the menace of starvation showed that, by the test of achievement, the Imperial system in Germany was failing, and so we find the Socialists becoming active in the development of peace propaganda.

In January 1916 the extremists founded the Spartacus League which aimed at destroying the war at the source, namely, industry. This league was in some ways a translation into reality of the reaction against the German war aims which was heralded by the writings of pacifists like Professor Sieper, Professor Quidde, Professor Walter Schücking, Professor Förster, and Hellmut von Gerlach. The Reichstag, during this period, played a decidedly minor part. It met at intervals largely to vote credits for the prosecution of the war, but it is significant that the minority in the Reichstag against the war should have increased very steadily from December 1914 to May 1916, largely under the influence of Karl Liebknecht. Thus in December we find Liebknecht, contrary to the party discipline of German Socialism, voting against the war credits. In April 1915 Liebknecht and a colleague again registered their disapproval, and Minority Socialists to the number of thirty left before voting took place.

The view of the Minority led by Haase, Bernstein, Liebknecht, and Ledebour was that the struggle had ceased to be a war of self-preservation and was being used by the Imperialists as a means of carrying out a widespread plan of Imperial conquest. At the end of 1915 the Minority definitely voted against credits, and in the spring of 1916 seventeen

further members of the Socialist party broke away, under the chairmanship of Haase, from the main body, while the remaining Majority Socialists
still supported the war.

The arrest and imprisonment of Liebknecht in May 1916 was the
beginning of a severe reaction against the war aims of the German
Government and especially the German military leaders. In June the
first strike occurred in the metal trades. It was inspired by extremists
working through the Spartacus League and had a definitely political
complexion.

At Christmas 1916, even after Roumania had been defeated and the
Austro-German armies had entered Bukarest, the movement in favour
of peace came to a head and some definition was attempted of German
war aims as compared with those of the Entente. To the proposal for
the restoration of a lasting peace put forward by Bethmann-Hollweg on
the 12th December the Entente replied in the negative on the 30th, and
even President Wilson had no success in his attempt to persuade the
belligerents to define the terms under which they were prepared to
consider peace. The intention of the German Chancellor was to influence
favourably neutral opinion and maintain peace with the United States,
but against this view that of Field-Marshal Ludendorff prevailed: that,
as a result of intensive submarine warfare, the war would be ended in a
short time with the exhaustion of the Allies' supplies.

At the beginning of 1917 the military leaders were still debating the
most extreme annexationist schemes. The struggle became one between
a military dictatorship and Parliamentary government, with the Chancellor and the politicians attempting to carry out effectively the principles
laid down by Bismarck in his handling of the national government. At
that time the Russian Revolution might have appeared a development
favourable to German aims, because it provided German democracy with
an example and a theory, but the reaction of the military side against
the extremists was merely intensified by the comparative failure of the
Allies in the battlefield during 1917. The early months in that year
showed a number of minor British victories on the Western front, but
they were accompanied by very severe losses at sea owing to the submarine
campaign, the collapse of Brusiloff's offensive in the East, which brought
to an end the Russian part in the war, and the disastrous experiment of
General Nivelle at the Chemin des Dames, which destroyed the morale
of the French army and put France out of the war for several months.
The advocates of peace and of revolution could point to the fact, however,
that the success of Germany and her allies was not complete in certain
psychologically important areas. It was difficult to maintain the Berlin-

E

Bagdad theory[1] in the face of the fact that the Turks had been forced to evacuate Bagdad in March 1917. The Bulgarians were weakening decidedly in the Balkans, and the new Austrian Emperor was determined to obtain peace if that were possible, negotiating in this matter with the Western Powers through his brother-in-law, Prince Sixte of Bourbon, who was serving in the Belgian army. In April 1917 the Austrians informed the German Emperor and his Chancellor that Austria could not hope to fight beyond the autumn of that year.

A further indication of a change in spirit resulting from the new atmosphere could be seen in the discussions held by the Socialists of the Majority and the Minority Parties with their foreign colleagues at Stockholm in June, where the Majority Socialists stated that they desired neither annexation nor indemnities and the Minority went as far as to advocate compensation to Belgium and a plebiscite in Alsace-Lorraine. On the 6th July Erzberger broadcast the Austrian memorandum and informed his fellow politicians in the Centre Party that there was no prospect of Germany winning the war. In July 1917 the Democratic opposition presented to the Reichstag a resolution in favour of peace put forward in the name of the Majority Socialists, the Centre Party and the Progressives. The reaction of the Emperor and his military advisers was strong enough to render it necessary for the Chancellor, Bethmann-Hollweg, to resign, and Germany found itself committed to continuation of the war.

The loss of Bethmann-Hollweg, who might have been an intermediary between the Democrats in their desire to impose constitutional methods on the Emperor and the military advisers who desired a dictatorship, was a serious loss to the cause of peace and of democracy in Germany. From that time onwards Imperial Headquarters were in control of the situation, and the new Chancellor, Georg Michaelis, acted as a nominee; but when the Reichstag Majority rose against his general indictment of the Minority Socialists as a revolutionary body and demanded a new Chancellor Imperial Headquarters retreated and Michaelis fell in the autumn of the year.

At that time the Reichstag might have affirmed its decision and imposed peace on Imperial Headquarters, but the elimination of the Russian and Roumanian enemy forces through the Treaties of Brest and Bukarest, the collapse of Italy at Caporetto in October and the penetration into Upper Venetia by the Austro-German troops once more gave some support to the view that a single additional effort on the part of Germany

---

[1] A slogan of Imperial German policy had been the building of a German-controlled railway from Berlin to Bagdad and the Mosul oilfields. See p. 168 (*Drang nach Osten*).

would bring victory. The purpose of the new Chancellor, Count Hertling, was merely to delay and to maintain some stability at home while
victory was being won on the battlefield. The expressed intention of the
Entente to enforce a bitter revengeful victory played into the hands of
the militarists and justified them in believing that the German people
would support their efforts to reach a decision on the Western front.

At the beginning of 1918 the revolutionary movement had reached
great proportions, even if it had not yet secured a hold on the interest or
enthusiasm of the masses. In January took place the great munition
strike, which was organized by the Spartacists and the Minority Socialists
and failed largely owing to the action of the trade unionists themselves,
who were still determined that the war should go on. The country as a
whole was not ready either to embark on revolution or to force on the
military autocracy a policy of peace. Events in France were favourable
to the policy of those who were determined to continue the war. The
attack at St. Quentin on the 21st March 1918, which led to the defeat of
the 5th British army and brought the Germans to within striking distance
of Amiens, the drive through the French forces along the line Soissons
to Rheims, which brought the German army to the Marne, aroused
expectations of a great military triumph; but the military position did not
improve beyond that point. As in 1914 the Marne proved the end of the
German offensive, while on the Italian front the Piave held up the
Austrian offensive and gave the Italian army time to reorganize itself. At
that time the position was ripe for the negotiation of peace on the part of
Germany, and this step was advocated very strongly by Kühlmann, the
Foreign Minister, in the Reichstag; but Hindenburg and Ludendorff
intervened to secure the dismissal of Kühlmann, and the stage was set for
the last great move by the military chiefs.

On the 15th July Ludendorff attacked on the Marne and stated definitely
that the capture of Rheims and the penetration through the Allied
defences beyond that city would end the war. But Rheims was not taken;
the Germans were forced across the Marne, and the Franco-British attack
of 8th August, which was the decisive victory of the war, brought with it
the defeat of Germany. This defeat destroyed the morale of German
Headquarters, and at a conference held at Spa on the 13th August,
Chancellor Count Hertling was empowered to negotiate terms of peace.
On the 8th September the military leaders expressed the opinion that the
fighting value of the German army had been so lowered by casualties and
by constant defeat since the 8th August that it could not be trusted to
carry out successful defensive operations, and Ludendorff advocated
immediate negotiations for an Armistice.

At the end of September came the successful Allied offensive in Macedonia, the collapse of Bulgaria and the re-entrance of Roumania into the war, bringing with it the virtual collapse of Turkey. On the 15th September Austria appealed for peace and Germany found herself isolated. Through the mediation of President Wilson and Prince Max of Baden, who was in charge of a parliamentary Cabinet dependent on a Reichstag majority inclusive of representatives of the Majority Socialists, the terms of peace were arranged and on 11th November the Armistice was declared.

Before this took place, however, the German Revolution had begun. On 30th October a mutiny broke out in the fleet at Wilhelmshaven, and by 3rd November the movement had gained Kiel and Hamburg. On 7th November Kurt Eisner proclaimed the Bavarian Republic and Germany was threatened with chaos. At this time the Majority Socialists, under Scheidemann, took control and issued an ultimatum to Prince Max that the Kaiser should abdicate. On 9th November the power was transferred by Prince Max to Friedrich Ebert, leader of the Socialists, and Wilhelm II, with all his theatrical love of display and of force, found himself in exile in Holland. A saddler ruled over a Germany which was no longer a machine dominated by Bismarck or by a military autocracy, but had become for the first time a democracy conscious of its own power but unconscious as yet of its responsibility.

On 10th November the first revolutionary Ministry was formed, Ebert, Scheidemann, and Landsberg representing the Majority Socialists, and Haase, Dittmann, and Barth the Independent or Minority Socialists; and it is significant that even at that time the influence exerted by the Workers' and Soldiers' Councils, which had come into existence everywhere on the Russian model, was comparatively slight. The Cabinet might announce itself as a 'Council of People's Commissaries' with an advanced Socialist programme, but it was decidedly more conservative than the progressive or advanced elements in the Revolution would have desired, and in this they represented more completely the German people than the revolutionaries pure and simple.

The war was liquidated by the signature of the Armistice, which nominally was based on President Wilson's Fourteen Points. It is significant that Erzberger should be the German signatory, Erzberger who was more the representative of the German middle class and professional type than the Socialist or Revolutionary. On 12th December the first Congress of Workers' and Soldiers' Councils took place, and this Congress gave an opportunity to the Spartacists to attempt to form an organized body in opposition to the Government; but the Congress supported the

Government and refused to admit Liebknecht and Rosa Luxemburg to its deliberations. In spite of this, dissensions broke out between the extremists and the conservative element in the German Government; Liebknecht's campaign against the Constituent Assembly and the advocacy of such an Assembly by the Majority Socialists were accompanied by the first indications of real revolution.

At that time the crisis was solved by the Government inviting the Congress to nominate three members of the Cabinet. The issue was then definitely between the Government and the Spartacists; and, on 4th January 1919, the former proceeded to remove Eichhorn, a left wing Independent in sympathy with the views of the Spartacists, from the office of Chief of Police. A general strike was declared, with the Independent Socialists' and Spartacists' approval, but it was put down by Noske, and, in the confusion, Liebknecht and Rosa Luxemburg were murdered. On 19th January the elections to the National Constituent Assembly were held, and they were remarkable in that they showed public approval of the policy of the Majority Socialists – a setback to extremists both on the left and the right, and a victory for constitutionalism. The Constituent Assembly met at Weimar, elected Ebert as President, and entrusted the formation of a Ministry to Scheidemann. The Ministry was based on a coalition of Majority Socialists, adherents of the Centre Party, and Democrats, accounting for 326 members out of a total in the House of 421. The extremists, however, were still active in various parts of Germany, notably in the Ruhr, Saxony, and Bavaria. The demand for nationalization of the Ruhr mines, backed by a general strike, was averted through the intervention of Government troops, and a number of sporadic revolts took place in the Rhineland, Thuringia, Saxony, Bavaria, where Kurt Eisner, who had attempted to form an independent Socialist State in Munich, was murdered in February.

By the end of May some stability had been introduced into the position, but the adverse effects of conciliation were soon to become evident when the Peace Treaty terms imposed by the Allies were understood by the German public. The action of the Government made an unbridgeable cleavage between the Majority and the Independent Socialists, and thus weakened the force of progress and of constitutionalism at a time when all its strength was required to meet the reaction caused by the Peace Treaty terms.

From 19th February to 11th August the Constituent Assembly at Weimar was engaged in drawing up a constitution for the new German Republic. The essence of the constitution was to be found in the combination of the principle of federalism with co-ordination through a central government. The Reich was given exclusive authority over foreign relations, citizenship, defence, coinage, customs, and posts, while it had final authority over civil and communal judicial procedure, public health, social legislation, insurance, railways, and public utilities. Apart from these things, the individual States had a fair measure of independence, but the Reich had always the right to question any of their laws whose activities affected the welfare of the entire country. The States were represented by a body termed the Reichsrat, which had certain privileges in the initiation and approval of legislation to be carried out by the Reichstag, while provision was made for the creation of a third body, the 'National Economic Council', which might be regarded as a sub-parliament composed of experts on economics, financial, and industrial matters. The duties of the President were carefully defined, and his position in the State regulated by reference to German parliamentary and political conditions. The President had within limited powers the right to dissolve Parliament and to appoint the Chancellor; but, as the Chancellor was in turn responsible to the Parliament, the right of the President in this case was restricted. The most important article in the constitution – an article which was invoked in 1931 – was that which gave the President dictatorial powers in the case of emergency regarded as rebellion or revolution on the part of the State or a party. The President could then govern by decree, but the decree was capable of being revoked by Parliament.

The second part of the constitution which defined the social obligations of the State and the part which the individual citizen should play in it, while it had no immediate administrative significance, was an almost exact definition of what the new German Republic and the new German civilization stood for.

There is nothing about it of the naïve idealism of which Germany has been and still is so prolific; it is emphatically the work of practical politicians who were no Utopians but were wise enough to reject the extremes of anti-Utopianism and to recognize the necessity of an idealist basis for development. The form of that development is variously conceived, but the end is the same – the harmonious development to full stature of every individual by the subordination of the individual to the community through his willing recognition that liberty, happiness, and moral goodness are perfected only when they are universally enjoyed. It is the work of men whose ideal of the State and of the citizen is service, and who honestly sought to build a new Germany.

Mid-way through these deliberations came the Treaty of Versailles with its alienation of Alsace-Lorraine from Germany. The Treaty of Versailles gave Eupen and Malmédy to Belgium, and compelled Luxemburg to withdraw from the Zollverein prior to being included in a Customs Union with Belgium. A plebiscite was to decide the fate of Northern Schleswig, while in the East the larger part of Posen, West Prussia and Upper Silesia were to be transferred to Poland. Danzig was made a Free City under the League of Nations, but within the Polish Customs Union. A corridor was created along the Vistula to allow Poland an exit to the sea. All German colonies were lost and were split up among the Allies as Mandates under the League of Nations. German South-West Africa was merged in the Union of South Africa. East Africa fell to Great Britain, France obtained almost the whole of Togoland and the Cameroons, the remainder in that area falling to Great Britain. Japan obtained German possessions in the Far East, north of the equator, while Great Britain secured New Guinea and the islands south of the equator. The German part of Samoa was given to New Zealand, Nauru to Great Britain, and the rest of the German territory to Australia. In this way the entire colonial acquisitions of Germany disappeared, largely in the British and French colonial Empires, the only proviso being that the League of Nations, through the Mandate system, could intervene to ensure equitable treatment of the population and prevent complete annexation.

The German army was reduced to 100,000 men, to be enlisted for twelve years, beginning in April 1920. The general staff was abolished and exact limits imposed on the munitions employed by the army. A belt of 50 kilometres on the east bank of the Rhine had to be entirely demilitarized, while the navy should be limited to six battleships, six cruisers, twelve destroyers, and twelve torpedo boats, with an establishment of 15,000 men. No submarines could be constructed. Heligoland was to be disarmed and the fortifications reduced, while no fortifications were allowed on the Baltic. In addition to this Germany had to surrender all her merchant fleet over 1600 tons, 50 per cent of those between 800 and 1600 tons, 25 per cent of all her fishing vessels, and had to construct ships to a total of 200,000 tons a year for five years for the purposes of the Allies. She had also to bear the cost of the armies of occupation and agree to the sale of all German property in allied countries. The Kiel Canal was to be opened to all countries and all ships on equal terms, and the great German rivers were to be placed under International Commissions.

To ensure that these provisions would be carried out the Allies would occupy German territory for fifteen years on the left bank of the Rhine, including a number of bridge-heads on the right bank, and evacuation of this occupied territory would take place in three stages. In the event of Germany being unable or unwilling to fulfil her obligations the evacuated area would be reoccupied. Germany and her Allies had specifically to admit their responsibility for the war, and were required to make reparations in accordance with a total sum which should be fixed by an International Commission before the 1st May 1921; but by that date one thousand millions were to be paid, the remainder being liquidated in thirty years. Part of this payment could be made by reparations deliveries in kind.

In the ensuing negotiations, when the Germans attempted to obtain some alleviation of these proposals, largely on the ground that they did not adhere to the Fourteen Points of President Wilson on which the Armistice had been based, Germany was unable to break down the resistance of France, supported by President Wilson, and the one concession made was that, before Upper Silesia should be given to Poland, the inhabitants should be allowed to give their views through a plebiscite. The only other concession of any importance allowed Germany within four months of the signature of the Treaty to offer a lump sum in settlement of her liabilities.

It is unnecessary to describe the effect on Germany of the Treaty, and the difficulties which were encountered by the German Government and above all Erzberger, Scheidemann, and Payer[1] in their attempt to obtain acceptance by the German people on the one hand, and to modify the attitude of the Allies on the other. The Government had also to contend with intrigues, first by the Poles in Eastern Germany, and by the French army in the Rhineland – intrigues which aimed in the latter at the creation of an independent republic of the Rhine and the Palatinate. In spite of the difficulties the Treaty was signed, and came into force on 10th January 1920. Two months later an attempt was made by a group of reactionaries under Kapp and Jagow, Bauer and Lüttwitz to upset the German Government, and to put in its place a more reactionary body with largely dictatorial powers. In the struggle which ensued, where Noske, representing the Government, was in direct opposition to Lüttwitz – a struggle which centred largely in Berlin –, prompt action by General von Seeckt and the successful exercise of his power to call on the loyalty of the army and strike at the centre of revolution and reaction made the Kapp revolt a failure.

It is difficult to attach much importance to the developments which intervened between 1920 and 1924. In the elections for the first Republican Reichstag, carried out on 6th June 1920, the Moderate and Progressive

[1] (Von) Payer belonged to the *Volkspartei* and was Vice-President in Graf Hertling's Cabinet.

Parties received a fairly severe defeat. The Majority Socialists held only 112 seats as against 163 in the previous Government; the Democrats, 45 as against 74; the Centre Party, 68 as against 89. All of these Parties were responsible for the signature of the Peace Treaty and had carried out the Revolution. The Parties, either to the Right or to the Left, which had criticized the Treaty on the lines that it had not gone far enough[1] and were against Germany's adhesion, increased markedly their representation. The Nationalists secured 56 seats as against 42; the People's Party 62 as against 22, and the Independent Socialists 81 as against 22. The election was a definite proclamation of the German people that it did not agree to the conditions which had been imposed on it by the Allied Powers, and heralded that period of passive resistance which rendered necessary the Dawes Plan in 1924.

The history of Germany in the latter half of 1920 and the whole of 1921 is linked up with reparations. The official Allied policy on this matter was communicated to the Germans at Spa in July 1920, and elaborated in closer detail three months later at Brussels. These two conferences did obtain some slight information regarding the financial position of Germany, but they were still influenced by the political unrealities and prejudices of the war period, and took no notice of even the most elementary economic principles. At the end of January 1921 the final terms were announced by the Allies, working largely under the domination of France, and they were communicated to the German representatives in London on 1st March. The German delegates in London put up determined opposition – opposition of despair because they knew that the internal situation in Germany would not allow them to return successfully without having obtained many considerable modifications in the Allies' terms. The Allies, however, insisted on the text of their ultimatum, and stated that if their proposals were not accepted by the 12th May 1921 the French would occupy the Ruhr. While negotiations were preceeding the German Government was defeated, and a new Government under the leadership of Dr Wirth formed, composed of the Parties which had carried through the Revolution and signed the Treaty of Versailles; and, in this case again, they were forced to accept the Allies' terms, including even the fantastical sum of £6,600,000,000 put forward as the total to be paid on reparation account. The Wirth Cabinet was strengthened on the industrial side by the inclusion of Walter Rathenau as Minister of Reconstruction, an agreement was made between Rathenau and Loucheur for the regulation of deliveries in kind from Germany to France, and a first instalment of seven and a half million pounds of the fifty million

[1] That is, not reactionary nor radical enough.

pounds demanded in the Allies' ultimatum was found; but political conditions in Germany, accompanied by a recrudescence of trouble consequent on exhaustion of industrial expansion brought artificially into being by the inflation of the currency, made the financial position extremely difficult.

Bavaria was in a state of armed commotion resulting from the activities of Ludendorff and Adolf Hitler. The state of tension between the Reich and Southern Germany came to an acute point when Erzberger was murdered in the Black Forest in August 1921. His assassination passed by without causing any real expression of horror or sympathy in Southern Germany. The feeling was general that the statesman who had negotiated the Peace Treaties and had signed the Armistice was guilty of treason in any case, and deserved assassination. The stage was prepared at that time for the trial of strength between the Republican forces in Germany and the Separatists in Bavaria. The virtual loss of Upper Silesia, however, made Germany almost united in indignant protest and postponed the struggle. The mark continued its collapse, and the Allies summoned a conference at Cannes to clear up the reparations situation and obtain some measure of financial stability. The Cannes Conference was completely abortive owing to the attitude of suspicion adopted by France, while the change of Government in the latter, whereby Poincaré replaced Briand as Prime Minister, meant the introduction of blank reaction into European politics and the intensification of the financial and industrial crisis. The International Conference which was held at Genoa in April 1922, three months after Cannes, was rendered wholly ineffective by the attitude of opposition adopted by Poincaré, while the Treaty made between Russia and Germany at Rapallo, governing trade relations, came at an unfortunate time for those who, like the British Prime Minister, were attempting to introduce some reason into the reparations negotiations.

In July 1922 the Wirth Government informed the Reparations Commission that a financial catastrophe was in sight, if the Allies insisted on obtaining from Germany large sums which could only be rendered available through the sale of German securities and German marks and the consequent further depreciation of the German currency. Germany demanded, therefore, a moratorium to cover the years 1923 and 1924, as well as the remaining five months of 1922, and they were supported in this view by the British representative on the Reparations Commission. Poincaré advocated, on the other hand, the acquisition of productive guarantees such as the State forests and State mines in the Ruhr. It was obvious by that time that the French were determined to occupy the Ruhr.

On the 10th January 1923, on the insecurely founded claim that Germany had defaulted on reparations deliveries in wood and coal, the French and Belgian Governments declared Germany to be in default and sent a Control Commission backed by an army. The Italian Government was represented by a few engineers who left the territory in February, and the struggle was confined, therefore, to Germany, France, and Belgium. The German Government, in April, guaranteed up to 80 per cent of the total loss incurred by industrial undertakings in making forced reparations deliveries – which was equivalent to making resistance complete; the Government, on 14th April, gave guarantees to cover the cash requirements of the iron and steel works and made good losses incurred in forced reparations deliveries. On 12th June a similar arrangement was made with the coal companies. On 27th September the German Government declared passive resistance at an end; on 7th October the Otto-Wolff concern came to terms with the Control Commission for coal deliveries, followed on 1st November by Krupp, while the German Chancellor, during the period 20th October to 13th November, entered into negotiations with the Mining Association at Essen to begin again reparations deliveries. On 23rd November agreements covering brown coal, chemicals, and other products ensued. The Ruhr occupation entered, therefore, into a new phase, and a return to normal conditions of production took place by degrees. The stand taken by General Dawes on 21st March 1924, that no good could result from the labours of the Commission of Experts unless the Ruhr were evacuated, contributed to a change in the attitude of France and Belgium, and the acceptance by Germany of the Dawes Report made evacuation possible. On 10th August 1924 the Herriot Government decided to terminate the Ruhr occupation. Such in short is the history of the Ruhr adventure.

The Ruhr adventure, which led to the downfall of the Cuno Cabinet, and the abandonment of the policy of obstruction and of passive resistance, brought into prominence Gustav Stresemann, who formed a Cabinet in August 1923 to clear up the situation. The Stresemann Government was on the whole reactionary, especially in social policy, but it had sufficient strength to restore order inside of Germany, and it was successful not only in quelling the Communist upheaval in Saxony, but in destroying easily the pretentions of the Hitlerites, who had proclaimed in Bavaria a Republic with Hitler as President and Ludendorff as acting Dictator. The Hitler movement was defeated largely through internal dissension, two of the principal commanders, Kahr and Lossow, refusing to co-operate in the extreme measures proposed by the reactionaries.

The second great achievement of the Stresemann Government was the

stabilization of the mark through the Rentenbank and the issue on 15th
November of Rentenmark notes not backed by gold but by a form of
mortgage on the entire real estate of Germany. The introduction of the
Rentenmark rendered possible in advance the financial reforms proposed
in the Dawes Plan some months later. On 22nd November the Stresemann Government was defeated through a combination of extremists
on both the right and left flanks, and in the new Cabinet, in which Wilhelm Marx functioned as Chancellor, Stresemann went to the Foreign
Office. Such was the effective beginning of the activities in international
politics of one of the most notable and one of the most successful Foreign
Secretaries that Germany has ever had. The history of Germany from that
period onwards is largely the history of the efforts made by Stresemann
to carry out a policy of fulfilment of the Peace Treaties joined to conciliation, not only of the opposition inside Germany, but also of the former
enemies of the Republic. While German Chancellors changed, Stresemann as Foreign Secretary remained, and it should not be forgotten that
the year during which the Stresemann policy was most effective, namely
1924, was a year when reaction reached the highest point in Germany
and the country threatened to be split up into opposing Communist and
Monarchist factions.

The first most important movement towards the political restoration
of Europe after five years of folly, such as we have described, was the
Report of the Dawes and McKenna Committees appointed by the
Reparations Commission on the 3rd November 1923 to study methods
of balancing the Budget and stabilizing German currency and to suggest
plans for repatriating capital which had flown out of Germany since the
conclusion of the war. The proposals of those Committees are summarized
later in this chapter as belonging to economic development; but, as some
part of them required a change in the German constitution, they had
important political repercussions. In the election which took place after
the publication of the Dawes Plan the Nationalists obtained 106 seats as
against 67 in the previous Parliament, while the Government Parties all
lost ground: the Centre Party from 68 to 65; the People's Party from 66
to 44; the Democrats from 39 to 28; and the Bavarian People's Party
from 20 to 16. The Communists won 62 seats, and the Socialists lost 73,
their representation being now only 100. In spite of this the Dawes Plan
was accepted on 29th August by the Government, and the new period of
stabilized economic and political conditions set in.

A further critical stage in German politics took place at the end of
February 1925, when Ebert the President died suddenly. In the resultant
elections the candidate put forward by the Nationalists, Field-Marshal

von Hindenburg, was successful, and it was felt that the transition to Monarchism was now only a matter of time; but the election of Hindenburg meant the complete defeat of Nationalism owing to the qualities of character and of resolution possessed by Hindenburg himself. The extremists had not counted on a sense of duty which would consider loyalty to the Republic as an act of faith and an act of honour, and which could not be qualified by any suggestion of disloyalty; and so, during its most critical period, 1925-31, the German Republic found its greatest strength and its worthiest commendation in the character and the policy of the Field-Marshal who had striven most bitterly in the war to carry out the Imperialistic aims of the old Imperial régime.

Through the Dawes Plan Germany obtained some measure of liquidaticn of international financial difficulties and could look forward to a programme of industrial and financial reconstruction without interference from France. It was essential now to obtain in the political sphere some small measure of consolidation and stabilization. Such a measure would be based on international arrangements similar in inspiration to that of the Dawes Plan – arrangements which would meet the French desire for security and allow Germany to take once more its proper position as one of the leading European Powers represented in the League of Nations.

The first real attempt to introduce such a stabilizing factor was the Protocol, which was produced at Geneva largely to meet French views; through it the machinery of the League would be used to implement the League guarantee of territorial integrity and the League desire to maintain perpetual peace. The Geneva Protocol was merely a translation into international politics of the ancient doctrine that peace could only be preserved by a sufficiently large army and a sufficiently active and powerful navy. The Protocol, rejected by the British Labour Government, was disposed of finally by Mr Austen Chamberlain at Geneva in March 1925.

The second measure was that which aimed at the creation of an internaional political pact to stabilize Franco-German relations. The offer made by Stresemann to France at the beginning of 1925 covered the joint guarantee by both countries of the integrity of the frontiers established by the Versailles Treaty. It did not guarantee the French system of political alliances, since it applied purely to the western frontier of Germany. In this matter Streseman was strongly supported by Great Britain, and his proposal made it impossible for France to retire on guarantees which might be prepared by the League of Nations. No more effective guarantee than that given by Germany could be imagined. As a condition of French acceptance, however, Germany was required to enter the League of Nations – a move which suited the policy of Stresemann particularly well; and so conditions were established for the preparation and signature of the Treaty of Locarno on 16th October 1925.

Under this Treaty not only were Germany, France, and Belgium pledged to maintain the western frontiers established by the Versailles Treaty, but an additional guarantee was given by both Britain and Italy. It would be difficult to imagine a more complete international regulation of political questions arising out of the war treaties than Locarno; but the Treaty had the elements of failure in it largely through the fact that it did not refer in any way to the eastern frontier of Germany. The entrance of Germany into the League of Nations was obstructed by a series of intrigues which aimed partly at reducing the value of Germany's admission to the Council through increase of the permanent membership of such a Council by the inclusion of Spain, Brazil, China, and Poland, and partly by postponement of admission. In September 1926, however, the victory of Stresemann in rehabilitating Germany among the Powers was complete, and it was possible from that time onwards for that country to use the League of Nations to settle grievances and maladjustments which previously were not considered. Thus we find Germany using her influence later in criticism of the Mandates possessed by the Powers over the former German colonies. During this time Stresemann had to encounter very severe criticism from the Nationalists and even from those less extreme circles which still remembered the consolidation of the German Empire and regarded the loss of Alsace-Lorraine merely as temporary. Stresemann's renunciation of Alsace-Lorraine was taken as treason by the extreme irredentists. Events supported Stresemann – so much so that on 16th November 1925 the Allies announced a considerable reduction in the occupation forces, a revision of conditions governing occupation, and the evacuation of the Cologne zone. On 27th November, against the opposition of the Nationalists, the Fascists, and the Communists, the Locarno agreement was passed by the Reichstag, and on 1st December Dr Luther and Herr Stresemann signed the agreement in London.

Between the end of 1925 and the admission of Germany into the Council of the League of Nations with a permanent seat on 28th September 1926 and the crisis which intervened in 1931 the political history of Germany is punctuated by few exciting moments. International complications were still present, largely as the result of the continued occupation of parts of Germany. The Stresemann policy of conciliation had, however, its reward when, following on the recommendations made in the Report of the Agent-General for Reparation Payments in December 1927, the Assembly of the League at Geneva in September 1928 discussed the possibility of settling finally the reparations problem and evacuating the Rhineland. It was decided on 16th September to set up a Committee of Experts to clear up the reparations difficulties, and on 8th January 1929 the Reparations Commission appointed the Committee representative of Great Britain, France, Italy, Japan, Belgium, and Germany. The American members were Owen D. Young and J. P. Morgan, and the British Sir Josiah Stamp and Lord Revelstoke, Sir Charles Addis taking the place of the latter when he died suddenly during the negotiations. The final report known as the Young Plan was completed on 22nd May 1929.

The International Conference which met at The Hague from 6th August to 31st August 1929 caused a very severe, if short-lived, period of tension, largely between Great Britain and France. In this case one could trace some measure of co-operation between French and German industrialists and economic advisers in the political as well as industrial spheres. The Young Plan may have caused certain differences of opinion between Great Britain and France, but it did not affect other than favourably the position of Germany, which had obtained a double advantage:

The definite reduction in the total annuities payable to the Allies, and greater flexibility in their application;

The complete evacuation of the occupied territories – an evacuation which was to be completed before the summer of 1930.

On 3rd October 1929 Gustav Stresemann died, within sight of the conclusion of his life's work; and the second Hague Conference, which sat from 3rd January to 20th January to work out in detailed agreements and schedules the Young Plan, set the coping stone on his achievement during six years.

ECONOMIC DEVELOPMENT

The introduction of the general tariff of 1879 which, in addition to protecting in some measure German agriculture, was the first real attempt to apply a tariff on scientific lines to the whole of German production, was really the beginning of large-scale modern German industry as we understand it now. One cannot, however, affirm that the closer organization of the basic industries took place after the introduction of such a tariff, and it is permissible to regard it not as a revenue, but rather as a protective measure. The tendency in German industry to form national monopolies through the machinery of the cartel had already been fairly clearly shown. Thus, one can find traces of the tendency towards monopoly before 1860, but the great period of the cartels in their first purely experimental stage was between 1873 and 1889, when severe trade depression undoubtedly forced industrialists into discussion of proposals for closer co-operation. The principal characteristic of cartel policy in its elementary state was that of price control, with a certain measure of exploitation of the consumer, and the insecurity of the position was such that few of the original cartels thus created before 1890 survived into the twentieth century, and the further trade depression which ensued after 1890 was a period of liquidation.

The second phase took place from the beginning of the century onwards, and one may regard the cartel as it functions now as a twentieth century product. The crisis of 1900 to 1903 could no longer be regarded as a crisis affecting individual industries and individual firms in an industry, but as a testing time for the central organizations which had been created. Competition had been eliminated in practically all of the basic industries of Germany. In the period prior to 1890 can be found many of the capitalist organizations which have reached such enormous proportions now. The limited liability company in industry, financed with ordinary share capital, took form from 1870 onwards. In engineering practically all companies of any importance were registered after 1870, and the average dividend paid on shares over the twenty years ending 1900 was slightly over 7 per cent. The chemical industry, which began in the 'fifties, entered its first phase of expansion in 1870. The *Interessengemein-schaft der Farbenindustrie* linked up the *Badische Anilin- und Sodafabrik* and *F. Bayer & Company* in 1873. A second group comprising the *Höchster Farbwerke* and *Leopold Cassella & Company* was constituted also in 1873, and *Meister, Lucius & Brünning* in 1880. The great companies controlling the chemical industry date from this period, and in no case did the industry as a whole pay less than 10 per cent before 1900. The electrical manufacturing industry in the firm of the *Deutsche Edison Gesellschaft*, now the A.E.G., dates from 1883, and the Siemens organization a little earlier. The textile and paper industries came into their first period of expansion also in the 'nineties, and it is significant that all of those industries, which, at that time, might be regarded as entirely modern, yielded a net income of rather more than 7 per cent. It is necessary to quote this yield merely to show that this first great period in modern German industrial history was remarkably profitable, and was such as to justify much investment of capital and the development of very large marketing organizations both at home and abroad.

It is significant, also, that the industrial expansion which began in the 'nineties and continued unabated almost up to 1913 should have coincided with a period of political decline. There is no doubt that the political prestige of Germany since the dismissal of Bismarck had fallen very steadily, and through the awkward handling of international questions it had rendered difficult the extension or expansion of German industrial products in markets outside of that country. At practically no time during this period were political and economic policies in harmony. One can find a certain justification in this divergence. The world, especially from 1900 to 1913, was becoming definitely aware of the rising industrial and economic significance of Germany. Great Britain and France, especially, could see an enormously powerful industrial organization in the act of creation – an organization which could carry out effectively the Imperialistic aims of the German Government; and the accusation was freely advanced that Germany's industrial expansion was based on the desire to create an enormously powerful fighting machine. It is legitimate to question this interpretation.

Some conception of this forward movement may be obtained from trade statistics. Over the period of depression, 1875 to 1889, German imports only rose from 3,528,000,000 marks to 3,899,000,000 marks, while her exports rose from 2,492,000,000 marks to 3,165,000,000 marks, an improvement of about 40 per cent in exports and only about 8 per cent in imports. From 1890 to 1913 a very rapid expansion took place. Imports rose from 4,146,000,000 marks to 10,770,000,000 marks. Exports expanded even more rapidly from 3,327,000,000 marks to 10,095,000,000 marks – an increase of more than 200 per cent. The increase in exports was even greater than that registered by the United States, where the corresponding figures were 845,000,000 dollars in 1890, and 2,429,000,000 dollars in 1913. In Great Britain, the increase in exports was very much less, from £328,000,000 in 1890 to £635,000,000 in 1913, and in France, from 4,437,000,000 francs to 8,421,000,000 francs. These figures illustrate the emergence of two great Powers in international trade, Germany and the United States. The German achievement was greater than that of America largely through the circumstance that its exports had been based on the products of her staple manufacturing industries and not on shipments of raw materials or cereals, as in the case of the United States. In finished goods, for example, German exports in 1913 were more than twice those of the United States, and were moving up rapidly to the British level.

The change in international economic values caused by this rapid industrial expansion may have led in itself to severe political complications, and it was not unaccompanied by very serious difficulties in the financial sphere. It was not in any sense a steady, uninterrupted movement of expansion. It was broken by periods of fairly severe stress; above all, between 1892 to 1894, 1900 to 1901, and 1907 to 1908. These years were, of course, years of difficulty in almost every country, but in some ways they were aggravated by the unstable credit position of German industry. A notable characteristic of this time was the very rapid industrialization of the country, and the increase in the large manufacturing unit. Thus, between 1895 and 1907 we find the number of factories in the chemical industry increasing by about 10 per cent, but the number of workers employed by 50 per cent; an increase in the metal and engineering industries of 5 per cent, and more than 50 per cent in the number of employees, while the corresponding figures were for the paper industry 30 per cent and 50 per cent; in the building industry 45 per cent and 55 per cent. The textile industry showed a decline of 7 per cent in the number of factories, and an increase in employees of 15 per cent. To give the exact figures, the number of workers in the engineering and metal working industries rose from 561,000 to 1,134,000; in the chemical industry, from 111,000 to 165,000; in the paper industry, from 145,000 to 219,000; in the wood-working industry, from 471,000 to 649,000; in the leather industry, from 139,000 to 185,000; in the food industries, from 981,000 to 1,210,000; in the clothing industries, from 655,000 to 825,000; and in the mining and allied industries, from 537,000 to 740,000.

The total figures given in the various censuses from 1882 to 1925 show the upward movement in industry quite clearly. In 1882 the number of persons engaged in industry and workshops was given as 5,702,000; in 1895 this figure had risen to 7,458,000; in 1907 to 9,831,000, and in 1925 to 13,239,000. In 1882 industry supported 35 per cent of the total population; in 1895, 39 per cent; in 1907, 41 per cent, and in 1925, 41·3 per cent. To all intents and purposes the industrial configuration of the country was established and did not markedly change thereafter, the growth in population being accompanied by a corresponding growth in the number of industrial workers, the one difference in 1925 being an increase in the workers actually employed in industry, and a decrease in the number of dependents on these workers.

During this period Germany was building up a powerful export trade based partly on actual organization and partly on the investment of capital. In 1890 German capital invested abroad, represented largely by loans and long-term credits, amounted to about £500,000,000, but in 1913 it had risen to £1,000,000,000, while to these figures should be added capital investment in manufacturing plants, merchanting and financial organizations, which would probably be about £400,000,000 in 1890 and about £600,000,000 in 1913, so that the total investment on foreign account rose from £900,000,000 to about £1,600,000,000. The direction of such investment was quite different from that of Great Britain or France, inasmuch as about two-thirds went to Europe and one-third overseas, the principal debtor countries in Europe being Austria-Hungary, Russia, Turkey, and Roumania, and, in overseas countries, the U.S.A., South America, British South Africa, and other British colonies. German direct investments in plants and agencies overseas were to be found principally in Russia and south-east Europe, the U.S.A., South America, and the Middle East. This investment corresponded in some measure to the orientation of political policy before the war. Great Britain directed its capital investment predominantly to British possessions, South America, and the Far East, all of them countries within her colonizing influence; France to Russia and her own colonies; so that one can see in the financial sphere a delimitation of influence very similar to that created in the political. It was a remarkable circumstance that Germany should have been able to develop much of her export trade with the countries thus acting in competition in foreign capital investment, Great Britain, the United States, and France. To this circumstance must be attributed much of the strength and much of the weakness of the German post-war financial situation. German banks had very early adopted a policy of direct co-operation with industry and in many cases were holders of large percentages of the ordinary share capital of manufacturing concerns. The banks had, therefore, direct interest in advancing German trade, and so we find industrialists adopting very early the principle of fairly lengthy credits as a means of developing export trade, above all in South America and the Far East. We find also German banks financing such credits through the acquisition of short term credits in Paris and London, creating thereby the dangerous principle of borrowing short and lending long. Such a principle made the German banking system peculiarly sensitive to international credit crises or to international economic depressions. It made it also vulnerable to attacks of a political nature. Thus we find the German political situation very seriously weakened by developments in the financial sphere. The withdrawal of French credits at the time of the Morocco crisis in 1911 caused difficulties, industrial and financial, within Germany, and was a factor dictating the withdrawal of Germany from this adventure. Again, minor crises of the same type, based on withdrawals of credits resulting largely from political complications, were to be found in the beginning of the century and in 1914. The American crisis of 1907 and 1908 also made for a weakening of credit resources at the disposal of German industry.

While, therefore, Germany was able to increase considerably her capital investment, she was not absolutely sound in many of her movements, and financially laid herself open to dangerous attacks. Politically, she had to advance loans to Allies whose credit was not sufficiently high to allow them to obtain such loans internationally. After the Morocco crisis and the Balkan Wars Germany found herself constrained, for example, to give loans to Austria-Hungary and Turkey which could not be quoted on the Bourse; but, in general, politics entered very slightly into capital investment, so much so that new Russian securities were introduced to the Berlin Exchange in the summer of 1914. German financial policy was, however, characterized by the capacity to make use effectively of the credit facilities created by Great Britain and France, especially Great Britain. If we analyse the period intervening between 1907 and 1913, we discover only one year in which the balance of gold shipments as between Great Britain and Germany was favourable to the former, namely, 1907, and only three years in which German shipments were in excess of British from 1899 onwards, the three years being 1905, 1906, and 1907, all three years of depression. At its lowest point Germany shipped about £5,000,000 to Great Britain, while British shipments over the period 1907 to 1913 averaged about £7,000,000 annually. In general, however, the statistics show that even before the war Great Britain was really the centre of finance for a considerable portion of German trade. It is important also to note that over the period 1898 to 1913 the total German gold holding should have increased much more rapidly than the British. It rose from 2,515,000,000 marks to 3,875,000,000 marks, an increase of 1,360,000,000 marks, while the increase in the British holding, calculated in marks, amounted to about 800,000,000 marks, from 2,274,000,000 marks to 3,068,000,000 marks in the same period. During those fifteen years France increased her holding from 3,257,000,000 marks to 5,422,000,000 marks, the increase being equal to that of Great Britain and Germany combined. The two countries which were responsible for the greater part of the increase in world gold accumulation were the United States and France.

The great expansion of German industry was rendered possible during the period 1898 to 1913 not merely by the use of international credits and the close association of German banks and industrial undertakings, but also by the more general adoption of the cheque system, trade bills, and other methods which rendered unnecessary the actual exchange of gold or currency. While, therefore, the total volume of production in the country increased very rapidly over those fifteen years, there was less demand for gold than would have been necessary if those changes had not taken place. In 1898 the total volume of currency in circulation was valued at 4,022,000,000 marks as against a gold holding of 2,515,000,000 marks, the gold cover being, therefore, 62·5 per cent. In 1913, at the end of the period, the currency in circulation had risen to 6,553,000,000 marks and the gold cover had fallen to slightly less than 59 per cent. One can trace a fairly rapid expansion in the currency, largely to finance a rising market, so much so that in 1898 the currency in circulation was about 11·6 per cent of the national income of 34,700,000,000 marks. In 1912 it had risen to 13·9 per cent, and during the year of deflation, 1913, fell again to 13·2 per cent. The prosperity of Germany can be seen also from the expansion in the national income. In 1898 it had risen to 37,800,000,000 marks; in 1900 to 41,200,000,000 marks, and expanded rapidly from that period right up to 1913 when it stood at 49,700,000,000 marks.

The population itself during the fifteen years had risen by rather less than 20 per cent; the national income by 43 per cent; the currency in circulation by 63 per cent; foreign trade, as represented by exports, by 170 per cent; national savings, as represented by the holdings of the savings banks, by 270 per cent; and capital invested abroad by over 100 per cent. During this period prices showed a long-term upward movement. They were in 1898, using a basis of 100 for the average of the years 1901 to 1910, 93; in 1900, 100; fell during the three depressed years 1901 to 1903 to 92, and in 1913 stood at 113. During those fifteen years there were a series of short-lived booms, namely, at the end of the century, in 1907 and in 1912; but, on the whole, the price movement was favourable, not only to the increasing industrial production of Germany, but also to the development of the cartel system in organization and administration. This rise was sufficient to render agriculture profitable, so much so that at the outbreak of the war in 1914 Germany could count on a very strongly organized and prosperous agricultural basis − a factor of very great importance indeed in maintaining the German resistance to the blockade declared by the Allies.

In the world this period was one of rising prices and rapidly increased industrial activity. It was characterized by the equipment of the colonies and of the South American Republics when communications were being opened up with the constant demand for engineering, iron and steel and transport products, and the great wheat centres, notably Canada and the United States, were entering into the phase of mass harvests and central marketing. The latter had not yet reached the position where, through mechanization, they could reduce costs so greatly as to endanger the stability of agriculture in the principal European countries. There was a measure of stability, both national and international, which made for a definite improvement in the German standard of living and in the prosperity of every part of the population. German industry, through the influence of the great cartels, especially in coal mining, iron and steel, chemicals and potash, through the initiative of industrial leaders like

Emile Rathenau, Werner von Siemens, Kirdorf, Thyssen, Ballin, and Krupp, moved forward not only in its task of equipping the immense industrial machine in Germany, but also of conquering newly developed markets where German engineering and technical skill could find free play. Large scale modern production began in the 'nineties with the realization of Thyssen's plans for developing the potentialities of Lorraine in conjunction with the Saar and the Ruhr, the careful planning of Krupp round the great steel centre of Essen, and the linking up of communications throughout the entire Lorraine, Saar, and Ruhr region. Lorraine, with the new Thyssen works established at Hagondange, the Gelsenkirchen works at Esch, the Klöckner works at Knutange, and the Rombachar works on the border between it and the Saar, could show some of the largest and most modern installations in the world. Similarly, in Luxemburg, the Ruhr industrialists established great iron and steel plants —among them, the Differdange works of the Stinnes concern and the Burbach-Eich-Dudelange group. This period was characterized by the emergence of Berlin as a powerful engineering centre, especially in electrical manufacture and general engineering, by the consolidation of the chemical industry and by the rapid development of Upper Silesia. When during the war Walter Rathenau was entrusted with the task of organizing German industry in war production, he found that the preparations for those years had created for him an instrument which could be applied with little modification. The cartels had already brought together manufacturers in the basic industries and introduced the principle of operation as a common unit. The great trusts had already come into existence in chemicals, and enormously powerful companies controlled electrical manufacture and electricity supply. The only industries in which some definite co-ordination was required other than that which had already been general were textiles, general engineering, and to some extent also paper. The effort of Rathenau was concentrated more on them than on the industries which had already been brought together through the cartel system.

The effect of the Peace Treaties was fourfold:

I.—They destroyed the Ruhr-Luxemburg-Saar-Lorraine economic unit which had been brought to a high state of development by German industrialists, and through this alone rendered necessary a new period of adjustment which could not fail to be a source of difficulty not only for Germany but also for Europe;

II.—They reduced through territorial losses the earning capacity of Germany by about 11 per cent, the national income by a very similar figure, and deprived the great engineering centres of Berlin and

Nuremberg of many of the sources of raw and semi-finished materials;

III.—Through reparations and the financial demands of the Allies they rendered the task of maintaining currency stability and financial liquidity extremely difficult if not impossible;

IV.—Through the cession by Germany of the greater part of her mercantile fleet, a high percentage of the rolling stock and the liquidation of German property abroad, the capacity of Germany to re-establish foreign trade, and above all international credits necessary to such trade, was severely restricted.

The least important of these facts were undoubtedly the second and fourth. The loss of territory, notably Lorraine, the Saar, and, in 1922, Upper Silesia, undoubtedly reduced supplies of essential raw materials and combustibles; but the raw materials in question were not a monopoly of the territories taken away. They were among the most abundant in world trade and could be obtained from other sources. In time, also, it would be expected that France would of its own accord try to re-establish the economic links which had been constructed before the war, if only to derive from the ceded or controlled territories a full measure of profit. German policy was directed, therefore, towards the realization of higher efficiency in manufacturing methods, especially in the iron and steel industry, so that the comparatively higher price of imported raw materials could be neutralized. The loss of the Saar and Upper Silesia was made good by development of other sources of industrial power. Economy took the form of reduction in raw materials wherever possible, reduction of the consumption of fuel through electrification and the realization of greater supplies of energy from the establishment of super-power stations in the coal-fields in the Rhineland and the centre of Germany, from the more effective exploitation of water-power resources, from the widespread electrification of industry and of transport. Recovery of production took the form of reconstitution of the great manufacturing combines, especially in the coal-mining, iron and steel, and heavy engineering industries, with an orientation towards the interior of Germany and away from Lorraine, the Saar, and Luxemburg; the reconstitution of the cartels which had broken up during the period of inflation and the restoration of currency stability; the active participation of the individual States and the Reich itself in industrial undertakings supplying essential raw materials or energy to German industry. Thus we find a series of State undertakings, notably in Prussia, Saxony, Bavaria, Baden, Württemberg, undertaking the construction of main transmission systems, linking up new water-power or brown coal generating stations with the centres of industrial activity, the Reich itself obtaining control over companies manufacturing aluminium, electro-metallurgical products, and chemicals. These developments, which came to a conclusion about 1927, brought Germany into a much stronger position than before the war. The output of her principal industrial products had surpassed the pre-war level, and she had an equipment which was probably superior to that obtaining in any other country in the world.

On two occasions at least industrialists had been able to benefit from political developments. First of all, they were indemnified for the loss of their manufacturing concerns in Luxemburg and the Saar. During the period of inflation in 1921, 1922, and the first nine months of 1923 they were able to carry out very large extensions of productive capacity, put in new plant, and equip new factories at a capital cost which the progress of inflation reduced to nothing. One can perhaps distinguish a third occasion, between 1927 and 1931, when Germany, acting under the belief that her productive machinery should be improved to permit of reparations payments, was able to obtain a very large volume of long-term and short-term credits in foreign countries, above all, Great Britain and the United States, the greater part of which went again into industrial construction. It was estimated that, at the end of 1929, the total sums raised by Germany in this way since 1924 amounted to slightly less than £650,000,000, £350,000,000 being represented by long-term loans, about £60,000,000 by the sale of German securities and control in German industrial firms, banks, and other institutions, to foreign interests, and about £240,000,000 by short-term credits. At the end of 1930, consequently, the capital invested in German industry, public utilities, housing, public works, was probably greater than in any other industrial country, with the exception of the United States, and since 1924 the interest on such capital was calculated to lay a very heavy prior charge on the total volume of industrial production. The fact that £240,000,000 represented short-term credits which could be liquidated at any time, and the greater part of which had been used for financing trade, made for uncertainty. German industry, at the end of 1927, had more than made good the loss caused by the Peace Treaties and was in a strong position, but in 1931 it had reached an unsound credit position owing to the fact that the majority of industrial plants were seriously over-built, over-equipped, while loans and credits had not been stabilized to the point where adjustment could be made effectively on a long-term basis.

The German cartel system had been almost completely reconstituted by the end of 1925, and it had been extended to form international agreements to cover steel, pig iron, chemicals, steel products, heavy electrical generating plant, artificial silk, and even certain sections of the paper trades. During the period of crisis, however, in 1929 and 1931, the cartel system passed through a strain very similar to that experienced during the years of inflation. It was adversely affected by the rationalization movement which tended to concentrate output in very large units, above all in the iron and steel, chemical and electrical manufacturing and potash industries, and it was unable to keep up the level of German prices against the precipitous fall which had taken place in world prices and commodities. At the end of 1930, therefore, there were indications of a severe internal crisis in German industry resulting from excessively ambitious plans brought to maturity since 1927. By the middle of 1931, the credit collapse took place, and it was found that some form of reconstruction and reorganization would be necessary to liquidate inflation in capital expenditure represented by equipment far in excess of the needs both of Germany itself and of the world's markets as a whole.

The policy of industrial development *à outrance* was paralleled in communications and above all shipping. At the end of 1930 the German mercantile marine had a tonnage actually in excess of the highest figure recorded in the pre-war years, and German shipping lines began to compete very determinedly for passenger traffic, especially on the Atlantic between the United States and South America and Europe. In all of these lines competition was already so keen internationally that there was a definite surplus of shipping even under prosperous international trading conditions such as obtained during 1929, and into this difficult area German lines entered. It was doubtful whether in this direction also the ambition of Germany had not gone beyond economic justification.

In other forms of communication very large schemes were put into operation, notably in wireless and in civil aviation and in airship construction, and in the majority of such services revenue-earning capacity was dependent in large measure on the maintenance of a high standard of activity within Germany and a steady improvement in trade and communications throughout Europe. In few cases had the capital invested in these services reached a stage where earnings could meet annually the interest and funding charges.

On the whole, however, the recovery of Germany from the war and from the inflation period was practically complete at the end of 1927, and a new series of problems came into existence from that year onwards. It is difficult to establish statistically the increase in the total German production, since no records have been made. One can, however, use the figures given in connection with the turnover tax. In 1924 the total turnover subject to tax amounted to 76,700,000,000 marks; it rose in a straight line to 134,300,000,000 marks in 1928, an increase of 80 per cent;

remained stationary at this latter figure in 1929, but as the result of trade depression fell in 1930 to 119,000,000,000 marks, and in the first half of 1931 to 48,000,000,000 marks, a decrease in 1931 of 19 per cent below the corresponding figure for the first half of 1930. If 1924 is compared with 1930 the increase was almost 50 per cent at a time when prices were falling fairly steadily, and the population had increased by only slightly more than 1·5 per cent. There was consequently very considerable improvement in the wealth and the standard of living of Germany even if, as the result of mechanization and rationalization, the excess of labour unemployable in the country should have risen to slightly more than 3,000,000 workers – an excess which under normal trade conditions would not usefully be absorbed.

While industrially Germany was creating for herself a very powerful position it cannot be said that financially a similar movement took place. The ostensible reason for this was primarily the necessity to meet reparations payments, but reparations were not the only cause of German financial insecurity. Other causes were the inability and unwillingness of German industrialists and even financial institutions to invest their surplus permanently inside Germany itself. On at least three occasions the credit situation was weakened by the action of German nationals in abandoning the mark and purchasing foreign securities. Those three occasions were in 1921, at the opening of the inflation period, in 1923, and in 1930 and 1931.

The history of public and even private finance in Germany since the conclusion of the war is linked up very closely with reparations. German policy during the war was in itself calculated to create a difficult situation. Instead of imposing additional taxation and meeting some part of the cost of the war the German Government preferred to raise its requirements in the form of loans with the addition of a very large increase in the emission of Treasury Bills. At the end of the war the total debt had risen to 147,000,000,000 marks, 89,000,000,000 marks being represented by funded debt and the remainder by Treasury Bills. Taxation had redeemed only one-tenth of this total. The funding of the sum of 55,000,000,000 marks of floating debt represented in itself a formidable problem which, handled unscientifically, would lead to inflation and depreciation of the mark. In addition to this factor there was a very large increase in currency in circulation. At the beginning of the war it amounted to about 7,000,000,000 marks, and at the end to about 33,000,000,000 marks. It was necessary, therefore, to carry out a very severe deflation policy, not merely to bring the currency in circulation to a reasonable level, but also to reduce the volume of the floating debt. Funding of the entire debt, long term and short term, would require the annual surplus of not much less than £380,000,000 per annum. While the gold reserves of the country had fallen to about 2,300,000,000 marks, the holdings of German investments abroad had been reduced to 5,450,000,000 marks. One can see that Germany had practically very few resources even at that time to sustain the national credit structure and to finance foreign trade. To this was added the demands of the Allies for reparations, fixed in 1921 at the fantastic figure of 132,000,000,000 marks. The annual debt charges of such a sum added to the surplus of the German internal debt amounted to at least £850,000,000 – a figure which no country in the world, not excluding the United States, could have supported without national bankruptcy.

The Treaty of Versailles took away most of her productive assets as represented by mercantile marine, railway rolling stock, and industrial areas. The income from foreign investments, which was before the war about £75,000,000, had shrunk to practically nothing, and Germany was confronted by severe exhaustion of all the credit supplies necessary to maintain economic activity in her population. The payments made direct to the Allies on reparations, namely, 1,000,000,000 marks in August 1921, resulting from the London Conference, forced the Reichsmark down to 181 to the dollar in October 1921. The second payment of 368,000,000 gold marks, following on the Conference at Cannes, and the moratorium of March 1922, depreciated it further to 670 to the dollar in July. The transfer of 254,000,000 marks to Belgium in August 1922 depreciated the mark to 4,500 to the dollar, while the invasion of the Ruhr completed the disaster. It is remarkable that such a small sum as £81,000,000, which represented the total reparations transfers to the Allies, should have destroyed the value of the mark, but one must add to this the effect of the transfer on the part of German industrialists of their funds abroad. Certain theorists have stated that this flight from the mark was more immediately responsible for the collapse of German credit than the reparations demands themselves. In any case, the war itself had brought the country to such a position that drastic reduction of debt charges was necessary either through repudiation of part of the debt or depreciation of the mark itself. The disappearance of the mark in August 1923 eliminated all debt inside Germany, national and private. It reduced the loan charges on industry to practically nothing and left industry in the possession of enormously valuable fixed assets as represented by plant and machinery without any corresponding capital investment charges.

For this result the entire German people paid very bitterly, and above all the middle classes. The general standard of living during the three years 1921-24 was probably lower in Germany than in any other country in Europe. It is only necessary, for example, to look at the consumption of wheat and cereals. In 1922, at the lowest point in the financial depression, the consumption of rye amounted to 5,700,000 tons, compared with 10,300,000 tons in 1913. The consumption of wheat, barley, oats show even greater falls than that recorded for rye and was less than half of that recorded in 1913. In 1923 the consumption of meat stood at 1,920,000 tons, compared with 3,100,000 in 1913 and 3,300,000 in 1929. The decline in the consumption of beer was in the same rates as that of cereals. The whole German people found themselves impoverished and deprived of all the advantages which had been obtained over the great period of German expansion from 1890 to 1913. The history of Germany since the end of 1923 is really a history of an improvement in the standard of living up to, and in certain cases beyond, the pre-war level. In 1929 one could state that, in the majority of food products and cereals, the pre-war standard had been surpassed. This result must be attributed to the determined effort that was made to raise industrial production up to pre-war standard, and above all to the period of stability which was introduced by the Dawes Plan.

The Dawes Plan proposed certain very definite reforms, bearing principally on the methods by which the budget should be balanced in Germany. The Reichsbank should act as a central credit and finance institution, and the German economic organization be brought to a point where it could supply the Government with a sufficient surplus to meet the reparations demands imposed by the Plan itself. The changes determined were the recovery of German credit, the elimination of the political factor as far as possible from the main public services contributory to reparations and to financial control, namely, the railways and the Reichsbank, and the maintenance of the gold standard with a stabilized mark in Germany. The reorganization of the Reichsbank was perhaps the most significant development. The Reichsbank became specifically independent of the State, with the right to control the circulation of currency in Germany, to facilitate financial transactions, and to utilize capital placed at its disposal. For fifty years it would have the sole right in Germany to issue bank-notes, but the notes already issued by the four private banks remained unaffected. The Reichsbank was empowered to raise its capital to 400 million marks, but its present capital transferred to the new gold basis should not exceed 100 million marks. Other regulations dealt with the ordinary discount business of the bank on the usual lines, with the important proviso, however, that the Reichsbank could grant working credits to the State only for a minimum period of three months at a time with a limit of 100 million marks, and at the end of the financial year State indebtedness towards the bank should be liquidated. All financial transactions of the State should pass through the Reichsbank, which could grant credits to the German railways and the German post not exceeding 200 million marks for both. The Bank was not permitted to advance credits to the Reich, but the latter would have a reparations account which could not go beyond 2000 million marks without the consent of the Bank. The currency in circulation should have a gold cover of 40 per cent, three-fourths of which should be actually gold. In the event of a lower ratio being adopted the Bank would require to pay duty to the State and raise the discount rate. The government of the Bank itself was to be vested in a Direktorium, the President of which was elected by the General Council, composed of fourteen members, seven German, and one each nominated by Britain, France, Italy, Belgium, United States, Holland, and Switzerland. The voting arrangements permitted of special consideration being given to German interests, and in this way the international element was toned down. The Reichsbank became, as a result of this scheme, the main element in German financial policy, and its very constitution made inflation for political purposes impossible.

The functions of the Gold Discount Bank, commissioned in March 1924 to finance trade and deal with commercial credits, passed into the hands of the Reichsbank; and from October 1924 onwards one could see in operation one banking policy carried out by one all-powerful institution removed effectively from the control of the State. In much the same way the control of the State railways was taken away and vested in a private company in which the Allies would be represented, but the action of the State in acquiring all the shares of the company was tantamount to renewal of national control within the form of a private industrial undertaking. In the latter case the main preoccupation of the Dawes Committee lay in abolishing a régime of waste, in restoring efficiency to administration, and in realizing more satisfactory profit margins, while in the former the recovery and the consolidation of the national credit were held to be more than anything else fundamental to the economic salvation of the country.

Other changes of less importance were envisaged, but the two already indicated were decisive. A special Reparations Commission, under the chairmanship of Mr Parker Gilbert, an American representative, came into operation to collect reparations dues and exert some advisory control over German financial policy, especially where it affected the delivery, actual or future, of reparations. Under the Dawes Plan Germany had to pay in reparations in a full year 2500 million marks (£125,000,000), but

for the first years of the scheme lower contributions would be exacted –
1000 million marks in 1924-25, 1220 million marks in 1925-26 and in
1926-27, 1750 million marks in 1927-28, and 2500 million marks thereafter. In the first year the new Reichsbank was set up, the German budget
balanced, the railways transferred to a private company with a capital of
15,000 million marks, with 11,000 million marks in bonds bearing interest
at 5 per cent with 1 per cent Sinking Fund, and industrial debentures
created to the value of 5000 million marks under similar interest and
sinking fund conditions. The Dawes Plan remained in operation until
1930, when the Young Plan began to take effect.

The essentials of the scheme put forward by the Young Committee
covered:

Assessment of the annuities to be paid each year beginning with the
seven months' period ending 31st March 1930.

The separation of the annuities into conditional and unconditional
payments through the creation of an international bank termed the
Bank for International Settlements, to ensure the transfer of these
annuities to the creditor countries and carry out the functions of an
international clearing house for international war debts – not merely
between European countries, but between European countries and
the United States.

The drastic reduction in the value of reparations deliveries in kind from
759,000,000 marks in the first year to the extinction of such deliveries
in the tenth year, payment for such reparations deliveries to be made
by the Bank for International Settlements.

Abolition of the machinery set up under the Dawes Plan for the
supervision and collection of annuities from Germany.

Provision for the mobilization of the unconditional section of the
annuities.

For the seven months ending 31st May 1930 a total of 743,000,000
marks were to be paid which, added to receipts under the Dawes Plan for
the previous five months, would give a total equivalent to that due under
the first full year of the Young Plan. The average value of the annuities
over the thirty-seven years to 31st March 1966 would be 1,989,000,000
marks plus the charges required for the Dawes loan of 960,000,000 marks
raised in 1924. In the year ending 31st March 1931 1,708,000,000 marks
would require to be paid; in the succeeding year 1,685,000,000 marks; and
the highest point would be reached in 1966 with 2,429,000,000 marks.
For the ensuing years, when payments would decrease to nothing, special
preparation would require to be made. Of the total annuities in any year,
660,000,000 marks, including the amounts required for the service of the

Dawes loan, would be unconditional, and would not be subject to post-ponement. Payment of the conditional section could be postponed on application by the German State, three months' notice being required, this provision being substituted for the transfer guarantee operative under the Dawes Plan. It was proposed also that, in the event of such a suspension being declared, France should guarantee to pay into the Bank for International Settlements the sum of 500,000,000 marks. This provision was destined to cancel in some measure the special position granted to France in connection with the payment of unconditional annuities where 500,000,000 marks out of 660,000,000 marks were due to be assigned to that country. The provision for commercialization applied to unconditional annuities and allowed France to raise capital sums in the international money market based on the revenues of the German railways and in this way capitalize part of the total unconditional annuities due to her. Advantage was taken of this provision to raise in the summer of 1930 the total sum of £60,000,000, the greater part of which went to France, and this was responsible in that year for putting out of balance the international exchange position and might be regarded as a contributory factor to the credit crisis which took place in the summer of 1931.

THE YEARS OF CRISIS

The Young Plan imposed a temporary solution to the reparations problem, but it made no allowance for an intensification of the world economic crisis in 1931, and it was evident that some modification would be necessary if the principle of reparations were to be retained. The Young Plan fixed absolutely the annuities to be paid, and abolished the index which allowed the Dawes Plan to take advantage of any considerable fall of prices to reduce the total payable and establish in this way some relationship between the actual output of the German people and the burden represented by reparations.

In 1931 a catastrophic fall in wholesale prices took place. Thus in December 1929 the index, using 1913 as a basis of 100, stood at 134·3, but in the middle of June 1931 it had fallen to 112·6, so that payments under the Young Plan had really increased by 16 per cent. At the end of 1931 wholesale prices had fallen to 106·6, so that if the Young payments had been continued the final increase would have been more than 20 per cent.

We can examine in turn favourable and unfavourable factors in the German situation as it developed during 1930 and 1931. Favourable factors were undoubtedly to be found in foreign trade, in the national savings, and in industrial equipment. Thus German exports rose from

9,291,000,000 marks in 1925 to 13,483,000,000 in 1929, an increase of 45 per cent in value, and 53 per cent in volume. In 1930 they fell slightly to 12,036,000,000 marks, and in 1931 to 9,600,000,000 marks. All these figures are inclusive of reparations deliveries. Imports rose from 12,362,000,000 marks in 1925, to 13,447,000,000 marks in 1929, shrank to 10,393,000,000 in 1930, and to 6,632,000,000 marks in 1931. The favourable balance of trade was, consequently, in 1929 36,000,000 marks, in 1930 1,743,000,000, and in 1931 2,968,000,000 marks. The total of payments under the Young Plan for reparations in 1931 was about 1,650,000,000 marks, inclusive of deliveries in kind, so that the favourable balance of trade alone was almost equal to twice the total required for the service of reparations, if attention is devoted purely to cash transfers.

Against those figures should be placed the enormous foreign borrowings of Germany over the period 1924 to 1930 inclusive, where we find that Germany imported long-term capital and credits amounting to about 7,200,000,000 marks (£360,000,000), allowance being made for capital repayment and for discounts, and obtained short-term credits amounting to 5,000,000,000 marks (£250,000,000), while to this last total should be added sundry credits not immediately ascertainable amounting to about 2,800,000,000 marks (£140,000,000), or the total on short-term account of 7,800,000,000 marks (£390,000,000). The total German borrowings, therefore, were equal to £750,000,000. Against this must be placed payments on reparations account amounting in the seven years to 10,300,000,000 marks (£515,000,000); but from this total should be deducted 4,010,000,000 marks representing deliveries in kind and about 900,000,000 marks representing reparations services and payments such as the cost of the armies of occupation which were not subject to transfer, so that the net reparations payments entering into the balance of accounts were about 5,390,000,000 marks (£270,000,000). The excess of German borrowing over reparations payments was consequently £480,000,000, and it was used to renew and improve the economic equipment of the country and finance an enormous export trade. In 1931 the position was aggravated through further enormous borrowings on short-term account which raised the total under this head to more than £600,000,000 and the aggregate of all indebtedness other than reparations to more than £1,150,000,000. On 6th December 1930 the Statistical Department of the Reich estimated the total foreign indebtedness of Germany at about 28,000,000,000 marks (£1,400,000,000), over 11,000,000,000 marks (£550,000,000) being represented by short-term indebtedness. German foreign investments were given as 8,800–10,800 million marks (£440,000,000–£540,000,000).

The increase in the savings of the German people was also a factor making for financial strength. In 1925 the deposits of Savings Banks and similar institutions amounted to 2283 million marks, but at the end of 1930 they stood at 14,000 million marks, more than six times that recorded in 1925. They are still less than in 1913, but one must take into account the increase in the industrial investment habit by the people, the increase in insurance, and, to some extent, the increase in stock exchange speculative activity. If allowance is made for all those figures, Germany in 1930 had reached a level of production, of capital investment of savings, of material well-being, which was decidedly higher than that reached during the best years of the period between 1890 and 1913.

Industrial equipment, which was very largely financed by imported capital, had reached a stage where the leading industries were in possession of the most modern and most powerful productive capacity in Europe, and were able to take advantage of very large resources for the control of the home market and for the development of exports. One indication of this can be found in the statistics of nominal capital of German firms. At the end of 1925 such capital was given as 19,121,000,000 marks, and at the end of 1930 24,189,000,000 marks. The average dividends paid by those companies, excluding banks and insurance, over the period was about 6·5 per cent, while the results of the companies recorded in the first quarter of 1930 gave an average dividend of 7·7 per cent, the most profitable industries being found in electrical manufacture, metal working, engineering, sugar, brewing, real estate companies, and iron and steel, all of them belonging to industries deriving benefit from greatly increased public expenditure on buildings, public works and services, and expenditure incurred by public utilities such as electricity supply. Germany, at the end of 1930, had reached a position of very considerable prosperity, above all in industry. Even companies reporting in the first quarter of 1931 paid a dividend of 5·27 per cent, so that the crisis had not yet affected industry. It had been calculated that, inclusive of industry, the increase in capital realized in Germany over the period 1924 to 1930 was in excess of £2,400,000,000, a figure very similar to that realized in Great Britain. In 1930, despite the crisis, only 5·8 per cent of industrial companies were in possession of foreign interests.

Unfavourable factors were to be found in the political and financial situation, and in the incredibly stupid and inhuman economic policy of the Government. The growth of Hitlerism, financed in its very early stages by German industrialists who saw in it a means to undermine the position of labour, was a factor which served most of all to weaken the international credit status of Germany; and in the elections held in

F

September 1930 the Hitler movement showed an enormous increase, not only in votes, but also in representation in the Reichstag. The National Socialists (Hitlerites) gained 95 seats, their representation in the Reichstag being 107, while the total vote recorded in their favour was 6,500,000, or 30 per cent of the electorate. The trial in September 1930 of three officers of the Reichswehr on charges of treason gave Hitler an opportunity of expressing in the most determined fashion his political policy – repudiation of all war debts and treaties, and complete refusal to admit Germany's guilt. Early in October a Stahlhelm demonstration at Coblenz before the ex-Crown Prince and General von Seeckt, and the declared intention of the Hitlerites to demand a plebiscite for the dissolution of the Prussian Diet, caused profound uneasiness in France and Great Britain.

From that moment onwards, Hitler dominated the political scene to a greater degree than Chancellor Heinrich Brüning, who succeeded Stresemann in 1929; and he emerged at dramatic intervals to show his strength. Thus on 30th May 1931 140,000 'soldiers' of the Stahlhelm paraded at Breslau before the ex-Crown Prince and King Friedrich August of Saxony, and made an imposing gesture against the corridor and Poland. On 9th July Hitler and Hugenberg (National Socialists and Nationalists) joined forces; on 21st July Hitler and Hugenberg sent a telegram to Brüning denouncing any arrangement with France resulting from the Hoover moratorium; on 9th August the Stahlhelm referendum on the dissolution of the Prussian Diet secured only 37 per cent of the necessary votes instead of 50 per cent and failed; on 11th October a mass demonstration was held at Bad Harzburg, and on 12th October Dr Schacht criticized adversely, apparently with justice, the accounts of the Reichsbank as not truly representative of the financial position, and on 17th October the Nazi storm troops, over 70,000 in strength, demonstrated at Brunswick for two days. On 26th November the plan of action of the Hitlerites for the seizure of political and economic power was published, a week after a document had been found in Hesse describing Nazi arrangements in the case of a civil war or Communist rising. Hitler repudiated the Hesse memorandum on 4th December and declared himself in favour of constitutionalism and international co-operation, provided that political debts were cancelled. The German administration should be simplified and all but essential imports barred out.

The German home political situation had degenerated into a race between Dr Brüning and Hitler over the prostrate body of the German people.

To Hitler's threats Dr Brüning answered by Decrees signed by a docile President. On 28th March national and State authorities were vested with drastic powers to overcome political violence, deal with fire-arms, and suppress newspapers publishing anti-national or anti-religious matter; on 17th July a further decree controlled press agitation; but on 10th August such control was vested only in the Reich and not in the States; on 7th October the inviolability of person and home was removed where persons were found in possession of fire-arms; and on 8th December the wearing of political uniforms and badges was forbidden and more rigid control of fire-arms imposed. In the words of Dr Brüning: 'The political leadership of the German Reich and the representation of its interests abroad will remain hereafter exclusively in the hands of the President and of the Constitutional Government', i.e. Dictator Brüning-Hindenburg. In January 1932 an attempt was made by Dr Brüning to ensure the co-operation of Hitler in repudiating war debts and reparations, but it failed.

The struggle between Dr Brüning and Hitler found its repercussions in the financial situation. Withdrawal of credits, largely on the part of France and Holland, and later U.S.A., began in the late autumn of 1930: between the General Election and 15th October 437,500,000 marks in gold had been exported; and at the beginning of July 1931 the Finance Minister stated that 3,000-4,000 million marks of foreign exchange had been withdrawn. In June President Hindenburg appealed direct to President Hoover, with the result that, on 20th June, the latter proposed a moratorium of one year on all war debts; and on 5th July agreement was reached by all the countries concerned, France insisting on the un-conditional section of the Young Plan being maintained but granted as a loan to the German Railways. The moratorium came too late to avoid a crisis in Germany, even if the Bank for International Settlements should have advanced to the Reichsbank a re-discount credit of 400,000,000 marks (£20,000,000) and the Federal Reserve Bank 200,000,000 marks at the end of June.

The North German Wool Company failed with a loss of 200,000,000 marks on 8th July, involving the Darmstädter und National Bank, which closed its doors on 13th July. The scheme for a joint guarantee of 500,000,000 marks put forward by 1000 industrialists was legalized by Presidential decree on 8th July and taken over by the Gold Discount Bank, but it had no effect on the situation. A further decree allowed the Reichsbank to reduce the gold covering for notes to 30 per cent, and to permit in this way an increase in circulation of about 2,000,000,000 marks; and the discount rate was raised to 10 per cent, the Reichsbank assuming control of foreign exchange dealings. All banks were closed for two days and reopened on 16th July, but from 20th to 23rd July no bank could pay out more than 100 marks daily in one account, and no exchange bureau more than 100 marks per week. On 25th July a special 'Acceptance and Guarantee Bank', formed by the Government and eleven banks with a capital of 200,000,000 marks, came into activity to facilitate the return to normal and allow resumption of business by the Darmstädter und National Bank. On 3rd August a group of industrialists advanced 43,000,000 marks to the latter in return for shares valued at slightly less than this amount, and the Government took up 300,000,000 marks of new pre-ferred shares issued by the Dresdner Bank, also in difficulties. The British and American and later the French, Dutch, and Swiss banks agreed to allow their credits to remain in Germany for six months. New decrees controlling foreign exchange, cash payments, and cheque clearings (50 per cent of a depositor's account up to a maximum of 16,000 marks), deferring also payments by Savings Banks to 10th August, were issued.

Normal banking operations were resumed on 5th August for the first time since 14th July; but, in the interval, the Government had secured control of the banking system, and the crisis ended with a suspension of repayment of foreign short-term credits, a rigid control of foreign exchange, and, as a consequence, of German foreign trade, and super-vision of all banking operations. In three weeks the Brüning Government had carried out nationalization of finance more complete than even the Soviet had attempted, and, with this weapon in hand, could meet with confidence the Hitler menace.

Two committees were set up by the Bank for International Settlements, one under the chairmanship of Albert Wiggin, representing the Federal Reserve Board, to study the conversion of German short-term credits into long-term loans and assess the immediate additional credits required by Germany, and the second, under the chairmanship of Dr Beneduce of Italy, to study the question of reparations in the light of the financial crisis in Germany. The latter committee was demanded by the German Government in a note on 19th November. The first committee was appointed on 31st July, and reported in the first fortnight of August; the second, appointed on 25th November, reported on 23rd December. The analysis of the financial and credit position of Germany by the Young Plan Advisory Committee showed that the payment of reparations could not be resumed on 1st July 1932, that the repayment of commercial debts should be facilitated if German credit internationally were to recover, and that the crisis was only part of an international problem which could only be solved by international action. On the other hand the Committee accused Germany of extravagance and misdirection of capital investment, especially foreign capital, and uttered the significant statement: 'The release of a debtor country from a burden of payments which it is unable to bear may merely have the effect of transferring that burden to a creditor country which, in its character of debtor, it, in its turn, may be unable to bear.' The analysis was, by implication at least, hostile to Germany, and as such was received by Dr Brüning and the German press.

On 11th December negotiations were opened in Berlin between the German and creditor banking interests concerned in the moratorium on short-term debts due to expire on 2nd February 1932, and it was announced on 23rd January 1932 that the 'standstill' agreement would be prolonged until 28th February 1933. The report of the Foreign Creditors' Committee, which carried out the negotiations, contained a further survey of the German financial situation wherein it was shown that the value of short-term credits covered by the agreement was 5,360,000,000 marks. It cast some doubt on the estimates of short-term debts submitted to it by German interests – considerably in excess of the estimate of 8,000,000,000 marks shown in the Basle Report of August 1931 – and suggested that only a small part of this addition (namely, 4,000,000,000 marks) could be considered. Such items as debt of German subsidiaries to foreign parent corporations, funds invested in fixed assets and not easily realized, and debts of German parent corporations to foreign subsidiaries as well as participation in German firms in the nature of advances were included, and no one could legitimately classify them as short-term debt. In plain words, the true statistics of indebtedness were as difficult to establish as German reparations payments since the conclusion of the war, and political propaganda had distorted both fact and relation. It was announced later that a small German Foreign Debt Committee consisting of a representative of the Government, a representative of the Reichsbank, and three representatives of German economic life would be set up to advise the Government on foreign indebtedness and foreign exchange control.

The deflationary policy of the Government was initiated on a large scale by the publication of a revised economic plan on 30th September 1930, to make good the estimated budget deficit of £37,000,000 for the current year. The plan provided for a reduction of 20 per cent in the salaries of all Ministers and deputies, Federal and State, and 6 per cent in those of civil servants receiving more than £75 a year. Unemployment insurance would be made self-supporting, contribution being raised to 6½ per cent of the wage paid, one-half by employers and one-half by employees. Minor adjustments followed, all aimed at reducing incomes and undermining still further the position of labour. Reductions in wages were announced in the majority of industries, above all in engineering and metal-working, where a strike was declared in Berlin on 15th October, and in coal mining, where the employers' association proclaimed a reduction of 8 per cent to take place on 15th January 1931. After a number of sporadic strikes on 2nd January, the Ministry of Labour imposed a reduction of 6 per cent. The second move took the direction of an Emergency Decree promulgated on 4th June 1931, to make good a further Budget deficit, and to realize about £90,000,000; taxes of 1 per cent to 5 per cent were imposed on wages and salaries above £60 a year, persons under twenty-one and agricultural workers were excluded from unemployment relief, a further 4 per cent to 8 per cent was cut off civil servants' salaries. A further decree gave the Government absolute powers to reduce prices, wages, railway freights, and interest rates – the decrease in wages being 23 per cent – , and increase taxes on turnover.

In finance arbitrary powers were also obtained and put into force: on 19th September the Government assumed control over the banks, created new and more stringent legislation for public companies with the addition of a special court to deal with serious cases of defalcation, fraud, and concealment of taxable revenue and foreign exchange holdings, and invited subscription to a loan of 250,000,000 marks to be issued by the railways. On 1st August 1931 the Foreign Exchange Decree came into effect regulating all transactions above 3000 marks requiring the sale and purchase of foreign exchange for trade purposes, and on 2nd October all holders of foreign exchange were forced to surrender their holdings to the Reichsbank, the amount exempted being only 200 marks. On 1st December a presidential decree empowered the Government to vary import duties at will until the meeting of the Reichstag on 23rd February 1932. In addition to those measures the Government, through excessive protectionist devices, virtually prohibited imports of cereals and other agricultural products, doubled taxation on sugar, and, in January 1932, imposed a ban on butter imports, with the further prohibition represented by anti-dumping duties on products from countries with depreciated currencies, principally Scandinavia and Great Britain.

In less than sixteen months the German Government had virtually destroyed the home market in Germany through deflation of a savagery unexampled in history, destroyed all the privileges and advantages secured by Labour since 1919, raised the cost of food-stuffs to fantastic heights, and imposed a régime of impoverishment on the entire German people. The horrors of inflation were as nothing beside the horrors of deflation in the sacred name, not of reparations, but of unprincipled industrial imperialism.

At a time when political difficulties were acute, especially with France, and German statesmen were proclaiming their inability to pay reparations, industrial policy led to developments which could only intensify international distrust and which strengthened the hand of France. The proclamation of the Austro-German Customs Union on 25th March 1931 was followed by the launching of the cruiser *Deutschland* at Kiel on 19th May. Commercial treaties were concluded with the Irish Free State, Hungary, Roumania, and Russia, among other countries, allowing for special privileges in the interchange of goods. Exports to Russia received further stimulus through an agreement on 18th April 1931 to finance Russian purchases to the value of 300,000,000 marks; the 'Ifago', a credit institution created by the Government and the leading banks to finance imports to Russia to a total of 200,000,000 marks, was renewed; and it was stated in August that orders amounting to 635,000,000 marks had been placed by Russia in the first seven months of 1931, 170,000,000 marks in July alone.

At the end of January 1932 the financial and political situation in Germany had become clarified to some considerable degree. On reparations, the Brüning declaration of 9th January, to the effect that Germany could not pay reparations and that any attempt to enforce such payment would lead to a severe crisis, not only in Germany, but in the whole world, showed definitely to France that negotiation would be useless, and the International Conference on reparations, which was due to meet on 25th January at Lausanne, was postponed until June. Dr Brüning had, in this statement, definitely overtaken Hitler, and there was very little left in the Hitler programme which had not already been incorporated, either in the decrees of the Brüning Government or in the statement of the Chancellor. An attempt to ensure the co-operation of Hitler in the unanimous nomination of Hindenburg as President for another year failed, largely because Hitler felt that, in doing so, he would be abandoning the principle of political liberty and independence which alone was left to him after Brüning had neutralized his policy in economic and financial matters.

One can, therefore, regard the German Government as successful in its attempts to eliminate reparations and avoid payments on a very heavy proportion of private debts as well. It had, through assumption of dictatorial powers, forced down wages in Germany to a level where production costs were so low that German industry could compete with almost every other country in the world in export trade. It had, through its agricultural protection, through its rigid control of foreign exchange, and through its special measures to counteract imports from countries with depreciated currencies, eliminated foreign competition from the German market and handed over the whole of the German people to industrial interests. On the other hand, it had destroyed the German home market, so that at the end of January 1932 almost six million workers were unemployed, industrial production was less that 60 per cent and a number of the leading municipalities were in a state of actual or potential bankruptcy. The social and cultural advance of Germany since the war was obliterated, schemes for improved public services and social betterment were postponed indefinitely, and the German people found themselves deprived of almost every liberty or privilege which, in a modern State, are necessary to the public welfare. The liberty of the home, of association, of expression, of investment, of travel, and of consumption had gone, the Press was effectively muzzled, and the State had complete control over the banks. The State also decided wages and working conditions, while it had dissociated itself entirely from the relief of unemployment, transferring the burden direct to the workers themselves and to local authorities.

The history of Germany during the years of crisis has been the history of the sacrifice of the German people to the struggle between Hitler and Brüning for political supremacy.

BIBLIOGRAPHY TO CHAPTER IV

Barnes, Harry Elmer. *Genesis of the World War*. New York and London, 1927

Brandenburg, Erich. *From Bismarck to the World War: A History of German Foreign Policy, 1870-1914*. Oxford, 1933

Dawson, W. H. *The German Empire, 1867-1914, and the Unity Movement*. 2 vols. London, 1919

Dawson, W. H. *A History of Germany*. London, 1928

Gooch, G. P. *Germany*. Modern World Series. London, 1925

Gooch, G. P. *History of Modern Europe, 1878-1919*. London, 1920

Gooch, G. P. *Franco-German Relations, 1871-1914*. London, 1923

Gooch, G. P., and Ward, Sir A. (Ed.) *Cambridge History of British Foreign Policy*

Gooch and Temperley. *British Documents on the Origin of the War, 1898-1914*

Grey, Lord. *Twenty-Five Years, 1892-1916*. 1925

Grey, Lord. *Selected Speeches on Foreign Affairs*. 1931

Grey, Lord. *German Diplomatic Documents, 1871-1914*. Selected and translated by E. T. S. Dugdale. 1928-31

      Vol.   I.   *Bismarck's Relations with England* (1871-90)

      Vol. II.   *From Bismarck's Fall to 1898*

      Vol. III.   *The Growing Antagonism* (1898-1910)

      Vol. IV.   *The Descent to the Abyss* (1911-14)

Hammann, Otto. *The World Policy of Germany, 1890-1912*. London, 1927

Harms, Bernhard (Ed.). *Strukturwandlungen der Deutschen Volkswirtschaft*. 1928

Heuss, Theodor. *Friedrich Naumann. Der Mann, das Werk, die Zeit*. Tübingen, 1948

Ludendorff, Erich von. *My War Memories*. 2 vols. London, 1919

Lutz, Ralph Haswell (Ed.). *The Fall of the German Empire, 1914-1918: Documents of the German Revolution.* Stanford University Press, U.S.A., and Oxford University Press, 1932

McFadyean, Sir Andrew. *Reparations Reviewed.* 1930

Preller, Ludwig. *Sozialpolitik der Weimarer Republik.* Stuttgart, 1949

Quigley, H., and Clark, R. T. *Republican Germany.* 1928

Schultze-Pfaelzer, G. M. *Deutsche Geschichte, 1918-1933. Vom zweiten Reich zum dritten Reich.* 1933

Temperley, H. M. V. (Ed.). *History of the Peace Conference of Paris.* 6 vols. 1920-24

Toynbee, Arnold J., and others. *Survey of International Affairs* (1920-23, 1924, 1925, 1926, 1927, 1928, 1929). 1925-30

Veit, Valentin. *Deutschlands Aussenpolitik von Bismarcks Abgang bis zum Ende des Weltkrieges.* 1921

Veit, Valentin. *Geschichte der Deutschen.* 1947. Translated by O. Marx as *The German People from the Holy Roman Empire to the Third Reich.* Knopf, New York, 1946

William II. *My Early Life.* London, 1926

Ybarra, Thomas Russell. *Hindenburg, the Man with Three Lives.* New York, 1932

CHAPTER V

GERMAN HISTORY FROM 1931 TO 1937[1]

THE struggle for supremacy between Brüning and Hitler, which in 1931 (pp. 149-51, 156) was taking on definite contours, ended with the crushing victory of the Nazi leader and a transformation of German government and life so vast and complete that at the present time, when the final phase has not been reached, anyone who deals with it can do little more than attempt an explanation of the ideals and aims which made it possible. One thing is certain: no statesman in the whole range of German history has made such sweeping changes as Hitler has done with the ease of a magician; and no German King or Kaiser has ever wielded such power.

We can see now that Brüning represents the transition between the international Socialism which framed and attempted to work the Weimar Constitution and the ruthless tyranny of National Socialism. Brüning's inability to weld Parliamentary parties into a majority forced him in 1930 to twist Article 48 of the Constitution into an interpretation which justified his new device of governing by 'emergency decrees' (Notverordnungen) issued by a 'presidential cabinet' (Präsidialkabinett); that is, in effect, by the personal authority deposed by the President in the Chancellor, who was thus independent of the Reichstag. Brüning was not a dictator; but he had begun to govern dictatorially. He failed mainly, not because he adopted this autocratic method, but because he came into conflict with the autocratic tendencies of the Junker clique behind Hindenburg. Brüning's positive achievements were afterwards ignored; but it is a literal fact that he smoothed the way for Hitler, above all by contriving the reduction of wages.

On 5th May 1932 Hindenburg's period of seven years as President was due to expire, and an attempt was made to persuade Hitler to agree to an

[1] This chapter is left pretty much as it was written in 1937. To have changed present or perfect tense to past would have ruined the mood and tensity of the style and whatever vividness the picture may have of something ever-present in our minds in those anxious days. The exposition of the racial and political theories then in the forefront of interest have now historical and literary interest; one would rather expand than suppress them.

extension (p. 155); for this to be possible under the Constitution a majority of two-thirds was needed, and this could only be done with Hitler's support. Hitler, supported by Hugenberg, refused; and an election for the Presidency was therefore necessary. Hugenberg, the leader of the German Nationalist Party (*die Deutschnationalen*) and of the industrialists (from 1909 to 1918 he had been Chairman of Directors at Krupps, was the owner of the Scherl Press, which published the *Lokalanzeiger* and *Die Woche*, and he controlled the Ufa – Universal Film A.G. – the largest German film company), had supported Hitler in resisting the acceptance by the Reichstag of the Young Plan, and thereafter he was closely associated with Hitler and with von Seldte, the founder and leader of the Steel Helmets. Technically Hitler was not eligible as a candidate for the Presidency: not only was he not a German of the Reich, but he was actually without nationality, for he had been deprived of his Austrian citizenship for having joined the Bavarian army as a volunteer on the outbreak of the war. German citizenship was, however, contrived for him: the Government of Brunswick, which was controlled by the Nazis, appointed him a member of their legation at Berlin; and on 27th February his candidature was officially announced. It was a dramatic event: a man of the people, a man who had earned his living as a bricklayer's labourer, one who had risen in the war to no higher rank than that of corporal, a ranting demagogue credited with criminal tendencies, to challenge the victor of Tannenberg, the time-worn idol of the nation! Two other candidates, Colonel Duesterberg for the German Nationalists and the Steel Helmets and Thälmann for the Communists, were already in the field. The results of the election on the 13th March were indecisive: Hindenburg did not pull off the required absolute majority. In the supplementary election Hitler, being refused facilities for reaching the electors by wireless, made the first of his breathless and legendary flights over Germany (*erster Deutschlandflug*): in subsequent flights he more than doubled his first record of speeches in twenty-one cities. Hugenberg had withdrawn in favour of the Nazi leader, who on 10th April obtained 13·41 million votes against Hindenburg's 19·35 million and Thälmann's 3·70 million: Hindenburg had thus an absolute majority, and was elected for a second period of seven years.

In the meantime an attempt to suppress the SA and the SS had been in preparation. The SA (= *Sturmabteilung*) had been founded in Munich in 1921 as a body of stalwarts whose duty it was to protect speakers of the party, throw out interruptors, and assist in the dissemination of propaganda. They had been organized by Flight Captain Hermann Göring, who during the war had taken over the command of Richthofen's famous 'circus'. Since the war he had earned his living as a pilot and official of aviation companies in Denmark and Sweden, and he had helped immensely to get the movement on its feet in Munich; he had, moreover, marched with Hitler and Ludendorff in the *Putsch* of November 1923. The SS (= *Schutzstaffeln*) had been established in 1925, when Hitler seemed to be losing control of the SA, to act as the Leader's personal bodyguard; from their black cap with a death's-head they came to be known as 'the Black Corps'. As a counterpoise to the Nazi formations the democratic parties had in 1924 established their own body of drilled fighters, the *Reichsbanner Schwarz-rot-gold*; and in 1931 this had been reorganized as the 'Iron Front' (*die Eiserne Front*). In November 1931 a document had been seized at the Hessian manor of Boxheim; it formulated the plan of action of the Hessian Nazis in the event of a Communist rising (p. 150), and this was taken to be a general plan of the Nazis. According to the Boxheim document the SA was to take over the reins of government, confiscate all revenues, and shoot all who resisted. Nazi headquarters disclaimed responsibility; but there was reason to fear that the document correctly stated Hitler's prepared plan; and all that has happened since proves that his simple and rock-firm device is to use fear of the Communists as an excuse for his lightning strokes – his strategy ever since the almost comic failure of his first and only attempt at armed revolt has been openly to proclaim the 'tactics of legality'; that is, to acknowledge the authority of the law and to rely nominally on a majority of votes, and then, in a crisis which, in view of the post-war self-assertion of the workers, might be calculated as certain to come, to thrust himself forward as the saviour of society. This expectation rather than definite proof was no doubt behind the suppression by a decree, dated 13th April 1932, of SA and SS as being 'a private army'. An immediate result of this was that in the elections of 24th April for the Landtag in Prussia, Württemberg, Anhalt and Hamburg, the NSDAP[1] came out as the strongest party (in Prussia they won 162 out of 422 seats). In the Reichstag there were violent attacks on the Government, as a result of which General Groener, who was made the scapegoat for the measures against the militant bands, was forced to resign as Reichswehr Minister, though he continued to act as Minister of the Interior. There were now four Ministries vacant, and Brüning was thus at the head of a Rump Cabinet. When on 28th May the Attorney-General (*Oberreichsanwalt*) in Leipzig rejected as insufficiently proven the charge of treason brought by Carl Severing, the Prussian Minister of the Interior, against the NSDAP, it was clear that Brüning was near his fall. On 28th May there was the first tentative meeting

[1] = *Nationalsozialistische Deutsche Arbeiterpartei.*

between Hitler and the Centre deputy Franz von Papen; Hitler promised
that the NSDAP would 'tolerate' any cabinet that von Papen might
form, provided that the decrees forbidding the SA and the SS and the
wearing of uniforms were rescinded, and that the Reichstag were dissolved. On the 30th of May Hindenburg refused to sign an emergency
decree presented by Brüning, because it contained provisions for the
compulsory disappropriation of Junker estates in East Prussia to provide
farms for settlements. Brüning thereupon resigned. On 1st June von
Papen, on the recommendation of General von Schleicher, was appointed
Chancellor, and formed a presidential cabinet. General Kurt von
Schleicher's influence at this time, wielded more or less in the dark, was
due to his friendship with Colonel von Hindenburg, the President's son,
an old companion in arms of his. Von Schleicher was second to General
Groener in command of the Reichswehr, and since his chief was palpably
discredited the striking power was practically in his hands.

Franz von Papen was closely associated with the great industrialists as
well as with the Centre Party, and was a member of the Herrenklub;
owing to these associations the cabinet he headed was nicknamed 'the
Barons' Cabinet' (*Kabinett der Barone*). He was remembered in England
for the scandal he had created when, as Military Attaché at Washington,
his portfolio had been discreetly detached from his person while he was
sitting in an omnibus; its contents had led to his expulsion from the
United States. Von Papen is the perfect type of a German gentleman;
more led than leading, he was no match for a *Draufgänger* like Hitler. That
the settlement of the War Debts question at Lausanne in 1932 – it was
arranged that Germany was to make a final payment of three milliards of
marks – fell to his period of office was more a chronological accident than
a personal achievement; we have seen that it had been manœuvred by
Brüning. An initial contretemps was Hitler's withdrawal, in writing after
an interview with von Schleicher, of his promise of 'toleration'; von
Papen, however, carried out, on 14th June, the revocation of the decrees
against the SA and the SS. On 4th June the Reichstag had been dissolved
and new elections fixed for 31st July – to the disgust of Hitler, who wanted
an immediate trial of strength. The result gave Hitler 230 seats as against
107 in the previous Reichstag.

On 17th November von Papen's cabinet resigned, and Hitler was
summoned by telegram to Berlin. Hindenburg, however, refused to
accept Hitler's terms, and von Schleicher was appointed Chancellor,
Minister of Defence, and Commissioner for Prussia. Hitler's determined
adherence to his policy of all or nothing, correctly calculated as the sequel
proved it to be, now met with resistance from several of the leading men

of his party, who were eager for cabinet rank; the party at that time happened to be financially in very low water, and indeed it was only saved in the nick of time by subsidies from the industrial magnates and (it is said) from the ex-Kaiser; at all events Gregor Strasser, the chief organizer (*Reichsorganisator*) and business manager of the NSDAP, was not perhaps so self-seeking as he was supposed to be when he refused obedience to his chief and negotiated for office with von Schleicher. Hitler acted with his usual fierce decision; Dr Wilhelm Frick[1] submitted humbly, and the incorruptibles closed round their Leader, so that the only result of the dangerous defection was that Strasser – a brilliant orator, and one of the few intellectuals of the party – was eliminated.

On 9th December the Reichstag adjourned and never reassembled. Negotiations lasting from the 17th to the 28th January led to an agreement between Göring, von Papen, Hugenberg, and von Seldte. It was foreseen that von Schleicher's period of office as Chancellor would be short; as a matter of fact he ran on a rock at the very start by telling Hindenburg – who, after he had been presented by the nation with the East Prussian estate of Neudeck, was the largest landowner in the country – that he would carry out Brüning's plan for sequestering the bankrupt estates in East Prussia. On 28th January the President refused his signature to a decree presented by von Schleicher for the dissolution of the Reichstag without fixing a new election; whereupon the Chancellor resigned. Von Papen was commissioned by Hindenburg to conduct negotiations with Hitler, who finally agreed to the President's conditions – Baron von Neurath to remain at the Foreign office and General von Blomberg to be brought from Königsberg to be Reichswehr Minister. On 30th January 1933 – a red-letter date – Hitler was appointed Chancellor, and the victory so tenaciously fought for was celebrated by a torchlight procession of the SA through the Brandenburg Gate and the Wilhelmstrasse past Hindenburg and Hitler. History will see in this picture the old President already outclassed and in the shadow; he had never been more than a heavy figure propped up by a more or less factitious reputation and moved to and fro by those who explained his policy to him. And yet Hitler's victory was at the time questioned by those who underestimated his power of hammering a wedge: to all appearances Hugenberg had the best of the bargain, for, apart from the President's nominees, who were spirit of his spirit, he was himself Minister of Agriculture (*Reichsminister für Ernährung und Landwirtschaft*), while Graf Scherwin von Krosigk was again Finance Minister, and von Papen Vice-Chancellor and again Commissioner for Prussia. Von Seldte was given the Labour Ministry. Göring

[1] See p. 171. From 1933 he was Reich Minister of the Interior.

was ostensibly, as Minister without portfolio (*ohne Geschäftsbereich*) kept in the background, but he was ready to pounce, and it is now clear that his prospective function was, above all, to thrust his weight under von Papen and remove this lath from the control of Prussia; on 10th April he became Prime Minister of Prussia and Minister of the Interior, and on 28th April he took over a newly created department, the Ministry of Aviation, as head of which his aim was bound to be to make Germany supreme in the air. The most interesting appointment perhaps was that of Dr Goebbels, who was to prove that mass psychology was a more vital sphere of influence than the task given provisionally to the Conservative parties of handling trade and finance. His title was 'Minister for the Enlightenment of the People and for Propaganda' (*Reichsminister für Volksaufklärung und Propaganda*). '*Kein Mensch muss müssen*', Lessing had said; Goebbels' privilege it was to prove that the German people, in their own conviction the most intelligent and the best-educated in the world, would fanatically believe anything that they were told they *must* believe. Hitler, Göring, and Goebbels have often been referred to as the Nazi Triumvirate; and though they are by no means the intellectuals of the party the description is apt. If Hitler is the man of few and shockingly naïve but pregnant ideas, the man of daring and determined plans, of lightning decision and of ruthless action; if Göring is the brave, abrupt soldier, unsparing in speech, a monumental figure not unlike von Hindenburg except that he is a driving rather than a driven force; then Goebbels completes the two by his insidious cunning, his contemptuous reading of the nation's mentality, his tinsel glitter of phrase and pageantry. He is the perfect advertiser, the showman who devises the endless succession of pictures, the eternal pose, the tumult and the shouting. His Ministry controls press, wireless, films; and that is a mere outline of his province. His most typical performance, perhaps, was his prohibition, in December 1936, of literary, musical, and art criticism, with the proviso that 'appreciation' (in the Nazi sense of course) is permitted to writers over thirty. Lessing, Macaulay pointed out, was the greatest critic in Europe; he could not exist in the Germany of today. Goebbels, who had been a pupil at Heidelberg of the Jewish critic Friedrich Gundolf, had himself written a feeble autobiographical novel[1] (*Michael*, 1933), and done journalistic work for his party; in his *Kampf um Berlin* he has described how as District Leader (*Gauleiter*) he won the capital for the Nazis. He exercised great influence as editor of the Berlin daily *Der Angriff*, which he founded in 1927. He is a man of insignificant physique (he has a crippled foot); nevertheless 'the Nazi Fouché', as he has been called, has

[1] One point stressed is that Christ was not a Jew.

an uncanny fascination, complicated by the fact that his qualities are unmistakably those which his party revile in the Jews.

Notorious in the early 'twenties was the rivalry for the Leadership between Hitler and Göring. In 1923 Göring as Commander of the SA had an army of 15,000 men at his beck and call, and to counter his thinly veiled plans a shock troop (Stosstrupp Hitler) was formed as a personal safeguard; this in time developed into the SS (p. 159). In 1927 a man under suspicion for embezzlement and other misdemeanours, hitherto subordinate to Gregor Strasser (p. 162), was promoted to be leader (Reichsführer) of the SS. It was Heinrich Himmler, who had carried the flag in Hitler's 1923 Munich *Putsch*. He had joined the SS in 1925. He was a man with lustreless eyes hidden behind his pince-nez and with the toothbrush moustache that gave Hitler's face a certain *hauteur* but lent no lift of fierceness whatever to Himmler's flat, mean features. His mean face fitted his apparently self-effacing disposition; he was prominent, but he did not, as the other leaders programmatically did, seek the limelight; rather he lived simply and even meanly; he was more of a rat-catcher than a swashbuckler. In 1933 he was put at the head of the secret police (*Geheime Staatspolizei*, shortened to *Gestapo*), which had been formed on 27th April 1933; and in 1936 he was made head of the whole German police force. As police dictator Himmler was one of the bloodiest tyrants in history. He worked in close touch with Goebbels, and both were ever on guard against Göring.

A department closely related to that of Goebbels was given to Bernhard Rust, who on 4th February was appointed Minister of Culture in Prussia; personally a man of sterling personality he is to be pitied for the task imposed on him of Nazifying schools and universities. Equally tragic was his Nazification of the German Academy of Literature (*die Deutsche Akademie der Dichtung*), which had been founded in 1926; having eliminated the Jews he was left with a skeleton and very dulled Academy. Another important appointment was that of Dr Schacht, who on 16th March replaced Dr Luther as President of the Reichsbank; on 30th July 1934, he became *Reichswirtschaftsminister*. One of the most important members of the party, Rudolf Hess, did not attend the meetings of the cabinet till June. His relations to the Führer are still somewhat obscure – he reminds one of the Jesuit confessors of old French kings; on 27th April he was given the title of Hitler's Deputy (*Stellvertreter*). He is one of the oldest friends of Hitler, and is no doubt the guardian if not the instigator of the Leader's plans; the guardian too of his secrets – and of his private life. Joachim von Ribbentrop came into prominence later as (from 24th April 1934) Peripatetic Ambassador; a man with long English connections he was the most suitable man who could possibly have been chosen as Ambassador to London, and his appointment as such in 1936 was welcome. He had acquired social polish in his capacity as a wines salesman for Henkell of Cologne; but he soon forfeited the comparatively favourable impression he made at first by giving the Nazi salute at Court and by similar outrages on good taste. Walther Darré did not join the Cabinet (as Minister of Agriculture) till June: he succeeded Hugenberg when the latter was, as the Americans say, pushed off. His work for farmers and peasants is outstanding, and will be lasting; in the cultural sense he will be remembered for the currency he gave to the catchword *Blut und Boden* to drive home the idea that as the soil is so is the blood[1]; though part and parcel of the racial theory this shibboleth is the stamp for that vast expansion of *Heimatkunst* (pp. 24, 331-2) in which Nazi litera-ture is for the most part running to waste.

Here is the place to attempt a characterization of the leader of this startling cabinet and an interpretation of his policy. His character is easily intelligible in the light of his origins, upbringing, and early experiences, discreetly veiled rather than revealed in his autobiography, *Mein Kampf*; he is a peasant by extraction, but his father had risen to be an excise official (*Zollbeamter*), and was able to send his boy to the Gymnasium at Linz. What Hitler says of his congenital resistance to orthodox education and particularly to the teaching of history does not cover up the fact that he failed to pass his leaving examination; and even his self-implied genius for drawing and architecture is not confirmed by his rejection as a student of architecture at Vienna (see p. 555). His campaign for a robust race and his emphatic subordination of mental culture to physical fitness does not hide the fact that he himself is congenitally feeble: he had inflamma-tion of the lungs at school, and his glaring personal peculiarities (he com-bines hysterical audacity with a retiring shyness and a certain awkward-ness) are not altogether to be explained by his war wound 'in the upper part of the thigh' and by his having been gassed. The charge of his enemies that he is uneducated is ill-founded; but he is in the main self-educated – i.e. he absorbed his mass of doctrinaire theories from an omnivorous reading of popular (mostly journalistic) literature. It would be impossible to deny him a streak of genius, morbid as this may be; the astonishing thing is that it should have taken him as far as it has done – if we say, for instance, that Bismarck was a genius we have not only his political record to justify the statement, but this is borne out by the dignity

[1] His books *Das Bauerntum als Lebensquell der nordischen Rasse* and *Neuadel aus Blut und Boden* are given prominence in the official list of 'the first hundred books for National Socialist Libraries'.

and distinction of his oratory, whereas Hitler's *Mein Kampf* and speeches betray a calculating and combinative but uncultured mind. The explanation is that Hitler has not so much directed a current as been borne along by it: he happened to be the most determined demagogue to preach that national feeling which seethed to boiling-point under the sting of defeat and defiantly asserted Germanic superiority over the rest of the world. Hitler had the trick of stating this conviction in the simplest terms, and of supporting it by a naïve display of illusory logic, with the main points cleverly brought into the light by typographical devices and margination. *Mein Kampf* is literally the Nazi Bible. All Germans on being married must possess this strange book (since 1936 even when married by German consuls abroad). And its sale has gone into millions. For the intelligence of events in Germany since the accession to power of Hitler *Mein Kampf*, the two volumes of which appeared in 1925 and 1927 (it was partly written in prison after the 1923 *Putsch*), is essential, painful as it is to eat one's way through its unshapen mass and its crass journalese. One by one as time goes on we see its concatenated items carried into effect; and now that the Treaty of Versailles has been reduced to a blank what remains to be seen is whether the grandiose schemes of territorial expansion it holds in prospect can be carried out as programmatically.

There is in *Mein Kampf* not a shred of originality except in the calculated forcefulness of the presentation: the doctrine is entirely derived, and the sources might easily be tabulated, say in a doctor's dissertation. Apart from Gobineau, Lagarde,[1] Houston Stewart Chamberlain, and Moeller van den Bruck,[2] there are two intellectuals[3] who gave definite shaping to Hitler's mentality and views in his tyro days as an agitator at Munich: these are Dietrich Eckhart and Alfred Rosenberg. Eckhart, a capable journalist, put what polish was possible on Hitler's literary and oratorical style; he translated *Peer Gynt* and wrote historical plays; and, since he died in prison after the Munich *Putsch*, he ranks as one of the martyrs of the movement. His memory is kept green by his song *Deutschland erwache!*, the call to arms of the movement, with its brazen clangour and clashed anger an excellent onomatopoeic rendering of the tocsin. Alfred Rosenberg is perhaps, as far as theories are concerned, the architect in chief of

[1] Paul de Lagarde (1827-91): *Deutsche Schriften* (1886); reprinted as *Schriften für das deutsche Volk*, 2 vols., 2nd ed., 1934. Extracts published in *Lagarde als Künder des Dritten Reiches* (Langenscheidt, Berlin).

[2] He familiarized the term 'das Dritte Reich', the 'Monumentalität' of which is to come from '*der preussische Stil*'. The idea of 'der Führer' owes something to his classification of famous Germans – '*gestaltende, entscheidende, führende Deutsche*,' etc. His *Der Preussische Stil* is one of the first 'hundred best books' of the Party.

[3] Hitler's intercourse with Siegfried and Winifred Wagner (from 1923) will be prominent when the facts of his life are published.

the Nazi movement. And yet he is a German from beyond the frontier (*ein Auslandsdeutscher*): really in fact and mentality a White Russian. Born at Reval in 1893, he was during the war a student in Russia, and met Hitler while a refugee at Munich. To his influence is to be ascribed much of the Russia-ward trend of Hitler's policy. The task still allotted to this long-sighted schemer, as is indicated by his title of Director of the Extra-Political Ministry and his functions as director of *Kraft durch Freude*, that arrangement for the conveyance of culture on the cheap to the working-classes by means of theatres, concerts, travel, etc., is to keep intact the sum and substance of Nazi doctrine; this he helped to clarify, particularly as regards the Racial Theory, in his cleverly written *Der Mythus des 20. Jahrhunderts*; and he keeps the pot boiling as editor of *Nationalsozialistische Monatshefte* (founded by Hitler in 1930). Rosenberg is notoriously hostile to Christianity, and those who seek to replace Christ by Wodan (in all seriousness – Ludendorff and his wife actually edit a fortnightly pagan journal, *Am heiligen Quell deutscher Kraft*) – find support in him.

But, if the Nazi doctrine derives from idea-twisters like Rosenberg, for the gospel cut and dried we must go to *Mein Kampf*: here we have the simple faith against which doubt is heresy. The book is an *olla podrida* in the literal Spanish sense; but the ingredients may be ladled out and classified. There is a scathing denunciation of Austria as a country effete because of eternal misgovernment and of too weakly resisted Slav encroachment, to be saved and kept German only by incorporation in the Reich. Indeed, all the German minorities over the frontiers must be made one with Germany; this, however, can only be done by a regenerated Fatherland. And this regeneration of the Fatherland is the passionate plea which the whole book serves. There can be only one purpose for this regeneration, this moral and physical *Wandlung*: the establishment of the superiority of the German race, and hence the restoration of the German Empire not merely in its pre-war glory but in the glory for which it was predestined by its very qualities of blood and brain; the establishment, in short, of what is religiously hailed as 'the Third Kingdom'. 'Das Dritte Reich' is not merely the rebirth of the Empires founded by Charlemagne and Bismarck, it is in a deeper significance the culminating third stage of Mysticism (1. *Läuterung*, 2. *Erleuchtung*, 3. *Vollendung*; or 1. *Seelenerschütterung*, 2. *Bekehrung* or *Umkehrung*, 3. *Wandlung*). It was an idea much worked by the Expressionists (p. 346), to whom stage 1 was represented by the Great War, stage 2 by post-war pacifism, stage 3 by that sacrifice of self to the common good which is the theme of so many notable books (pp. 348, 416). To the Nazis stage 2 is the mental travail in the agony of defeat which gives birth to the national system of stage 3, in which perfection is attained by the sacrifice of self to the regenerated state; a final transformation, not necessarily contradictory to Expressionistic *Wandlung*, for the common good is, according to the Nazis, not born in the travail of the individual's own soul (which, however, in true mysticism it must be) but conferred on him (like grace by the Catholic Church) by a State perfected by the *Wandlung* of individuals. And thus Hitler takes rank with the Pope: 'just as the Roman Catholics consider the Pope to be infallible,' says Göring, 'so the National Socialists consider Hitler to be infallible.' It is, therefore, not blasphemous to hail him as *der Erlöser* (the Saviour).

Hitler's scheme of regeneration begins with the hardening of the body. He preaches Rousseau's 'back to nature' gospel; but Rousseau's sanitarian ideal is in the new Germany to be a rigidly enforced State policy: fitness for war is the main purpose of life for males; to produce such males is the only purpose of life for a sanitarily fitted woman. Physical training must be crowned by early marriage, in order to root out prostitution and syphilis, evils which are characteristically laid at the door of the Jews as *Mammonisierung der Liebe* and *die Judenkrankheit*.

The cardinal political doctrine is that a country with not enough land for its population is entitled by the law of nature to take land from a country in the contrary case, and that any race which has the power to seize such land is entitled by the law of nature to do so. Hitler points out with an ominous emphasis that German colonization has only been permanent on land taken from the Slavs (pp. 1, 67, 71, 74), and he argues therefore that the Germans must begin again where they stayed their trek six centuries ago. 'We stop the eternal migration of the Germans west or south', he proclaims, 'and look to the east.' To this project Hitler and his paladins persistently and consistently return; and the general interpretation of the obsession is that the lands in view are the Ukraine and those districts of Russia on the Black Sea which are regarded as German(ic) territory because they were once occupied by the Goths. The rescue of German minorities might be taken in in such a stride, whether the way leads to the mouth of the Danube through Czechoslovakia or brings back the Polish corridor and Danzig and Upper Silesia.

National Socialism[1] is a cleverly devised term to indicate a synthesis of the symbols or labels adopted in pre-totalitarian days by the main parties in the State, the proletariat on the one hand and the middle and higher classes on the other. The Socialists, that is the 'common' people, were to be converted (by persuasion or by force) to the national ideal, and the

---

[1] The term *nationalsozial* was first used by the parson politician (Pfarrer) Friedrich Naumann; in 1896 he founded the *Nationalsozialer Verein*, later *Nationalsoziale Partei*.

Nationalists were to be cured of their hostility to the 'people'. Since no thinkable concessions on either side could bridge the division, the only cure for this unnatural hatred was to make the two parties one party. The task might have seemed impossible; but Hitler – who, as we know from *Mein Kampf*, interpreted the aim of English propaganda during the war as the creation of an obsession by pitiless repetition – was aware that it was merely a question of inducing a desired state of mind in the mass of the people, or, in the more intelligent section of the community, a limitation of the idea of *Wandlung* from international to national; and he was helped by the fury of the nation when the French occupied the Ruhr, by the destruction of the currency and of savings which followed, by the presence of French coloured troops in the Rhineland with the bastardization which, he alleges, left its visible mark on the province, and by the persistent refusal to grant Germany equality of status (*Gleichberechtigung*) at the Disarmament Conference. Year after year the Germans were being treated as a conquered and humiliated race: Hitler's method was to hammer it into them (*einhämmern* is a favourite term of his) that by the evidence of ethnology and history they were the salt of the earth, and that with determination and adequate preparation not only might all losses be made good but room provided for expansion by that final break through which their race, hemmed in in the centre of Europe, had always been trying to force. A scapegoat was found for the humiliation of defeat: the Jews, in their aim to dominate the world, had sold the Germans through their financiers, and had poisoned the minds of the masses by organizing them in Trade Unions; the Revolution of 1918, that proverbial 'stab in the back', was the work of Jewish demagogues. The Jews were parasites, 'plant-lice', unable to live save by sucking the blood of their betters; the time had come to shake them off and cleanse the body politic; and Hitler promised that when he came into power 'heads should roll in the sand'. The Jews, statistics showed, formed less than 1 per cent of the population; but not only was finance practically a monopoly of theirs, but in the medical and legal professions, at the universities, and elsewhere they filled an undue proportion of the highest posts. In literature and journalism the case against them was irrefutable: the most prosperous publishers, the best newspapers, were Jewish; and therefore non-Jewish writers had less chance of being boomed. (That writers like Gerhart Hauptmann and Thomas Mann owed their success to the enterprise or genius of Jews like S. Fischer and Max Reinhardt was overlooked.)

In the gigantic plan of mass conversion the main argument was from the first the Racial Theory. There was nothing new in this teaching.

Gobineau,[1] confirmed by Vacher de Lapouge, had proclaimed that 'the Aryan race, and in particular the Teutons, are the true creators of culture and leaders in the world'. Houston Stewart Chamberlain[2] had popularized the idea, but he had pointed out that mixture with other races leads inevitably to degeneration and decay; and this was confirmed by the pessimism of Oswald Spengler, who in his *Der Untergang des Abendlandes* (2 vols., 1918-22) demonstrated that civilization completes itself, and therefore exhausts itself, in the satiety of cities. The proof absolute of Aryan superiority came with Alfred Rosenberg's *Der Mythus des 20. Jahrhunderts* (1930). With him racial intermarriage is heightened to the tub-thumping term 'blood pollution' (*Blutschande*):[3] this served for branding sexual intercourse with Jews, or with semi-Jews, as the unforgivable sin. Rosenberg (himself, like Hitler, merely an astute popularizer of the speculations of scholars) follows up the investigations of Hermann Wirth, who in his *Der Aufgang der Menschheit* (1928) and *Die heilige Urschrift der Menschheit* (1930) has attempted to trace the wanderings of a primitive Nordic race over the earth. Wirth's argument is that myths are not, taking them as a whole, the spontaneous growth of different races, but that they have one origin and have then migrated: where we find the same myth, therefore, we have a proof that the primitive race which can be shown to have produced that myth had migrated with it to whatever place it is found in. Thus the solar myth does *not* represent a common stage of civilization, but must have had its birth in a country where the sun was a cosmic experience; that is, in the extreme north. Following the solar myth we thus find that the Nordic race once sailed those ships of theirs with the swan and dragon prows to the shores of the Mediterranean, to India, to Oceania; and that on land they roamed to Central Asia, Turkestan (where an Indo-European language, Tocharic, was discovered early in the twentieth century), and thence to China and Japan; and by way of North America to the land of the Mayas in South America. The Nordic boat with swan's neck and trefoil is found in pre-dynastic Egypt, and those who rowed in it were the blonde and blue-eyed Amorites, the sons of Enak, who wandered by way of Syria to Babylon. The Berbers

[1] Comte Joseph-Arthur de Gobineau (1816-82): *Essai sur l'inégalité des races humaines* (1853-55).

[2] Houston Stewart Chamberlain (1855-1927): *Die Grundlagen des 19. Jahrhunderts* (2 vols., 1899-1904); *Rasse und Persönlichkeit* (1925). Hitler met him at Munich in 1923. The base of his philosophy is the idea of the self-willed regeneration of a nation ('*völkisch-seelische Erneuerung*'), possible in the creative Aryan race, which is contrasted with the inferior Semitic race. One of his main points is that Christ was not a Jew (see p. 163).

[3] The title of his book *Blut und Ehre: ein Kampf für deutsche Wiedergeburt* is sufficiently indicative.

of North Africa are fair-skinned and blue-eyed. Egyptian reliefs of 2400 B.C. show fair-skinned, red-haired and blue-eyed men – the blonde Libyans whom Pausanias mentioned. Thus it is clear that the Nordic race overran North Africa. Jerusalem itself was founded by the Amorites, and they formed the Nordic stratum in Galilee, whence Jesus sprang; Jesus was thus of Nordic race, and *not* a Jew. Signs for writing were invented by the Nordic race; and the rock drawings of the Stone Age in Sweden represent the first stage of the linear script of the pre-dynastic Egyptians, from which all other writing in the world is derived. Thus (*Q.E.D.*) all culture is Nordic, and was conveyed in the following waves: that of the Atlantides across North Africa; that of the Aryans to Persia and India, with Dorians, Macedonians, Latini in their wake; the German Migration of the Nations; and lastly the colonization of the world by the Germanic or Germanized West of Europe. Italy was conquered by successive waves of Nordic invaders: Stilicho, Alaric, Odoacer, Theoderic, the Lombards; the Normans seized Latin lands; and therefore the Italian Renaissance was Nordic, for, as Ludwig Woltmann has shown in his *Die Germanen und die Renaissance in Italien* (1905), 63 per cent of the great figures who made it were blonde.

All this reads like a fairy-tale; but it was corroborated by numerous ethnological popularizations[1] by Hans F. K. Günther; this gentleman was (against the will of the faculty) appointed by the Government of Thuringia a professor at Jena when, in January 1930, Dr Frick had the honour of being the first Nazi to be appointed a Cabinet Minister; at the induction of this specifically Nazi professor Hitler had marched in the inevitable torch-light procession. Günther, sagely cock-sure, fixed the primitive home of the Nordic race in Central Europe;[2] the chief argument for this is that a Thuringian type of cord-ornamented pottery (*Schnurkeramik*), dating from the Neolithic Age, can be followed eastwards through Europe. The Nordic race as it migrated would then transfer its culture to the races it conquered; and this process is termed *Aufnordung*. The reverse process of *Entnordung* is now in operation, and for economic reasons: the Nordics, since they have the most responsible positions, restrict their families, while the lesser tribes are prolific and encroach in waves of increase which not only threaten the predominance of the Nordic race, but, since culture is Nordic only, threaten to engulf culture itself. The only remedy is a deliberate breeding process coupled with

[1] *Rassenkunde des deutschen Volkes*, 13th ed., Munich, 1919. *Rassenkunde Europas,* 3rd ed., Munich, 1929.

[2] Hermann Hirt (*Die Indogermanen*, 1905-7) for linguistic reasons fixes the *Urheimat* in the North German plain; C. Schuchardt in his *Alteuropa in seiner Kultur- und Stilentwicklung* (3rd ed., 1935) places it in Thuringia.

instruction (*Aufklärung*) of the Nordics in their own racial supremacy. It is remarkable that this process of re-Nordification had been stressed by a Jew, Walter Rathenau (pp. 125, 138), in his books *Reflexionen und Aufsätze* (1908) and *Zur Mechanik des Geistes* (1913), and that he too had called for 'Nordification of the West'.

But the current conception of Aryan and Nordic – two distinct ideas beautifully fused and confused – is derived mainly from *Mein Kampf*. Hitler ignores the culture of the Hungarians and the Finns, ethnologically members of an Asiatic race (Günther argues that they are so *aufgenordet* by admixture that they may be classed as Nordics!); to him, as to Houston Stewart Chamberlain, the yawning gap is between Aryans and Jews. Hitler divides mankind into those who create culture (*Kulturgründer*), those who carry culture or on whom culture is imposed (*Kulturträger*), and those who destroy culture (*Kulturzerstörer*). Only in the Aryans is culture innate. Those who bear culture on their backs are races like the Chinese and the Japanese; if Europe and America were to perish, Japanese barbarity would pierce the veneer of culture that hides it today. Ancient Chinese and Japanese culture was created by that first Aryan wave which came from Turkestan; the proof of this is the ossification which ensued when actual contact with the vivifying race had been lost. Aryan culture has been conveyed in the course of history by conquest; and wherever the Aryan conquerors have mixed their blood with the conquered race they have decayed as a result of the pollution. But all is well so long as the conqueror – '*die staatenbildende Herrenrasse*' – keeps his distance and uses the inferior race as machines: e.g. thus the Pyramids were built. Enslavement of inferior races is a necessary part of the Aryan manifestation of culture: the Aryans must use and direct the soulless machine. Indeed, since the inferior race is what it is, it is happiest in its condition of enslavement to the Aryan.

This doctrine of lord and slave obviously derives from Nietzsche (pp. 313-4 ff); but another of the popular books of recent years confirms it from a new angle. L. F. Clauss in his *Die nordische Seele* (2nd ed., 1932) classifies not so much by facial marks as by spiritual traits (*das Seelische*); he divides humanity into 'the productive man' (*Leistungsmensch*) – that is the Nordic race – and the 'self-effacing man' (*Enthebungsmensch*); the one grips the world, the other slips it (activity and passivity). Action alone, Goethe said, can satisfy a German; achievement surpasses thought; contemplation is Buddhistic; that is, Nihilistic. The Nordic must ever be roaming; and therefore the world is his. He has 'will to space' (*Raumwille*). The Germans have the will to space but not the space they will, as Hans Grimm has shown in one of the most influential novels of recent years, *Volk ohne*

Raum (1926); the will to space, it follows, is an integral part of Nazi policy, and explains the agitation for the return of Germany's colonies, which is at this moment in the forefront of interest.

Integrally interwoven with the Racial Theory is the adoption of the Swastika banner, which Hitler devised in 1920 as the symbol of the Nazi movement[1] (on 12th March 1933 it was given equal rank with the old Imperial flag; by decree of 15th September 1935 it supplanted the black-white-red banner). It is true that the swastika (*das Hakenkreuz*) is found in Egypt, Greece, India, China; but this, we are to understand, is simply because it migrated thither like the solar myth; the symbol, actually a scythed wheel, is defined by the Nazi Germanists as a 'solar rune of victory' (*Sonnen- und Siegrune*). In Hitler's own words the new flag was to embody will-power together with reverence for the hoary past of the race.

Hitler began his rule on the day after his appointment as Chancellor by fixing new elections to the Reichstag for 5th March; and on the same day he announced, in his first wireless speech, his two four-year plans of reconstruction. In Prussia the Communists worked into Göring's hands by calling a general strike and by rioting; he issued a decree prohibiting demonstrations. But Communist demonstrations and no more did not fit in with the plan which, as we have seen, was with good reason ascribed to the Nazis; and there is grave suspicion – though from the nature of the case there can be no proof – that they in malice prepense contrived the excuse they needed for establishing a dictatorship. At all events on the 27th of February the Reichstag was destroyed by fire. Marinus van der Lubbe, a Dutch Communist (a mere boy, and hardly *compos mentis*) was arrested on the spot; on the following day Torgler, a Communist member of the Reichstag, was arrested; and on 9th March three Bulgarian Communists, Dimitroff, Popoff, and Taneff. During the trial, which lasted from 21st September to 23rd December, Göring and Goebbels rather made inflammatory speeches than gave evidence. Van der Lubbe was condemned and executed; the others were acquitted because the evidence was inconclusive. On the day after the fire the Communist Party was declared illegal, Göring arrested 4000 Communist deputies and functionaries, and entirely suppressed all Communist and Socialist newspapers. Another step was to establish concentration camps in which, as Dr Frick put it, Marxists were to be trained to be useful members of society. On 24th February there had been a domiciliary search in the Karl Liebknecht House in the Bülow Square in Berlin (on 8th March it was rechristened 'Horst Wessel House', in honour of an SA leader – the author of the Horst Wessel Lied, which became the Party hymn – who had been shot by

[1] Jörg Lechler, *Vom Hakenkreuz: Die Geschichte eines Symbols*. Leipzig, 1934.

Communists on 14th January 1930); it was announced that the incriminating documents there found would be made known, but this was never done, and there is good reason to think that none were found, as the Communists knew what to expect; that plans were found for the burning of the Reichstag, and for the Communist rising spoken of, is extremely unlikely. An official communiqué published in the *Frankfurter Zeitung* the day after the fire stated that persons with torches had been seen in the Reichstag when the fire was discovered, and that the police could not arrest them because they slipped away, apparently through the subterranean passage which bears the central heating apparatus from the Reichstag to Göring's official residence as President of the Reichstag. Other statements were forthcoming that the Reichstag fire had been devised by Goebbels as an 'electoral bomb', and that Göring was the incendiary. At all events the result of the elections for the Reichstag on 5th March evidenced the propaganda value of the fire and the alleged Communist danger: the NSDAP won 288 seats as against 196 in the previous Reichstag; and, with the German Nationalists and the Steel Helmets, they had now an absolute majority. The Communists, of course, could not sit. The Party also obtained an absolute majority in the elections for the Prussian Landtag,[1] which were held on the same day.

The system of dual government by Reich and Landtag in the separate States had always given rise to friction, particularly in Prussia, the largest State. Franz von Papen, when Chancellor, had been faced with an awkward situation: the Social Democratic Prime Minister Otto Braun and his Minister for the Interior, Carl Severing, were still *de facto* at the head of affairs, although *de jure* they should have resigned, as they had been defeated in the Landtag, and it was only as Commissioner for Prussia that Papen could proceed to remove Braun and Severing and their officials; resistance was threatened, but a squad of policemen proved to be all that was required to seize the Government offices and to put an end to democratic government. Papen, as Commissioner for Prussia once again, completed this cleaning up process. In any case Göring acquired complete control by establishing an auxiliary police force in Prussia, made up of members of the SA, the SS, and the Steel Helmets; to them he issued his famous 'order to shoot' – any policeman who shot and killed his man, he said in the instructions issued, would be exonerated, while failure to shoot would be investigated.

The Nazis now seized power in the Free Cities and in the other separate States. The only place where opposition seemed likely was Bavaria: here

---

[1] Diet; the legislative body of one of the German States comprising the Reich. The Reichstag is the all-German Parliament.

the Government had proclaimed that any Commissioner sent from Berlin would be arrested at the frontier; the Commissioner appointed, however, was General von Epp, a Bavarian already in the country; and on 10th March he took possession of the Government building and entered on his duties. On 12th March Hitler flew to a completely Nazified Munich (the city was in 1935, as a special honour, declared to be the headquarters of the NSDAP); and in the speech he made here the word *Gleichschaltung* was used for the first time. It is a word difficult to render: 'co-ordination' is far less vivid, and 'unification' is too abstract; it means that the States can only be units of the Reich, and that all these units must be *forced* into cohesion. *Gleichschaltung* was, however, not limited to welding what had always been a heterogeneous group of States into a homogeneous whole, but was applied to all phases of citizenship and of life physical and mental, to build up the very simple but never in all history realized 'totalitarian State' (*Totalitätsstaat*) – one for all and all for one. What it actually led to was the tyranny of an idea, the crushing of all individuality. On 31st March a law was passed to codify this *Gleichschaltung* as applied to the States.

On 21st March, at noon, the newly-elected Reichstag assembled in the Garrison Church at Potsdam, and was addressed by Hindenburg and Hitler. Goebbels staged a spectacular finale: while the deputies waited in hushed suspense the old President with his heavy tread descended to the vaults to pray at the sarcophagus of Frederick the Great. In the afternoon the deputies reassembled in the Kroll Opera House in Berlin; and here on 23rd March the Act of Authorization (*Ermächtigungsgesetz*) was passed, which had the effect of abrogating a great part of the Weimar Constitution – that infamous thing (it had been drawn up by a Jewish jurist, Dr Preuss).

On 1st April occurred a day's boycott of the Jews, ostensibly as a punishment for Jewish agitation ('*Greuelpropaganda*') abroad. It had been arranged by Julius Streicher, the District Leader of Franconia, a man of evil repute, whose typical line of attack, in his newspaper *Der Stürmer*, was to depict the Jews as sexual maniacs. The boycott was only limited to one day because of the fear that a prolonged boycott might result in financial chaos. The boycott was followed on 10th May by a holocaust on the public squares of Marxist and Liberal books, seized by students in public libraries and elsewhere. Goebbels gave his official blessing to the destruction of this 'filth' – which included first-class literature, e.g. books by Heinrich Mann, who was one of the first to undergo the punishment decreed for democrats unrepentant in exile: such people were to be denationalized (*ausgebürgert*), with confiscation of their property wherever it could be seized. Einstein suffered this fate; Thomas Mann, though he removed to Paris at once, was spared until December 1936. The persecution of the Jews culminated in a law passed on 15th September 1935 'for the protection of German blood and German honour', i.e. prohibiting mixed marriages with non-Aryans. Officials with any Jewish ancestry, even remote, were dismissed wholesale; service in the war and (technically at least) appointment before 1918 was alone counted a safeguard.

The Party was now firmly fixed in the saddle, and the only danger of a fall came in 1934, when an armed rebellion prepared by Major Röhm, Chief of Staff of the SA, was crushed by the swift action of Hitler, who on 30th June flew in the night from Bonn to Munich and arrested the ringleader. Röhm was shot with others of the conspirators. There was a 'purge' in Berlin, too; von Schleicher, whose implication in the plot is to say the least dubious, was shot with his wife when SA men burst into his study. Von Papen was in danger, but was spared. Röhm was one of several men of immoral character who have rendered signal service to the NSDAP; he was an intimate friend of Hitler from the first. A brave soldier, he was too self-assertive not to resist when the promotion he expected was denied him; for him, however, higher office was out of the question, for he was a notorious paederast. Röhm, an outspoken Nietzschean, had been at least frank: 'nothing is more false than the so-called social ethic', he had declared; 'I will on no account be reckoned among the "moral men".' If there could be anything to the credit of Nazi doctrine it would be that it does imply clean living, partly no doubt from the athlete's sense of Spartan discipline, but certainly also from a religious sense that duty to the Fatherland must couple moral integrity with physical fitness. The tyrannical Nazi dragooning of life and all the phases of it did perhaps mean, in some aspects and phases of life, a cleansing of morals, and with that a purification of literature and art, which for all their brilliance were before the Nazi régime often sensational and too daringly obscene. Röhm's particular vice, and incest, were favourite themes of even the best literature; and although to us particular works may appear merely like a doctor's handling of disease it is possible to understand, if not condone, Goebbel's too comprehensive word 'filth'.

The death of Hindenburg on 2nd August 1934 served for the most spectacular funeral, in the monument prepared for him at Tannenberg, known to history. Hitler at once abolished the title of President, and himself assumed the functions of the office with the official title of 'Führer und Reichskanzler'. The usual plebiscite confirmed this step by a majority of nearly 90 per cent.

It would be tedious to follow the successive stages by which all political parties except the NSDAP were suppressed. The voluntary dissolution of the German Nationalists on the 28th June 1933 brought with it the elimination of Hugenberg from the Cabinet. The process was rounded off by the law of 14th July 1933 which declared that only one party was legal. The Trade Unions had their property confiscated; and on 2nd May 1933 they were all welded together as *Die Deutsche Arbeitsfront*, provision being made for the cultural improvement of the masses by the branch department *Kraft durch Freude*. On the following day compulsory labour service was decreed.

For *Gleichschaltung* to be quite totalitarian it would have to co-ordinate all the religious sects. But attempts in this direction have met with heroic resistance. The crazy revival of ancient Germanic paganism is in consonance with the official demand that the ancient Germans must no longer be described in historical manuals as barbarians; and the orientation of the 'German Christians' – that is, the Nazi Protestant party – is tainted with this archaeological patriotism. The Old Testament, they assert, must be discarded *in toto*; and as for the New Testament, Christ must be transformed to a militant personality. The trouble is, of course, that Christ was a pacifist; for which reason he was transformed ages ago by the Old Saxons in their epic *Der Héliand* (p. 214). Lagarde was a theologian; but he had written: 'Palestine is no concern of ours – to return to (our national) antiquity means progress.' And therefore, say the German Christians, not the holy places of Palestine must be visited but the holy places of Germany. In this grotesque attempt to Nazify Protestantism the chief agent has been Ludwig Müller, who came from East Prussia (where he was chaplain to the Reichswehr) with General von Blomberg, and in due course was elected Reich bishop.

The Catholics found it prudent to make a series of compromises; but on religious ground they could not by the very nature of their faith budge an inch. A concordat with the Pope was signed on 8th July 1933 – after the suppression of the Centre Party – by the terms of which the clergy were forbidden to take part in political affairs. 1937 opened with a joint protest by the three Catholic Archbishops in a pastoral letter: while promising Hitler their support in his struggle with Bolshevism they significantly expressed the hope that when Bolshevism, State enemy No. 1, was exterminated the Catholic Church would not be attacked as State enemy No. 2. It is well known that the Nazi government regard with great apprehension the power which the Catholic Church is bound to exercise over the minds of its faithful.

The NSDAP had promised that if they were elected they would do away with unemployment, which had gone from bad to worse. On the surface, the promise was fulfilled: on 31st December 1932 there were 5·77 millions unemployed; by the summer of 1935 this had been reduced to below 2 millions. This good showing is no doubt due to a great extent to the rearmament programme, and to such semi-military measures as the construction of great motoring roads (*Reichsautobahnen*), a favourite project of Hitler's. The stress of poverty was also relieved by the plan of help for the winter (*Winterhilfswerk*) announced in September 1933 by Goebbels: millions of marks have been collected winter by winter by this system of free giving quickened by moral compulsion.

Advanced health legislation has been carried through; for instance, a law passed in 1935 forbade marriage with hereditarily diseased persons; a certificate of fitness for marriage (*Ehetauglichkeitszeugnis*) is required. Compulsory sterilization of the unfit is a provision.

The thorny problem of rearmament (*Aufrüstung*) led to the notification by Germany on 19th October 1933 of her intention to leave the League of Nations as a protest against not being accorded equality of status at the Disarmament Conference; a step approved on 12th November by a plebiscite. Conscription was reintroduced on 16th March 1935. Other conditions of the Treaty of Versailles were one by one defied; and the process of liberation from these galling shackles was completed when, on 7th March 1936, Hitler announced to the Reichstag that German troops had just marched into the demilitarized zone of the Rhineland. As an excuse for this thunderbolt he pointed to the recent alliance of France with Soviet Russia; this, he declared, was in effect a violation of the Treaty of Locarno. Germany's full sovereignty over her own territory being now established, Hitler made tentative but nebulous proposals for securing peace, and even hinted that Germany, if these proposals were worked out, might return to the League of Nations. The British reply was a detailed *questionnaire* asking for a precise statement of Germany's intentions; to this no reply has been forthcoming. The usual plebiscite approved Hitler's defiant move. The last blow at Versailles, the denunciation, in November 1936, of the international control of German rivers, elicited merely formal protests; the next step was the declaration in January 1937 that in future foreign warships would only be allowed to pass through the Kiel Canal if permission had previously been obtained. British diplomacy may be assumed to be far-seeing in its faintly-protesting attitude to these progressive violations of a treaty which could not possibly be enforced on a Germany in process of arming to the teeth; French indignation was helpless, but flared up when, on 18th June 1935, a Naval Treaty negotiated by von Ribbentrop was signed in London; by the terms of this German naval strength was limited to 35 per cent of our own, except in submarines.

On 26th January 1934 a Ten Years' Pact of peace and non-aggression was signed with Poland; and this postponed – rather than settled – the vexed questions of the Corridor and the German minority in Upper Silesia. Danzig, however, was completely Nazified by a gradual process, and no settlement save by incorporation with the Reich seems possible. The incorporation (*der Anschluss*, to use the familiar term) of Austria with the Reich seems – for economic as well as racial reasons – as inevitable as that of Danzig; but this logical solution is rendered impossible by the hostility of Italy and the Danubian States. The growth of the Nazi Party in Austria synchronized with that in the Reich, and their activity, supported as it was by the Nazi organization in Munich, led to constant friction with the Reich; this came to a head May-June 1933, when a fee of 1000 marks was exacted from Reich Germans visiting Austria, while from the Austrian side Theo Habicht, the Press attaché at the German Embassy in Vienna, was expelled; however, he continued his open help of the Austrian Nazis from Munich. On 25th July 1934 there was a Nazi Putsch in Austria; and Dollfuss, the Chancellor, was murdered. This caused such a wave of disgust throughout the world that the German Government thought fit to dismiss Habicht, and to send von Papen as special ambassador to Vienna; this eliminated the former Chancellor from a cabinet in which he was out of place. Thereafter relations between Austria and the Reich gradually improved, and culminated in a Gentleman's Agreement of non-interference signed on 11th July 1936.

The plebiscite, held in accordance with the provisions of the Treaty of Versailles, 13th December-January 1935, to decide whether the Saar should return to the Reich, preserve the *status quo*, or be incorporated with France, resulted in a majority of over 90 per cent in favour of the Reich; and the province was solemnly reincorporated on 1st March.

The Four-Power Pact (*Viermächtepakt*) proposed by Mussolini and signed in Rome on 15th June 1933 proved to be illusory: it made any revision of the Treaty of Versailles contingent upon the agreement of each of the signatory Powers. During and after the Abyssinian War Germany and Italy moved closer to each other, and in 1936 – the Austrian bone of contention being left lying – they came to an agreement the terms of which are a matter of speculation. What is certain is that both these Fascist Powers are allied, however loosely, by a common determination to root out Bolshevism at home and elsewhere. The advantages of a military alliance with Italy had been stressed by Hitler in *Mein Kampf*; and the formation of a Central European league in which a docile Austria is the link is one of the great dangers now to be reckoned with; the hope of its frustration rests in the ineradicable Roman Catholicism of Austria and the shiftiness of Italy.

Any outside historian distributing light and shadow over the Nazi picture is likely to leave an impression of gloom. There is a temptation to compare the present attempt to redeem a galling defeat with the heroic regeneration which closed the Napoleonic Wars. The spirit which animates both is that of Kant's categorical imperative: *ich kann, denn ich muss.* The national regeneration of 1813 left the mind free, more free than it had ever been; its very essence was criticism of government; it was the mind of independent thinkers constraining the government, not the government machine destroying, for the sake of the machine, the activity of individual minds; and for that very reason the rehabilitation of the nation and the race was glorified by a burst of splendour in literature and philosophy, whereas today literature and philosophy are forced to flow in channels made by a government to whom literature and philosophy and all other arts, and science itself, and (if they can get their way) even religion, are merely means of propaganda. The struggle is, therefore, between spirit and the machine. History has no sense except as the record of the victory of the spirit of man. *E pur si muove. . . .*

BIBLIOGRAPHY TO CHAPTER V

Bartlett, Vernon. *Nazi Germany Explained.* Gollancz, London, 1933
Braun, Otto. *Von Weimar zu Hitler.* Europa-Verlag, Zurich and New York, 1940
Clark, R. T. *The Fall of the German Republic.* Allen & Unwin, London, 1935
Fabricius, Hans. *Geschichte der nationalsozialistischen Bewegung.* Berlin, 1935
Heiden, Konrad. *A History of National Socialism.* Methuen, 1934
Hitler, Adolf. *Mein Kampf.* 1925-26
Mowrer, Edgar. *Germany puts the Clock back.* A Penguin Special. 1933, revised ed., 1938
Papen, Franz von. *Der Wahrheit eine Gasse.* Paul List, Munich, 1952
Reynolds, R. T. *Prelude to Hitler.* London, 1933
Roberts, Stephen H. *The House that Hitler built.* Methuen, 1937
Rosenberg, Alfred. *Houston Stewart Chamberlain als Verkünder und Begründer einer deutschen Zukunft.* Munich, 1927
Rosenberg, Arthur. *History of the German Republic.* Methuen, 1936
Severing, Carl. *Mein Lebensweg.* 2 vols. Greven, Cologne, 1950
Wheeler-Bennett, J. W. *Hindenburg: The Wooden Titan.* Macmillan, 1936

CHAPTER VI

GERMAN HISTORY FROM 1937 TO 1952

I. Final Preparations for War, 1937-39

IN his speech to the Reichstag to celebrate the fourth anniversary of his accession to power Hitler announced that the period of surprises was over. It was in 1937, however, that the Führer made up his mind to reveal the fundamental aggressiveness of his foreign policy in ways which he knew were bound to make war all but inevitable. The rearmament of Germany was by now well advanced. Economic preparations had been inaugurated when the Four-Year Plan, which was intended to make the Reich self-sufficient in raw materials, was announced at the Nuremberg Party Congress on 9th September 1936. Göring was made responsible for the execution of the new Plan, which brought him into conflict with Dr Schacht (p. 164), at that time Minister of Economic Affairs as well as President of the Reichsbank. As such Schacht had enormously increased the economic pressure which the Germans could exert abroad, especially in South-eastern Europe. After the slump years the peasant countries were thankful for Germany to buy up their corn; only later did they find that she could or would pay them in nothing but her own industrial goods, including all kinds of arms. Before long they found themselves more than half dependent upon her economic and military system.

The political prospect was encouraging to Hitler. The Spanish Civil War created dangerous friction between the Powers in the West, while providing useful rehearsals for the Luftwaffe. Once again, the Führer held, the decadence of the British and French was evident. Mussolini's reference to a Berlin-Rome Axis in his speech in Milan on 1st November 1936 was followed by his pompous visit to Germany at the end of September 1937; from that time Hitler knew that the Italian alliance was ready to his hand whenever he should wish. This knowledge contributed to the pronouncements he made to the secret military conference which he summoned to the Reichskanzlei in Berlin on 5th November 1937. On this momentous occasion he proposed to implement the cardinal political doctrine of *Mein Kampf* (p. 168) in a war of conquest, to begin not later than 1943-45, but probably earlier.[1] As a preliminary operation, Austria and Czechoslovakia, which to his Austrian mind were inseparable, must be completely subjected to Germany. Of Japanese friendship Hitler had already made fairly sure with the anti-Komintern Pact of 25th November 1936; this was joined by Italy on the day after the Führer's military conference of 5th November 1937.

The next step forward was to oust Schacht from the Ministry of Economic Affairs, where, it was considered, he had not been co-operative over the Four-Year Plan: on 26th November 1937 Walther Funk[2] took over the Ministry, Schacht remaining at the Reichsbank until the first winter of the war. This promotion of Party Member Funk pointed the way to the big step taken on 4th February 1938 when several key positions were captured from the old conservative nationalist type which had formed the major part of Hitler's governmental coalition in 1933 (pp. 162-3). Now Ribbentrop was made Foreign Minister in Neurath's place; at the same time Blomberg (p. 162), Minister of War, and Werner Freiherr von Fritsch, the Commander-in-Chief[3] were dismissed to make place for Hitler himself, with Keitel as *Chef des Oberkommando der Wehrmacht*; Wilhelm Keitel and Alfred Jodl, his next in command, were known to be good Nazi yes-men. The only non-Nazi to remain in an important post was Schwerin von Krosigk, who had been Minister of Finance under Brüning, and who lasted to the end; it was always said that he had too many unmarried daughters to take any risks with his job.

The changes made on 4th February 1938 were of great importance in the development of Hitler's power. On 30th June 1934 he had eliminated a number of potential enemies and in particular the leaders of the SA, the amorphous body of followers on whose shoulders he had been raised to become Chancellor. The Army chiefs imagined that the defeat of the SA spelt their own victory, even over Hitler himself. But with the death of Hindenburg, scarcely more than a month later, Hitler had made himself Supreme Commander, and from that moment all the Armed forces were obliged to swear an oath of personal loyalty to him. In February

---

[1] See *Documents on German Foreign Policy* 1918-45. Series D. Vol. I. No. 19 (the Hossbach Memorandum).

[2] Funk had been for a few months at this Ministry (*Reichswirtschaftsrat*) with Dr Gottfried Feder, who from 1918 onwards had thundered against the enslavement of the national economy by the payment of interest to the banks. Feder's catchword was: '*Brechung der Zinsknechtschaft ist das Herzstück des Nationalsozialismus*'; capital he divided into '*raffend*' (Jewish) and '*schaffend*' (Aryan).

[3] Fritsch was the old type of German staff officer, upright and retiring. He went to the Polish front with his old regiment in 1939 and, as is generally believed, chose to be killed on the battlefield. He was made Commander-in-Chief, Army, in 1935.

1938, and again in December 1941 and July 1944, the significance of this oath was to be sharply felt.

If 30th June 1934 was a Pyrrhic victory for the Reichswehr, the victors in the long run were Himmler and the other SS chiefs, masters of cruelty such as Reinhard Heydrich. Of all the Nazi leaders Reichsführer der SS Heinrich Himmler, dreaming his runic dreams behind his pince-nez, seemed perhaps the most absurd. Yet it was he who organized Hitler's Reich on the basis of the sadism of the Nazi concentration camps, the control of which, together with that of the secret police, he took over from Göring in the course of 1934. It was he who organized the blackmail by means of which Blomberg and Fritsch were disposed of, the latter in defiance of the Army's indignation. And it would be he whose name would strike terror throughout Hitler's Europe in the war that was to come.

Since the Austro-German Agreement of 11th July 1936 (p. 179) Nazi pressure upon Austria had steadily increased, and von Papen, as Hitler's diplomatic representative in Vienna, intrigued incessantly against the Schuschnigg régime, which he hoped to undermine rather than to crush. It was thought that he, too, as a member of the old Junker set, would lose his post (as did Hassell, the German Ambassador in Rome) on 4th February 1938; but instead he succeeded in arranging that Schuschnigg should be brought to Berchtesgaden for an interview with Hitler. This famous encounter took place on 12th February; at the end of it the brow-beaten Schuschnigg was presented with a seven-point ultimatum which was bound to destroy Austrian sovereignty in everything but name. The Austrian Federal Chancellor provisionally signed the so-called Berchtesgaden agreement, but in his slow way he was determined upon defensive action to the last. On 9th March he announced that a plebiscite would be held on the 13th to give the Austrians the chance to express their wish with regard to the independence of Austria. Hitler was waiting for a pretext and had no intention of allowing a relatively uninfluenced vote to take place; thus the German Army was ordered to invade and occupy Austria at daybreak of 12th March. Mussolini, who had still in some quarters been expected to object, responded to Hitler's messages to Rome with a telegram in which he said: 'My attitude is determined by the friendship between our two countries, which is consecrated in the Axis.' Previous Nazi talk of Austrian autonomy was forgotten and Austria was annexed to Hitler's highly centralized Reich. Vienna, a centre of distinguished Jews, was quickly subjected to Himmler's persecution; the Catholic Church was more gradually victimized. The unfortunate Schuschnigg was arrested at once and maltreated for the next seven years.

It was the Czechoslovak turn next. Since 1935 the Germans in Czechoslovakia, latterly known as the Sudeten Germans, had been organized by the Nazis in the Reich,[1] and pressure upon the Czechs had proportionately increased. With the Austrian *Anschluss* the Czechoslovak situation was brought to a head. After a secret interview between Hitler and the Sudeten German leader, Konrad Henlein, on 28th March, the latter increased his demands at a speech he made at Karlsbad (Karlovy Vary) on 24th April; as in the demands put to Schuschnigg at Berchtesgaden, Henlein claimed for his followers the right to profess Nazi beliefs which obviously involved the elimination of Czechoslovakia, a multinational and basically liberal state. During the second half of May the Führer completed his plans for its destruction 'as from 1st October at the latest'.[2] The Runciman mission, which the British Government chose to send to mediate between the Czechs and Sudeten Germans, suited Hitler's plans well, since it diverted attention without in any way affecting his determination. At the Nazi Party congress from 6th to 12th September the Führer made clear his aggressive intentions against President Beneš and the Czechoslovak Republic, and from the middle of the month a Sudeten German Free Corps became active along the frontier for the 'Protection of the Sudeten Germans and maintenance of disturbances and clashes'.[3]

At this juncture Chamberlain startled the world by offering to visit the ruffianly ruler of Germany, his junior by twenty years, in order to plead with him for peace. It was only when Mussolini took up Chamberlain's plea for a conference that Hitler, in fear of complete isolation, agreed to meet the Duce, Chamberlain, and Daladier to discuss the Sudeten German question at Munich on 29th September 1938. The agreement reached there in the early hours of the next morning forced the Czechs to surrender broad fringes of their country to Germany, but left them with the nominal independence of the central area they retained; shorn of its defences it lay in fact at Hitler's mercy. Far from being satisfied the Führer was exasperated at having been prevented from a display of force. Within three weeks of the Munich Agreement he signed a directive preparing for the invasion of the Czechoslovak rump state, and on 15th March 1939 he seized upon a flimsy excuse to occupy Prague and proclaim a 'Protectorate' over the Czechs, whom, he had said, he never wished to rule. Thus the first part of his programme had been carried out at the price of revealing his perfidy to the world. If his racial theories could be

---

[1] This was furiously denied at the time but admitted later.
[2] See *Documents on German Foreign Policy 1918-45*. Series D. Vol. II. No. 221.
[3] See Trial of the Major War Criminals before the Internat. Milit. Tribunal. Vol. III, p. 79 (Nuremberg, 1947).

so lightly discarded, was it not above all a destructive lust for power which drove him relentlessly on? If this were so the danger had indeed become very great, for the banks and the industry controlled by Vienna and Prague provided him with the economic domination of all Eastern Europe between Germany and the U.S.S.R. while huge armament concerns like the Skoda works at Pilsen were now directly under his rule.

Hitler's only disappointment at this time was provided by the lack of war fever in Germany. Goebbels' unceasing propaganda, propelled in every direction with the help of every device, fired the Nazi Party and its youth; but the general public had cheered Chamberlain and peace, not the military parades, in September 1938. The Jewish bogy, therefore, was served up again when a German diplomat in Paris was murdered by a Jew. In November 1938 a large-scale pogrom followed in Germany; it disgusted the Western world, especially Britain and the United States, but the Führer paid no heed.

Since his visit to Rome early in May 1938 Hitler had been pressing for a military alliance with Mussolini, who, however, until the beginning of 1939, feared too greatly the strength of anti-German feeling in Italy. In spite of the seizure of Prague the Fascist Government now plunged ahead, and on 22nd May 1939 the Steel Pact was signed in Berlin. Armed with this frankly aggressive alliance, which bound each partner to march if the other should merely become 'involved in warlike complications', Hitler at another secret conference on the following day proclaimed to his military chiefs his decision 'to attack Poland at the first suitable opportunity'. (Although he was to use Danzig as his pretext for war he stated at this meeting that 'Danzig is not the subject of the dispute at all'.)[1] A still more important part of his preparations was, perhaps, the tentative advance he had made to the U.S.S.R. since the beginning of the year. The Russians were ready enough to partition Poland with Germany, and after prolonged negotiations a German-Russian non-aggression Pact was signed in Moscow on 23rd August 1939; a secret Protocol was attached by which Hitler agreed, if it came to it, to divide Poland with Stalin, and in addition to let the Russians do what they wished with the Baltic States and Eastern Roumania. In return Hitler gained only the temporary advantage of isolating Poland and – as he felt convinced – of further demoralizing the Western Powers, who had themselves been negotiating for an anti-German agreement with the U.S.S.R. Ignoring constant warnings from Italy that his attack upon Poland would inexorably bring about a general war with France and Britain as his enemies, Hitler annexed Danzig and ordered the invasion of Poland – without any declaration of

[1] Trial of Major War Criminals. Vol. II, pp. 279, 280.

war – at dawn on 1st September 1939. Two days later the Western Powers, in view of their undertakings to Poland since the previous spring, declared war on Germany. The French proceeded with slightly less conviction and some hours' delay caused by Georges Bonnet's interest in a fresh offer from Italy to mediate. But the British correctly objected to mediation if Hitler's armies remained on Polish soil, and the Führer was in no mood to withdraw. Documentary evidence makes clear that he was determined that no one should rob him of his war this time. The Nazi quibble that the West provoked war because the Western Powers observed the convention of declaring it is unacceptable. Yet within five years of the end of the war the legend of the British stab in the back was already established in Germany.

II. GERMANY AT WAR, 1939-45

The Germans did not march singing into the war in 1939, as they had done twenty-five years before. For all Hitler's flair and fascination, and the *élan* of the Party, there was a foreboding of disaster, especially in Berlin. The feeling was widespread that it would end as it had ended before; to have Britain as one's enemy, to all but the very young, spelt blockade and starvation.

Although the Nazi Party had its doubters, particularly with regard to the pact with the Kremlin, it is nevertheless probable that the majority of its members were well enough satisfied. The *Parteigenossen* apart, the majority of the nation was ill-informed and uncritical and well accustomed to follow its leader. The Nazis had extended their power with the primitive instruments of fear and the hope of reward, and people counted on advancement through the war. It was a more popular conception to have a swipe at the Poles than to fight the Czechs, for the Germans had lived since Versailles with the hope of annexing Danzig and the 'Corridor', whereas the Sudeten country had belonged to the Habsburgs and meant little to them. If the Poles could be beaten quickly and the British and French then placated, as Hitler said, nothing could be more satisfactory. The majority of the nation, it should be added, was kept by the Nazi 'élite' from any knowledge of the esoteric Nietzschean doctrine of ruthlessness privately preached by the Führer and practised by the SS. On the other hand, a great many people long before the war had a shrewd notion of what went on in the concentration camps or KZ, although part of Himmler's system was to shroud it all in mystery and to prevent people from talking or even thinking about what they knew by filling them with an ill-defined dread of the consequences.

There was never an organized movement of German resistance to the

Nazi régime, never even a serious strike comparable with that of the Fiat workers against the Fascists in Turin in March 1943. A few German Communists managed to survive through the Hitler period, but their organization had really been broken in 1933, and they were paralysed by the pact with Russia from 1939 to 1941; later Harro Schulze-Boysen[1] of the German Air Ministry worked with a spy-ring called *Die Rote Kapelle* until he was arrested and executed. Promising Socialist leaders like Carlo Mierendorf had long ago disappeared into concentration camps; and, though a large Social-Democrat party re-emerged in 1945, its members were on the whole remarkably inactive during the war. Moderate anti-Nazi feeling crystallized around certain Catholic and Protestant bishops and pastors who, in view of Pastor Niemöller's[2] arrest in 1937, expressed their criticism of the Nazis with understandable caution and exemplary patriotism; during the war the Catholic Bishop, Galen, of Münster and the Protestant Bishop, Wurm, of Württemberg were among their leaders. There were in addition small groups of anti-Nazi intellectuals, such as that around Rudolf Pechel, the editor of the *Deutsche Rundschau*. This review he managed to use for camouflaged attacks upon tyranny – in the manner of the intellectual rebels in eighteenth-century France – until his arrest in 1942. By and large the opposition had no political influence and was of course more gravely handicapped once war had come; but it preserved the noblest standards of western humanity by, for instance, rescuing many individual Jews from cruel persecution at the risk of terrifying penalties.

It remains to consider the attitude of the bureaucracy and the Army. The civil servants had stuck to their jobs;[3] those who criticized the Nazis maintained that they kept some braking power in office, while they would not merely starve but lose all influence if they resigned.[4] This was true, though the influence of those who remained was rarely felt except perhaps in the Foreign Office. The Foreign Service, with its external contacts, was freer, even with SS Führer Ribbentrop at its head; it was, however, subject to the surveillance as well as the rivalry of his personal

---

[1] He was married to one of the Eulenburgs; together they were executed in December 1942.

[2] Dr Martin Niemöller had opposed the election of Müller (p. 177) as Reich bishop and had refused to conform to the Nazified type of church service which had been instituted. After serving as a submarine commander in the First World War he joined the Nazis, but left them to fight their doctrine of the unified Aryan church and assumed the leadership of the 'Confessional Church' (*Bekenntniskirche*), the six principles of which were promulgated at a synod held at Barmen in May 1934. His services attracted great crowds; but in 1937 he was sent to a concentration camp.

[3] Two senior members of the Foreign Service resigned.

[4] See Erich Kordt: *Nicht aus den Akten*. Union Deutsche Verlagsgesellschaft, 1950.

staff (*Büro-Ribbentrop*) at home and abroad. Though Ribbentrop's people were often members of the SS, the Gestapo under Himmler and Heydrich developed its own foreign service, or system of foreign espionage and fifth column preparations abroad, well before the outbreak of war. With the Reichswehr intelligence service, the *Abwehr*, also in the field, rival German agents seemed sometimes to trip over one another.

Before the war certain German diplomats, notably the brothers Theo and Erich Kordt,[1] had tried occasionally to stiffen the attitude of the British Government towards Hitler by such hints as they felt able to drop. But, like the rest of their colleagues, they were so greatly obsessed by their conviction that the Treaty of Versailles was an unmitigated evil and Germans permanently superior to Slavs, that they repeatedly found themselves in opposition only to Hitler's person, not his policy, and were therefore alarmed when the policy received a rare check. Economically the Treaty of Versailles had proved disastrous, but politically the establishment of the new successor states was a not unjust historical tribute to the evolution of the Slav nationalities during the nineteenth century. As for the moral superiority of the Germans, with Hitler at their head that claim was reduced to absurdity.

The non-Nazi Reichswehr leaders were paralysed by similar contradictions. Hitler had achieved their own aims, but by methods which surprised or shocked them. It had been fairly clear from the beginning that nothing but military power could overthrow him. But a German military coup against the Führer meant a violation of the oath each soldier swore to him. After endless discussion of the difficulties Generals Beck, Witzleben and Halder decided to arrest Hitler in September 1938, until the news that Chamberlain was on his way to Germany destroyed their resolution; Beck resigned soon after. The extraordinary luck of Hitler seemed to thwart the generals again and again. They were frightened of his popularity, especially with the younger officers. Once the war had begun they were paralysed at first by Hitler's successes, which made it more difficult to move against him, and later by his failures, which might make their action seem treacherous. Thus until 1944 army opposition to Hitler remained hypothetical.

The German attack upon Poland was overwhelmingly successful, the Polish Army being annihilated within a few weeks and Poland divided, according to their secret pledge, between Hitler and Stalin. But when the Polish victory failed to bring peace with the West the gloom in

---

[1] Theo was Chargé d'Affaires in London, 1938 and 1939. Erich held various diplomatic posts, but his most important appointment was *Chef des Ministerbüros* in February 1938, when Ribbentrop became Foreign Minister.

Germany returned in spite of this longed-for reckoning with the Poles. A feeling of isolation, which easily afflicts the Germans, was strong – the Italian Ally had not marched, and friendship with Russia was *unheimlich*. The Army, moreover, and through soldiers on leave a large part of the public, was aware of a new and distasteful factor in the situation. The professional soldiers had maintained decent discipline in Poland, but SS forces[1] had followed on their heels and had perpetrated systematic atrocities against the helpless population of the conquered country; it was the SS which set up the German administration in Western Poland, the so-called Warthegau which was annexed to Germany, and the 'General-Government' in central Poland, of which Hans Frank[2] became Governor. It was for the SS, the non-Nazi officers bitterly reflected, that they appeared to have fought.

The Nazi Party, however, and those most susceptible to its influence, were confident; and, after the strange, blank winter of 1939-40, in the spring their confidence was justified. In April the Germans overran Denmark and Norway, in May they invaded Holland and Belgium, broke through the Maginot line at Sedan and drove a wedge between the Franco-British forces, of whom the northern group retreated via Dunkirk to Britain. On 5th June Hitler ordered an offensive against Paris; by 17th June the French had begged for an armistice which was signed at Compiègne on 22nd June. Blitzkrieg indeed! Hitler had achieved the impossible against the senior experts' advice – it has been said that he had triumphed over his generals as completely as he had triumphed over the French. Neither the last war nor 1870 had brought such sensational success. Inevitably there was a tremendous *Siegesrausch*, with the cheapest and most violent German chauvinism and hero-worship uppermost. The Germans, it was confidently claimed, would now be recognized as the master race of Europe, with the rest of the peoples as their underlings, the British having humbly begged for peace; and it was all thanks to the Führer and the Führer alone.

Far from ending the war, however, the Nazi victory over France seemed rather to begin it. Mussolini had rushed into war a week before France surrendered, and he now made greedy demands which were not compatible with the coaxing to which Hitler wished to treat the Pétain régime. Fascist claims also clashed with the price General Franco asked for his alliance. Ungrateful for having been allowed to escape from

---

[1] Himmler gradually expanded the SS into a separate army under his control, the *Waffen S.S.* fighting formations thus being added to the secret police.

[2] In his capacity as Law Leader he had once told a congress of jurists that every judge, before delivering judgment, should ask himself: 'How would the Führer judge in my place?'

Dunkirk, the British, with a new Churchill Government, refused to acknowledge their defeat; indeed they refused to acknowledge that the French were beaten, for they encouraged General de Gaulle to set up the standard of a free France in London. Hitler commanded his officers to prepare Operation Sea-Lion (invasion of Britain); in order to win a preliminary air supremacy the Luftwaffe attacked London and the ports in August, but German losses were far heavier than those of the undermanned R.A.F., and in September Göring lost the air-battle of Britain. On 17th September, two days after a Victory-over-Britain march through Berlin had been planned, Hitler postponed Operation Sea-Lion indefinitely – only a feint was to be kept up. Goebbels, Ribbentrop and Himmler were each of them glad to find that Göring's position with the Führer was never quite the same.

Now Hitler was an Austrian who thought essentially in terms of German expansion down the Danube and to the East (*der Drang nach Osten*), and it may be that he was less disturbed by the tenacity of the British than by that of the Russians. Stalin wasted no moment, once he had learnt of the collapse of France, to redress the balance of power by an ample interpretation of his secret agreements with Germany. As the Germans entered Paris the Russians entered Kaunas and Vilna, and they had soon spread over the three Baltic states; at the beginning of July they invaded Roumania and annexed Bessarabia and part of Bukovina. On 27th September Japan was persuaded to sign a Tripartite military alliance with Germany and Italy which was worded so as to be aimed against the United States, not the U.S.S.R. Yet in calling off his attack upon Britain Hitler had already decided to beat Russia first, and Molotov's visit to Berlin in November served only to harden the decision.

If the Führer had determined to attack Russia, he wished first to subject diplomatically the small countries which still lay between him and Stalin. Control of the positions of Hungary and Bulgaria, like control of the metals of Yugoslavia and the oil of Roumania, were essential, and they were all to be forced into vassalage by adherence to the Tripartite Pact. The disastrous Italian attack upon Greece at the end of October 1940 not only distorted Hitler's programme but shook the prestige of the Axis. It was followed in March 1941 by a rising in Belgrade, a national upheaval of the Serbs headed by some Air Force officers, which swept Prince Paul's régime away and which brought into power there an anti-German régime. In December 1940 the Führer had fixed May 1941 for his assault upon Russia. But on 6th April 1941 German forces were diverted into the Balkan peninsula for a preliminary liquidation of Yugoslavia and Greece, and it was not until 22nd June 1941 that the Germans invaded the U.S.S.R.

German success against an exhausted Greece and an unprepared and divided Yugoslavia was overwhelming, and Hitler's dominion was extended again. Each extension meant new jobs and new supplies, which restored the attractions of war even if Yugoslavia could not provide the German officers with the champagne and other delicacies of France. Nor before 1942 did the war spell deprivation to the German civilian population. German soldiers all over Europe were sending things home. On the assumption of a short war an all-out production effort had not yet been demanded. In the general post which the New Europe involved, German labour needs were readily supplied by a stream of foreign labour from the occupied countries to Germany. Originally the foreign workers were supposed to be volunteers, but increasingly they came to be the victims of denationalizing or punitive SS action and later the haphazard prey of SS press gangs. Finally Gauleiter Fritz Sauckel became the master of what were in effect nearly five million foreign slaves.

With the attack upon Russia the Germans as a whole were probably more thoroughly united with their Führer than they had been since the end of the Polish campaign. Wiser prophets referred gloomily to the downfall of Napoleon, but the ordinary people were congenitally willing to believe in the Russian menace and almost relieved that the flirtation with Communism was over. For the first three or four months the advance eastwards was phenomenal, but then in November victory eluded the infinitely successful Hitler outside Moscow, and the German armies suffered terribly from lack of preparation for the cold. On 19th December 1941 the indignant Führer made himself Commander-in-Chief (Army) in Brauchitsch's[1] place and virtually dismissed Bock and Leeb; Rundstedt had retired earlier in the year and Halder stayed on until the following September. The Führer's conquest of the old army was at last complete. Meanwhile the Japanese had attacked Pearl Harbour. Thus by the end of the year the second great war had become world-wide; and, remembering 1917, many Germans shivered slightly at the significance of the belligerency of the United States. Muttered phrases about being destroyed by one's own victories – *wir siegen uns zum Tode* – were often to be heard.

Not only had Göring lost ground, but in May 1941 Hitler had been rudely startled by the flight to Scotland of his old friend and Deputy, Rudolf Hess, who was always a little mad. The Nazi régime was in fact

[1] Promoted General-Leutnant in 1933; he specialized in political and economic questions.

reinforced by his disappearance, since this gave greater importance to
Hess's assistant, Martin Bormann, a hard-working and ruthless fanatic
who succeeded as well as anyone – except, perhaps, the notorious Dr
Morell – in making himself indispensable to Hitler. Early in 1942 Todt[1]
was killed in an accident and was succeeded by Albert Speer (see p. 556)
as Minister of Armaments, and from this time on war production was
reorganized and greatly speeded up, civilian life being proportionately
affected. In May 1942 Heydrich, second only to Himmler in the SS, was
murdered in Prague, whither he had been sent to intensify the Nazi Reign
of Terror: this was the first major act of defiance from the occupied
countries. In this year, too, a deterioration in Hitler's health became
evident and there were whispers that Morell kept him going with drugs.
People also began to notice that a good-looking young woman called
Eva Braun, who had been an assistant to his friend, the photographer
Hoffmann, was often in the Führer's company; it was she who was later
to become his wife, only to join him in suicide.

The battle raged backward and forward in 1942 until the Allied landing
along the coast of Morocco and Algeria early in November, which followed close upon Montgomery's defeat of the hitherto triumphant
Field-Marshal Erwin Rommel at El Alamein; it synchronized also with
the halting of the Germans before Stalingrad. It was this autumn which
precipitated the great and complicated German crisis of the year 1943. By
February of that year, when Paulus surrendered at Stalingrad, it was clear
that Germany had not so much gained a barren victory as suffered a great
and costly defeat at Russia's hand; the indispensable oil-wells of the
Caucasus had been attained only to be lost. In July the Allies landed in
Sicily and Mussolini was dismissed by the King of Italy, who then
came to terms with the enemy. The British-American air war against
Germany had by now become intense.[2] The German public was shaken – it
knew fear as it had perhaps never known it before. Yet whether, without
Himmler's reign of terror, the mass of the people would have deserted the
régime it is difficult to guess[3] on account of certain shortcomings on the
Allied side. In January 1943 the demand for unconditional surrender made
by Roosevelt and Churchill at their meeting at Casablanca stiffened

---

[1] Fritz Todt was a gifted engineer who became Hitler's road-builder and, one
might say, his Vauban, for he also constructed Hitler's most important fortifications.
He was allowed to dispose of an army of his own workers, the OT (*Organization
Todt*).

[2] Though the damage inflicted on German industry, cleverly decentralized, was
not yet great.

[3] Germans listened a good deal to the B.B.C., in spite of the death penalty, but
out of curiosity at least as much as from serious hostility to the régime.

German resistance. In April the discovery of the Katyn murders provided Goebbels, as he gleefully acknowledged, with unusually convincing propaganda against Russia. The Allies failed to follow up their advantage in Italy, and Hitler sent SS man Otto Skorzeny to effect a dramatic air-rescue of the Duce. As for the air-raids, most Germans became hardened to the ordeal, and the indiscriminate tendencies of 'Bomber' Harris and of American daylight raids made the Germans forget that it was they who had begun air-raids with the intention to terrorize. Germany itself now employed foreign labour by the million, and people began to think uneasily of the end of the war when the Army might still be spread over Europe, the prey of partisans, while the foreign labourers at home joined forces and attacked the German civilian population. In these circumstances the ordinary German seemed to steel himself with a kind of schizophrenic desperation, conscious of the dangers yet determined not to be so.

An intelligent and more scrupulous minority was aware of what Hitlerism meant, either in the shape of the German occupation of Europe, the kidnapping of labour and the massacring of hostages, or in that of the concentration camps soberly described by Dr Kogon, their seven-year victim, in *Der S.S. Staat*. By 1943 it was also known that the SS were engaged in the process of exterminating the Jews of all Europe by gassing them.[1] The genuine anti-Nazis held that here was no room for compromise: Germany would be best served by the destruction of Hitler even if this meant Germany's defeat. Early in 1943 several magnificent leaflets of protest were circulated by two students in Munich, Hans Scholl and his sister Sophie, whereupon they and their associates were executed. Meanwhile Karl Goerdeler, an ex-mayor of Leipzig, had been working to link up the various anti-Nazi groups, a risky proceeding in itself made more so by Goerdeler's indiscretion. He and the ex-Ambassador Hassell (p. 183) tried in vain to get the Generals to move; but the Army chiefs had waited too long and were demoralized by their dependence upon Hitler and Hitler's largesse. A few younger officers, several in Admiral Canaris' *Abwehr*, where they were indirectly helped by their chief until Himmler got rid of him in February 1944, worked out a plan with the retired General Beck. It had become clear that only Hitler's death would end the efficacy of the oath of loyalty to his person. A bomb placed in his aeroplane in March 1943 failed to explode. After this Count Stauffenberg, an officer who had been wounded in North Africa, was chosen as

[1] According to the evidence laid before the International Military Tribunal 1945-46, it is estimated that the total number of Jews murdered by the Nazis was about six million.

the agent of the conspirators; his opportunity came when he was appointed Chief of Staff to General Fromm, Commander-in-Chief Home Army. On 20th July 1944, a few hours before the resurrected Mussolini was due to visit Hitler's HQ at Rastenburg (East Prussia), Stauffenberg[1] caused a bomb to explode in the Führer's presence, a bomb which, however, while killing four others, only slightly wounded Hitler; the conspirators' plans were nipped in the bud by the quick action of Goebbels and of a Nazi commander called Remer.

The effect of the attempt of 20th July 1944 was devastating. Hitler's fanaticism had now become semi-mad. On the one hand he buoyed himself up with the evidence that he was indeed Fortune's darling if he had survived this attempt upon his life; on the other he vowed to intensify the terror upon which his rule was based – above all a fearful revenge was to be taken upon the traditional officer class which had once done so much to raise him to power. At the same time members of the various groups of civilian recusants, who had, through Goerdeler, been drawing a little closer to each other, were arrested *en masse*. Judge Roland Freisler, presiding over the People's Court, excelled himself in anathematizing the victims rather than in extorting public confessions.[2] Many like Witzleben (p. 188), Hassell, Goerdeler were executed, often with odious barbarity; many others were crowded into the concentration camps where men of all nationalities were now massed together for six or eight more months in pain and misery.

Early in June 1944, just over six weeks before Stauffenberg's failure and almost at the moment when the Allies liberated Rome, the Anglo-American forces had landed in Normandy; and on 23rd August Paris was liberated. In the East the Russian armies were advancing steadily, much of Yugoslavia was in the hands of the Communist Partisan leader Tito, and Roumania came over to the Allies. It was useless for Hitler to forbid the Germans to fall back. It was in vain for him to force the Ardennes offensive at the end of the year. His hopes were based upon two circumstances which were, it is true, not wholly illusory. He believed that the clash of interest between the Western Allies and the U.S.S.R. would break up the coalition against him, and he believed that his new weapons, rockets and the new type of U-boats, would turn the tide of war.

---

[1] There were three brothers Stauffenberg, scions of an old noble family; Graf Claus made the attempt on Hitler's life; Graf Berthold, murdered after the attempt, is the 'B. v. St.' to whom Stefan George dedicated one of the poems of *Das Neue Reich*; Graf Alexander, professor of medieval history at Munich University, survives and is the author of *Der Tod des Meisters* (1948), in which the illness, death and burial of Stefan George is described in nobly cadenced Georgian verse.

[2] Thus providing a striking contrast with Communist political trials.

But, while the rockets and U-boats came too late, it was too early for the East-West split. The occupied countries had risen with zest against the Germans and many of the bravest of their leaders were Communists: in 1945 the wave of enthusiasm for Russia was still potent in Europe, and if Roosevelt's confidence in Stalin was not shared by all Americans it continued to bear fruit for months after the President's death in April. Indeed it contributed to the holding back of the American forces which could have liberated Prague at the beginning of May; instead the capital of Bohemia, that key position, the last important town to which the Germans clung, was occupied by soldiers of the U.S.S.R. Hitler had killed himself one week earlier (30th April 1945) as the Russian troops fought their way into Berlin. Goebbels killed himself and all his family at the same time.

The history of the Germans from 20th July 1944 until Admiral Dönitz, appointed by Hitler to succeed him, surrendered unconditionally on 7th May 1945 from Flensburg, was in the nature of a nightmare. As the enemy closed in on all sides many Nazi leaders, including Himmler and Heydrich's successor, Ernst Kaltenbrunner, had tried for some months to negotiate behind Hitler's back, especially with the West. A few stalwarts planned to hold out in an Alpine redoubt; others, the werewolves, began to organize clandestine resistance for the future. Old men were pressed into the Volkssturm, children manned the A.A. batteries. For the people as a whole life was a grim conglomeration of devastating air attacks, overwork, shortages, with refugees streaming in afresh before the Russians. Everyone seemed to be an evacuee, or to live in a cellar, or both. The Nazis had intended to unite all the German minorities in Europe by the expansion of Germany; now the minorities were united by having been uprooted and brought 'home' to Germany, either by Hitler's command, like the South Tyrolese and the Baltic and Bessarabian Germans, or later because the populations drove them out along with or soon after the retreating German troops. At the last Hitler ordered the destruction of everything that might serve the enemy; but from Albert Speer downwards people rather thought of what they could save. When it came to the final abysmal collapse, those who were not overwhelmed by despair more than half welcomed the Anglo-American troops.

III. GERMANY SINCE THE WAR, 1945-52

When Stalin, Roosevelt and Churchill met at Yalta in February 1945 they announced – in reply to Goebbels' cries to the contrary – : 'It is not the intention of the Allies to destroy or enslave the German people.' With regard to the future frontiers of Germany, Austria and Czechoslovakia were of course to be fully restored, while Poland, in return for the loss of eastern territory to Russia, was to be allowed to expand westwards. Later, at Potsdam, this expansion was defined as permitted up to the Oder and western Neisse until such time as a final peace treaty might confirm the arrangement or not; at Potsdam, also, it was agreed that Königsberg with the adjacent territory should go to Russia 'subject to expert examination of the actual frontier'. At Yalta it was agreed to include France with the three Great Powers which were to occupy Germany. The zones of occupation had already been mapped out by a European Advisory Commission, and by an agreement signed on 2nd May 1945 a French zone was wedged in which caused a division of Württemberg and Baden between the Americans and the French.[1] On 5th June the four Allied Commanders-in-Chief met in Berlin, which was still in solely Soviet hands, to confirm a plan according to which each of the four Powers should hold a sector of the German capital, although it lay wholly in the zone allotted to the Russians; the Western Powers, however, failed to exact a Russian guarantee of the land and water communications between their respective zones and their sectors of Berlin. In the first few days of July 1945 American and British troops moved into Berlin.

The three main principles laid down at Yalta for the future treatment of Germany were: that the German military machine should be destroyed; that National-Socialism should be wiped out; and that those who had committed the worst crimes associated with it should be brought to trial. The Big Three – this time it was Truman who represented the United States – met again at Potsdam on 17th July to develop their policy on Germany more positively; by the end of the conference early in August Attlee had replaced Churchill. No legal German authority of any kind now remained. Instead it was confirmed that the Commanders-in-Chief should be the supreme authority in each zone 'and also jointly, in matters affecting Germany as a whole, in their capacity as members of the Control Council'. This sanguine trust in future unanimity was part of the Big Three Policy of that time, a policy intended to preserve the unity of Germany within the Yalta framework; the Potsdam Agreement (clause 14) declared that: 'During the period of occupation Germany shall be treated as a single economic unit.' There were, however, at least three centrifugal influences which quickly came into play. The first was the inevitable difference in *Weltanschauung* between the Western Powers and the Soviet Union. The second was the decision to establish no central German authority for the time being, but to educate the Germans to

[1] The division was ended in 1952, when the *Süd-West Staat* was formed out of Württemberg and Baden.

democratic life through local beginnings; that is, to decentralize administration by setting up rural and communal councils within the separate *Länder* which could later be joined in a federal union; the very first *Kreis* and *Gemeinde* elections were held in the U.S. zone in January 1946. The Americans in particular emphasized the advantages of decentralization; they desired it in the economic life of Germany as well in order to break up the huge industrial concerns such as the *I.G. Farbenindustrie*, which had done so much to facilitate the aggressions of Hitler. Thus the Americans were caught in something that looked like a paradox: the advocacy of uniformity of treatment with a parallel decentralization of administration – if the one were real the other was likely to be simulated. A third centrifugal influence was that of France, which had not been represented at Potsdam. The French, on the one hand, had regretted the unification of Germany ever since 1870, and, on the other, would have liked to detach the Saar (for themselves) and the Ruhr (under international control) and, if possible, an autonomous Rhineland. For reasons of this kind a frequent veto from France made difficulties in the early days of the Control Commission.

On 8th August 1945 legal representatives of the four Occupying Powers signed an agreement in London by which they laid down the procedure to be adopted in the trial of the twenty-four major war criminals of Nazi Germany – one, Martin Bormann, could not be found – which was to inaugurate the denazification of the Germans. The trial opened at Nuremberg on 20th November 1945. Göring and his fellows were accused of crimes against peace, war crimes, crimes against humanity, and of conspiring to bring about the whole Nazi assault upon the world. The Allies had captured large numbers of documents which revealed the enormities of National Socialism to an extent which many of its worst enemies would otherwise have dismissed as incredible. On the whole the Nazi leaders, who were given an equitable chance of defending themselves, cut a poor figure; only Göring showed spirit and fought cleverly both for his own life and for the Nazi cause. Judgment was delivered on 30th September 1946; and the verdicts were pronounced on the following day, when Göring, Rosenberg, Ribbentrop, Kaltenbrunner, Frick, Hans Frank, Sauckel, Streicher, Seyss-Inquart, Keitel and Jodl were sentenced to death; the executions followed on 16th October, but Göring poisoned himself the night before.[1] Hess, Funk and Raeder were sentenced to

[1] Robert Ley and Krupp had also been among the twenty-four defendants, but Ley had committed suicide in October 1945, while Krupp's trial was postponed because he was seriously ill. Ley, as *Führer der Arbeitsfront*, had controlled compulsory labour and done away with the trade unions. Krupp von Bohlen was the great industrialist who produced armaments at Essen; see p. 138.

imprisonment for life, and Speer, Schirach, Neurath and Dönitz to periods of imprisonment varying from ten to twenty years; Schacht, Papen and Fritzsche were acquitted. This trial was followed by others which involved Schwerin von Krosigk, Weizsäcker (who had been State Secretary in the Auswärtiges Amt), Krupp and a number of generals, while each of the occupied countries was entitled to bring to trial Nazis who had committed crimes mainly upon their territory. Of the subsidiary trials that of Weizsäcker and his associates (before an American court), which was aimed at the collaboration of the former German Foreign Office with the Nazis and which lasted from January 1948 to April 1949, was perhaps the most interesting. Weizsäcker was condemned to seven years' imprisonment, but was released in 1950 and died not long afterwards.

The effect of the trials was weakened by at least three factors. Lawyers were uneasy at the application of a new international code retrospectively, while the German public protested that the Russians had no right to sit in judgment on the Germans; the general German attitude was to say: 'this is only happening because we lost the war'. The process of weeding out Nazis from the public services was handed over to the German courts in March 1946. Too often it led to the penalization of harmless and unimportant people, who were thus unnecessarily alienated by their new 'democratic' experiences; at the same time more dangerous people preserved sufficient influence to arrange their own exoneration, often by paying favour to ill-informed representatives of the Occupying Powers.

The year 1946, when the Germans were most aware of the trials, was a year when the after-effects of the stunning blow of 1945 were perhaps most acutely felt. Out of the ruins, the physical, mental and moral chaos and nothingness, the Allies had first of all to re-create some kind of administration, fitting their own armies into the picture as well. While the Americans and British brought their own food, the French and Russians expected to live off Germany; the British zone, which included the Ruhr, was by far the hardest hit. Peace thus began as a period of near starvation and black-marketing, while the foreign occupation inevitably intensified the already grim lack of housing. The foreign workers dispersed more easily than had been thought possible, but nevertheless many were left as 'Displaced Persons'. Furthermore all kinds of German refugees from other countries continued to amass themselves in Germany, especially Germans from Poland, Czechoslovakia and Hungary – the Potsdam Protocol had agreed to their expulsion provided it were orderly and humane, but this proviso was frequently neglected. It proved extraordinarily difficult to start up industrial production with the working people half-starved and crowded in unheated cellars; indeed everything was paralysed by the inability and unwillingness of the Ruhr miners to produce on anything approximate to the normal scale. Economic revival was further impeded by fear of reparations and the dismantling of industry, by the weakness of the currency and peoples' preference for barter, and also by the division of the country into four separate zones between which communications were neglected.

Meanwhile Russian policy in the Soviet zone included a sweeping land reform with expropriation of the Junkers and other more or less Communistic steps; at the same time German industrial plant was removed to the U.S.S.R. as reparations,[1] and the food supplies which had formerly come from East to West Germany were sent to Russia instead. Since it was impossible to contrive a common economic policy with the Russians, the Americans pressed with growing persistence for a merger of the American with the British zone; in fact the 'bi-zone' (*vereinigtes Wirtschaftsgebiet*) was inaugurated on 1st January 1947. On 25th February, as part of the same administrative reorganization, a decree was signed for the dissolution of Prussia. Thus the Junkers and their world had gone, to make way for better things, as it was hoped. The Council of Foreign Ministers, which had functioned at intervals since it was established by the Potsdam conference, accepted the decision to abolish Prussia in March.

This time the Council of Foreign Ministers met in Moscow from 10th March to 24th April 1947. It began by discussing the reparations claimed by Russia, the distribution of German coal and the level of German industry to be permitted in the future. It then went on to the question of the relations of a future central Government in Germany to the *Länder* – it happened that *Länder* elections had been held throughout the American zone in the previous December, and were fixed for April and May for the British and French zones respectively. The Foreign Ministers failed to agree over economic and political issues alike, the Russians urging the establishment of a strong central Government for Germany; the question of a German Peace Treaty was also brought up in vain. On 21st April the three Western Powers made a separate agreement on coal. When the Foreign Ministers met again in London at the end of the year the French gave way and agreement was reached on the level of steel production – $11\frac{1}{2}$ million tons per annum – to be allowed to Germany. Finally the Russians protested over what in their view already amounted

---

[1] According to the Potsdam Agreement, the U.S.S.R. was entitled to the removal of equipment, even from the Western zones of Germany, in return for the delivery of certain raw materials within five years.

to the setting-up of a West German state in connection with the Marshall offer of American economic aid to Europe.

As in Europe so in Germany the Marshall offer in June was decisive in dividing West from East. The American-British bi-zone had already seemed to justify the Russian reproach that the Western Powers were unfaithful to the principle of German unity as embodied in the Potsdam Agreement. But even if the Russians would have accepted Marshall Aid for Eastern Germany the Americans could scarcely wish to supply facilities which seemed more likely to be used to help Russia, directly or indirectly, than the Germans. Western Germany, whose heavy industry they regarded as the economic key to Europe, the Americans were determined to include in their offer of aid; but it must be a Western Germany free from Russian interference and economically stable. This meant a reform of the currency, which had dwindled into meaninglessness, being more or less replaced by Allied cigarettes; wages were mostly paid in kind and normal commerce was suspended. The French having dropped more and more into line, the three Western Powers at the beginning of 1948 were already discussing an Occupation Statute for Western Germany, while the Russians were in a state of constant protestation over this neglect of German unity. Their protests could always be expressed physically by causing difficulties for the traffic between Western Germany and Berlin. Not long after the Western authorities had established the *Bank deutscher Länder* independently of Eastern Germany and with the obvious intention of a Western currency-reform move, a Russian pilot collided intentionally as it appeared with a British plane which crashed near Gatow (the British air-port for Berlin) in consequence. This was on 5th April 1948 and was felt to be a threat to Western air communication with Berlin. On 18th June 1948 the Western Powers notified the Russian authorities of the currency measures they had decided to introduce, by which every holding of 100 *Reichsmarks* (beyond the first 60 at par) was converted into 6½ *Deutschemarks*; thereupon they found their land traffic facilities with Berlin immediately cut down. The Russians replied in two notes of 20th and 22nd June, after which they completely blockaded the Allied sectors in Berlin from their three zones in the west, and behaved as if the quadripartite government of Berlin were at an end. The dispute was made a little more acid by the desire of the Russians to impose their own new currency, which they themselves had decided to introduce into their zone, upon all the sectors of Berlin, which they claimed as a part of their zone if they were to accept a division of Germany. It seems probable that they believed that their blockade could not now be resisted. Thereupon the Western Allies decided upon a counter-blockade and inaugurated an 'air lift' from 25th June; thus for nearly a year, until 12th May 1949, they kept their sectors of Berlin supplied by air with increasing success, but of course at an alarmingly heavy financial cost. When the Russians finally lifted the blockade they had suffered a notable defeat, partly expressed in the West Berlin elections in December 1948, which showed an impressive Socialist (i.e. anti-Communist) majority; on the other hand the anomaly of a divided Berlin within the Russian zone remained to symbolize the problem of Germany. The introduction of currency reform was generally regarded as the final breakdown of the Potsdam programme: 'for the time-being at least,' wrote the *Economist* on 26th June 1948, 'there are two Germanies, East and West'.

After the currency reform, although many individuals were greatly impoverished, Western Germany quickly became remarkably prosperous. This prosperity, however, was based on *laissez-faire* principles, permitting great inequality. Unemployment remained considerable because of the refugees from Western Poland and Czechoslovakia and the constant stream from Eastern Germany; altogether there were about eight million German refugees in Western Germany early in 1952.[1] The contrast between the social systems of the West and the East emphasized the division between the two Germanies. The fear of unemployment was oppressive in the West, and led to clashes with the Occupying Powers over the dismantling of former war industries, many of which were in the British Zone. After dismantling had been called off the chief evidence of the occupation was to be found in the splitting up of the biggest industrial concerns into smaller units. The ownership of the Ruhr industries remained indeterminate.

The three Western Allies[2] and the West Germans now set to work to draw up an Occupation Statute in conjunction with a constitution for Western Germany. The Statute was published on 10th April 1949, and the Basic Law (*Grundgesetz*) having been accepted by a Constituent Assembly at Bonn on 23rd May, the West German Federal Republic was declared to be in existence from that midnight. On 14th August 402 deputies were elected to the *Bundestag* (Federal Diet) by universal suffrage; the twelve *Länder*, including West Berlin, were represented by three or more of their Ministers (according to the size of their populations) in the *Bundesrat* (Federal Council); the West Berliners, who made the number up to 45, were present as observers, but could not vote. The *Bundesrat*

---

[1] By that time an impressive number of them had been absorbed into West German industry; the problem was aggravated by the high proportion of refugees from the East who wanted agricultural work.

[2] Only at this stage was the French zone completely *gleichgeschaltet* with the other two in the West.

had little power beyond a right to delay federal legislation for a short time; its acquiescence was not needed, except in the case of federal laws concerning taxation (*Steuern, deren Aufkommen den Ländern oder den Gemeinden ganz oder zum Teil zufliesst*). On the other hand much legislation was left to the single-chamber parliaments of the *Länder*. On 12th September Theodor Heuss was elected Federal President and, three days later, Konrad Adenauer Federal Chancellor.

Although the history of Eastern Germany[1] is of little interest from this time, since it was scarcely distinguishable from that of the rest of the Communist-controlled states, it should be mentioned that a competing East German constitution came into force on 7th October 1949. It created a *Volkskammer* and *Länderkammer*; the latter, unlike the Western *Bundesrat*, in a very subordinate role. Grotewohl was elected Minister-President of Eastern Germany with Ulbricht as his deputy: the President of the People's Democracy with its headquarters at Pankow was Wilhelm Pieck, a Communist leader of Weimar days. Like most of their counterparts in Western Germany, Pieck, Otto Grotewohl and Walter Ulbricht were all elderly men: they were all, of course, members of the dominant Socialist Unity (Communist) Party, though other parties were nominally allowed to exist.

The new Western Federal Republic was geographically reminiscent of Napoleon's Confederation of the Rhine, deprussianized, federal, and predominantly Catholic.[2] It aroused no enthusiasm; indeed its resumption of the *Schwarz-Rot-Gold* flag of 1848 and of the Weimar Republic seemed to invite failure. All nationalistically-minded Germans – the big majority – regarded the new state as an artificial makeshift to fill in time until a united unitary Germany should re-emerge, stretching to Königsberg in the east and perhaps beyond Vienna in the south; indeed the Preamble to the *Grundgesetz* hinted at much the same thing.[3] Heuss and his wife[4] were

---

[1] The Germans call the Soviet Zone Mitteldeutschland or – now – the D.D.R. (Deutsche Demokratische Republik). Ostdeutschland they reserve as the name of the western territories of Poland, Silesia, East Pomerania, and also East Prussia.

[2] Eastern Germany, on the other hand, was predominantly Protestant; the Protestants in Western Germany, indeed, accused Dr Adenauer of indifference towards the division of Germany on this account.

[3] In the *Bundesbahn* the maps which were put up showed Königsberg as German territory occupied by the U.S.S.R. and Pomerania and Silesia of course as German territory occupied by the Poles. Further, as the years passed, the irredentism of the refugee Sudeten Germans was increasingly supported by certain members of the Federal Government, particularly members of the F.D.P. (see below). The fact that none of these territories were likely to be returned to Germany except at the cost of a third world war seemed to make no difference.

[4] Elly Heuss-Knapp, well known in *Bekenntniskirche* (p. 187, n. 2) circles. She died in 1952.

respected anti-Nazis and enlightened intellectuals, but their influence was restricted. Adenauer, even after he had proved his political ability, was unpopular except in strongly Catholic circles; he was disliked as old and retrograde, he was accused of having been a Rhenish separatist after the first war and as such was suspected as the tool of the Occupying Powers. Finally his insistence upon a sleepy country town such as Bonn for Federal capital instead of Frankfurt, the town where the Emperors had been crowned from 1562 to 1806 and a great modern city, was also regarded with frowns.

Of the 402 seats in the *Bundestag* the Chancellor's party (the Christian-Democratic Union, known as Christian-Social in Bavaria, and hence abbreviated as C.D.U./C.S.U.) held 140; it was a hybrid party with strong Catholic tendencies. With 131 seats the Social-Democrats could pull almost the same parliamentary weight – in a *Land* like Hessen they were in the majority. The thing they seemed chiefly to have taken to heart was the Social-Democrats' handicap, in the last days of Weimar, in not being able to compete with the chauvinistic demagogy of Hitler. Consequently the Social-Democrats of the *Bundesrepublik* indulged in excessive nationalism. This cue was given by their leader, Dr Kurt Schumacher,[1] whose sufferings in Nazi concentration camps had sharpened the knife of his policy; but many of his followers, too, were content to gain kudos by abusing Dr Adenauer as untrue to German unity. Though only 15 Communists were elected to the *Bundestag*, the Socialists were frightened of losing influence to them and their East German allies, should Socialist enthusiasm for German unity seem less than theirs. In 1952, for instance, they took the lead in the nationalist agitation for the reincorporation of the Saar, which the French had made autonomous within the French ecomonic area, within Germany.

The mainly Socialist *Deutscher Gewerkschaftsbund*, with some special encouragement from the British authorities, was soon reconstructed as a powerful organization. After some two years' campaign against the resurgent employers, the trade union leaders in May 1951 succeeded in pressing through the *Bundestag* legislation which established the *Mitbestimmungsrecht* of the workers' representatives in heavy industry, a share in the management in fact. It is too early to judge whether this is working out as its sponsors intended or whether, as some critics claim, the men's representatives are easily outmanœuvred by the other side.

Dr Adenauer's chief partners in the Government coalition were members of the *Freie Demokratische Partei* (F.D.P.), which with 52 deputies

---

[1] He died in the summer of 1952 and was succeeded as leader of the S.P.D. by Erich Ollenhauer, who had lived in London during the war.

could hold the balance between the chief Government party, the C.D.U., and the Social-Democrat opposition. The F.D.P., which was supported by left-wing liberals like Heuss himself at the beginning, became increasingly *Deutschnational* as time passed. Providing some of the strongest economic influences in the administration of the Federal Republic, it was instrumental in the return to a *laissez-faire* economic policy with its successes and its drawbacks. Indeed the keynote in the life of the Federal Republic was *Restauration*, back to old men and old ideas, with more than a suggestion of 1815 and Metternich. Strictly speaking, the return was a return to the standards of Kaiser Wilhelm II's reign, back to the attitudes of the Prussian Junkers who had been so ostentatiously abolished. The West German administration was staffed, not with outspoken Nazis, but with the *deutschnationale Alte Herren* or 'Old Boys' of the traditional *Studenten-Corps*. And, since times were hard unless one could get into industry, the new generation of students began again to accept the precepts and even the practices[1] of the *Alte Herren* in order to inherit their jobs in the bureaucracy. As in much of the rest of Europe after two tremendous wars, there was more indirect corruption than in the times to which these people wished to return. Justice was again administered in a Hindenburg-Hugenberg spirit, while the police combined this approach with that of a number of SS people who had somehow remained in their ranks.

This state of affairs encouraged the political apathy of many Germans. A small number of idealists clung to the promise of the federation of Europe, while some industrialists welcomed the Schuman coal-and-steel plan in 1950,[2] expecting to become its dominant members. A more common reaction, however, was to feel as exasperated as rank-and-file Nazis had done in the days of Papen's Cabinet of Barons. Dislike of the Occupation and of the Adenauer régime combined with fear of the U.S.S.R. to encourage many people to feel that if Hitler made the mistake of losing the war, most of his notions were sound. It was astonishing to find how essentially Nazi were the chance comments one heard. It was no longer admitted, for instance, that the Nazis had murdered millions of Jews; at the same

[1] Although duelling had been forbidden by various authorities, from 1950 on it was surreptitiously resumed.

[2] This was a proposal made by the French Foreign Minister for the pooling of all the heavy industry of Western Europe with regard to prices and management. In 1952 the six Powers, France, Western Germany, Italy, Holland, Belgium and Luxemburg, finally established the Coal-and-Iron Community which Monsieur Schuman had envisaged, with its headquarters at Luxemburg; there was talk of moving from there to Saarbrücken later, when France and Western Germany should have reached an understanding on the Saar.

time the attitude was: 'And what if they did?'[1] The neo-Nazis still seemed negligible, because that kind of discontent is ineffectual until a mass leader expresses it, and men like Loritz, Dorls and Remer chiefly squabbled among themselves. The Communists progressively lost ground in Western Germany, particularly after the Korean conflict had begun.

The Korean War in 1950 accentuated the division of Germany anew and suggested to the Occupying Powers and to the West German Government that the Federal Republic might at any moment be invaded from East Germany. The Americans became convinced that without German military divisions the West could not be held. In the next two years, therefore, since the hope of arriving at a German Peace Treaty in company with Russia had repeatedly failed, the Western Powers worked out their own equivalent in the Contractual Agreements of 1952 and prepared for the inclusion of Western Germany in the European Defence Community. After the pains to which the Potsdam powers had gone to disarm Germany totally, the Western Powers felt compelled to ask the Germans to put on their uniforms once more, while the German response for long remained the notorious 'Ohne mich'. After 1945 there were always a good many Germans who believed that the surest path back to unity lay in neutrality between East and West, while neo-Nazi theorists played with the idea of a fresh alliance with Stalin as the prelude to a third war against the West – they believed that ultimately, as Ley had once said to Ciano, 'the Germans can easily tame Slavs everywhere'.

On 10th March 1952 the Russians had marvellously confused the issues by presenting a fresh Note to the Allies in favour of a German Peace Treaty, a Note which diligently exploited German susceptibilities. For it suggested that the terms of the Treaty should include the end of partition, the withdrawal of the occupying armies within one year, and that Germany should be allowed such German forces as her defence might require: further, the Treaty was to be drawn up with the participation of an all-German Government based on the elections throughout the country of which there had long been talk. In spite of these seductive suggestions, and in the teeth of strong Socialist opposition, Dr Adenauer persuaded the Federal Parliament to approve the various steps necessary in order to incorporate Western Germany in the West European organizations against which the Russian Note was aimed. Notes on a German Peace Treaty passed backwards and forwards between the West and the

---

[1] The Adenauer Government did, however, succeed in putting through a treaty for reparation to Israel in 1952; the negotiations were carried on in secret.

U.S.S.R. for the next six months, the West insisting that the first step must be genuinely free elections throughout both Germanies.[1]

[1] At the moment of going to press there is a noticeable change in spirit due to the extraordinary prosperity which has to some extent counteracted Nazi tendencies. The Nazis are also now deflected into championing *die Vertriebenen.*

BIBLIOGRAPHY TO CHAPTER VI

Bullock, Alan. *Hitler – a Study in Tyranny.* Odhams, 1952

Clay, Lucius. *Decision in Germany.* Doubleday & Co., New York, 1950

Davidson, Basil. *Germany – What now?* Frederick Muller, London, 1950

Dulles, A. W. *Germany's Underground.* Macmillan, New York, 1947

Goebbels Tagebücher, ed. Louis Lochner. Atlantis Verlag, Zurich, 1948 (English translation published by Hamish Hamilton)

Goebbels, the Man next to Hitler. Diary notes by R. Semmler. Westhouse, 1947

Hassell, U. von. *Vom andern Deutschland.* Atlantis-Verlag, Zurich, 1946

Hitler's Table Talk, 1941-44. Weidenfeld and Nicolson, London, 1953

Kogon, E. *Der S.S. Staat.* Karl Alber, Munich, 1946

†Kordt, Erich. *Wahn und Wirklichkeit.* Union Deutsche Verlagsgesellschaft, Stuttgart, 1947

Kordt, Erich. *Nicht aus den Akten.* Union Deutsche Verlagsgesellschaft, Stuttgart, 1947

*Meissner, O. *Der Schicksalsweg des deutschen Volkes.* Hoffmann & Campe Verlag, Hamburg, 1950

Namier, L. B. *Diplomatic Prelude.* Macmillan, 1948

Namier, L. B. *In the Nazi Era.* Macmillan, 1952

Nettl, J. P. *The Eastern Zone and Soviet Policy in Germany 1945.* Oxford University Press, 1950

*Papen, Franz von. *Memoirs.* André Deutsch, London, 1952

Pechel, R. *Deutscher Widerstand.* Eugen Rentsch, Zurich, 1947

†Schmidt, Paul. *Statist auf diplomatischer Bühne.* Athenäum Verlag, Bonn, 1949

Shirer, W. *A Berlin Diary.* H. Hamilton, London, 1941

Speeches of Adolf Hitler 1922-39, edited by Norman H. Baynes. Oxford University Press, 1942

Speidel, General Hans. *We Defended Normandy.* Herbert Jenkins, London, 1951

Stolper, Gustav. *Deutsche Wirtschaft 1870-1940.* Stuttgart, 1950. (As *German Economy, 1870-1940: Issues and Trends.* Allen and Unwin, 1940)

Survey of International Affairs: *Hitler's Europe, 1941-45.* O.U.P., 1954

Trevor-Roper, H. R. *The Last Days of Hitler.* Macmillan, Second Edition, 1950

Two excellent articles by the Industrial Correspondent of the *Times* on German Industrial Recovery, published on 22nd and 23rd February, 1952

*Weizsäcker, E. von. *Erinnerungen.* Paul List Verlag, Munich, 1950

Wheeler-Bennett, J. W. *Munich.* Macmillan, 1948

Wheeler-Bennett, J. W. *The Nemesis of Power.* Macmillan, 1953

Wilmot, Chester. *The Struggle for Europe.* Collins, London, 1952

Wiskemann, Elizabeth. *The Rome-Berlin Axis.* O.U.P., 1949

Wiskemann, Elizabeth. *Czechs and Germans*. O.U.P., 1938
Wiskemann, Elizabeth. *Germany's Eastern Neighbours*. O.U.P., 1956
Zeller, Eberhard, *Geist der Freiheit*. Hermann Rinn, Munich, 1953

    † *Mit Vorsicht zu geniessen*
    * Strongly tendentious

SOME OFFICIAL PUBLICATIONS:

Akten zur deutschen auswärtigen Politik 1918-45, pub. Imprimerie nationale Baden-Baden; or alternatively
Documents on German Foreign Policy, pub. H.M. Stationery Office, 1949. Series III, Vols. 1-6, deal with Munich and events leading up to the attack upon Poland.
Documents on British Foreign Policy 1919-39. Series III. (Vol. 2 deals with Munich.) H.M. Stationery Office, 1951
Trial of the Major War Criminals before the International Military Tribunal. Nuremberg, 1947-49
Nazi Conspiracy and Aggression. U.S. Government Printing Office, Washington, 1946
Nazi-Soviet Relations. Department of State, Washington, 1948
Monthly Reports of the Control Commission. Also background letters
Die Volksvertretung. Handbuch des deutschen Bundestags. Cotta'sche Buchhandlung, Stuttgart, 1949
Führer Conferences on Naval Affairs. Published by the Admiralty, 1946-47

CHAPTER VII

GERMAN LITERATURE TO 1748

A COMMON language and literature unite the German and Austrian nations and the German Swiss. A sprinkling of German-speaking communities was once found in the Baltic States, in Yugoslavia (Gottschee), in Roumania (Transylvania), and in Russia as far as the Lower Volga, where the Germans formed a Soviet republic. A small number of Pennsylvanian 'Dutch' settlers have kept their Palatine dialect in the New World. The Netherlanders of Holland, Belgium, and the Union of South Africa, the Frisians, the Scandinavian nations, and the English, all of whom belong by their origins to the same cultural unity as the Germans, remain outside. On the territory of Germany itself are found the last relics of Frisian in marsh-girt moors of the Saterland in Oldenburg, on the islands of Heligoland, Föhr, Amrum, and Sylt, and a strip of the Slesvig coast; a network of waterways has preserved the cohesion of the Wends or Sorbs in the Spreewald, last remnant of those Slavonic peoples who once extended to the Lower Elbe, where even in the eighteenth century fishermen could talk Polabian.

Community of language masks considerable diversity of race. The Scandinavian countries, the Finnish coast, the Baltic islands, the North German plain, Friesland, Northern Holland, and the southern and eastern regions of Great Britain are inhabited predominantly by a relatively tall, fair-haired, grey or blue-eyed, long-skulled population, which – according to modern ethnologists – includes two stocks: the one rather thick-set, square-faced, and often ash-blonde, called Falians (from Westphalia) by the Germans, and Dalians (from Dalecarlia) by the Swedes, and the other of sparer and lither build and yellow hair, the well-known Nordics. Dark, short round-heads belonging to the Alpine or 'Ostisch' race occupy the centre, and are flanked to the west by the Rhenish peoples, whose typically 'Frankish face' points to admixture with the race known as western, Atlantic, or Mediterranean, those slender dark long-heads we meet in Spain, France, and Wales. A link with south-eastern Europe is the Dinaric people of tall stature and rugged aspect, prevalent in the Tyrol and southern Bavaria.

Before the Christian era the northern blondes probably spoke a language sufficiently homogeneous to be understood by all the northern tribes right from those who had crossed the Rhine shortly before Caesar's Gallic wars to the coast dwellers of what are now Esthonia and Finland. We call this language Primitive Germanic, other appellations being Teutonic and – with Schütte and Jespersen – Gothonic. It is a member of the far-flung Indo-European family of languages, but differs from the others by its concentration of stress on the root or significant syllable in substitution for the mobile Indo-European stressing and especially by consistently carrying through that shift of the Indo-European plosive consonants, which has given us, e.g. *fee, horn, two, three, corn,* as against Latin *pecu, cornu, duo, tres, granum.* From the Celts of the Rhineland, Alsace, Swabia, and Helvetia, Germanic may have drawn a few metallurgical terms, e.g. *iron,* a witness to the influence of the La Tène culture of the Iron Age about 400 B.C., and administrative words like *Reich, Amt, Geisel, Eid.* Traders from the south-east may have brought us *path* and perhaps through Dutch *pea*-jacket (*Pfad* from Old Iranian and the dialect form *Pfeid,* 'shirt', from Thrace or Asia Minor). In return Germanic gave – probably not before the consonantal shift – a few words to Finnish and the Slavonic languages.

The uniformity of Germanic was destroyed by migrations. From Scandinavia Goths and Burgundians settled in the region of the lower Vistula, leaving a trace of their names in Gothland and Bornholm. The Goths moved on to the Black Sea, where – in modern Bulgaria – Visigothic literature flourished in the fourth century in the Bible translation of Bishop Wulfila. In the Crimea people were still talking Gothic in the sixteenth century, over a thousand years after the downfall of the Goths in the west. With Vandals, originally from Jutland, and Burgundians the Goths constitute the East Germanic branch, nearest akin to the North Germanic which includes Norwegian, Icelandic (from the ninth century), the now obsolete Norse of the Orkneys and Shetlands, Danish, and Swedish. The remaining group, West Germanic, comprises English and its nearest congener, Frisian, and 'deutsch', an inclusive term for the unshifted Low Franconian represented chiefly by the Flemish dialects, Low Saxon of the North German plain, and the shifted High German. Dutch is fundamentally Low Franconian influenced by Frisian and Low Saxon; its literary language, like that of the Scandinavian countries, has drawn a great deal on German.

Just as Germanic diverged from Indo-European, so High German has split off from West Germanic. Between the fifth and seventh centuries A.D. occurred a consonantal shift, most intense in the south among

Alemans and Bavarians, and weakening as it proceeded northward, which gives us the shifted High German forms *zu*, *Pfeife*, *Wasser*, *machen*, *treiben*, as against Low German (and English) *to*, *Piep*, *Water*, *maken*, *driewen*. The differences of incidence of this sound-shift, together with certain features of the vowel system, supply criteria for the larger dialect divisions within High German, viz. (1) Central German, which includes the dialects of the Middle Rhine and Moselle as well as Thuringian, Upper Saxon, and Silesian, and (2) Upper German, which embraces Alemannic (Alsatian, Swabian, Swiss-German), and Bavarian (including Austrian). These larger regional divisions correspond roughly to old tribal differences; their subdivisions are often found to depend upon much later manorial and ecclesiastical delimitations. The Rhine has been a great highway for the propagation of High German in the west, and the Danube in the south-east.

From the chronological point of view it is convenient to distinguish the following periods of High German language and literature: Old High German (OHG), from the first written documents about A.D. 750 to about 1050, then Middle High German (MHG) from 1050 till roughly the latter part of the thirteenth century, when New High German begins to emerge more clearly. The middle of the seventeenth century marks linguistically the beginnings of Late Modern German. OHG ceases when the final vowels ă, ĕ, ĭ, ŏ, and ŭ have become merged in a flat ə, written *e*. Within MHG dialects of the south-east begin to diphthongize *wîn* to *Wein*, *hûs* to *Haus* and *friunt* [*frünt*] to *Freund*, and those of the centre to monophthongize *dienen* [diənən] to *dienen* [dinən], *muot* to *Mut*, and *müede* to *müde*, and to lengthen the short vowels preceding the syllable boundary in *săgen*, *lĕben*, *sĭgen*, *lŏben*, *jŭde*. The combination of these features gives New High German its distinctive appearance. The merging of central and south-eastern peculiarities was completed in the Imperial and provincial chancelleries, especially in the fifteenth and early sixteenth century – the Imperial office at Prague being at the meeting-point of dialect boundaries. Luther deliberately adopted phonetic forms from the Upper Saxon chancellery e.g. South German diphthongs, Central German monophthongs and Upper rather than Central German consonants; but in vocabulary, syntax, idiom, and style he adhered to the usage of East Central Germany. A compromise language of this kind was found convenient by the printers even of Augsburg and Strassburg, and Protestantism superimposed a standard High German (associated with Meissen in Saxony and hence called 'Meissnisch') on the Low German dialects of Hamburg, Bremen, and the north. Catholic Austria and Reformed Switzerland tended to keep aloof from the conventional literary language till the eighteenth century, but the wish to secure a larger audience (as the Swiss Haller tells us) and the great prestige of Lessing, Goethe, Schiller, and a host of other writers of the standard, brought about unity.

It is noteworthy that Modern German does not spring directly from those unifying tendencies in the late twelfth and early thirteenth century which constituted a Middle High German 'Dichtersprache'. Here the dominating influence was the south-west, but in any case the unity was guaranteed by renunciation rather than adoption: poets eschewed rhymes which would lose their rhyming purity in other dialects and words which seemed to them boorish or old-fashioned. Only occasionally did they borrow forms from each other. Fixation in writing tends to consolidate a language by the reaction of a traditional spelling against phonetic adaptation, and even in the OHG period we can see the strong influence of a great scriptorium like that of the Abbey of Fulda. It is also quite likely that the Rhenish Franconian apparently spoken at the Carolingian court stood a little apart from the local dialects, for educated men influence each other and mark themselves off from the populace.

Loan-words, i.e. fully assimilated foreign words, buoy the channels of influence from foreign nations. Rome was the great teacher of the West Germanic tribes, who learnt from her much of military organization, commerce, viticulture, agriculture, gardening, fruit-growing, poultry-farming, building, furnishing, cooking, clothing, navigating, and governing. Witnesses are such words as *Strasse, Kampf, Wall; kaufen* (caupo, 'innkeeper'), *Pfund, Speicher, Saumtier, Esel, Maultier; Wein, Kelch, Kelter, Trichter, Flasche, eichen, mischen; Flegel, Wanne, Stoppel; Pfirsich, Pflaume, Kirsche, pflanzen, impfen, pfropfen, pflücken; Flaum, Käfig, mausern; Mauer, Ziegel, Fenster, Keller; Tisch, Schemel, Spiegel; Koch, Pfanne; Socke, Schürze; Anker, Riemen; Kaiser, Kerker, Zoll.* In the OHG period, Slavonic fur traders gave *Zobel* and *Kürschn[er]*. The Christian missionaries brought numbers of Latin and Greek words from *Pfaffe* and *Kirche* to *Engel* and *Priester*; English may have suggested *Ostern*. In the twelfth century French chivalry gave *Turnier, Abenteuer, Fee, Forst,* etc.; and the suffixes *-ei* and *-ieren*. Brabant knights gave the unshifted *Wappen* for *Waffen*. The Humanists have left many words connected with school and university life, e.g. *Aula, Dekan, Kolleg, Quästur,* etc. Italian musical and commercial terms, Spanish military terms, and French expressions of politeness and gallantry found a lodgment in German as in other European languages, but the 'Fremdwort' or unassimilated foreign word has been combated with varying success right from the seventeenth century. In our own day we see how the adoption of English and American terms (especially in sport, tailoring, hotels, etc.) is contemporaneous with the elimination – by administrative action – of many foreign words, e.g.

those used formerly on the railways or in the post-office (*Eindeutschungs.*

For the replenishment of the native stock of words, OHG glossator)
and translators performed a service in developing the processes of affix-
derivation, e.g. by *-ung*, *-nis*, etc., and word-composition. Mystics have
left their mark in such significant expressions as *Eindruck, Einfluss, ein-
leuchten, gelassen*, and even *bloss* in its sense of 'merely'. In the eighteenth
century Wolff (see p. 436) added many apt German words to the vocabulary of logic and philosophy. Obsolete medieval forms like *Hain, Maid,
Minne, Hort* were revived in poetic diction in the age of the Storm and
Stress. Other native words came in through the lexicographers Adelung
and Campe. In syntax and style we find a contrast between slavish imitation of Latin constructions and more analytic Germanic phrases. The
great poets round A.D. 1200 had achieved a remarkable clarity and suppleness. Unfortunately the writers of the age of humanism and the baroque
often became involved in an incapsulated periodic style with such sub-
ordinationwithin subordination as puts an excessive strain on the attention
(see p. 237). From Lessing onward German has been gradually emanci-
pating itself from that tutelage. In particular the love of the *Volkslied* has
made its lyrical diction as limpid and as sincere as any in Europe.

Our knowledge of Germanic literature before the age of writing is
inferential and sketchy. It is unlikely that poets formed a professional
class in a population of scattered farmers and cattle-breeders, or of fishermen living on lonely halligs. At most, certain tribal groups would form
amphictyonies or groups for common worship, or hold assemblies for
righting wrongs and waging war. Men of great bodily strength or
personality were chosen as leaders and kept a retinue (Tacitus: *comitatus*,
OHG *druht*, whence *druhtîn*, 'lord') consisting of sons of yeomen, outlaws
(G. *Recken*), and professional fighters. Women, respected for their
wisdom, sometimes acted as priestesses. The old Indo-European god
of the sky, Tiu, identified by the Romans with their war-god Mars
(cf. *dies Martis, Tuesday*, Alem. *Ziestig*; *Dienstag* probably from [Mars]
Thingsus), was gradually displaced by Wodan, who first appears on
the Rhine (cf. Godesberg), and attained great importance in England
and the north. He is Mercurius Viator of the Romans, and was thought
to wear a long coat and broad-brimmed hat. The cult of Tiu or Ziu
long persisted in Alemannia, and he is mentioned – as the war-god
Saxnōt – as one of the gods to be renounced by the Saxons before baptism. The latter also had to give up Donar (Norse, *Thŏrr*), whose sacred
oak near Geismar in Hesse was hewn down in 723 by the English missionary St. Boniface. Of goddesses, Frija was the Germanic Venus;
Nerthus (Norse, *Njörðr*) was the earth-goddess worshipped by our

Anglian ancestors. A host of supernatural beings sporadically haunt medieval literature, especially the stories of the Nibelungen and Dietrich. There are giants and dwarfs, hoard-guarding dragons, nightmare-causing elves (*Alp*drücken), kobolds or house-sprites, nixies or water-sprites, fauns (OHG *scrato*), valkyries or battle-maidens, and such figures of destiny as Frau Holle, Frau Sorge, or the Schimmelreiter. The common Germanic word for Fate, OHG *wurt*, is perpetuated in the English *weird*. 'Charms', often consisting of an epic or narrative portion, depicting some analogous quandary, and an incantation formula or spell, have survived in English, Norse, and in High German. In OHG a manuscript of the tenth century at Merseburg preserves two charms, of which the first invites the aid of valkyries to free captive friends, and the second – a cure for sprain in a horse – brings in Fol, Wodan, Balder (?), Sinthgunt and her sister Sunna, Frija and her sister Folla. The incantation of the first is 'spring forth from the fetters, flee the foe!' and the lines alliterate. Unable to eradicate charms, the Church often christianized them. A Viennese charm prays Christ and St. Martin of Tours to protect the sheep-dogs from thief and wolf, and a Lorsch charm seeks the aid of Christ to prevent the loss of swarming bees. We find both blessings to promote good-fortune, e.g. for a departing traveller, and conjurations to remove evil, e.g. for a paralytic. Of other oral literature we learn something from Carolingian capitularies, in which the Church tells us what existed by specifying what it prohibited. English and German glosses of Latin literary terms supply us with suggestive compound words, but some of the latter are nonce-forms or of uncertain reference. Taking all this evidence in conjunction with allusions in the historians of the Goths, e.g. Ammianus Marcellinus and Jordanes, and with survivals in Norse and Old English, we feel safe in positing the following poetic types: gnomic and mnemonic verses and choric songs for weddings, sacrifices, marching, fighting, and rhythmic work in common. Though Tacitus refers to mythic songs in celebration of Mannus and Tuisco, and lays in praise of the hero Arminius, it is the Goths who are thought to have developed the eulogy of contemporary rulers and heroic lays based on the deadly feuds of past warriors. We hear that in 790 St. Liutger met a blind Frisian, Bernlef, who sang to the harp 'the deeds of the ancients and the struggles of kings'; passages in Beowulf show us what such songs were like. The only hero song in OHG, the lay of Hildebrand (MS. about A.D. 800 – original perhaps Bavarian overlaid with Low Saxon), tells with dramatic terseness of a duel between Dietrich's (i.e. Theoderic the Great's) henchman, Hildebrand, and his son Hadubrand, in the presence of the opposing armies. In the lost concluding portion, the father killed his son.

H

The *Hildebrandslied* is a convenient starting-point for the discussion of certain features of the hero-poetry. Its ground-theme – the tragic conflict between father and son – is international, occurring in the Persian story of Sohrab and Rustem, the Greek of Odysseus and Telegonus, and the Russian of Ilya of Murom. As in other heroic lays there is, however, a historical kernel, for Dietrich is the great Ostrogothic king and Otacher is his foe Odoacer. We assume that this struggle was sung by Goths, and passed on by them to Bavarians, just as we regard the story of the downfall of the Nibelungs as embodying a historical event of the fifth century, celebrated in a song passed by Goths to Bavarians. The poetic form of the *Hildebrandslied* is alliterative, like that of the lays in Old English and the Edda. Two half-lines or hemistichs are knit into one long line by the rhyming or 'staving' of the initial consonants of strongly stressed words (especially substantives and adjectives), e.g. *west*ar ubar *went*ilsêo | dat inan *wîc* furnam (cf. *west* over the *Wendel* sea | *war* took him forth), with two staves in the first half and one – usually the first stress – in the second half. Metrically the long line formed a unit, but we find in later alliterative verse a tendency to break off a sentence in the middle of the long line, start a new one, and carry over to the next. The Germanic principle of alliteration was used not only for hero-poetry, but for charms and other kinds. In OHG there have survived, besides the Merseburg charms, two Christian poems, the Wessobrunn Prayer and *Muspilli*, and in Old Saxon there is a Christian epic, the *Hêliand*. The so-called Wessobrunn Prayer contains the beginning of a cosmogony, which reminds us both of *Genesis* and of certain Norse poems and has a Germanic ring about it. It is Bavarian like *Muspilli*, which is a conglomeration of stories of the Soul's fate, firstly immediately after death, and secondly at the Last Judgment, where – following the Book of Revelation – Elijah must suffer death in a duel with Antichrist, and the blood dripping from his wounds causes a world-conflagration. The rough alliterative verse and the use of such words as *mittilagart* for 'earth' and *muspilli* for the final destruction are echoes from the heathen past. The *Hêliand* is in spirit and style much more akin to the Old English religious poems; it favours a heavier alliterative metre with '*Schwellverse*' with more than the usual number of beats, and builds complex sentence-structures. Christ is conceived somewhat like a Germanic prince, and His disciples as thegns, whose warlike ardour He sometimes curbs. Among the best passages in the epic are descriptions of the sea. The fragmentary Old Saxon *Genesis* is of particular interest because, even before its discovery at the Vatican in 1894, the German philologist Sievers had, in 1875, suspected its existence as the source of an interpolation in our English *Genesis* poem.

All the poems hitherto described were committed to writing in a Germany which had long been christianized. Though the Church set its face against heathen poetry, it is to monastic scribes that we owe the preservation of what we have. It was the Church, too, which adapted the Latin alphabet for the hard task of symbolizing High German sounds, and which schooled the German language, first by translation and then by original work. The making of manuscript books or codices for many centuries devolved upon monks. Their parchmenter steeped, scraped, pumiced, and cut the sheepskins; their scribes ruled the vellum thus prepared, and copied the text of the exemplar. Rubricators would insert coloured initials and headings, and the miniator, or illuminator, paint in a bright-hued miniature, sometimes on gold-leaf. The codex was then bound and placed in a library and catalogued. Both monks and nuns were encouraged to do scribal work, and it is not until the thirteenth century that we find lay craftsmen as copyists, e.g. in the scriptorium at Strassburg. In the fourteenth century the growing use of a cheaper material, paper (perhaps an invention of the Chinese, brought westward by Arabs), led to a greatly increased circulation of MSS. The invention of printing in the middle of the fifteenth century rendered scriptoria superfluous.

When written literature begins in Germany, with the so-called Keronian glosses produced at Reichenau about 750, all the tribes were christianized except the Saxons. The conversion of Clovis in 496 was followed by a series of missionary efforts, carried out first by Scottish and Irish monks (Fridolin, Columban, Gallus) in Alemannia, by Franks (Corbinian, Emmeram) in Bavaria, and by the greatest of all, a Devonian, Winfrith Bonifatius (Boniface), who evangelized and organized the Rhineland, Hesse, and Thuringia, and worked among the Frisians, who martyred him. Great centres grew up like St. Gall, Reichenau, and above all Fulda, modelled on the Benedictine Monte Cassino.

It was Charlemagne who gave the greatest impetus to learning and literature. He combined an interest in classical antiquity, as testified by his Academy of Frankish and foreign scholars, with zeal for Christianity and a warm love of German speech and poetry. In various enactments he set about improving the education of both clergy and laity. The Creed and Lord's Prayer had to be known in German prior to baptism. He wished boys to receive instruction either at the monastic or cathedral schools or from the village priest. The catechism, baptismal vows, confessions, and hymns were put into German, as well as the Gospels, e.g. a fitting together or 'harmony' of the gospels slavishly rendered at Fulda into the East Franconian dialect from a Latin MS. ultimately deriving from the work of an early Christian Syrian, Tatian. The much freer

Rhenish Franconian translations of the sixth-century tracts of Isidore of
Seville against the Jews and of St. Matthew's gospel in the Monsee-Vienna
codex are the highest achievement of German prose in the Carolingian
period.

Into poetry a monk of Weissenburg, Otfried, who had studied under
the great Latinist Hrabanus Maurus at Fulda, introduced a new principle,
that of end-rhyme in place of alliteration. He took it from Latin hymns,
where it occurs as early as the time of St. Ambrose, but for his rhythm
retained the Germanic principle of organization by stresses. The narrative
of his versified Gospel harmony trickles through a close-meshed sieve of
dedications and moral and allegorical commentaries. He has, however, in
his Latin preface, left us the first treatise on poetic theory to be written by
a German, and his leaden didacticism is lightened when he extols his
industrious and warlike Franks and describes the Annunciation and the
Christ-child in the manger. The Vienna MS. appears to have been cor-
rected by Otfried himself, and hence has the value of an original, a great
rarity in textual transmission. Of the short end-rhymed religious poems
subsequent to Otfried, the chief are a hymn to St. Peter with the refrain
Kyrie eleison, Christe eleison, a tersely written colloquy between Christ
and the Samaritan woman, and the legend of St. George, the first German
saint's legend. End-rhyme is used, too, for historical poetry. A poem by
a cleric celebrating the victory of King Louis III over the Normans at
Saucourt in 881 can be accurately dated, for in it he is represented as still
alive (actually he died in 882); in spite of its enthusiasm for the king and
a spirited passage describing the fight it cannot compare in vigour with
the English *Battle of Maldon.* A meeting between one of the Ottos and
a Duke Henry of Bavaria is the theme of a 'macaronic' poem, mingling
Latin and German, now in the Cambridge Song-book (see below).

Charlemagne had extended his civil and ecclesiastical jurisdiction to
the Lower Elbe and beyond. The Ottos continued their pressure eastwards against Slavs and Avars. Partly through their connections with
Italy and Byzantium – Otto II married Theophano, daughter of the
Emperor Romanos II – they fostered the growth of a Latin literature,
which shows great variety and a considerable modernity. The nun
Hrotswitha of Gandersheim near Brunswick wrote a series of religious
dramas influenced by Terence. A monk of St. Gall, Ekkehard, composed,
under the influence of Virgil, *Waltharius,* an epic of a Germanic hero, a
hostage at Attila's court, who is mentioned (as Waldere) in Old English
as well, and whose fame survived in Germany till the close of the Middle
Ages. It is written in hexameters, with a sprinkling of lines rhymed
between caesura and end of line. Among the so-called 'modi' such as we

find in the Cambridge Song-book, still preserved in the University library – perhaps the property of a Rhenish gleeman in the eleventh century – is an early beast story recounting the killing of a nun's donkey by a wicked wolf, an early *Lügenmärchen* (see p. 229) in which a Swabian is the liar, the story of the master-thief who stole his liver from St. Peter in heaven, and several love-poems (which some objector has tried to obliterate in the MS.), especially a dialogue between a nun and her cleric lover. Such friendships are referred to in another Latin poem in hexameters, *Ruodlieb* (composed in the monastery of Tegernsee about 1030), which also contains a Latin love-greeting sent by a woman to her knightly lover. With its German rhymes *liebes | loubes* and *wunna | minna* it is the earliest specimen of the secular love-lyric in Germany. *Ruodlieb* points forward, too, as being the earliest Court Romance, describing the adventures of a knight whom we see fishing and hunting and playing the harp, and follow through palace and castle and the country-side. Still earlier is the first beast-epic, *Ecbasis cujusdam captivi per tropologiam*, composed about 930-40 by a young monk at Toul to while away a period of detention. A straying calf is carried off by a wolf, and all the animals on the farm join in the chase. It is a praise of asceticism, for the calf is the monk and the wolf represents the lusts of the flesh. A story told by the wolf concerning a sick lion brings us near the famous Reynard the Fox, often used later for satirical purposes. About 1150 was written the Ghent Magister Nivardus' *Ysengrimus* ('iron-mask') and contemporaneously the French gleeman's *roman de Renart*. From the latter sprang two versions: a German *Reinhart Fuchs* (1180) by an Alsatian Heinrich, called 'der glîchezâre' or hypocrite (unless that refers to the fox!), and one by an East Fleming, Willem, in 1250. The latter was worked up in *Reinaerts Historie* (1375) and was added to by Hinrik van Alkmaar (1480), the Culeman fragments of whose work are in Cambridge. It finally appeared in the best-known version of all, the Low German *Reynke de Vos* (Lübeck, 1498); this was the work which Goethe turned into High German hexameters and published in 1794.

Even in clerical poetry these centuries brought changes. A monk of Jumièges is said to have inserted words into the gradual of the mass to help the choristers remember the jubilating notes of the Alleluia. These 'versus sequentes neumata' (neume=musical note) or 'sequentiae' are the free rhythms of the age. Nôtkêr the Stammerer and Tutilo did much to develop them at St. Gall.

Another Nôtkêr, nicknamed Labeo, 'the thick-lipped', likewise of St. Gall, was the last great writer of Old High German. A devoted teacher and skilful translator from Boethius, Martianus Capella, and Aristotle, he left German richer and more supple than it had ever been. His spelling-reform which distinguishes voiced and voiceless initial stop according to the nature of the preceding sound, e.g. *der bruoder* but *des pruoder*, indicates the possession of a sharp ear and systematic mind. After him the art of writing prose suffered an eclipse till it emerged triumphant in the middle of the thirteenth century in the sermons of the Franciscan preachers, David of Augsburg and Berthold of Regensburg.

The century between the accession of the Salic Emperor, Henry IV, and that of the Hohenstaufen, Frederick Barbarossa, saw a proliferation of religious poetry. Reaction against the worldliness of the age of the Ottos was intensified by a monastic movement towards extreme asceti-cism which arose among the Benedictines of Clugny, near Mâcon, towards the end of the tenth century, and spread through Lorraine to Western Germany, and even into Bavaria and Austria. Classical authors were laid aside. Man's duty on earth was to prepare for Eternal Life; though originally good he had become irremediably corrupted by the fallen angel Lucifer, from whose clutches not even Christ's redeeming death sufficed to free him. 'Remember death' is the watchword of ex-hortations and such pictures of its grotesque horrors as are given by the Austrian Heinrich von Melk (*Von des tôdes gehügede*, ab. 1160). Lax communities like those at Bamberg voluntarily submitted to a stricter rule, as we learn from the *Ezzolied* (about 1060), which recounts the story of man's striving from the 'anegenge', or beginning of things, to the 'urlôse', or redemption. Prayers, litanies, laments are put into verse. Biblical epics like the Viennese Genesis and Exodus afford a glimpse of peasant life. Balaam, Solomon, the youths in the fiery furnace, and Judith attracted poets. The first poetess known to us who composed her works in German, Frau Ava, an *inclusa* at the Convent of Melk, wrote on Christ, Antichrist, and the Last Judgment. Eschatological poems like the Hamburg *Doomsday* preach penitence; an Austrian *Himmelreich* depicts the joys of the after life 'per negationem', e.g. there is no baking, no clothing, etc., cf. Rev. vii, 16. The Saint's legend, novel of the devout, flourishes, and with it a visionary literature associated with the Irish saints, Patrick, Tundalus or Tnugdalus, and Brandan. If St. Albanus is a monastic Oedipus, then St. Brandan's tale of shipwrecks and marine adventures is like an Odyssey, and the tale of Tnugdalus like Dante's *Inferno*. Among the gems of this not too widely known clerical literature are the poems in praise of the Virgin, mother of mankind, whose sorrows, humility, purity and motherly compassion stirred the heart. After the institution of the Festival of the doctrine of the Immaculate Conception in Lyons about 1140 Cistercians and Praemonstratensians championed her cause in Germany. Hymns, sequences, and epics glorified her, often using an elaborate symbolism to body forth the mystery of Christ's birth, e.g. the unconsumed burning bush, Gideon's fleece, Aaron's rod, and the glass undamaged by the sunbeam's passage (*Melker Marienlied*, ab. 1140). One of the best hymns was composed by a nun at the convent of Arnstein on the Lahn (ab. 1150).

Between 1080 and 1110 a cleric wrote in Moselle Franconian a semi-historical, semi-legendary poem on Bishop Anno of Cologne, which we call the *Annolied*. The long historical preamble from the Creation till Anno's coming was utilized by Konrad – author of the *Rolandslied* (see below) – for his *Kaiserchronik*.

In the third decade of the twelfth century clerics turned to worldly themes. Between 1120 and 1130 a priest, Lamprecht, wrote his *Alexander* poem, using as his source the French tirades of Aubrei de Besançon and displaying in the description of the Indian expedition all the marvels of the East. He shows acquaintance with the Germanic story of Hilde (in the *Gudrun* poem). About 1130-33 a Ratisbon priest, Konrad, adapted the French *Chanson de Roland* and depicted the battle scenes in an unexpectedly spirited manner.

Between the worldly poetry of clerics and the Court Romance of the knights came a literature of a lower order grouped together as 'Spielmannsdichtung'. The term 'Spielmann', or gleeman, vaguely covers classes of professional poets and entertainers ranging from the acrobats, snake-charmers, tight-rope walkers, and mimes performing on the village green, or called in to brighten a gay festival in the castle, to those talented sons of knights and peasants forced to seek their living by attaching themselves temporarily to some lord who would keep and clothe them and then let them go *enwadele*, i.e. take to the road. One particular type of itinerant gleeman was the Goliards or *Vagantes*, consisting of priests without cures and students on the tramp.

The best worn theme of the Spielmann's romance is the often repeated abduction of an oriental beauty by a gallant knight. The Spielmann's diction abounds in *clichés* and in allusions to himself and challenges to his listeners. In the time of the Crusades it is not astonishing that he revels in tall stories of the fabulous beings of the East. Thus in *Salman und Morolf*, Solomon's wife is kidnapped by Fore (Pharaoh), and Morolf – the Spielmann – has to tax his brains to outwit her captors. When the Spielmann takes up legend he is not sparing of the miraculous. In *St. Oswald* a raven carries a love-message and a ring is found in a fish's belly; *Orendel* tells how Christ's seamless coat came to Treves.

Stylistically *König Rother* (1150-60) stands higher. The name goes back to the Langobard king, Authari, but it contains the story of Osanctrix and such fairy-tale motives as the one familiar to us from Cinderella, the fitting of shoes on a princess's feet. With *Herzog Ernst* we enter knightly literature in its more primitive and '*Spielmann*'-like beginnings. It combines historical reminiscence – inasmuch as Ernst's mother, Adelheid, is married to the Emperor Otto – with a fantastic travel yarn in which Ernst meets some men with crane's bills, others with flat feet and umbrella-shaped ears, and in which a magnetic mountain draws the rivets out of the ship and a curdled sea (*lebermer*) holds ships in a tight grip.

The true pioneer of Court Romance was a native of Maastricht, Heinrich von Veldeke, who relinquished his Low Franconian dialect in favour of Central German. Gottfried von Strassburg, a good connoisseur, tells us that he 'grafted the first shoot in the German tongue'. His *Enîde* became a model in point of the correctness of his language and the purity of his rhymes. He is a good representative of 'chivalry' in both epic and lyric.

'Chivalry' was a peculiar blend of medieval institutions and ethical conceptions ultimately traceable through French, Provençals, and Romans to the Greeks. The wars of the Hohenstaufen emperors demanded strong retinues of mounted fighters. Many of these were unfree 'ministeriales' or '*dienstman*', who might be rewarded for their services by grants of land. Konrad II made their feoffs hereditable, and Frederick Barbarossa excluded from knighthood all except the sons of knights. In the *camaraderie* of war, emperors and kings, princes, free yeomen and ministeriales felt their solidarity and developed a common outlook; 'ritter' was a name of honour and carried definite obligations. The aspirant to knighthood was taught to steel his body by jumping, running, throwing the spear, fencing, and jousting; to show good manners by serving at table and in the bed-chamber; to dance in a seemly manner and play chess; to play instrumental music; to speak foreign tongues, especially French, and to perform the various activities connected with hunting and hawking. Having been provided with sword, helmet, and mail for his vigil he was dubbed a knight at a grand ceremony called the '*swertleite*'. These customs owe a great deal to France, but it was the knights of Hainault and Brabant who were regarded as models. The ideal of knighthood was 'gentlemanliness' in the sense of the καλοκαγαθία and μηδὲν ἄγαν of the Greeks; i.e. to steer a middle course between monkish asceticism and boorish sensuality, to play one's part on earth without neglecting religious duties, and to move through life with some regard for æsthetic values. This aspiration was closely bound up with the new deference paid to women, almost amounting to worship, occurring in both romances and love-lyrics. The

Crusades enabled the knight to serve his religion in the way he could best understand. There was much social activity and ceremonial. Many knightly poets met together in the retinue of great patrons like the Landgrave Hermann of Thuringia, who drew them to the Wartburg at Eisenach; and there are legends of their poetic competitions.

The themes of the Court Romances were drawn from various literatures. Classical antiquity supplied the fall of Troy, the *Æneid* and *Alexander*. Late Greek novels yielded such stories of faithful friends as Athis and Prophilias. French *chansons de geste* were the sources of German poems on Roland and Count William of Toulouse. Most prevalent of all was the Celtic cycle, comprising the tale of a Pictish (?) prince Tristan, who loves the Irish wife of a Cornish king, that of Arthur and his Round Table, and Perceval, Gawain, and other seekers of the Holy Grail. For the German poets the immediate sources of these Classical, Byzantine, Carolingian, and Celtic stories were French.

Adapting the French originals of Chrestiens de Troyes and looking up to Veldeke as model, the Alemannic poet Hartmann von Aue (ab. 1170-ab. 1215) treated in the Arthurian romance of *Erec* the theme of the uxorious husband who becomes slack (*verlegen*) in his duties to the world, and in *Iwein* that of the neglectful husband who prefers adventure to the married state. Hartmann used religious motives in his romance of *Gregorius*, the papal Oedipus and Prometheus in one, and in *Der arme Heinrich*, based on a Latin 'exemplum' or homiletic anecdote which tells how the readiness of a peasant's young daughter to give her life's blood to heal her leprous master, Heinrich, results in his miraculous cure and their marriage. Both Longfellow and Gerhart Hauptmann have used this story. The crystalline purity of Hartmann's style delighted his contemporaries. His fluent and elegant colloquial passages bring him near to Chrestiens, whom he at times surpasses through his insight into mood and motive. He is interested in the external trappings of chivalry and can dilate on the good points of a horse, but he is also deeply concerned with the requirements of religion and piety.

Wolfram von Eschenbach, who counts himself a Bavarian, though the dialect of his native region of Ansbach is East Franconian, deserves to be mentioned with Dante as one of the most impressive poets of the Middle Ages. His thought is deep and searching and his manner is strikingly individual – so much so that Gottfried von Strassburg, more skilled in the setting of words, tells us – in veiled allusion – of a poet who zigzags like a hare, flings his words about like knuckle-bones, and uses the hocus-pocus of a conjurer claiming to produce pearls from dust. He apparently handles his sources pretty freely, as we see from his *Willehalm*, based on a no longer extant version of the French *Bataille d'Aliscans*. This is the story of a historic Count Guillaume's fight against the Saracens, in which he is ably seconded by Gyburg (Guitburga) – a reminiscence of the defeat of the Arabs at Narbonne in 793, adding features from the defeat of Abderrahman (= Terramêr) at Poitiers by Charles Martel in 732. With great sympathy Wolfram portrays Gyburg and a youth, Rennewart, who beneath his scullion's garb bears a noble soul and performs prodigious feats. The poem, too, breathes a remarkable spirit of tolerance for the Saracens. *Parzival* relates the story of a boy brought up in a secluded spot away from his peers, but whose inborn nobility shines forth even through his mistakes, and in many adventures after he has entered the world of chivalry. He seeks the Holy Grail, an object endowed with miraculous powers of healing and sustaining, the goal of the perfect knight's quest. While agreeing with Chrestiens' *Li contes del Graal* in the main lines of his poem, Wolfram combats his version and adduces the Provençal Kŷôt as his authority, an author unknown to us. Wolfram certainly appears – from his references to certain personages, his use of names and divergences in detail from Chrestiens – to have had access to other sources, but some of the unique features of his work are undoubtedly due to his own supreme originality. To him the Grail is a block of stone, which keeps an aged man alive and which causes food to be served to the Grail company; on its top a commandment is sometimes inscribed, and every Good Friday its power is renewed by a dove which lays upon it a small white wafer. Whereas the story of Parzival's youth is pretty clearly a Celtic folk-tale, the genesis of the Grail and its ritual is not yet established. In Chrestiens it may have been a Christian ciborium, and in a MHG poem, *Diu Krône*, by Heinrich von dem Türlîn, in which Gawan is the hero, the 'kefse' (capsa) is a box containing bread; some would, however, link up Wolfram's conceptions with the Mohammedan Ka'aba or stone of Mecca and with Gnostic speculations. *Parzival* shows Wolfram's psychological insight to the full in such varied characters as Parzival's gallant father, Gahmuret, his loyal mother, Herzeloyde, the gay Gawan, the disconsolate Sigune, Parzival's half-brother (the heathen Feirefîz) and many another. Parzival himself has in turn to cast off his boorishness by becoming conventional and worldly – in which state he fails to put the question 'what ails thee?' to the Grail king, and thus release him from his hurt – and then he has to learn through the bitterest experience to grow out of his worldliness and discover the spiritual nature slumbering in his deeper self. He wins because he shows *unverzaget mannes muot* and conquers that *zwîvel* or war within the soul, which balked him of the highest. One episode alluded to in *Parzival* – the love of Sigune for Schîânatulander, who was killed while trying to recover for her a precious collar from a fleeing brach – Wolfram has treated in a separate poem with four-line stanzas and a peculiar metre, a poem miscalled *Titurel*.

Of the three great Court Romancers, Gottfried, a citizen of Strassburg, is the most subtle artist. Music and the arts of 'courtoisie' are his element, love and gallantry stir him more than joustings. In *Tristan* the æsthetic predominates over the ethical; and he sympathizes with the lovers Tristan and Isolde, who are swayed by an overmastering passion which has crept into their hearts, not through the mere magic virtue of a love-potion drunk by mistake, but irresistibly and inevitably right from the moment of their first meeting. He follows the 'courtly' version of the Anglo-Norman poet Thomas (as does also the Middle English *Sir Tristrem*) rather than the rougher version represented in German by the Brunswick knight Eilhart von Oberg (ab. 1180), from whom ultimately Hans Sachs' *Tragedia* of 1553 derived. Both Thomas and Eilhart (whose version is close to part of the French Bérol version) go back to a verse *estoire*, which in turn is thought to go back to an equally hypothetical Anglo-Norman *Ur-Tristan*, composed about 1140-50. Several later poets tried to complete Gottfried's poem, left unfinished, but they cannot vie with him and fall back on Eilhart.

In his literary excursus Gottfried mentions one Court Romance with the highest praise, Bligger von Steinach's *Umbehanc*, i.e. tapestry, but it has not survived. Fortunately we need not fear that much besides is lost, for a later writer, Rudolf von Ems, supplies two further reviews of the literature of his age and that preceding, and most of the names he cites are represented in the extant literature. This Rudolf is a typical '*Epigone*' or successor of the classical writers, a man of versatility rather than depth, an admirer of Gottfried rather than himself an originator. Among his works are the anecdotal legend of *Barlaam und Josaphat* (ultimately derived from the story of the Buddha), a knightly romance, *Willehalm*, and a rhymed chronicle – the latter a genre which became rather prevalent. The bourgeois poet Konrad von Würzburg turns Janus-like back to the Court Romance and forward to the mastersingers. He is excessively didactic in a somewhat ill-digested, but remarkable collection of Marianic images, *Die Goldene Schmiede*, but he excels in such short versified tales as *Otte mit dem Barte* (when the Emperor Otto swore by his beard, he must keep his oath), and *Engelhart* (a tale of true friendship.) Both he and Rudolf were able to use Latin sources direct. One late poem, *Johan ûz dem Vergiere* (South Hessian gleeman's version about 1300), is remarkable as going back to a Netherlandish source.

By the heroic epic (*Heldenepos*) is meant that body of epic poetry composed in the twelfth and thirteenth centuries which draws its themes from the Germanic past, especially the age of migrations, and treats them in a style more archaic in words and constructions than that prevalent in the Court Romances. If some of its authors were knights, many were gleemen writing for the knight's entertainment. As Professors Ker and Heusler have shown in their treatises *Epic and Romance* and *Lied und Epos* respectively, their epics do not arise from the mere stringing together of a number of mutually complementary episodic lays; we no longer, for example, regard the *Nibelungenlied* as a collection of lays 'sung together'. The epics represent rather the stylistic elaboration or 'intumescence' – partially under the influence of the Latin epic – of some lay tersely narrating a whole plot, which the epic writer proceeds to deck out with supernumerary characters, secondary episodes, and lingering descriptions. In form the German hero-epics are often written in a stanza of four long lines with end-rhymes *aa | bb*; the first hemistich has throughout three lifts and ends in an unstressed syllable, whereas the second hemistich has three lifts, including one on its final syllable, except in the case of the last hemistich of all which is provided with four lifts. The material is of various origin: some epics go back to a tale of a Gothic king Ermanaric of the fourth century, some to the struggle of the Ostrogothic king Theodoric the Great with Odoacer for his kingdom in northern Italy (Dietrich of Bern, i.e. Verona; Rabenschlacht = battle of Ravenna), some to Frankish tales of Wolfdietrich, a son of the great Clovis, and of a prince Siegfried, who woos Brunhild and is murdered, some to the downfall of the Burgundians in 437, and still others to a tale of the abduction of Hilde, and her father's pursuit, a subject brought by Vikings from the Baltic to the mouth of the Rhine. Attila, still remembered as the scourge of God in the Norse poems, was regarded with a friendly eye by the Ostrogoths, who transmitted this impression to their Bavarian neighbours; his concubine Hildico, in whose presence he died in 453, became a Burgundian princess, Grimhild, sister of the Gunther who had perished in 437. The Latin epic *Waltharius* and the OE *Waldere* as well as a late MHG *Walther und Hildegunde*, tell of the successful escape of a hostage from Attila's court with a fellow captive, Hildegunde.

In the *Nibelungenlied* the tale of Siegfried's death is combined with that of the downfall of the Burgundians, which that death motivates. We are helped in reconstructing its previous history by the *Thidrekssaga*, a collection of stories made by a Norwegian at Bergen about 1250 from the mouth of Low German merchants. The 'downfall' appears to have constituted a separate epic, *Der Nibelunge Nôt*, written about 1170 on the basis of a supposed Bavarian lay of Kriemhild, of the seventh or eighth century, which in its turn derived through the Ostrogoths from a Bur-gundian lay. The poet of the *Nibelungenlied* took the *Nôt* and welded it with the material he had epicized out of a – perhaps – Rhenish lay of Siegfried's death, taking care to smooth the transitions. The *Nibelungenlied* has come down in a number of MSS., of which B (St. Gall) is taken as representing the oldest redaction, while C (Donaueschingen) has under-gone the influence of 'courtoisie'. The poem is followed by a lament for the dead in rhymed couplets known as *Die Klage*.

Of all the hero epics the *Nibelungen* was deservedly the m ost popular. The great variety, the poignancy of its scenes, its well-drawn figures seen in full development like Kriemhild and Hagen, the contrast between Kriemhild and Brunhild, the Burgundian brothers, especially young Gîselhêr, the courteous margrave Rüdegêr, forced by loyalty to his ruler to fight against those he has come to regard as friends, the brave minstrel Volkêr – all are unforgettable. Though there are allusions – in a speech of Hagen's – to a mythical background with a hoard-guarding dragon whose blood makes Siegfried invulnerable except at a spot where a leaf fell between his shoulders, and though Siegfried uses the invisible-making Tarnkappe in helping Gunther win the contests with Brunhilde, the drama as a whole is borne by human beings acting under the impulse of strong passions and not by mere figures of myth.

Like the *Nibelungenlied* the *Kudrun* epic is a conglomerate. Apart from a gleeman's Robinson-Crusoe-like prologue it consists of the story of the abduction of Hagen's daughter Hilde by a Danish king Hetel, who marries her, after a hard battle with the pursuing father, and of the story of their daughter Kudrun, likewise kidnapped, but by an unsuccessful suitor, whose mother sets her to menial tasks, until after many years she is rescued by her lover Herwig. In the Kudrun portion there is some repetition of motives from the Viking story of Hilde, but certain features and names appear to go back to the story of Dietrich's nephew Herbort (perhaps treated in a lost epic of ab. 1250) and to a ballad of the so-called Südeli-type, depicting the state of a woman torn between two suitors, but keeping faith with her betrothed. This Kudrun-epic – composed probably about 1230, in a stanza differing from the *Nibelungen* in the greater length of its last half line – is preserved only in the Ambras manuscript written in 1504-15 by Hans Ried of Bozen (Bolsano) at the behest of the Emperor Maximilian.

The Ostrogothic Dietrich-cycle is scattered about among a number of MHG epics and lays, of which some deal with pseudo-historical episodes and others are mythical. Among the themes of the former are Dietrich's flight, his struggle with Ermanarich (a ruler of 200 years earlier), who was substituted for the Otacher of the *Hildebrandslied*, the battle of Ravenna, the slaying of Attila's sons through the treachery of Witege (= Vidigoia, a Gothic ruler mentioned by Jordanes). The mythical poems tell of Dietrich's feats in freeing a maiden from a dwarf, Laurin, and in fighting against Tyrolese giants (*Eckenlied*); in *Sigenôt* the great Dietrich is actually held prisoner by a giant till freed by Hildebrand.

The Merovingian Wolfdietrich, the son of Clovis (himself called Hugdietrich), suffers from the intrigues of a traitor, Saben (OE Seafola), but is supported by a faithful henchman, Berchtung, and his loyal band of sons. About 1210-20 a MHG epic was composed bringing in further the story of a Russian hero, Ortnit, a dragon-slayer, whose kingdom, Nov*gorod* became associated with the Lago di *Garda*. The Merovingian lay developed on independent lines in France to the story of *Floovant* (Chlodowinc).

From some time between 1250 and 1280 dates a remarkable poem usually called *Meier Helmbrecht*, after the title to the text in the Ambras manuscript. It is the work of a gleeman, perhaps a farmer's son, but one familiar with the ways of courts. He sympathizes with the toiling peasantry against the reprobate knights and grasping clergy. Satirist and humorist though he is, he does not shrink from the tragic in this story of a farmer's son, who, spoilt by mother and sister, and heedless of his father's ripe wisdom, joins a band of robber knights and ends on the gallows. We gather from the poem that such tales as the fall of Troy, *Roland*, the *Rabenschlacht*, and *Herzog Ernst* were still popular and that it was the fashion to interlard one's speech with scraps of Flemish and even of Czech (due to Bohemian rule in Austria from 1246). We also learn something of life on the soil and of various social customs, e.g. in connection with marriage and the administration of the sheriff, in this still fresh and vivid poem.

The heroic epic and Court Romance were accompanied by a prolific output of lyric poetry (about 1175-1300).

The lyric of the German knights, the 'Minnesang', is uniform neither in form nor content. Austrian poets like the Kürenberger use a stanza of four long lines, in which each half line has three stresses, with the exception of the last which has four – in fact the same metre as in the *Nibelungenlied*; another, Dietmar von Aist, composed poems in rhymed couplets as in the Court Romance, but with assonances for some of the rhymes. On the other hand, the Frankish and Alemannic (Swiss, Alsatian) minnesingers have adopted the Provençal principal of tripartition of the stanza, in which two *stollen* of similar metrical structure (*Aufgesang*) are followed by an *Abgesang* of divergent structure, e.g. with a rhyme-scheme for the whole like *ab | ab || cdc* or *abc | abc || deef*. In content, too, there are important differences between the Austrian singers, whose art is often characterized as '*altheimisch*', and their West German contemporaries. In the Kürenberger's songs, it is the lady who woos the reluctant knight; she thought she had tamed him like her falcon, but he slipped the silken jesses and flew away. In Dietmar, too, it is the woman who, peering across a heath, sees a falcon flying free and thinks of her absent lover, sought by other women. The Kürenberger has both 'Frauenstrophen' and so-called 'Wechsel', i.e. a combination of a stanza put into the mouth of a woman with one attributed to the knight; but these groupings do not embody a real colloquy, but rather two monologues. As Uhland put it, such verses are like two distant evening-bells chiming together. There is, however, a dialogue in Dietmar's simple 'Tagelied' in which lovers say farewell to each other at dawn. Whether these less conventional songs of the Austrians link on to a native love-poetry or not, it is noteworthy that the Kürenberger mentions the 'huote', i.e. spies or 'merkære' set to watch over a lady's virtue, an office like that of the Provençal 'lauzangier'; and the Tagelied has its parallel in the Provençal 'alba'. The *sirventes* – a short satirical or occasional poem – may have been the source of some of the German poems; e.g. of political content, outside the love-lyric proper.

The 'canso' of the troubadours, written in the Langue d'oc with great formal dexterity, offers considerable variety within its limits of conventionality and its respectful attitude of feudal allegiance to the married women, who inspired it. Full of subtle reasonings, its studied elegance is occasionally relieved by irony and satire, and it comprises many types, of which several are found in German literature as well, e.g. the crusading song (*Kreuzlied*), represented by Friedrich von Hausen and Walther von der Vogelweide, and the 'planh' or threnody, e.g. Reinmar's lament at the death of Leopold. The 'tenso' and 'joc partit' developed the casuistry of love and the 'pastorela' sang the love of a poet for a shepherdess. The origin and spread of all this conventional poetry are still in dispute. Burdach attributes the first impulse to Arabic culture in the court-circle of Andalusia, whereas Brinkmann points to the influence on both Provençal and German lyric of medieval Latin love-poetry, fostered by an interest in Ovid taken by clerics, who sometimes even engaged in competition with the knights. It is also, however, indisputable that there are close resemblances between the Minnesang and certain Latin poems of the Goliards ('filii Goliae', i.e. of Goliath, or from *gula*, 'throat', i.e. spongers) or *Vagantes* such as are preserved in the *Carmina Burana* (Benediktbeuern MS. of first half thirteenth century), especially in the treatment of nature and the introduction of politics and occasional classical allusions.

Hartmann von Aue, Friedrich von Hausen, and Heinrich von Mohrungen may be taken as representative of Provençal inspiration in German
poetry, though all show some personal originality. Hartmann's lyric
poetry includes a *Kreuzlied* and some lines on worldly wisdom. Von
Hausen, who fell at Philomelium in 1190 on Barbarossa's crusade, in one
poem portrays the conflict between his heart, bound in love to a woman,
and his body, eager to fight the Saracen. Greatest of the Minnesänger
before Walther, Heinrich von Mohrungen, a Thuringian knight, brings
in more of the outer world and is of stronger utterance than his fellows.
His comparisons are apt and neat. The bemused lover is like a child
snatching at a mirror reflection and breaking the glass. A parrot or
starling would learn to say 'Minne' with greater speed than the lady of
his heart. However, he will not, like the nightingale, cease from singing
when the season of love is past, but like the swallow will sing whether
glad or sad.

The greatest Minnesänger is Walther von der Vogelweide. He learnt
the art of poetry and music at the Viennese court, where he spent happy
days mingling with an æsthetically responsive aristocracy. He gained
much from association with the Alsatian poet, Reinmar von Hagenau, a
pensive dreamer, but a deft and subtle weaver of lyric measures. On
Duke Friedrich's death he became a wanderer, and, perhaps through
contact with 'vagantes', was moved to compose songs of 'uncourtly' love
(*niedere Minne*) in praise of some village girl. A deep, heart-felt joy in the
glories of springtime, bright with blossoms and singing birds, and a
sprightly and frolicsome mood pervade these simply expressed songs, with
their cunning rhymes and melodious rhythms. The girls dancing on the
village green must lift the brim of their hat that he may see his loved one's
face. He lets a girl tell how she lay beside her lover under the linden-tree,
and he is proud to betroth himself with a glass ring instead of a queen's
gold. He did not, however, abandon *hohe Minne*, and continued to praise
the court ladies. He admires a woman of noble carriage as she moves
with stately dignity across the hall, a sun among the lesser stars. Just as
the troubadours praised their fair Provence, so Walther rejoices with
patriotic fervour in Germany, German breeding (*zuht*), and German
women. Walther was a religious and political poet as well as a singer of
love. He supported in turn Philip of Swabia, and then – on Philip's death
– the rival claimant, Otto, and finally the Emperor Friedrich II, from
whom he received a feoff at Würzburg, a home to 'keep the frost from
his toes'. He was no mere turncoat, for his main concern was to buttress
the might of Germany's rulers against the temporal (not spiritual) pretensions of the great pope Innocent III. At one time we hear of Walther

at the Landgrave's court at Eisenach; an entry among the travelling expenses of Bishop Wolfgēr of Passau in 1203 concerns the gift of a few 'solidi' to buy a fur coat to 'Walthero cantori de Vogelweide'. We do not even know his birthplace, but we suspect that he was a younger son of a ministerial knight.

During Walther's lifetime an Austrian, Neidhart von Reuental, amused his fellow knights by borrowing rustic themes from the old dancing songs. In the summer songs the girls are all agog and beg their mothers to let them dance on the green. One winter song tells how the table-trestles and chairs in the farm-house are pushed aside and the fiddler strikes up for the clod-hoppers to dance. One belle secures two partners and the dance ends in a free fight.

Even before Walther there had been gnomic or wisdom poetry of literary merit. A Rhenish gleeman, Hergēr, pities the homeless wanderer, worse off than a hedgehog. He sorrowfully notes that might is right in a struggle for a bone by two dogs, and that the wolf cannot change his ways even after he has become a monk. Playing a game of chess the wolf was so distracted by the sight of a sheep that he lost two castles for a pawn. Finest of all is his hymn of praise to God beginning 'Worts of the wood, grains of gold and all the abysses are known, O Lord, to thee'. Walther, too, imparts moral and religious teachings, e.g. in his praise of self-control, which makes a man able to slay lions and giants, and in his *Leich* which contains a pæan to the Virgin, barmherzec muoter'. A little later a Rhenish knight, Reinmar von Zweter, composed *Lügenmärchen* or nonsense-rhymes, e.g. 'I saw a crow catching pigs with a hawk in the brook', etc. Spervogel has left a specimen of the praeambulum (*Priamel*) in which a series of paralleled premises is epitomized at the end, e.g. he who seeks a friend when he has none, or tries to follow a track in melting snow, or buys goods without looking at them, etc., will live to regret his folly. Some of the pithiest wisdom-verses were gathered in the early part of the thirteenth century under the title *Bescheidenheit* (not 'modesty', but 'wisdom', 'discrimination'), attributed to an Alemannic gleeman, Freidank.

Towards the end of the thirteenth century the *Minnesang* began to ossify into the *Meistergesang*. The art of singing passed to glee-clubs containing both lay and clerical members. By the fifteenth century regular schools emerge, first at Mainz and then in many towns, especially Nuremberg, but not in the north. The apprentice to poetry – often a handicraftsman – was put through a rigid training, in the course of which he could graduate from 'Schreiber' through 'Schulfreund' to 'Dichter' and 'Meister' by observing scrupulously the rules set forth in the

Tabulatur'. Public singing and poetic competitions were held in a church, where the judges or 'Merker' disqualified candidates guilty of serious breaches of the rules, totted up the minor errors of those remaining and awarded the winner a silver chain with a medallion. Wagner has portrayed these practitioners in his opera, especially Hans Sachs, who has left numerous mastersongs. A 'Singschule' survived at Memmingen in Swabia till 1878.

A less regulated form of lyric is found in the 'Volkslied', an expression used by Herder to cover songs known in previous ages variously as 'Bergreihen', 'Gassenhauer' (now applied to vulgarized song-hits), and 'Reuterliedlein'. The term 'Volkslied' is now taken to imply popularization and a certain stylistic conformity to simpler tastes rather than to deny individual authorship. Goethe's *Heidenröslein*, Heine's *Lorelei*, Uhland's *Ich hatt' einen Kameraden*, and several songs by Hermann Löns (see p. 332) have become folk-songs in this sense, and in the older collections research has revealed that not only the Goliards' poems, but also some of the knightly love-songs have percolated down to the people, whose singers, however, have often profoundly modified them ('zersingen' is the term used). Important collections are the *Lochheimer Liederbuch* (1460), and that of the Augsburg nun, Clara Hätzlerin, in 1471. A naïve directness, a proclivity to animate nature, a love of dramatic dialogue, and a certain uncouthness of diction are common characteristics. The songs deal with the simple human themes of love and parting, loyalty and treachery, the joy of spring and burden of winter, and also such historical or contemporary events as the victory of the Swiss at Sempach (1386), or Robin Hood tales like *Der Lindenschmid* (1490). The archives at Freiburg im Breisgau contain over 125,000 specimens from medieval times till today.

In the first half of the fourteenth century arose a new prose literature, that of mysticism. Among the Dominicans, conversant with the neo-Platonic doctrines in their Christian adaptations by St. Augustine, were men who by meditation and contemplation sought ecstasy in a mystic union with God. To the great preacher Eckhart even Christ and the sacraments counted less than the mystic birth of God in the soul. He wrested from a stubborn German the means of expression for thoughts and experiences hitherto unformulated. His pupil, Seuse, or Suso (from his mother's name, his father's being von Berg), has been called the prose 'Minnesänger' of the clerics. He has left not only several mystical treatises, including *Das Buch von der ewigen Weisheit*, but also a biography of himself, written by a woman friend and revised by him. A third mystic, Tauler, who had studied Eckhart, proclaimed the omnipotence of God's grace and pleaded for a simple faith and against the growing abuses of the Church. Perhaps the most remarkable prose work of all is *Der Ackermann aus Böhmen*, written about 1400 in Bohemia. The author, Johannes von Saaz (or von Tepl), who had lost his loved wife, stages a disputation between a ploughman and Death, in which the ploughman turns against the older medieval view of life as a preparation for eternity and appeals to the Romans and even to Plato in support of the intrinsic value of life here and now. Death – not unlike the wise old father in *Meier Helmbrecht* – finally stresses the worth of a peaceful and active life and a clean conscience. In this work is seen the influence of Wycliffe's teachings disseminated by Oxford students and by the court circle of Queen Anne of Bohemia, daughter of the Emperor Charles IV and sister of King Wenceslas.

The court of Charles IV was, altogether, an important centre for the infiltration of the New Learning from Italy, and the consolidation of the modern written language. Burdach has shown the importance of the proto-notary and chancellor Johann von Neumarkt, and of the visits of Rienzi. The former compiled collections of model letters and formularies and was an industrious translator. In the meantime a more popular form of entertainment, the 'Schwank', was coming into vogue.

The 'Schwank' or *fabliau*, a humorous tale, in tone often coarse to the pitch of obscenity and in purpose insistently didactic, is well represented in rhymed couplets of the thirteenth, and in prose of the fifteenth century. Von der Hagen has gathered typical specimens of verse in his *Gesamtabenteuer*. The hero, e.g. the *Pfaffe Amis* of a bourgeois gleeman, Der Stricker, is often a clever trickster of his fellows. Later, the *Pfaffe von Kalenberg* – whose name survives in the French word for a pun, viz. *calembour* – emerges about 1470 and the better known *Till Eulenspiegel* – in reality a country lad from the Brunswick region who lived in the fourteenth century and whose pranks were originally narrated in Low German – appeared in a High German edition at Strassburg in 1515. The popularity of the prose tale received impetus, too, from translations of Boccaccio and of Leoni's *Fiori di virtù* made by the Nuremberg patrician 'Arigo' (Heinrich Schlüsselfeder); of Boccaccio, of Æsop's fables, and of the *Griseldis* of Petrarch by Heinrich Stainhöwel of Ulm, the last work having been introduced to Germans as early as 1436 by Erhart Gross of Nuremberg. Luther cultivated the fable, and the prose tales remained in favour, many being gathered together in such works as Jörg Wickram's *Rollwagenbüchlein* (1555), designed to while away the time on a coach journey, and Johannes Pauli's *Schimpf* (i.e. 'jest') *und Ernst* (1522), a treasure-trove of folklore. Of great interest are the successive developments of the Faust-story, which grew up round a certain Georg Faust (born at Knittlingen in Württemberg, in 1480, died at Staufen im Breisgau either 1539 or 1540), a scholar expelled from various university towns on account of his charlatanry. A few tales were told of him by the Nuremberger Christoph Rosshirt in 1570, but it is an anonymous text in a Wolfenbüttel MS. of 1575, perhaps derived from a Latin original, which formed the kernel of the most influential of the Faust-books, viz. the *Historia von D. Joh. Fausten* (1587), published by the Frankfort printer Johann Spies, who claimed to have received a MS. from a friend at Speyer. Spies, a strong Lutheran, points the moral of the story of an adventurer and debauchee, whose limbs are broken to pieces by the devil on the expiry of a twenty-four years' pact. From Spies are derived two branches of the Faust-tradition. Through an English version Marlowe was inspired to his drama of 1589, which was brought to Germany by English actors and eventually gave rise to Lessing's remarks in his seventeenth *Literaturbrief* and his fragmentary play, and maintained a somewhat changed existence in puppet-plays. In Germany, Spies's book was revised by Georg Rudolf Widmann, whose reflective and antipapal work appeared at Hamburg in 1599, this version in its turn being abridged in 1674 by Johann Nikolaus Pfitzer, who introduced the story of Faust's love for a simple girl. On Pfitzer is based the *Faustbuch des christlich Meynenden* (Frankfort and Leipzig, 1725), sold at fairs in editions on inferior paper, one of which fell into Goethe's hands.

Among other so-called 'Volksbücher' or chap-books which found their way into Elizabethan literature is *Bruder Rausch*. It came to England by way of Holland, appeared in 1572 as Friar Rush, and is the source of Dekker's *If this be not a good play, the Divell is in it* (1612), for it is the story of the havoc wrought by the devil in a monastery.

It is now time to survey the changes of taste and temper manifested in these developments. The decisive century is the fifteenth, poor though it is in poetic achievement.

The fifteenth century was a time of revolutionary change in religion, politics, economics, and general culture. With the decline of imperial and papal authority the knighthood crumbled away. Its outworn conventions gave way before coarseness and sensuality. The centre of gravity shifted to the towns, and money rather than landed property became the standard of value. Feudal territorialism grew to be less important than international commerce, especially with France, Italy, and the Netherlands. The townsman's characteristic virtues of sobriety, common sense, and practical efficiency gradually ousted the sensuous refinements of chivalry and the ascetic negations of monasticism. A rather gross conviviality among the worldly was set off among the more spiritual by a deep mystic yearning. Poetry gave place to prose, for with the spread of printing the habit of silent reading was preferred to recitation, and hence it was not so necessary to versify non-æsthetic works. The townsman first developed his literature from aristocratic models, but – significantly – he chose the ruder forms of chivalric poetry, e.g. the *Alexander* and earlier *Tristan*, prevalent before the spirit of moderation and tempered eroticism of the classical age. Prose romance had blossomed in Irish legends and tales, in the Welsh *mabinogion*, and in France before it came to Germany. After sporadic efforts – like the Low German *Lanzelet* of the thirteenth century – prose was for a time confined to historical and juridical literature, books of travel and natural history, saints' legends, sermons, and the writings of the mystics. In the fifteenth century the chief writers of prose romance were two women of high birth, Elizabeth of Nassau-Saarbrücken, who did not shrink from making a butcher's daughter the heroine of her *Hug Schapeler*, and a royal princess, Eleanor – daughter of James I of Scotland and wife of the Duke of the Tyrol – whose *Pontus und Sidonia* draws upon the Anglo-Norman story of Childe Horn. The great outburst of prose literature, however, came with the Reformation.

The literature of the Reformation spans the period between the nailing of the ninety-five theses against indulgences by Luther to the door of the castle chapel at Wittenberg in 1517 and the conclusion of the Pact of Augsburg in 1555. Partly in Latin, and partly in German, it is a literature of controversial pamphlets and broadsheets rather than of belles-lettres. As its aim was to inform, enlighten, uplift, or scourge, rather than to afford æsthetic delight, its language was apt to be heady and extravagant, but it helped to make German less stilted and less subservient to the fetters of Latin syntax. Its greatest writer, Luther, wrote militant articles of masterly clarity, e.g. *An den christlichen Adel deutscher Nation* (1520), in which he belabours the pretensions of papacy and priesthood; *Von der babylonischen Gefangenschaft der Kirche* (1520), which questions the validity of the sacraments; and *Von der Freiheit eines Christenmenschen* (1520), which exhorts the believer in Christ to seek direct communion with God. By his marriage with a former nun, Katharina von Bora, Luther founded the Protestant vicarage or manse; he showed his practical interest in conjugal problems in his sensible treatise *Von der Ehe*.

In contrast with Luther, humanism favoured a rather intellectualistic attitude to the conduct of life. Hence vice is stigmatized as folly in such poems of international repute as the *Narrenschiff* (1494) by the Strassburg humanist, SEBASTIAN BRANT (1457-1521), and in the *Narrenbeschwörung* (1512) by another Alsatian, the Franciscan THOMAS MURNER (1475-1537) who also satirized the Lutheran reformation as a monstrous piece of folly in his scurrilous poem *Von dem grossen lutherischen Narren, wie ihn Dr Murner beschworen hat* (1522). Yet another Alsatian, JOHANN FISCHART (1546–90), mocked at a prevalent superstition – the faith in the Old Moore's almanacs of the time – in his work *Aller Praktik Grossmutter* (1572–74). He is still better known for his coarse and exuberant imitations of Rabelais, and for his poem *Das Glückhafft Schiff von Zürich* (1576), in which he celebrates a journey made in record time by some Zurich citizens attending a shooting festival at Strassburg.

With the sixteenth century the drama grew in literary importance, and we must cast a glance at its previous history.

Serious drama had a religious origin. A portion of a service sung at one of the great Christian festivals was isolated and speech substituted for song with the retention of a few sequences and hymns. Drama gradually emerged through the creation of a 'scene', e.g. the introduction of the manger in France for the Christmas celebration, and the organization of 'tropes' (words introduced into the text of the mass) into dialogue as achieved by the monk Tutilo of St. Gall. 'Action' came into the Christmas celebrations with the rocking of the Christ-child by Joseph at Mary's bidding (like the Candlemas rocking of the baby at Blidworth), and the entry of the shepherds; at Epiphany there were the Three Wise Men and Herod as well. Eventually Christmas and Epiphany plays were amalgamated. The Easter Plays centred on the Holy Sepulchre, at which there was a colloquy between the three Maries. Passion Plays followed the events from the Last Supper to the burial; a comic element was introduced in a scene in which the Maries deal with an ointment-seller. The play best known today, that of Oberammergau, performed every ten years, dates only from 1634, the first text being the *Tragedi vom Leben und Sterben Jesu Christi* of 1662. The Bordesholm (Holstein) *Marienklage* of 1475 is a dramatization of Mary's lament for her Son; the *Ludus de Antichristo* (ab. 1160) and the Kremsmünster play of St. Dorothy in 1350 are dramatized legends. Sometimes the ending is happy, as when Faust's prototype, Theophilus, is saved by the Virgin's appeal to Jesus from the consequences of the devil's pact, or when Jutta (Pope Joan) buys release from damnation by choosing earthly disgrace. The inexorable doom of the ten foolish virgins in a play produced at Eisenach in 1322 drew a vehement protest from the Thuringian landgrave, Friedrich der Freidige.

As the number of actors grew, the scene was shifted to the market-place, which in at least one case had a balcony at one end representing Heaven, and was flanked by 'houses' (*aedes, Burgen, Höfe*), e.g. that of Pilate and that of Herod, roofed and curtained off as fixed stations for certain actors.

In the foreground was the gate of Hell for the 'harrowing'. In the case of the Corpus Christi processions of fraternities and guilds, *Fronleichnamsspiele* (cf. the English York and Townley plays) were performed at the halts. 'Moralities', so prevalent in England and France, had no vogue in Germany.

The Protestants looked askance at all the medieval mysteries, and the educated turned rather to the Latin dramas, written for performance at the humanistic gymnasia. These revived the ideas of Plautus and Terence. The general public was assisted by German arguments in rhyme. Starting with the Latin dramas of Dutchmen like Gnaphaeus and Germans like Jakob Wimpfeling (*Stylpho*, 1470) and Philipp Nikodemus Frischlin, a Protestant school-drama was built up, which gradually became germanized and continued to the end of the seventeenth century, when CHRISTIAN WEISE (1642-1708), headmaster at Zittau, wrote a series of German dramas (*Masaniello*, 1682). The Latin drama grew up again in the Catholic south and in the Rhineland among the Jesuits and, to a less extent, the Benedictines. Acting and recitations as a preparation for public life formed an important part of the school curriculum, and at the end of the school year a 'Schlusskomedie', composed and directed by the form-master of the 'rhetorica', was performed by a large number of scholars. The stage was lavishly decorated for banquets, weddings, and assemblies; music, ballets, and comic interludes were provided for an audience which included the highest and lowest. Ancient and modern martyrdoms, especially of Catholic missionaries, and events of Jewish history (especially the story of Judith) were the stock of these 'Jesuit dramas', which were filled with action and pointed to a definite moral aim. This was indicated in the form of the title, e.g. *Pietas Victrix sive Flavius Constantinus Magnus de Maxentio Tyranno Victor*. Tragic guilt consisted in pusillanimity and indolence, or a stubborn refusal to recognize the will of God. Death, though painted in all its morbid horrors in harrowing execution and torture-scenes, was conceived as a transfiguration. The drama was to inspire terror at the spectacle of dire suffering at the same time as compassion with the virtuous sufferer.

The *Fastnacht(s)spiel*, or carnival comedy, is traced back by some to the dramatized dances performed at heathen spring festivals, the fool with his slapstick representing a fertility dæmon holding a phallic symbol. In Germany it flourished during the fifteenth and sixteenth centuries, especially at Nuremberg, where a shoemaker, HANS SACHS, was its chief exponent. He has left us eighty-five plays, each consisting of about 360 *Knittelverse*, i.e. a 'freer' form with a line of from anything between 6 and 15 syllables and a 'stricter' form with 8-9 syllables, but frequent disregard of normal prose stressing. A close observer of human nature, with a gift for witty dialogue, he produced plays sustained by a manageable number of characters, which are still acted with success today, e.g. *Der fahrende Schüler im Paradies* (1550), *Der Bauer im Fegefeuer* (1552). On a lower level were the much earlier dramatic scenes (especially of a trial at law) enacted by the Nuremberg butchers' guild at their annual procession or *Schembartlaufen* (MHG *scheme*, 'mask'), and plays of the first half of the fifteenth century by two Nurembergers, HANS ROSENPLÜT and HANS FOLZ. Acted by apprentices in the street or market-place, these dramas were as inclusive as a modern revue and even less squeamish in their sexual and digestive allusions. Their last representative is Jakob Ayrer, who subsequently came under the influence of the *englische Komödianten*. The remarkable play in German, *The Comedy of the Crocodile*, a satire on the Nuremberg patricians, was performed towards the end of the sixteenth century.

English actors (*englische Komödianten*) paid a flying visit to Dresden in 1586. In 1592 Brown, Saxfield, and Bradstreet brought a troupe to Frankfort, and soon English acting secured bases in the Brunswick court at Wolfenbüttel and in the Hessian at Cassel, spreading later to Brandenburg and Saxony, but hardly touching Southern Germany. In a troupe consisting of 10-18 actors, and an orchestra of 6 instrumentalists, who could act as supers, the manager usually took the part of the clown (*Bouset, Stockfisch, Pickelhering*), as often he alone could 'get across' his jokes in German, and in that role he could save a dull piece from falling flat. Usually men played the women's parts. The arrival of the company at a town – sometime round market-day – on a fortnight's visit was heralded by a drummer and bill-poster; they unpacked their *Rüstwäglein* of its properties, and set up a stage of scaffolding in the town hall, schoolhouse, ballroom, or fencing loft. The stage was divided by curtains into a front and back stage, and a minstrels' gallery was sometimes erected. Blue hangings represented clouds, and there was a trap-door for the ghost. *Gammer Gurton's Needle* was one of the first dramas to be played at Frankfurt in 1592. Subsequently we hear of performances at various places of the *London Prodigal*, *The Jew of Malta*, *Romeo and Juliet*, *The Merchant of Venice*, *Dr Faustus* (1626, at Dresden and Leipzig), and many others, some of which eventually declined to the status of puppet shows. Verse was turned into broken German prose, with much ranting, moralizing, and gagging, and the action enlivened by a good deal of knock-about. These actors were often treated with esteem, and a few settled down – like Thomas Sackville at Brunswick – as respectable citizens. One German dramatist of note, JAKOB AYRER (1543-1605), learnt from *die neue englische*

Manier und Art to make use of the fool. His *Schöne Sidea* treats the same theme as Shakespeare's *Tempest*. He and others learnt much, too, from the English *Singspiele*, vaudevilles portraying scolds and cuckolds and diversified by jigs and pavans. Despite the importance of the English actors, however, Shakespeare is not known by name till a hundred years later.

The seventeenth century in Germany is the age of baroque. Just as in architecture and painting the baroque marks a reaction against the repose and forthrightness of the Renaissance in favour of an equipoise of antagonistic systems of stresses and a whole-hearted acceptance of ornament, so the literature tends to the tortuous, the antithetic, and the grandiloquent. Its time limits are roughly 1620 and 1710, within which development is noticeable from a stiff correctitude earlier on to the great verve and splendour in the 'Hochbarock' dramatists, ANDREAS GRYPHIUS (1616-64) and D. C. VON LOHENSTEIN (1635-83), reaching an extreme in the introduction of *Schwulst*, or bombast. A new style emerged in Spain in Guevara's *Libro aureo de Marco Aurelio* (1528), finding expression in England in Lyly's *Euphues*, based upon Sir Thomas North's translation *The Diall of Princes* (1577). The ultra-refined style (*estilo culto*) of LUIS DE GÓNGORA (1561-1627) passed by way of the Italian writers Marino and Guarini (*Il Pastor Fido*, 1585) into Germany. Certain affectations and pedantries of the followers of this new style are satirized by Molière in *Les précieuses ridicules*.

The age was partial to brilliant spectacles; its true expression is found in the opera, an importation from Italy – Rinuccini's *Dafne* was translated in 1627 – and in the drama, especially tragedy. Pompous and sententious, its drama heightens rather than portrays. This is due to the predilections of those officials of bourgeois parentage at the courts of minor princes in Northern Germany and Silesia, who devised and staged baroque dramas. Having been at a classical school and university, they revelled in classical allusions and in the figures of Roman history. It is understandable, too, that, at a time when trading companies were opening up India and the Far East, they should favour exotic themes, and that the events of the Thirty Years' War should leave a ground-tone of pessimism and a bent towards violent and harrowing scenes and the supernatural. Today the reader requires an effort to appreciate their plots and diction. The Alexandrines, with strong caesura and end-rhymes, verses teeming with epithets and far-sought metaphors, prove monotonous unless their impassioned feeling or stateliness are brought out by good declamation.

Among the baroque dramas we mention Gryphius' tragedies of martyrdom, *Catharina von Georgien* (1647), and *Ermordete Majestät oder Carolus*

Stuardus (1649) – which brings out our king Charles I's composure in bearing his fate – and (most typical) *Cardenio und Celinde* (1657), with its phantasms and corpses, its scenes of vengeance, and its highly moral conclusion. Daniel Casper von Lohenstein, with his six tragedies, e.g. *Cleopatra, Sophonisbe,* and *Ibrahim Sultan,* and his novel *Arminius,* was one of the heads of the so-called second Silesian school. His dramas mark a height till the advent of a cooler and 'correcter' type of drama favoured by Gottsched.

In prose fiction a new impetus came from Spain. The *Schelmenroman,* a novel of disreputable life, is a German development of the *novela picaresca*[1] which in the sixteenth century portrayed the social abuses of a Spain infested with beggars and adventurers. It was introduced at Munich in 1615 by Ægidius Albertinus' translation of the *Guzman de Alfarache* and at Augsburg in 1617 by Niclas Ulenhart's translation of *Lazarillo de Tormes.* The picaresque novel was followed about 1714 by the so-called *Avanturier*-novels copied from such Dutch models as NICOLAAS HEINSIUS' (ab. 1656-1718) *De vermakelijke* (entertaining) *avanturier* (1695), which tell how a man works his way up through life till he becomes a respectable citizen. Another type of Spanish novel, the vision or *sueño,* associated especially with the satirist Quevedo y Villegas, reached Germany indirectly by way of France; the impulse was not spent even in 1703 when the Welshman Elis Wynne wrote his *Visions of the Sleeping Bard.*

Of the picaresque novel the chief representative is *Der abenteuerliche Simplizissimus* (1669) of HANS (or JOHANN JAKOB) CHRISTOFFEL VON GRIMMELSHAUSEN († 1676). A Parzival-like boy, who has lost his home in the Thirty Years' War and is brought up in a wood by a hermit (in reality his father), is bandied about between the opposing armies till he acquires more than his share of worldly wisdom. Having found a temporary resting-place on a remote island, he is brought back in a sequel to become a maker of calendars. Vivid pictures are given of rich and poor, military and peasantry, forest, sea, and town; we learn much, too, of the witch-lore and demonology then rife. Above all the author sympathetically follows a character through a most variegated career and – except for the usual didactic and moral padding – does not let our interest flag.

Of the *sueño*-novelists the best known is HANS MICHAEL MOSCHEROSCH (1601-69), whose *Wunderliche und wahrhaftige Gesichte Philanders von Sittewald* (1642-43) shows up the demoralization of Germany due to the war and denounces '*à la mode*' tendencies to ape the French in speech, costume, and morals.

---

[1] The picaresque novel (from Spanish *picaro,* a rogue) had an international vogue.

Towards the turn of the century the most popular novels were those of gallantry modelled on the French. A good representative is CHRISTIAN FRIEDRICH HUNOLD – pen-name Menantes – (1680-1721), with his *Der europäischen Höfe Liebes- und Heldengeschichten* (1704), and *Satirischer Roman* (1705), which by its scandalous allusions to contemporary life in Hamburg caused the author's expulsion from that city. Such novels soon found a strong competitor in the *Robinsonaden* or German imitations of *Robinson Crusoe*. Defoe's work had been translated into German in 1719, a year after its appearance in England, and the market was soon flooded with stories of shipwrecked solitaries. The best is J. G. Schnabel's *Insel Felsenburg* (4 vols., 1731-43). Much later is *Der Schweizerische Robinson* (1812-27) by J. R. Wyss, well known to us as the *Swiss Family Robinson*.

The middle classes were well catered for by periodicals, inspired by Steele and Addison's *Tatler* (1709) and *Spectator* (1711). Selections and adaptations from them are found in a Hamburg journal, Johann Mattheson's *Vernünftler*, in 1713-14. The *moralische Wochenschriften*, as they were called, grew in popularity till after 1750. Lessing's attack in his *Literaturbriefe*, 48 et seq., 102 et seq. on the Copenhagen paper *Der nordische Aufseher* gave them a set-back, and they finally sank to the *Bauernfreund* level. The Zurich *Diskurse der Mahler* (1721-23) was the organ of the Swiss literary critics Bodmer and Breitinger, the Halle and Leipzig *Vernünftige Tadlerinnen* of their opponent, Gottsched. The Hamburg *Patriot* (1724-26) was of more general interest. Such journals aimed at the improvement of morality and education. They attack gaming, duels, lotteries, tufthunting, pedantry, and superstition. They stand up for the education of women, and are altogether powerful supporters of 'enlightenment'.

Within the seventeenth century falls the first treatise in German on 'Poetics': MARTIN OPITZ' (1597-1639) *Buch von der deutschen Poeterey* (1624). Largely dependent on Scaliger, Ronsard, and Heinsius, he discusses the nature of poetic invention and arrangement, and classifies the various kinds of poetry, describing tragedy as a majestic form which deals with sensational events occurring in a royal house, in contrast with comedy which deals with baser folk at their banquets, marriages, etc. Following upon the practice of Paul Rebhuhn's drama *Susanna* (1535), and the theory of the grammarian Johann Clajus (1578), Opitz rehabilitated stress as the governing principle in German metre, and did well in combating such extreme syncopation as *lieblchen* and epithesis as in the nominative *Sohne*. In diction he advocates clarity and warns against provincialisms and foreign words. His influence as critic remained unchallenged till Gottsched came. He had a genuine love of his native speech, as shown in his work *Aristarchus seu de contemptu linguae germanicae*

(1618), and revived a MHG work by publishing the *Annolied*. However, he was greater in theory than in practice, and was surpassed by certain lyric poets, several of whom formed the so-called *Königsberger Dichterkreis*. Between 1631 and 1640 a group of not more than a dozen friends would meet in a garden to discuss and recite poetry and listen to music. Opitz was their model, HEINRICH ALBERT (1604-51) their adviser in musical matters and a collector of their songs, and ROBERT ROBERTHIN (1600-48) their intellectual head. SIMON DACH (1605-59), with his gentle melancholy and engaging simplicity, was one of their best poets. One *bauer-lied*, or rustic love-poem, he has left us is the Low German song beginning *Grethke warumb heffstu mi | Doch so sehr bedrövet*, preserved with the music in a British Museum MS. The Low German *Anke van Tharau*, now a folk-song, is no longer attributed to him. The critical ideas of Opitz were disseminated by literary and puristic societies, of which the chief was the '*Fruchtbringende Gesellschaft*', founded in 1617 on the model of the Florentine 'Accademia della Crusca'. One of the chief opponents of '*à la mode*' speech was the Silesian FRIEDRICH VON LOGAU (1604-55), one of Germany's greatest epigrammatists.

Outside Königsberg, one of the most pleasing poets is PAUL FLEMING (1609-40), who, after travelling through Russia and Persia, was on his way to take up a medical post when he died suddenly in Hamburg. One can still enjoy such poems as *Ein getreues Herze wissen* and *In allen meinen Taten*, and his love-songs to his fiancée Elsabe Niehusen.

Some of the finest poetry of the century is to be found in church hymns, both Catholic and Protestant. A Jesuit professor, FRIEDRICH VON SPEE (1591-1635), who courageously opposed the monstrous procedure followed in witchcraft trials, gathered a number of simple and deep-felt hymns in *Trutz-Nachtigall* (1649), a work which owes its primary inspiration to the richly imaged Spanish mysticism of the lyrics of St. John of the Cross. The Protestant hymn-writers derive in unbroken succession from Luther, who had translated, adapted, and invented with great vigour. His famous hymn *Ein feste Burg ist unser Gott* is matched at the end of the Thirty Years' War by Martin Rinckart's *Nun danket alle Gott*, and above all by PAUL GERHARDT (1607-76), cf. especially *O Häupt voll Blut und Wunden* (1656), inspired by *Salve caput cruentatum*. Earlier hymnwriters often composed religious 'Kontrafakturen' of folk-songs. During the century the medieval mystics found a worthy successor in JAKOB BÖHME (1575-1624), the greatest mystic of Protestantism, who, in *Aurora, oder Morgenröthe im Aufgang* (1612) and other works, reflected upon the origin of things, the existence of evil and the revelations of God, influencing many devout people, including Sir Isaac Newton. He inspired in

Germany the Catholic poet JOHANN SCHEFFLER or 'ANGELUS SILESIUS', whose work *Der cherubinische Wandersmann* (1657) is, like Böhme's, theosophical and pantheistic in tendency.

In his *Critische Dichtkunst* (1730) JOHANN CHRISTOPH GOTTSCHED (1700-66) applied Boileau's standard of common sense to German poetry. With a zeal for order and truth, acquired from Christian Wolff (p. 436), he conceived poetry as based upon a set of irrefragable rules to be learnt by intellectual processes. Probability, moderation, sound instruction, were main requirements, and he decreed that the free play of the imagination in evoking the 'marvellous' must be rigorously curbed. Tragedy was to consist of a moral thesis embodied in a single story and sealed by an exemplary death. Despite the stiffness and lack of humour of his own drama *Der sterbende Cato* (1731) Gottsched helped Germany to appreciate the grandeur of French classical tragedy and to liberate drama, as a number of rather dull *Hofpoeten* or court laureates (Canitz, Besser, Neukirch, Pietsch) had liberated the lyric, from the tasteless 'marinism' (pp. 237-8) and bombast of the preceding age. In fighting for rationalism in poetry Gottsched found himself, on passing the zenith of his popularity, in the 'thirties, obliged to fight a rear-guard action on two fronts. Two Swiss writers, JOHANN JAKOB BODMER (1698-1783) and J. J. BREITINGER (1701-76), of Zurich, had, the one in *Abhandlung von dem Wunderbaren in der Poesie* (1740), and the other in *Critische Dichtkunst* (1740), defended the use of the imagination, having been inspired by Milton's *Paradise Lost* and the writings of such Italian critics as Muratori, and their works gained ground even among Gottsched's adherents.

In lyric the bridge between the baroque and modern is JOHANN CHRISTIAN GÜNTHER (1695-1723), a Silesian who, after a sadly wasted life, died at the age of twenty-eight. In his occasional poems he displays some of the baroque extravagances, but folk-song and student ditties have helped him to a simpler and more direct personal utterance in his love-songs and religious poems – he is, in fact, a forerunner of Goethe, who deplored the dissipation of so much talent.

In the Hamburg writer BARTHOLD HEINRICH BROCKES (1680-1747), who had started with over-reflective baroque poetry in a *Passionsgedicht* of 1712, subsequently set to music by Handel, nature suddenly bursts upon the view. Revelling in the sun and rain, the hills and more especially tinier objects like bright-hued insects and gay flowers, Brockes celebrated nature in a mood of quietistic trust in the providence of God. His *Irdisches Vergnügen in Gott*, which began to appear in 1721, had outstayed its welcome by 1747, when its ninth volume was issued. Meanwhile a nature-poet of greater depth had arisen in the Swiss physician, ALBRECHT

VON HALLER (1708-77), who, less complacent than Brockes, struggled with the problem of Eternity and of the origin of Evil. He revealed to his contemporaries the majestic beauty of the Alps and the sturdy simplicity of the Swiss mountaineers, thus providing a foil for the finicking art of rococo and an impetus towards the return to nature of a few decades later. By elaborate piecemeal description a picture was gradually built up, and his treatment of the gentian subsequently incurred the searching criticism of Lessing.

Gottsched's reputation waned during the 'forties. The chief collaborators on his journal *Belustigungen des Verstandes und Witzes* (founded 1741), e.g. the satirist Gottlieb Wilhelm Rabener; the critic JOHANN ELIAS SCHLEGEL, whose *Vergleichung Shakespeares und Andreas Gryphi* (1741), following close upon the translation of *Julius Caesar* (in alexandrines) by Caspar Wilhelm von Borck (German ambassador in London), showed an unwonted appreciation of Shakespeare; and JUSTUS FRIEDRICH WILHELM ZACHARIÄ (author of *Der Renommist*) seceded and from 1745 to 1748 ran a weekly called *Neue Beiträge zum Vergnügen des Verstandes und Witzes*, or more briefly, the *Bremer Beiträge*. The staff of the journal was reinforced by talents like GOTTLIEB WILHELM RABENER (1714-71), who practised a form of satire from which he amiably extracted the sting before he launched it; Gellert; Ewald von Kleist; Ramler; and one really great if difficult poet, Klopstock. CHRISTIAN FÜRCHTEGOTT GELLERT (1715-69) is to us today rather lovable as a man than worthy of high rank as a poet; but his fables and rhymed storyettes (*Fabeln und Erzählungen*, 1746) have always been and still are delightful to children; they have the melodious easy flow of his model, Lafontaine, but they are shorn of Lafontaine's pointed wit and sly malice; instead they have a wholesome plebeian morality which earned him the title 'praeceptor Germaniae'. CHRISTIAN EWALD VON KLEIST (1715-59), a Prussian officer who died of wounds received at the battle of Kunersdorf, imitated Thomson's *Seasons* in his *Der Frühling* (1749), written in hexameters with anacrusis (*mit Auftakt*); here for the first time in modern German verse nature is lyrically felt and visioned. KARL WILHELM RAMLER (1725-98) was given the cognomen of 'the German Horace' because of the careful closeness to rule of his versification, which is, however, by today's standards flat and hackneyed. The great master and moulder of rhythm was FRIEDRICH GOTTLOB KLOPSTOCK (1724-1803) (see next chapter); he indeed builded better than he knew, for his hexameters with their instinctive mastery of stress, though they may not scan to the classical pattern, have the natural and phonetic music of verse in free rhythms (see p. 380).

BIBLIOGRAPHY TO CHAPTER VII

(See also pp. 393 ff.)

Bach, Adolph. *Deutsche Namen Kunde.* 4 pts., 1952-54

de Boon, H. and Newald, R. *Geschichte der deutschen Literatur von den Anfängen bis zur Gegenwart.* Vols. I and II (till 1250). Munich, 1949

Bostock, J. Knight. *A Handbook on Old High German Literature.* Oxford. 1955

Coon, C. S. *The Races of Europe.* New York, 1939

Günther, Hans. *Rassenkunde des deutschen Volkes.* Munich, 14th ed., 1930

Jespersen, Otto. *Language. Its Nature, Development and Origin.* London, 1922

Much, Rudolf. *Deutsche Stammeskunde.* Sammlung Göschen. Leipzig, 1900

Ripley, W. Z. *The Races of Europe.* London, 1900

Schrader, O. *Die Indogermanen.* (Series *Wissenschaft und Bildung.*) Breslau, 3rd ed., 1918

Schütte, Gudmund. *Our Forefathers—the Gothonic Nations.* 2 vols. Cambridge, 1929-33

CHAPTER VIII

GERMAN LITERATURE FROM 1748 TO 1805

GERMAN literature from 1748 onwards presents a series of kaleido-scopic pictures made up of the diverse elements associated with 'classicism', 'romanticism', and 'realism' – words convenient as labels, even though the three varieties of art and outlook they indicate are neither entirely constant nor entirely different in their components. As the picture changes, the clearer, colder tints of classicism, the more glowing or sombre, intense or delicate hues of romanticism, the harder colours of realism, mingle in varying proportions. Each type in turn gains or loses ground, dominates the picture for a time, or becomes obscured, but is never entirely absent or in sole possession. Surveying the rapid changes during the century after Bodmer's essentially 'romantic' attack upon the Renaissance 'classicism' then in vogue, we see how the romantic elements gain ground till they outrival the classical at the time of the *Sturm und Drang*, then suffer a short eclipse, but predominate again during the 'Romantic Period', and to the end contribute appreciably to the general effect; we see, too, how the classical elements, purer ones supplanting those of the Renaissance and rococo kind, attain predominance towards the end of the eighteenth century, and afterwards make their presence felt sporadically; and how the realistic elements, hardly notice-able at first, become conspicuous during the *Sturm und Drang* years, catch the eye from time to time during the periods of classical and romantic supremacy, and finally become themselves predominant during the period of 'Poetic Realism'.

Eight years passed before Bodmer and his supporters could point to a German achievement illustrating adequately the vital truth of their prin-ciples. But in 1748 there appeared in the *Bremer Beiträge* the first three cantos of Klopstock's *Messias*, whose youthful author had set out to supplement Milton's *Paradise Lost* and *Paradise Regained*. Here was a sublime theme treated with religious fervour by a poet of bold imagi-nation. On steadily flowing hexameters the reader was borne first up to Heaven to hear mankind's redemption planned, then down to Hell to see the counter-plotting of Satan and his fellows, then up again to Earth to read of Christ on the Mount of Olives and Judas the Betrayer. These three cantos dwarfed all the light productions of the time. They did not, indeed, deserve all the enthusiastic praise with which Bodmer greeted them, for Klopstock's genius was essentially lyric, not epic. His limitations grew ever more apparent as the succeeding seventeen cantos slowly followed during the next twenty-five years. With few exceptions his characters are shadowy; lengthy dialogues and portrayals of feeling that lack variety retard the narrative; and the author moves in realms he cannot visualize. Yet there are passages of force and beauty such as no previous German had written. Though tedious to the modern reader, this grandiosely conceived epic was for long a household book in Germany, and was one of the earliest works to attract foreign attention to German literature.

It was as a lyricist that Klopstock did his best work. Disdaining what he called *den elenden Klingklang* of rhyme, he favoured in his 'Odes' forms modelled on, or reminiscent of, the lyric metres of classical antiquity. The absence of the melody of rhyme is partly compensated for by a skilful use of alliteration, assonance, and repetition; and though his style tends to be rugged and complex, and his muse to drop from ecstatic heights to sober, even dull, reflectiveness, his earlier poems and many of his later ones voice genuine feeling and lofty thought in forceful language and striking images. Religion, friendship, love, and patriotism were his main themes. His love poems struck a new note by their delicacy; but it was with his patriotic lyrics, including the bardic chants in his *Bardiete* (a trio of prose plays dealing with the national hero Hermann who destroyed Varus and his legions) that, inspired by Frederick the Great's victories, he broke fresh ground.

Klopstock's influence was disproportionate to the intrinsic merits of his work.[1] He appeared in an age ripening for revolution: from rationalism to idealism, from the intellectuality of French classicism to the spirituality of German romanticism; from the fetters of convention to the freedom of natural impulse. His example, therefore, provided stimuli whose effects were both immediate and lasting. Besides such imitators as the 'Ossianic' and 'bardic' poets of the 'sixties and 'seventies he had enthusiastic admirers possessing real talent. One group of these, among them JOHANN HEINRICH VOSS (1751-1826) and LUDWIG HEINRICH CHRISTIAN HÖLTY (1748-76), founded the Göttingen *Hainbund* in 1772, secured control of

---

[1] It has recently been shown that Klopstock influenced Rilke in his later years, both as regards form (the hexametric pattern of the *Duineser Elegien* and other late verse) and themes (that of *die Geliebte*, for instance, was taken over from Klopstock and Hölty).

the *Göttinger Musenalmanach*, and during the next few years published in it, besides work of their own, GOTTFRIED AUGUST BURGER'S (1747-94) famous ballad *Lenore* (1773) and many contributions from the young poets of the *Sturm und Drang*. But the more permanent effects of his work are more important. It is no exaggeration to say that Klopstock's works helped, directly and indirectly, to determine the metrical form, the style, the contents, and the spirit of much of the best German poetry from that time onwards. The hexameter, effectively used by Voss in his idyll *Luise* (1781-84), in his translation of Homer (*Odyssee*, 1781; *Ilias*, 1793) and in his *Idyllen* (in his *Gedichte*, 1785), and by Goethe in *Reineke Fuchs* (1794) and *Hermann und Dorothea* (1797), established itself as the normal epic metre; the rhymeless lyric was perfected under Goethe's touch, and has lived on; loftiness of diction, the use of expressive compounds, boldness of construction and imagery originated with Klopstock; he stimulated that interest in the nation's past which was to rejuvenate German poetry and provide endless sources of inspiration; he revived the spirit of individualism, showed that genius can rise above the theorist's rules, and introduced a new and higher conception of the poet's mission.

Apart from the working out of a German hexametric pattern there is modernity of lyric feeling and a development of native forms in the poetry of Hölty, who, when he died of consumption at twenty-eight, had written lyrics which remain as some of the most delicately felt and rhythmically sensitive in the German language, and in the more robust and popular verse, with its cheery optimism, of MATTHIAS CLAUDIUS (1740-1815), der Wandsbecker Bote as he called himself from the name of the newspaper he edited in a suburb of Hamburg. While Hölty gets close to the intimate moods of nature, Claudius continues the *Volkslied* in form and spirit, as does also Bürger, whose chief historical importance, however, lies in his renewal and extension of the ancient ballad (*Volksballade*), with Percy's *Reliques* (1765) as his direct incentive and inspiration; European Romanticism itself derives ultimately from the translation by Sir Walter Scott of his *Lenore*, which, with its dancing of ghosts in the moonlight and pervaded as it is with a sense of mystery quite new in literature, took Europe by storm. Bürger's love for his wife's sister is recorded in his poems to Molly and is the base of the theme in Jakob Wassermann's poignant novel *Das Gänsemännchen* (see pp. 294, 334).

While Voss's idylls, of which *Luise* is the best remembered, have the rough rural reality of the country life he intimately knew as a schoolmaster at Eutin, the Arcadian idylls (1756, 1772) of 'the German Theocritus', SALOMON GESSNER (1730-88), a Swiss from Zurich who lived in

Berlin, have an elegant artificiality which trims nature to the taste of drawing-room sentimentalists; his sighing shepherds are *Salonschäfer*, his coy milkmaids are not redolent of shippon and cheese. The artificiality is heightened by the delicate pencilling of the prose, for which Gessner, on Ramler's advice, had abandoned his first efforts in Anacreontic verse; and this prose of Gessner, with its smooth flow and the faultless roll and rhythm of its periods, marks a stage in the evolution of the genre, while at the same time it keeps for us today its old-world charm of rococo.

GOTTHOLD EPHRAIM LESSING (1729-81) supplemented Klopstock's work by his services to the drama. His genius was less original, and he was no poet; but he was an omnivorous reader, a skilful craftsman, an acute critic, and a hater of bigotry. His earlier plays are clever comedies in the French manner, worth mentioning here only because *Die Juden* and *Der Freigeist*, with their plea for religious tolerance, foreshadowed his last great work. At the age of twenty-six, however, inspired by Richardson's sentimental novel *Clarissa Harlowe*, and by Lillo's choice of a mere middle-class youth as the tragic hero of his *London Merchant*, Lessing defied Gottschedian convention and with his *Miss Sara Sampson* (1755) introduced the *bürgerliches Trauerspiel* into Germany. Immature as this work is, its novelty, its harrowing story of a gentle heroine poisoned by her libertine lover's discarded mistress, its very excess of sentimentality aroused widespread enthusiasm. But it was his *Emilia Galotti* (1772), a modernization of the story of that Virginia whose father slew her to save her honour, which actually established this genre in Germany. The characters and setting, though nominally Italian, were essentially eighteenth-century German; and the implied condemnation of the abuse of autocratic power appealed directly to the young rebels of the *Sturm und Drang*. Among their many tragedies of this type are Goethe's *Clavigo* (1774), audaciously based on a contemporary scandal made public by Beaumarchais to avenge his own sister; the Gretchen tragedy in *Faust*; and Schiller's *Kabale und Liebe* (1784) with its scarcely veiled attack on the Duke of Württemberg and his court. During the two generations of classical and romantic supremacy the *bürgerliches Trauerspiel* lived on – if we except Zacharias Werner's fatalistic *Der 24. Februar* (staged 1810) – only in the lower strata of dramatic production. But Hebbel's powerful tragedy of everyday bourgeois life, *Maria Magdalene* (1844), an indictment of antiquated and inadequate social and ethical ideas, and Ludwig's *Der Erbförster* (1850), a tragedy of obstinacy and impetuosity, linked the older *bürgerliches Trauerspiel* to the countless modern plays of this genre treating many themes besides love betrayed or thwarted by social barriers.

Lessing's finest achievement in drama was his *Minna von Barnhelm* (1767), the first German 'Comedy of Manners' – portraying in a group of typical representatives the military caste of the period – and the first of the few really great German comedies. Its truth to life, its genial humour, its freshness and frankness, its common-sense settlement of a point of honour, and its underlying plea for reconciliation between Prussia and Saxony after the Seven Years' War won it immediate success, and are still appreciated. His last play, *Nathan der Weise* (1779), owing partly to the influence of Shakespeare's technique, is faulty in construction; but it introduced blank verse (in place of the monotonous alexandrine) as a standard metre for serious drama, and, built up round the parable of the Three Rings, it has become world-famous as a convincing plea for religious tolerance.

As a critic and theorist Lessing came to the front at thirty years of age with his brilliant contributions to the new periodical *Briefe, die neueste Literatur betreffend*, launched in 1759 by the Berlin bookseller, FRIEDRICH NICOLAI (1733-1811). The seventeenth 'letter' contains his first attack on Gottsched and his recommendation of the English dramatists, especially Shakespeare, rather than the French, for his countrymen's emulation. This theme is elaborated more fully in the famous *Hamburgische Dramaturgie* (1767-69), which began as a series of critiques of the plays produced at the Hamburg theatre, but developed into a succession of treatises on a variety of dramatic topics, including the revaluation and reinterpretation of the (in those days sacrosanct) views on the 'three unities' and the 'purpose of tragedy' attributed to Aristotle. In his caustic denouncement of Voltaire and the French Classicists Lessing was rather a counsel for the prosecution than an unbiassed judge; but the work as a whole is a monument of wide knowledge, penetrating analysis, and sound judgment. Its influence on dramatic practice and theory can hardly be over-estimated; and like *Laokoon* (1766), which analysed the essential differences between the plastic and the poetic arts, it set up a new standard of critical discussion.

Equally important with Lessing as a contributor to *Briefe, die neueste Literatur betreffend* was MOSES MENDELSSOHN (1729-86), a Jew who had worked his way up from the dire poverty of his boyhood. He was the grandfather of Felix Mendelssohn, the composer. With his Platonic dialogues *Phädon, oder über die Unsterblichkeit der Seele* (1767) he earned rank as a popular philosopher, while his essay *Pope, ein Metaphysiker* (1755), written in collaboration with Lessing, shows up Pope's facile optimism ('Whatever is, is right') and proves with all the weight of logic that poet and philosopher are distinct species. Lessing, Nicolai, and Moses Mendelssohn were the chief representatives on the literary side of rationalism (*Vernunftglaube*) in the Voltairean sense; Nicolai's *Sebaldus Notanker* (1773), in form a novel but by purpose an attack on religion, is typical of the trend of thought which comes under the heading of *Aufklärung* ('enlightenment').

Contrasting with Klopstock and Lessing, both typical Germans, concerned above all with the forceful expression of ideas and principles, CHRISTOPH MARTIN WIELAND (1733-1813) represents that Latin strain, with its talent for lucidity, irony, elegance, and charming flights of fancy, which emerges most frequently in the Rhine districts. His chief domain was the epic, both prose and verse. A fervent pietist and admirer of Klopstock till he was thirty, he then came under the influence of Cervantes, whom he imitated in his satirical romance *Don Sylvio von Rosalva* (1764), and of the French and English rationalistic, satirical, and humorous writers, among them Voltaire, Rousseau, Diderot, Shaftesbury, Swift, Fielding, and Sterne. His *Agathon* (1766), a veiled autobiography depicting the conversion of a Greek youth from Platonism to a brighter and more worldly philosophy of life, inaugurated the long series of *Bildungsromane* which includes KARL PHILIPP MORITZ' (1756-93) *Anton Reiser* (1785-90), Goethe's *Wilhelm Meister* (1795-1829), and Keller's *Der Grüne Heinrich* (1855). Called to Weimar as tutor to the young Duke Karl August, he founded his periodical *Der teutsche Merkur*, and published in it *Die Abderiten* (1774), a satirical novel contrasting the narrow-minded stupidity of the petty bourgeoisie with the cosmopolitan wisdom of their travelled fellow-townsman Democritus, and *Oberon* (1780), a charming verse epic of fairyland and the days of Charlemagne, which was inspired by Shakespeare's *Midsummer Night's Dream*, and in its turn stimulated the Romanticists of the next generation. By his translation of this play in verse, and eleven others in prose (1762-66), he was the first to make Shakespeare readily accessible to German readers. Wieland's other numerous translations and original writings reflect predominantly the influence of France, Greece, and Rome. Broadly speaking his works form a side-current separated for a time from the main stream of development. The smoothness and lightness of his style, and the play of his wit, were appreciated and emulated; but during the *Sturm und Drang* years his influence was otherwise relatively slight, while his later influence was merged in stimuli from other sources.

In Wieland's *Agathon* there is cult of form as well as a personally motivated doctrine of life and art; in the novels of JOHANN JAKOB WILHELM HEINSE (1749-1803) there is inculcation of daring doctrine and of art theories, but form and plasticity are cast aside. Where Heinse's work is notable is that not only by its lubricity of theme it harks back to *Sturm und Drang*, but that at the same time it forecasts the *Künstlerroman* of

Romanticism and points far forward to our own days, certainly to expressionism (p. 346). A Thuringian, Heinse lived for three years in Rome and then launched on the world his notorious novel *Ardinghello oder die glückseligen Inseln* (1787), with its Italianate painters whose morality – or their denial of it – is that of the Renaissance (*Renaissance-moral*). This was followed in 1795 by *Hildegard von Hohenthal*, in which music and musicians create paradise for the ear as in *Ardinghello* painters had done for the eye. 'Man is a beast of prey', Heinse's lesson runs, and therefore the watchword is to live life to the full and to have strong nerves to stand the racket.

Klopstock, Lessing, and Wieland were still in their prime when the younger generation took the literary world by storm. The main attack came, not from the *Hainbund* in Göttingen, but from Strassburg, where JOHANN GOTTFRIED HERDER (1744-1803), an East Prussian, during the winter of 1770-71, fired Goethe's student circle with his own ideas and enthusiasms. Stimulated partly by Lessing's '*Literaturbriefe*' (cf. p. 248) and *Laokoon*, Herder had already published, before leaving Riga, his *Fragmente über die deutsche Literatur* (1767) and *Kritische Wälder* (1769). But while Lessing's attitude was objective, Herder's was subjective. Instead of cold critical analysis we find here glowing appreciations, as well as bitter denunciations, based on instinctive feeling. He insists on the supreme rights of genius; appeals in stirring tones for originality, for work independent of foreign models and truly national in form and spirit; and contrasts the spontaneous *Naturpoesie* of Homer and the Bible with the less inspiring, more sophisticated *Kunstpoesie* of Virgil. In 1773 appeared what has been called the manifesto of the *Sturm und Drang* – five essays collected under the title *Von deutscher Art und Kunst*, two of them by Herder, who took in the one Ossian and the folk-song, in the other Shakespeare, as examples justifying his enthusiasm for *Naturpoesie*. With his *Volkslieder* (1778-79), reissued as *Stimmen der Völker in Liedern* (1778-79), a collection of folk-songs from many lands, some German, the rest admirable reproductions of foreign originals, he concluded his mission as the rejuvenator of German poetry. From his time onwards the *Volkslied* has repeatedly been a source of new life and freshness and simplicity for the lyric and ballad. Of his later works, the *Ideen zur Philosophie der Geschichte der Menschheit* (1784-87) and *Briefe zur Beförderung der Humanität* (1793-97) are noteworthy as introducing the conception of man's history as the progress, determined by an inner force of divine origin, of the primitive child of Nature towards an ideal of true humanity; and his posthumous *Der Cid* (1805), an epic based on old Spanish verse romances, again shows his genius for reclothing foreign originals in German garb.

Herder's influence was only one of many factors combining to produce the *Sturm und Drang* movement, which was not confined to his Strassburg circle. Similar and parallel influences had been at work throughout Germany before 1770. Some have already been indicated. Others were: JOHANN GEORG HAMANN's (1730-88) ideas of genius in his *Sokratische Denkwürdigkeiten* (1759), a main source of Herder's own inspiration; Young's defence of originality and genius in *Conjectures on Original Composition* (German translation 1760); HEINRICH WILHELM VON GERSTENBERG's (1737-1823) appreciation of Shakespeare in his *Briefe über Merkwürdigkeiten der Literatur* (1766-70); and Rousseau's revolutionary doctrines and summons to 'return to Nature'. The *Sturm und Drang* was essentially a revolt of youth against the deadening cold of rationalism and the fetters of antiquated and intolerable traditions, conventions, and rules. It expressed itself partly in social unconventionalities, but mainly in a literary revolution in which 'originality', 'force', 'genius', and 'freedom' were favourite war-cries. Hence the terms *Geniezeit* for the period more usually named after FRIEDRICH MAXIMILIAN VON KLINGER's (1752-1831) play *Sturm und Drang* (1776), and *Original- und Kraftgenies* for the youthful rebels themselves. Isolated works that defied established canons, such as Gerstenberg's tragedy *Ugolino* (1768), depicting realistically a whole family's death by starvation, but lacking dramatic action and conflict, were followed by a spate of daring and tempestuous plays, novels, and poems beginning with Goethe's *Götz von Berlichingen* (1773), slackening after a few years, regaining force with Schiller's *Die Räuber* (1781), and ending with his *Don Carlos* (1787). Among their outstanding characteristics were: the flouting of all literary canons; attacks on the social, moral, and political order; insistence on the rights of the individual; a Titanesque defiance of authority; the glorification of champions of freedom and great leaders of men; a sense of unity with Nature; enthusiasm for more primitive ages; interest in the common people; a free use of the popular idiom; revival of the forms and style of the folk-song; a strongly subjective attitude to the themes chosen; spontaneous outbursts of feeling and passion, often extravagantly expressed; and a frequent introduction of realistic detail. Some of the more notable works belonging to, or influenced by the *Sturm und Drang* are *Die Soldaten* (1776), a lurid play depicting garrison life, by JAKOB MICHAEL REINHOLD LENZ (1751-92), whose *Anmerkungen übers Theater* (1774) first defined the essential difference between ancient tragedy, with its background of Destiny, and the modern tragedy of character; Klinger's tragedy *Die Zwillinge* (1776), based like Johann Anton Leisewitz' *Julius von Tarent* (1776), which the youthful Schiller so greatly admired, on the favourite theme of the hostile brothers; HEINRICH LEOPOLD WAGNER'S (1747-79) *Die Reue nach der Tat* (1775), a tragedy of class prejudice, and *Die Kindermörderin* (1776), a realistic treatment of Goethe's Gretchen theme; and Bürger's ballad *Der wilde Jäger* (p. 246). But the two great original geniuses of the movement were Goethe and Schiller.

If *Von deutscher Art und Kunst* was the manifesto of the *Sturm und Drang*, its first signal success was JOHANN WOLFGANG VON GOETHE'S (1749-1832) *Götz von Berlichingen* (1773), the first of the countless *Ritterdramen* that help to link the *Sturm und Drang* with the Romantic Movement proper. It is a free dramatization of the autobiography of one of those predatory and feud-loving minor nobles, who, even in the early sixteenth century, still resisted centralized law and order; and the hero is idealized as a great-hearted champion of individual freedom struggling vainly against the wiles of courtiers and dying for a lost cause in a degenerate age. All the dramatic unities are defied, and stage requirements are disregarded (the scene changes 55 times, involving over 30 different stage settings!); but the breathless succession of stirring and touching episodes, in which figures of all classes speak a realistic prose suited to their parts, grip the reader's interest, and give a picture of the age glowing with life. The faults of this 'most beautiful and captivating monstrosity', as a contemporary critic called it, are mainly exaggerations of what Goethe then thought to be characteristic of Shakespeare's technique; its merits are due mainly to the vigour and naturalness that Herder had taught him not to restrain, to his wonderful power of visualization, and to his practice of using his writings as vehicles for confessions that unburdened his soul. It is this subjectivity that makes his psychological novel *Die Leiden des jungen Werthers* (1774) so absorbing and convincing. The romantic, sensitive, morbidly intro-spective youth who pours forth in these letters the story of his hopeless love for his friend's betrothed expresses to a great extent the feelings of Goethe himself when he loved Charlotte Buff. But Goethe had a firmer mental balance than his Werther; he always stands above the figures he creates to mirror sides of his own nature. Werther's suicide – suggested by that of Goethe's acquaintance Jerusalem in similar circumstances – represents, like the fickle Weislingen's tragic end in *Götz von Berlichingen*, the fitting poetic outcome of a situation akin to, but not identical with, Goethe's own.

Goethe's *Sturm und Drang* years, those preceding his call to the Weimar Court in November 1775, were his most prolific period. To them belong, besides *Götz* and *Werther* (which brought him immediate, enduring, and world-wide fame), his tragedy *Clavigo* (1774), in which the faithless lover is punished, like Weislingen, by death; his *Stella* (1776), a play daringly unconventional in its original *ménage à trois* solution of the eternal triangle problem; several slighter works, among them satires, farces, and vaudevilles; fragments of what were to have been titanic tragedies on Mahomet and Prometheus; the first, but still uncompleted, version of *Faust, Part I*, bold in conception, rebellious in spirit, by turns romantically poetic and unsparingly realistic in treatment (most of it preserved by a fortunate chance in the so-called *Urfaust*, a manuscript copy made by Fräulein von Göchhausen of the Weimar Court); part of *Egmont*; and frequent outbursts of lyric song. Of these many have never been surpassed; especially those inspired by his love for the simple country pastor's daughter, Friederike Brion, and for his fiancée of a few years later, Lili Schönemann, the fashionable daughter of a Frankfurt banker. Some, like *Heidenröslein* and *Der König in Thule*, have the simple charm of the folk-song; *Mit einem gemalten Band* combines rococo daintiness with genuine feeling; in *Willkommen und Abschied* a lover's impetuosity and tenderness are united effectively with unsurpassable lines descriptive of nature; *Mailied* pours fourth an ectasy of living, loving, and unison with nature; *Meine Ruh ist hin* and *Rastlose Liebe* are direct and perfect expressions of heart-ache and restlessness and longing. But many other themes moved him to lyrical expression. *Prometheus*, with its bitter defiance of the gods and bold self-reliance, breathing the very spirit of the *Sturm und Drang*, and *An Schwager Kronos*, a terse and forcible picture of eager youth's ideal of the journey of life, may be mentioned as outstanding examples.

A very different spirit pervades the poetry of Goethe's first ten years in Weimar. Responsibilities hastened the maturing of his outlook on life; Frau von Stein's influence helped to teach him restraint; memories of bygone happiness and faithlessness haunted him; the classics strengthened their hold on him; Italy drew him more and more strongly. His finest lyrics of this period (such as *An den Mond*, *Über allen Gipfeln*, *Der Fischer*, *Erlkönig*, *Mignons Lieder*, *Lied des Harfners*, *Seefahrt*, *Gesang der Geister über den Wassern*, *Harzreise im Winter*, *Das Göttliche*, *Grenzen der Menschheit*, *Der Sänger*, *Meine Göttin*) reflect elegiac moods and the growth of a soberer, more detached, more altruistic, more philosophic attitude to life and art. Administrative duties and other distractions prevented the real completion of any but minor works during this period of transition. But when he seized his opportunity and fled to Italy in 1786 *Egmont* had long been 'nearly finished'; his 'classical' drama, *Iphigenie*, had been staged in its first prose version (1779) and been recast in iambics and again in rhythmic prose; two acts of *Tasso* existed in prose; and from his intimate connection with the Court theatre had sprung the greater part of a novel vividly descriptive of the actor's calling: *Wilhelm Meisters theatralische Sendung*, a fragment bearing much the same relationship to the complete *Wilhelm Meister* as the *Urfaust* does to *Faust*.

Just when Goethe was entering on his 'classical' period, FRIEDRICH VON SCHILLER (1759-1805) gave a new impetus to the *Sturm und Drang* with his *Die Räuber* (1781), an outburst of youthful fire and fury, tempered by idealism, that spread his fame through Germany, and in a few years through Europe. In spite of its crudities this revolutionary tragedy, whose noble-minded hero Karl Moor, a victim of his brother's base intrigues, defies the law as the leader of a robber band, is clearly the work of a born dramatist with an instinct for stage effects and necessities – the first essentially dramatic genius of German birth. Voicing the spirit of the age, and depicting robber exploits such as were still remembered, it united the appeal of actuality with dramatic and theatrical effectiveness, and thus marked a new stage in the development of German drama. The much weaker tragedy *Die Verschwörung des Fiesko zu Genua* (1783) champions republican ideals in a sixteenth-century Italian setting; but the 'bürgerliches Trauerspiel' *Kabale und Liebe* (1784) combines a strong love interest with open attacks on social evils of the day in Germany.

By temperament a preacher and reformer, Schiller regarded the stage as his pulpit; as early as 1785 he published the essay later entitled *Die Schaubühne als eine moralische Anstalt betrachtet*, to the influence of which the German theatre owes much of its prestige as an educational institution. This essay, like so much of his work from 1785 to 1791, appeared first in his periodical *Rheinische Thalia* (continued as *Thalia, Neue Thalia*), in which can be seen how he, too, outgrew the *Sturm und Drang* and turned with zest to classical studies. His poem *Die Götter Griechenlands* (published in Wieland's *Merkur* 1788) voices this new enthusiasm; but the drama *Don Carlos* (1787), written like Lessing's *Nathan* in blank verse, is the most important imaginative work of this period of transition. Beginning as the tragedy of a prince's passion for his father's bride, it becomes a plea for cosmopolitan humanitarianism, with the prince's friend as spokesman and real hero, and ends as a tragedy of court intrigue. From the historical researches undertaken while writing this play developed his *Geschichte des Abfalls der vereinigten Niederlande* (1788), and this led to his appointment, on Goethe's recommendation, as professor of history in Jena. For some years he now devoted himself mainly to the study of history and – stimulated by Kant's three epoch-making 'Critiques' (1781-90), with their purely idealistic basis and argument – of philosophy. The outstanding immediate results of these studies were his colourful *Geschichte des dreissig-jährigen Krieges* (1793); a number of essays on æsthetics, including the one republished later as *Über naive und sentimentalische Dichtung* (first version 1796), and a series of philosophic lyrics, among them *Das Ideal und das Leben* and *Der Spaziergang*, which opened up a new domain for poetic treatment. But it was not until his friendship with Goethe had ripened that he returned to imaginative literature as his life's work.

Goethe, meanwhile, had spent nearly two years in Italy, studying both nature and art: observing deliberately the life around him as well as examples of the 'noble simplicity and quiet grandeur' (*edle Einfalt und stille Grösse*) that JOHANN JOACHIM WINCKELMANN (1717-68)[1] had taught his contemporaries to see in the works of classical, especially Greek, antiquity; completing his own development along the path he had already begun to tread; cultivating objectivity, restraint, and a broad humanism. His literary output during these years was small, if we except the material (consisting largely of letters to Frau von Stein) later embodied in his *Italienische Reise* (1816-17). But he wrestled again with *Faust*, making changes and composing new portions, and eventually publishing *Faust, ein Fragment* (1790). He also finished *Egmont*, recast *Iphigenie* in its final blank verse form, and made some progress with *Tasso*, completing it shortly after his return to Weimar. His *Egmont* (1788) and *Torquato Tasso* (1790) reflect his transition from the rebellious individualist of former years to the mature advocate of personal responsibility and social obligations. *Egmont* was probably first conceived as a tragedy somewhat similar to *Götz*, having as its hero a dashing and generous-hearted young prince driven on by a 'demonic' force and dying as the guiltless victim of black tyranny; but it became a tragedy of irresponsibility and lack of foresight and judgment; and while Götz dies defeated Egmont goes to his death sustained by a vision prophetic of his country's liberation. In *Tasso*, begun when Goethe was already growing maturer, but still felt keenly the dissonance between the sensitive poetic temperament and the world's hard materialism, we see the author's sympathy largely transferred from the original hero to the representatives of social propriety and humane culture. Both *Tasso* and *Iphigenie auf Tauris* (1787), in which the Greek legend is infused with the modern humanitarian spirit, and truth succeeds where deceit would have failed, emphasize the refining, healing, and redeeming influence of noble womanhood, and are imperishable monuments to Frau von Stein. These two dramas, with their simplicity of plot and structure and characterization, their restraint, the harmonious flow of their verse,

---

[1] Winckelmann's *Gedanken über die Nachahmung der griechischen Werke in der Malerei und Bildhauerkunst* (1754) and his masterpiece *Geschichte der Kunst des Altertums* (1764) laid the foundations for the scientific study of art; he based his interpretation on climate, landscape, and racial character.

and their insistence on humane ideals, inaugurate the brief predominantly 'classical' period of German literature.

Returning to Weimar, Goethe found he had outgrown his former friends. He lived in comparative seclusion with Christiane Vulpius, his love for whom inspired the *Römische Elegien* (1789), devoted much of his time to scientific studies, and published treatises, including the one on *Die Metamorphose der Pflanzen*, now famous in the annals of science. But, apart from a few inferior products of his experiences during the German campaign against the French revolutionaries, poetic inspiration failed him till he came under the spell of Schiller's infectious enthusiasm. His acceptance, in 1794, of Schiller's invitation to contribute to the periodical *Die Horen* led gradually to a firm friendship that proved mutually stimulating. The first important outcome of Schiller's encouraging appreciation was the remodelling and extension of *Wilhelm Meisters theatralische Sendung* into *Wilhelm Meisters Lehrjahre* (1795-96), in which the hero's original goal, the foundation of a national theatre, is exchanged for a new one: perfected self-development as a useful member of society. As a novel this *Bildungsroman* lacks vitality and continuity; some of its figures are shadowy symbols; but its discussion of *Hamlet* is one of the landmarks in Shakespeare criticism, its expositions of the author's views on art and life and education had an enduring influence, and its introduction of a quasi-masonic secret society and other 'Romantic' features won it a popularity that lasted for a generation. It was in 1796, however, that the relations between the two poets became more intimate as they collaborated in writing their *Xenien*, two-lined epigrams appreciative of great writers of the past and scathingly derisive of the self-satisfied mediocrities of the time. Over four hundred were printed in Schiller's *Musenalmanach*, raising a storm which cleared the air and left Goethe and Schiller supreme in the world of literature. The next year proved their title to this supremacy. It saw the publication of Goethe's idyllic epic in hexameters, *Hermann und Dorothea* (1797), a delicately idealized, but objectively clear, story of village life touched by the dark shadow of the French Revolution, the heroine who becomes Hermann's bride being one of a company of refugees. It was also the famous *Balladenjahr*, in which the *Musenalmanach* contained a first series of imperishable ballads, among them Goethe's *Der Schatzgräber*, *Der Zauberlehrling*, *Die Braut von Corinth*, *Der Gott und die Bajadere* (all showing in their form and in their pointing of a moral the influence of Schiller), and Schiller's *Der Taucher*, *Der Handschuh*, *Die Kraniche des Ibykus*, and *Der Gang nach dem Eisenhammer*. And it was the year in which, constantly urged on by Schiller, Goethe resumed work on his *Faust*, deciding to give it a deeper and wider significance, to depict in

Faust not merely the insatiable thirster after genuine knowledge, but the representative of Man as a whole, with his weaknesses and his strivings towards an ideal goal. The work proceeded slowly and intermittently; it was not until the year after Schiller's death that the First Part, with the *Zueignung*, the *Vorspiel auf dem Theater*, the *Prolog im Himmel*, and the various gaps of the *Fragment* filled up, was ready for publication as *Faust, Erster Teil* (1808).

Except for his work on *Faust*, and a few genuinely inspired lyrics (e.g. *Euphrosyne*, an elegy on the death of a promising young Weimar actress), Goethe's poetic production from 1798 to 1805 was not on his highest level; he was again concerning himself mainly with artistic theories and scientific studies. Schiller, on the other hand, in spite of repeated illness, won success after success during these last seven years of his life. In his *Musenalmanach auf das Jahr* 1797, and elsewhere, he continued to give to the world his philosophic lyrics and impressive ballads (among them *Der Kampf mit dem Drachen*, *Die Bürgschaft*, *Das Eleusische Fest*, *Das Lied von der Glocke*, *Hero und Leander*, *Der Graf von Habsburg*), while at the same time raising the German drama to a level it had never before attained. His study of history now bore poetic fruit in the magnificent tragedy *Wallenstein* (1800), with its brilliant prelude *Wallensteins Lager*, in which we see a vivid picture of the soldiery of the Thirty Years' War, and its two further parts *Die Piccolomini* and *Wallensteins Tod*, containing the real dramatic action. Ambition and distrust of the Emperor's intentions have tempted Wallenstein into taking the first steps towards treason; he finds himself irresistibly driven forward by the consequences of his own acts; the moral forces that he and those who urge him to conclude his pact with the Swedes have underrated so blindly show their strength; his faith in the stars and prophetic dreams proves illusory; he finds himself deserted by all but a handful of staunch supporters, condemned by his favourite, the young idealist Max Piccolomini, and betrayed by the man he had thought his closest friend; an old wrong he had done to one of those who appear to remain true to him recoils on his own head; and the approach of his new allies hastens on the final tragedy of a man whose real nobility has shown itself in his misfortune and won our sympathy. In *Maria Stuart* (1801) Schiller shows equal skill in gaining our sympathy for a heroine whom suffering and true repentance have ennobled and purified; she herself regards her death as an atonement for Darnley's murder; but her real dramatic guilt lies in her strong claim to the English crown, and her tragic end is brought about by jealousy and intrigue. 'Classical' though these two works are, using the term in a broad sense, they show a growing influence of that Romantic Movement which was already on the point of carrying all before it. And his next play, *Die Jungfrau von Orleans* (1801) is rightly described by Schiller himself as a 'romantic tragedy'. Inspired by a chivalrous desire to vindicate Joan's good name against the patriotic libels of Shakespeare and the rationalist slanders of Voltaire, Schiller makes her not merely an honest visionary like Shaw's St. Joan, but the fulfiller of a genuinely divine mission. For one brief interval earthly love fills her with a sense of guilt, destroys her miraculous powers, and leads to her capture; but she conquers her passion, breaks her fetters, rejoins her friends, and dies on the field of battle, her mission accomplished. *Die Braut von Messina* (1803), in which Schiller returns to the theme of the hostile brothers, is a not entirely successful attempt to blend characteristic features of modern and ancient drama by introducing into a tragedy of character the idea of an inexorable Fate and adapting the Greek chorus to modern stage requirements. But his last completed play, *Wilhelm Tell* (1804), with the whole Swiss people as its real 'hero,' is (in spite of the criticisms to which its last act is open) a dramatic masterpiece that deserves the popularity it has always enjoyed. His *Demetrius*, which handles the psychology of a pretender to a throne, remained a fragment at his death; it has the promise of a masterpiece. More in the nature of work dashed off to keep the Court Theatre at Weimar going were several adaptations: *Turandot* (1801; see p. 490), an experiment in the *commedia del'arte*, but with its native wickedness and flippancy weighted with Schiller's moralizing sentiment and pathos; Shakespeare's *Macbeth* (1880); and Racine's *Phedre* (*Phädra*, 1805).

Schiller's death in 1805 (which called forth Goethe's moving elegy entitled *Epilog zu Schillers Glocke*) is generally taken as marking the close of the 'classical' age of German literature. It was, indeed, he who had been for years the leading representative of definitely classical tendencies and of the broadly humane spirit associated with them; but during those years Romanticism had already begun to assert the dominance it was to maintain for a generation.

In striking contrast to the ring and resonance of Schiller's mainly didactic and cultural verse is the muted mellifluous flow with its dreamy undertones – comparatively speaking the lyrical modernity – in the elegiac poetry of FRIEDRICH VON MATTHISSON (1761-1831) and JOHANN GAUDENZ VON SALIS-SEEWIS (1762-1834); they are in the line of Hölty rather than of Schiller. Matthisson's central theme is the mutability (*Vergänglichkeit*) of all mortal things; both poets brood over ruins, graveyards and tombstones. Descriptions of Swiss landscapes – for the first time since Haller (p. 242) – provide a noble background for their nostalgic moods of meditation.

CHAPTER IX

GERMAN LITERATURE FROM 1805 TO 1880

THE word Romantic was imported from England to the Continent with the sentimental novel of Sterne and Richardson. It was thus applied to the prodigality of feeling and extravagance of language which aroused the hostility of the *Aufklärung* and made it, in its origin, a term of contempt. But under the influence of Rousseau, who wrote of the 'romantic' Alps, its meaning was gradually modified into admiration for wild, natural scenery, for ruined castles and picturesque cities, until 'romantic' was applied indiscriminately to situations and persons, travels and memoirs, pictures and music. It thus acquired the 'universal significance' which seemed to Friedrich Schlegel the chief characteristic of the new art. It was first used by Novalis as a label for the school of criticism and poetry which arose in Jena in the early 'nineties of the eighteenth century. Through the agency of the *Athenäum* and the critical lectures of the brothers Schlegel, Romanticism became a catchword of European importance.

Romanticism was in its origin not inimical to Classicism: Goethe, with *Wilhelm Meister*, Kant with his critical idealism were the progenitors of the movement. Even Schiller gave it an unexpected fillip with his 'romantic' drama *Die Jungfrau von Orleans*. But where Goethe had learned from Kant to accept the ultimate world of reality as unknowable to the senses, the Romanticists sought to attain to its mysteries with the help of the transcendental philosophy of Fichte and Schelling. Classicism was concerned primarily with man in his social setting, Romanticism with nature in which man was but one link. Classicism had learned the lesson of renunciation and moderation in this circumscribed world of reality; Romanticism longed for reunion with the ultimate cosmic forces of the universe.

In art and poetry the Romanticists returned in theory to Herder's thesis of historical development, in practice to the irrationalism and intemperance of the *Sturm und Drang*. Hence, on the one hand, their burning interest in the artistic products of other peoples, be they Greeks, Latins, or English – on the other, the mysticism and formlessness of much of their imaginative work. In this sense the Romanticists are the antagonists of the *Aufklärung*, and Nicolai and Kotzebue[1] were the chief butts of their wit. And, while they respected Lessing's critical brilliance, they condemned the attitude which considered the Greeks as the supreme arbiters of taste for all times and all peoples. They would, in particular, have nothing to do with the severance of the genres proclaimed in *Laokoon*: poetry and music, painting and sculpture were all interchangeable manifestations of the poetic spirit. Tieck wrote poems that have no significance beyond their music, A. W. Schlegel paraphrased pictures in his *Gemäldesonette*, Hoffmann was the first to apprehend colours in music, Heine spoke of *ein Meer von blauen Gedanken*, Schwind (p. 523) painted a symphony in four movements.

The critical tenets of Romanticism were formulated by the brothers Schlegel in their short-lived journal *Athenäum* (1798-1800), and especially in their several 'Lectures' on poetry and art. But the real creative geniuses of the movement were WILHELM HEINRICH WACKENRODER (1773-98), TIECK, and NOVALIS (FRIEDRICH LEOPOLD VON HARDENBERG, 1772-1801). In *Herzensergiessungen eines kunstliebenden Klosterbruders* (1797) and *Franz Sternbalds Wanderungen* (1798) Wackenroder and Tieck gave poetic expression to the Romantic glorification of art and music. Novalis's *Hymnen an die Nacht* (1800) preach the cult of mystic sensuality. His novel *Heinrich von Ofterdingen* (1799-1802) is the very incarnation of Romantic 'Sehnsucht' (symbolized by the *Blaue Blume*), while an essay, *Die Christenheit oder Europa* (written 1799, published 1826), helped to start a revival of Catholicism which was one of the characteristic features in European life of the nineteenth century. An ever increasing number of the Romanticists themselves became converts to the ancient faith.

The chief creative work of AUGUST WILHELM SCHLEGEL (1767-1845) was his translation of Shakespeare (1797-1810), which he left to Tieck's daughter and Wolf Graf von Baudissin to finish (1825-33). It is the most successful rendering into another language of the work of a great poet, mainly because no one had ever penetrated into the form and contents of another literature with such fine perception and feeling. The Romanticists were generally most felicitous in their translations: Tieck and A. W. Schlegel both made masterly renderings from the Romance languages, and Friedrich Schlegel opened a whole new field of poetry for Western Europe by an epoch-making work, *Über die Sprache und Weisheit der Indier* (1808). This book raised many an echo in German literature, and inspired even Goethe with the latter-day poetry of the *Westöstlicher Divan* (1819). RÜCKERT and PLATEN followed in its train with their 'ghasels' and 'makamen'. The most popular collection of original poetry is FRIEDRICH

[1] See note 1, p. 279.

BODENSTEDT's (1819-92) *Die Lieder des Mirza Schaffy* (1851), which had reached the 264th edition by 1917. LUDWIG TIECK (1773-1853), in the wake of his friend Wackenroder, also endeavoured to recapture the Germanic past. He had already rejuvenated some of the old chap-books in the *Volksmärchen von Peter Leberecht* (1797), and his *Minnelieder aus dem schwäbischen Zeitalter* (1803) were the starting-point for the new science of Germanic philology.

In *Lucinde* (1799) FRIEDRICH SCHLEGEL (1772-1829) broached many a problem of social and moral reform which afterwards became a commonplace of European literature. FRIEDRICH ERNST DANIEL SCHLEIERMACHER, the Protestant divine, also advocated the claims of feminism in his *Vertraute Briefe über Lucinde* (1800) and the *Katechismus der Vernunft für edle Frauen* (1800). But Schleiermacher's chief importance lies in the Romantic definition he gave to religion in the *Reden über die Religion* (1799) as 'feeling and taste for the infinite'.

Romantic ideas dominated German literature for the next fifty years from various centres. From Heidelberg was issued the magnificent collection of Volkslieder of ACHIM VON ARNIM (1781-1831) and CLEMENS BRENTANO (1778-1842), *Des Knaben Wunderhorn* (1806-8), in which, true to Friedrich Schlegel's precepts, the whole German people is represented in its widest aspects. The apparent simplicity and naïveté of the *Wunderhorn* rendered it a prime favourite among later Romanticists, and even Goethe acknowledged its charm. These national tendencies were furthered by Joseph von Görres with his *Der Rheinische Merkur* (1814), which Napoleon himself grudgingly acknowledged as 'a fifth great power'. The world-famous tales of the brothers GRIMM (*Hausmärchen*, 1812-22), and the *Deutsche Sagen* (1816), also owe their inspiration to the same movement.

Some of these Romanticists formed the nucleus of a new circle in Berlin which comprised in addition the poets Fouqué, Wilhelm Müller, Eichendorff, Chamisso, the dramatist Heinrich von Kleist, the philosopher Adam Müller and the jurist Friedrich Karl von Savigny. Berlin, where not long before the philosopher Fichte had preached the necessity of a national education in the interests of the State (*Reden an die deutsche Nation*, 1807-8), was a hotbed of German patriotism and of revolt against Napoleon. Kleist and Adam Müller edited the *Berliner Abendblätter* as the organ of the 'Christlich-deutsche Tischgesellschaft', to which many of these poets belonged. And from afar ERNST MORITZ ARNDT (1769-1860), with whom these patriots were in touch, fulminated against the French in the *Nordischer Kontrolleur*. Thus, when the critical year 1813 arrived it found a united Germany, and the revolt against Napoleon was felt as a holy war. Most of these poets joined the army as volunteers, and sang its deeds in fervent song. The real poet of the Wars of Liberation was Arndt, and his *Kriegslieder* (1813) most successfully catch the spirit of manly vigour and sacrifice which inspired the German armies. Some of these poets scored an even greater success in the more legitimate sphere of the pure lyric. WILHELM MÜLLER's (1794-1827) *Wanderlieder* and his pleasantly sentimental *Lindenbaum* are immortal in Schubert's settings, ADALBERT VON CHAMISSO's (1781-1838) *Frauen-Liebe und Leben* are still sung to Schumann's music, while JOSEPH, FREIHERR VON EICHENDORFF (1788-1857) wrote some of the greatest songs in German poetry: *O Täler weit, o Höhen* and *Wem Gott will rechte Gunst erweisen* have been carried round the world in Mendelssohn's settings.

A third and perhaps more fruitful centre of German Romanticism was formed in Swabia under the leadership of LUDWIG UHLAND (1787-1862) and comprised among its members JUSTINUS KERNER and GUSTAV SCHWAB. Uhland made a name both as a scholar and a politician. His *Gedichte* (1815) fill but a small volume, but to his contemporaries they seemed 'the culmination of the Romantic lyric'. The modern world gives the palm rather to EDUARD MÖRIKE (1804-75), only remotely connected with the school, whose gentle spirit, fervent love of nature and quiet humour are admirably reflected in his poetry.

The other-worldliness of Romanticism, its neglect of form and its unpractical view of life necessarily militated against its success in the drama, and Tieck's *Genoveva* (1799) and *Kaiser Octavianus* (1804) are failures, even if splendid failures. But in HEINRICH WILHELM VON KLEIST (1777-1811) it possessed a dramatic genius of the first order, morbid though his outlook upon life might be and far-fetched his plots. Three of his works, the rather grim comedy *Der zerbrochene Krug* (1811), the romantic play *Das Käthchen von Heilbronn* (1810), and the patriotic drama *Der Prinz von Homburg* (1821), have won a permanent place in the affection of the German people. Kleist is accounted by many as the greatest dramatist of modern Germany: his whole work, dramas as well as novels, is the expression of an elementary, tragic conception of life which eventually led him to suicide: there exists on earth no absolute justice, no absolute love, and his characters are bound to perish in their heroic efforts to attain either. This pessimism seemed to Goethe merely morbid, but to a modern generation schooled in the horrors of two wars Kleist appeals with ever-increasing force. For, despite the pathological nature of their themes, Kleist has succeeded in his *Penthesilea* (1806-8) and *Die Hermannsschlacht* (1808), by the artistry of his language and the tautness of the dramatic organisation, in subjugating the intractable material to his artistic purpose. Perhaps the best, certainly the most modern, of his plays is *Amphitryon* (1807), with its delicate probing into a woman's soul. In contrast the dramas of ZACHARIAS WERNER (1768-1823), though not without psychological interest, lack realism. Only once did he obtain more than a passing success with *Der 24. Februar* (produced 1810, published 1815), in which fate is cleverly symbolized by fatal requisites and an unlucky date.

It was in the novel, and especially in the short story, that Romanticism achieved its greatest distinction. Again Goethe's *Wilhelm Meister* (1795-96) was the chief inspiration. The fullness of life which it represents, the breadth of outlook and, above all, its stressing of the irrational aspects of existence (symbolized by the mysterious figures of the Harper and Mignon), all contributed to making it the favourite book of the Romanticists. JEAN PAUL (Friedrich Richter, 1763-1825) is patently indebted to it in his first novel *Hesperus* (1795). In spite of exaggerations and digressions no author was more popular than Jean Paul, at the time when Goethe and Schiller were read by the few. The time has passed when, with Carlyle, we spoke of Jean Paul as 'one of the chosen men of Germany and of the world', but his loving portrayal of the little things of life, the whimsical humour akin to tears, his tenderness and pity for the frail and weak, long endeared him to the middle classes both in Germany and England. The same unpractical outlook on life characterizes the heroes of most Romantic novels from *Heinrich von Ofterdingen* down to that supreme glorification of idleness, Eichendorff's *Aus dem Leben eines Taugenichts* (1826). The tradition of *Wilhelm Meister*, in which art and love are the chief formative influences on the hero, has persisted in German literature, and even had some repercussion abroad; Tieck's *Der junge Tischlermeister* (1836) belongs to this category, as do also Mörike's *Maler Nolten* (1832) and Gottfried Keller's *Der grüne Heinrich* (1854).

Goethe, too, first naturalized the Italian *novella* by his *Unterhaltungen deutscher Ausgewanderten* (1795), but it was the Romanticists, by their theory and practice, who decided the popularity of its German imitation. F. Schlegel, in his studies on Boccaccio, and Tieck in *Gesammelte Schriften* (XI, 86), both stressed its anecdotal and unique character, the novelty of the subject matter, the importance of the crisis, the gently ironic attitude, the unexpectedness of the solution. But few of Tieck's own *Novellen* came up to his precepts, apart from *Die Gemälde*, *Die Verlobung*, *Die Reisenden*. His *Märchen*, on the other hand, have won a permanent place in literature: *Der blonde Eckbert*, *Der Runenberg*, *Die Elfen* are convincing stories of the immanence of the supernatural in men's daily lives. The real master of the Romantic *Novelle* was Kleist: his *Michael Kohlhaas* (1821) is a dramatic story told with superb artistry and concentration:

Die Marquise von O, Die Verlobung auf St. Domingo, Das Erdbeben in Chili, Das Bettelweib von Locarno are all brilliant examples of his power to treat an unheard-of, even monstrous occurrence with the same perfect command of subject and language. E. T. A. HOFFMANN[1] (1776-1822) exaggerated the 'unexpected' element which, according to Goethe, is the Novelle's chief characteristic, into the grotesque, and obtained his most telling effects from the juxtaposition of the supernatural with reality, as in *Der goldene Topf* (1813) and *Nussknacker und Mausekönig* (1821). No mean musician and a brilliant caricaturist, Hoffmann is at his best in the description of the artistic temperament; and he has given a sympathetic portrayal of his own in the eccentric figure of Kapellmeister Kreisler in the *Kreisleriana* (1814). His grotesques won him a European reputation, and he exerted great influence on the French and English Romantics and beyond to the 'hallucinated' heroes of Franz Kafka in our own day. His name was most fittingly immortalized in the tuneful opera of Offenbach *Les Contes d'Hoffmann*. Through Hoffmann the *Künstlernovelle* became very popular. Music was the favourite Romantic art, and it is significant that two of the greatest stories of the time should have had a musician as their heroes – a sorry one in Grillparzer's *Der arme Spielmann* (1848), a supreme artist in Mörike's *Mozart auf der Reise nach Prag* (1852-53). Other *Novellen* are reminiscent of the more realistic treatment of Tieck: Achim von Arnim's *Der tolle Invalide* (1818), Hoffmann's *Das Fräulein von Scuderi* (1819) and Annette von Droste-Hülshoff's *Die Judenbuche* (1842); the two latter both precursors of the modern detective story, as are too Fontane's *Unterm Birnbaum* (1886), Raabe's *Stopfkuchen* (1891), Ricarda Huch's *Der Fall Deruga* (1917). Still others tend to break with the accepted form, and approach the *Märchen* – the distinction between *Märchen* and *Novelle* is often hard to draw. The beautiful *Hyacinth und Rosenblütchen* (1802) of Novalis, Clemens Brentano's *Aus der Chronika eines fahrenden Schülers* (begun 1803, published 1818), *Das Märchen von dem Rhein und dem Müller Radlauf* (1846), and *Gockel, Hinkel und Gackeleia* (1838), and Fouqué's *Undine* (1811) are all tales of delightful fancy. Both Goethe in his *Märchen* (1794), and Tieck in his *Phantasus* (1812-17) had shown the way. Brentano's *Geschichte vom braven Kasperl* (1817), on the other hand, shows the two genres running fluid the one into the other. Eventually the closed form of the *Novelle* broke up altogether, and in the hands of Gottfried Keller and Conrad Ferdinand Meyer broad, general problems of life and the historical background gradually submerged the single anecdotal theme.

While Romanticism was in no sense antagonistic to Classicism –

[1] He was christened Ernst Theodor Wilhelm, but he substituted Amadeus for Wilhelm, because of his love of Mozart.

Friedrich Schlegel himself began as a fervent admirer of Greek literature – it yet broke definitely with the one-sided conception of Winckelmann's *edle Einfalt und stille Grösse*. Herder and Goethe had both emphasized the *edle Menschlichkeit* of the Greeks, and Goethe's *Iphigenie* is his noblest tribute to eighteenth-century humanitarianism. Helena remained for Goethe his whole life long a symbol of Greek beauty. But to FRIEDRICH HÖLDERLIN (1770-1843) the Greeks were primarily an ideal national community in which nature and man were in perfect harmony. It was for such a vision of ancient Hellas that the hero of the epistolar prose romance *Hyperion* (1797-99) longed in vain; but it is realized artistically in the ode *Archipelagos* (1800). The Germans, too, Hölderlin declared, could attain to this ideal synthesis would they but listen to the voice of the seer (*Gesang der Deutschen*). It is only by offering the divine spark of his individuality as a sacrifice to the oneness of nature that man can hope to attain again to the harmony which he has destroyed by the very fact of his existence. Such is the theme of his unfinished drama *Empedokles* (1797). It is this mystic pantheism which makes Hölderlin a Romantic in spite of his classical sympathies. There is already present in his work an orgiastic trait (in his translation of Sophocles for instance) which led him to imagine a synthesis of Christ and Dionysus in the ode *Brot und Wein* (1801). Nietzsche was only carrying the idea further when, in *Die Geburt der Tragödie aus dem Geiste der Musik* (1872; see p. 445), he emphasized the tragic, pessimistic substratum of Greek culture which he described as Dionysiac in contrast to the Apollonian harmony of Goethe's or Schiller's gods of Greece. These contrasting views of the Greeks still find an echo in the literature of today: side by side with the hysterical *Elektra* of Hofmannsthal and the brutality of Werfel's *Troerinnen* we have the serene, harmonious conception of human beauty in Stefan George's *Hirten- und Preisgedichte* (1895).

FRANZ GRILLPARZER (1791-1872), too, sought a common norm between ancient Hellas and modern Europe; but his Greeks, like Hölderlin's, are romanticized. Grillparzer kept aloof from schools and cliques, and his sympathies, both literary and political, were with the eighteenth century, his outlook upon life was that of the cosmopolitan Voltaire. He was proud of being an Austrian and a Viennese, and of being able to look back on centuries of international culture of the Danube monarchy. His historical plays are a glorification of the Habsburgs: *König Ottokars Glück und Ende* (1825), *Ein treuer Diener seines Herrn* (1830), *Ein Bruderzwist in Habsburg* (1873). *Die Ahnfrau* (1817) is a *Schicksalstragödie* on the model of Zacharias Werner's *Der 24. Februar* (p. 363), in which fate is again symbolized by the coincidence of dates and the use of fatal instruments.

It is written in trochaic tetrameters, a favourite metre of Grillparzer's derived from Spanish tragedy (of which he was an expert critic) and which he used again in his most popular play *Der Traum ein Leben* (1817-34), a *Märchendrama* of the type introduced by his countryman FERDINAND RAIMUND (1790-1836), and founded on the local pantomime. He now turned to classical subjects, the better to bring out the disproportion of art and reality which made his own life wretched. Like Goethe's *Tasso*, *Sappho* is a *Künstlertragödie* (1818). It shows the poetess, like Grillparzer himself, unable to descend from the heights to partake in the common experiences of mankind for which she longs. An even greater discord ruins the life of Medea, the heroine of *Das goldene Vliess* (1820), while Hero in *Des Meeres und der Liebe Wellen* (1831), after vacillating between renunciation and passion, finally gives herself up entirely to love. Grillparzer wrote one comedy, *Weh' dem, der lügt* (1838), so serious in tone that it failed when first performed, and caused Grillparzer to withdraw still more into himself. But the spirit of kindliness and humanity, of tolerance and unselfishness and generous good-humour which pervades the play gives it a high place in the dramatic literature of Austria.

The same overwhelming pessimism also looms over the work of NIKOLAUS LENAU (1802-50); for him, too, the time was out of joint, and his poetry, both lyric and dramatic, suffers from Romantic subjectivity. But occasionally he emerges from this morbid introspection into an objective view of life and nature which makes his *Schilflieder* some of the most perfect lyrics of modern times. The musicality of his verses has attracted musicians to set them to music more often than those of any other German poet except Heine. ANNETTE FREIIN VON DROSTE-HÜLSHOFF (1797-1848), acclaimed by many as the greatest German poetess, was inspired by her native Westphalia to write her 'Heidebilder' (*Gedichte* 1844), which still rank amongst the best of German nature lyrics. The poetry of FRIEDRICH RÜCKERT (1788-1866) runs the whole gamut of the lyric: love poems, nature poems, even ballads; and he was adept in the handling of foreign metres. His *Kindertotenlieder* (1834), his *Liebesfrühling* (1823) and many gems from the *Weisheit des Brahmanen* (1836-39) are still remembered, not only for their virtuosity, but for their genuine poetry. AUGUST GRAF VON PLATEN-HALLERMÜNDE (1796-1835) was generally inimical to Romanticism and parodied the *Schicksalstragödie* in *Die verhängnisvolle Gabel* (1826). His poetry is on the whole intellectual rather than emotional and, though some of his ballads ('Das Grab im Busento', 'Der Pilgrim von St. Just') are still found in every German anthology, his best work was done in the formal perfection of the sonnet (*Sonette aus Venedig* 1825).

German Romanticism dominated most of the nineteenth century, and its influence persists even today. It brought home to Europe the universality of Goethe's genius, and for the first time in history established a temporary predominance of the German spirit. It realized to some extent Goethe's vision of a World Literature which should unite all peoples and countries in a community of intellectual interests. The remainder of the century is thus either the fulfilment of, or the reaction to, Romanticism.

The chief bond which united *Das Junge Deutschland* was the conscious opposition to the prevailing Goethe idolatry and to the mysticism and irreality of Romanticism. The first definite attempt to bring art and literature down to earth once more was made by a group of young hotheads known by this designation. But few of these Young Germans, apart from Heine, possessed more than talent, and their work only rarely rises above good journalism. The theoretician of the movement, LUDOLF WIENBARG (1802-72), definitely (in his *Ästhetische Feldzüge*, 1834) recommended treating politics and social problems as literature. LUDWIG BÖRNE[1] (1786-1837), with his *Briefe aus Paris* (1832-34), breathed the fire and flame of the Revolution he had just witnessed in France. Consequently the work of most of this group has a distinct polemic tendency: KARL GUTZKOW (1811-78) attacks orthodoxy in *Maha Guru, Geschichte eines Gottes* (1833), and conventional morality in *Wally, die Zweiflerin* (1835), Catholic ultramontanism in *Der Zauberer von Rom* (1846) and *Die Ritter vom Geiste* (1850). But his best work is in the drama: *Uriel Acosta* (1847) is still effective on the stage as a plea for religious tolerance. *Zopf und Schwert* (1844), on the other hand, is a heavy comedy of intrigue reeking too much of beer and tobacco. *Der Königsleutnant* (1849), founded on a celebrated episode in Goethe's youth, was once very popular on the stage, but, in spite of many humorous touches and telling points, is now only read in schools. HEINRICH LAUBE's (1806-1884) interests were also primarily in the theatre, and he accomplished good works as director of the Viennese Burgtheater. Laube also composed numerous dramas of his own. *Graf Essex* (1853) is in the style of the grand historical dramas of Schiller, whose *Demetrius* he also furnished with a conclusion. He wrote one novel of more than passing interest: *Das junge Europa* (1833-37), which affords remarkable insight into the social and political background of his time. THEODOR MUNDT (1806-61), on the other hand, would be forgotten today but for his connection with Charlotte Stieglitz, whose tragic suicide he commemorated in a sympathetic *Denkmal* (1835); the wife of another poet of Jung Deutschland, Heinrich Stieglitz, she killed herself in the hope of rekindling her husband's dormant genius.

---

[1] Name adopted by Löb Baruch when he was converted to Christianity.

Among the members of the Young German school condemned for their subversive tendencies by the notorious edict of the Bundesrat in 1835 was included HEINRICH HEINE (1797-1856). But his interest in the movement was chiefly that, as a Jew, he was an outcast in the eyes of German officialdom. He was driven into opposition and exile when he would much have preferred to live as a respectable bourgeois. Hence much of his cynicism and bitterness was a personal reaction to injustice and persecution. In his affectation of romantic irony he was at the same time the literary heir of that age of pessimism which had begun with *Werther* and culminated in Byron. He finally found a congenial home in the Paris of Louis Philippe. To the outside world Heine is the greatest German lyric poet after Goethe, a judgment to which the Germans themselves have never subscribed, estranged as they are by his political heresies, his French sympathies, his mockery of all they hold sacred, his lapses into bad taste and loose morality; or simply, like the hot-headed patriot Wolfgang Menzel,[2] or Hitler's National Socialists, out of sheer prejudice against 'all Jews and Frenchmen'. But granted that much of his work is pure journalism, that his poetry is often spoiled by misplaced sarcasm, there yet remains sufficient great poetry in the *Buch der Lieder* (1827) and the *Romanzero* (1851) to render his name immortal. The German public, as apart from the critic, has no doubt as to his greatness, and *Die Lorelei*, *Die Grenadiere*, *Du bist wie eine Blume* have become veritable *Volkslieder*, while German musicians, with Schumann at their head, have set his poems more often than those of any other German poet.

Closely related to *Das Junge Deutschland* was a group of politically-minded poets whose songs are prophetic of the coming revolution of 1848: an Austrian aristocrat, Graf Auersperg (pseudonym ANASTASIUS GRÜN) had led the way with the *Spaziergänge eines Wiener Poeten* (1831), Heine had followed suit with his *Zeitgedichte* and the satiric epic *Deutschland, ein Wintermärchen* (both 1844); Georg Herwegh with the *Gedichte eines Lebendigen* (1841); FERDINAND FREILIGRATH with *Ein Glaubensbekenntnis* (1844) and *Ça ira* (1846); HOFFMANN VON FALLERSLEBEN with his *Unpolitische Lieder* (1840-42); FRANZ VON DINGELSTEDT with the *Lieder eines kosmopolitischen Nachtwächters* (1841). But apart from the *Weberlied* of Heine, and the *Von unten auf* of Freiligrath there is little of permanent value in this political poetry.

The failure of the Revolution either drove these poets into exile or

---

[2] It was chiefly Menzel who, by his denunciation of the Young Germans in his *Literaturblatt*, first drew the attention of Metternich to the movement, and was thus responsible for the notorious decree of the Bundesrat in 1835 which suppressed it.

forced them to compromise with the ruling powers. Others, like GUSTAV FREYTAG (1816-95), continued the liberal traditions of 1848. His three-volume novel *Soll und Haben* (1855) is not only a panegyric of the middle classes at the expense of the nobility but one of the best examples of the German *Bildungsroman* (see p. 256). His comedy *Die Journalisten* (1854) is a plea for political reconciliation, but it is also one of the few good comedies in German literature, still vital today through its humorous situations and clever dialogues. FRIEDRICH SPIELHAGEN's (1829-1911) *Problematische Naturen* (1861) still glorifies the liberal heroes of 1848, but his novel *Hammer und Amboss* (1869) foreshadows the coming revolution of the proletariat: GEORG HERWEGH (1817-75), the friend of Lassalle, gave the Socialist movement its war-cry in the famous *Bundeslied für den allgemeinen deutschen Arbeiterverein* (1864), with its stirring call to the general strike: *Mann der Arbeit aufgewacht!* | *Und erkenne deine Macht!* | *Alle Räder stehen still* | *Wenn dein starker Arm es will.*

Of the poets of revolution none was more unrestrained in his life and work than the North German CHRISTIAN DIETRICH GRABBE (1801-36). His wild imagination – made the wilder by the alcoholism which brought him to an untimely grave – found expression in a play *Herzog Theodor von Gothland* (1827), which in stark horror and lust of destruction outdoes the worst excesses of the *Sturm und Drang*. Grabbe sought out examples in history of individuals at enmity with themselves and with life: Sulla, Hannibal, Arminius, Barbarossa, Napoleon. But behind this belated Storm and Stress was real dramatic power, and *Don Juan und Faust* (1829) is remarkable for its effective fusion of two famous legends. In spite of much rant and bombast and some transgressions against good taste, Grabbe has drawn a convincing and, at times, moving, presentation of the struggle of two demonic personalities for the same woman.

The transition from literature to politics is best seen in the work of GEORG BÜCHNER (1813-37), the eldest child of a distinguished family of writers which comprised amongst its members a materialistic philosopher (Ludwig; p. 271) and an early champion of women's rights (Luise). Virtually unknown during his life except as a political agitator, he was rediscovered after the First World War and acclaimed as the precursor of expressionist drama. (It is significant that Kasimir Edschmid re-edited his *Gesammelte Werke* as late as 1948.) A born demagogue, he anticipated Marx by his proclamation of class warfare: '*Friede den Hütten, Krieg den Palästen!*'; he was forced to flee from Germany and died in exile. He was introduced to literature by Gutzkow, but, though in the violence of his themes he showed affinities to *Das Junge Deutschland*, in the terse, staccato, ecstatic, convulsive expression of them he uses a language that is entirely his own. Foiled in politics he turned to literature, and *Dantons Tod* (1835) and *Woyzeck* (not published till 1879) are both powerful dramas of revolution which foreshadow the supremacy of the proletariat. The former has all the excitement of Schiller's first drama, and its hero, eloquent agitator and fiery cynic, lofty idealist and loose liver, is drawn from the poet's own heart. The latter, the tragedy of a common soldier, is a moving portrayal of a primitive herd-man broken by a cruel fate on a hostile and callous world indifferent to the sufferings of the underdog. By the dissolution of the action into a succession of self-contained scenes Büchner is not only the heir of the ballad technique of Goethe's early plays (*Götz* and the *Urfaust*) but also anticipates the modern cinema. Through the opera of Alban Berg, *Woyzeck* (first performed in 1923), he has attracted universal attention. If these two dramas foreshadow the coming of realism, *Leonce und Lena* (1836) is a return to the literary comedy of Tieck and Brentano, but with a political twist. The Novelle *Lenz* (1836) can still hold the modern reader by its penetrating study of the wayward, irresponsible, perverse yet brilliant genius, Goethe's quondam friend as seen through the eyes of Büchner the brain specialist. Büchner's early death in 1837 robbed the world not only of a promising physician, but of one of the most talented dramatists of the modern world.

It is customary to dismiss as dilettanti or *epigoni* the group of poets and art lovers (they went under the name of 'Das Krokodil') whom Maximilian II collected around him in Munich after his accession to the Bavarian throne in 1848. And indeed little of the poetry of HERMANN LINGG (1820-1905), GRAF ADOLF FRIEDRICH VON SCHACK (1815-94), JULIUS GROSSE (1828-1902), HEINRICH LEUTHOLD (1827-79), MARTIN GREIF (1839-1911) rises above virtuosity. But both EMANUEL GEIBEL (1815-84) and especially PAUL HEYSE (1830-1914) possessed real poetic talent. The former is still remembered by the lofty thought and formal perfection of the patriotic *Heroldsrufe* (1871), inspired by the German victories of the war of 1870-71. Among his non-political poetry one song at least has achieved immortality: *Der Mai ist gekommen, die Bäume schlagen aus*. Among the hundred or more *Novellen* of Heyse (the first collection appeared in 1855) there are surprisingly few masterpieces. He rarely succeeded in fusing the beauty of form which he had learned from his Italian masters with objectivity of outlook as in *L'Arrabbiata* (1855) or *Villa Falconieri* (1887). He did good work as a translator from the Italian and also achieved distinction as critic of the *Novelle*. In the preface to the *Deutscher Novellenschatz* (24 vols., 1871 *seq.*) he propounded the celebrated *Falkentheorie* derived from the salient importance of the falcon in one of Boccaccio's stories. He argued from this that the *Novelle* should possess

one central conflict to which the action should always revert. JOSEPH
VIKTOR VON SCHEFFEL (1826-86) stood in close relation to the Munich
group and suffered from the same sentimentality. But his humorous
verse romance *Der Trompeter von Säkkingen* (1854), although nowhere
rising to great heights of poetry, is a freshly and vividly told, pleasantly
romantic story. Scheffel's humour is of the jovial, boisterous, obvious
type; his collection of student songs, *Gaudeamus* (1867), admirably
represents the traditional beer-drinking (*feuchtfröhlich*), amorous side of
German academic life usually associated with the Corps-student and with
the University of Heidelberg: *Alt Heidelberg du feine!* The collection
Frau Aventiure (1863) also contains some fine lyrics.

The Munich school forms a convenient bridge to the second literary
movement of the nineteenth century, Poetic Realism. According to
Otto Ludwig, who invented the term, the main function of poetry was
to represent life, but life only as it was worthy of artistic permanence.
Der poetische Realismus stands for truth, but, unlike later Naturalism, it
insists on beauty. In another sense it derives from Young Germany,
especially through its interests in social and moral problems; it differs from
it in so far as it believes in evolution (Darwin's *Origin of Species* appeared
in 1859) rather than revolution. It is positive in its tendencies rather than
negative, and finds its political ideals in the liberalism that the Continent
was gradually assimilating from England. Unlike Romanticism, it considers the individual primarily as the member of an ordered society; and
like Classicism, of which it is the ninteenth century equivalent, it deals
with the world of reality rather than with the world of dreams. Consequently, it draws its chief inspiration from the exact sciences, and has
little use for speculative philosophy. ERNST HAECKEL (1834-1919), in his
Natürliche Schöpfungsgeschichte (1867), considered all living organisms
under the aspect of historical evolution. LUDWIG BÜCHNER (1824-99)
emphasized the material aspect of life in a popular scientific work, *Kraft
und Stoff* (1855), in which the phrase occurs: 'Der Mensch ist, was er isst.'
LUDWIG FEUERBACH (1804-72), the philosopher of the movement (Gottfried Keller sat at his feet as a student in Heidelberg), taught hedonism
and, like Stuart Mill in England, saw the ideal in the greatest happiness
of the greatest number. LEOPOLD VON RANKE (1795-1886) built up
history on the solid foundations of ascertained fact, and DAVID FRIEDRICH
STRAUSS (1808-74), applying similar critical methods, endeavoured to
disentangle the historical figure from the myth and legend with which it
was overlaid in *Das Leben Jesu* (1835, translated by George Eliot in 1846).

Poetry is thus, according to this school, chiefly concerned with social
problems and psychological development, and it deals with actual people

in real settings. Hence the interest attaching not only to the townsman, but above all to the peasant and his characteristic habits and speech, as being nearer to nature. Till comparatively recently BERTHOLD AUERBACH (1812-82) passed as the actual founder of a new genre with his *Schwarzwälder Dorfgeschichten* (1843-54); but the critics had forgotten the fine tale, *Der Oberhof,* buried in KARL LEBERECHT IMMERMANN's (1796-1840) *Münchhausen* (1839); and they had underestimated the novels of peasant life by the Swiss parson JEREMIAS GOTTHELF (Albert Bitzius, 1797-1854), a contemporary of Auerbach. Gotthelf gives proof of real understanding and sympathy for the worker on the soil, and his objective treatment (*Wie Uli, der Knecht, glücklich ward,* 1841; *Uli der Pächter,* 1849) makes Auerbach's once famous stories seem artificial and sentimental by contrast. Auerbach found many imitators, but none more competent than OTTO LUDWIG (1813-65), in whose hands the *Dorfnovelle* became a magnificent study of psychological realism: *Die Heiterethei* (1854), *Aus dem Regen in die Traufe* (1857), *Zwischen Himmel und Erde* (1856). GOTTFRIED KELLER (1819-90) was an even greater master of the realistic short story. His early training as a painter had sharpened his vision, and his two cycles *Die Leute von Seldwyla* (1856-74) and *Züricher Novellen* (1878) still charm by their truth to nature, their romantic setting, and their serene humour. Keller marks the transition between Romanticism and Naturalism, and in the autobiographical novel *Der grüne Heinrich* (1854, revised version 1879) he has set forth his own development from Romantic æstheticism to social-political realism. Salvation both for the individual and society lies in truth to nature: what is natural is good.

Keller's humour never forsakes him, even in the most tragic situations, confident as he is that truth must ultimately win through. But it was only after repeated attempts that WILHELM RAABE (1831-1910) emerged from the pessimism of *Der Hungerpastor* (1862-63), *Abu Telfan* (1868) and *Der Schüdderump* (1867-69) to the serene optimism of his model, Jean Paul. But then he wrote some of the best *Novellen* in German literature: *Des Reiches Krone, Else von der Tanne, Holunderblüte, Alte Nester, Das Horn von Wanza,* in which life even at its bitterest is treated with idyllic tenderness, loving detail, and kindly humour. FRITZ REUTER (1810-74) had learned from bitter experience that life is hard and unjust – he had spent seven years in a fortress as a political prisoner – but in spite of all he never lost faith in its ultimate goodness. *Ut mine Stromtid* (1863) – Reuter, like his compatriot Klaus Groth, wrote in Low German – is a masterpiece of realistic description, and in *Ut mine Festungstid* (1863) he can bear to look back without bitterness on the harshness of his imprisonment.

The Austrian novelist ADALBERT STIFTER (1805-68) has only become known to a wider public since the publication between 1901 and 1928 of his Collected Works in 21 volumes. He is a typical representative of the Austrian reverence for tradition and of Austrian quietism. In his young days he consorted with the Viennese circle of the Vormärz[1] which included Grillparzer, Grün and Lenau. Repelled by the revolution of 1848, he retired to the provinces, settling finally in his native Bohemia, where, in a fit of maniac depression, he put an end to his life. His æsthetic creed is contained in the introduction to the collection of stories *Bunte Steine* (1853), in which, like Jean Paul before him, he proclaims the greatness of every-day happenings, of the trivial and infinitely small as revealing the everlasting and infinite reality of which they are the symbol. In true Romantic fashion he sought the harmony of man with nature, and found it in the lives of the country folk he knew in his Bohemian mountains, in the idyllic landscapes in which they lived, and in the daily occurrences which ruled their lives. He can thus best be assigned to 'Poetic Realism', which, indeed, he was the first to define theoretically. His best-known novel, *Nachsommer* (3 vols. 1857), has often been compared to *Wilhelm Meister*, with which it has the pedagogic theme in common. But it has none of the universal sweep of Goethe's *Erziehungsroman*, and Stifter is concerned with the integration of his hero into the family rather than into society. His tranquil outlook upon the world (so different from the psychosis which ruined his life) is best seen in the historical novel *Witiko* (1865-67), in which he dreams of a utopian Bohemia united into a happy land of Czech peasants and feudal German overlords under the aegis of a Catholic dynasty; a beautiful illusion, out-of-date before it was glimpsed, and destined to be shattered on the hard reality of historical events. Stifter's own favourite story was *Die Mappe meines Urgroßvaters* (1841 ff), which he rewrote no less than four times in his quest for perfection. It expresses his faith in the basic forms of human existence which he recognized as the 'simple life'. Stifter has long been acknowledged as a stylist and by no less a master than Nietzsche himself, and it is this, in conjunction with his insistence on universal human values, which turns him from the poet of the narrower sphere of *Heimatkunst* into a literary figure of European stature.

THEODOR STORM (1817-88) began as a Romantic, and his earliest Novelle *Immensee* (1850) is loose in composition and elegiac in tone. Gradually he fell under the spell of the new psychological realism, and gave pictures of German life, past and present, which are distinguished by perfection of form, tenseness of composition, and a rare delicacy and depth of characterization. Many of Storm's stories have won a permanent

---

[1] The period before the March revolution in 1848. See p. 83.

place in German literature: *Beim Vetter Christian* (1874), *Pole Poppenspäler* (1874), *Psyche* (1875), *Carsten Curator* (1878), *Die Söhne des Senators* (1880), *Der Schimmelreiter* (1888).

A number of Storm's *Novellen* dealt with the German past and, indeed, under the influence of the rising historical school under von Ranke, Georg Waitz, Friedrich Wilhelm von Giesebrecht, Heinrich von Sybel, history began to play a part of increasing importance in the novel. WILLIBALD ALEXIS (Wilhelm Häring, 1798-1871) had written some admirable stories of Prussian history in imitation of Walter Scott; and WILHELM HAUFF (1802-27) had glorified his own beautiful Swabian countryside in *Lichtenstein* (1826). Scheffel made the tenth century live again by modernizing the thoughts and characters of his *Ekkehard* (1857). WILHELM HEINRICH RIEHL (1823-97) sought to represent imaginary characters against the background of a definite period: his *Kulturgeschicht-liche Novellen* (1856) are, however, better history than they are novels, and the same is true of the eight volumes of Gustav Freytag's *Die Ahnen* (1872-80), which present the story of a German family from about A.D. 400 to 1848. Finally, in the hands of GEORG EBERS (1837-98) and FELIX DAHN (1834-1912), the novel became a vehicle for scholars to parade their learning. They hoped to render history palatable to the general reader by the description of stirring events or the introduction of a love episode. *Eine ägyptische Königstochter* by Ebers (1864), however, won European fame and was popular with our Victorian ancestors. Dahn's *Ein Kampf um Rom* (1876) is a sensational account of the final struggle between Goth and Greek in Italy, and was once the favourite light reading of the young student of Germanic philology.

On a very different plane of artistry are the novels and stories of CONRAD FERDINAND MEYER (1825-98). As a Swiss, Meyer was heir to both German and French culture: from the former he derived fullness of content and depth of thought and feeling; from the latter the power of sensuous perception and plastic expression. The German victories of 1870 brought to him the consciousness of his German nationality and strengthened his individualistic and psychological tendencies. JAKOB BURCKHARDT's (1818-97) *Die Kultur der Renaissance in Italien* (1860) provided him with the social and historical background for the great individualists whom he takes as his heroes. His best *Novellen* are set in the gorgeous pageantry of the Renaissance: *Jürg Jenatsch, Der Schuss von der Kanzel, Das Amulett, Die Versuchung des Pescara, Angela Borgia*. *Der Heilige* takes us back to the troublous times of Thomas à Becket, and is to some extent a reflection of the conflict between the Church and the State under Bismarck known as the 'Kulturkampf'. Meyer is one of the few Germans who have united romantic content and realistic form into a harmonious whole. He, at all events, justified the term *poetischer Realismus*.

A similar synthesis was also achieved by the leading dramatist of the movement, FRIEDRICH HEBBEL (1813-63). He, too, had started from the Young German school, in opposition to the classical drama of Schiller, in which he saw nothing but an artificial creation lacking in national content and deep conception of personality. He is conscious of the disproportion of life rather than of its harmony; and, like Hölderlin in his *Empedokles*, he is haunted by the agony of existence, of the dualism between the individual and the universal. The tragedy of life consists for Hebbel in the constant battle between man and the universal law, in the contradictions of life for which there is no solution. Hebbel claimed that his drama was more closely akin to that of the Greeks than to that of Shakespeare; not character, but fate conditions tragedy, pitiless fate which crushes the innocent and guilty alike. But Hebbel was primarily a poet and not a thinker, and it is a mistake to exaggerate the philosophic content of his work. His early dramas *Judith* (1841) and *Genoveva* (1843) owe more, however, to the social theories of *Das Junge Deutschland* and to the monomania of youthful heroes of the *Sturm und Drang* like Götz or Karl Moor than to Sophocles. In one sense, however, *Judith* marks an epoch in the European drama: by insisting on individuality rather than character Hebbel discovered a new motive for dramatic action. Judith slays Holofernes, not as the enemy of her people, but because he has most wantonly outraged her individuality. Hebbel has well been called the Frauenlob[1] of modern German literature, after the medieval minnesinger who had placed the social worth of woman above her sex.

Hebbel's was a strong sensual nature, and practically all his plays turn on the sex conflict. *Genoveva* is personal as few of his dramas are: in Golo he has represented his own sexual life, torn between his duty to Elise, his mistress, and a sudden passion for a passing acquaintance. There is also a strong 'confessional' element in *Maria Magdalene* (1844), the tragedy of common life which he had reproduced from his own experience. Klara dies a voluntary death because she cannot reconcile her actions with the accepted code of morality. Hebbel claimed in his *Vorwort* that he had thus raised the *bürgerliche Tragödie* to universal significance, whereas Schiller, in *Kabale und Liebe*, had been content with the purely external and temporary conflict of *mésalliance*.

---

[1] Heinrich von Meissen (*c*. 1250-1318), one of the later Minnesänger, was given the name of Frauenlob because in a contest of song he maintained that *Frau* (lady) was a nobler term than *Weib*. He founded the first Meistersängerschule in Mainz, where he was borne to his grave by ladies.

From now onwards the action of Hebbel's dramas takes place in an unnatural philosophic world of his own. It seemed to him that the tragic conflicts between man and woman, or between the individual and society, took on universal significance from being set at turning points in the history of civilization. Hebbel was always a recluse; and, as he confessed himself, he had little contact with life. Thus, subtle and brilliant as are the dialectics of *Herodes and Marianne* (1850), and psychologically faultless as is the action once the premises are granted, yet there is no pretending that either Herod or his consort have any connection with real life. The situations imagined by the dramatist are so obviously unreal, the characters so exceptional that they scarcely arouse sympathy. The frictions and misunderstandings, the possessive jealousy and false pride inherent in every union of sensitive souls lead to tragedy for Hebbel only because he will admit of no compromise.

The setting of Hebbel's next play is reminiscent of Kleist's *Das Käthchen von Heilbronn*, but it is only outwardly that *Agnes Bernauer* (1852) is Romantic. Its problem is modern: it is the conflict of the individual with the State and the tragedy of beauty which conditions its own ruin. *Gyges und sein Ring* (1856) is even more a fiction of the mind than *Herodes und Marianne*. Hebbel deliberately flouts everyday experience, and accepts the magic story of the ring in order to bring about the tragic conflict. It is difficult to believe that Rhodope, the dreamy Oriental, acts from any other motive than outraged propriety, and that Kandaules is actuated by anything nobler than vanity. In *Die Nibelungen* (1862) Hebbel comes down to earth and succeeds, by reducing the supernatural element and the ruggedness of the medieval epic, in making the story humanly comprehensible to the modern world.

The intellectualism, the artificiality of Hebbel's drama have necessarily limited the range of his influence. To academic circles, indeed, he offers many an interesting æsthetic and critical problem, and the 'literature' on Hebbel has grown to vast proportions. But to the masses he scarcely appeals at all, and his plays are rarely seen on the German stage. *Agnes Bernauer* and *Die Nibelungen* are still read in schools, but from historical rather than æsthetic motives. And yet, in its day, Hebbel's drama had some repercussion in European literature, and Ibsen once expressed surprise that he should be hailed as a pioneer in the country that had nurtured Hebbel. In *A Doll's House, The Lady of the Sea, John Gabriel Borkman*, the central thesis is, as so often in Hebbel, the rights of the individual. Hebbel's influence on the succeeding generation of Realists thus came through the intermediary of a foreign dramatist rather than direct.

While the theoretical background of Hebbel's drama was uncertain and fluctuating, the work of Otto Ludwig (p. 272) is rooted in the solid reality of Shakespeare. His *Shakespearestudien* (1871), though full of brilliant *aperçus*, led him to a one-sided, prejudiced view of Schiller. *Die Makkabäer* (1854) is scarcely a great historical tragedy, but *Der Erbförster* (1850) is set against the real background of Ludwig's own Thuringian countryside, and admirably illustrates the author's precepts that poetry must show the truth of life, and that each man makes or mars his own destiny. But the play is overladen with sensational elements derived from his favourite author E.T.A. Hoffmann and the *Schicksalstragödie*.

With superb aplomb and egotism RICHARD WAGNER (1813–83) pro-claimed the accomplishment of the Romantic dream: the merging of all the arts, music, poetry, miming, painting into one *Gesamtkunstwerk* and for a moment he believed, with Nietzsche, that he had outdone the Greeks. So strong was his belief in his own genius and in the ethical value of its message for mankind that he bore down all opposition by the sheer force of his personality. Yet though his influence has been immense, it belongs to the history of music rather than to that of literature; and even here it has not gone unchallenged. Nietzsche turned against the god he had adored and pointed to his immoderation, his morbidity and vulgarity, his ruthlessness, fanaticism and self-assertion. Thomas Mann, himself a great musician, has taken up the cry and deplored the tendencies to chaos which he discerns in his work and which seem to him to reflect the chief danger of the German character. It is at least certain that Nazism seized on his glorification of the Nordic myth and turned it into one of its most blatant and obnoxious instruments of propaganda.

K

CHAPTER X

GERMAN LITERATURE FROM 1880 TO 1954

IN a sense it is possible to say that the literature of the period 1880-1954 begins with the *bürgerliches Trauerspiel* (p. 247), in which for the first time in literature middle-class characters are depicted as capable of tragic emotion. This development continues practically without interruption; for even the characters of the classical period belong for the most part to the middle classes: *Werther*, *Tasso*, *Wilhelm Meister*, and *Faust* illumine essentially the same problems of artistic mentality as those of Thomas Mann's fiction; the theme even of Schiller's *Don Carlos* is that political liberalism which ferments in the writings of *Jungdeutschland*, moves the hectic tides of Spielhagen's novels, and is distorted in the communistically crazy preaching of universal brotherhood in the expressionism which followed the First World War. In the main lines this literature of a century and a half is a gradual fading, culminating in the *reductio ad absurdum* of Thomas Mann's *Königliche Hoheit*, of the glamour in which monarchs and nobles had lived a charmed life, and a corresponding intensification of the mental life of men belonging to all classes of society.

The drastic change of ideals at the beginning of our period had been gradually prepared; indeed, though the performance of Gerhart Hauptmann's *Vor Sonnenaufgang* in 1889 can be used as a landmark in the same way as the production of *Hernani* is used in dating the first crashing victory of the French Romantic movement, in reality it only marks the date when the existence of a new orientation in literature was forced on the consciousness of the nation at large. The origins of the new doctrine are to be found in Gutzkow, who preached 'the emancipation of the flesh'; in Spielhagen, who continued Gutzkow, particularly in his hostility to existingforms of government; and in the 'poetic realism' of such writers as Otto Ludwig and Gottfried Keller.

The state of literature in 1880 was respectable but stagnant. In lyric verse the scholarly poets of the Munich school had achieved a perfection of form which is apt to weary by its monotony and lack of rude masculinity; its themes were decent but hackneyed; and even the outer appearance of the volumes was used to typify it in the term of opprobrium,

278

Goldschnittlyrik, cast at it by the new school. A flood-tide of verse tales in facile rhythms had followed Scheffel's *Trompeter von Säkkingen* (1854); JULIUS WOLFF (1834-1910) continued to pour out his rhymed romances till near the end of the century. The exhaustion of the novel is seen in two genres, that of the sentimental tale which had its strongholds in the family journals (particularly *Die Gartenlaube)* and the historical novel, the so-called *Professorenroman* or *archäologischer Roman.* The vogue of the historical novel is to be explained by the hypertrophied race-consciousness which was the result of the victories of 1870: from the glory of the present novelists like Gustav Freytag and Felix Dahn turned to the glories of the past; the conquest of Italy as related in Felix Dahn's *Ein Kampf um Rom* (1876) symbolized the superiority over the decadent, slothful, and shifty romance nations of the unspoilt Germanic tribes. The historical novel, in so far as it renewed the historical novel of Scott and Willibald Alexis by packing it with palatable erudition, had elements of novelty; the historical drama, on the other hand – it was christened *Oberlehrerdrama* or *Epigonendrama* – is resurrected Schiller progressively debilitated; ADOLF WILBRANDT's (1837-1911) *Der Meister von Palmyra* (1889), however, points ahead by its use of allegory. The theatre had existed mainly on the *Sitten- und Thesenstück,* which was, on the one hand, a continuation of the *Familiendrama* of Iffland and Kotzebue, and, on the other hand, an imitation of the machine-made plays of Sardou and *hoc genus omne*; PAUL LINDAU (1830-1918) was one of the chief purveyors.[1]

Another consequence of the Franco-Prussian War was the sudden affluence of wealth, particularly in Berlin; in the Prussian capital there was an orgy of building and of speculation (*Gründertum*); it is depicted in Spielhagen's novel *Sturmflut* (1876). Berlin, mightily magnified, had become a European city conscious of its significance; it became a literary centre to which authors streamed from the provinces; and the wealth of the upper and trading classes was matched by the grovelling poverty of the working population. But the workers were at the advent of their rise to power; Spielhagen's *In Reih und Glied* (1866) had already been a Socialistic novel, with a hero clearly modelled on the Socialist leader, Ferdinand Lassalle (1825-64); labour and capital had faced each other as

---

[1] Two writers of flimsy farces of this generation have scored successes in England: we know Gustav von Moser's (1825-1903) *Der Bibliothekar* as *The Private Secretary,* and Oskar Blumenthal's (1852-1918) *Im weissen Rössl* as *White Horse Inn.* Since the days of August Wilhelm Iffland (1759-1814) – *Verbrechen aus Ehrfurcht* (1784), *Die Jäger* (1785) – and August von Kotzebue ('kɔtsəbu:; 1761-1819) – *Menschenhass und Reue* (1789) – theatre managers have had to rely for revenue on this *Trivialdramatik*; mostly pictures of family life with ostensibly a moral tendency; thus Sudermann (p. 304) helps to pay for producing Ibsen and Gerhart Hauptmann.

irreconcilable forces in the same author's *Hammer und Amboss* (1869); and henceforward Marxism[1] is to be reckoned with as a literary ferment. With Socialism goes a wave of pessimism, in stark contrast with the racial optimism of the historical novel. Goethe had overcome the *Weltschmerz* of *Werther*, though the teaching of *Faust* is still *Entsagung*; in the romantic period *Weltschmerz* had blended with Byronism; Schopenhauer (1788-1860) made pessimism a philosophic system the influence of which on literature was profound. It was not definitely displaced till Nietzsche's doctrine of the superman passed into the neo-romanticism of the impressionists; and even here it still acts as a secondary influence, for the neo-romanticists take over the moods of the French symbolists, who had themselves been profoundly influenced by Schopenhauer. Into this stream of pessimism flowed a new current, deriving from Darwin's doctrines of the struggle for existence. Darwin's laws of heredity and environment (*Milieu, Umgebung, Umwelt*) immediately provided catchwords for literature; even Gunther in Wilhelm Jordan's *Die Nibelunge* (1868-74) selects his *Bettgenossin* with an eye to *Zuchtwahl*. Darwin's theories, supplemented by the teaching of ERNST HAECKEL (1834-1919),[2] were to revolutionize the conception of society, and, as a vision of irresistible cosmic forces, were already in 1880 shaking the crass utilitarianism which, as the accepted view of life, had accompanied the accession to wealth of the great cities. Wilhelm Scherer (1841-86), professor of German literature at the University of Berlin, was one of the first to proclaim the coming domination of science; he had declared that natural science was the '*signatura temporis: . . . sie drückt der Poesie ihren Stempel auf. Die Naturwissenschaft zieht als Triumphator auf dem Siegeswagen einher, an den wir alle gefesselt sind*'.

These changes of outlook would, no doubt, if they had been left to themselves, have worked their own way to a new expression. But Germany, always receptive to ideas, has at all stages of new development in her literature caught the vivifying fire from abroad. Now, while Marx and Darwin were working so to speak under the surface, ideas came in with a rush from three foreign sources: Russia, France, and Norway. Much as in the eighteenth-century Rousseau had forced on literature a change of front with his paradox of 'back to nature', Tolstoy now, with his denunciation of the depravity of the cultured classes and his preaching

---

[1] The first volume of Karl Marx's (1818-83) *Das Kapital* had appeared in 1867 (see pp. 360 and 442).

[2] Haeckel's *Die Welträtsel* (1899) popularized his system of Darwinistic evolutionism. It is essentially the gospel of materialism; but in *Der Monismus* (1892) he had attempted to link science with religion by deriving moral goodness (i.e. ethics) and the cult of beauty (i.e. æsthetics) from the recognition of ultimate truth (see p. 444).

of asceticism, raised a new ideal, and turned attention to the misery of the poor. His *Might of Darkness* (1886) was a powerful influence. Dostoieffsky, with his minute and relentless psychology and his strange characters, pointed to new directions. Zola, following up Taine's theory of *milieu*, proclaimed that the meticulous methods of science should be applied to literature, that an author should give a slice of life seen through a temperament. Zola's procedure, deliberately photographical, seemed the denial of poetry and inspiration; in actual result, however, he achieves the effect of poetry by his gigantic symbolism. Ibsen, too, in the plays of his maturity, made a show of the abnegation of poetry in the shorn plainness of his dialogue; but he again in his latest plays wedded an illusory realism to a mystical and wistful symbolism. The stark ugliness of Tolstoy's picture of life reappears in the first period of naturalism. Zola is more than anyone else the acclaimed model of the first naturalists, both in drama and the novel. Ibsen lends form and substance to the dramas of the iconoclasts; he himself, however, had continued the problem plays of Hebbel (see pp. 275-6), and there is thus in the naturalistic plays which are modelled on those of Ibsen a chain of continuity with a link forged across the sea.

Another strongly emphasized feature of the new naturalism is hostility to the doctrines of Christianity. This is, however, nothing new in German literature. There is anti-sectarian feeling in Gottfried Keller's *Der grüne Heinrich* and in Spielhagen's *Problematische Naturen*; and the anticlerical atmosphere of Paul Heyse's *Kinder der Welt* (1873) had been denounced as the glorification of Sodom and Gomorrah. Anticlericalism goes together with the assertion of the rights of the senses (Gutzkow's 'emancipation of the flesh'); there had been much of this doctrine in Paul Heyse's long novel *Im Paradiese* (1876), and it is preached *ad nauseam* by the naturalists and, indeed, by the succeeding schools down to the present day; only in individual authors is there a questioning of this placing of morality beyond the pale of reason, as in Thomas Mann (e.g. *Fiorenza*). It is true that, although passion is hailed as sovereign, there is at the beginning of naturalism a kind of eugenic denunciation of individual vices, e.g. drunkenness in Hauptmann's *Vor Sonnenaufgang*; but even Hauptmann's drunkards, in his later plays, illustrate the general sentiment that: *tout comprendre c'est tout pardonner*. The argument runs that since mentality is shaped by *milieu* and hereditary tendencies, above all by the sexual impulse, man's will is not free; and, since the will is not free, morality is not absolute (i.e. a law for all), but relative (a law possible or impossible according to physical constitution, mentality, and environment). Action is due to nerves; and since men are not responsible for their nerves they are not responsible for their actions.

Two poets of the older generation belong more or less to the new schools of naturalism and impressionism, Theodor Fontane and Conrad Ferdinand Meyer (see p. 274), the former by virtue of his realism and the relativity of his moral judgments, the latter by his use of symbol and his handling of history and renaissance themes. C. F. Meyer, whose collected verse appeared in 1882, used history to veil the intimate problem of his own personality, and so cunningly that symbolism and psycho-analysis had to make their impress on criticism before the hidden import of his verse as of his tales could be unravelled.

THEODOR FONTANE (1818-98) was, like his forerunner as a writer of tales of Brandenburg, Willibald Alexis (1798-1871), of Huguenot descent.[1] He had lived a busy life as a journalist when, at the age of sixty, he began to write novels. His social novels deal mainly, and with complete freedom from prejudice, with three problems: *das Verhältnis* or liaison between gentleman and working-class girl, *mésalliances*, and adultery. *L'Adultera* (1822) is a tale in which a woman is seen gliding, not passionately but inevitably, into adultery with a baptized Jew; the husband has the good qualities of that husband from whom Dorothea Veit ran away to Friedrich Schlegel, but she feels the physical repugnance which Irene in *The Forsyte Saga* feels for Soames; she is made to feel – her own children recoil from her – that she has outraged society, but in the end she is forgiven even by the husband she has deserted; her action is questioned, but not judged; there is indeed symbolic reference to Tintoretto's picture of Christ and the woman taken in adultery. 'Don't take it more tragically than need be, and don't worry too much about the old nasty theme of guilt and punishment' – these words on the last page show the modern attitude of the forthcoming novels. The central theme of *Irrungen, Wirrungen* (1888) is a *Verhältnis* between an officer and a working-class girl – '*das landesübliche Techtelmechtel*', as it is called in Otto Erich Hartleben's *Rosenmontag*; the girl is practical and far-sighted, and gives up her lover, marries one of her own class, and lives – happily? In the girl's leave-taking there is a dramatic poignancy as of the old ballads Fontane loved – he wrote some of the best (modelled on our old Border ballads) in German literature: 'And so', she says, 'this is the last time I shall hold your hand in mine?' After *Irrungen, Wirrungen* the naturalists claimed Fontane for their own, and he with his wise old generosity acknowledged their right to a place in the sun. They were writing *Berliner Romane*[2] which are now

---

[1] The novelist pronounced his name as [fɔn'taːn]; [fɔn'taːnə] is common.
[2] The typical novels of contemporary Berlin life are Paul Lindau's trilogy *Der Zug nach dem Westen* (1886), *Arme Mädchen* (1887), and *Spitzen* (1888); Fritz Mauthner's

forgotten; his remain. In *Effi Briest* (1895) a young girl marries an old lover of her own mother; he is a man of high position who is rather above her than with her; she falls to a lover rather from boredom than from passion, and returns to her paternal home to die; there is no pronouncement that she was guilty. Here again Fontane shows forces working, but does not judge those who are overcome by these forces. *Frau Jenny Treibel* (1892) shows him at his best as a sly humorist: Frau Jenny is a parvenue with a mouth full of enthusiasm for higher things and an unerring sense of what is good and practical. Frau Jenny is ridiculous, but delightful; the irony lights up, but does not corrode. In Fontane's descriptions of the Prussian nobility, as in *Die Poggenpuhls* (1896), which shows the family of a dead officer struggling to keep up appearances, the irony touches very lightly. Fontane has a limited range of characters – junkers, officers, dear old aunts, gardeners, clergymen –, but his types are sharply individualized by his masterly handling of dialogue; his technique depends largely on conversation or on self-expression in monologue and correspondence. R. M. Meyer calls Fontane 'the first consistent realist in German literature'; this is not quite correct: Fontane, it is true, is not a 'poetic realist', because he is without Romanticism (except in his ballads), but he differs from the 'consistent' naturalists because he is worlds removed from *Armeleutepoesie*; the working classes only come into his work as foils to his gentry; his affinities with the new school are in tone rather than in texture – they show, not so much in his realism as in his large-hearted attitude to social problems, or, to repeat the catchword, in the relativity of his morality.

Two other forerunners of naturalism, Ludwig Anzengruber and Marie von Ebner-Eschenbach, are of very high rank in literature. The naturalistic drama really begins with LUDWIG ANZENGRUBER (1839-89), the dramatic effectiveness of whose plays is partly due to his training as an actor. He was a Viennese; i.e. a city man with a good knowledge of village life and a more or less artificially acquired knowledge of dialect – an advantage for stage purposes. He had learned something from Auerbach, another townsman who made village tales his province; but, unlike Auerbach, he gets inside his peasants; and what he really continues is the old Viennese

Berlin W (1886); Hermann Heiberg's *Dunst aus der Tiefe* (1890). The Zolaesque tendencies have as much sociological as literary interest in Max Kretzer's (1854-1941) bitter novels of the Berlin proletariat (*Die Betrogenen*, 1882; *Die Verkommenen*, 1883). Kretzer's *Meister Timpe* (1888) has for its theme the crushing of the small independent craftsman by the mass production of factories; in his *Das Gesicht Christi* (1897) the Saviour moves as a symbol of pity among the poor of Berlin. A group of novels unrolls an unedifying picture of the Bohemian life of the metropolis (Karl Bleibtreu's *Schlechte Gesellschaft*, 1885), with mightily bosomed *Kellnerinnen* towering over quailing poets.

Volksstück (Mozart's *Magic Flute* is such a local play), which he modernizes by dropping the fabulous elements and some (but not all) of the irrelevant music, while still keeping the sensational machinery, thunder and lightning playing round the catastrophe, bullets whizzing in a gloomy gorge, etc. He made his reputation with *Der Pfarrer von Kirchfeld* (1870), which shows his qualities and his limitations. The hero Hell (a symbolic name), a perfect priest in a Tyrolese village, has reformed his parishioners, who idolize him, but his enlightenment is looked upon by the village lord (whose name, Graf von Finsterberg, symbolizes his obscurantism) as heterodoxy, and the play ends with Hell being summoned to appear before his ecclesiastical superiors. He is shown to be dangerously in love with a picturesque maiden who helps his quaint old housekeeper with the housework; but he is in complete control of himself, though his kindly treatment of the girl is misconstrued. The play is a discussion of the moot topics of the day: marriages between Protestants and Catholics are shown to be natural; and, above all, the action drives home the moral that it is cruelty to priests to forbid them to marry. *Der Pfarrer von Kirchfeld* is, therefore, at once a problem play, pointed social criticism, and an attack on sectarian religion; where it lags behind is in the naïve technique; this is frankly melodramatic, but with its strange atmosphere as of a world of dream it is far removed from vulgarity. The peasants speak an easily intelligible dialect, and speak it naturally; here, too, Anzengruber is a pioneer. The characters of *Der Pfarrer von Kirchfeld* are charming but childlike; the following plays show an advance in intensity of characterization. The hero of *Der Meineidbauer* (1871) is a kind of village Richard III; there are sensational scenes, but the action grips; and the belief of the Meineidbauer that he is safe in sin till the catastrophe shows that the devil, not the Lord, has guarded him so long, carries him along in an inevitable course to destruction. *Das vierte Gebot* (1878) comes nearest of Anzengruber's plays to the naturalistic formulas, and was acknowledged by the naturalists as a masterpiece.[1] It is as much an arraignment of existing morals as Sudermann's *Sodoms Ende*: a turner and his bawdy wife bring up their daughter as a whore, and their son ends as a murderer; another character sells his daughter to a rascal; such is the world in which people are bidden to obey the fourth commandment.[2] The priest asks the murderer before he is executed whether he forgives his parents; 'No!' he answers; 'to many a man it is the greatest misfortune to be brought up

---

[1] It was far too modern for the Vienna of 1877 (the censor mangled it), and only began its victorious career when produced by the *Freie Bühne* in Berlin in 1890.

[2] The Lutheran church has the Augustinian enumeration, with the first and second commandment run together.

by his parents; if you tell scholars in school to honour father and mother, tell parents from the pulpit to be fit for it.'

There is the Shakespearean blending of comedy in Anzengruber's tragedies; in the comedies proper fun runs riot, and the quaint characters – they are like nothing on earth, but in their Tyrolese setting they are as real as goitre – are a perpetual delight. *Die Kreuzelschreiber* (1872) are villagers who have been persuaded to affix their crosses – they cannot write – to a document which is in intent an attack on Holy Church; the priest now orders the wives to withhold marital rights, and peace is only restored by the mother wit of Steinklopferhanns, who tells the wives that their husbands are to make a pilgrimage to Rome – with the unmarried women of the village. Moral: priests should not interfere in family affairs. The hero of *Der G'wissenswurm* (1874) suffers from pangs of conscience because once on a time he had played loose with a girl; he recovers his peace of mind when he comes across her as a farmer's wife and happy mother – and she shows him the door; and when his old sin, in the shape of a merry girl, locks him in her arms and warms him like sunshine. Moral: morality should not be implacable, and conscience should not make cowards of us all. In *Doppelselbstmord* (1876) a pair of star-crossed lovers bury their parents' strife by making them believe they have committed suicide; they are discovered committing matrimony on the high mountains. *Jungferngift* (1876) glides gaily along the edge of obscenity: a rich lover is shied off by a story, only faintly offensive in a *fabliau* or a Viennese *Volksstück*, that the lady is strangely cursed – the first carnal touch of her brings death.

Anzengruber was equally a master of the *Dorfnovelle* or village tale. In *Der Schandfleck* (1876) he handles the theme of ungrateful children tormenting an old man, a village Lear, who finds refuge with a bastard child (the *Schandfleck*). The heroine of *Der Sternsteinhof* (1883-84), a masterly character study, sets her cap, poorest wench of the village though she is, at the richest farmer's son, and, a village Helen sticking at nothing, with her '*ehrfurchtgebietende Immoralität*' a Nietzschean unawares, achieves her end; she then shows herself to be a capable housekeeper, and rules her conquered realm with stern and implacable justice.

MARIE VON EBNER-ESCHENBACH (1830-1916), who is at her best where she describes the life of her native province of Moravia, is naturalistic in her rendering of *milieu*. The world of her tales (*Dorf- und Schlossgeschichten*, 1883 and 1886) is that of the Austrian nobility to which she belonged, but she also describes with innate sympathy the life of peasants and servants attached to the nobility; like another aristocrat, George Sand, she inclines with a sympathy akin to Socialism to the labouring poor; one of her main themes is the starvation of the mind by unfavourable environment and hereditary failings. She achieved fame with *Ein Spätgeborener* (1875), and her best novels were written in the two following decades. Although her marriage was childless, no one has ever described children better than she did. One of her best novels, *Das Gemeindekind* (1887), has for its hero a boy who is the son of a murderer, and whose mother is in prison; he has the whole village against him, but wins through by strength of character and by following the precept to requite evil with good. Marie von Ebner-Eschenbach shares the didactic tendency of the writers of village tales; her great lesson is that duty comes first and must be performed as much by a countess (*Unsühnbar*, 1890) as by a servant (*Božena*, 1876); not love, therefore, but renunciation is the chief thing in life. According to her, love is rare. What is essential for the well-being of the human race is not love of individuals but love of one's fellow-men. 'I look on love', she says, 'as the most cruel of all the means which an angry Deity has invented for the punishment of His creatures.' Perhaps for this reason she often keeps her lovers apart.

A forerunner of a different sort was Duke Georg von Meiningen, who had set himself as the task of his life to reform the German stage. Not the least important step in this programme was his morganatic marriage to one of the actresses of his Court theatre; she with him superintended the rehearsals, drilled the company, and selected the plays, while the Duke himself did the scene-painting. Both launched into historical research work to ensure accuracy of *mise en scène* and costumes; and, as far as possible, furniture actually used at the time the plays represented was procured. This cult of realism on the stage went so far that in the production of ALBERT LINDNER's (1831-88) *Bluthochzeit* (1871; an *Epigonendrama*), which deals with the massacre of St. Bartholomew, the whole theatre was so full of real powder that the actors could scarcely speak for hoarseness and the spectators got sore eyes. The Meiningers were the forerunners of Max Reinhardt in this stage realism, as well as in their handling of crowds, which with them were an active part of the picture, not an inert mass. One of the great events in the history of the German stage was the visit, in 1874, of the Duke of Meiningen's company to Berlin, where they produced Shakespeare's *Julius Caesar*. This was the beginning of the reform of the Berlin Theatre.

A further stage in this reform was the establishment in 1883 of Das Deutsche Theater in Berlin. The director appointed was ADOLF L'ARRONGE (1838-1908). Adolf L'Arronge has some importance historically as a dramatist, and he might be classified as a link between the *Sitten- und Thesenstück* and the naturalistic drama; his plays owed their vogue to their careful though not rigidly realistic painting of Berlin life, especially of the mushroom plutocracy which was to be more drastically pilloried in Sudermann's *Sodoms Ende* and Heinrich Mann's novel *Im Schlaraffen-land*; and it was L'Arronge who first, though with a different moral, laid hold of the contrast between *Vorder- und Hinterhaus* and created a new type of play which culminated in Sudermann's *Die Ehre*. In the history of the German stage L'Arronge will always figure prominently. The great work of his life was his management of the Deutsches Theater. L'Arronge gradually worked out his schemes of reform. He combined the scenic splendour of the Meiningers with the noble declamation, the cult of poetry in the spoken word, for which the Burg Theatre at Vienna had, under Heinrich Laube's management, become famous. He revived Shakespeare and Goethe and Schiller, and took down from the library shelves the noble dramatic poems of the later classics, Kleist and Grill-parzer and Hebbel, and gave them at last a definite and enduring place in the life of the nation.

Another event that was destined to be of the greatest importance in the history of the drama was the establishment in Berlin in 1889 of the *Verein Freie Bühne*. The name was suggested by Antoine's *Théâtre libre*; whereas, however, the Parisian theatre was dependent for its existence on its box-office takings, the *Freie Bühne* aimed at producing plays with no popular appeal but new in inspiration. Among the founders of the club were MAXIMILIAN HARDEN (1861-1927), the editor of *Die Zukunft*, Heinrich and Julius Hart, and PAUL SCHLENTHER (1854-1912); OTTO BRAHM (1856-1912) was the director. The first play produced by the *Freie Bühne* was Ibsen's *Ghosts*; it was soon followed by Hauptmann's *Vor Sonnenaufgang*. But the first dramatic successes of the period fell to tragedies that are really *Epigonendramen*, iambic verse plays in Schiller's manner. The first of ERNST VON WILDENBRUCH's (1845-1909) successes had been *Die Karolinger* (1881), which centres round the quarrels of the grandsons of Charlemagne. Wildenbruch, a scion of the Hohenzollerns on the wrong side of the blanket (his father, the German consul at Beirut in Syria, where the poet was born, was the son of Prinz Louis Ferdinand), had served as a Prussian officer, and had abandoned the army for a career in the civil service. Of his 'Hohenzollern plays' the most interesting is *Die Quitzows* (1888); here he makes concessions to the naturalistic dogma by intro-ducing the Berlin dialect – a chronological impossibility, since at the time of the action of the play (it describes the subjection of the unruly nobles of the March of Brandenburg by the newly imported Margrave Frederick of Nuremberg) *Plattdeutsch* was spoken in Berlin. There is an attempt to combine the grand historical style with up-to-date realism in the double drama *Heinrich und Heinrichs Geschlecht* (1896), in which the German Emperor's humiliation at Canossa provides a sensational scene. The action of Wildenbruch's plays rushes along and culminates in such dazzling stage effects; but they are poor as literature, owing to the naïve characterization; the characters are lyrically exuberant puppets, and the construction, instead of building up to a climax, reels from sensation to sensation. Wildenbruch, in his desire to be abreast of the times, joined company with the naturalists; in two of his plays, *Meister Balzer* (1892) and *Die Haubenlerche* (1890), he outwardly followed their formulas.

The victory of the new realism which we have seen coming was being prepared by the beginnings of a new criticism. The early history of naturalism is that of two groups, one in Berlin and the other in Munich, each with a militant organ of its own. The Berlin naturalists gather round the brothers HEINRICH (1855-1906) and JULIUS HART (1859-1930), who launched the campaign in their review *Kritische Waffengänge* (1882-84). Of this review only four numbers appeared; the campaign was fought out in *Die Freie Bühne*, which was later *Die Neue Rundschau*. The organ of the Munich group was *Die Gesellschaft* (1885-1902), founded and edited by MICHAEL GEORG CONRAD (1846-1927), who was one of the first devotees of the cult of Zola; he planned a series of novels of Munich life on the scale of the Rougon-Maquart cycle, but got no farther than diffuse sketches (*Was die Isar rauscht*, 1887).

In lyric verse the revolt was heralded by an anthology published in 1884 in Berlin: *Moderne Dichtercharaktere*. It was prefaced by two introductions intended as a manifesto, one by HERMANN CONRADI (1862-90) and the other by KARL HENCKELL (1864-1929) – brave words calling for new characters to write the new verse, but surprisingly empty. The poems of the anthology, as a matter of fact, present no innovation of form; what is new is the prominence given to 'modern' subjects, mainly in the direction of *Grossstadtpoesie*. Hermann Conradi had a certain originality; his note is that of half-disgust with the debauch into which his sensual nature hurled him down from the heights to which his intellect strove; this note lends a pathetic interest – for he died of pneumonia at the age of twenty-eight – to his book of verse *Lieder eines Sünders* (1887), with its sulphurous defiance as of Tannhäuser prisoned in the Venusberg, in the *mons veneris*: '*Ich ringe krampfhaft mich zum Licht empor* – | *nach süssen Sünden dürsten meine Sinne* – | *vor meinen Augen reisst der Nebelflor* – | *und unersättlich feir' ich dich, Frau Minne!*' Conradi's half-tragic, half-ridiculous fate, together with the partially realized intensely personal style of his novel *Adam Mensch* (1889), revived interest in him in the days of expressionism. Karl Henckell, as time went on, assumed the role of poet laureate of the Socialists. Of the other poets of the anthology, few were destined to win lasting fame; but Otto Erich Hartleben (p. 308), who distinguished himself later as a dramatist and humorist, was represented with odes in the ancient Greek style, and Arno Holz contributed poems which, though traditional in form, are excellent in their genre-painting.

ARNO HOLZ (1863-1929) it was who, in conjunction with his friend JOHANNES SCHLAF (1862-1941), put the match to the gunpowder. Arno Holz, an East Prussian, had begun as an imitator of Geibel, but in his volume of verse *Buch der Zeit* (1885), though the form is traditional, there is already *Armeleutepoesie*. Holz has described in his work *Die Kunst: ihr Wesen und ihre Gesetze* (1890-92) how he discovered 'consistent realism'. On his return from Paris, where he had studied Zola's critical writings, he had taken rooms with his friend Schlaf in a Berlin suburb, and there he came across a boy's drawing of a soldier on a slate; to anybody else it might have been a camel, to the boy it was a soldier; the boy had failed in the first place because his tools were inadequate, and in the second place because he did not know how to handle the tools he had. From this Holz deduced his famous law: *Die Kunst hat die Tendenz, die Natur zu sein. Sie wird sie nach Massgabe ihrer Mittel und deren Handhabung.* That is: art differs from nature only in the means of representation. There are as many forms of art as there are means of representing it. Since art strives to *be* nature, the stern aim of art must be to be 'consistent', or unswerving in the exact reproduction of nature. In illustration of this truth, Holz and Schlaf wrote three *Novellen*, which were published in 1889 as *Papa Hamlet* by Bjarne P. Holmsen. The name of the alleged author reflects the popularity at that time of Scandinavian writers. Papa Hamlet is an old actor who is always declaiming passages from *Hamlet*; when his baby Fortinbras cries he puts a pillow over its face; in the end he stifles the child. The characters of the three tales are grey ordinary beings; it is a chunk of daily life narrated with photographic reality. Zola had defined art as life seen through the artist's temperament; Holz eliminates the artist's temperament and, in intention, photographs like a camera, with no apparent interest either in his characters or in their speech, which he gives in fragments and disjointed. The best of the tales is the third: *Ein Tod*, the description of a night passed by students at the death-bed of a comrade who has been wounded in a duel. Here the unfinished sentences and the three full stops to represent the unspoken words produce an atmosphere and admirably suggest the sleepy crawling of the night-hours. This style is known as *Sekundenstil* (the term was first used by Adalbert von Hanstein in his book *Das Jüngste Deutschland*, 1900), i.e. a style which laboriously produces the impression of every ticking second of time; it is a minute notation of trains of thought and sensuous impressions which points forward to psycho-analysis and the 'waves of consciousness' novel of our time. *Papa Hamlet* owes its importance in the history of literature principally to the fact that Gerhart Hauptmann in his first play, which was dedicated to Bjarne P. Holmsen, '*dem konsequentesten Realisten*', copied the externals of its style, i.e. *Sekundenstil*.

In the first of the three tales, *Papa Hamlet*, there was so much dialogue that it approached drama. The two friends then provided their model for a naturalistic style of drama in *Familie Selicke* (1890), which was staged by the *Freie Bühne*, and of which Theodor Fontane said: 'Here the roads part; here old and new separate.' A father comes home drunk and goes to sleep on the sofa while his family are watching by the bed-side of a sick child. The child dies; the daughter has to tell a theological student, the lodger, that she cannot marry him, as she will be needed at home to keep the peace between her drunken father and suffering mother. The language is in the Berlin dialect and the strictest *Sekundenstil*. Schlaf continued to write naturalistic dramas (*Meister Ölze*, 1892; *Gertrud*, 1897). Meister Ölze, a carpenter in a Thuringian village, suffers from an evil conscience: in days gone by he, with the help of his mother, has murdered his father. His stepsister suspects him of the crime, and she tortures him to death – not a very difficult task, for he is consumptive. He wishes to save his soul (like an Irish villain) by making his son a clergyman, but the son boasts of his atheism. Schlaf's loosely connected sketches of rural scenery *In Dingsda* (1892) and *Frühling* (1894) deviate in the direction of lyric prose; ostensibly they show the reaction to nature of a Berlin naturalist on his escape to the country; really they continue the old style of German rural sentimentality with a tang of peevishness added. They were followed by a trilogy of novels (*Das Dritte Reich*, 1900; *Die Suchenden*, 1901; *Peter Bojes Freite*, 1902) which foreshadow the idea of the expressionists that man should be recreated (*Wandlung*).

Arno Holz relaxed his austerity and scored one popular success with his drama of school life, written in collaboration with Otto Jerschke, *Traumulus* (1905); the straining of the educational machine in Germany had led to an epidemic of suicides among school children, and the problem of educational methods, both as regards teacher and taught, became so acute that there was repeated discussion of it in literature. Three other plays related in theme are Wedekind's *Frühlings Erwachen* (1891), Otto Ernst's *Flachsmann als Erzieher* (1901), and Georg Kaiser's *Rektor Kleist* (1905).[1]

---

[1] There are distressing pictures of school life in Thomas Mann's *Buddenbrooks*, Heinrich Mann's *Professor Unrat*, Friedrich Huch's *Peter Michel* (1901), *Freund Hein*

Holz planned a *magnum opus*, a cycle of twelve plays; of these he completed *Sozialaristokraten* (1896), a literary satire; *Sonnenfinsternis* (1908), the tragedy of the artist; and *Ignorabimus* (1912), the tragedy of the poet. In these later plays Holz sets himself the gigantic task of fixing the inner rhythm of everything that is spoken by every character: accentuation and gesture are not to be those of the author, nor those of the actor, but of the given character at a given moment controlled by a given emotion.

In *Revolution der Lyrik* (1899) Holz declared war against established form in lyric verse, and the rhythmic theories here propounded shape the vast mass of the impressionistic verse collected in *Phantasus* (1898-1916). All previous verse, says Holz, had been metrical; this metrical form he smashes ('*zerbreche ich*'), and he replaces it by its diametrical opposite, rhythmical form ('*Rhythmik*'). Rhyme and stanza vanish; the 'natural and necessary rhythm' constitutes the poem, which turns on an invisible central pivot (*Mittelachse*). Thus: *Der Mond steigt hinter blühenden Apfelbaumzweigen auf* is in prose; but

> *Hinter blühenden Apfelbaumzweigen*
> *steigt der Mond auf*

is verse rotating round an invisible central pivot. Sceptically regarded this might seem to mean that any reciter may turn prose into verse by modulating his voice before and after a pause (traditionally: caesura); or that any compositor can arrange prose as verse by what Holz calls an 'acoustic picture'. Truth to tell, these poems in free rhythms (a term Holz rejects) depend for their effect on their inherent poetry, their grotesque humour, their vivid pictures. The poems of *Phantasus* are often delightful if individually interpreted, but Holz has forced them into a kind of *Légende des siècles* which is at the same time a kind of apology for his own career. Somewhat incongruous by reason of their masterly handling of rhyme are the volume of baroque verse *Dafnis* (1904), a pastiche of seventeenth-century anacreontics with dualistic undertones, and *Die Blechschmiede* (1902 and 1921), a book of riotous paradistic verse.

Arno Holz was all his life long a fanatical theorist experimenting out in the cold. The harvest of the new idea was reaped by Gerhart Hauptmann and his disciples. GERHART HAUPTMANN (1862-1946) was born in the Silesian health resort of Obersalzbrunn; his father was the landlord and owner of the hotel *Zur Preussischen Krone*. Silesian birth and upbringing and the events of his youth are of importance in the work of

---

(1902) by Emil Strauss, and J. C. Heer's *Joggeli* (1923). Hermann Hesse's *Unterm Rad* (1905) has a ring of reality in its gentle unfolding of the processes of mental exhaustion.

this poet, for his use of Silesian dialect belongs to the history of the
development of literature, and his adolescence comes into the subject-
matter of work after work. He was educated at Obersalzbrunn, and then
(1874-78) at the *Realschule* of Breslau. He was so negligent or unreceptive
at his studies that he was sent to his uncle's farm to learn practical farming.
But he was too dreamy for this business and was taken back and, in 1880,
sent to study sculpture at the *Kunstschule* at Breslau, from which he was
sent down for insubordination. Then he joined his brother Carl, who was
studying at the University of Jena; here he attended lectures by Haeckel.
Too restless for methodical study, he set out on a sea voyage from Hamburg to Spain and Italy; and made a last attempt at being a sculptor in
Rome, where he had an *atelier*. His travel impressions made up his first
book of verse, *Promethidenlos* (1885), an imitation of *Childe Harold*;
noteworthy in the book is the marked sympathy with the outcast. On
his return Gerhart married Marie Thienemann, a well-to-do woman,
whose means enabled him to live in Erkner, a Berlin suburb. His studies
here were mainly scientific or economic; he read Darwin and Karl Marx.
His social feeling was in the best sense religious: at the base of it was the
goodness of his mother, who had been brought up in the Moravian creed.
He planned an epic on Jesus of Nazareth; it remained an idea, but his
religious conception (in the main pity for suffering humanity) materialized
years later in his novel *Der Narr in Christo Emanuel Quint*. In 1887 his
short story *Bahnwärter Thiel* appeared in *Die Gesellschaft*; a man who
tends a railway crossing is incapacitated by sexual dependence on his
virago of a wife. In these moods of social pity the theories of Holz
unlocked Hauptmann's creative power: *Sekundenstil*, he thought, gave
him the means of showing truth by depicting humanity in the raw; plan,
development, selection, effect were not needed; what the artist had to do
was to let situation follow situation; the situation would be vivid because
actual, and pregnant with meaning because all life is full of tragic pity.
He had been present at the historical performance in 1887 of Ibsen's
Ghosts in Berlin, and had been deeply moved. He set to work and produced *Vor Sonnenaufgang* (1889). Alfred Loth, a Socialist agitator, comes
to a Silesian mining village to do research in economic conditions. He is
invited to stay in the home of a farmer enriched by the working of mines
under his fields. The farmer is a dipsomaniac; his wife is unchaste; one
of his two daughters, also alcoholic, does not appear on the stage, as she
is expecting her confinement; the other, Helene, pure in spite of her
environment, falls in love with Loth, the first clean man she has met.
Loth, still unaware of the general degeneration of the family, makes a
love-match with Helene; but when he learns the state of things he breaks

off the engagement and goes away – for he is a teetotaller and believes in heredity –, and Helene kills herself with a hunting-knife.

Vor Sonnenaufgang was produced on the 20th of October 1889 in the Lessing Theatre, Berlin, under the auspices of the *Freie Bühne*. It was a battle like that of *Hernani*. The excitement culminated when a physician, at the moment when Helene's sister is near her confinement, and there is a call for a midwife, threw a pair of forceps on the stage. The play was hissed and acclaimed and discussed for weeks after. Naturalism had arrived. The vogue in literature of scientific determinism was established; i.e. the conception that the will is rendered powerless by heredity and *milieu*. Moreover, a new dramatic technique opened new vistas. Monologues and asides were declared antiquated. Stage directions were like a catalogue. The idea that a play should have a 'hero' gave way to the conception (*Heldenlosigkeit*) that since the drama portrays men, and since men are weaklings, the purpose of the dramatist is not to weigh out a calculated sum of 'tragic guilt', but to arouse a tender pity for pathetic humanity; life is tragic because it is life, not because it is guilty.

But, since all the processes of art tend to become mechanical, the naturalistic drama, from the start, adopts an external machinery which makes it as stereotyped as the French classical drama. This rigid framework is as gaunt as anywhere in *Vor Sonnenaufgang*. It is an 'analytical drama' (*Drama des reifen Zustandes*): as in Ibsen's plays the characters are fixed (*fertige Charaktere*); i.e. they are not developed by the action of the drama, which is merely the unfolding of a catastrophe prepared by the course of events prior to the first act. The naturalistic drama is one, not of action, but of situation. Scenes or 'processes' from the lives of human beings are shown, not in shapely acts (in some naturalistic plays, e.g. *Das Friedensfest*, acts are called *Vorgänge*), but shapelessly fluid and cut off *in processu* by the fall of the curtain. There is neither beginning nor end, but just a 'chunk of life'.

Into the moral decrepitude of the Silesian mining village steps a 'saviour from afar' (*der Retter aus der Ferne*), another ingredient of the naturalistic drama as of Ibsen's plays. In Hauptmann's next play, *Das Friedensfest* (1890), it is a man who is on the verge of nervous collapse who is to be saved by a healthy woman sweeping in from the outer world. A physician had married a woman inferior to him in intelligence, and friction ensues; this is a favourite theme of Hauptmann's, who (like Wedekind and Thomas Mann) constantly rehandles the same problem. The doctor had abandoned wife and children when one of his sons, Wilhelm, had slapped his face. Wilhelm is engaged to a healthy girl; but, conscious of his hereditary handicaps, he hesitates to marry her (as, to quote an instance familiar from literary history, Grillparzer for the same reason had hesitated

to marry his *ewige Braut*). However, there is a family gathering to celebrate the engagement, and during the rejoicings father Scholz unexpectedly returns. Wilhelm begs his father's pardon for having slapped his
face; there is a general reconciliation; but the father dies of apoplexy.
The final result is left in doubt: will Wilhelm marry Ida, and will the
hereditary disease yield to her care; or is tragedy inevitable?

The third play, *Einsame Menschen* (1891), handles the triangular marriage
(*Ehe zu Dritt*), which ruined the poet Bürger, which Goethe handled with
unintentional comic effect in *Stella*, Maeterlinck tediously in *Aglavaine et
Sélysette*, Ernst Hardt with intentional comic effect in *Schirin und Gertraude*
(1912; a dramatization of the old legend of the man with two wives, *Der
Graf von Gleichen*), and Jakob Wassermann in his novel *Das Gänsemännchen*. Johannes Vockerat is married to a woman intellectually beneath
him (like the wife in *Das Friedensfest*); as a woman of means, she can give
him creature comforts and the opportunity of living a student's life, but
not intellectual comradeship. He is *l'homme incompris*; even his parents
do not understand him, for they are pious and orthodox, and he is a
disciple of Darwin and Haeckel. Into his quiet home comes a girl student
from Zurich (*der Retter aus der Ferne*); *she* understands Johannes, and he
falls in love with her; his wife despairs; Anna has to leave, and Johannes
drowns himself. The outlines show a similarity with Ibsen's *Rosmersholm*,
but (though it was a tenet of naturalism that personal interest should be
eliminated) the inspiration was no doubt that which later found symbolic
expression in *Die versunkene Glocke*. In any case, *Einsame Menschen* is a
study of neurasthenia, just as *Das Friedensfest* had been a study of heredity
and *Vor Sonnenaufgang* a study of alcoholism.

With *Die Weber* (1892) Hauptmann achieved European fame. The
poverty-stricken condition of the Silesian weavers was at that time a
topical question, and Hauptmann, himself the grandson of a Silesian
weaver, studied the situation in his native mountains. There had been a
revolt of the weavers in 1844; and this past revolt Hauptmann used to
create the social drama of the present. There is no 'construction' in the
accepted sense: the play consists of a series of pictures of abject misery.
Naturalistic *Heldenlosigkeit* has here an interesting development: there is
no individual hero, but the weavers collectively are the hero – each
individually insignificant, but as a mass a sweeping force. *Die Weber* is
the first play in which 'mass psychology' is successfully handled; here
the mass does indeed express itself as a unity; all the individualities coalesce
in an entity. How successfully Hauptmann has realized the conception
can be seen by a comparison with Schiller's *Wilhelm Tell*: Schiller's idea
was to make the Swiss people the hero of his play, but, since the Swiss

people are expressed by William Tell (in the limelight), William Tell is the hero, not the Swiss people. The revolt is crushed; but morally the weavers are victorious. Whether *Die Weber* marks an actual advance in dramatic technique is a moot question; the opposite view is that the innovation is in the direction of making the drama epic (*Episierung des Dramas*); i.e. minute but haphazard and loosely billowing description of *milieu* takes the place of action selected and concentrated by a controlling mind.

The enslavement by sexual needs (the Samson motif) sketched in the short tale *Bahnwärter Thiel* finds deepened expression in *Fuhrmann Henschel* (1898). A Silesian carter has sworn to his dying wife that he will never marry their servant Hanne. But he cannot live without a wife, and he succumbs to Hanne's wiles. She is untrue to him, and he hangs himself. *Fuhrmann Henschel* and *Rose Bernd* (1904) are *bürgerliche Trauerspiele* which differ from Hauptmann's earlier plays in two important respects: the characters are developed by suffering, and their fate is not fixed by outside forces (heredity and *milieu*), but depends on volition; the characters are free to decide what their actions shall be; in other words, they are not puppets. Thirdly, there is a clean-cut ending (a catastrophe in the old sense) to both plays; we know that the gods have done their worst with Henschel and Rose Bernd. In *Rose Bernd* Hauptmann handles a favourite motif of the *Sturm und Drang*: Rose is the frenzied mother who murders her new-born baby; it is the eternal tragedy of woman sexually pursued and helplessly yielding.

German literature has only half a dozen or so of classical comedies; Hauptmann's *Der Biberpelz* (1893) is one of them. It has a certain similarity to Kleist's *Der zerbrochene Krug*: in both comedies there is a culprit whose transgressions are investigated in court; but whereas in *Der zerbrochene Krug* the culprit is the investigating judge himself, whose cross-examination of innocent parties unravels his own guilt, in *Der Biberpelz* the judge is a pompous fool who is led by the nose by the culprit, the egregious washerwoman Frau Wolffen. This lady, unshakable in her brazen effrontery, gets the court bailiff to hold a lantern while she steals wood; to the judge she is the pattern of honesty. *Der rote Hahn* (1901), a sequel to *Der Biberpelz*, was a fiasco. *College Crampton* (1892), a study of alcoholism, is a kind of comedy, but the humour touches tragedy. The dipsomaniac is this time a professor of painting; the weakness of the play is that, whereas we are to believe that Crampton is a genius debased by alcohol, we see the effects of the alcohol but no evidence of the genius. Crampton has given way to drink because his wife did not understand him; he is another *homme incompris*, like Johannes Vockerat. There is again, as in *Das Friedensfest*, a contrast with a healthy family, who set the old man up in a sort of way in an atelier; there is, however, no solution of the problem, but (as in *Das Friedensfest*) the question is left undecided whether kindness and contact with normal beings can effect a cure; or, in other words, is disease a fault or is it fate? *College Crampton* is the carefully executed portrait of an artist; similar portraits of artists variously tormented and never understood by their (Strindbergian) wives are *Michael Kramer* (1900), *Gabriel Schillings Flucht* (1912) with its pictures of sea and dunes on Hiddensee, and *Peter Brauer* (1921). In *Michael Kramer* (as in *Das Friedensfest*) there is the conflict between son and father so dear to the expressionists.

An event of considerable importance in the history of the German theatre was the appointment in 1894 of Otto Brahm, one of the stalwarts of naturalistic propaganda, as director of the Deutsches Theater in Berlin; this theatre now became the temple of the Hauptmann cult. Here in 1896 Hauptmann's historical tragedy *Florian Geyer* was produced. It had been planned as a tragedy of the first magnitude: Hauptmann's intention was to apply the technique of the naturalistic drama on a large scale. In other words, it was in *Sekundenstil*, though (ostensibly at least) in the archaic language of the period depicted. It is the tragedy of the Peasants' Rebellion of 1525, unrolled in a series of loosely connected scenes; and the peasants as a mass are the hero, though the play takes its name from one of their leaders. To Hauptmann's immense sorrow the play was ill received; his grief is symbolically woven into the poetry of *The Sunken Bell* – '*Im Tale klingt sie, in den Bergen nicht*', the bell of his art rang in the lowlands but not on the heights. Criticism between the two wars gave the play much higher rank.

The reason for the immediate failure of *Florian Geyer* lay partly in a reaction of taste – neo-romanticism was beginning –, partly in the inherent weakness of the naturalistic conception of tragedy: in *Florian Geyer* we have a series of dissolving views which do not rivet the attention. But Hauptmann had already struck out into new paths: in *Hanneles Himmelfahrt* (1893) he had combined naturalism with the time-old *Märchendrama*, the three essential ingredients of which – dream, allegory, supernatural beings – here harmoniously link and fuse. Hannele, the fourteen-year-old daughter of a drunkard in a Silesian village, runs away from her father's ill-treatment and tries to drown herself, as her mother had done before her, in the village pond. She is rescued, and is taken by her teacher to the workhouse; in the dreams of her fever, which pass over the stage, she sees Bible texts and fairy-tale fancies realized, with herself as the heroine in the magical white light of it. The awakenings of puberty lend a chill warmth to her visions: her teacher is the Saviour, whom she is to wed. The angel of death stands, black-robed and black-winged, in the room, sword in hand; a hunch-backed village tailor comes and robes her in a bridal dress of white silk, and puts glass slippers on her feet: the angel lifts his sword and vanishes: Hannele is dead. Angels lay her in her coffin; a stranger who resembles the village teacher bids her rise: she kneels at his feet: he takes all her lowliness from her, and angels take her to Kingdom Come.

Verse of great beauty had mingled with the naturalistic prose of *Hannele*: it is by the beauty of its verse that *Die versunkene Glocke* (1896) lives and will live. Only the old witch speaks in (Silesian) dialect, and even this is verse. All the naturalistic stock-in-trade (except the ethics of the rights of passion) is dropped: there are long resonant monologues, the only reality is folded in the spirals of a defiant symbol, and the inspiration is intense personal experience and mental conflict. The heroine Rautendelein (Silesian for *rotes Ännlein*) is the first of the red-haired girls who – symbols of art, beauty, mystery, the lure of Bohemian genius – bewitch the heroes of Hauptmann's plays; it is well known that the model was Hauptmann's second wife, a gifted violin-player. The lesson of the play is that the artist must live in loneliness, out of society, but in communion with nature, here symbolized by sprites of woodland and water who have the quaintness of Böcklin's mythical figures – the *Nickelmann* rising, reeds in hair, from the well and snorting like a seal; the *Waldschrat*, a horned and goatfoot satyr. Heinrich the bell-founder has cast a wonderful bell which is to ring glad tidings down to humanity from the church on the mountains; on its way uphill the satyr upsets the cart and it tumbles into the mountain lake (the physical elements of nature – *Elementargeister* – are hostile to mental striving); Heinrich drags himself to the witch's hut, where he is tended by Rautendelein, with whom he is happy and inspired; the Philistine forces (parson, schoolmaster, barber) fetch him back to the village; but he cannot live there, and he finds his way back to the mountains to die on a last kiss of Rautendelein, who has joined the old watersprite at the bottom of his well (beauty, denied the struggling tormented artist, is the prey of primitive brute strength). Beauty at which all hands snatch, and which is crushed by the grasp of force, is the symbol, too, of the weird play *Und Pippa tanzt* (1906); Pippa (the name was taken from Browning) – frail as a Venetian goblet of cut glass – is rescued from those who pursue her by a consumptive apprentice on his way through the packed ice and snow of the Riesengebirge to the fairy world of Venice. She dies; Michel (i.e. *der deutsche Michel*, the dreamer, the poet) goes blind, but he sees Venice, and Pippa dances in his dreams: beauty, which shatters in the grasp of force, is only seen and possessed by the blind. In three plays Hauptmann goes back to the old German period. *Der arme Heinrich* (1902) dramatizes the legend of the knight sick with leprosy who is told that only the blood of a maiden can save him; the daughter of the farmer at whose house he has found refuge offers the sacrifice (the stirrings of puberty move her as they did Hannele), but the knight, transformed morally by the miracle of love he beholds, stays the surgeon's knife, is cured by the grace of God, and weds the maid. In *Kaiser Karls Geisel* (1908) there is a contrast of senile eroticism[1] (in Charlemagne) with constitutional nymphomania in a girl of sixteen; the ethic problem is (as in Hebbel's *Agnes Bernauer*) whether one whose life is claimed for the public good has a right to personal indulgence. In another medieval drama, *Griselda* (1909), Hauptmann turns the irritating old legend of wifely humility into a somewhat brutal study of masochism. The plays on legendary subjects (the heroine is usually a half-grown girl) have been classed as *Balladendramen*; one such play, *Winterballade* (1917), is actually called a ballad in the title; it is the dramatization of a tale by Selma Lagerlöf (as *Elga*, 1905, is a dramatization of Grillparzer's tale *Das Kloster bei Sendomir*). With *Der weisse Heiland* (1920), which derives largely from Eduard Stucken's novel *Die weissen Götter* (1918), the scene shifts to Mexico: Montezuma welcomes Cortés as the 'White Saviour' promised by old legend; but he himself is the Saviour, who is tortured and put to death by the Spaniards for greed of gold and in the name of religion. The undertone is poignant: in the almost sick denunciation of atrocities perpetrated in the name of fanatic patriotism and religion is to be heard Hauptmann's own disgust in the war years. *Schluck und Jau* (1901) had transferred the main idea (life is a dream) of Christopher Sly's lordship to Silesia; *Indipohdi* (1920) is closely modelled on *The Tempest*: Prospero, dethroned by his son, has been wrecked on a Pacific island, where he is hailed by the Indians as the long-promised White Saviour. With him is his daughter (red-haired), who has grown up on the island; hunting an eagle on the mountains she meets a youth who turns out to be her own brother, wrecked in his turn; she falls in love with him, and proclaims her intention of living with him, even when she learns the relationship. [Incest becomes a favourite theme at this period; it occurs, e.g., in Leonhard Frank's *Bruder und Schwester* (1929), Hesse's *Demian* (1919), Fritz von Unruh's *Ein Geschlecht* (1917), Thomas Mann's *Wälsungenblut* (1921) and *Der Erwählte* (1951), Max Brod's *Lord Byron kommt aus der Mode* (1929), Kasimir Edschmid's *Lord Byron* (1929).] The old magician, rather than

---

[1] A pre-Freudian sketch to be compared with the cruelly elaborated studies of Georg Kaiser (see p. 349).

sanction human sacrifices, which he had abolished, ascends a volcano, and (like Hölderlin's *Empedocles*) descends into the crater: his son and daughter are to rule united. *Veland* (1925) dramatizes the legend of Wayland the Smith, but it is not a *Märchendrama* proper, if only because, like *Griselda*, its ground theme is that of sadism; Veland enslaves Bödwild by twisting her hair round his fists and raping her; he 'bends her like a bow', as it is a man's prerogative to do, and therefore she worships and loves him. In this feeling of love for a strong man's cruelty there is masochism again; but there is also the theme of the self-liberation of workers from bondage: Veland, the first bird-man of Germanic legend, frees himself by making wings to fly with. The play has the rushed tempo of expressionism (p. 346 ff). We have Masochism again in *Dorothea Angermann* (1926): a parson's daughter is seduced by a cook, and she loves him with an abject devotion because he drags her through the mud. *Vor Sonnenuntergang* (1932) is a study of senile eroticism: a septuagenarian is rejuvenated by his passion for a young Kindergarten teacher, and commits suicide when placed by his family under legal restraint.

In the 'thirties Hauptmann produced a chain of what may be called romantic plays, somewhat light or even flimsy in texture, dream-like or phantastic: *Die goldene Harfe* (1932), *Das Hirtenlied* (1935) are of this type. *Hamlet in Wittenberg*[1] (1935) complements the novel of the following year, *Im Wirbel der Berufung* (p. 330); in the play Hamlet as a youth of nineteen, already pathologically complicated and a libertine, proposes to marry a gipsy; one motif is that of the contact of royalty with commoners (Hauptmann's son married a duodecimo princess). Medieval folklore and legend provide the matter of *Die Tochter der Kathedrale* (1939) and (Hauptmann's last comedy to be completed) *Ulrich von Lichtenstein* (1939), in which an old Minnesinger roams the land dressed in women's clothes and parading as Frau Venus, as he does in the strange verse epic he wrote about himself and his antics.

In 1907 Hauptmann visited Greece, and described his experiences in *Griechischer Frühling* (1908). This journey deepened his conception of pagan myth, and gave a new sunniness and plasticity to his work, as in the play of the return of Ulysses to Ithaca: *Der Bogen des Odysseus* (1914). This Ulysses drama has something of the sunny mood of Homer; the action is mythical and impossible, but the interest never flags. Typically the opening scene is outside a farm with a swineherd rubbing his bow with tallow. These pleasantly contriving gods of Homer yield the stage in a tetralogy of Greek plays, written during the Second World War, to the dark chthonic deities of pre-Aeschylean Greece. Hauptmann

---

[1] One of Karl Gutzkow's (p. 267) first plays was a *Hamlet in Wittenberg*.

on his visit to Delphi had come to the conclusion that 'the bloody root of tragedy lies in blood sacrifices'; and his Iphigenia, as the priestess of the moon-goddess Hecate, offers human sacrifices as part of the ritual to which she is dedicated. Following up the outlines in Goethe's *Italienische Reise* of a projected drama with the same title, Hauptmann had first written *Iphigenie in Delphi* (1941), which is chronologically the fourth of the tetralogy; he had then added *Iphigenie in Aulis* (1944); then followed the two centre pieces, *Agamemnons Tod* and *Elektra*, both in 1947. The *Atriden-Tetralogie* has clearly the psychopathic mood of the war years, and what is revealed is that in the cruelty and lust of destruction of our own day we have the survival, masked by illusory religions and spurious passions such as false patriotism, of primitive states of mind; Agamemnon has the brain-storms of a dictator who for self-aggrandisement sacrifices all that should be dear to him.

In his 'prentice days Hauptmann had written a short tale, *Der Apostel* (1890), at once a prose poem and a subtle presentment of religious mania. The kernel of the story is a dream of the *unio mystica*: the 'apostle' dreams that Jesus appears to him, and that the apparition cures him of the strange sensations of his brain. This dream and the results of it are repeated in *Der Narr in Christo Emanuel Quint* (1910). In this novel Hauptmann has taken up the subject of his early short story, and, repeating some of the details, has worked out a more prosaic exposition of religious mania. Many Messiahs have appeared in the world, and Hauptmann lights up, sympathetically, the genesis and growth of their delusions, as well as the effect of their preaching on credulous minds. It is perhaps unfortunate that the career of his hero is so closely modelled on that of Jesus; for even to freethinkers who take the book as it is meant, as an interpretation of the Gospels, the taking over of fact after fact – for instance, the hovering doves when Quint is baptized – will seem too obviously inartistic; while to some, of course, the story will be blasphemy. Again, the novelist has kept too close to science to keep the illusion of art; the events are so scientifically possible that they are improbable. The Moravian atmosphere of Silesian mountain villages, however, the atmosphere of Silesian pietism in which Hauptmann grew up, is wonderfully well reproduced; we are made to feel that religious revivals are just as inevitable among these weavers and tillers of the soil as they are in Wales. In *The Fool in Christ*, as in other books by Hauptmann, there is a struggle between the spirit and the flesh; but Emanuel Quint conquers the flesh by persuading himself that he is a spirit. This belief explains his teaching. He thinks that the Lord's Prayer is an address to the Ghost – that is, to the God-Spirit in man. It is with the spirit, therefore, that he baptizes. But he that is baptized of the spirit is born again of the spirit, and is therefore the Son of God. Quint merely wishes to save men from their dead selves – i.e. their bodies – by making them spirits, or God; but his hearers do not follow his admirably simple reasoning. To the learned among them it seems laby-rinthine madness; to the starving peasants it seems to be the self-glorifi-cation of the Messiah, and as such they worship him, forming a community which wallows in mad orgies till he forbids them to read the Bible, the source of their delusions and selfish hopes. Quint is a prophet preaching in the wilderness; what his disciples want is not the kingdom of the spirit but better times. In the end he wanders about Germany, knocking at doors and saying he is Christ; and he is last seen in the mountains of Switzerland. When his corpse is found after the spring thaw there is a sheet of paper in his pocket, and on it, still legible, are the words: 'The mystery of the kingdom?' With this query the book ends.

Apart from the religious and psychopathic problems, there is much that is interesting in *The Fool in Christ*. There is an autobiographical element: Kurt Simon is clearly a picture of Hauptmann as an agricultural student; none the less self-portraiture is Dominik, the Breslau student whose teachers will not allow him to come up for his examination 'on the ground of moral delinquency'. The period of Quint's appearance is set about 1890, a time when all Germany was in a ferment; and we have transparent portraits of celebrities of that time and after, e.g. Peter Hullen-kamp is the hallucinated poet PETER HILLE (1854-1904), the picturesque vagrom man among the naturalists.

There is an autobiographical substratum, too, in Hauptmann's second long novel. In 1884, while studying sculpture in Rome, he had been laid up with an attack of typhoid fever, and probably his life was saved by his *fiancée*, who came from Germany to nurse him. Ten years later he visited America. These are the two experiences which form the ground-work of *Atlantis* (1912). There is much else that is obviously autobio-graphical; probably the hero Friedrich von Kammacher, whose experi-ments in bacteriology have ended in a fiasco, is as much Hauptmann himself as Vockerat is in *Einsame Menschen* or Heinrich in *Die versunkene Glocke*. While Friedrich's scientific reputation was being torn to shreds his wife had gone mad; these two threads which the Parcae had woven into his life had snapped; but a third thread, his passion for a little vampire of a dancing girl, is still whole. He takes a berth on a steamer by which she is travelling to New York; and more than half of the book is taken up with the life on board the *Roland* till it is rammed by a derelict, with the escape of a boatful of passengers, including the doctor and his dancing girl, and with their rescue by a schooner. Minute as the description is, there is not a moment's languor; and accounts of actual shipwrecks by survivors seem illusory after the unerring balancing of psychological states which even Hauptmann could probably not have written if he had not been a pupil of Forel.[1] Moreover, the events as described are strangely prophetic of the disaster to the *Titanic*, which occurred shortly afterwards. In New York, Friedrich whistles his dancing girl down the wind, joins a circle of artists, and takes lessons in sculpture, at which he had tried his hands in his youth, from Eva Burns. But he cannot free his mind from the experiences of the shipwreck, and he would have become a maniac if the 'poisons and putrid matter' in his body had not ended his consciousness by an attack of typhoid fever. He is nursed back to life by Eva Burns, and his hysterical wife having in the meantime died to make way for the 'healthy woman' of so many of the novels of the period [e.g. Gustav Frenssen's *Klaus Hinrich Baas* (1909)], he returns with her to Europe.

A Greek paganism which literally amounts to phallus-worship gives a disquieting fascination to the novel *Der Ketzer von Soana* (1918). The hero is an Italian priest in Ticino, who, to unite himself with a beautiful girl, herself the child of incest, forsakes his creed and lives as a goatherd. The intention – Eve rules all, and there is no help for it – sounds ecstatic or hopeless according to attitude from the words in which the poet, who as he descends the mountain meets the woman coming up, describes her: 'She rose up from the depths of the world – and she rises and rises, into eternity, as the one into whose merciless hands heaven and hell are delivered up.' That is, a man cannot escape love. That woman cannot deny herself to love is demonstrated with sly irony in *Die Insel der grossen Mutter* (1924). A ship is wrecked on the coast of a South Sea island: only the women escape, with one lovely boy. The women establish a matriarchy. In due course babies arrive: there is an Indian god on the island. The first child is looked upon as Messiah. As the boys grow up they are banished to Manland, whence in due course they return to conquer their willing mothers and sisters. *Phantom, Aufzeichnungen eines ehemaligen Sträflings* (1922) describes the inner life and transformation of a criminal. The hero of *Wanda* (1928) is yet another of Hauptmann's alcoholic artists: he pursues a vampire of a girl, who prefers to be attached to a circus.

Anna (1921) is a rural idyll, like *Hermann und Dorothea*, but in dreadful hexameters, much worse than the trochees of *Der weisse Heiland*. It is autobiographical in its outlines: the hero goes to a farm managed by his uncle to learn the business of agriculture. There is a girl at the farm, Anna, with whom he falls in love; she denies herself to him because she is honest, and has already fallen to the lad's uncle, a slimy drunkard.

---

[1] August Forel's *Die sexuelle Frage* (1904) had considerable influence on our period.

She is sacrificed in holy wedlock to a very greasy Moravian brother. In the two volumes of *Das Abenteuer meiner Jugend* (1937) Hauptmann records the story of the first twenty-five years of his life. There is auto-biography, too, in the two volumes of *Das Buch der Leidenschaft* (1929-30), in the novel *Im Wirbel der Berufung* (1936), in the Novelle *Die Spitzhacke* (1930), and in *Der grosse Traum* (1942), an epic poem in terza rima. The epic poem in hexameters *Till Eulenspiegel* (1928) has its personal element in so far as it shows forth Hauptmann's detestation of war.

In every literary movement that pushes forward to extremes there is a group of cautious adherents who trail along with them something of the paraphernalia of the old school. They are followers, but not pioneers. In the period of naturalism they are classed, as far as the theatre is con-cerned, as *Kompromissdramatiker* (Sudermann, Fulda, Halbe, Otto Ernst), but they feuilletonize the novel just as much as they blend old and new in the drama. Both in drama and novel the typical pseudo-naturalist is HERMANN SUDERMANN (1857-1928). Born in East Prussia, he migrated to Berlin, and made a hit in 1887 with his novel *Frau Sorge*, an East Prussian variation of the Romeo and Juliet theme[1] which already shows the salient features of Sudermann's novels: his characters are shown in grim contest with conditions imposed upon them by the sins of others. *Frau Sorge* is the story of a poor boy with a bad father; the dice of fate are loaded against him, but he works his way to success. It is a *Bildungs-roman* with a restricted framework: whereas the *Bildungsromane* of the classical and romantic periods took their hero through phases of mental development to a high stage of culture, the idea of *Frau Sorge* is success by work. In this it follows Freytag's *Soll und Haben* and Julian Schmidt's dictum blazoned thereon that the novel must seek the Germans where they are at their best, at their work. It was to have a long series of success-ful imitations, the best known of which is Gustav Frenssen's *Jörn Uhl* (1901). *Frau Sorge* is generally recognized as the progenitor of Frenssen's tale, but it does not seem to have been noticed that there is a striking similarity between *Frau Sorge* and Marie von Ebner-Eschenbach's *Das Gemeindekind* (1887); in both tales the progress of the hero is shown from childhood upward; he has to suffer for the sins of his father; and in both tales there is symbolic use of a '*Lokomobile*'. How loosely attached Suder-mann is to consistent naturalism can be seen by a comparison of the two novels: whereas Marie von Ebner-Eschenbach is consistently scientific in her consideration of the effects of heredity (the ending, as cautious as

---

[1] A favourite motif of *Dorfnovelle* and *Bauerndrama*, e.g. Keller's *Romeo und Julie auf dem Dorfe*, Auerbach's *Erdmute*, Anzengruber's *Der Meineidbauer* and *Doppel-selbstmord*.

that of Hauptmann's *Das Friedensfest*, leaves it questionable whether the boy will overcome his hereditary tendencies or not – he relinquishes love because he is conscious of homicidal passion), Sudermann, after letting his hero overcome his adversaries by a show of physical courage (as Ebner-Eschenbach does), ends with romantic happiness. The headlong rush of action of Sudermann's narration is seen at its best in *Der Katzensteg* (1889); the period is that of the Napoleonic wars, but the interest is psychological, not to say erotic (the hero loves his dead father's sweetheart).

The success of *Vor Sonnenaufgang* was disputed; the first overwhelming success in drama of the new movement was that of Sudermann's *Die Ehre* (1889). Looking backward now, one can see that the success may have been due, not to the identification of the drama with the naturalistic movement, but to its skilful combination of the old stage technique with the new social feeling. It was a modernized *bürgerliches Trauerspiel* with the traditional contrast of classes, conflict between children and parents, augmented by a cynical valuation of sexual 'honour'. The scene is a house in Berlin; the front part is inhabited by a rich man, and the rear by the family of a man who is employed in the rich man's factory. The situation (*Vorderhaus und Hinterhaus*) became famous. There is a son and a daughter in each family; in the symmetry of the play (a dramatic chiasmus) the daughter of the rich man and the son of the poor man have risen above class prejudice, while the son of the rich man and the daughter of the poor man are moral degenerates; the good daughter and the good son are lovers; the poor man's daughter has been seduced by the rich man's son. The mouthpiece for the idea of the play (culture's elastic conception of 'honour') is Graf Trast, who has had to give up his career as an officer because of his inability to pay a gambling debt; he has since made a fortune in business. The end is that the naughty girl is paid off, while the son from the rear (a good match because he is Trast's heir) marries the girl at the front. As things are, the dishonoured girl will have a better chance of making a decent marriage (she has a dowry) than if she had been a virgin; Trast, who points this out, says that he is as raw as nature and as cruel as truth.

Die Ehre is, after all, constructed on the French model, and is in the line of Scribe and Sardou: Graf Trast is the *raisonneur* who voices the idea round which the characters turn. To this careful French technique Sudermann owed the success of the majority of his plays; when he deserted it, as in his comedy *Die Schmetterlingsschlacht* (1895), to attempt *milieu*-painting, he failed entirely. The production of his second play, *Sodoms Ende*, was at first forbidden by the police; when it was produced in 1890 it turned out to be a crass picture of just that stratum of Berlin society which bought theatre tickets and made or damned plays. Sodom is the Berlin society of the day; a young painter is seduced and debased by a rich dame; he comes home drunk in the dead of night and violates his foster-sister, a mere child; she rushes out and drowns herself, and he dies of hæmorrhage. The next play, *Heimat* (1893), is well known in England as *Magda*: Sarah Bernhardt and Mrs Pat Campbell played the title-role. The characters are not really new: there is an old retired officer ('*der polternde Vater*'); his daughter, who had run away from home and now comes back as a famous singer ('the woman with a past'); and the man who seduced her when she was a girl, now a man of position. The latter is willing to marry a *prima donna*; and when the father hears the whole story he sees no other way out; the lady, however, has developed more than her chest; she despises the man who had abandoned her; her father levels a pistol at her, but has an apoplectic fit, and falls dead before he can pull the trigger. *Heimat* has again the traditional elements of the *bürgerliches Trauerspiel*: conflict between father and daughter, between passion and respectability, between social strata (here middle-class society and Bohemianism). It is a notable contribution to that feminism which begins with the *Lucinde* literature (see p. 261) and in the drama with Grillparzer's *Sappho*.

LUDWIG FULDA (1862-1939) has that mastery of form which goes to the making of a first-class translator; and possibly his translations of Molière and Rostand will live longer than his own plays, though *Der Talisman* (1893) and *Der Sohn des Kalifen* (1896) have importance in the revival of the verse *Märchendrama*. Fulda, though there was nothing in his composition (rather that of the cloistered scholar) of social pity, attempted a naturalistic drama in *Das verlorene Paradies* (1890), in which workmen strike and get what they want because their spokesman wins over the employer's daughter. MAX HALBE (1865-1944) brought the landscapes and the mentality of Eastern Germany with contrasts of German and Polish character into the naturalistic play. His *Der Eisgang* (1892) symbolizes in the breaking of the ice on the Vistula the loosed flood-tide of Socialism sweeping away all rotten barriers. Halbe's *Jugend* (1893) was one of the great successes of the period. The scene is in Poland, in the home of an old Catholic priest; with him lives his niece, a girl of eighteen, the child of an unmarried mother. A cousin, who is just about to go to the university, comes on a visit. The two young people are left too much alone, and the girl goes the same way as her mother had done; her half-brother, a species of idiot, aims a bullet at the student; it misses him, but kills the girl. What was new in the play was the psychology of adolescence:

these young people awakening to the facts of life expressed their feelings in language not unnatural but charged with poetry; and there was an air of reality and inevitability in the events, which in the girl's case might be explained by the laws of heredity.

To Hauptmann's school belong the plays of GEORG HIRSCHFELD (1873-1935), who at the age of twenty-three made a hit with *Die Mütter* (1896), and those of Gerhart's brother, CARL HAUPTMANN (1858-1921): *Marianne* (1894), *Die Waldleute* (1895), *Ephraims Breite* (1898). Carl Hauptmann's *Die Bergschmiede* (1902) is a symbolistic *Märchendrama*; his novel *Mathilde* (1902), the heroine of which, a factory lass, arrives at a broad contentment in the humdrum existence of her class, is naturalistic; his *Einhart der Lächler* (1907) follows the type of the *Bildungsroman*, but continues the development to the death of the hero, who is said to be modelled on Gerhart Hauptmann. Wolfram von Eschenbach's *Parzival* (often called the first of the *Bildungsromane*) has been described (adequately to friend or foe) as the story of a perfect fool; and the idea of a simple soul winding his devious and dubious way through the labyrinths of a mysterious world to the clear heights of contentment is the kernel of *Einhart der Lächler*, who never loses the smile of his simple nature.

FRANK WEDEKIND (1864-1916) cannot be called a naturalist because: (*a*) he has no pity; (*b*) the characters and action of his plays are not observed, but invented, i.e. they are caricatures of reality or quite fantastic; (*c*) the form of his plays is not analytic, but synthetic, a film-like sequence of scenes or pictures, as in the old *Sturm und Drang*, with an illusory division into acts. Wedekind is the creator of a new genre, the grotesque drama of manners, and in this respect, as in his rejection of the accepted canons of decency, he is the acknowledged prophet and forerunner of expressionism. The butt of his vitriolic attack is conventional morality, but he himself, in repeated self-interpretation through the mouth of his characters, claims to be a moralist, and, incredible as it seems to us, the claim has been upheld by the most serious academic critics of Germany. The explanation no doubt is that he came in on a flood-tide of popularity after his death as a critic of pre-war society; but one asks whether the circus-proprietor who offered Karl Hetman, the hero of *Hidalla*, obviously intended by Wedekind as a portrait of himself, a post as clown, was radically wrong in his estimation; the only objection is that his clowning is too vile for laughter. His influence on literature, however, both as regards form and substance, cannot be minimized. With Strindberg he provided a new eroticism; but whereas Strindberg represents woman as subjugating man by the patient exercise of low cunning, to Wedekind she is a scintillating snake who fascinates and poisons but can be tamed by brutality, which is the best thing for her (in the famous prologue to *Erdgeist* man is the tamer with the whip). To Wedekind as to Strindberg woman is the source of all suffering; but while Strindberg hates her Wedekind sadistically adores her and paints her as irresistible, even when she is (literally) smeared with the blood of her victims. She is the 'earth-spirit' who draws down the mind of man to the dust; but in the dust man is happy, for 'this bliss of the senses is the beam of light that pierces the night of our existence'. It is the cosmic urge, and it is holy, for it serves 'the morality of beauty'; regeneration of the race should come from this love – resistless and therefore mystical – of the beautiful body of soulless woman. Even a prostitute is divine, for she is flesh; copulation in a brothel is, in the sulphurous light of Wedekind's hallucinations, a *unio mystica.*

With this apostolic preaching of sex goes a corrosive criticism of institutions and cherished ideals. *Frühlings Erwachen* (1891) initiates a long series of works by other writers in which parents and teachers are accused of keeping children at the critical stage in ignorance of the facts of life. During a storm a schoolgirl of fourteen takes refuge with a schoolboy in a barn; she is to have a baby – to her great surprise –, but dies of means used to procure abortion – of anæmia according to her decent gravestone. It is the fantastic atmosphere of the play which counts in literary history: a schoolboy who fails in his examination commits suicide and, with his head under his arm, meets, in the churchyard, the boy who is responsible for the baby; the latter, instead of following him into the grave, follows a *vermummter Herr* (= Wedekind), who comes along to explain the idiocy of existence. *Erdgeist* (1895) is the very shrine of Wedekind's eroticism; round the heroine Lulu, a symbol of soulless woman, a mixture of vamp and vegetable, dance lovers like moths round a flame. In the sequel, *Die Büchse der Pandora* (1904), long condemned by the censor, Lulu has degenerated into an object bought and sold; in the gruesome scene – very fine as Grand Guignol – at the end she is slit open in a London attic by Jack the Ripper. She shares this thrilling death with a countess who has clung to her with the devotion of a dog and the torments of unsatisfied Lesbian love. *Hidalla* (1904) records the squabblings of a sect – 'The International Union for the Breeding of Beautiful Thoroughbreds' – who swear to give themselves in love at first asking to any fellow-member: a deed of public service in the interests of the race, since all are eugenically certified. Only the secretary, Karl Hetman, is deformed and queer; since, however, he has an intellectual fascination the full-blood females in sheer illogical perversity gravitate to him. *Der Kammersänger* (1897) is a short sharp scene, showing a tenor beset by nymphomaniac admirers; as he has to catch a train he says good-bye to the last somewhat rudely; she shoots herself – but he cannot miss his train.

Wedekind was a clown, but not (strictly speaking) a humorist. The humour in the drama of the day is represented by JOSEF RUEDERER (1861-1915) with *Fahnenweihe* (1894), LUDWIG THOMA (1867-1921) with *Moral* (1909), OTTO ERICH HARTLEBEN (1864-1905), and OTTO ERNST (1862-1926). In Hartleben's comedy *Hanna Jagert* (1893) a Marxist flaunting of free love counters the Nietzschean concept of the strong personality; his sentimental tragedy *Rosenmontag* (1900), one of the great stage successes of the period, shows up the caste feeling and the brazen profligacy of Prussian officers. There is more lasting merit in his lyric verse (*Meine Verse*, 1895). Otto Ernst gave an impetus to the revival of the *Bildungsroman* with his to a great extent autobiographical *Asmus Sempers Jugendland* (1905), *Semper der Jüngling* (1908), *Semper der Mann* (1916), the hero of which rises from the working-classes to be an elementary teacher – a rank which in Germany (since Jean Paul wove the village schoolmaster's life into cloud-rapt idylls) has been associated with culture and influence. Himself an elementary schoolmaster before he became an author, Otto Ernst satirized educational pedantries in his comedy *Flachsmann als Erzieher* (1902), in *Jugend von heute* (1900) the megalomania of would-be supermen in the literary world, and in *Gerechtigkeit* (1902) blustering journalists.

Consistent naturalism did not very long hold the field as the movement of the day; before it had lost its strangeness it was challenged by a new movement, that of symbolism, neo-romanticism or impressionism (three names for much the same thing); and gradually naturalism merges with these new currents, some poets shifting as mood dictates from one style to the other. Impressionism is partly a reaction from naturalism, but to a great extent it derives from French symbolism, which was itself a reaction against two completely different styles, naturalism and Parnassianism; in Germany, however, the manner of the French Parnassians is imitated, e.g. by RICHARD VON SCHAUKAL (1874-1942), at the same time as that of the symbolists; i.e. the sculptured or pictorial Parnassian style blends with symbolist infolding of meaning.

Impressionism in painting loosely assembles light effects round blurred outlines. So, too, literary impressionism produces (to quote Schiller's summing-up of Klopstock's nebulosity) a given state of mind without the help of a given subject. In a word, impressionism produces *Stimmung*, mood, atmosphere, *état d'âme*, or any other shibboleth that will adumbrate enjoyment passing into a folding, feminized receptivity with the questioning functions of the intellect flooded and stilled by excited pulses.

It is a law of physics that action and reaction are equal and in opposite directions. The direction which impressionism gives to art is away from nature. Hermann Bahr interpreted the phase somewhat whimsically: the poet or painter, he says, is the mirror in which nature is reflected; or nature as we see it in the work of art is not seen directly but reflected in a temperament. If the temperament is abnormal, the reflection will be abnormal; but it will be art. Moreover, according to naturalistic theory nature must always appear the same in art, for art must be a photographic reproduction of nature; art would thus be infinitely monotonous; according to impressionistic theory, on the other hand, the reflection of nature in art differs as infinitely as artists differ in temperament. Only vision is true. A child watches its mother in a green shade and says to papa: 'Mama has a green nose!' Papa says it only seems so, but the child knows better, it says what it sees. Papa knows too much; his superior knowledge corrects his vision. In reality we never see anything as our intelligence tells us it is. But the appearance which intelligence says is untrue is beautiful; and art portrays the beautiful, which *is* the real, only the real is *underneath* it. '*Am farbigen Abglanz haben wir das Leben*', wrote Goethe.

Impressionism first appears as programmatic in Hermann Bahr's novel *Die gute Schule* (1890). HERMANN BAHR (1863-1934), an Austrian from Linz, had just arrived in Berlin after a stay in Paris, where by this time the symbolist doctrines were the latest thing. The hero of the novel is a young painter who, after eating red salmon in green sauce, is pursued by these colours. The sub-title is *Seelische Zustände*, and this is symptomatic; the notation of a state is here transferred from the outer to the inner world. In *Die gute Schule* Bahr shows his uncanny flair for coming fashions; he is the herald of every new movement, and, if he did not actually turn the course of literature, he has at various stages been the first to point out the change in direction (*Zur Kritik der Moderne*, 1890; *Die Überwindung des Naturalismus*, 1891; *Expressionismus*, 1914). The term *die Moderne* (= *Modernismus, Modernität, der moderne Zeitgeist*) was brought into vogue by him. It is as an impressionistic essayist that he has done his best work, but his plays have importance; some (*Der Krampus*, 1902) are in the manner of the Viennese *Volksstück*; others are problem dramas (*Sanna*, 1905); and *Das Konzert* (1911) is a rollicking farce with the picture of a musician pursued by neurotic women.

Up to 1889 the trend of thought had been strongly 'social democratic', towards the masses. August Bebel was a force in the land. In 1889 the news was spread that Friedrich Nietzsche was mad, and his ideas began to be discussed in all quarters. A reaction set in towards individualism; 'the right of the strong', 'the will to power', 'the superman' became catchwords.

L

FRIEDRICH NIETZSCHE (1844-1900) was a Saxon like Lessing and Wagner, like Lessing a parson's son, and like Klopstock an *alumnus* of Schulpforta. His first book, *Die Geburt der Tragödie aus dem Geiste der Musik* (1872), reads strangely in the light of his later work: it is passionately reasoned propaganda for Wagner's 'music drama'. It is an interesting link in the chain of æsthetic theories; and while it buttresses Wagner's critical writings – *Das Kunstwerk der Zukunft* (1850), *Oper und Drama* (1851) – it supplements Schiller's classical division, in *Über naive und sentimentalische Dichtung*, of poetry into *naiv* (i.e. spontaneous) and *sentimentalisch* (i.e. reflective). Schiller had defined *das Naive* as the oneness of mind with nature, and *das Sentimentalische* as the conflict of mind with nature. Nietzsche derives art from the contest between Apollo and Dionysus; just as man and woman, though contraries and in constant strife, generate humanity by a periodic reconciliation, so the union of *apollinisch* and *dionysisch* generates art. Apollo is form, plastic art, rationalism, subjective creation; Dionysus is formlessness, music, mysticism, intoxication creating in the forgetfulness of self (*Selbstvergessenheit im Rausche*). Art fluctuates between two extremes of perfect form and formlessness, between classical architecture and music, between fixed and unfixed. Between these two extremes – the two worlds of intoxication and dream (*Rausch und Traum*) – there is an ascending gradation in music, lyric verse, epic, plastic art, architecture towards fixity of image, each image (*Abbild*) being an Apolline dream-shape, or the will to existence as phenomenon of what is in the world beyond sense shapeless. Dream shapes that which is shapeless in chaos; the Greek gods themselves are dreamed visions of pure limbs in a vaporous void. This dream-world of lovely illusion (*der schöne Schein*) is limited, and therefore calm; but intoxication is limitless, and therefore orgiastic. Judgment is calm, but ecstasy is drunken. All creation of life is in ecstasy; what is not created in ecstasy is without life; life can only come of life; calmness, even 'health', is barren, dead.[1] The calm shapers of vision – the Apolline or subjective poets – scorn Dionysiac orgies as morbid; little they know how livid and ghastly (*leichenfarbig und gespenstisch*) their 'health' looks when the glowing life of Dionysiac revellers reels past them. Apollo is raised above nature, not one with nature; but nature joins the mad rout of Dionysus: panther and tiger pace under his yoke; in Dionysiac frenzy man is one again with nature, he dances upwards into the air, he floats on enchanted clouds like the gods. Apollo is the artist with measuring mind and shaping hands – shaping an idolon; Dionysus drunk is

---

[1] Nietzsche has no inkling of Thomas Mann's insistent teaching (the biological fact) that creation kills the creator; that creation, while the highest manifestation of life, is also the beginning of the death of life (see pp. 338, 340).

more than artist, he is god, he is art itself; his frenzy of rapture creates the noblest work of art – man magnified and panting in passion. Now these two opposite ideals of *Traumkunst*, or shaping vision, and *Rauschkunst*,[1] or creation in ecstasy, are united in the ancient Greek tragedy, which springs from the chorus of satyrs; for in Greek tragedy Apollo shapes, in a symbolic vision, the oneness with nature of the drunken reveller. Music is the highest of the arts; for, though it shapes no visions, it expresses that ancient pain (*Urschmerz*) felt by man when by the process of becoming man he was wrenched from synthesis with the eternal. Music is the echo thrilled with pain of a lost divine harmony. And therefore the nearer to music, the more divine is verse. It follows that lyric verse is next in beauty to music; though by the very nature of lyric verse the lyric poet sings of self, he sings his intoxication with self, and is therefore Dionysiac. (In illustration one might say that Burns's poem *To Mary in Heaven* would be merely local gossip if it were not an echo in music of the *Urschmerz*.) The *Volkslied* clings in close imitation to music, and is thus the ideal of a poem, which merely expresses what in music is not expressed. The epic poet, on the other hand, is lost in contemplation of images or shapes. Music symbolizes the universe (*Musik ist Weltsymbolik*). As Wagner said, civilization is eclipsed by music as lamplight is by the sun's radiance. Art saves man from Buddha's denial of life; in utter disgust with life man is rescued from the horrible by the sublime and from the absurd by comic laughter. Greek art was saved by the chorus of satyrs. To the Greek the bearded satyr was nature; and whereas the flute-playing shepherd of modern pastorals was a pretence of nature, the Greek satyr was true man; not in Gessner's *Salonschäfer*, but in Hauptmann's *Waldschrat*, Nietzsche might have urged if he had read *Die versunkene Glocke*, is nature real and redolent. The regeneration of myth which was the inspiration of Greek tragedy was killed by Euripides, with his explanatory prologues, and by Socrates, that spinner of theories; stripped by logic (or rationalism) of music and mysticism, tragedy dies. But in German music (Wagner is meant) there is an awakening of the Dionysiac spirit, and a rebirth of (German) myth.

Nietzsche next, in 1873, launched an attack on David Friedrich Strauss[2] (1808-74) (*David Strauss, der Bekenner und der Schriftsteller*), whom he angrily dismisses as a '*Bildungsphilosoph*'; that is, a scholar who does not seek truth, because he thinks truth has already been found by the mighty dead, a slave of barren learning, not a creator. His next work, *Vom Nutzen*

---

[1] Ideas vital for the intelligence of literature after 1890 (see pp. 337, 346).
[2] His *Der alte und der neue Glaube*, which has been called *Die Bibel des Bildungsphilisters*, had appeared in 1872 (see pp. 271, 429).

und Nachteil der Historie für das Leben (1874), continues the attack on contemporary ideals of culture. The study of history, he proclaims, is useless unless it is a fertilizing process creating the future: history studied on the principle '*fiat veritas, pereat vita*' makes man passive, retrospective, a living lexicon, a eunuch. History reduced to knowledge has lost its germs like corn ground to flour. Thus contemporary culture is not culture, but a knowledge of culture; it produces scholars and philistines, but not men who, fighting history or the reality round them, make history. Thus, in these two books two new ideals are proclaimed: a new culture and new man. These two books were negative; the two next, *Schopenhauer als Erzieher* (1874) and *Richard Wagner in Bayreuth* (1876), are positive. New man can be imbued with the new culture in the school of Schopenhauer, and in Wagner's operas new man can be seen realized. The four works mentioned were collected under the title *Unzeitgemässe Betrachtungen*: '*unzeitgemäss*' is what Schopenhauer and Wagner teach us to be, that is, hostile to circumambient reality, to the time we live in; they were men who, instead of bending their backs to the golden calf – pseudo-culture, a scarecrow hung with rags – wandered out into the wilderness and feared not to be alone. Real culture is a life-force surging from the heart and transforming the whole organism into a perfect unity.

The great crisis in Nietzsche's life was his loss of faith in Wagner, when the latter, as it seemed to Nietzsche, 'collapsed before the Christian cross'. His *Menschliches, Allzumenschliches* (1878), published as his health broke for good (he had been infected with syphilis by a contact in 1866), bears evidence of the mental storm and stress through which he had passed. It is, like all Nietzsche's books written after this crisis in his life, a collection of aphorisms. Nietzsche here shows a violent reaction against current literature, both in its form and substance. The form was the natural outcome of the mode of composition. Nietzsche, doomed to death but with the will to live, lived in the open air and jotted down his ideas as they came. He never rounded his philosophy into a system: it remains in rudimentary form, aphorisms shot into shape, clear by force of repetition and hammering in, but not logically fitted in section by section. It has the freshness of mountain air and the poetry of surprise, as of sudden vistas opening out from a scaled height; it has a Biblical familiarity of style studded with Hebrew parallelisms and variation. In *Unzeitgemässe Betrachtungen* there had been drastic disillusionment; in *Menschliches, Allzumenschliches* even the illusions he had kept have gone. There are two kinds of poetry, we are told now: one (for mature men) is quiet and harmonious, the other (for women and children) is passionate and chaotic.

The ideal poet is he who bodies forth types of the future: healthy, glad and beautiful men.[1] This poet's landscape is bathed in the light of a sun which lights up cobwebs in the mystic cave, rends the iridescent dreams of the romanticist, and shows up every metaphysical system that ever was as a mirage.

From *Menschliches, Allzumenschliches* and the following works Nietzsche's *Weltanschauung* has to be pieced together by the reader, who must disregard contradictions: seen from a scaled peak boulders flatten themselves out in the vast sweep of the slopes. Science, we are told, gives insight and calls for nobler natures than poetry and music – these are leaves falling in autumn, the swan-song of departing things. The highest state of the soul is a glad, roguish seriousness; and therefore Socrates was wiser than Christ. Men of old were glad; men of today merely shun pain; our descendants must be like our forefathers, and for this 'conscience' and the idea of 'evil' must be done away with. The prick of conscience is like a dog's bite in a stone; it is silly; the will is not free, and all is necessary. In nature there are no contradictions, only grades of difference. There is no basic difference between good and evil.

Humanity has gone backwards since Christianity crossed the world's threshold. The rebellion of slaves against ancient philosophy was completed by Christianity, which enthroned the emotions love, fear, hope, and faith. Christianity by the trick of 'love' became lyric religion, by the trick of 'hell' it drew the timid into its fold. Its character was oriental and feminine; it identified misfortune and guilt, whereas antiquity was familiar with the idea of free and guiltless misfortune. Christianity brought pity, that canker that has eaten into man's marrow. Christianity's altruistic morality – 'love thy neighbour' – is the morality of the helpless: it has ever been the foe of the strong, the lonely. No instinct is in itself moral, the same instinct can develop (e.g.) into cowardice or humility – and submission to morality is not moral. It may be called forth by slavishness or despair! The morality of the slave is not the morality of the strong man. Morality is obedience to prevailing laws; free man is immoral. They were the strong, evil spirits that led man upwards. Morality is nothing more than the instinct of the herd. There must be a new adjustment of the table of values (*eine Umwertung aller Werte*). But for that a new man is needed who can stand like a giant among pygmies. The driving force in history is the will to power (*der Wille zur Macht*; not, as in Schopenhauer's system, the will to live) in individuals as in nations.

Also sprach Zarathustra (1883-91) brings into relief the ideal figure of

[1] '*Das Ziel ist der starke und schöne Mensch.*' Richard Wagner: *Die Kunst und die Revolution* (1849).

the great lonely man who breaks down all old values and replaces them by new, shows the steps that lead up to the superman. In *Also sprach Zarathustra* we are told that men are not equal and never will be.

Through all history, runs the main thread of Nietzsche's argument, there has been a bitter contrast between two contrary ideas of morality, between the morality of the rulers and the ruled, the morality of masters and the morality of slaves, the former characterized by the definition of values 'good – bad' (*gut – schlecht*), the latter by that of 'good – evil' (*gut – böse*). Nietzsche explains the origin and definition of values of these two moral principles in *Jenseits von Gut und Böse* (1886), and *Zur Genealogie der Moral* (1887). The highly-placed, high-minded man looked upon himself and his actions as 'good', that is, first-rate, in contradiction to the lowly-placed, low-minded man and *his* actions: by means of this 'pathos of distance' he created values and the names for them. This is the origin of the terms 'good – bad'. [Nietzsche was guided by somewhat slippery etymologies, e.g. the fact that *schlicht* (= plain) and *schlecht* (= bad) are originally the same word.] Slave morality had a different origin. A chiasmus of equivalents therefore arises:

1. Morality of master: Good – bad
                          ><
2. Slave morality: Good – evil

That is, what in the morality of the masters was good was evil in slave morality. To the slave the mighty lord is 'evil'; i.e. 'evil' to the slave is 'good' to the lord. The masters are optimists, the slaves are pessimists. Slave morality was spiritualized and refined by the priests, for the caste of priests were weaklings, and it was in their interests to turn the original statement of values upside down. The rebellion began with the Jews, that hate-filled race of priests, and the function of Jews in history was continued by Christianity: Judea conquered Rome. The ideal of antiquity came to life again at the Renaissance,[1] but the two great plebeian revolutions, the German and the English reformation first, and then the French revolution, tumbled the ruined temples of antiquity to the ground, and on them the nineteenth century built its appalling barracks for workmen.

The ruling element of Christianity is altruism. It makes virtues of weaknesses and brands the strong, glad man as a criminal. It glorifies all those qualities by means of which it can maintain itself in the struggle for existence: charity, pity, self-sacrifice. An ascetic ideal which is hostile to life! 'Bad conscience' is merely the suppressed striving for freedom of an enslaved race; the instincts they exercised when free they must now,

[1] Impressionism turns to the *cinquecento* for themes (see pp. 232-3, 314, 325).

as slaves, resist and brand as evil. This race of 'conscience'-stricken slaves devised religious conceptions of sin against God; they conceive God as the extreme contrast of their suppressed but still stirring instincts; these instincts they interpret as sin against God, their sufferings they interpret as punishment for the sins with which they identify 'bad conscience'. It was religion's most eventful *tour de force*; the weakling thus became a criminal, but the will was saved, and life had a meaning; it was the will *against* life, against the body, against the world, against beauty and happiness. And therefore away with 'bad conscience' and pity and ascetic ideas! We must be 'good Europeans', who have outgrown Christianity. Let us return to the clear-cut distinction of good (or strong) and bad (or weak). By the will to truth we shall find the way to the other side of good and evil, till the first-born of the new time come, the new Zarathustra, the blonde beast[1] – like the dawn over the sea. Then, in the new Dionysiac age of gladness, with truth realized, the division into lords and slaves will be no more, for we shall all have crossed the bridges from ape to man and from man to superman. Equality will have been reached, not by depressing the strong and proud, but by elevating the weak and humble. Not to be happy in Heaven, to be happy on earth is the watchword of the new culture.

The quintessence of Nietzsche's thinking is thus seen to be the permanent elevation of the type man. But this fiery optimism is chilled by one philosophical shudder: the doctrine of eternal recurrence, which Nietzsche substitutes for eternal life after death (*die ewige Wiederkunft, die Wiederkehr des Gleichen*): the number of possibilities is limited, but time is unlimited; everything, therefore, must repeat itself, and therefore man must inevitably follow superman.

In verse, impressionism had actually begun a year before the publication of the naturalistic manifesto in *Moderne Dichtercharaktere* (p. 288); DETLEV VON LILIENCRON's (1844-1909) *Adjutantenritte* had appeared in 1883. Impressionism, which succeeds naturalism, might therefore be shown to have begun before naturalism. There is even symbolism or double sense in Liliencron's 1883 volume: he is fond of a quizzical glance at death or of a light-hearted but penetrating reference to man's mutability in the permanence of nature; but the lesson is suggested, not expressed. *Holsatia non cantat* was an old saying; but Detlev von Liliencron is another in the list (Hebbel, Klaus Groth, Theodor Storm) of poets of the first rank born and reared in Schleswig-Holstein; and he closely follows Theodor Storm (as Timm Kröger and Gustav Frenssen follow him) as a delineator of his native province; the virile martial note which the title of his first

---

[1] '*die prachtvolle, nach Beute und Sieg lüstern schweifende, blonde Bestie*'.

volume announces is doubled and relieved by the most vivid descriptions of *Marsch* and *Geest*, of the leagues of rolling heather by oozy mud flats (*Watten*) bared by the ebb of the tide on the eastern coast of Holstein. Liliencron had served as an officer in the wars of 1866 and 1870; had there gathered the experiences which went to the making of his best prose work: *Kriegsnovellen* (1894); had retired and found official occupation in such out-of-door posts as Captain of Dikes on his native heath. *Adjutanten-ritte* revealed him as one of the new characters which *Moderne Dichter-charaktere* were calling for to create the new verse; and the new leader was found far from all *cénacles*, absolutely unconscious of theory and pro-gramme, creating the new style out of the freshness of his originality. In the historical panorama of German verse Liliencron stands out as one of the most significant poets. Intellectually his range is low; that is, he was no thinker. But he makes history by his style. This marks an advance or a new direction in two main aspects. Firstly, he flouts poetic diction. He accomplishes the reform – an abandonment of traditional artificiality in favour of a language new-coined to pass current in a new, less idealistic life – for which Conradi and his merry men had been clamouring; but whereas they had carried on with the old style of language, Liliencron renews the language of verse without premeditation by the mere trick of abolishing such devices as the *Dichter-e* (*spielet* for *spielt*), and above all by admitting as poetically effective words from everyday life (such as *Büro*, *Zigaretten*, *Einglas*) previously regarded as too tawdry for the purpose. The second main element of his style is what is now interpreted as impressionism: Liliencron gives, not (like the naturalists) a drab section of a continuous state, but momentary, very vivid impressions of some-thing unusual, or a series of such impressions with everything unnecessary eliminated. The difference is that between a photograph and a film; the naturalists freeze life, Liliencron shows it in flashes of movement. This verbal magic is enhanced by other qualities, above all by his delightful rough humour, which may come out in a juggling with words (*Tigert er auf dich heraus,* | *Tatz' ihn! wie die Katz die Maus*), or in a startling pretence of coarseness (*Das war der König Ragnar,* | *Der lebte fromm und frei.* | *Er trug gepichte Hosen,* | *Wie seine Leichtmatrosen,* | *Die rochen nicht nach Rosen,* | *Das war ihm einerlei*); he is a master, too, of sound-painting (*die Quelle klunglingklangt*) and of metaphor (*Ein Wasser schwatzt sich selig durchs Gelände; Es schleicht die Sommernacht auf Katzenpfoten*). Liliencron's way-wardness unshapes but lends a charm to his higgledy-piggledy 'epic' *Poggfred* (1896-1908), in the style and stanza of Byron's *Don Juan* slowed down in the more serious parts by *terza rima*. The title is Low German for 'frog's peace', a pious fiction for the poet's country mansion (more likely his abode at the time was in plain lodgings at Altona); the poem is a panorama of the memories and fancies of the poet's life shaped as humorous episodes or allegorical visions.

The familiar contrast of Goethe and Schiller as naïve and sentimental is seen again in Liliencron and his friend and neighbour RICHARD DEHMEL (1863-1920). Liliencron's verse was spontaneous, Dehmel's was excogitated, sometimes tortured; his poems, he himself says, 'vollziehen sich aus Gefühlen, | Die den ganzen Menschen aufwühlen'. In another image Dehmel compared himself to an eagle rising heavily, but, once risen, floating freely; and the image adequately indicates the majestic sweep of his verse at its best. Liliencron's verse is sensuous; that is, it gives impressions of reality through the senses; Dehmel's verse (Erlösungen, 1891; Aber die Liebe, 1893; Weib und Welt, 1896; Die Verwandlungen der Venus, 1907) is idealistic; that is, concerned with ideals or ideas – his poetry comes from the processes of his thought probing his conception of the universe. The root of Dehmel's conception of the cosmos is sexuality, which he transfigures in the white heat of his ecstasy into a kind of religious mysticism ('Wollust zur Welt'). This sanctification of the sexual instinct as cosmic urge – Dehmel calls himself in an almost blasphemous image triebselig – should be historically interesting, even to those whom it might repel, as the logical outcome of Darwin's doctrines electrified by the Dionysiac call to joy of Nietzsche. There is the further influence of Strindberg, and still more of a strange Pole who wrote in German, STANISLAW PRZYBYSZEW-SKI (1867-1927), the typical exponent in German of Satanism. According to Dehmel, man is ripest when he is nearest to nature, i.e. in the act of love; love is a divine duty. Love is the elimination of the antagonism of 'I' and 'all'; it is both consciousness of self and forgetfulness of self, 'die Rundung des eignen Ich im All zum All'. This erotic pantheism is perhaps best grasped as a system in the epic Zwei Menschen (1903), in which man and woman grow into each other and out beyond themselves, their individuality becoming universality, their I the world. A hostile critic might say that in the episodes of Dehmel's verse Nietzsche's will to power is twisted into will to sin; and indeed Dehmel refuses to shun experience, since all experience is the way to God (Noch hat keiner Gott erflogen, | der vor Gottes Teufeln flüchtet; or again: Ich habe mit Inbrünsten jeder Art | mich zwischen Gott und Tier herumgeschlagen). It would be easy to find apparent brutality in Dehmel; e.g. Da du so schön bist, muss ich dich begehren, | denn alle Schönheit ist mir freies Gut. | Da du so schön bist, will ich dich zerstören,| damit es nicht ein andrer tut might be placed in the same category as Liliencron's lurid poem Bruder Liederlich – if it were not that the reply of the woman in this Wechsel of two perfect stanzas reveals the psyche of the female, self-surrender and pride that makes a conquest of the victor. Dehmel is not, like Nietzsche (who was syphilitic), and like Strindberg (who was exhausted), a contemner of women; to him woman is equal with man as a worshipper in the temple in which the divine service is the act of love. As a new force in verse Dehmel ranks equally with Liliencron; his language is sometimes forced, sometimes in questionable taste; but he is a master particularly of rhythm and metaphor, in the nice balancing of vowels and the evocation of colour by assonance: notice (to give one example) the livid effect of *Über Russlands Leichenwüstenei | faltet hoch die Nacht die blassen Hände.*

Liliencron and his immediate followers, such as GUSTAV FALKE (1853-1916), were entirely German in tradition. OTTO JULIUS BIERBAUM (1865-1910), the most popular poet of the period (*Irrgarten der Liebe*, 1901), gave a lighter lilt to old rhythms and was hardly touched by foreign styles. Dehmel assimilated French symbolism but remained German to the core;[1] his matter is Nietzschean touched up with decadent refulgence. In STEFAN GEORGE (1868-1933) and his school the French influence is – at all events till the end of the century – predominant. Reminiscences of the German Romanticists, however, and still more of Hölderlin, deepen the French ultra-refinement of George; and two German poets with whom he has striking affinities are Platen, an artificer of verse equally patient though with tools less delicate, and Conrad Ferdinand Meyer, an aristocrat equally feminized by French culture, one who in an equal degree was pained by contact with crowds and who likewise veiled his personal experiences in recondite symbols. Something, too, of the atmosphere and colouring of the English Pre-Raphaelites and æsthetes illumines the Mallarmean scroll of George, in whose work are renderings of Rossetti, Swinburne, and Ernest Dowson. This poetry of George and his school is, literally, *l' art pour l' art* (*Artistenkunst*), and they are officially classed as *die Artisten*. Whatever they printed was at first available only to their own exclusive circle; the journal in which their poems appeared, *Blätter für die Kunst*, was privately printed and distributed from 1892 till 1899; after 1899 the works of the group were made accessible to the *profanum vulgus*, who were, however, kept at a distance by certain devices: rules of punctuation were ignored, nouns began with small letters, words unknown to dictionaries abounded, and word-order was problematical. George's verse is thus like a legal document in which the pith of the meaning,

---

[1] That is, Prussian, or in other words with a worship of power and a ruthlessness (*Schrecklichkeit*) due possibly to a Slav admixture; he was born at Wendisch-Hermsdorf in the Spreewald. One of the secrets of his style is a Germanic control of Slav hysteria.

because it is so vitally important, is guarded by being run on without stops and bound to words which have a hieratic sense distinct from the sense they have in common use.

Historically the importance of Stefan George lies in his uncompromising rejection of naturalism. This takes several directions. The novelist CONRAD ALBERTI (1862-1918) had said that for the purposes of art the death of the greatest hero is on a level with the birth-throes of a cow; Stefan George will have none of these levelling doctrines – he returns to the Romantic conception of heroes and choice spirits, and accepts the Nietzschean table of values. He spurns concrete reality: to him the work of the intellect is more real than the reality of the senses. The essential reality is that which is created by the mind of the artist: 'one should not', he says, 'look for an original or source (*Urbild*) of a poem in humanity or landscape: this has been so transformed by art that it has become insignificant to the creator himself.'

The outstanding achievement of George is in his creation of a new language for poetry. Poets were in despair because all phrase was hackneyed, because all words were worn with use (*'Sprachverzweiflung'*): George allocates these abrased words so cunningly in his setting that they are coined anew; they are the old words and rhymes, but used as they have never been used before. Compounds he handles like an architect rearing a gorgeous edifice (e.g. *das trümmergrosse Rom*). He thus refines his metal (to use his own image) till it becomes *eine grosse fremde dolde | geformt aus feuerrotem golde | und reichem blitzendem gestein*. This new refinement and ornamentation of language is needed, he says, because 'we will have no invention of stories, but a reproduction of moods; no meditation, but a picture; no entertaining, but an impression'. The peril of this attitude – or pose – is that form becomes paramount: 'The worth of a poem is fixed,' says George, 'not by the meaning of it – for then it might be wisdom, learning – but by its form'; the poet's task is thus to produce by means of form, or in other words by sound and rhythm (*'jenes tief Erregende an Mass und Klang'*), a mood (*Stimmung*) which is not bound to sense or substance; we thus get a process akin to that of music. George, therefore, paints with vowels, or plays on them as a pianist plays on keys; he tangles his constructions; he swathes the inner meaning of the poem in a floating veil of symbol. As (to use the image of one of his poems) the linked figures frozen in a dance under dead boughs in the complicated pattern of an Oriental carpet come to life, some evening or other, with the dead boughs stirring, chilling the spectator's sense with their mystery revealed, so the secret woven intricately into the poem comes with the gift of its beauty – but not at call, not at any hour accustomed; to the many it comes never, and rarely to the rare (*Des Sehers Wort ist wenigen gemeinsam*). Poetry is thus esoteric, a priestlike evocation, only for the adept in the ivory tower.

In his first trilogy of verse – *Hymnen*, 1890; *Pilgerfahrten*, 1891; *Algabal*, 1892 – there is a pilgrimage of the poet's mind to the temple of beauty built by Heliogabalus, that late Roman emperor familiar from Verlaine's inverted sonnet, in history a byword for effeminate corruption, in George's mutation of values a great artist because ruthless and contemptuous of the crowd. ('Neronism' or *Ich-Anbetung* now becomes a familiar aspect of literature, derived in part from the writings of Maurice Barrès.) Algabal is at the same time Ludwig II of Bavaria, who had built such a temple; and he is the poet himself robed in royal state, priest and king, lonely and magnificent. In *Das Buch der Hirten und Preisgedichte* there is an escape into the pastoral peace of antiquity, in *Buch der Sagen und Sänge* into the knightly romance of the motley middle ages.[1] *Das Jahr der Seele* (1897) has the tones and moods of other poets of George's group, MAX DAUTHENDEY's (1867-1918) strangely coloured landscapes. In *Der Teppich des Lebens* (1899) there are hints of a change-over from Romance over-refinement to the German tradition: 'Rome vast in ruin' yields pride of place to the aroma of oaks and vines in blossom by the green Rhine; George comes thus from the past of myth and legend by way of ideal Germany to the real present; it is indeed to a large extent by his last four books (*Der siebente Ring*, 1907-11; *Der Stern des Bundes*, 1914; *Der Krieg*, 1917; *Das neue Reich*, 1928) that he has won acknowledgment as a representative poet of his nation, as (to many admirers) the greatest German poet of recent times. Not only does he in these later books, Dantesque in their wrathful austerity, return to his own people as a belated wanderer laden with wisdom, but, lashing materialism in art and life, he sees in spirit (in *Der Stern des Bundes*) the crash coming, and by his insistent call for a more intense culture of the intellect and a new love ('*das neue Heil kommt nur aus neuer Liebe*') proves himself the prophet of expressionism: '*Und Herr der Zukunft (bleibt), wer sich wandeln kann.*' That George is conscious of his transformation (*Wandlung*, to use the great catchword of the expressionists) he shows by the (shall one venture to say amusing?) picture he draws of a Stefan George already legendary, the coldly cruel sybarite singer in the ivory tower, a legend to which he denies authenticity: 'I was held to be a prince drunk with unction, who, gently cradled, counted his tacts in slender grace or cool dignity, in pale solemnity earth-remote.'

---

[1] In one volume as *Die Bücher der Hirten- und Preisgedichte, der Sagen und Sänge und der hängenden Gärten* (1895).

Problematic and in some ways disturbing in *Der siebente Ring* is the idolization of a beautiful boy, Maximin, whom George met in Munich. George's prose essays are collected in *Tage und Taten* (1903). Important for the literary history of the period is *Briefwechsel zwischen Stefan George und Hugo von Hofmannsthal* (1939).

Of Stefan George's disciples and associates (*der Kreis um Stefan George, die Georgianer*) those who have permanent importance tended to move away from him and to strike out on original lines. KARL WOLFSKEHL (1869-1948), a picturesque Jew who had been a fellow pupil of George at Darmstadt, studied Germanic philology and wrote epics on medieval themes (*Wolfdietrich, Thors Hammer*). He died in exile in New Zealand, where he wrote his two last poems, *Hiob oder die vier Spiegel* (1950) and *An die Deutschen*, the latter a vindication of himself and his ancestors as, *quand même*, Germans tried and true. Another Darmstadt man, ERNST BERTRAM (1884-) was for many years a professor at Cologne University. His poetry (*Gedichte*, 1924; *Das Nornenbuch*, 1925; *Der Rhein*, 1927; *Das weisse Pferd*, 1936) idealizes old Germanic culture, German rivers and cities. In his book of essays *Deutsche Gestalten* (1934) he brilliantly interprets Klopstock, Goethe, Kleist, Stifter, and his *Nietzsche: Versuch einer Mythologie* (1919) shows the same qualities of insight and analysis. The typically Georgian critic, FRIEDRICH GUNDOLF (1880-1931) – yet another Darmstadt man – has such a reputation for exhaustive interpretation that the term 'heroic criticism' has been applied to his work; it shows, not only immense scholarship but a style so dazzling and an argumentation so infolded and subtle that it needs heroic effort to follow up. In his translation of Shakespeare (*Shakespeare in deutscher Sprache*, 10 vols., 1905-14) there is ample evidence of his own mastery of Georgian verse style, though his diction is clear and the sense of his original not obscured. There is much of the Georgian devotion to refinement of form in the poetry and verse translations of RUDOLF BORCHARDT (1877-1945) and ALBRECHT SCHAEFFER (1885-1950), whose æsthetic novel *Helianth* (1920) is in point of form and style one of the most daringly experimental works of the period.

The influence of the Dane J. P. JACOBSEN (1847-85) is very manifest in many directions, notably in the dream-like procession of the years of boyhood in RAINER MARIA RILKE's (1875-1926) prose tale *Die Aufzeichnungen des Malte Laurids Brigge*. New is the definition of verse in this book: poems, says Rilke, are not feelings, but experiences; and of his poems it is true that each is the unfolding of an intense mental experience, not, however, with the nerves of it exposed and quivering in the psychoanalytic manner, but moved into the magic light of the non-sensuous.

Even his maidens who, in *Die frühen Gedichte* (1902), pray to the Virgin Mary, have their stirrings of maternal desire transfused in a mystic devotion as clean and tender as starlight. Rilke in each succeeding volume reveals himself more and more as a consummate master of verse form. Like George, he veils with a new mystery ('as with festal raiment') *'unscheinbare Worte, die im Alltag darben'* ; and he is unsurpassed in rhymecraft, in the intricate linking of sentences, and in the folding over of verse lines to give snake-like suppleness to the pattern of the stanza. As a symbolist he is to be ranged with the Austrian school of Hofmannsthal; the scion of an old Roman Catholic family, Prague was his birthplace, as it was that of Max Brod and Franz Werfel. But, above all, Rilke was a mystic and a God-seeker, and as such the expressionists rightly claimed him as their own; he was the first of the poets to grow out of the Nietzschean conception of the hero and to proclaim the new Franciscan ideal of humility.

Das Stundenbuch (written 1899-1902, published 1905) moulds the impressions of Rilke's two visits to Russia in April-June 1899 and May-August 1900. This *Book of Hours* is as classical an expression of German mysticism as *Der Cherubinische Wandersmann* (1657) of Angelus Silesius. It is the most intensely religious poem since Francis Thompson wrote *The Hound of Heaven*; but whereas in Thompson's poem God is pursuing man, in Rilke's man is wrestling for and with God. God is in all things that one loves: *Ich finde Dich in allen diesen Dingen,* | *denen ich gut und wie ein Bruder bin.* Delicately expressed is the idea that God is multiform and permeates all: *Oft wenn ich Dich in Sinnen sehe,* | *verteilt sich deine Allgestalt;* | *Du gehst wie lauter lichte Rehe,* | *und ich bin dunkel und bin Wald.* The daring images flash with the vividness of lightning against black cloud, fade into each other, and leave the feeling of human helplessness whelmed in darkness, with glimpses, and with the tentacles of the soul groping for God. Curious (but in consonance with old Germanic tradition of painting and poetry) is the familiar attitude to God: he is addressed as 'old apple garden', 'whiskered peasant', 'hairy one', 'the whispering rusty one stretched out sleeping on all the stoves'.

In August 1900 he visited the painters' colony at Worpswede near Bremen; here he met the sculptress Clara Westhoff, whom he married in 1901. But in 1902 he left his wife and went to Paris, where from 1902 to 1906 he was secretary to Rodin, whom he interprets in *Auguste Rodin* (1903). Rilke's association with Rodin gave a new direction to his work, but the transition appears already in his book of verse *Das Buch der Bilder* (1902); here mysticism blends with description of things seen. The influence of Worpswede is palpable: these poems are 'pictures'; or rather they are impressions and sensations (*Erlebnisse*), each of which is shaped to a picture. In these poems, which interpret things without him, Rilke is already shaping that objectivity which makes his next books of verse, *Neue Gedichte* (1907), *Der neuen Gedichte anderer Teil* (1908), something of a new genre in literature. The predominating influence is that of Rodin; it is seen particluarly in poems which have statues or architecture for their theme. The *Neue Gedichte* are now famous as '*Dinggedichte*' ('And Rilke whom *die Dinge* bless', sings W. H. Auden, 'The Santa Claus of loneliness'). Goethe had long since defined the concept: '*der Künstler*,' he says, '*gibt die Dinge, der Dilettant seine Gedanken und Gefühle, über die Dinge.*'   The poem *is the thing*, not talk about it. The *Dinggedicht* is conceived objectivally, and is not the poet speaking himself into the 'thing', but the 'thing' speaking iteslf into the poet.

The little narrative poem *Weise von Liebe und Tod des Cornets Christoph Rilke* (1906) is, for Rilke, light in texture; there is no more in it than one short night of love granted, on campaign, to an imaginary noble ancestor of the poet. Very popular, too, is *Das Marienleben* (1913), known also in the musical setting of Hindemith. For the great series of poems which are still to follow, the *Duinese Elegies*, one book of prose is in some ways a preliminary stage: *Die Aufzeichnungen des Malte Laurids Brigge* (1910). In 1904 Rilke had visited Denmark, and there are some Danish ferments in this long outpouring of fears and fancies in diary form. Malte is a Danish youth, the scion of an old family of aristocrats. He is living alone in one room in Paris and suffering from anxiety neurosis; indeed he is very near to mental derangement. His observations on what passes around him alternate with reminiscences of the time when he was a boy. But Malte, it is clear, is Rilke calling back his own years of childhood; and it is, moreover, palpably a revelation of the poet's congenital malaise and of his shrinking from rough contacts and crowds. The book is simply Rilke in search of himself. But also of Rilke in search of God. Indeed the two quests are the same; for Rilke's God is only his own perfected personality. His mysticism is, therefore, realistic because it is the inner illumination of a 'thing', a pathetic human being.

The period of Rilke's life from 1914 to 1921 was one of mental exhaustion, and the springs of his genius ran dry except for plans, fragments, and translations. His Elizabeth Barret Browning's *Sonette aus dem Portugiesischen* (1908) were followed by *Portugiesische Briefe* (1915), the letters of the Portuguese nun Marianne Alcoforado.

The work of Rilke's later years – of '*der späte Rilke*', as the term goes – is so individual and startlingly new in conception as in form that it has had an influence no student can miss on the poetry of Europe and in particular of America. The form of his *Duineser Elegien* (1923), so called because they were begun, in 1912, at the Castle of Duino in Istria, is basically in rough hexameters, distantly modelled (one may assume) on the hexameter of Klopstock's *Messias*, which Rilke is known to have studied zealously from 1909 onwards. These *Duinese Elegies* were not finished till ten years later at the Castle of Muzot in Valais, which had been placed at his disposal by an admirer. In the *Elegies* there is mysticism, but not really religious or even philosophical mysticism as usually defined; the poems wrestle with the mystery of existence, and seek to unravel the relation of life on earth to whatever spiritual survival there may be beyond life; but in the poems at their deepest what matters is not so much their sense and purport as the expression, in (very often) the loveliest and the strangest verse, of the soul of a very great poet. The *Elegies* were followed by the *Sonette an Orpheus* (1923), in which the doctrines of the *Elegies* are concentrated to a mystic gospel. Orpheus is the poet in whose mouth human existence is 'rhythmic happening', a paean of praise. In Rilke's intention there is here and in the tenets of the *Elegies* a doctrine of salvation for mankind; but the agent of this salvation is the poet as a new Saviour of his fellow-men.

Rilke's lyric range is yet again extended by his posthumously published *Späte Gedichte* (1934), with their intensified and now once more melodic renderings of moods and meditations in his last four years in his Valaisan valley. Vitally important for students are his letters and diaries: *Briefe und Tagebuchblätter aus der Frühzeit 1899-1902* (1931); *Briefe aus den Jahren 1902 bis 1906* (1929) include correspondence with his wife and with Lou Andreas-Salomé, who had also been a great friend of Nietzsche.

Another God-seeker was CHRISTIAN MORGENSTERN (1871-1914), who developed from a disciple of Nietzsche and Ibsen (whose poems he translated) into a Christian mystic. In his earlier verse – *Galgenlieder*, 1905; *Palmström*, 1910 – he launches quaint, pathetic attacks on materialism and intellectual culture; he makes mathematical absurdities look logical, and turns everything topsyturvy by taking *das Wort* to be *das Ding an sich*. Interstices are removed from the laths of a fence; a knee goes wandering through the wide world because the man has been shot away in the war, 'round and round'; and the sea-gulls all look as if their name was Emma. He defines the pantheism of his later volumes (*Einkehr*, 1910; *Ich und Du*, 1911; *Wir fanden einen Pfad*, 1914): 'Weder "ich" bin, noch jener "Baum" ist, sondern ein Drittes, nur unsere Vermählung ist.' Break up things and the ideas of them: the rest is silence – which is God. The world is the marriage in God of 'I' and 'thou'.

Artistenkunst is of the Rhineland and the French border: George's esoteric art centres in the Rhine province, Darmstadt, Frankfurt-am-Main;

Friedrich Gundolf died as a professor at Heidelberg; Ernst Bertram was a professor in Cologne. But the victories of symbolism were won, as far as the world at large is concerned, not along the Rhine, but in Vienna. Not for the first time in the history of German literature, Austria now leads: in criticism (Hermann Bahr), in aphorism (PETER ALTENBERG, 1859–1919), in the lyric (Richard von Schaukal, R. M. Rilke), but above all in the lyric drama. Voluptuous Vienna, between the nations, takes into its literature moods from all its neighbours and becomes international, the more easily as its greatest writers are Jews or half-Jews who have the typical Viennese mentality (soft and cynical and half-despairing – Vienna is the city of suicides), and are yet, with their limitless receptivity, half-Italian, or half-French, or half-Slav.

HUGO VON HOFMANNSTHAL (1874–1929), the great-grandson of a Jew, has a world-wide fame as a dramatist, but he is essentially a lyrist (*Gesammelte Gedichte*, 1907; *Nachlese der Gedichte*, 1934), even in his dramas. The immediate model for the neo-romantic lyric drama is Maeterlinck, whose influence on Hofmannsthal is marked: both are creatures with blank misgivings in a world unrealized; both, in weary rhythms, ask wistful questions that they leave hovering in space. But Hofmannsthal far outclasses Maeterlinck and any of the French symbolists in the gorgeous colouring as in the supple sensuousness of his language; here his model is d'Annunzio, whose erotic sensationalism he also has. The new style has already a dazzling beauty in the dramatic sketches: *Gestern* (1892), the hero of which, a sick artist seeking new sensations like Huysman's Des Esseintes, is Hofmannsthal's first Renaissance type, and *Der Tod des Tizian* (1892), a panegyric of beauty on the lips of Titian's pupils in the hour of his death, the very manifesto of German symbolism – the town seen far below is transfigured to beauty by distance, though ugliness and vulgarity dwell there, and mad folks with bestial; 'even their sleep is not like ours with the purple blooms and golden serpents in it: theirs is the dim somnolence of oysters'. These two playlets are masterpieces by a boy of seventeen. The artistic temperament of the sterile dilettante is tragically illuminated in *Der Tor und der Tod* (1894): to the hero, Claudio, in his study, crowded with precious objects of art, comes Death, playing a violin – not a skeleton, but a god of the soul kin to Dionysus and Venus; Claudio cries out that he is not ready – '*Ich habe nicht gelebt*'; Death calls the shades of his mother and the discarded love of his youth, and Claudio, before he falls dead at Death's feet, realizes the emptiness of his selfish life. The playlet is interesting by its imitation of Faust's monologue before the Easter bells ring out; Faust, too, had lived away from life; what *is* life? Claudio, whose malady was that which the expressionists were soon to

revile as the *summum malum, Trägheit des Herzens*, learns too late that life
is only realized in the consciousness of the shadow of death. Three 1897
dramas, *Der Kaiser und die Hexe, Der weisse Fächer, Das kleine Welttheater*
come closer to the exigent problems of life – the will to live, renunciation
–, while *Das Bergwerk zu Falun* (1906), a dramatization of E. T. A. Hoffmann's tale, has a mythical element: a sailor worn with experience of
the brute world goes over, at the bidding of the Queen of the Mountain,
to the spirit realm. Of the three plays of *Theater in Versen* (1899) *Die
Hochzeit der Sobeide* has its scene in Persia, *Der Abenteurer und die Sängerin*
is Venetian, and *Die Frau im Fenster*, a dramatization of d'Annunzio's
Sogno d'un mattino di primavera, is the herald of a series of revenge dramas.
There is a Venetian mood, again, in two of Hofmannsthal's comedies:
Cristinas Heimreise (1910) and *Florindo* (1923), while another comedy,
Der Schwierige (1921), almost belies this poet, who in his person and his
moods is the very embodiment of Vienna, by having its scene in his native
city. But it is post-war Vienna; and in this period of depression and
frustration his moods were changing and his weary mind was turning
churchwards.

Hofmannsthal's original plays are sealed with Stefan George's dictum:
'We will have no invention of stories – only moods' – they are intense
moods. There is no conflict and no development. The real dramas of
Hofmannsthal – real because he takes over the conflict and action that he
found in them – are his adaptations, not so much of English plays (*Das
gerettete Venedig*, 1905, from Otway, and *Jedermann*, 1912, his version of
Everyman) as his modernizations of ancient Greek tragedies: *Alkestis*
(1894), *Elektra* (1904), *Ödipus und die Sphinx* (1906). In these Greek plays
Hofmannsthal, instead of refining the motives of the characters, makes
them far more barbarous than they are in the original versions, intending,
no doubt, to be more true to nature. Elektra – obviously closely kin
to Oscar Wilde's neurotic Salome, the muse and pattern of all that is
most daring in this neo-romantic eroticism – avenges not only her murdered father but her own thwarted erotic impulses, and, shrieking madly,
haunts the back courtyard of Agamemnon's palace. Stains of red light,
falling from a fig-tree like blood-stains, cling round her when she first
comes on the stage. It is not from Sophocles that the description of
Clytemnestra comes: 'Her sallow, bloated face in the glaring torchlight
shows yet more pallid above her scarlet robes; she leans upon a waiting-
woman, who is clad in dark velvet, and upon a staff of ivory; she is
covered all over with jewels and talismans, her arms are heavy with
bracelets, her fingers are stiff with rings.'

Hofmannsthal's *Das Salzburger Grosse Welttheater* (1922), produced on the Domplatz at Salzburg, is not so much an imitation of Calderon as a renewal of the theocentric drama of the seventeenth century; its holy beggar is now the poet's type of modern man. Hofmannsthal now felt that his mission was to be the teacher of his fellow Germans, and his last play, *Der Turm* (1925), holds forth his post-war dictum: *Kraft ist Glaube*. '*Erziehen*', we are told, means '*herausziehen aus der Tiernatur*'. The story which drives home the moral lesson is closely similar to that of Caspar Hauser (p. 335); a prince in a mythical Poland is brought up as a prisoner in a tower, and away from the world is nearer to God.

By his libretti Hofmannsthal won world-wide fame and keeps it. They were set to music, as *Elektra* was, by Richard Strauss. *Der Rosenkavalier* (1911) is the best known; the others are *Ariadne auf Naxos* (1912), *Josephs Legende* (1914), *Die ägyptische Helene* (1928), *Arabella* (1935).

As a prose writer Hofmannsthal had no grip in his fiction. In *Das Märchen der 672 Nacht* (1904) we have again the young æsthete whose wealth keeps him from life. *Die Frau ohne Schatten* (1919) is a *Märchen* from *The Arabian Nights*; it is spun out thinly over the idea that there should be no sex relations in marriages intended to be childless. The best of Hofmannsthal as a prose writer is in his essays, criticism, addresses, and letters (*Die prosaischen Schriften gesammelt*, from 1907 onwards, 4 vols.). In *Unterhaltungen über literarische Gegenstände* (1904) and in the lecture *Der Dichter und diese Zeit* (1907) he deals with the functions and the mission of the poet.

In the occult verse of Stefan George the mist is woven into the words; in that of ALFRED MOMBERT (1872-1942) it lies clinging over them, but shifting to reveal strange glimpses of the *Urwelt* or chaos, of planets rising half-formed from blind seas, with a spirit-being ('the sea-gull shoots freely through his body') ranging through the seething clouds: the poet-creator, or God, with *logos* nesting in his hair. At a cursory glance at this weltering vapour the wary reader may well say: *blauer Dunst* pure and simple; but with Mombert familiarity breeds a distant, if not effortless, comprehension. The terror is in the ideas, not in the language; this is of the simplest: it is even very often like the babbling of a child. Nor is there intricacy of rhythm or even the melody of rapt music: it is all rather prose poetry lifting here and there into ghost-like incantation. The early poems of *Tag und Nacht* (1894) have the lure of simplicity; the later verse (*Der Glühende*, 1896; *Die Schöpfung*, 1897; *Der Denker*, 1901; *Die Blüte des Chaos*, 1905) can only be (like Einstein) an acquired taste. The quintessence of Mombert is offered by himself in *Der himmlische Zecher: Ausgewählte Gedichte* (1909, 1922). *Der Held der Erde* (1919) is a mythically transfigured vision of the First World War. 'Symphonic dramas' is the name he gives to the trilogy

Aeon, der Weltgesuchte (1907), *Aeon, zwischen den Frauen* (1910), and *Aeon vor Syrakus* (1911); Aeon is the genius of humanity wedded at Syracuse, in the face of the teeming east and at the cradle of the seafaring nations, to Semiramis, the mother of peoples. Here all is symbol: thus Aeon is 'between two women' as in temporal dramas, but of these women one is Chaos and the other Form, or Gothic art (unformed and therefore to-be-shaped) and Greek art (formed and perfect). One would need the imagination with which Francis Thompson credits Shelley to run wild over the fields of ether with Alfred Mombert, to tumble about in the reek of chaos, with one's head between the lances of the lightning, and to see the butterfly moon, diamond-green, floating over the skies. But even the too wary reader might pick out broken fancies from the litter of Mombert's creation, and take a joy in their uncanny evocations.

Mombert, a Jew, resided at Karlsruhe and Heidelberg. ARTHUR SCHNITZLER (1862-1931) was born in Vienna, and lived there, as a practising physician and famous author, all his life. One might say of him at once that he would have been an adept in psycho-analysis if this had not been elaborated as a system by another Viennese Jew, SIGMUND FREUD (1856-1939). Schnitzler attempted the naturalistic play with *Freiwild* (1896) and *Das Vermächtnis* (1898), but for his other plays he turned his back on the proletariat, keeping only the working-class girl – *das süsse Madl* – as a toy for his men about town. His psychogrammatic playlets are something quite new. In form they tend to be novelettes in dialogue form – more or less the French *causerie* as cultivated by (e.g.) Paul Hervieu. But there is nothing French in the substance or mood of the plays: Schnitzler does, it is true, handle his characters as puppets – one cycle of plays (*Marionetten*, 1906) indicates this by the title; but probably he owed nothing more than suggestion to Maeterlinck's *drames pour marionettes*; Schnitzler's characters are only marionettes in the sense that they are creatures of nerves and impulse ('*Stimmungen unterworfen*'); they have no will, the will that moves them is in the purpose of the universe, not in them. Another Viennese, Grillparzer, had represented life as a dream and dream as life; and so does Schnitzler. His leit-motif is that life is an actor's make-believe. That make-believe and life flow into each other is the idea of one of the most effective of his playlets, *Der grüne Kakadu* (1899): French aristocrats meet nightly in a low tavern to watch actors (a new sensation) making believe that they have committed atrocious crimes; on the night the Bastille is taken they still, with death at their throats, think the frightfulness is play-acting; here, indeed, the dream is life. All Schnitzler is in *Anatol* (1893), a cycle of one-act plays which fixed his reputation from the start as a cynic of 'melancholy cheerfulness'; Anatol is the *viveur* of so many other of his plays and tales, not (to misquote Dryden) cursedly confined to one, but lighting the extinguished torch (or rather candle) of one love instanter at the bosom of the next. For *Anatol* a boy of eighteen – Hofmannsthal – wrote a prologue of beautiful verse, very famous, the sad formula of all this Viennese impressionism: *Also spielen wir Theater, | Spielen unsre eignen Stücke, | Früh gereift und zart und traurig, | Die Komödie unsrer Seele, | Unsres Fühlens heut und gestern, | Böser Dinge hübsche Formel, | Glatte Worte, bunte Bilder, | Halbes, heimliches Empfinden, | Agonien, Episoden. . . . .* This *halbes Empfinden* is perhaps only once in Schnitzler's work intensified to full feeling: in *Liebelei* (1895); a youth has had a dangerous liaison with a married woman, has freed himself and attached himself to the usual *süsses Madl*, but is killed in a duel by the husband of his former love; the girl cannot at first realize that what she thought was love was *Liebelei*, and when she does she commits suicide. In *Literatur* (1902) Schnitzler comes nearest to the accepted idea of comedy: there is real fun in the gradual discovery by two lovers who have separated that each has embodied the love-letters of the other (copies having been kept of what each wrote as well as the replies) in novels actually in the press. Schnitzler's dialogue is nowhere more brilliant than in *Literatur*; in his tales and novels there is the same sparkle of wit, the same delicate rendering of nuance, but the filling in of the narration makes them less perfect and life-like than the plays. One of the short tales, *Leutnant Gustl* (1901), is the long monologue of an officer who is about to commit suicide because he has been insulted; it is very much like the 'waves of consciousness tales' of these later days.

To let KARL SCHÖNHERR (1869-1943) follow Schnitzler is illusory: the only reason is that they stood together, though on different planes, as the typical Austrian dramatists of their day. Schönherr really follows Anzengruber; he (a Tyrolese) finds his dialect-speaking characters in the same mountain villages, and he, too, mixes old-world sentimentality and ruthless realism. His comedy *Erde* (1908) is grim indeed in its black lines as of an old woodcut. The tenseness of the action and (for a German audience) the involved humour depend on the peasant custom that the father is lord of the house till the eldest son marries; to him the father must then relinquish his rights. In *Erde* the son cannot marry till the father dies; at the beginning of the play hope dawns that he may soon be gathered unto his fathers, for he is kicked by a horse, orders his grave, has his coffin made; and while he is bedridden the son makes a cradle and (the housekeeper anticipating the joys of possession) the baby for it; but the old peasant is indestructible, he has touched the earth he loves and sprung up renewed. In *Glaube und Heimat* (1910) there is warm feeling; the period is that of

the Counter Reformation; the order has come that Protestants are to be
driven out of the country, and Tyrolese peasants die clinging to Luther's
Bible. The idea which animates the play is that of reconciliation between
the two creeds – that tolerance the sweet reasonableness of which Anzengruber had shown in *Der Pfarrer von Kirchfeld* and which Baronin ENRICA
VON HANDEL-MAZZETTI (1871-1955), another Austrian writer (a native of
Styria), found compatible with her Roman Catholic orthodoxy when
she wrote her novels of the Counter Reformation, *Jesse und Maria* (1906)
and *Die arme Margaret* (1911), with their distinguished rendering of
the baroque atmosphere and the linguistic strangeness of the period
depicted.

   To go from Vienna to CARL SPITTELER (1845-1924), who in 1919 was
awarded the Nobel prize for literature, is like an escape to mountain
heights, particularly if we begin with his chief work, *Der Olympische
Frühling* (1900-10), an epic in bumping alexandrines, into which ancient
mythology is thrown as into a melting-pot to be created anew both
as a vision of ideal Switzerland, snowy Alps and radiant pastures, and
as an expression of the endless struggle with evil of mind and morality
lured to unscalable heights by beauty. For his first philosophical epic,
Prometheus und Epimetheus (1881), Spitteler had devised a startling Whitmanesque style (ostensibly prose but lyrically tensile) which had so much
in common with Nietzsche's *Also sprach Zarathustra* that it was taken to
be an imitation of it, especially as both works agree in their cult of the
strong personality. As a matter of fact, it had been published two years
before Nietzsche's string of charmed aphorisms, and it has been suggested
that Nietzsche, who at all events referred to Spitteler as 'the finest æsthetic
writer of his day', may have been the borrower, both as regards Biblical
style and ideas. Spitteler's *Literarische Gleichnisse* (1892) and *Balladen* (1896)
are parables and allegories; his more specifically lyrical poems are in
Schmetterlinge (1889) and *Glockenlieder* (1906); the quaintness of their
symbolism (e.g. the Duke of Bells goes out to meet the King of Noon
and spreads at his feet a carpet of undulating melody) fits the Swiss
hardness of the verse.

   Another cosmic epic of grandiose beauty is THEODOR DÄUBLER's
(1876-1934) *Das Nordlicht* (1910). Däubler, an Austrian from Trieste, here
creates his own mystically conceived mythology: the earth, a dark star,
will shine out in brightness when the races who dwell on it are lit by the
inner radiance of religious love; we are pilgrims to the sun, taking the
earth with us; the epic is thus informed by the altruistic ideal of the
expressionists, one of whose guides and prophets Däubler is.

   Spitteler's work – except for his Novelle *Conrad der Leutnant* (1898), which embodies this Swiss poet's contribution to the problem of realism in fiction and belongs, though written in detachment from the school, to the history of naturalism – is a return to classical tradition; the best of it brings Hölderlin's neo-Hellenism out of the dream-world of glimpsed ideals into the clear refulgence of modern thought firmly reared on the rock of logic. A reaction from both the naturalistic and the symbolist drama to the clear-cut outlines and the three unities of classical form was championed in theory and practice by PAUL ERNST (1866-1933) and WILHELM VON SCHOLZ (1874-). Paul Ernst, with *Der schmale Weg zum Glück* (1903), had written one of the outstanding *Bildungsromane* of our period, and, going back for his inspiration to the old Italian tales, had done much for the rejuvenation of the Novelle (*Italienische Novellen*, 1902). His tragedies (*Demetrius*, 1905; *Brunhild*, 1909; *Ariadne auf Naxos*, 1912) are austerely and coldly classical. Wilhelm von Scholz's *Der Jude von Konstanz* (1905) and *Meroe* (1906) are neo-classic plays with something still of neo-romanticism; and this poet showed by his later development that his heart was not in the classic business: he struck out into mysticism, occultism, and related pseudo-scientific studies. Occultism and spiritism play a great part in the sensation-mongering of a group of writers who are, historically regarded, in the direct line of development from E. T. A. Hoffmann and Edgar Allan Poe; they represent the 'grotesque-demonic' side of romanticism. The typical writers of this group are GUSTAV MEYRINK (1868-1932) and HANNS HEINZ EWERS (1871-1943). Meyrink, a Jew of Prague, satirizes the automatism of organized society in one of the most curious of modern tales, *Der Golem* (1915), the scene of which is in the ghetto of Prague.

The *Dorfnovelle* continued its development. Auerbach had given the village tale a classical habitation in the Black Forest; it was here continued by HEINRICH HANSJAKOB (1837-1916), the *Stadtpfarrer* of Freiburg im Breisgau. The chief writer of such stories in our period was PETER ROSEGGER (1843-1918), who lived in Graz, and described the simple lives of the peasants in his native province of Styria. The *Dorfnovelle*, though a long-established genre, had already the features identified with the literature of a new movement to which the name of *Heimatkunst* was given; this was at once a reaction against naturalism and a continuation of it. The naturalistic and impressionistic novel had tended to restrict itself to the life of towns, particularly of Berlin, Vienna, and Munich; this literature was, moreover, rather international than national. An attack on this *Grossstadtliteratur* was launched about 1900 by Fritz Lienhard (an Alsatian) and Adolf Bartels (from Dithmarschen). What they demanded from the writers of *Heimatkunst* was that the author should describe the life of his own particular province. This, it was thought, would make the novel *deutschnational* or *heimisch*: born of the soil and redolent of the soil (*Schollendichtung*), national in its ideals as in its traditions. The movement, which in England produced the regional novels (Hardy for Wessex, etc.), was a spontaneous development due to a heightened love of locality; and in Germany, too, the development would have been inevitable without the fanatical propaganda which merely made it conscious of its tendencies. The most obvious development was the change of scene from urban to rural; but, strictly speaking, a town is just as much *Heimat* as a village, so that the main difference is that whereas the naturalistic novel devotes itself to the proletariat and the brain-workers, *Heimatkunst* prefers for hero the horny-handed tiller of the soil, stolid and grimly determined, throwing himself on manual labour (as the hero of Ebner-Eschenbach's *Das Gemeindekind* does) 'like a lion on his prey'. In any case, *Heimatkunst* is an integral part of naturalistic and impressionistic literature; it is governed by the same cult of externals; the essential thing is the rendering of *milieu*; character is more than ever shaped by surroundings. The great success of *Heimatkunst* was *Jörn Uhl* (1901), by GUSTAV FRENSSEN (1863-1945, see pp. 303, 315). Other novelists of *Heimatkunst* are TIMM KRÖGER (1844-1918) and HELENE VOIGT-DIEDERICHS (1875-1952) for Schleswig-Holstein, LULU VON STRAUSS UND TORNEY (1873-1948) for Westphalia, HERMANN LÖNS (1866-1914) for the Lüneburger Heide,[1] WILHELM SCHÄFER (1868-1952) and JOSEF PONTEN (1883-1941) for the Rhineland, Hermann Stehr for Silesia, ERNST ZAHN (1867-1952) and J. C. HEER (1859-1925) for Switzerland.

The *Milieuromane* written by the women of the period expand the psychological novel by the introduction of the writer's own physiological experiences. The typical example is GABRIELE REUTER's (1859-1941) *Aus guter Familie* (1895), which shows the outbreak in a spinster of long-suppressed sexual impulses. Her *Tränenhaus* (1909) deals with the right of any woman to motherhood. The intellectual equality of women with men (to Nietzsche the height of absurdity)[2] was fought for by HELENE BÖHLAU (1859-1919), who had begun with humorous descriptions of life in Weimar in the classical period and shortly afterwards (*Ratsmädelgeschichten*, 1888), in her novels *Der Rangierbahnhof* (1895) and *Halbtier* (1899). The heroine of *Der Rangierbahnhof* is intellectually superior to her husband, but the physical drawbacks attendant on womanhood in

---

[1] His *Der Wehrwolf* (1910), one of the most popular novels of our period, gives a vivid picture of life on the Lüneburger Heide during the Thirty Years' War; an English translation, *Harm Wulf*, appeared in 1931.

[2] The German universities were not opened to women till 1896, and even then some professors refused to lecture to them.

marriage deny her the full development of her genius as an artist; it is the Sappho motif of mind shackled by bodily needs. Marriage, moreover, destroys the artist: genius lives on the heights, not in the kitchen. The physiological basis of love is revealed with ruthless sensationalism in the novels of CLARA VIEBIG (1860-1952), particularly in *Das Weiberdorf* (1900), which (like other novels of this fearless – or calculating? – writer) is notable for its handling of mass psychology: the men of a village in the uplands of the Eifel live away from home, working in the industrial districts of the Rhine; on their periodical returns the starved women, so to speak, devour them. Though Clara Viebig had written much of her best work before *Heimatkunst* became a catchword, her novels are 'regional'; some describe life in the Eifel district and the Rhineland (she was born at Treves): *Kinder der Eifel* (1897), *Die Wacht am Rhein* (1902), *Das Kreuz im Venn* (1908). *Das tägliche Brot* (1902) describes the life of a servant-girl in Berlin. One of her best novels is *Das schlafende Heer* (1904); it brings out the never-resting racial conflicts in the vast melancholy of the Polish plains. *Töchter der Hekuba* (1917) is a war novel poignant with its revelation of starvation and suffering on the home front.

HERMANN STEHR (1864-1940) is above all a visionary, a mystic probing the subconscious and seeking religious certainty, missing it in *Der begrabene Gott* (1905) (the God buried within us), but finding it in *Drei Nächte* (1909) and in his most famous tale *Der Heiligenhof* (1917), the scene of which is laid in Westphalia; in some sort it is a companion volume to Hauptmann's *Emanuel Quint* – both novels continue the ancient Silesian mysticism of JAKOB BÖHME (1575-1624), and in both hallucinations and fixed ideas constitute religion. Stehr, with his type of the new *Seelenmensch*, is already the *Gottsucher* of the expressionists; the *Wandlung* of which they are so fond occurs with illogical suddenness in *Der Heiligenhof*: as soon as the hero, a Berserker type of farmer, discovers that his little girl is blind, he is reformed and earns for his farm the name that provides the title for the book. The mystical idea is that which Gerhart Hauptmann weaves into *Und Pippa tanzt*: only the blind see; or, in other words, the outer reality seen by the eyes of the body is corruption, the inner reality visible to the soul is imperishable beauty. In the life behind life, and there alone, is the peace that passeth understanding, and clarification is a process that must come out of one's own deeps (*Selbstheiligung*) – the idea of salvation by another was invented by priests, but the muddiest pool grows clear of itself when peace comes to it within itself. His last trilogy of novels, *Nathanael Maechler* (1929) and *Nachkommen* (1933) was to record the vicissitudes of a German family from 1848 to our own day (in one volume as *Droben Gnade, drunten Recht*, 1952); the third volume did not appear.

Some of the tales at least of JAKOB WASSERMANN (1873-1934) may be ranked as *Heimatkunst*; born at Fürth, he describes Franconia, and with great intimacy Nuremberg; in *Die Juden von Zirndorf* (1897) and other tales he is the accredited interpreter of the spiritual and physical environment of the Franconian Jews, as GEORG HERMANN (1871-1943)[1] with his notable novel *Jettchen Gebert* (1906) is of that of the Jews of Berlin. But, since Wassermann was a Jew, his native province was not so much Franconia as a world of ideas, unctuously oriental to a great extent in substance and presentment, although in his autobiographical sketch *Mein Weg als Deutscher und Jude* (1921) he has energetically asserted his claim to all the German heritage of soul and language. The declared aim of his laboured writing is to bring about the birth through tribulation of spirit of 'the new man', simple, humble, and good, who calls himself brother to the outcast, and will kneel (in *Christian Wahnschaffe*, 1919) even to a criminal who has raped and murdered a little girl. (A murderer is innocent, runs the argument in Stehr's *Der Heiligenhof*, in the depths of his soul, just as on the ocean bed there is peace while tempests rend its surface; we shall see that the expressionists proper show that not the murderer but the murdered is guilty.) Wassermann's didactic tendency clearly runs parallel with that of Hermann Stehr, but there is a wide disparity in their technique: Stehr leads up to his *Seelenmensch* by inner experiences which illumine and purify the soul they awaken; Wassermann's characters are transformed in a welter of crass sensationalism which has elements of Eugène Sue or of the *Police Gazette*. If only by reason of this lurid excitement and concentration on physically criminal types one is forced to question the permanent value of Wassermann's writings. Of interest there is no lack; the obvious reason for his comparative failure is that the cerebrally evolved characters act, not dynamically, but to illustrate the theory (proclaimed in *Christian Wahnschaffe*) that to reveal humanity the novelist must 'sink himself into sick souls', unveil what is secret and hidden by 'inquisition' – i.e. by psycho-analysis. The novelist must know everything about human beings, 'for they, you see, are the mystery and the terror. ... To go to one, always to a single one, then to the next, and to the third, and know and learn and reveal and take his sufferings from him as one takes out the vitals of a fowl.' (What remains of a fowl when the vitals are taken out?) Wassermann's high seriousness disarms criticism, but the novelist who makes it his business to unravel vitals is apt to be hallucinated, like the worshipper who gazes on Buddha's navel. His

[1] He was murdered in the concentration camp at Auschwitz.

Caspar Hauser oder die Trägheit des Herzens' (1908) is perhaps his best novel; it is hardly so good as a less known novel, Karl Röttger's *Kaspar Hausers letzte Tage.*

Stehr's obstinate seeking for a new religion and Wassermann's programmatic Buddhism (Christian Wahnschaffe abandons wealth) are symptomatic of the change that takes place in the novel after 1900 in the choice of hero: the decadent *Nervenmensch* of (e.g.) HEINZ TOVOTE's (1864-1946) tales makes way for the great personality (Nietzsche's *Adelsmensch*), or (later) for the *Gottsucher*. Felix HOLLÄNDER's (1867-1931) *Der Weg des Thomas Truck* (1902) is a landmark: the hero learns by experience to subordinate self to the common good, and finds bliss in *das Dritte Reich* (see p. 348). These novels of the new century are, since they describe the development of the hero from youth to maturity through weal and woe, *Bildungsromane* or *Entwicklungsromane*; but the best of them are so intensely personal that they have been classified as *Bekenntnis- und Bildungsromane*: in their pages the author reveals himself.

The work of the two brothers Heinrich and Thomas Mann has from first to last this blending of confession and mental evolution, and at the same time criticism of society, gently ironic in the work of Thomas, corrosive in that of Heinrich, who has been called the German Juvenal. The two brothers are scions of an old patrician family of Lübeck. Their mother was a Brazilian creole, a skilled musician; she is the 'southern' mother, passionate and artistic, who in Thomas Mann's novels stands in stark contrast to the solid and practical German temperament of the men of the old stock. In Thomas the German temperament prevails and controls his slow, carefully considered and polished style with its sad rhythms; in Heinrich the romance blood is credited with the hectic rush of the sentences, with his gorgeous colouring, and with his Italianate rut of passion.

HEINRICH MANN (1871-1950) reveals his own personality, particularly in his *Novellen*, by those of his characters who are artists and poets. Mario Mavolto in *Pippo Spano* (one of the short tales of *Flöten und Dolche*, 1904-5) is self-portraiture; he is a poet who, forced to observe life, remains outside it; this disgust with art is again expressed in *Die Göttinnen* by the painter to whom it would be happiness if he could contemplate beauty without having to paint it. Art is reviled as 'a perverse debauch' that enervates its victim to such an extent that he is incapable of real feeling. Heinrich Mann's novels may be divided into two classes; the first class, the scenes of which are mostly in Germany, are caricature in the grotesque genre, in intent social criticism and culminating in a kind of political propaganda; the second class are as a rule localized in Italy, and, though they may be classed as *Bekenntnisromane*, since they reveal the author's orgiastic mind, are riotous pæans of life lived at fever heat in a world where common sense and goodness and pity do not count. *Im Schlaraffen-land* (1901) caricatures and excoriates the stock-jobbers and literary hacks of Berlin; it is a picture of Sodom in which all the sinners are not worth a decent man's kick. The hero, obviously modelled on Maupassant's Bel-Ami, is a *littérateur* who lives by love. *Professor Unrat* (1905), well known as the film *The Blue Angel*, has for hero a grotesque schoolmaster who, tracking his pupils to a tavern where they wait on a light o' love, is himself drawn into her coils, marries her, loses his post, and avenges himself on his fellow-citizens, his former pupils, by luring them through his wife to debauch. The picture is repulsive; but Heinrich Mann is applying the method of Balzac: by exaggeration he aims at showing the terrific power of instincts and of passions latent in any respectable individual; a Philistine or an immaculate Methodist is a potential monster of vice; for, since virtue is vice reversed, intensity may be equal in a different direction, just as rising (according to the observer's standpoint) is falling upwards. The psychological and personal trend of Heinrich Mann's work develops, like that of his brother, in the direction of the regeneration of society by democracy; his political and social satire culminates in the trilogy *Das Kaiserreich* (*Der Untertan*, 1914 – the officials; *Die Armen*, 1917 – the proletariat; *Der Kopf*, 1925 – state policy), a scathing denunciation of the Wilhelminian state which is all the more daring as the first novel of the series was in course of publication when war broke out. In *Zwischen den Rassen* (1907) Heinrich Mann fights out the conflict in his own blood between north and south, spirituality and sensuality. In *Die Göttinnen oder die drei Romane der Herzogin von Assy* (1902-3), his most ambitious work, all this southern fever seethes into delirium. To blame his creole blood for the ravishing rut of it all is hardly scientific; much of it is due to his residence in Italy and still more to his cult of d'Annunzio, who, moreover, appears, thinly disguised, as one of the characters. 'I have discovered a new genre,' one of the characters proclaims, 'the hysterical Renaissance!' This term hits the nail on the head: the characters are weaklings to whom their perversities are heroic strength; the keynote of the trilogy is the discord between desire and capacity. As in a German novel written a century before, J. J. W. Heinse's *Ardinghello* (p. 250), the wickedness is a phantasmagoria, not a ruthless unfolding of strength as in the authentic history of the *cinquecento*. Conrad Ferdinand Meyer, himself a weakling worshipping the strong, had delineated Renaissance voluptuaries with the credibility of a historian; Heinrich Mann sees only one side of their mentality: worship of beauty unhampered by the moral law, and therefore lust, not love. The scene is set on a vast scale – the Duchess rules by right of beauty from Dalmatia to Venice, Rome, Naples – but the inner meaning shrinks: she is in the first novel Diana achieving freedom, in the second Minerva ruling the realm of ideal beauty in art, in the third Venus seizing joy (*Freiheitssucht, Kunstfieber, Liebeswut*) – but in reality as the novel shapes we see her, in the first two novels empty and aching, and in the third Venus vulgivaga and nothing more. Nietzsche's doctrine of Dionysiac joy is here like a cup drained to the dregs: a boy is loved to death at Capri; there are violations and sadism; there is a bout of Lesbian love by experts staged and watched like a boxing-match; a robust English dame, Lady Olympia, moves through the tale, coming from the ends of the earth and emerging at parties to whisper, with a velvet voice, to some stranger or other: *Heute nacht sind Sie mein Geliebter – . . . Meine Gondel wartet*. But the trilogy stands out in the history of literature both by reason of its extreme tendency and of its style. It stands on the threshold of expressionism, first because it is the *ne plus ultra* of Nietzschean *Schrecklichkeit*, and therefore nearest to the inevitable reaction from ideals of picturesque depravity dear to impressionism; and, secondly, because the style, so feverish that it rushes along in a succession of pictures, has passed beyond the coldly gemmed and chiselled style of impressionism, and is already *Rauschkunst*, the ecstatic style which presents life (*das rasende Leben*) in cinematographic flashes.

Nothing could be more different from the whipped haste and the darting radiance of Heinrich Mann's style than the quiet flow and the guarded flame of THOMAS MANN's (1875-) writings. The ever-recurring theme in his tales (short and long) is the glaring contrast between the normal man (*der Bürger*), who is fit to live (*lebenstüchtig*), and the artist or poet (*der Künstler*), who is not fit to live (*lebensuntüchtig, 'unheilbar unbürgerlich'*). Thomas Mann's artist is another version of Schnitzler's over-ripe decadent; but whereas Schnitzler's creature dies under kisses as under a gradual anæsthetic, Thomas Mann's artist is tortured by the inescapable contemplation of his normal fellow-men with blue eyes and the rosy glow of health and no self-consciousness. The 'citizen' is cased in his insensitive skin as in thick armour; he lives a charmed life, while the artist, to whom beauty is full of arrows, is assailed and driven despairing into the lonely corners of self-contempt. The artist is shut out inexorably from life; he is an outcast, a cripple, often an attitudinizing fraud. Something of this strange conception of the artist may be due to the vogue about 1900 of Lombroso's *Man of Genius*; but it is also by way of reaction from the old romantic worshipping of the poet as one born in a golden clime, dowered with heaven knows what, ambrosial-locked, adulated, in short Tennyson or Paul Heyse or Wedekind's Kammersänger, or Hofmannsthal's Titian. There is only one previous author with whose interpretation of the tragedy of the artist Mann's can be compared. But in Gottfried Keller's *Der grüne Heinrich* the lesson that life lies away from dream and mental effort is rather to be gathered by the wise than thrust to the front of all eyes; Keller's significance here is rather in the example of his own life – he, a great and sensitive artist, turned his back on art and letters and did his tedious duty for years as *Staatsschreiber* of Zurich. To go further back, Goethe was lost for years in the common round of duties useful to his fellow-men: was he then a traitor to his genius or, for a period, sane?

Thomas Mann began with the short stories *Gefallen* (1894) and *Der kleine Herr Friedemann* (1898). He wrote *Buddenbrooks* (1901) when he was twenty-five; it made him a reputation which he has progressively con- solidated. It is a story of the parallel decay in the fortunes of a merchant's family in Lübeck and in the capacity for life of the members of it as succeeding generations take on more and more of the polish of culture. Through all Thomas Mann's work winds the grey thread of this idea that degeneration is the fruit of culture, that with culture goes physical decay. One ghastly detail recurs with unpleasant frequency: the carious teeth of the cultured; the last of the Buddenbrook dynasty suffers agonies and in the end dies from diseased teeth. Two of Mann's characters (the author Spinell in the short story *Tristan* and the fat, degenerate husband in *Luischen*) are beardless in manhood (like Conrad Ferdinand Meyer before his Indian summer). It is in this conception of catastrophe springing not from the classic conception of 'tragic guilt' or the romantic conception of uncontrollable passion, but from a natural and inevitable process like that of seeding after flowering, that Thomas Mann is an innovator; to have proved with a slow, painstaking logic supported by all the evidence of science that culture is death (and with this idea he interweaves the still more tragic conception that love is death) is to have earned a secure seat with the immortals who have struck out into new paths in literature. The lesson is, in *Buddenbrooks* as in the following stories, enforced by an intricate use of symbol; e.g. though the Buddenbrooks die guiltless and in utter decency the last head of the firm, the immaculate senator Thomas, falls into a puddle in the streets and is brought home stained and bleeding to die; or, in plain terms, physical decay brings back the flower of gentility to the gutter. The technique of the novel is on the whole masterly, with its slow contrasts of character and its minute rendering of the *milieu* of an ancient Hanseatic city; faulty, perhaps, is the Dickens-like caricature of the eccentrics and villains; and very dubious is the use of leit-motifs, i.e. the wearisome repetition of facial and personal peculiarities and tricks of diction and gesture. This not only tends to bore if not irritate the reader, it limits the characters; that is, at a certain moment they *must* say a certain thing or make a certain gesture – they are bound up in the piffling trammels of their personal habits instead of having unrestricted freedom of movement and self-revelation. To this practice, however, Thomas Mann keeps; thus in *Königliche Hoheit* Imma always speaks 'with pouted lips', and the Grand Duke always sucks his upper lip.

The most poignant expression of the artist's tragedy, perhaps, is in *Tonio Kröger* (1903), the story of the Lübeck boy with a correct father and an exotic, passionate mother; he strays into art and longs to get back to decency, and is not surprised that when he returns as a famous author to his native city he is arrested under suspicion of being a criminal. The collection of short stories *Tristan* (1903) contains more than one acknowledged masterpiece. Asceticism and joy in life, or in other words dualism, are the theme of the short tale *Gladius Dei* and of the literary drama *Fiorenza* (1905). In *Gladius Dei* a religious fanatic declaims against the flaunting indecencies and the display of physical beauty in Munich, the typical art-city of our days; in *Fiorenza* Savonarola faces and defies Lorenzo de' Medici, while Florence, symbolized as the courtesan Fiore, has to choose between the two, between ascetic spirituality (*Geist*) and art that snares the senses. In *Königliche Hoheit* (1909) the individualism of the impressionists turns to the altruism which the expressionists were soon to proclaim: a prince (with a withered hand – bold symbolism before 1914!)[1] stands for the artist or unusual character; he achieves salvation by sacrificing himself for the good of the community. The problem of the extraordinary personality here finds its solution, which is (in Mann's own words) that turning of the mind to democracy, common service, companionship, love, which had been proclaimed in the previous year in Heinrich Mann's novel *Die kleine Stadt*.

The problem of the artist is handled with painful incisiveness in *Der Tod in Venedig* (1913): a German author, ripe in years, with his work already in the schoolbooks, goes for a holiday to Venice; here, to his own horror, he falls in love with a beautiful boy, cannot tear himself away, dies.[2] The negative solution is positive in scope: the romantic adulation of beauty is shameless ('*liederlich*'); the hero, if he had not been a romantic artist, might have controlled himself, might have left Venice and returned to duty. The septentrional artist is softened and corrupted by the balmy south; but there is peril, too, in the indolent and consciousless

---

[1] Kaiser Wilhelm II was born with a withered arm. [2] See p. 321.

east: the boy is a Pole, and smitten already with an incurable disease. The meaning of *Der Tod in Venedig* is clear enough in the hero's communings with himself: beauty, virtue, wisdom are, as Plato taught, divine; but of these only beauty is at once divine and visible to the senses; and, since the artist works by the apperception of the senses, beauty is the artist's way to the spiritual. But how can he whose way to the spiritual goes through the senses attain wisdom and dignity? Is not this a devious way of sin that is bound to lead astray? The poet cannot take the way to beauty but Eros joins him as guide. . . . Poets are like women, passion is their exaltation, and their yearning must be for love. Mann's grim picture of the doomed artist is relieved by his interpretation of Schiller's character in the short tale *Schwere Stunde* in the volume of Novellen *Das Wunderkind* (1914): it is the physical incapacity caused by the overweight of mind that isolates the artist; but the true artist, conscious of his frailty, but also of the nobility of his task, develops the 'heroism of weakness' (*Heroismus der Schwäche*): Schiller, too, is doomed by disease, and realizes how terrible his fate is when he compares himself with Goethe; but he finds consolation in the thought that it is harder to be a hero than to be a god. Here, too, there is an acknowledgment by Mann that the artist may be god-like and raised above critisicm: Goethe, '*der Göttlich-Unbewusste*', creating by inspiration and not by knowledge, is worlds away from the man of letters to whom creation is a craft learned by rote and practised in tortured isolation.

This preoccupation with the problems of degeneration and disease culminates with Thomas Mann in his vast symbolic interpretation of life: *Der Zauberberg* (1924), perhaps the most deeply planned novel since *Wilhelm Meister*. Hans Castorp, the last scion of a patrician family in Hamburg, comes on a visit to his cousin, who is a patient at a sanatorium for consumptives at Davos; he comes for three weeks, he remains seven years, and leaves the place to fall in the First World War – rescued by a great cataclysm, returned from dream to duty. The Magic Mountain is a symbol of Europe before the First World War; the novel is a questioning of all culture. The Magic Mountain is the world of the dead: the doctor in charge is Rhadamanthus, all reckoning of time is lost, the inmates eat greedily (it is a life from copious meal to meal), and fall in love, the diseased with the diseased. Hans Castorp is in love with a Russian lady (Madame Chauchat): that is, the cultured love beauty – but beauty is only the phosphorescence of a dead body. This is the old medieval view of life which we call dualism. Life itself, Hans Castorp discovers, is the equivalent of death: for life is a process of decomposition just as takes place in the body after death; the only difference is that in life there is chemical renewal.[1] Disease quickens the greed for food and love: so does culture. Hans is X-rayed: he sees his skeleton. But he keeps consciousness of the world of duty; there is a contrast between the bright daylight of the world of duty without and the soft moonlight in which he lingers hallucinated; afar is manly dignity, on the Magic Mountain there is Claudia Chauchat (like *Vrou Werlt* of medieval days), '*schlaff, wurmstichig und kirgiesenäugig*'.

It took Thomas Mann sixteen years to complete his Biblical tetralogy: *Die Geschichten Jaakobs* (1933), *Der junge Joseph* (1934), *Joseph in Ägypten* (1936), *Joseph der Ernährer* (1942). The action of *Lotte in Weimar* (1939) returns ostensibly to modernity – the date is 1816 –, but the foundation matter is still myth, the myth or legend of *The Sorrows of Werther*. The main theme, however, is that of a writer's loss of productivity as the pitiless years take their toll. Lotte visits Goethe in Weimar and finds him, not so much aged as lost to life, as life is in female fancy. Goethe as we see him, stiffened and sterile, in *Lotte in Weimar*, exemplifies one of the main tenets stated in Mann's next novel, *Doktor Faustus* (1947): 'Choose good, you vegetate; choose evil, you attain knowledge and you create.' The narrator is Serenus Zeitblom, Ph.D., a grammar school teacher. In the two years from 1943 to 1945 he writes down the story of an old schoolfellow and lifelong friend, Adrian Leverkühn, who had died in 1940. They had studied together at Halle; Zeitblom philology, Leverkühn theology. Very clear in the story is the contrast of *Bürger* – Zeitblom, and *Künstler* – Leverkühn. Or, otherwise contrasted, they typify *Moralismus* – *Ästhetentum*. Leverkühn's study of theology at Halle is the first approach to the atmosphere of the Faust legend; however, he changes over to music. Zeitblom writes during the course of the Second World War; he is an anti-Nazi, but finds it prudent to keep quiet. The main idea of the book is that Dr Faustus is Germany, the collapse of which is symbolized in the last musical works of Leverkühn, *Apocalipsis cum figuris* and *Wehklag Dr. Fausti*.

In *Doktor Faustus* Mann had outlined the plot of a musical composition by Leverkühn: *The Birth of Pope Gregory*; this points forward to his next novel, *Der Erwählte* (1951), the story of yet another nominal sinner. The source is the epic *Gregorius* by the Middle High German poet Hartmann von Aue, a medieval counterpart of the Greek legend of Ödipus; that is to say, it is a handling of the involuntary incest theme. The legend is treated ironically; that is, it is intended to be entertaining rather than morally uplifting.

[1] *Der Trieb unserer Elemente geht auf Desoxydation. Das Leben ist erzwungene Oxydation.* Novalis.

M

Notable as Thomas Mann is for richness of invention and sheer distinction of style it is a question whether he ranks appreciably higher than
a woman (with a very masculine mind), RICARDA HUCH (1864-1947).
She belonged to a Brunswick family, but lived in Switzerland, and was
noticeably influenced, particularly in her earlier work, by Gottfried Keller
and Conrad Ferdinand Meyer. Her first novel on a large scale, *Erinnerungen von Ludolf Ursleu dem Jüngeren* (1893), lives by reason of its
lyrical style with its sad, sated rhythms; it set the model for neo-romantic
prose as Hofmannsthal's *Der Tod des Tizian* and *Der Tor und der Tod* set
it for verse drama. The story itself is irritatingly decadent; it runs its
hectic course in that Dionysiac cult of beauty the peril of which was to be
shown forth by Thomas Mann's *Der Tod in Venedig*; there is the familiar
ostentation of illicit love as the right of personality. As in *Buddenbrooks*,
the main tenor of the tale is the decay of a Hanseatic patrician family,
this time in Hamburg, but (since the style is in pointed hostility to the
naturalistic formula) without that weaving in of business affairs which
makes *Buddenbrooks* as good a commercial novel as Freytag's *Soll und
Haben*. Ricarda Huch breaks new ground as much by her regeneration
of the historical novel, which had been begun by the regional writers, as
by her elaboration of a lyrical prose style; she frees the former from
restrictions of locality and raises it to epic grandeur and timeless significance in *Die Geschichten von Garibaldi* (1906-7), *Merkwürdige Menschen und
Schicksale aus dem Zeitalter des Risorgimento* (1908), and *Das Leben des
Grafen Federigo Confalonieri* (1910). She makes Garibaldi a symbol of
genius, isolated (in Thomas Mann's sense) by his own 'difference from
the others' (*Anderssein*), prone to excess, and inevitably the tool of inferior
but coldly calculating minds (Cavour). In her prose epic of the Thirty
Years' War, *Der grosse Krieg in Deutschland* (1912-14), we have her new
conception of history rather than of historical fiction brought to fruition:
in her vision of these vast events – since her aim is to portray, not individuals, but a whole period with its inner impulses, its mass psychology,
its cumulative devastation – she does not bring the great leaders out in
stark relief – that is, she practises *Entpersönlichung* –, but lets them take
their place (even Gustavus Adolphus and Wallenstein) as actors controlled
by the drama rather than controlling it, as scene billows after scene in the
ocean of happenings with no ordered beginning and no clear-cut ending.

In the new historical novel we get a symbolic interpretation of history.
Whether there is always the advance which is claimed on the archaic
Professorenroman of Dahn and Ebers (p. 274) is open to question; MAX
BROD's (1884-) *Tycho Brahes Weg zu Gott* (1916), for instance, is in style
hardly less naïve than that of Ebers. A difference in the problem there

certainly is: whereas the archæological novel made a show of erudition, the new historical novel illuminates, in intention, the state of mind of the character of people famous in history. Moreover, whereas the archæological novel portrayed the hero and his period as chronologically isolated, the new historical novel interprets the present by shifting its problems to olden times. In *Tycho Brahes Weg zu Gott* there is a contrast of two types of intellect: the onrushing Danish astronomer and the cool and patient Kepler; it is a history, not of stirring events, but of Tycho's brain-storms ending in a moral victory by complete abnegation of self (*Wandlung*); it is the seeking of God that matters, not the scientist's seeking of truth. Mysticism read into history appears, too, in the novels of ERWIN GUIDO KOLBENHEYER (1878-): in *Amor Dei* (1908) he interprets Spinoza; in his trilogy *Paracelsus* (1917-25) the sixteenth-century alchemist; in *Meister Joachim Pausewang* (1910) the Silesian mystic Jakob Böhme; in *Heroische Leidenschafteon* (1929) Giordano Bruno. WALTER VON MOLO (1880-) drew energetic pictures of Schiller in *Der Schiller-Roman* (1912-14) and of Frederick the Great in *Der Roman meines Volkes* (*Fridericus*, 1918; *Luise*, 1919; *Das Volk wacht auf*, 1922). The cinematographic biographies of EMIL LUDWIG (1881-1948) with their pseudo-Carlylese are borne along on this tide. The historical novels of LION FEUCHTWANGER (1884-), *Jud Süss* (1925), *Die hässliche Herzogin* (1926) and *Erfolg* (1930) owe their sales to their massed filth; they show little originality: Wilhelm Hauff had written a novel on the subject of *Jud Süss*, and the daughter hidden away in a rural bower and discovered by the sovereign is the heart of Conrad Ferdinand Meyer's tale of Thomas à Becket (*Der Heilige*); the two queens in *Die hässliche Herzogin* are obviously the traditional German conceptions of Elizabeth of England and Mary of Scotland.

That *Bildungsroman* and *Bekenntnisroman* are two distinct types would appear from the comparison of (say) Carl Hauptmann's *Einhart der Lächler* with HERMANN HESSE's (1877-) *Peter Camenzind* (1904), a kind of inverted *Künstleroman*: the artist here divests himself of his artistry and levels himself to the humdrum existence of the ordinary mortal; here we have not (as with Thomas Mann) the contrast with the tortured mentality of the artist of the happy normal being, but a sheer decadent surrender of personality. Domiciled in Switzerland, a hotbed of psycho-analysis, Hesse was himself treated, in 1916, by a pupil of Jung, when he fell ill as a result of mental stress during the war; he then wrote a series of typically psycho-analytical novels. In *Demian* (1919) - as in FRIEDRICH HUCH's (1873-1913) *Mao* (1907) - there is a minute delineation of states of adolescence as determined by the uprooting which school life means and by the chemical changes in the body before and after the shock of puberty.

Siddharta (1923) is an attempt to weave what is on the face of it Indian philosophy, but is in the heart of it a considered Bolschevization of morality, stage by stage, into the story of a boy's relations to his father and the world. The problem of split personality and the quest of the *Urmutter* which is the fundamental inspiration of *Demian* as of the following novels derives both from Hesse's psycho-analytical training and from his study of JOHANN JAKOB BACHHOFEN's (1815-87) book *Das Mutterrecht* (1861), the substance of which is that the dualism of human life is due to the never-ending conflict of the mother-principle with the father-principle. This conflict is more clearly defined in *Narziss und Goldmund* (1930). Of the two heroes of the novel Narziss represents the father-principle—intellect, reason, logic, order, morality, asceticism –, while Goldmund represents the mother-principle – nature, love, primal urges, the Aphroditic *jus naturale*. The synthesis of these opposites is symbolically achieved in *Das Glasperlenspiel* (1943). This story of the bead-game shows, round about the year 2400, mathematics and art in unison contriving control of the functions of existence.

The ground-work in the novels of ALFRED DÖBLIN (1878-), a physician in Berlin, is science and philosophy. He came to the fore during the First World War with his Chinese novel *Die drei Sprünge des Wang-Lun* (1915); the son of a Chinese fisherman founds a sect of the poor in spirit and teaches that 'to be weak, to endure is the pure way'; the hero 'jumps' from passivity, which is holiness, to action, and back again to holiness. Döblin's long historical novel *Wallenstein* (1920) is still actuated by Chinese philosophy; but here the problem of to do or not to do is represented by the contrasted characters of Wallenstein as the principle of action and the pathologically conceived passive Emperor Ferdinand. *Wadzeks Kampf mit der Dampfturbine* (1918) comes to epic grips with machinery; *Berge, Meere und Giganten* (1924: new edition as *Giganten*, 1932) in a nightmare of activity raging mad gives us the age of the superman with machinery supreme, A.D. 2700-3000. The technological novel had scored its most popular success with BERNHARD KELLERMANN's (1879-1951) *Der Tunnel* (1913), in which the building of a tunnel under the Atlantic is described. But while *Der Tunnel* uses engineering in Jules Verne's way to provide the elements of an exciting story, *Berge, Meere und Giganten* subordinates the story to the problem of the mechanization of the cosmos; it is the idea of Samuel Butler's *Erewhon* that machinery is destined to become master of man. As the slave of machinery, man goes to battle with nature: with the fire of Iceland's volcanoes he frees Greenland from ice; but nature turns on him and puts him in his proper place – down with the beasts of the earth; the *Wandlung* to a new humanity is not to be achieved

by an ascent of man to god over an enslaved nature but by a humble
return of man to nature. *Berlin Alexanderplatz* (1929), the life-story of a
bully (*Zuhälter*) in Berlin, is notable as the pioneer waves-of-consciousness
novel; the hero, unjustly charged with the murder of a prostitute, is
released from prison, tries to reform, but, after a period in a lunatic
asylum, ends as a low-class porter. The three following novels were
written in exile. In *Die Babylonische Wanderung oder Hochmut kommt vor
dem Fall* (1934) a Babylonian god experiences the comicality and the
misery of existence here below. *Pardon wird nicht gegeben* (1935) pictures
post-war conditions and the perils of proletarian and Nazi ideology; a
middle-class profiteer is induced by his dominating mother to give up
the revolutionary convictions of his youth for safety's sake; problematically considered his natural development is thwarted by family interference. There is complex symbolic inference and a destructive
analysis of cultural and political tendencies in our own days, as well as of
religious pretence through the ages, in Döblin's next book, the vast
South American trilogy which in its moods and pitiless probing of racial
domination is largely the fruit of Döblin's suffering in exile. In the historical sense the trilogy is an epilogue to Eduard Stucken's *Die weissen
Götter* (p. 298) and Gerhart Hauptmann's *Der weisse Heiland* (p. 298);
these describe the conquest of Mexico, while *Das Land ohne Tod* (1936),
the first volume of Döblin's trilogy, is a panorama of the conquest of
Peru. Just as the Aztecs in Mexico welcomed Cortés as the 'White
Saviour', so the Incas see in the Spaniards the fulfilment of age-old
prophecies of the coming of strange gods: this they see realized in the
pale skins and the bearded faces of the invaders, in their horses, and their
fire-spitting tubes laden with death. There is a stark contrast of these
happy and innocent 'pagans' with the 'religion' of the Christians; actually
there is only one true Christian among them – Las Casas. In the second
volume, *Der blaue Tiger* (1936) – the blue tiger is the beast of destruction
of Indian saga – the Jesuits make their historic attempt to institute humane
colonization, but are thwarted by secular policy. The third volume, *Der
neue Urwald* (1936) applies a parallel to the conditions of today, and drives
home the lesson that the barbarians are the whites. *November* 1918 (1939)
is a blend of historical chronicle and fiction; in four volumes with the
titles *Der Zusammenbruch, Verratenes Volk, Heimkehr der Fronttruppen, Karl
und Rosa* the events from 22nd November to December 1918 are portrayed. The revolution is a failure; inevitably so, for individual action is
motived by illusion and self-deception.

Politically the First World War marks the end of a period, 'the age of
imperialism', which began with the accession of Kaiser Wilhelm II in

1888. In literature the war is a disturbing force, but it does not mark a break in development; it accelerated and intensified expressionism, which had begun before 1914. The war literature itself is either naturalistic or expressionistic, or both together. Expressionism is only the naturalism of poets who again select their reality as the poetic realists had done, and who flood their reality with their own passion. There is the same reversal of fashion in literature as in abstract thought and painting: just as Ibsen is eclipsed by Strindberg and Wedekind, Manet and Renoir yield pride of place to Van Gogh, while the ideas of intuition as certainty, of life as movement, of the *élan vital*, of creative development, come in with the acceptation of Bergson, and are reinforced by the phenomenology or *reine Wesensschau* of EDMUND HUSSERL (1859-1938), who teaches that what matters in things is not their *existentia* but their *essentia*.

The naturalists had aimed at photographic reproduction of nature; the cry of the expressionists is: *Los von der Natur!* The naturalists had been, in intention, outside what they described (though, of course, their sympathies appeared in their choice of matter); and their matter might be in its presentation as dull as life; in other words, the matter was not animated by mind (*Geist*). The expressionists demand both feeling and mind: in other words, they are both passionate and brilliant. They put their own passionate hearts into their matter and flood it with light; that at least is their intention. 'Be ecstatic!', they cry: and the result is *Rausch-kunst* (see p. 311), which expresses *das rasende Leben*, life in fevered haste to exhaust existence. Since, as Bergson teaches, only time that has lived has permanence, and since there is no life with sluggishness of heart (*Trägheit des Herzens*), the expressionists live their life with a fiery heart full to overflowing; and their expression of this life is '*ein geballter Schrei*', a clenched cry of ecstasy, a spate of ideas too fierce and young for dignity, so rushing and rapid that they would be profaned by beauty of form – there can be no calm and patient shaping in the white heat of ecstasy. In short, the idea is to give the palpable essence of things, their qualities sharply intensified, not their appearance in reality.

The expressionists cry for a more real reality: but to them reality is not the outer world, it is the inner world of thought and vision. Thought is real, for it exists. The momentary semblances of naturalism are not real; what is real is not the image of time, but the very essence of it. The outer world presents itself through the eyes of the mind, but what the expressionists render is not reality as seen by eyes, but as seen, with the eyes as a gateway, by the mind. The expressionist creates his vision just as the composer creates his music: neither need be anything like anything ever seen or heard in nature; but they exist, for they are seen and heard. Art reproduces things seen; i.e. art is vision fixed on paper or in marble or in colours. But what is vision? The eye is an intermediary between the outer world and the mind: the eye *passively* receives the vision of reality, but conveys this vision to the mind, which *actively* receives, i.e. transforms this reality – differently according to individuality. There is an apparent distortion (the eye of the body cannot see all six sides of a cube at the same time, the eye of the mind can), but the image attempted – all representation in space of inner vision can only be approximate – is that of an instantaneous conception inwardly visualized. In literature much of this expressionistic distortion might be traced back to the *unanisme* of Jules Romains, who (e.g.) visualized the morning debouchment at a city railway station 'as poured out of a bent full bottle's neck', or said of man and wife in bed (Parisian *gourmands* we hope) that their bellies 'swell out towards each other like two clouds'. It is not far from this to Hanns Johst's (p. 389) description in *Der König* (1920), one of the typical expressionistic plays, of streets filled like bowels with dysentery, though one is minded of the drunken man's vision in the old song: *Strasse wie wunderlich siehst du mir aus!*

In the expressionistic drama there is a continuation of Hauptmann's innovation in *Die Weber* and *Florian Geyer*: the characters are not extraordinary individuals, but types representing groups and masses; and since they are symbols they are given no names, but appear as 'the father' (that is, any father), 'the son', 'first sailor', 'second sailor', 'the clerk', etc. The characterization is not by stage directions, but by what is said and done on the stage. The language, following the theory that expression must be '*geballt*', i.e. frantically concentrated like strength in a clenched fist, is grotesquely ungrammatical – conjunctions and articles fall out, sentences are syncopated, separable verbs obstinately cling together – and the clause is reduced to rudimentary forms, differing, however, from the *Telegrammstil* of the naturalists in that whereas the latter indicated the conversational carelessness of mental apathy, a scattering of small shot, the expressionistic shortening comes from the swiftness of ecstasy or frenzy, the whizzing of a bullet straight at the mark.[1] In dramatic construction there is a return to antiquated technique: monologues reappear, verse and prose alternate, rhyme heads off a climax. For the looseness of construction and stylistic grotesqueness of these plays the models were found, not only in Strindberg and Wedekind, but in the *Sturm und Drang* dramas of Lenz and Klinger, and particularly in Georg Büchner's (p. 269) *Woyzeck* (1879). The new technique appears in REINHARD JOHANNES SORGE'S (1892-1916) *Der Bettler* (1912); on a stage illuminated by searchlights

---

[1] *Schreidramen* was a term applied to these 'ecstatic' explosions.

the walls of a café recede and the hero recites his lines against the purple night-sky; or he turns to the spectators and harangues them. In the lyric, too, there is a break-up of form: with OTTO ZUR LINDE (1873-1938) and the poets who wrote for his review *Charon* (1904 ff) there is a reaction against the cult of form of George's school; and ERNST STADLER (1883-1914), who is fond of the long billowing Whitmanesque line, aims at verse like ploughed clods.

The ethics of expressionism can be stated in a few catchwords. '*Nicht ich sondern du*', or '*Wirbewusstsein*', means altruism or love of others. Freethinkers, but thrusting forward a fanatical pretence of religion, the expressionists are 'seekers of God' (*Gottsucher*). They claim to have the ecstatic belief in God of Klopstock, the ecstatic faith in humanity of Schiller in his green youth; in their cry for the brotherhood of races and their reconciliation they repeat Schiller's *Millionen seid umschlungen!* They accuse the pre-war Germans of having gone to sleep on *Trägheit des Herzens*; this state they replace by *bewegte Fülle des Herzens*. That man is an intermediary form between two kingdoms (*ein Zwischenwesen zweier Reiche*) is expressed by the idea of *das Dritte Reich* explored by Johannes Schlaf in the trilogy of novels thus called (p. 290), but discussed, too, by Ibsen in *Emperor and Galilean*, and logically involved in Lessing's *Die Erziehung des Menschengeschlechts*. *Wandlung*, or moral transformation, impossibly sudden frequently as in Masefield's *The Everlasting Mercy*, may be explained as psychic discontinuity, and no doubt owes something to Freud: there is in all of us a series of 'I's' any one of which may come to the surface as another is submerged. The enthusiasm for freedom takes intense symbolic form in the frequent use of the son-father motif.[1] Postwar youth held their fathers responsible for the war, but the revolt against parental authority had long been brewing – it went with the swift growth of the *Jugendbewegung* which sent the youth of the country hiking in gay bands. Son and father fight out their quarrel with the lyric logic loaded against the parent in WALTER HASENCLEVER's (1890-1941) drama *Der Sohn* (1914); only a convenient fit of apoplexy saves the father from being shot by his son.[2] 'It is the old song against injustice and cruelty', cries the son; father is to son as King Philip was to Don Carlos. This literary spirit of revolution had its share in the smashing

---

[1] This conflict begins earlier with a more reasoned sociological import in Samuel Butler's *The Way of all Flesh*; here the father represents 'the conscious' (acquired qualities, tradition), and the son 'the unconscious'.

[2] Other 'son-father' dramas are Hauptmann's *Friedensfest*, *Michael Kramer*, *Indipohdi*; Peter Hille's *Des Platonikers Sohn* (1896); Hermann Burte's (1879-) *Katte* (1914); Georg Kaiser's *Die Koralle* (1917); Anton Wildgans's (p. 352) *Dies irae* (1918); Arnolt Bronnen's *Vatermord*.

of the old régime; but it quickly degenerated into political communism.

The programme of the expressionists was proclaimed by KASIMIR EDSCHMID (pp. 374, 385) in *Expressionismus in der Literatur* (1919); he demands, not 'rockets', but (in harmony with Bergson's theory of emotion as permanent) *dauernde Erregung*; i.e. a work of art must be one whole ferment of ecstasy. Another master of the expressionistic short tale and novel is KLABUND (1891-1930), whose Novelle *Der letzte Kaiser* (1923) is strangely beautiful.

But it is in the drama that the grotesque suggestiveness of expressionism forces its claim to at least historical significance. Disciples of Wedekind are Paul Kornfeld, Carl Sternheim, and Georg Kaiser. PAUL KORNFELD (1889-) turns away not merely from reality but from psychology, which, he says, tells us as little as anatomy does of the nature of man, who is 'the mirror and shadow of the eternal and God's mouth'; reality is a mistake, the truth is raptness of soul (*Beseeltheit*). CARL STERNHEIM (1878-1943) in his comedies shows up the respectable middle classes, to which by birth he belongs (he is a banker's son); to him the *Bürger* is not Monsieur Homais, slippered and sleek and harmless, but a loathsome blend of venomous toad, braying ass, and scarecrow. In his treatise *Tasso oder Kunst des Juste Milieu* (1921) he pillories Goethe himself as a petty Philistine! His most characteristic work is to be found in a series of eleven comedies, written 1908-22, and grouped under the ironic title *Aus dem bürgerlichen Heldenleben*.

GEORG KAISER (1878-1945) was certainly a gifted dramatist; he was steeped in the routine of the theatre, and did not stand above sensational effects, but he had the daring of the pioneer and a skill in the symmetrical handling of symbol which makes even his failures interesting. His first plays were studies, influenced by Freud, of sexual states. *Die jüdische Witwe* (1911) shows a Judith unwillingly chaste; her marriage with an old man has not been consummated, and her people reward her for slaying Holofernes by making her a Virgin of the Temple, privileged to tread the Holy of Holies with the High Priest; in him she at last finds her man. Through *König Hahnrei* (1913) Tristan and Isolde move almost as hallucinated automatons, while the interest is concentrated on the senile erotic impotence of King Mark. In *Von Morgens bis Mitternachts* (1916) Kaiser pursues his idea that industrial man is an automaton: a bank-clerk turned by routine into a calculating machine runs out into life – with 60,000 marks from the till; only to find, between morn and midnight, that money buys nothing worth having. In *Koralle* (1917) a millionaire envies his secretary, who (a clergyman's son) can look back to the Paradise of a happy childhood; they are the image of each other, but the secretary's identity is marked by a coral on his watch-chain; the millionaire shoot; the secretary, puts the coral on his own watch-chain, is condemned for the murder of himself, but is happy. In the two parts of *Gas* (*Gas I*, 1918s *Gas II*, 1920), Kaiser deals with the problem of the mechanization of humanity by factory labour; but the son of the millionaire who tries to liberate these mechanized slaves fails lamentably: they will not relinquish, for healthy natural labour amid the fruit and flowers of the field, the quick gain that machines bring them. Faultlessly symmetrical and gruesome in its Wellsian glare of futuristic science is *Gas II*, which ends with the extinction of all and everything by a pellet of poison gas. The 'new man' stands four-square to the blasts of fate in *Die Bürger von Calais* (1914): when six volunteers are called for to be delivered up to King Edward, seven come forward; one too many means that one may hope to survive; the sacrifice for the city would thus be a gamble; but one of the seven slays himself to end the conflict. He is the new man who is born: he who readily sacrifices himself for others. The play is notable for the chiselled majesty of its language; it is as monumental and rugged in words as Rodin's group is in bronze. As an exile in Switzerland Kaiser wrote an anti-Nazi play *Der Soldat Tanaka* (1940); the hero is a Japanese private soldier who suddenly realizes what a horrible business soldiering is. Thereafter Kaiser turned, like Gerhart Hauptmann in his final stage, to Greek themes; his 'Hellenic trilogy' (1948) *Zweimal Amphitryon, Pygmalion*, and *Bellerophon* is in iambic verse. It might be shown that the 'classical' form in these Greek dramas is negatived by an absolutely modern and brutal form of realism which is, or is not, compensated for by Kaiser's specific symbolism or playing with ideas (*Denkspielerei*), whereas Hauptmann comes nearer to the traditional form of German classical drama on (more or less) the Greek pattern.

ERNST TOLLER (1893-1939) pairs with Kaiser as a Communistic dramatist; but while Kaiser would lift up the proletariat and liberate them from the deformation of routine labour, Toller descends to them wholeheartedly and identifies himself with their aims and hatreds; where Kaiser uses politics for the drama, Toller uses the drama for politics. In *Die Wandlung* (1919) a soldier, who by patriotism has earned the respect of his fellow-countrymen, casts off all outward honour to be born again as pure man calling, in love, his brothers to revolution. *Masse Mensch* (1920) discusses the question whether murder in the cause of progress is to be tolerated or not; the State that murdered by means of generals was Moloch, and so are the masses if they murder for the sake of a cause. In *Die Maschinenstürmer* (1922) the mass of the workers are the collectivist hero. The revolutionary propaganda is taken back to the Luddite riots in

England; it proclaims Kaiser's doctrine that machinery makes men automatons and destroys the soul.[1] *Der deutsche Hinkemann* (1923) is bitter with disillusionment; a war veteran returns, with his virility shot away, to his wife. In 1919 Toller was imprisoned for his share in Kurt Eisner's *coup d'état*, and during his incarceration he wrote his poem *Das Schwalbenbuch* (1923): a pair of swallows make their nest in his cell, and he describes their summer life. In *I was a German* (1934), written as a political exile in English, and in *Eine Jugend in Deutschland* (1934) Toller tells his own story. He hanged himself in New York in 1939.

The Communism in the plays of Toller and other *Aktivisten* is interesting in its revelation of the mentality produced by the collapse of the militaristic system. The war at sea found its dramatist in REINHARD GOERING (1887-1936); the action of his *Seeschlacht* (1917) takes place in the turret of a cruiser before and after the battle of Jutland; the conflict is between duty and revolution; the seven sailors fire the guns rather than rebel, because it is easier to obey, but the ideas of mutiny are not so much political as bound up with the question of intense individual life calling away from an impersonal fate that rolls its slaves round and round as cogs in a grinding wheel. The action of *Skapa Flow* (1919) is before and after the sinking of the surrendered German fleet. Goering committed suicide in 1936.

The war on land finds its most lyrical expression in the verse plays of FRITZ VON UNRUH (1885-). He had begun, while serving as a Prussian officer, with two tragedies, *Offiziere* (1911) and *Louis Ferdinand, Prinz von Preussen* (1913); both have actually the same problem as Heinrich von Kleist's *Der Prinz von Homburg* – whether an officer is entitled to act contrary to his instructions, even when success is achieved by insubordination. The experience of the war turned von Unruh into a pacifist. The revulsion from war, which was to become a general feature of German literature in this period, began as early as 1914 with his dramatic poem, written in the field, *Vor der Entscheidung* (published 1919). The prose epic *Opfergang*, written during the fight for Verdun in 1916, was published in 1918. *Ein Geschlecht* (1917), a verse drama, is a phantasmagoria of orgiastic passions let loose by war: there is a tragic mother,[2] two of whose sons have been condemned to death, one for cowardice and the

---

[1] Man as the slave and ultimately the victim of machinery is the subject of *Der Mensch und die Technik* (1931) by Oswald Spengler (1880-1936), who in his famous book *Der Untergang des Abendlandes* (1918-22) had argued that the victory of the city means the ultimate extinction of civilization. See p. 447.

[2] The problem of the mother (*das Mutterthema*) had come to the fore with Georg Hirschfeld's *Die Mütter* (see p. 306): mother lures son home again from mistress. It occurs in Toller's *Die Wandlung*.

other for violating women (he cannot conceive why the individual in
war should not have the same right to cut through law that the State has);
he even rages with incestuous desire for his sister, who feels the same
flame. Sister and brother curse their mother, in whom they see merely
a tool of the State producing sacrifices for the State. In the sequel, *Platz*
(1920), the restoration of order is shown to depend on the victory of
expressionistic ethics: humanity must turn away from mechanized civilization and find salvation in the love of all for all. *Stürme* (1923) continues
von Unruh's fight for his concepts of a new ethical doctrine which grants
freedom of the will even in sexual relations, while *Heinrich von Andernach*
(1925), in essence a contribution to the millenary celebrations of the
Rhineland in history, calls for peace among the nations the world over.
In *Bonaparte* (1927) the proclamation of Napoleon as Emperor is stultified
by his judicial murder of the Duc d'Enghien. His novel, *Fürchtet nichts*
(1952), is a sensational handling of the love affair of the Empress Anna
Iwanowa in the eighteenth century; the action and the title convey a
direct appeal to the Germans of today not to be afraid of the tyrants who
grind them down, and to make no concessions to them. In his Renaissance novel *Die Heilige* (1952), based on the revelations of St. Catharine of
Siena, the saint, determined to save the soul of an atheist painter, feels an
inrush of earthly feeling in his corporeal presence; 'this is the grave', he
tells her in her cell; she, who is represented as bearing the stigmata of
Christ on her body, must choose between the call of a body standing in
masculine beauty before her and the dream shape of a mystical idea. But
the novel is starred with a motto from Balzac: 'Facts are nothing. They
do not exist. Nothing remains to us but ideas.' Thus in von Unruh's
work generally, crude and violent as it may often seem, the driving force
is the mysticism of ideas mightier than the raw reality of law and custom.

Some lyric poets of great promise in this period were cut off in early
youth. GEORG HEYM (1887-1912) was drowned when skating on the
Havel; GEORG TRAKL (1887-1914) and ERNST STADLER (1883-1914) were
early victims of the war. (For Trakl see p. 380.) Heym (*Der ewige Tag*,
1911; *Umbra Vitae*, 1912) sang demonic gloom into his pictures of great
cities (Berlin is meant); PAUL ZECH (1888-1946), too (*Die eiserne Brücke*,
1914), is haunted by Verhaeren's nightmare of tentacular towns. Trakl's
verse (*Gedichte*, 1914) is German in tradition and elegiac in Hölderlin's
sense. In Stadler's poems (*Der Aufbruch*, 1914) the programme of the
expressionists breaks through as regards revolt against both form and
substance.

The outstanding exponent of Viennese expressionism in the drama
and in lyric verse was ANTON WILDGANS (1881-1932), who was for a time

director of the Burgtheater; his first play, *Armut* (1915), is crudely naturalistic; his famous *Dies Irae* (1919), another handling of the son-father conflict, is toned down to what was defined as *Halbexpressionismus*; *Liebe* (1919) treats the pathetic dying down of the erotic urge in the married life of ageing couples.

To the group of activists belonged BERT(OLT) BRECHT (1898-1956) with his dramas *Trommeln in der Nacht* (1922) – the background is the Communist ('Spartakus') rising of 1919; *Im Dickicht der Städte* (1924; the 'thicket' is Chicago); *Leben Eduards II von England* (1924; an adaptation of Marlowe's tragedy). *Dreigroschenoper* (1928) – a great success as drama, opera (set to music by Kurt Weill), and film – is basically an adaptation of *The Beggar's Opera*, but is drastically reshaped to a Marxist exposure of the capitalistic society of today, and, with its songs distilled from Villon and Kipling, parodies heroic opera. *Dreigroschenroman* (1934) is a variation by way of a novel. This genre of *epische Oper*, as Brecht terms his innovation, is continued in *Aufstieg und Fall der Stadt Mahagonny* (1929), which satirizes the barbarism of great cities. Today Brecht is known as a poet committed heart and soul to Communist propaganda; typical of this is the very title of his play *Badener Lehrstück* (1929). In *Die Massnahme* (1931) we have what is now the stereotyped 'confession' of a Communist before he is executed. There is the same spirit in *Die Mutter*, a play which dramatizes one of Maxim Gorki's novels. *Der Flug der Lindberghs* (1930) is a paean to man and the elements he conquers. *Die heilige Johanna der Schlachthöfe* (1932) in a final tableau parodies Schiller's *Die Jungfrau von Orleans*: a Salvation Army lassie perishes because she fails to convert the capitalists who run the slaughter houses of Chicago. See p. 497.

In JOHANNES R. BECHER's (1891-1958) revolutionary drama *Arbeiter, Bauern, Soldaten* (1919) a whole nation is transformed to goodness and sets out 'to God' with the spectators of the play; all march except the All-Highest. Today Becher ranks with Bert Brecht as the laureate of the East German Democratic Republic. His work has been mainly lyrical: *Die hungrige Stadt* (1927) throws a lurid light on class distinctions in capitalistic cities; *Ein Mensch unserer Zeit* (1930), a selection of his verse and prose, is prefaced by an exposé of the poet's development. Another volume of selections is *München in meinem Gedicht* (1946); *Wir -Unsere Zeit* (1948) is a selection from Becher's work generally with an introductory essay by the Communist critic Georg Lucács. *Abschied* (1941) is a novel, obviously autobiographical, which unfolds the life in Munich of a boy with a Pan-German father; there is a son-father conflict with the son breaking away to progressist ideology.

The dramatic work of FERDINAND BRUCKNER (1891-) – like Wildgans,

Bronnen and Oskar Kokoschka, Viennese by birth – marks the beginning of a new movement known as *die Neue Sachlichkeit*; the term denotes an intention to get back to things as they are and to pathology that a physician might recognize as at least problematically possible. The writers of this 'New Factuality' or 'New Functionalism' do indeed aim at atomistic exactitude, but the reality which their psychic probing seeks may be trammelled in the inmost depths of consciousness. Sexual crises and perversions form the staple of Bruckner's *Krankheit der Jugend* (1926); in *Die Verbrecher* (1928) he lights up the misery of a block of flats which symbolize God's house of many chambers. His experimenting interested London audiences when his *Elisabeth von England* (1930) was produced at the Cambridge Theatre in 1931; the love element is weak (the Essex-Elizabeth motif discussed by Lessing still baffles all who attempt it), and the documentation is no doubt that of Strachey, but the doubling of the action – one side of a cathedral in London and the other in Spain, with the action alternizing or synchronizing, Protestants and Catholics praying to one (?ironic) God – had at least the effect of novelty. Of Bruckner's later plays *Timon* (1932) is gloomed by the pessimism of Shakespeare's *Timon of Athens*; *Die Marquise von O.* (1933) dramatizes Kleist's Novelle; in *Napoleon I* (1936) the Emperor philanders with women who are intellectually his superiors; in *Heroische Komödie* (1938) Madame de Staël fights for freedom in love and elsewhere. His *Pyrrhus und Andromache* (1952) weds the matter of Euripides to the form of Racine; *Früchte des Nichts* (1952), which shows forth the hopelessness of youth at the end of the Second World War, completes a series united in the volume *Jugend zweier Kriege* (1947); here *Krankheit der Jugend* and *Die Verbrecher* are followed by *Die Rassen* (1933), the theme of which is the mental conflict of a student who loves a Jewish girl.

'Explosive diction' or frantic expressionism runs through the plays of OSKAR KOKOSCHKA (1886-); in *Mörder, Hoffnung der Frauen* (1907) and *Orpheus und Eurydike* (1918) the problem is that of 'senseless desire from horror to horror, insatiable circling in empty space' caused by the splitting of humanity into sexes.

Kokoschka is a painter as well as a poet; ERNST BARLACH (1870-1938) was a famous sculptor (mostly in wood), and the characters of his dramas (*Der tote Tag*, 1912; *Der arme Vetter*, 1918; *Die echten Sedemunds*, 1920; *Der Findling*, 1922; *Die Sündflut*, 1924; *Der blaue Boll*, 1926; *Die gute Zeit*, 1930; *Der Graf von Ratzeburg*, 1951) are like figures massively sculptured, awkward and hampered because left in the rough, but lifted as though by the wind or the breath of God in their folds; they belong to two worlds, earth-bound as 'creatures of this side' but as 'creatures of the other side' hearing 'the rustling of the blood of a higher life behind the ship's planks of everyday custom'; they are thus ghosts, but in the flesh. Barlach attempts to interweave – with the delicacy, the cruelty, and the intricacy of a spider's web – the unseen with the seen in a new creation of myth. In *Der tote Tag* the problem of a mother's relations to her son is viewed from a totally different angle from that of Hesse in *Demian*: a very physical mother and a son in whom spirituality stirs live in the great hall of a house with a cellar attached; the son's father is a god ('all sons have their best blood from an invisible father'); the mother wishes to keep her son tied to her apron-strings, by cellar and kitchen and broom; she would fain have him 'a suckling grown up' (Herzeloyde in the same way would have prisoned Parzival to the warmth of her breast, if angels from afar had not lured him forth); '*Sohneszukunft*', says the mother in Barlach's play, '*ist Muttervergangenheit*'; and when the invisible father sends a magic steed (Sonnenross) to spirit the lad into radiance she stabs it to death in the night; for, she says, 'the son who rides forth on a steed comes back hobbling on a beggar's staff' – as her long-vanished husband does during the action of the play, blind with gazing on misery and with, for sole possession, a stone which symbolizes sorrow; 'a man', she says, 'is he who takes up the sorrow of others.' Sonnenross being slain, no dawn comes, but dense darkness swathes all – the 'dead day' of home and cradling mother love. Materialism has put out the light of idealism.

It is doubtful whether even the best of the post-First World War novels can be reckoned as literature. *Im Westen nichts Neues* (1929), by ERICH MARIA REMARQUE (1898-), belongs to the anti-war literature of Communistic expressionism. There is more thought and some relation to literature in ARNOLD ZWEIG's (1887-) *Der Streit um den Sergeanten Grischa* (1926-27). Of the lyric poetry inspired by the war the best was by a group of workmen poets, of whom HEINRICH LERSCH (1889-1936), a coppersmith from the Rhine, and KARL BRÖGER (1886-1944) may be mentioned.

The most noted of the poets of expressionism was FRANZ WERFEL (1890-1945), a Jew from Prague. The very titles of his collections of poems indicate their tendency: *Der Weltfreund* (1911), *Wir sind* (1913), *Einander* (1915), *Gerichtstag* (1919), *Beschwörungen* (1923). His collected verse, *Gedichte aus den Jahren 1908 bis 1945* (1948), includes satirical poems on Hitler. There is anti-war feeling in this lyric verse; *Die Troerinnen*, his adaptation of the *Trojan Women* of Euripides, shows by implication the utter senselessness of war; all the post-war disillusionment is here, but also the lesson that duty bids us cling to life when all seems lost, and that to be good is better than to be happy. *Der Spiegelmensch* (1920) is a trilogy of rhymed dramas, the action of which portrays the conflict between man's two souls: the *Seins-Ich* and the *Scheins-Ich* or *Spiegel-Ich*. Werfel's tale *Nicht der Mörder, der Ermordete ist schuldig* (1920) deals with the son-father motif. (Georg Kaiser, too, in *Hölle, Weg, Erde* (1919) had shown that the victim of a would-be murderer was guilty of the crime.) The drama *Paulus unter den Juden* (1926) deals with the problem of Jesus and the Jews. The doctrine of 'love thine enemy' is the theme of the tragedy *Juarez und Maximilian* (1924), a contrast of monarchical and republican ideas in Mexico, and of the 'novel of the opera' *Verdi* (1924), in which Verdi and Wagner are contrasted. For Thomas Mann Wagner is an inspiration breathing through '*die wissende Wehmut der Sterbensreife*'; to Werfel he is decadent over-ripeness. There is keen psychological probing in the later novels: *Der Abituriententag* (1928), *Barbara oder die Frömmigkeit* (1929), *Der gestohlene Himmel* (1939; title changed 1948 to *Der veruntreute Himmel*). *Die Geschwister von Neapel* (1931) is a searching study of the effects of Fascism. *Das Lied von Bernadette* (1941) was written to fulfil a vow made by Werfel when, in 1940, he found sanctuary in Lourdes.

In Franz Werfel expressionism culminates. But his later work, clinging as it does to clear facts (e.g. *Verdi* is impeccable musical history and criticism) moves in the direction of *die Neue Sachlichkeit*.

LITERATURE 1914 TO 1954

One of the main ferments in the literature of recent years and of today is existentialism (see p. 346). Of this there are many aspects, simply because the writers classed on broad principles as existentialists interpret *existentia* each in his or her own way. The philosophical and religious tenets derive ultimately from the Danish writer Søren Kierkegaard (1813-55). In Germany the concepts of existentialism have been defined and expounded by Karl Jaspers (1883-) and Martin Heidegger (1889-); both concern themselves with the real Being (*Sein*) of self and things, and they seek to eliminate whatever opposition there is between self and things. There are diverse currents in the Protestant existentialism of KARL BARTH (1886-), who is very influential as a theologian; and RUDOLF KASSNER (1873-) with such works of his as *Die Moral der Musik* (1905) and *Grundlagen der Physiognomik* (1922) has helped to shape the ideological content of poets and essayists such as Fritz Usinger; see p. 385. There is also the very extensive reflex action of foreign existentialists, particularly of the French author Jean-Paul Sartre with his novel *La Nausée* (1938), etc. See p. 386 and for principles involved pp. 450-1.

One aspect or phase of existentialism which is very much to the fore today, especially in the novel, is simultaneity (*Doppelbödigkeit*). Man is made up of two entities: (1) his visible body, which makes contact with the world in space through the medium of his senses, and (2) an invisible mind which has no contact with space but is conscious of time. Actually the pedigree of *Doppelbödigkeit* flings back to Joyce's *Ulysses*. It is really a question of creation on two planes of consciousness (*Gestaltung auf zwei Ebenen*). Man is conscious of time past, present, and future; and thus in his consciousness past, present, and future are one; in this sense of time the novelists here concerned nestle in varying degrees of closeness to Proust. But the lighter variants take over the technique of Virginia Woolf as well as of Thomas Wolfe, Thornton Wilder, and Ernest Hemingway. The main principle is that there is an existential contradiction between what is said and what is thought, and thus we have the two phases of *Sagen und Meinen*. There may also be an existential contradiction between what one does and what one feels (*Tun und Empfinden*). What is essential is to reach the inner nature of the speaking character; the accepted term is *er-innern*. The gospel text is Kierkegaard's: '*Die Bewegung der Entwicklung geht nach innen, nicht nach aussen; die Szene ist innen, nicht aussen, ist eine Geisterszene.*'

We have this *Geisterszene* in the writings of FRANZ KAFKA (1883-1924), who was born in Prague as the son of Jewish parents. At Prague University he switched over from language and literature to law. One of his fellow-students was Max Brod (p. 342), who, after Kafka's early death from consumption, published his friend's works and wrote his biography. After taking his degree in 1906 Kafka was an insurance official, but had time to follow his literary leanings. Consumption forced him to relinquish his post in 1917; he had seven years free for writing before his death. In Kafka's relations with his father there was the son-father conflict of the expressionists; this is clear from his *Brief an den Vater* of 1919; here he says: 'My writings are about you.' There is personal revelation, too, in his *Tagebücher* (1951), in which he describes his work as '*Darstellung meines traumhaften inneren Lebens*'. His contacts with the Prague Jews, whom he met in the literary cafés of the town, helped to shape him, while his contact with Christian officialdom made him feel that he was an outsider in the hostile world without him. In his diary he wrote that 'one becomes aware of how every person is lost within himself beyond hope of rescue'; he was an introspective, and within himself he was aware of a prison from which there is no escape. His contacts with the Prague Jews induced his literary beginnings; in particular Gustav Meyrink (p. 331) specialized in horrific tales of unearthly happenings (*Grotesken*). In Kafka's stories, however, the horrors are not worked up for effect on the readers' nerves; they are intensified metaphysical symbols. Max Brod persuaded him to publish a volume of short passages, *Betrachtung* (1913). In the short story

Die Verwandlung (1915) a commercial traveller wakes up one morning to find that he has been transformed into a man-sized slimy insect; he crawls about the room and hangs down, feet upwards, from the ceiling (in his letter to his father Kafka describes himself as *Ungeziefer*). The son-father conflict is the base of *Das Urteil* (1916); a son drowns himself at his father's bidding. In *In der Strafkolonie* (1919) we read of an explorer who inspects a machine which kills a man by engraving a sentence into his flesh; the victim does not know what his crime is – but 'he will feel it in his body'. In *Ein Bericht für eine Akademie*, one of the sketches of *Ein Landarzt* (1920), a monkey is trained at Hagenbeck's Zoo and reports on his transformation (*Wandlung*) to man. Max Brod, Kafka's executor, ignored his friend's testamentary instructions that his works, except several specified short stories, were to be burned, and fame, soon to be world-wide, followed the publication of a trilogy of novels: *Der Prozess* (1925), *Das Schloss* (1926), and *Amerika* (1927). These novels were unfinished; perhaps in Kafka's conception they were bound to be, for they each represent a quest for the infinite, and the infinite cannot be reached. In *Der Prozess* Josef K., a bank official, is called before a court that sits continuously, but no progress is made – that is, the trial is *zeitlos*, out of time. The hero of *Das Schloss* has been appointed to the post of surveyor at a castle, but when he arrives he is told that no surveyor is required; to keep going he accepts a post as janitor at the village school. As a surveyor in the castle he would be fulfilling his higher destiny, whereas as a school janitor he is sundered from the better life he seeks. In *Amerika* a boy of seventeen has been seduced by the servant at his home, a woman of thirty-five. The story of his seduction makes it clear that he is not so much innocent as an innocent; he is *der reine Tor* of the medieval legends. He has adventures in the glamorous panorama of the New York we know from the Charlie Chaplin films such as *City Lights*, and one might have fancied some influence of these if they had been in existence when the novel was written. What matters in Kafka's work is not the story but the meaning. Very tangible is the lesson that man is prisoned in life here below; and this tragedy of man comes, not from guilt, but because he is doomed not to know. We have lost Paradise, not because we have sinned, but so that we shall not eat of the Tree of Life. The reality we seek is the world of the spirit; the world of the senses is evil which we cannot escape in our quest for the divine, of which we should be part if there were synthesis of divine and human. If we fail to obtain entrance to the Castle, or whatever is the symbol of the Beyond, our life is one of frustration; and Kafka visualizes this frustration in tale after tale; and indeed the mass of his work has been described (by Hans Egon Holthusen) as one great myth of frustration. In the short story *Vor dem Gesetz* (incorporated in *Der Prozess*) a petitioner all his life long argues and deals with a door-keeper to obtain entrance, and shortly before he dies the doorkeeper tells him: '*Dieser Eingang war für dich bestimmt. Ich gehe jetzt und schliesse ihn.*'

Close to Kafka is HERMANN KASACK's (1896-) allegorical novel *Die Stadt hinter dem Strom* (1948), somewhat in the nature of Albert Camus' *La Peste* (1947). It is not so much the city of the dead that is chronicled as an intermediary station where those who have crossed the river make a stay before their dissolution; in them there is still a flickering glimpse of the last events of their lives. Existence is visioned between two realms of nothingness, an existence without illusion that nevertheless affirms its state of being, although (as in *Le Mythe de Sisyphe* of Camus) it is conscious of the hopelessness of all effort and (like Sartre's dwellers in his *Huit clos*) is imprisoned in a hell of its own making. The interplay of life and death is an integration in Rilke's sense, and the co-ordination of the two dimen-sions of time and space in the City of the Dead could hardly have been thought of before the advent of the theory of relativity. Equally close to Kafka is *Der Webstuhl* (1949), again a picture of the mechanized hell of the totalitarian State, which by the laws of its being necessarily disintegrates. What is described is the weaving of a carpet in which a country's life is centred. Originally the carpet was a ritual symbol, but with the course of time the sense of the ritual has faded, and what remains is mechanized repetition. Kasack again lashes out at dehumanized State institutions in his last novel, *Das grosse Netz* (1952). He is also a dramatist: *Die tragische Sendung* (1920); *Die Schwester* (1926); *Vincent* (1924; the theme is the relation to world and time of Vincent van Gogh). His lyric verse is collected in *Das ewige Dasein* (1943).

There is again a ghostly and twilight atmosphere superimposed on realism in the work of ERNST KREUDER (1903-), in his short stories *Die Nacht der Gefangenen* (1939) as in his novels *Die Gesellschaft vom Dachboden* (1946) and *Die Unauffindbaren* (1948). 'The Undiscoverables' are an anarchistic set who have fled from drab reality to live in a world of fantasy and dream beyond the bounds of space and time. There is again juggling with space and time and reality fused with dream in the poetry (*Gedichte*, 1947), dramas (the action of *Die Rotte Kain*, 1949, takes place '*mindestens zehntausend Jahre vor dem bekannten Bibelereignis*'), and in the prose of ERNST NOSSACK (1901-). Something of Kafka's depiction of life as a nightmare occurs, too, in the fiction of HEINZ RISSE (1898-). His novel *Wenn die Erde bebt* (1950) has guilt and atonement for the basic problem. The theme is carried on in the novel *So frei von Schuld* (1951) and the short stories *Schlangen in Genf* (1951) and *Feldmäuse* (1951).

In the later work of ERNST JÜNGER (1895-) there is something of the mystic idealism of Ernst Kreuder's questing of the ideal city or of the ideal State, but the heart of his work is 'heroic realism'. And this holds good even of the dream imagery of his later mythological allegories, to which the term 'magic realism' has been applied. Indeed the whole of his work can be classed as heroic realism, but only in the sense that in his conception of it heroism is real; it is the age-old mark of the German character; it is cruel because it is real. And also: heroic leadership is the prerogative of the higher and the cultured classes; in other words Ernst Jünger is an aristocrat to his finger tips; his sum and substance is the recovery in the face of the democratic uplift of our days of conservative supremacy and domination. At sixteen he ran away from school, made his way to Marseilles, and enlisted in the Foreign Legion, from which he was in due course released by family efforts; this escapade he describes from the mellow retrospect of maturity in his *Afrikanische Spiele* (1936). In 1914 he joined up as a volunteer, was frequently and seriously wounded in trench warfare, and was awarded the *Ordre pour le mérite* for his fearless leadership of his men. During the Nazi régime he was in contact with resistance circles, but escaped arrest. It is significant that after the Second World War he was forbidden to write; in public estimation he was still the fervent militarist who had made his reputation by his war diary *In Stahlgewittern* (1920; in 1942 the title was changed to *Ein Kriegstagebuch*). This was followed by *Der Kampf als inneres Erlebnis* (1920), *Das Wäldchen 125* (1925) and *Feuer und Blut* (1926). The title of *Die totale Mobilmachung* (1931) trumpets the sense of the text: the total mobilization of mankind is called for to build up totalitarian government. *Der Arbeiter* (1932) portrays the fashion and functioning of the totalitarian State, which by reason of its concern for totality can take no account of the individual soul and therefore must give no room to Christianity. The God of *Der Arbeiter* is Technique. We have here a determined and well reasoned reduction to absurdity of the tenets of Karl Marx; freedom, runs the argument, means stripping oneself of self, is labour not for self or personality, but as one merged in a mass, as 'a type'. This Fascist doctrine – in essence the sanctified tradition of Prussian class supremacy – is further expounded in *Blätter und Steine* (1934). In *Das abenteuerliche Herz* (1929), another book of essays, he comes to grips with post-war moods and tendencies. The revised edition of the book issued in 1938 reveals a change of spirit and a full appreciation of western culture. This *Wandlung* comes out more clearly in the visionary speculations and the self-revelation of *Auf den Marmorklippen* (1939); he has had his fill of the totalitarian State and what he gives us here is a post-Fascist attack, veiled in dream-symbolism, on

Nazi tyranny. It is an allegory of an ancient culture destroyed by a tyrant and his sub-human myrmidons. Now we hear of a trinity of Word, Might, and Spirit, which supplants the trinity of War, Might, and Power of the earlier works. And the greatest power in the new trinity is the Word, which cannot exist without *Geist und Freiheit*. Moreover those who proclaim the Word are individuals, who have no place in the massed totality of *Der Arbeiter*. And the way to self-realization for the individual is the cultivation of the Beautiful. In form, *Auf den Marmorklippen* is one of the pioneer works on the principle of *Doppelbödigkeit*; the scene is contemporaneously in the region of the Lake of Constance, Dalmatia, and Burgundy, and the period is simultaneously that of classical antiquity, of Germanic pre-history, the Middle Ages, the Renaissance, and the present. All this mirrors the development of Europe; and it is very noticeable that Jünger now acknowledges the validity of religious faith; faith is a help in the pessimism that is inevitable in the face of perpetual evil, but the great comfort is that evil and catastrophe cannot quell the spirit of man: '*die Stunde der Vernichtung ist stets die Stunde des Lebens.*'

Ernst Jünger served as an officer from start to finish of the Second World War, and part of his experience of it is covered by *Gärten und Strassen* (1942). Since the book betrayed sympathy with the sufferings of the French it was banned. It is made up of diary entries (1939-40) covering the preparations for war and the advance through France. Here Jünger faces up to the facts and fierceness of war, as he does courageously and clearly in *Der Friede* (1948), which circulated secretly in sheets; and here, too, he finds his way back to Christian concepts of love and charity. Another volume in diary form is *Strahlungen* (1949); the entries run from 1941 to 1945, and were written in Paris, Russia, and Germany. The works that follow the Second World War are intended to be a gospel of salvation for Germany; at a time when 'the only cathedrals that remain are those formed by the cupolas of folded hands' the only hope lies in spiritual regeneration. Jünger sets his face against the nihilism of the masses in *Über die Linie* (1950), which upholds the cultural ferment of Eros and the creative impulses of art and literature. In *Der Waldgang* (1950) we have a picture of the homeless individual of today, who resolutely crosses the meridian of nihilism (*Nullmeridian*) to reconquer freedom.

The threads of *Auf den Marmorklippen* are taken up again in *Heliopolis* (1949), an allegorical novel more or less in the line of Kasack's *Die Stadt hinter dem Strom*. This 'city of the sun' is pictured as spiritually more real than those our earth has known. The action takes place between the overthrow of the first world empire and the foundation of the second. Actually the chronicle of our own time is interwoven in this vision of the future which – by the victory of truth, of freedom, of love – is bound to come. It is the world of Superman. In the world of fierce conflict between Landvogt and Proconsul (Hitler and Hindenburg), between Demos and *die Edeltrefflichen*, the problems of Germany today are set out in clear lines.

As a travel writer Ernst Jünger followed up *Atlantische Fahrt* (1947) with *Myrdun. Briefe aus Norwegen* (1948) and *Ein Inselfrühling. Ein Tagebuch aus Rhodos* (1949). In the essay *Sprache und Körperbau* (1947) we have the culmination of his musings on the mysteries of language, of the Word which, he says, is 'the sword-blade of meaning'; this interest in the symbolic magic of sound goes back to *Lob der Vokale*, one of the essays of *Blätter und Steine*, and recurs in other works. Jünger is indeed so conscious an artificer of language and style that he has been charged with a lack of spontaneity; his handling of words, it is suggested, is contrived to convey excogitated nuances of meaning. The more general view is that as a stylist he is ultra-refined and that, though he lacks the subtlety of (say) Hermann Hesse, he is one of the great craftsmen of recent years.

ROBERT EDLER VON MUSIL (1880-1942), a native of Klagenfurt who lived in Vienna, ranks as the most systematic exponent of 'magic realism'; in other words he is in the same category as Joyce and Proust. He toiled for twenty years at his masterpiece, the waves-of-consciousness novel *Der Mann ohne Eigenschaften* (Vol. 1, 1931; Vol. 2, 1933). The book was rewritten several times; and, though it runs to over 2000 pages, it was still unfinished when he died suddenly at Zurich, where he had found asylum after the *Anschluss*. Though by his technique of *Doppelbödigkeit* and his *existentieller Widerspruch* (there are two sides of everything, and truth is only achieved when these two sides are contrasted and balanced) Musil ploughs the same furrow as Joyce, he angrily rejected the imputation that he was indebted to anybody; and indeed he was far too original to need discipleship. He was an exact scholar in philosophy; and so it is not surprising that throughout his immense work we have psychological two-dimensional probings into the inner consciousness and the subconscious currents of his characters. What action there is takes place in the year of destiny 1913-14; and it is concerned with the social contact of characters who have formed a committee in Vienna to prepare for the celebration there of the Emperor's jubilee. The honorary secretary of the committee is Ulrich, an ex-cavalry officer. Ulrich has shed his qualities; that is, he has cast off all the acquired prejudices which today make up the pattern of culture, the idea being that a man, if he is to be himself and not just the type convention requires, must do without qualities which represent no driving force of individuality. Having shed his qualities, Ulrich is in a state of existence out of time and space. Why should qualities which falsify the world exist? This and other such problems are posed, poised, dissected, and analysed with ruthless psychological insight into the inanity of all that by the laws of logic is not congenitally part of personality. A man who sheds his qualities, the lesson runs, is potentially in possession of all qualities. The world will be built up not by types and patterns, but by men strong in their sense of power welling up from deep within them.

Another Viennese writer, HERMANN BROCH (1886-1951), wrote one of the best essays we have on Joyce: *James Joyce* (1936). After some trouble with the police he escaped to America, where, after naturalization, he was appointed professor of German at Yale University. He died in 1951 at New Haven. His first novel, *Die unbekannte Grösse* (1933), is conventional in plot and treatment; but he went over to the polyhistoric form of fiction as handled by Joyce, Proust, and Kafka in his trilogy *Die Schlafwandler* (1931-32), a long drawn out chronicle which dissects middle-class German life from 1888 to 1918. The first volume, *Pasenow oder die Romantik 1888* (1931), shows a period dominated by the military class. The commercial magnate in this first section is taken over into the second volume, *Esch oder die Anarchie 1903* (1931), to face his contrary, an anarchist book-keeper. The latter appears again in the third volume, *Huguenau oder die Sachlichkeit 1918* (1932), and is reduced to ruin by a deserter who has turned business man and is successful in all his nefarious dealings. From stage to stage of the triptych we see the decay of values and the disintegration of religious faith. Joyce's technique of inner monologue is effectively handled in Broch's masterpiece, *Der Tod des Vergil* (1945); this prose poem – for it is nothing less – is indeed one of the most brilliant of those visionary existential tales in which past, present and future are one dimension (*Zeitlosigkeit*). Virgil, on the point of dying, looks back wistfully on the stages of his development as man and poet, and in discussions with friends brands his *Aeneid* as a failure because it swerves from truth and falls short of perfection in what is humanly and poetically vital; for in these last hours the world, to which the true God is about to come, is revealed to the poet as a mystery rich beyond speaking, ruled by eternal love. The three-dimensional conception of time is again the groundwork of *Die Schuldlosen* (1950). The period chronicled is the period which follows that of *Die Schlafwandler*, 1918 to 1933, and 'the guiltless' are average types who, with one war and the time before it to look back to and another projected, are callous and passive and not conscious that their ethical indifference creates the atmosphere for the totalitarian state which looms ahead.

MANFRED HAUSMANN (1898-) is an existentialist on the Protestant side; he was a freethinker converted to Christianity by his study in his riper years of Kierkegaard and Karl Barth. The son of a manufacturer in Kassel, he was for a time a factory worker, and was then a pupil of Gundolf at Heidelberg. His early work runs in impressionistic grooves of experience and adventure in the outer world. He began with *Novellen*; those of *Demeter* (1936) have autobiographical interest. He leapt into fame with his *Lampioon küsst Mädchen und kleine Birken* (1928), the tale of a tramp who roams the roads of the world, a lover of lasses and nature that is fresh as they are. Very noticeable in the fiction that follows is the influence of the Dane Jens Peter Jacobsen and particularly that of the Norwegian Knut Hamsun. There is a pensive mood of romance still flushed with the ebullience of younger years – as compared, that is, with the life-worn weariness of his great exemplar Knut Hamsun – in the *Novellen* of his *Salut gen Himmel* (1929). In 1929 he travelled in the United States and described his experiences in his travel book *Kleine Liebe zu Amerika* (1930), and after his return a new zest in life comes to the fore in his novel *Abel mit der Mundharmonika* (1932). In the tale *Quartier bei Magelone* (1941) he is back in Germany, in the Palatinate. Hausmann's religious *Wandlung* is the substance of his *Einer muss wachen* (1951), the second volume of his *Gesammelte Schriften*, a collection of essays, letters, and speeches; now he is at grips with the inner problem of existence and finds the only possible solution in absolute acceptance of Christianity. The shock of conversion had been conveyed in the short story *Der Überfall* (1947), now the leading Novelle of *Gesammelte Erzählungen*, the fourth volume of the *Collected Works*. A young poet is called out to one of his friends, a glass-painter, who, he hears, has suddenly gone out of his mind; it turns out that the *Überfall* has been spiritual: '*Er hat mich überfallen*', whispers the glass painter. 'Who?' the visitor asks, and the reply is: 'God.' Among the problems discussed in *Einer muss wachen* is that of marriage; and this is the theme of the novel *Abschied von der Jugend* (1937), which unrolls experiences of wife, husband and another during a trip round Iceland. The novel typifies for Hausmann his own farewell to youth and the deepening of his spiritual life. His lyric verse (*Jahreszeiten*, 1924; *Jahre des Lebens*, 1938; *Alte Musik*, 1941; *Füreinander*, 1946) is collected in *Gedichte* (1949), the first volume of his *Collected Works*; it has distinction and the thematic individuality of his fictional work. *Marienkind* (1927) and *Lilofee* (1937) dramatize two of *Grimm's Tales*. *Worpsweder Hirtenspiel* (1946) and *Der dunkle Reigen* (1951) are mystery plays; the latter, following Hofmannsthal, renews the medieval genre of the Dance of Death.

'Magic realism' as applied to the later novels of Hermann Hesse, in which, though the milieu is fantastic, the psychology is basically real, is a dubious term. It is a question whether it fits Ernst Jünger's mythical explorations of the present day (p. 360), if only because his conception of realism is ideal, not real; HANS CAROSSA (1878-1956) it fits exactly. For his symbolic interpretation of life is psychologically and literally true under its halo of dream; it is visionary, but what the vision bodies forth in a world of fancy exists in everyday life. His own designation of himself is that he is a healer; he decided early that as a writer he would handle language as he handled *Heilgifte* (a favourite word of his) in his practice as a doctor; it is the poet-healer, he says, that a nation needs; and he is a *Lichtbringer*, a giver of light. The finest possible praise of him – it is common – is that of all modern authors he is the nearest to Goethe. He comes nearest to Goethe because both, as poet-scientists, interpret life biologically – thus in the boy and youth of Carossa's autobiography there are the stages of development by metamorphoses that there are in Goethe's plant. In the autobiography as a whole we have the same background as in *Dichtung und Wahrheit*, but the pattern of Goethe's tale is too fixed to literal fact to be Carossa's model; actually this is nearer to Goethe's *Die Wahlverwandtschaften*, with its doctrine of 'elective affinities' or inner relationship (*Bezüge*) between person and person. Chronologically and primarily Carossa is to be classed as an expressionist; but as such he is essentially a symbolist; in his autobiography he himself in person is the great symbol for his message to the world; and throughout his writings he uses scientific phenomena – fauna, flora, etc. – as symbols. Prominent, too, in his fixed technique are recurrent symbolic happenings – *doppelte Zeichen*, as he calls them –, double recordings or double phenomena. These symbols are often recondite, but all converge in the one great lesson that from the chaos that follows wars a new world must be born in which mind will rule – Carossa's *Königreich der Seele*, or (with a term that he takes over from Stefan George) the Third Realm (*das Dritte Reich*) of the spirit. (See also pp. 290 and 416 ff.)

Carossa did not relinquish his practice as a doctor till the end of the 1930's. His first work, apart from the poem *Stella Mystica* (1907) and a thin volume of verse (*Gedichte*, 1910), appeared when he was thirty-five; it was *Doktor Bürgers Ende* (1930), a tragic tale which is glaringly modelled on Goethe's *Werther*. In 1922 appeared the first volume of his autobiography, *Eine Kindheit*; this was followed in 1928 by *Verwandlung einer Jugend*; and the two sections were in 1933 published together as *Kindheit und Jugend*. At the outbreak of war Carossa immediately volunteered, and his experiences as an army doctor are described in *Rumänisches Tagebuch* (1924: from 1933 title is *Tagebuch im Kriege*). The sense of this war diary is that Carossa amid the crash of civilization sets about the work of reconstruction; in this sense it breaks ground for *Der Arzt Gion* (1931), in which the heroic way is shown to be the healing of the mental and moral degradation that comes in the wake of war. *Führung und Geleit* (1933), the fourth volume of the autobiography proper, gives the story of Carossa's development as a writer. The autobiographical content of *Geheimnisse des reifen Lebens* (1936) is obvious, but in its details problematical. *Das Jahr der schönen Täuschungen* (1941) gives the autobiography from the beginning of Carossa's university studies in 1908 to the end of his first year as a medical student. *Aufzeichnungen aus Italien* (1948) is made up of highly sensitive impressions of travel. *Ungleiche Welten* (1951) is a fresh section of the autobiography; the first section deals with the whole period of Nazi rule and the three years after it; in the second part, *Ein Tag im Spätsommer 1947*, we have a symbolical interpretation of the whole sense and purport of the first part. In 1947 came a little volume of new verse, *Stern über der Lichtung*; these poems are now included in the new edition of *Gesammelte Gedichte* (1948).

Since 1920 there has been a striking revival of Roman Catholicism in Austria as a literary ferment, and it has gained momentum since the end of the Second World War. The most notable of the converts whose ardour of faith is the inspiration and almost the sum and substance of their new work is FELIX BRAUN (1885-), a Jew by race and in days gone by a close friend of the galaxy of writers, mostly freethinking, who made the Austrian literature of their period world-famous – Rilke, Hofmannsthal, Schnitzler, Stefan Zweig, and the rest. He distinguished himself by lyric verse in the taste of the day: *Gedichte* (1909), followed by *Das neue Leben* (1913), *Das Haar der Berenike* (1919), and *Das innere Leben* (1925). Of his plays the tragedy *Tantalos* (1917) is fittingly in verse; also Greek in theme are *Aktaion* (1921) and *Der Tod des Aischylos* (1926), while *Esther* (1925) and *Die Tochter des Jairus* (1950) are Biblical. His Novellen and legends are gathered together in *Laterna Magica* (1932). Austrian through and through is *Der unsichtbare Gast* (1924), which unrolls the ruin of Austria between the years of 1913 and 1919. The conviction that this national ruin, which threatens from without and within, can be remedied only by religion is obviously the driving force of Felix Braun's work of recent years. Thus *Die Taten des Herakles* (1921) swathes the myth of Hercules in a blanket of Christian mysticism; the deeds of the Greek demigod are ingeniously fitted to the formative experiences of a young Roman patrician, who in Greece meets St. Luke and other disciples, is converted, and perishes in his fight with a Numidian lion in Nero's circus. *Der Stachel in der Seele* (1950), a labyrinth of mystical doctrine, was completed during the poet's exile in England; it is an endlessly winding interpretation of Catholic doctrine, a Dantesque vision of a Purgatory here below. The mortal seeks religious conviction in his probings through the night of the soul, *la noche oscura* of Spanish mysticism; and the sting in the soul is nature (*das Natürliche*): what is in man and is his nature but is alien to God. The inspiration of the dream-like prose of *Briefe in das Jenseits* (1952) is that we all have communings with our dead loved ones; here the communings are shaped in epistolary form, which allows commemorative recordings, and has thus autobiographical interest. There had been an autobiographical fundament in *Der Schatten des Todes* (1910); there is at least the first part of the poet's autobiography, the story of his youth, in *Das Licht der Welt* (1949). The title is revealing: the dark night of the soul is dispersed by the Saviour, the Light of the World. We have the obsession of this image once again in *Die dunkle Nacht der Seele* (1952), possibly the loveliest translation in any language of the mystical lyrics of St. John of the Cross, which centuries before had inspired the *Trutz Nachtigall* of Friedrich von Spee. As a critic Felix Braun is represented by *Verklärungen* (1916), *Deutsche Geister* (1925); of particular interest are the essays of *Das musische Land* (1952), in which there is discussion of the differences between the literature of 'the land of the Muses' – that is, Austria – and that of North Germany.

East Prussia and the Baltic provinces have played a great role in German literature from the time of Hamann, Herder, and Lenz; over the turn of the present century we have had the two brothers from Courland, the novelist GRAF EDUARD VON KEYSERLING (1855-1918) and the philosopher GRAF HERMANN VON KEYSERLING (1880-1946); and in the present generation we have the two popular novelists Frank Thiess and Werner Bergengruen, both from Riga, the capital of Latvia. FRANK THIESS (1890-) is one of those who, while influenced by expressionism and, in their later work, by existentialist tenets, are in the main impressionists and realists. As good a term as any is *transparenter Realismus*; this is used for writers, such as Hermann Hesse too, whose base of realism is in the main ideological and is illuminated by what Thiess calls '*die Scheinwerfer der Erkenntnis*'. Thiess – whose mother, an Eschenbach, is said to have been a descendant of Wolfram – began with *Der Tod in Falern* (1921), the tale of a dying town, and won through to fame with *Die Verdammten* (1922), an epic unfolding of the decay of the Baltic aristocracy; the theme is incest of brother and sister. In *Angelika ten Swaart* (1923) we find the 'associative thinking' and word symbolism of existentialism; e.g. the name of the American research worker in medicine who marries Angelika, a Dutch aristocrat of aristocrats, is Morr; this by verbal suggestion verified by the course of the action is *mors, la mort*, or even *Mord*; and the pith of the meaning is: to the bride in the marriage night comes Death in the shape of the bridegroom; for he induces physical changes that bring the beginning of death. But the association of ideas is more complicated than this: to Angelika, Morr is a stranger; he is plebeian; and yet, as life fades, she realizes that she loves the father of her child. Death loves Life, and in the end Life loves Death. In *Frauen-raub* (1928) we have a daring exploration of sexual states: an architect marries a frail girl of nineteen; she is a disappointing bride: she can only give her husband excitement, not surrender –, for she has been physically spoilt by a Lesbian affair with an older woman. *Das Tor der Welt* (1926) explores the sexual awakening of a group of sixth form boys and girls in a small town in the Harz; here again we have word symbolism and the rest; e.g. *Gymnasiast* is related to γυμνός, 'naked'. In *Der Weg zu Isabelle* (1934) a German in the south of France has an affair, in 1914, with the daughter of a French officer who will not hear of their marriage. The lovers are torn asunder by the outbreak of war; the girl gives birth to a female child. Twenty years later the German learns that the mother had been killed by bombs, but he discovers a girl who in the light of evidence seems to be his daughter, and as such he adopts her and takes her to Germany. But she has led a loose life; sexual experience is in her blood; and she tells her presumed father that she would love him sexually even if she were sure he was her father. It turns out that he is not, and the presumption is that he marries her, though this is not stated. From a rapid indication of Thiess's field of fiction it might seem that he pounces on sensational best-seller themes; this is, however, far from the truth; he is a psychiatrist and he probes quietly and deep. The '*keusche Entblössungen*' of *Der Weg zu Isabelle* led to his rejection by Nazi critics on the score of morbidity, though *Tsushima, der Roman eines Seekrieges* (1936), which shows the heroic inception of the modern might of Japan, might have been expected to rehabilitate him.

WERNER BERGENGRUEN (1892-) was born, as the scion of a patrician house, at Riga. His name (-gruen is Swedish *gren*, 'branch') indicates the Swedish provenance of the family; it will be remembered that Latvia was once a province of Sweden. During the Nazi period several of his books were banned; later he was placed under surveillance but allowed to write. He emigrated from Munich to Achenkirch in the Tyrol, from where, in 1945, friends managed to smuggle him to Switzerland. At Achenkirch he had written resistance poems which were duplicated and surreptitiously passed from hand to hand in Germany, as were also resistance poems of Ernst Wiechert; Bergengruen recited his poems at clandestine meetings. His first novel was *Das Gesetz des Atum* (1923), which has autobiographical elements. *Der goldene Griffel* (1931) is a novel of the inflation, with a criminal as central figure; here Bergengruen sketches out his main tenet, amplified in the work that follows, that evil can be overcome by spiritual means. His aim, he says, is: '*die ewigen Ordnungen sichtbar machen.*' There is deep religious faith in his work, and much of his apparent patience with wrong-doing is to be explained by his conversion in the late 1930's to Roman Catholicism; what we find is that contrast of evil and good which comforts converts; it is the dream-lore, the poetry of Catholic doctrine. If we are to believe Bergengruen, God reconciles conflicting forces, and evil must be accepted as belonging to God's way with men. In *Der Grosstyrann und das Gericht* (1935) the problem of Nazi Germany is transposed to the Renaissance period in a small Italian State. Bergengruen's very personal technique – too mathematically devised and elaborated – is perhaps best exemplified in a novel which was banned by Goebbels, *Am Himmel wie auf Erden* (1940). The period is that of the Elector Joachim I of Brandenburg, who was fanatically opposed to Luther, and the twin towns of Berlin and Koelln are the scene. The tone is Catholic, and the theme is the disintegration of life through fear (as in Nazi days!). A second deluge is prophesied by the State astrologer, who has read the coming event in the stars. He tells only the Elector, who also dabbles in astrology; arks are built, and there is general chaos. The young chamberlain sends his fiancée to a safe place; for this betrayal of the secret he is condemned to death by the Elector, and before his death he realizes that he who is afraid is not perfect in love. The Elector himself flees, but returns to stay with his people. And there is no deluge. The novel was begun in 1931 and finished in the summer of 1940, when a new catastrophe was impending. Bergengruen is a master of the Novelle, in which he is influenced by E. T. A. Hoffmann. The starting-point mostly conforms to Goethe's definition of a Novelle as '*eine sich ereignete unerhörte Begebenheit*', but Bergengruen's unheard of event is a manifestation of eternal laws, the effect of which tends to be, not so much a chance happening as a religious *Wandlung*, a moral regeneration which does not always carry conviction; it is rather fixed up or *ausgeklügelt* than inevitable. The best appreciated of the separate Novellen are those of the collections *Die drei Falken* (1937), *Schatzgräbergeschichten* (1943), *Hornunger Heimweh* (1942). As a lyric poet Bergengruen is best known for his *Dies Irae* (1945), the anti-Nazi poems of which were written in the Tyrol and privately circulated. But his lyrical work is mostly religious in tone and substance; *Die Rose von Jericho* (1946), *Die verborgene Frucht* (1938), *Der ewige Kaiser* (1937), *Die heile Welt* (1950) variously convey the religious message which is the burden of his prose and his, if anything, too tamely personalized interpretation of the existentialist doctrine of world and being.

ERNST WIECHERT (1887-1950) is another popular writer who should be adjudged regionally: he is the novelist *par excellence* of East Prussia, the laureate of the vast forests and heathlands in which he grew up as the son of a forest ranger. As a secondary teacher at Berlin he came into conflict with the government, was sent in 1934 to the concentration camp at Oranienburg, and from there transferred to Buchenwald; five months later he was released, but prevented from publishing anything. His autobiography is contained in *Wälder und Menschen* (1936), the story of his boyhood, and *Jahre und Zeiten* (1949). His first novel, *Die Flucht* (1916), has also autobiographical elements; the hero, a teacher, flees from a loathsome world to the forests of Masuria and commits suicide. There is the same conflict with the world of today in the novels which follow: *Der Wald* (1922), *Der Totenwolf* (1924), *Die blauen Schwingen* (1925). In *Der Totenwolf* Christianity is specifically charged with life's misery, but this disgust with the world changed to a certain acceptance of Christian feeling, though not of Christian doctrine as the Church teaches it, when, as the term goes, he found grace. From now on there is a note of appeasement in his tales; his characters face up to death and devilry, and healing is found in shouldering the burdens life imposes; the lesson runs that not God, but man, decides. There is some show of a reasoned reconciliation with life in *Der Knecht Gottes Andreas Nyland* (1926), the story of a clergyman who throws up his living to walk the ways of Christ among stricken humanity, but comes to grief. The religious self-abasement, as it seems to some, of this first stage of Wiechert's mature period has been branded as escapism; and indeed by comparison it marks a softening of the hard post-war doctrine of reclamation of the race and of the Fatherland such as we find it in the writings of Ernst Jünger. Wiechert's new idealization of nature and of nature-like man comes out in the Novellen of *Der silberne Wagen* (1928) and *Die Flöte des Pan* (1930), and his spiritual rebirth informs *Die kleine Passion* (1929), the hero of which, Johannes, is told as a boy by his mentor that what decides is 'blood'; not in the sense of sex instinct, but with the meaning that any man acts potentially as his blood, or the imperative force of his physical nature, impels him. This is by now Wiechert's deterministic doctrine; life is decided by blood (spiritual heredity or race-transmitted qualities). In Wiechert's concept blood with heredity as its corollary is one of the three saving forces of existence; the other two are loneliness (or concentration on one's chosen task in aloofness from distractions), and nature. It might be argued that if development of character is thus predetermined the processes of the *Entwicklungsroman* must be ruled out. At all events, beautiful in some ways as *Die kleine Passion* is, it affords proof positive that Wiechert's gospel of the inherent rights of the strong personality is morally and socially impossible. On the side of technique the intrigue is inventively poor; if the novel is to be ranked high – and this holds good of other novels of Wiechert – it can only be because of its mastery of language, its wealth of allusion, its *Bilder, Düfte, Klänge* (to use Wiechert's own way of putting it), the basic common sense of its rebellion against ingrained prejudice and Biblical illogicality. *Jedermann* (1931) is a sequel; it recounts the experiences of Johannes in the war. Wiechert's theme of escape from misery, which is the base of *Jedermann*, is more mythically handled in *Die Magd des Jürgen Dostocil* (1932); the hero is an East Prussian ferryman on the Memel, a primitive gifted with second sight, and with age-old pagan beliefs piercing through his crust of Christianity. The ingrained heathen qualities surviving in these fastnesses of nature give the story with its inwoven symbolic undertones a luring charm. The hero of *Die Majorin* (1934) returns, after twenty years' service in the Foreign Legion, from a prisoners' camp in Africa and lives an outlaw's life in an East Prussian forest, till he is won back to faith in life by a great-hearted woman. *Die Hirten-novelle* (1935) is today classed as one of the finest short stories in German literature. This tale of a shepherd lad of sixteen, who guards the flocks of a lonely East Prussian hamlet on the frontier, is marvellously fitted detail by detail to the Bible story of David, though the note is of halcyon peace till the war comes, with the Russians, and Michael is killed as he tries to save a lamb that has strayed from where he has hidden flocks and the village folk. *Das einfache Leben* (1939) introduces a third period of maturity: the gospel of the second period is still the staple, but it is reasoned more logically and with less acerbity of argument. Sex is clean cut out; the tone is throughout austere and noble. The manuscript, written after the Buchenwald experience, was recovered from a tin box in the garden. It is ostensibly a post-war novel, and the aim is rehabilitation after the catastrophe of the First World War; but the war that is coming is foreshadowed, although Nazi activities are for discretionary reasons kept out of the picture, while Communists and Stahlhelm are episodically in the foreground. There is the same spirit of redemption by love and labour in *Die Jerominkinder* (2 vols., 1945 and 1947), in which there is again a delightful evocation of life in a lonely East Prussian village. Wiechert's last novel, *Missa sine nomine* (1950), describes the fate of three brothers of the old nobility during and after the war. One of the three is obviously a self-portrait; on his release from a concentration camp he gradually, in the loneliness of nature, finds his Christian faith and realizes that God has created good and evil for man to choose between them.

There is a hectic tempo and a heaping up of lurid horror touched up by expressionistic psychology in the historical novels of ALFRED NEUMANN (1895-1952). He made his reputation with *Der Teufel* (1926), a melodramatic handling of Olivier le Daim in his relationships with Louis XI and his court. The background of *Rebellen* (1927) and its sequel *Guerra* (1928) is formed by the Carbonari risings in Italy. 'The tragedy of the nineteenth century' is unrolled in a trilogy of novels which chronicle the life and times of the Emperor Napoleon Bonaparte: *Neuer Cäsar* (1934), *Kaiserreich* (1936), *Die Volksfreunde* (1941). *Es waren ihrer sechs* (1944) deals with a rebellion of students against Hitler during the war. The erotic extravagance of Alfred Neumann's *Königin Christine von Schweden* (1935) is equalled in the historical novels of the Viennese writer ROBERT NEUMANN (1897-); *Sintflut* (1922) plays round the antics of financiers in the Vienna of our day, while the satire of *Die Macht* (1932) is aimed at the Nazis. In 1933 he emigrated to England and wrote in English (*Blind Man's Buff*, 1949); several of his novels (*Die Kinder von Wien*, 1948; *Die Puppen von Poschansk*, 1952) have been translated from English into German. There is a scholarly handling of history and a fine Jewish culture in the novels of BRUNO FRANK (1887-1945). His *Tage des Königs* (1920) is a well-documented study of Frederick the Great, who also dominates the scene in *Trenck, Roman eines Günstlings* (1918), a lively picture of Prussian rococo. *Politische Novelle* (1928) shows the absurdity of the plea that antagonism between France and Germany is inevitable. In *Cervantes* (1935) there is effective satire on Spanish misgovernment and anti-Jewish legislation; *Chamfort erzählt seinen Tod* (1937) is the *vie romancée* of this French aphorist; *Der Reisepass* (1937) is yet another denunciation of the Nazi régime by an émigré (to the United States). Several of Bruno Frank's dramas were successful on the English stage; of these *Zwölftausend* (1927) throws a lurid light on the sale by a German princeling of 12,000 of his subjects to England as cannon fodder; *Sturm im Wasserglas* (1930) – James Bridie's *Storm in a Teacup* (1937) – caricatures a platitudinous dictator; in *Nina* (1931) a film star, for love of her husband, sacrifices her glamorous career, which is taken over by a double.

LEONHARD FRANK (1882-), a Würzburg man, has been loosely classed as 'a vulgarizator of expressionism', and indeed what remains of the mood and method of the movement in his work is no bar to common and immediate enjoyment. His ideal of humanity is in any case the *profanum vulgus*, whose sterling qualities he reveals in tales bristling with event, feeling, and humour. He himself began as a factory worker. His first success was *Die Räuberbande* (1914); it describes the escapades of a band of youths whose heads have been turned by the Wild West stories of Karl May. Four of them turn up again after the war in *Das Ochsen-furter Männerquartett* (1927). *Karl und Anna* (1928) is one of the most original of the *Heimkehrerromane* (p. 377); *Bruder und Schwester* (1929) is yet another incest novel; *Der Mensch ist gut* (1918) is a sequence of anti-war Novellen with a Communistic groundwork, and *Die Jünger Jesu* (1950) is a Communistic rehash of *Die Räuberbande*; here, in Würzburg after the war, the rich are robbed to keep the poor going.

The fading out of expressionism in the 'twenties is, chronologically considered, a return to normality. But there are divergent aspects; there is sense and system in the idealism of Carossa and in the reconstructive fervour of Ernst Jünger; the very essence of it is that, after all, life is worth living. The only question is whether the lesser *gesundete Expressionisten* have not with their fine frenzy sacrificed their daring and therefore their newness; realism may be magic or it may be ordinary. As typical writers of the *volte-face* we may consider Hans Franck and Kasimir Edschmid (or Eduard Schmidt, to give him the name he had as a boy).

HANS FRANCK (1879-) typifies a return even to classical norms: in his plays at all events he is in the direct line of Hebbel, while in his novels his aim is to embody Hegelian ideology, mostly by contrast of siderial and tellurian elements. Thus in his novel *Das dritte Reich* (1921) the dualism of *Jenseitigkeit* and *Diesseitigkeit* is visioned by contrasting a *Gedanken-Denker* with a *Dinge-Denker*, and Franck asks whether there is not a 'third empire' in which the two are one. Such syncretism is the goal, too, of a later novel, *Sebastian: Der Gottsucher* (1949), the hero of which, first a Catholic and then a Lutheran, renounces both these dogmas to dream of a Church in which all that is basically true in all religions shall meet and fuse. In the novel *Meta Koggenpoord* (1925) – the heroine is a portrait of Rilke's friend, the painter Paula Modersohn-Becker – we have Franck's rejection of naturalism as a mere transcription of phenomena and of expressionism as a mere preaching of ideas. Many of his Novellen are of the first water, in particular those in the collection *Der Regenbogen* (1927) and the tale of Johann Sebastian Bach, *Die Pilgerfahrt nach Lübeck* (1935). There is fine literary interest in the 'Droste-Roman' *Annette* (1937). After his historical dramas *Der Herzog von Reichstadt* (1910) and *Herzog Heinrichs Heimkehr* (1911) Franck made a hit with his *Godiva* (1919), in which he takes the side of the husband against the wife, who resists insistence on marital rights. There is sex psychology in *Opfernacht* (1921) and *Martha und Maria* (1922).

N

The rejection of expressionism is most pronounced in the late work – that which is widely read today – of KASIMIR EDSCHMID (1890-), who had himself, in *Über den Expressionismus in der Literatur und die neue Dichtung* (1919), drawn up the programme of the movement and, in the short stories of *Das rasende Leben* (1916), defined its aim in the phrase '*das Leben furchtbar packen wie eine unendliche Geliebte*'. There is the same ferment of ecstatic feeling and style in the tales of *Die sechs Mündungen* (1915) – actually the pioneer work of expressionistic prose –, and in the novels *Die achatenen Kugeln* (1920), with their scabrous eroticism, and *Die gespenstischen Abenteuer des Hofrats Brüstlein* (1926; title later *Pourtalés Abenteuer*, 1947), while *Lord Byron: Roman einer Leidenschaft* (1929) probes with some show of documentation into the poet's passion for his half-sister. Edschmid began to free himself from expressionism in *Die Engel mit dem Spleen* (1923), a novel in E. T. A. Hoffmann's manner. The reversal is complete in the novel *Sport um Gagaly* (1927), a glorification of the sportsman's life, and in Edschmid's numerous travel books from *Das grosse Reisebuch* (1926) and *Basken, Stiere, Araber* (1926) to *Bunte Erde* (1948). The tales of *Hallo Welt* (1930) and the novels *Deutsches Schicksal* (1932) and *Das Südreich* (1933) have this multi-racial texture, while *Feine Leute oder die Grossen dieser Erde* (1930), with its pitiless exposure of international high finance on the Lido, interweaves geographical enlightenment with its portraiture of scamps and their loosely living women of the *haute élite*. In his later work indeed Edschmid stands out as an inveterate globe-trotter, and his matured philosophy of existence is a sane and practical internationalism. He is at his best in his books of Italy: *Italien – Lorbeer, Land und Ruhm* (1935), *Gärten, Männer und Geschichte* (1939), and in his description of tropical lands: *Afrika – nackt und angezogen* (1930), *Glanz und Elend Südamerikas* (1931). Some of the best of his work is his latest: the four short stories of *Im Diamantental* (1948); his biography of *Albert Schweitzer* (1949); his novels *Das gute Recht* (1946), which has an autobiographical substratum, *Der Zauberfaden* (1949), a chronicle of the Rhineland silk industry, and *Wenn es Rosen sind, werden sie blühen* (1950), the hero of which is Georg Büchner, whose *Gesammelte Werke* (1947) he edited.

Of the novelists who have made the Second World War their theme none reaches the height of Ernst Jünger. Of the influences discernable *L'homme révolté* of Camus and Hemingway's novels stand out; Ernst Jünger's *Strahlungen* (1949) and *Über die Linie* (1950) also count. The first of these novels to appear were by writers who for the most part had fought as privates and who, to begin with at least, were Communists – Theodor Plievier, Hans Werner Richter, Walter Kolbenhoff in particular. The representative novel of this *Anklageliteratur* is Plievier's *Stalingrad*.

THEODOR PLIEVIER (1892-), born in Berlin, was a sailor and then a rancher in South America. From 1914 to 1915 he served in the German navy and was one of the leaders of the sailors' revolt at Wilhelmshaven. In 1933 he fled to Russia, and in the Second World War he was a member of the committee Freies Deutschland. In 1945 he returned to Germany with the Red Army and in 1947 settled at Wallhausen on the shores of the Lake of Constance. He had made his reputation with *Des Kaisers Kulis* (1929), the theme of which is a revolt of sailors after Skagerrak and in which he gives vent to his personal resentment, as he does too in *Der Kaiser ging, die Generale blieben* (1932). *Stalingrad* (1945) was written in Russia during the war; it was finished a year after the battle. Since his conviction then was that to be a prisoner of the Russians was to be saved the main tenor of the book is shot with illusion. *Stalingrad* relates the fate of an army and is built up of information collected on the battlefield, from diaries and letters, and from conversations with prisoners of war. It gives a credible description of the actual battle, but in intention and effect it is a symbol of the destruction of German military power. In form it is a sequence of pictures with the horror of the happenings so heightened as to produce the maximum effect of shock on the reader's nerves. The language is sometimes ungrammatical – *Kolportagestil* is not an unfair term; and generally it is sensational – e.g. *Brüllen* is a favourite word. For the critic the problem is whether it is a novel proper or just journalese reporting ('*Reportage*'); the author dubs it both 'novel' and 'chronicle'. If it is to be judged by construction (*Aufbau*) and form it is hardly a novel, not so much so as Tolstoy's *War and Peace*. It is the raw material of history loosely shaped to a gigantic symbol; it has been classed as 'a monumental morality'. *Tatsachenroman* hits it off best perhaps. The *dramatis personae* are types, not characters; and therefore there is no psychology, but just man in the mass and massed effects which, as such, are sensational. The colonel of an armed division and a gravedigger stand out from the rest. The gospel presented is that the individual does not exist; what does exist is *Massemensch* (to quote the title of Ernst Toller's play), the mass made up of men who count only as counters in the mass. There is the same mood and method in Plievier's following fiction: *Das gefrorene Herz* (1945) lashes out at the madness of war; *Im letzten Winkel der Erde* (1945) exposes the exploitation of labour in the saltpetre mines of Chile and brings in personal experience of Chile and its coast as Plievier had done in his earlier novel *Zwölf Mann und ein Kapitän* (1930) and as he does in *Haifische* (1949), a sequel to *Im letzten Winkel der Erde*. *Deutsche Novelle* (1947) shows an individual at grips with fate in the period from 1918 to 1945. *Moskau* (1952) is on the grand scale of *Stalingrad*, but falls below it; even the language has lost brutality, and there is some attempt at balancing, for both sides of the front come into the picture. Of the other novels which denounce the war *Hinter Gottes Rücken* (1948) by BASTIAN MÜLLER (1912-) has its scene of action in Germany and the occupied countries in the period 1938-46; the author began as a goatherd and described his early struggles in *Die Eulen* (1939). HANS WERNER RICHTER (1908-), the son of a fisherman on the island of Usedom, had a hard struggle with privation in youth; notorious for anti-Nazi speeches, he had to flee to Paris in 1933, but was driven by hunger to return to Berlin in 1934. Forced into the army in 1940 he was taken prisoner in 1943 and was sent to a camp in the United States. His novel *Die Geschlagenen* (1949) begins in Italy; its highlight is the battle of Monte Cassino. His second novel, *Sie fielen aus Gottes Hand* (1951), describes the experiences of a bundle of characters of different nationality, including a Jewish cobbler boy from Warsaw, in the period 1939 to 1950. WOLFGANG BORCHERT (1921-1947) had a short life of intense suffering; he was condemned to death for defeatism, but released; in 1944 he was jailed in Moabit. He wrote a verse play (*Draussen vor der Tür*, 1947; the leading character is a *Heimkehrer* from Siberia), Novellen (*Die Hundeblume*, 1948; *An diesem Dienstag*, 1948) and poems (*Laterne, Nacht und Sterne*, 1946); the helplessness of the individual during the war period fills his work. There is something of Borchert's despairing mood in Heinrich Böll's (1917-) *Der Zug war pünktlich* (1949): it is the tale of three days and nights spent by men on leave from the front; there is the same despair, of privates serving or wounded and sent home (*Heimkehrer*), in the short stories of his *Wanderer, kommst du nach Spa* (1950); his novel *Wo warst du Adam?* (1951) brands the idiocy of war. WALTER KOLBENHOFF (1908-), the son of a labourer, threw up his job as a factory worker when he was seventeen and tramped Europe as a street singer; he was then a journalist in Berlin, fled to Denmark in 1933, was pitched into the German army in 1942, and went through the hells of Sebastapol, El Alamein and Monte Cassino; in 1944 he was captured by the Americans, and while a prisoner wrote his novel *Von unserem Fleisch und Blut* (1947); his theme is the misery of those who hate the Nazis and are forced to fight; *Heimkehr in die Fremde* (1949) is another *Heimkehrerroman*.

More than at any previous stage of literary history the women writers of today form a group divergent often in outlook and uptake from their male compeers. They are best grouped by region and by religion as well as by school of literature. If we go by period of theme we find that their interpretation or criticism of life tends to be linked with the records of history; that is, their bent is towards the historical novel or the *vie romancée*. Of the older generation HELENE VOIGT-DIEDERICHS (1875-1952), the novelist of Schleswig-Holstein, has kept persistently to *Heimatkunst*; her characteristic work is foreshadowed in the tales of her *Schleswig-Holsteiner Landleute* (1928), expanded in 1926 and rounded off in 1928 by *Schleswig-Holsteiner Blut*, Novellen taken over from *Leben ohne Lärmen* (1903) and *Nur ein Gleichnis* (1910). The *Volksleben* of her province is finely rendered in her novels *Regine Vosgerau* (1901) and *Dreiviertel Stund vor Tag* (1905), and the awakening of maidenhood and a maid's yearning for motherhood is nowhere more healthily conveyed than in her book of memories *Auf Marienhoff* (1925). INA SEIDEL (1885-) has distinction as a lyric poet (*Gesammelte Gedichte*, 1937; *Gedichte*, 1950). Her most popular earlier tales (*Das Haus zum Monde*, 1917, with its sequel *Sterne der Heimkehr*, 1923) stand out by their insistent handling of woman's importance in family life; her speciality is the relationship of brothers and sisters (*Brömseshof*, 1928; *Renée und Rainer*, 1928; *Der Weg ohne Wahl*, 1933). *Das Labyrinth* (1922) is a painfully Freudian study of Georg Forster, the Sanscrit scholar who first translated *Sakuntala*. Her masterpiece is *Das Wunschkind* (1930), which explores and lights up the ideal of military devotion in the Prussian mentality. *Lennacker* (1938), like *Brömseshof*, is a *Heimkehrerroman*.

The Catholic women novelists are mostly Austrians; for the North GERTRUD FREIIN VON LE FORT (1876-), a Westphalian, is the outstanding representative. She, the descendant of Huguenot immigrants, did not enter the Roman Church till 1926. Her conversion provides the substance of her novel *Das Schweisstuch der Veronika* (1929); *Der Kranz der Engel* (1946) is a sequel. There is a strong Catholic bias too in her historical novels *Der Papst aus dem Ghetto* (1930), *Die letzte am Schafott* (1932), *Das Reich des Kindes* (1934), *Die Magdeburgische Hochzeit* (1938). ELIZABETH LANGGÄSSER (1899-1950) in her verse (*Der Wendekreis des Lammes. Ein Hymnus der Erlösung*, 1924; *Die Tierkreisgedichte*, 1935; *Der Laubmann und die Rose*, 1947) dreams ecstatic feeling into Catholic ritual and symbol. In her novel *Das unauslöschliche Siegel* (1946) a freethinking Jew accepts baptism, but belief and salvation come after long tribulation from the miraculous action of the mystic ceremony. There is the same mood in the short stories of *Das Labyrinth* (1949), while *Märkische Argonautenfahrt* (1950) symbolizes spiritual healing in the persons of seven wanderers from Berlin after the havoc of 1945, who find their way together to the convent of Anastasiendorf in the March of Brandenburg, their 'golden fleece' of salvation. PAULA GROGGER (1892-), a Catholic of Styria, is a disciple of Enrica von Handel-Mazzetti (p. 330); her novel *Das Grimmingtor* (1926) unrolls the saga of her native village during the Napoleonic invasion, while *Der Lobenstock* (1935) is just the plain love story, packed with pathos and meaning, of a simple girl. Faith has its mysteries, and its miracles too, in her numerous legends: *Die Räuberlegende* (1929), *Der Antichrist und unsere Liebe Frau* (1949), and many others. PAULA VON PRERADOVIČ (1887-1951) will be remembered as the author of the new national anthem of the Bundesrepublik of Austria: *Land der Berge, Land der Ströme*. As a lyric songster she began full-fledged with *Südlicher Sommer* (1929); this is verse directly inspired by the racial and landscape poetry of Istria and Dalmatia, where, though she was Viennese born, her youth was passed. Her poetry is collected in *Verlorene Heimat* (1949) and *Schicksalsland* (1952). Great originality and experimental courage – modernist innovation with outwardly an old technique – show in her novel *Pave und Pero* (1940); it is a *vie romancée* based on the correspondence (in the 1850's and thereabouts) of the author's grandfather, a general in the Austrian army and the national poet of Croatia, with his wife. Of her other work *Königslegende* (1950) is in substance a Serbian ballad in prose, while in *Die Versuchung des Colomba* (1951) the Irish missionary is visited on the island of Iona by a girl from the heathen wilds of Donegal; she had been betrothed to him as a child and now she comes to claim her man and her children. She hangs a bundle of aromatic herbs round his neck; they are bewitched, and he is nearly swept off his feet; but when they are removed he is a saint again, and she dies a penitent on a barren rock off Iona.

The Communist woman novelist is ANNA SEGHERS (1900-). She made her reputation with *Der Aufstand der Fischer von St. Barbara* (1928); it has marked originality of style and handling, but the relentless depiction of the hard life in a small fishing port in Brittany is rather romancified than realistic; the village whore, for instance, plies her trade with too much femininity to be physically possible; the build-up of the tale is by episodes, sharply limned and often jagged, and the total effect is film-like. Communist doctrine forms the staple of the novels *Die Gefährten* (1932), *Der Kopflohn* (1933), *Weg durch den Februar* (1935), *Die Rettung* (1937). Her masterpiece is *Das siebte Kreuz* (1941); it describes the flight of seven prisoners from a German concentration camp just before the outbreak of the war and in its totality gives a stirring picture of the whole Hitler period. This was followed by *Die Toten bleiben jung* (1949) and by four collections of Novellen: *Der Ausflug der toten Mädchen* (1948), *Hochzeit von Haiti* (1949), *Die Linie* (1950), *Die Kinder* (1951).

After Carossa's *Kindheit und Jugend* JOSEF LEITGEB's (1897-1952) *Das unversehrte Jahr* (1948) is the loveliest story of childhood and youth in recent literature. The story, which, like so many German autobiographies, recalls the thrill of first communion and the evolving experiences of school life, runs on to the school-leaving age; the outbreak of the First World War is imminent. The district lies near Innsbruck, where Leitgeb lived, and Tyrolese life is described with intimate realism tempered with fine poetic feeling and relieved by a delightful humour that never descends to coarseness and brutality. The book is, however, hardly to be classed with the South German *Bauernnovelle*: the boy's father is a railway official, and the contacts are rather with cultural avocations, the outlook being that of a lyrically attuned youth with feelings quivering forward to the most delicate expression of colouring and symbol. There are the same subtle rhythms and the same delicately toned response to the shifting moods of nature in Leitgeb's book of essays *Von Bäumen, Blumen und Musik* (1947), and in the prose of *Trinkt, O Augen* (1942). There is a considerable autobiographical fundament in the novel *Christian und Brigitte* (1938): a teacher who has served in the war comes to an Alpine village and here finds love and his true self. *Kinderlegende* (1934) is the tale of another Tyrolese boy who, in the 17th century, is put to death as a 'Hexer'. Mastery of form is one's first impression from reading Leitgeb's verse: *Gedichte* (1922), *Musik der Landschaft* (1935), *Vita somnium breve* (1943), *Lebenszeichen* (1943), *Sämtliche Gedichte* (1953). Though he pays tribute to Trakl and Walt Whitman he is consciously traditional in theme as in form, and in his deepest musings he is always crystal clear. There is an uprush of tragic feeling in his last book of verse, *Lebenszeichen*, in which, in the pressure of his own experience – he served as an intelligence officer in the Ukraine – he lashes out at the folly and fury of war. He records his impressions of the Ukraine in *Am Rande des Krieges* (1942); and his *Fünf Erzählungen* (1951) have the same factual fundament.

KARL HEINRICH WAGGERL (1897-), who was born at Bad Gastein but has made his home at Wagrain in the Salzburg country, found his feet with his novel *Brot* (1930), which shows the influence of Knut Hamsun's *Segen der Erde*. Village life forms the staple of *Schweres Blut* (1931), while *Das Jahr des Herrn* (1934) has autobiographical elements. Unmarried mothers come into the texture of *Mütter* (1935), and the two wars into *Und wenn du willst, vergiss* (1950). His Novellen have their scenes in the Salzburg localities of his homeland, which he describes in *Wagrainer Tagebuch* (1936). His legends – *Kalendergeschichten* (1937), etc. –, more or less in the manner of Gottfried Keller's *Sieben Legenden*, are naïve rather than subtle; for the most part they assume the possibliity of miracles in the life of today and for this reason tend to be foolish to non-Catholics; but *Die Schöpfung*, with its quaint and humorous picture of the seven days of Creation, is delightful. Waggerl's racy humour is at its best in his for a great part anecdotal short stories; *Fröhliche Armut* (1948) tells the story of his boyhood in the Gasteiner Tal; and the tales of *Die Pfingstreise* (1946) and *Drei Erzählungen* (1952) are also autobiographical. His botanical avocation comes out in *Das Lob der Wiese* (1950), while *Heiteres Herbarium* (1950) is a book of flower aquarelles with a commentary in humorous verse. *Kleines Erdenrund* (1951) by Hanns Arens is an introduction to Waggerl's work in anthology form with commentary.

In lyric poetry the development in recent years has been in a direction which by-passes hackneyed traditional forms in favour of stanzaic irregularity and free rhythms. Only the sonnet remains much as it was (except that line length may be shortened). The ballad of Liliencron's pattern with its ring of fighting fierceness is by now an archaic genre; its last exponent was BÖRRIES FREIHERR VON MÜNCHHAUSEN (1874-1945); his various volumes were collected in *Das Balladenbuch* (1924); his poems of personal experience are in *Das Liederbuch* (1928) and *Idyllen* (1933). Famous for her ballads, too, is the East Prussian poetess AGNES MIEGEL (1879-): *Gedichte* (1901; title changed to *Frühe Gesichte*, 1939); *Balladen und Lieder* (1907); *Gedichte und Spiele* (1920); *Gesammelte Gedichte* (1927); *Herbstgesang* (1932). Like Agnes Miegel typically North German was OSKAR LOERKE (1884-1941); the tendency since his death has been to give him high rank, say midway between Annette von Droste-Hülshoff and Wilhelm Lehmann; all three are past masters in the delineation of the landscapes of their homeland, all three with hard clear lines and vivid but discreet coloration. Loerke bends over from impressionistic notation to expressionistic involution of meaning; he has a highly personal cipher, and this spells difficulty to those who would read as they run. His verse, for the most part pantheistic and didactic (*Gedichte*, 1916 – title changed to *Pansmusik* in 2nd ed., 1929; *Atem der Erde*, 1930; *Der Silberdistelwald*, 1934; *Die Abschiedshand*, 1949) has the deeply thought out imagery which gives rare qualities of style to the prose of his novels (*Der Turmbau*, 1910; *Der Oger*, 1921) and his Novellen.

There is no trace of North German rural robustiousness in the expressionistic lyrics and prose reveries and sketches of ELSE LASKER-SCHÜLER (1876-1945), 'the Black Swan of Israel', if we may use the title awarded her when in Nazi days she fled from Berlin to Jerusalem to be some sort of national Hebrew poet. Her *Hebräische Balladen* (1913) have pathological modernity; *Dichtungen und Dokumente* (1951) contain a good cross-section of her ever varied work with its strange moods and fancies.

One poet of the expressionistic phase whose influence on the *Gegenwartslyrik* is very discernible is GEORG TRAKL (see p. 352), an Austrian of Salzburg. He is a Baudelairean poet whose diseased mind draws *nouveaux frissons* from the tints of decay ('*Verwestes gleitend durch die morsche Stube*').

His verse (*Gedichte*, 1913; *Die Dichtungen*, 1917; *Gesamtausgabe*, 1949; *Aus goldnem Kelch*, 1939) has a thrill for sensitive minds with its new rhythms, soft and mellow and with dying falls – '*Tönend von Wehmut und weichem Wahnsinn*'; '*mond'ne Kühle*'; '*elfenbeinerne Traurigkeit*'; '*Und leise tönen im Rohr die dunklen Flöten des Herbstes*'. Another poet who faded out in his twenties, GEORG HEYM (p. 352) – 'the German Rimbaud' – also influenced poets who followed him; none, perhaps, more than GOTTFRIED BENN (1886-), though as regards form rather than content. Benn's liking for modern French poetry may be congenital – his mother was French Swiss, but is more likely to be because by temperament and vocational training he is a surrealist with a sharp and cutting intellect that pierces straight to the core of phenomena. In his *Probleme der Lyrik* (1951) he discusses the origins of the lyric of today and derives it from Verlaine, Rimbaud, Valéry, Apollinaire and the surrealists with André Breton and Louis Aragon as pathfinders. But as a surrealist Benn has outstripped all the rest in the ruthless and raw cruelty of his interpretation; he has a very simple idea that appearances are ectoplastic with *das Nichts* beneath them; he is therefore classed as a nihilist, with nihilism in the philosophic sense as his poetic creed, bound up with the corollary that progressist concepts of development are mythical. But *das Nichts*, he argues, is supplanted by art, which creates from the very wilderness of chaos; nihilism is therefore productive; the poet's or the artist's task is to keep his eyes fixed to Being as it is, not to imagined idols; and his aim must be to express, not the thing itself, but his contact with the thing. What the poet has to see and figure is the Being (*das Sein*) of the thing. Such figuring is by means of art, and for this '*Montagekunst*' or '*Artismus*' of expression – which results from an adjustment (*Ausgleich*) of art and life, of mind and history – a '*Doppelleben*' is necessary. Benn's nihilism is thus in effect a disintegration which leads to an integration, and the final result is a transcendence which consists of the recognition of reality and the expressing of it in the new form. Benn's apparent pessimism – life is a matter of instinct and fate depends on chance – is extraneous to creative art. One essential fact in Benn's poetic make-up is that by profession he is a doctor of medicine – he began as an army doctor and after the first war he was a specialist for skin and venereal diseases in Berlin. Certainly his method of treating reality is that of a surgeon. Nothing could be more humanly dreadful – and at the same time as verse effective – than such poems of his as *Mann und Frau gehn durch die Krebsbaracke* ('*Bett stinkt bei Bett. Die Schwestern wechseln stündlich*'). With such poems as this it is no wonder that his first book *Morgue* (1952) brought him to the fore. The best introduction to his work for those who dare to venture into it is his volume of selections *Trunkene*

Flut (1952) together with his autobiographical and self-interpretative
Doppelleben (1950). His early verse, collected in, *Gesammelte Gedichte*
(1927), is completed by *Ausgewählte Gedichte* (1936), *Statische Gedichte*
(1948), and *Fragmente* (1951). There is the same crass realism in Benn's
Novellen (*Gehirne*, 1946). In his book of conversations *Drei alte Männer*
(1949) he explores the existential situation of today, and in his descriptive
sketches and critical or philosophic prose he diagnoses the symptoms of
decay: *Fazit der Perspektive* (1930); *Nach dem Nihilismus* (1932); *Der
Ptolomäer* (1949); *Ausdruckswelt* (1949); *Frühe Prosa* (1950); *Essays* (1951).

There is no reason to say that modernity of outlook or of vision is
bound up with irregular form; there is indeed a group of poets – we may
call them traditionalists or neo-classicists – who express the moods of
today in classically chiselled moulds (Hans Franck, Joseph Leitgeb, Hans
Leifhelm). But there is likely to be a subtle modulation of rhythm which
reveals a new relation to nature (Wilhelm Lehmann), or to social problems (F. G. Jünger), or even to religion (R. A. Schröder, Josef Weinheber).

RUDOLF BINDING (1867-1938) was one of the most refined of the neo-
classical poets; there is the mark of a distinguished personality but little
originality in his *Tage* (1924), *Ausgewählte und neue Gedichte* (1930), *Die
Gedichte, Gesamtausgabe* (1937), and in the war poems of *Stolz und Trauer*
(1922). His legends and Novellen, too, have the restraint of the neo-classic
pattern: *Die Legenden der Zeit* (1909), *Die Geige* (1911). With Binding as
a neo-classic stands RUDOLF ALEXANDER SCHRÖDER (1878-); or rather,
since in his earlier verse he uses Greek metres, he is a neo-Hellenist.
Schröder has considerable historical importance, for instance as co-founder
of the journal *Die Insel*; and he has in recent years been loaded with
honours from all quarters. He swept all before him when, as the greater
poets of his generation passed away, he continued his mass production
and established himself as a facile translator (*Homers Odyssee*, 1910; *Die
Ilias*, 1943; Virgil's *Hirtengedichte*, 1924; Horace's poems, 1935; also
translations of Shakespeare, Pope, Aubrey Beardsley, T. S. Eliot; translations of Molière and Racine and of Dutch and Flemish classics). Above
all he is recognized, after his rebuilding of the hymnal lyric of Paul Gerhardt and Paul Fleming, as – literally – the laureate of the Protestant
community. His more personal lyric work ranges from *Unmut* (1899),
Lieder an eine Geliebte (1900), *Gesammelte Gedichte* (1912), *Deutsche Oden*
(1914; patriotic verse), *Heilig Vaterland* (1914; weak war verse) to the
religious verse of *Widmungen und Opfer* (1925), *Mitte des Lebens* (1930), *Weih-
nachtslieder* (1947). *Die weltlichen Gedichte* (1940) collects his secular poetry,
Die geistlichen Gedichte (1950) his religious verse. The story of his youth is
told in *Der Wanderer und die Heimat* (1931) and *Aus Kindheit und Jugend*

(1934). His attitude to religion is enunciated in *Zur Naturgeschichte des Glaubens* (1936), while *Dichtung und Dichter der Kirche* (1936) has importance for hymnology. *Reden und Aufsätze* (1939) deal with translation problems and include essays on Hofmannsthal, Rilke, Binding, and other friends of his.

Another poet who combines extreme modernity of theme with traditional form is FRIEDRICH GEORG JÜNGER (1898-), the brother of Ernst Jünger. The verse of his first volume, *Gedichte* (1934), follows the moulds of Klopstock and Hölderlin; in *Der Taurus* (1937) he shows himself a master of the narrative elegy. *Der Missouri* (1940) and *Der Westwind* (1946) are flanked by the twin volumes *Die Silberdistelklause* (1946) and *Weinberghaus* (1947), both in 4-feet trochees, a line of which he makes great use; they reflect the bucolic peace of his Swiss retreat at Überlingen. *Die Perlenschnur* (1948) was followed by *Gedichte* (1950), a collection from previous books. In *Iris im Wind* (1952) there is a note of elementary cheerfulness. Taking him all in all the outstanding quality of his verse is energy; his main motifs are fire, fierceness, violence; to him the motive spirit of all life is flame: '*Fuoco sei, to pyr, das Feuer | Dir mehr als alles andere teuer.*' With this goes his withering contempt for the masses; he is indeed an out-and-out aristocrat, to whom the great enemy today is Demos, whom he compares with rats; or with grubs that gnaw at the roots of life. As a writer of fiction he began late with the short stories of *Dalmatinische Nacht* (1950) and *Die Pfauen* (1952); the three tales of murder in the latter may derive from his early experiences as a *Richter*. Of his essays *Über das Komische* (1938) is audacious in its negative approach to all comic elements in literature. In other essays (*Griechische Götter*, 1943; *Titanen*, 1944; *Griechische Mythen*, 1947) there is idealization of Greek concepts. *Grüne Zweige* (1951) relates the saga of his life till he threw up law for writing.

Formally considered neo-Hellenism finds its most determined expression in the work of JOSEF WEINHEBER (1892-1945); there is strict classical form, particularly in ode and elegy, in his *Adel und Untergang* (1934) and *Späte Krone* (1936). His three previous volumes of verse – *Der einsame Mensch* (1920), *Von beiden Ufern* (1923), and *Boot in der Bucht* (1926) – had fallen flat. There is the pith of his verse in the three books of selections *Vereinsamtes Herz* (1935), *Selbstbildnis* (1937), and *Dokumente des Herzens* (1944). *Wien wörtlich* (1935) is a volume of dialectal verse which is redolent of the free and easy life and the glib garrulity of Vienna, while *O Mensch, gib acht* (1937) interprets old customs and the legends of the zodiac. *Zwischen Göttern und Dämonen* (1938) is made up of forty odes. *Kammermusik* (1939) presents 'musical poems' adapted to the note of the instruments required. *Hier ist das Wort* (1947) is a posthumously published book into which

Weinheber's doctrine of prosody is inwoven; the final section consists of twelve poems which bring into high relief events in the cultural life of Vienna. Of his essays, *Im Namen der Kunst* (1936 attempts an enunciation of the function and philosophy of poetry, while *Über die Dichtkunst* (1949) deals with his own development as man and poet. His novels *Das Waisenhaus* (1925), *Nachwuchs* (1927) and *Gold ausser Kurs* (written 1932-33, published 1953) have autobiographical interest.

WILHELM LEHMANN (1882-) was from the first appraised as a poet *sui generis* and intrinsically of the first order. But it is only in recent years that this perception has pierced through. Lehmann's verse is difficult; he is specifically and intensively a *Naturdichter*, and in the strict sense that his continuous theme is nature both for itself and as symbol his verse may be so recondite that for full comprehension a knowledge of botany and of animal life is needed. Lehmann is a poets' poet; and as such he is read and appraised by most of those who write verse today. There is no doubt that his direct influence can be traced in much of contemporary verse; there is, for instance, the same mythical interpretation of nature in the verse of Elizabeth Langgässer (p. 377); and there is something of his chthonic concepts in ODA SCHÄFER's (1900-) *Irdisches Geleit* (1946) and *Kranz des Jahres* (1948) as also in MARTIN KESSEL's (1901-) *Erwachen und Wiedersehen* (1940) and *Gesammelte Gedichte* (1951). It is now a matter of literary history that Lehmann's first volume of verse, *Antwort des Schweigens* (1935), resulted in the founding of a new school of poetry, 'die naturmagische Schule'. Lehmann's own key to his lyric practice is, quite simply, 'Bestehen ist nur ein Sehen'; that is: to live, we must look; the existential principle of lyric creation is to *see* what nature shows and to bring one's own personal observation into relation with what the great poets of all times have observed and dreamed into their verse. The real key to his creative power is that by the magic of his verbal rendering he transforms the world he sees. The outcome is a magic illumination of words: the word represents the thing, but the thing is transformed by the poet's representation of it. It is word magic rather than nature magic. At first glance the facture of Lehmann's verse and stanzas is traditional, but the quickest reading brings home to the reader that there is everywhere the new handling of a radically new poet. Nor is there any change in form and texture as new volumes appear – *Der grüne Gott* (1942), *Entzückter Staub* (1946), *Noch nicht genug* (1950). In Lehmann's fiction, too – *Der Bilderstürmer* (1917), *Die Schmetterlingspuppe* (1918), *Weingott* (1921), *Ruhm des Daseins* (1953) –, he is a nature poet.

KARL KROLOW (1915-) acknowledges the influence on his lyric manner of Droste-Hülshoff; this is less evident than that of Rilke, Trakl, and

Wilhelm Lehmann. In the mass his verse is in the wake of Wilhelm Lehmann's cult of the interrelation of man and nature, but with surrealistic undertones and existentialist ideology. *Gedichte* (1948) is a volume of selections, with his first two books, *Hochgelobtes gutes Leben* (1945) and *Auf Erden* (1949), as the staple. In *Heimsuchung* (1949) there is sometimes a poignant personal note; *Selbstbildnis mit der Rumflasche* is Baudelairean: in the mesh of drunken dream the flask in the poet's hand swells out to a vessel that sails blessedly along under tropical heavens, on to Jamaica and the lips of negresses at the rim of the Paradise beyond this world. *Die Zeichen der Welt* (1951) is confessedly coloured by Krolow's contacts with Lorca, Supervielle, Eluard, and Auden.

FRITZ USINGER (1895-) began as a member of *Die Dachstube*, a group of young revolutionary poets and artists grouped around Joseph Würth, a master of handpress printing in Darmstadt; other members of the circle were Kasimir Edschmid (p. 374) and ANTON SCHNÄCK (1892 -). *Gedichte* (1940) is made up of selections from his previous work; this was followed by *Das Glück* (1947) and *Hesperische Hymnen* (1948). His important essays on the literature of today are collected in *Das Wirkliche* (1947) and *Geist und Gestalt* (1948).

'Regional poetry' is the conventional term for quite a galaxy of poets (Max Mell, Richard Billinger, Karl Heinrich Waggerl in the forefront) who for the most part sing and describe their narrower homeland. With these, though his regional affinities are not primary, may be ranged GEORG BRITTING (1891-), a Regensburg man by birth but resident in Munich, the poet of the Lower Bavarian countryside. He began with expressionist plays (*Der Mann im Mond*, 1920; *Das Storchennest*, 1921; *Paula und Bianca*, 1922) and then went over to Novellen; *Valentin und Veronika* and *Der Eisläufer*, both 1948, reprint tales from previous volumes. His experience of war service comes into the weft and woof of his one novel, *Lebenslauf eines dicken Mannes, der Hamlet hiess* (1932). Hamlet wages war in Norway on behalf of his stepfather, and the chronicle adumbrates the poet's own reactions as a soldier to the humbug which launches armies to torture and death. The style and language of the novel, expressionistically strange but sensuous and highly coloured, wends along wearily with the faint pulse and rhythm of dream. His books of verse are *Gedichte* (1930), *Der irdische Tag* (1935), *Rabe, Rose und Hahn* (1939), *Lob des Weines* (1944), *Die Begegnung* (1947), *Unter hohen Bäumen* (1951). His earlier lyric manner, more or less rooted in expressionism, quickly develops to the solid shaping of his later verse, which varies in mood rather than in its general tenor. The structure of the verse is hard and firm, sometimes rough; traditional forms are broken up to give, not free rhythms, though these occur sporadically, but freedom to lengthen or shorten lines or to tail a stanza with an extra line. Already in *Der irdische Tag* we have the poet's full panoply. The forefront of what is presented is the exterior world as the year runs its changes of scene and feeling round the gardener's calendar. The procession of the seasons has been worked out by many poets since James Thomson; in Britting's sequences it is all new because the vision is new and regional: these are the seasons centred on the Danube – always '*der Strom*' (*die Isar* is less lovingly given its name). *Die Begegnung* is a chain of seventy sonnets, which in substance renew and vary the medieval Dance of Death in language tuned to the hard sharp-cut contours of the old woodcuts of the *danse macabre*.

Women poets of distinction are ODA SCHÄFER (p. 384); MARIE LUISE KASCHNITZ (1901-; *Gedichte*, 1947; *Zukunftsmusik*, 1950); RUTH SCHAUMANN (1899-; *Der Knospengrund*, 1924; *Das Passional*, 1926; *Der Rebenhag*, 1927; *Klage und Trost*, 1947; *Ländliches Gastgeschenk*, 1949).

Several poets may be grouped at the end of this survey of the lyric as innovators in so far as they fall into line with the international tendencies of today. Of these HANS EGON HOLTHUSEN (1913-) began with *Hier in der Zeit* (1949); the title indicates the stark actuality of the themes. The first poem of the volume, *Trilogie des Krieges*, in a loose hexametric form, is the first attempt – it was written in 1946 – to give poetic form to the mentality of the five years of war. But the persistent note is that of existentialism. There is still the pang of the war in some of the poems of *Labyrinthische Jahre* (1952); in the first, *Acht Variationen über Zeit und Tod*, the doctrine of the identity of past, present, and future is quickened by flash-lights on the Nazi régime. The pattern of the verse is not repellent if it is realized that it is fitted to the sense of the poem and to the revelation of the sense by flashes; the most characteristic poems are those in the rough hexametric shaping of Rilke's latest work. Stretches of apparently flat prose are broken by a sudden rush of tensely phrased and lovely imagery. The poetry is in the totality of the poem; and even the totality of a single poem is merely a fragment of a great doctrine of mystic truth, a gospel which in these labyrinthine years of our wandering through the 'Waste Land' of existence brings comfort and intelligence of the way we go and to where. Holthusen's existentialism has the Protestant stamp of Kierkegaard and Karl Barth; he has been at pains to stress his aversion to the French decoction of Heidegger represented chiefly by Sartre. He deals with these problems in the essays of his *Der unbehauste Mensch* (1951).

Among poets who have earned recognition in the last few years RUDOLF HAGELSTANGE (1912-) stands out both for brilliantly imaged presentation of ethical ideas and as a daring innovator of form. He began with *Venezianisches Credo* (1948), a cycle of sonnets written in the north of Italy at the end of the war, when he was a soldier in the service of a Führer whose creed he loathed. There is still the shadow of the war years over *Es spannt sich der Bogen* (1943) and *Strom der Zeit* (1948). *Meersburger Elegie* (1950) has less of the decorative impressionistic pattern of the earlier verse, but is noticeably influenced by the line variation and free stressing of Rilke's *Duineser Elegien*. 'Die zarte Sibylle am steinernen Turme', whose life is inwoven in the problematic arabesque of the poem, is Annette von Droste-Hülshoff; the elegy plaintively evokes her caged and cabined life, her patrician bondage in the Castle of Meersburg on the Lake of Constance. Hagelstange reaches full maturity and indeed mastership in his *Ballade vom verschütteten Leben* (1952). The ballad dirges a new saga – the saga of Dust. The plain newspaper source is transcribed at the head of the poem: in June 1951 it was reported from Warsaw that an old bunker had been unearthed near Gdynia – Danzig of old, Gotenhafen in Hitler's trumped-up saga; into the light of day tottered two soldiers, whose outlet had for six years been barred by a bomb; they had been kept alive by a vast and varied store of food and drink. As there was no water they had washed themselves in cognac. They had lived in an inferno more torturing than Dante's hell, for it was merely the long drawn out fading of hope and the rotting of mind and body.

There is a hard note of personal experience – he was an American prisoner of war – in the verse of GÜNTER EICH (1907-; *Gedichte*, 1930; *Abgelegene Gehöfte*, 1948; *Untergrundbahn*, 1949). Existentialism is not glaringly prominent in the lyric verse of HEINZ PIONTEK (1925-); he rather, with Günter Eich, represents a new type of drastic realism which is transformed to symbolic significance by the total import of the poem; his lyrics are collected in *Die Furt* (1952) and *Die Rauchfahne* (1953). A pathetic interest attaches to the poetry of HANS LEIFHELM (1891-1947); born a Westphalian (in München-Gladbach) he lived in Graz, the capital of Styria, and then, as an exile, in Italy. The perfect workmanship of his verse (*Hahnenschrei*, 1926; *Gesänge von der Erde*, 1933; *Lob der Vergänglichkeit*, 1949) makes him a poets' poet. There is a typical North German hardness in his rhythmic pattern, but it has more musicality than that of Annette von Droste-Hülshoff, to whom he has been likened, and his panorama of the seasons in his fine Styrian landscapes is worked out with a painter's fullness of detail.

Of the humorous poets of today the best known is ERICH KÄSTNER (1899-), famous for his tale of *Emil und die Detektive* (1936); he has himself anthologized his verse in *Lyrische Hausapotheke* (1938). Very popular, too, is the rollicking verse of Eugen Roth (1895-): *Ein Mensch* (1935), *Die Frau in der Weltgeschichte* (1936), *Der Wunderdoktor* (1939), *Mensch und Unmensch* (1948). He also writes serious verse, for the most part wistfully recording the seasons' moods: *Traum des Jahres* (1937), *Rose und Nessel* (1951); and Novellen: *Das Schweizerhäusl* (1950), tales and anecdotes from the years of his boyhood in Munich. Buffoonery runs riot in the rhyming of the itinerant cabaret mime Joachim Ringelnatz (1883-1934), whose pet pose was that of a drunken sailor; his seafaring in early years provided him with the matter of his *Kuttel Daddeldu* (1920). His *Clownerien* are collected in . . . *und auf einmal steht es neben dir* (1950); a good approach is *Ausgewählte Gedichte* (1950). Another Brettl-Dichter was Fred Endrikat (1890-1942); he began with *Die lustige Arche* (1935), a '*Tierfibel für Jung und Alt*', and continued with *Höchst weltliche Sündenfibel* (1939), *Liederliches und Lyrisches* (1940), and *Der fröhliche Diogenes* (1942). *Verse und Lieder* (1949) is a selection.

The revival of the historical drama begins with Wolfgang Goetz's (1885-) *Gneisenau* (1925). His *Kavaliere* (1930) handles the love story of Ludwig I, King of Bavaria, with the dancer Lola Montez. Where Goetz attempts other than German history he falls off, as in *Robert Emmet* (1927) or *Kuckuckseier* (1934), which pictures Shakespeare in country retirement in his old age. His great success after *Gneisenau* was *Der Ministerpräsident* (1936); the Prime Minister is apparently modelled on Bismarck. *Kampf ums Reich* (1939) portrays Fieldmarshal von Arnheimb as the pattern of a statesman during the Thirty Years' War. Goetz has also written popular fiction. In *Reise ins Blaue* (1920) the British government sends, at Napoleon's request, a bevy of girls to St. Helena to amuse the band of devotees still with him. *Das Gralswunder* (1926) is a comic story of the film world. He has also written critical work: *Du und die Literatur* (1951), and biographies: *Napoleon* (1926), *Goethe* (1938), *Mozart* (1941), *Schiller* (1944).

Though Curt Gotz (1888-) is a namesake and almost of the same age as Wolfgang he is at the opposite pole of dramatic creation. Curt's set purpose is to entertain, at whatever level, not to inculcate Prussian virtues. There is the lightest possible touch in the five grotesque sketches of *Nachtbeleuchtung* (1919) and in *Menagerie* (1920). There is a species of family relationship running from the comedy *Ingeborg* (1921) through the three one-act plays of *Die tote Tante* (1924) and the comedy *Das Haus in Montevideo* (1946). In *Dr. med. Hiob Prätorius* (1932) a doctor is on the track of the bacillus responsible for silliness. There is the same irresponsible sensationalism in the 'legend' *Tatjana* (1949) and his erotic novel *Die Tote von Beverly Hills* (1951).

HANNS JOHST (1890-) began with full-blast expressionism (p. 347) and *Pubertätsdramatik* in *Der junge Mensch, ein ekstatisches Szenarium* (1916). The subject of *Der Einsame* (1917) is the alcoholic ruin of the dramatist Dietrich Grabbe, while in *Der König* (1920) we have a picture of conditions in Germany – conflict of community and Kaiser – instanced in ancient Greece. Johst pleads for a return of religious or humanitarian faith in *Propheten* (1923), in which Luther represents the idea of the hero's community with the race to which he belongs, while his *Thomas Paine* (1927) was acclaimed as a glowing expression of the sacrifice of the individual self in propaganda for a nation's coming greatness. In *Schlageter* (1933), the action of which pictures the resistance to the French occupation of the Ruhr, frenzy is brutalized. His fiction serves the same political and social ideals: *Kreuzweg* (1922), *So gehen sie hin* (1930).

HANS JOSÉ REHFISCH (1891-) was at one time dubbed '*der Sudermann der neuen Dramatiker*'. During the Second World War he was a lecturer in sociology in New York and edited the emigrants' journal *In Tirannos*. He began with the neo-romantic drama *Die goldenen Waffen* (1913), the theme of which is the fight of Ajax with Ulysses. Plays which followed were *Die Heimkehr* (1918); *Das Paradies* (1919); and *Deukalion* (1921), in which the hero with his wife survives the Deluge. A great success was *Chauffeur Martin* (1921), the hero of which revolts against God because in complete innocence he has run over a man. The comedy *Die Erziehung durch Kolibri* (1921) was in 1924 rechristened *Die Libelle*. The tragicomedy *Wer weint um Juckenack?* (1924) had international success. Typical of Rehfisch's touch on the pulse of theatre-goers is *Hände weg von Helena* (1951); the heroine is highly tickled by attempts at artificial insemination. More solid than the ruck of these plays and based on historical study is the novel *Die Hexen von Paris* (1951), the story of the Marquise de Montespan.

The plays of HANS HENNY JAHNN (1894-) have to be considered for tentative study if only because, revolting as they often are, they are symptomatic. Because of the sexual extravagances of his themes Jahnn has earned the title of *Prophet der Unzucht*. His first plays illustrate his declared conviction that 'man is capable of anything'. The hero of his *Pastor Ephraim Magnus* (1919) seeks God by way of torture and throttles his sister because of her incestuous love for him. Incest is again the theme of *Der gestohlene Gott* (1923) and abnormal sex relations are the subject of *Der Arzt, sein Weib, sein Sohn* (1922). In *Die Krönung Richards III* (1921) Richard murders in the exasperation of his rage at the decay of his own body, and Queen Elizabeth murders the boys she has enjoyed. His *Medea* (1926) has the eyes torn out of a messenger who comes with bad news. Discussion of Jahnn flared up again when in 1948 *Armut, Reichtum,*

Mensch und Tier, written in 1934, was performed: a Norwegian farmer if rent by a mystic love for his horse and is tragically caught between two women. The defence of Jahnn, who is an ultra-respectable organ builder in Hamburg, is that he is trying to pierce to the very roots of Freudian complexes; and if he is given credit for experimental psychiatry he at least deserves consideration by the side of Ernst Barlach. There is experimentation in Jahnn's novel *Perrudja* (2 vols., 1929), a pioneer attempt in the manner of James Joyce's *Ulysses*, and still more in the trilogy of novels *Fluss ohne Ufer*. The first volume, *Holzschiff* (1937), is a gruesome tale of happenings on a ship out at sea; the nature of these mysteries is revealed in Vol. 2, *Die Niederschrift des Gustav Anias Horn* (1949). Vol. 3, *Epilog*, will appear in 1954.

CARL ZUCKMAYER (1896–) began with outrageous expressionist plays: *Kreuzweg* (1920) and *Pankraz oder die Hinterwäldler* (1925), the latter a play of the Wild West. In 1939 he found a refuge in the United States, where he ran a farm in Vermont Hill. In 1947 he returned to Germany. His comedy *Der fröhliche Weinberg* (1925) was awarded the Kleist prize because it was the first breakaway from the nebulosity of expressionism to life as it *might* be lived. From now on Zuckmayer ranks as a *gesundeter Expressionist*. The hero of *Schinderhannes* (1927) is a captain of robbers in the Rhineland in Napoleon's days; the doctrine is frankly soaked with the Socialism of today; the real robbers are Church and State, while Schinderhannes takes nothing from the poor. *Der Hauptmann von Köpenick* (1931) is a relentless exposure of Prussian militarism before the outbreak of the First World War; an out-of-work cobbler who has spent most of his life in prison steals a captain's uniform, walks into a town hall, arrests the mayor, and walks off with the civic cash-box. Zuckmayer's great success is *Des Teufels General* (1946), which throws a lurid light on conditions in Germany just before the United States came into the war. *Der Gesang im Feuerofen* (1950) is in some sort a return to the ecstatic upsurge of expressionism: German military police set fire to a castle in which a French resistance group are gathered; Zuckmayer again lights up the depravity of a period, but also the power of resistance which is sure to win through in the end. His powers as a dramatist come out also in his fiction (*Der Bauer aus dem Taunus*, 1927; *Herr über Leben und Tod*, 1938; *Der Seelenbräu*, 1945). As a lyric poet he is represented by *Der Baum* (1926), which is reprinted in *Die Gedichte* (1948). Autobiographical are *Pro Domo* (1938) and *Second Wind* (1940; in English only).

BERNT VON HEISELER (1907–) began with one-act plays which are collected in *Kleines Theater* (1940). His first full drama, *Schill* (1934), presents the Prussian patriot Ferdinand von Schill, who raised a rebellion against Napoleon. *Das letzte Geheimnis* (1931) uses motifs of Calderon, while *Des Königs Schatten* (1939) is modelled on one of Goldoni's plays. Von Heiseler was forbidden to publish after his tragedy *Cäsar* (1941) had shown open conflict between dictatorship and democracy resulting from the murder of Caesar by Brutus. *Der Bettler unter der Treppe* (1942) has a crusader for hero; *Philoktet* (1947), modelled on the drama of Sophocles, calls for truth even in politics. The very titles of some of von Heiseler's plays indicate that thematically he has recourse to Renaissance and neo-romantic material, which he may bring into relation with problems of today. A great effort is his *Hohenstaufentrilogie* (1948); the prelude is *Die Stunde vor Konstanz* (1939), and the centre piece *Kaiser Friedrich der II*. is completed by *Der Gefangene*, with the death of Enzio. *Semiramis* (1943) harks back to the draft of a play by Calderon. In *Das Neubeurer Krippenspiel* (1945), produced in aid of the restoration fund of the Frauenkirche at Munich, religions which differ in doctrine collaborate for a good cause. *Das Haus der Angst* (1950) satirizes existentialism: the princess imprisoned in Bluebeard's castle undergoes all the stages from *Daseinsangst* onward of this doctrine of today. Von Heiseler's unquestioning Christianity, which gives tone and substance to the pith of his plays, emerges too in his lyric poetry: *Wanderndes Hoffen* (1935) and *Spiegel im dunklen Wort* (1945; a selection). He has written biographies: *Stefan George* (1936), *Kleist* (1939); and in *Ahnung und Aussage* (1939) he interprets Kleist, Hebbel, Mörike, and poets of today. In fiction he has to his credit the short stories *Die Unverständigen* (1936) and *Erzählungen* (1943) and a novel of Tyrolese peasant life, *Die gute Welt* (1938).

FRANZ THEODOR CSOKOR (1885– ; pronounce Tschokor) attacked the Nazis and had to take refuge in Poland and, in successional escapes after that, in Roumania, Serbia, and Dalmatia, to find safety at last in Italy after its occupation by the Allies. He belongs to Vienna by birth and there he again resides. He entered literature with the ballads of *Die Gewalten* (1912) and the verse of *Der Dolch und die Wunde* (1918) and *Das schwarze Schiff* (1947). *Ewiger Aufbruch* (1926) is a selection of his ballads, and *Immer ist Anfang* (1952) is his collected verse. In Austria he is classed as one of the first of living dramatists. His plays followed in quick succession: *Die Sünde wider den Geist* (1912), *Der Baum des Erkenntnis* (1917), *Die rote Strasse* (1918), *Die Stunde des Absterbens* (1919), *Ballade von der Stadt* (1926). His drama on the fate of the revolutionary poet Georg Büchner, *Gesellschaft der Menschenrechte* (1929), and *Besetztes Gebiet* (1930), which deals with passive resistance in the Rhein-Ruhr district after the First World War, were substantial successes; of lighter texture were *Die Weibermühle* (1931), a typically Austrian Zauberstück, *Gewesene Menschen*

(1932), and *Der tausendjährige Traum* (1933). His most successful play, *3. November 1918* (1936), shows the collapse of Austria and the partisan fighting which continued in Carinthia. *Gottes General* (1948) dramatizes the life of Ignatius Loyola. There is variety of theme in *Jadwiga* (1939), *Satans Arche* (1940), *Wenn sie zurückkommen* (1941), *Kalypso* (1946). *Der verlorene Sohn* (1946) is the direct outcome of his stay in the Dalmatian island of Korčula, where he was imprisoned by the Italians till his liberation by the partisans of Tito of Yugo-Slavia; it deals with the impact of the war on a peasant family and the ensuing rupture of family ties. Problematic and controversial (as regards the possibility of production on the stage) is *Pilatus* (1948); Christ does not appear, but Pilatus (we are told in the preface), ready as he may be to die for Jesus, will not find it possible to change his life for him. This is the idea of the play, and it applies to the post-war conditions of today. Csokor's *Als Zivilist im polnischen Krieg* (1939) and *Als Zivilist im Balkankrieg* (1947) have permanent emotional interest. *Über die Schwelle* (1938) is a book of Novellen, and *Ein Reich gegen die Welt* (1952) is a novel dealing with the Münster Anabaptists, with a passionate application to the problems of today.

Another successful Austrian dramatist is ALEXANDER LERNET-HOLENIA (1897-). After his expressionistic *Demetrius* (1925), with the theme we know from Schiller's unfinished tragedy, he went over to satirical comedies (*Erotik*, 1927, etc.). Of his novels *Die Standarte* (1934) is related to Rilke's *Cornet*. His lyric verse, influenced by Hölderlin and Rilke, is collected in *Gedichte 1939-1945* (1946).

MAX MELL (1882-) is associated with the revival of the medieval mystery and morality play, which had begun with Hofmannsthal's *Jedermann*. Born at Marburg an der Drau in Styria he grew up in Vienna. He began with Novellen: *Lateinische Erzählungen* (1904), *Die Grazien des Traums* (1906), *Jägersage und andere Novellen* (1910). His best short stories he selected for the collection *Das Donauweibchen* (1938). The tone and temper of his mystery plays are foreshadowed in his verse tale *Die Osterfeier* (1921) and take shape in *Das Wiener Kripperl von 1919* (1921). His masterpiece is *Apostelspiel* (1924), at once a mystery play and a peasant drama (*Bauernspiel*); that is, one with primitive peasants for players in a rough village location. With *Die Sieben gegen Theben* (1932) Mell turns to regular drama in blank verse. His greatest effort is *Der Nibelunge Not* (1942), in rough-hewn verse of four beats to the line. Of this, the first part, *Rache*, was produced during the war and was acclaimed as a Teutonic epic drama worthy of the heroic spirit of the day. The second part, *Kriemhilds Rache* (1951), is generally admitted to fall off because the spirit of it has something of the preaching quality of the peasant moralities which are, in sober truth, Mell's province by right of conquest. As a lyric poet he sings the revolving seasons of Styria in *Das bekränzte Jahr* (1911) and joy in earth in *Gedichte* (1919). *Gedichte* (1928) is a selection.

RICHARD BILLINGER (1893-) was to have been a priest, but blossomed out into a poet – the prolific poet and dramatist of Upper Bavaria. In *Asche des Fegefeuers* (1931) he tells the story of his upbringing as a village *Heiligenbüblein*. There is a strong religious element as well as pulsing melodrama in his peasant plays; *Knecht* (1924), *Das Perchtenspiel* (1928), *Rauhnacht* (1931), *Rosse* (1931), *Der Gigant* (1937) give the general note; the motive force is raw heathen passion under a thin crust of Christian discipline, and this holds good, too, of his peasant tales: *Das Schutzengelhaus* (1934), *Lehen aus Gottes Hand* (1935), *Das verschenkte Leben* (1937). Billinger deserts the peasant play in his comedies *Stille Gäste* (1933), *Lob des Landes* (1933), *Melusine* (1941), *Der Galgenvogel* (1948), and in his dramas *Gabriele Dambrone* (1941), *Die Fuchsfalle* (1914), *Das Haus* (1948). His lyric poetry (*Lob Gottes*, 1923; *Über die Äcker*, 1923; *Gedichte*, 1929; *Nachtwache*, 1935; and *Holder Morgen*, 1942) is collected in *Sichel am Himmel* (1949). The pith of this lyric outpouring is symbolization of Catholic ritual flanked by vignettes of farming life and age-old village custom, but there is here and there a flash of communistic revolt, as in *Gebet der Knechte und Mägde*, and there is the crude criminal passion of the peasant plays in such a poem as *Knechtsballade*.

Two other Austrian novelists now well to the fore are FRANZ NABL (1883-; *Ödhof*, 1911; *Die Galgenfrist*, 1921; *Ein Mann von gestern*, 1935; *Die Ortliebschen Frauen*, 1936) and HEIMITO VON DODERER (1896-; *Ein Mord, den jeder begeht*, 1938; *Die erleuchteten Fenster*, 1950; *Die Strudelhofstiege*, 1951). His masterpiece is *Die Dämonen* (1956). There is a tendency to class von Doderer as the direct successor of Robert Musil.

BIBLIOGRAPHY TO CHAPTERS VII-X

LANGUAGE

Bach, Adolf. *Geschichte der deutschen Sprache*. Heidelberg, 4th ed., 1949

Behaghel, Otto. *Geschichte der deutschen Sprache*. Vol. 3 of Paul's *Grundriss der deutschen Sprache*. Strassburg, 5th ed., 1928

Behaghel, Otto. *Die deutsche Sprache*. Vienna and Leipzig, 1904. 8th ed., 1930

Behaghel, Otto. *Deutsche Syntax*. Heidelberg, 1923 ff

Bithell, Jethro. *German Pronunciation and Phonology*. London, 1952

Brooke, K. *An Introduction to Early New High German*. Blackwell, Oxford, 1955

Collinson, W. E. *The German Language Today; its Patterns and Historical Background*. London, 1953

Curme, George O. *A Grammar of the German Language.* New York, 2nd ed., 1922; 7th printing 1952

Dal, Ingerid. *Deutsche Wortbildung.* Halle, 1947

Dam, J. van. *Handbuch der deutschen Sprache.* Groningen, 1937

Der grosse Duden: Wörterbuch und Leitfaden der deutschen Rechtschreibung. Leipzig, 1929 ff, 15th ed., 1957

Farrell, R. B. *Dictionary of German Synonyms.* Cambridge, 1953

Frings, T. *Grundlegung einer Geschichte der deutschen Sprache.* Halle, 1948. 2nd ed., Halle, 1950

Glinz, H. *Die innere Form des Deutschen: eine neue deutsche Grammatik.* Berne, 1952

Henzen, W. *Deutsche Wortbildung.* Halle, 1947

Kluge, F., and Goetze, A. *Etymologisches Wörterbuch der deutschen Sprache.* Berlin, 15th revised ed., 1951

Krahe, H. *Germanische Sprachwissenschaft.* 2 vols. Sammlung Göschen 238 and 780. Berlin, 1948

Paul, Hermann (ed. H. Stolte). *Kurze deutsche Grammatik.* Halle, 1949

Priebsch, R., and Collinson, W. E. *The German Language.* London, 1934. 2nd. ed., 1946 (reprinted 1952; 4th ed. revised, 1958)

Schwarz, Ernst. *Die deutschen Mundarten.* Göttingen, 1950

Schwarz, Ernst. *Deutsche Namengebung. I. Ruf- und Personennamen.* Göttingen, 1949. *II. Orts- und Flurnamen.* Göttingen, 1950

Stolte, H. *Kurze deutsche Grammatik auf Grund der fünfbändigen Grammatik von Hermann Paul.* Halle, 1949

Sütterlin, Ludwig. *Die deutsche Sprache der Gegenwart.* Leipzig, 5th ed., 1923

Tonnelat, E. *Histoire de la langue allemande.* (Collection Armand Volin.) Paris, 1927

Walsh, Maurice O'Connor. *A concise German etymological Dictionary.* London, 1954

HISTORIES OF LITERATURE

Annalen der deutschen Literatur. Geschichte der deutschen Literatur von den Anfängen bis zur Gegenwart. Herausgegeben von H. O. Burger. Stuttgart, 1951-52

Bartels, Adolf. *Geschichte der deutschen Literatur.* 3 vols. Leipzig, 1924-28

Biese, A. *Deutsche Literaturgeschichte.* 3 vols. Munich, 25th ed., 1930

Francke, Kuno. *German Literature as determined by Social Forces.* New York, 6th ed., 1903. (In German: *Die Kulturwerte der deutschen Literatur.* 2 vols. 1910, 1923)

Friederich, Werner P. *An Outline History of German Literature.* New York, 1951

Robertson, J. G. *A History of German Literature.* Edinburgh, 2nd. ed., 1931

Scherer, W. *Geschichte der deutschen Literatur.* Berlin, 4th ed., revised and edited by O. Walzel, 1928

Vogt, F., and Koch, M. *Geschichte der deutschen Literatur.* Leipzig, Neudruck in 3 vols. 1926-30

Waterhouse, Gilbert. *A Short History of German Literature.* London, 2nd ed., 1952

Ehrismann, Gustav. *Geschichte der deutschen Literatur bis zum Ausgang des Mittelalters.* 3 vols. Munich, 1918, 1922, 1935

Müller, Günther. *Deutsche Dichtung von der Renaissance bis zum Ausgang des Barock.* Potsdam, 1927

Schneider, F. J. *Die deutsche Dichtung vom Ausgang des Barocks bis zum Beginn des Klassizismus* (1700-85). (In *Epochen der deutschen Literatur.*) Stuttgart, 1924

Stammler, Wolfgang. *Von der Mystik bis zum Barock* (1400-1600). (In *Epochen der deutschen Literatur.*) Stuttgart, 1927

Alker, Ernst. *Geschichte der deutschen Literatur von Goethes Tod bis zur Gegenwart.* 2 vols. Stuttgart, 1949-50

Bieber, H. *Der Kampf um die Tradition: die deutsche Dichtung von 1830 bis 1880.* (In *Epochen der deutschen Literatur.*) Stuttgart, 1928

Cysarz, H. *Von Schiller bis Nietzsche.* Halle, 1927

Stammler, Wolfgang. *Deutsche Literatur vom Naturalismus bis zur Gegenwart.* Breslau, 1924. 2nd ed., 1927

Walzel, O. *Die deutsche Dichtung seit Goethes Tod.* Berlin, 2nd ed., 1920

Walzel, O. *Deutsche Dichtung von Gottsched bis zur Gegenwart.* In *Handbuch der Literaturwissenschaft,* ed. O. Walzel. Potsdam, 1928

Wiegler, Paul. *Geschichte der deutschen Literatur von der Romantik bis zur Gegenwart.* Berlin, 1930

RACIAL HISTORIES OF LITERATURE

Baechtold, J. *Geschichte der deutschen Literatur in der Schweiz.* New ed., Frauenfeld, 1919

Ermatinger, E. *Dichtung und Geistesleben der deutschen Schweiz.* Munich, 1933 Vol. 2, 1953

Jellinghaus, H. *Geschichte der mittelniederdeutschen Literatur.* (In the *Grundriss.*) 3rd ed., 1925

Kindermann, Heinz. *Wegweiser durch die moderne Literatur in Österreich.* Innsbruck, 1954

Krauss, R. *Schwäbische Literaturgeschichte.* 2 vols. Freiburg, 1897-99

Nadler, Josef. *Literaturgeschichte der deutschen Stämme und Landschaften.* 4 vols. Regensburg, 1912-32. 4th ed., 1938-41

Nadler, Josef. *Literaturgeschichte Österreichs.* Salzburg, 2nd ed., 1951

Nadler, Josef. *Literaturgeschichte der deutschen Schweiz.* Leipzig, 1932

VALUABLE WORKS OF REFERENCE

Körner, Josef. *Bibliographisches Handbuch des deutschen Schrifttums.* Berne, 3rd ed., 1949

Kosch, W. *Deutsches Literaturlexikon.* 2 vols. Halle, 2nd ed., 1928-30. Vol I, 1949, Vol II, 1953

Kindermann, Heinz, and Dietrich, Margarete. *Taschenlexikon der deutschen Literatur.* Stuttgart, 1951

Lennartz, Franz. *Die Dichter unserer Zeit. 250 Einzeldarstellungen zur deutschen Dichtung der Gegenwart.* Stuttgart, 5th ed., 1952

Merker, P., and Stammler, W. *Reallexikon der deutschen Literaturgeschichte.* Berlin, 1925-31

FROM MYSTICISM TO GOETHE

Series *Deutsche Literatur,* ed. Kindermann, Heinz:

   Kindermann, H. *Volksbücher des sterbenden Rittertums.* Leipzig, 1928

   Flemming, W. *Das Ordensdrama.* Leipzig, 1930

   Flemming, W. *Das schlesische Kunstdrama.* Leipzig, 1930

Benz, Richard. *Deutsches Barock. Kultur des 18. Jahrhunderts.* I. Teil, Stuttgart, 1949

Bruford, W. H. *Germany in the Eighteenth Century. The Social Background of Germany.* Cambridge, 1935

Butler, E. M. *The Tyranny of Greece over Germany.* Cambridge, 1935

Dilthey, W. *Das Erlebnis und die Dichtung.* (Lessing, Goethe, Novalis, Hölderlin.) Berlin and Leipzig, 1916

Ermatinger, E. *Barock und Rokoko in der deutschen Dichtung.* Leipzig, 1926

Garland, H. B. *Storm and Stress.* London, 1952

Gundolf, F. *Shakespeare und der deutsche Geist.* Berlin, 7th ed., 1923

Hettner, H. *Geschichte der deutschen Literatur im 18. Jahrhundert.* Ed. G. Witkowski. Leipzig, 1929

Kommerell, Max. *Der Dichter als Führer in der deutschen Klassik.* Berlin, 1928

Korff, H. A. *Geist der Goethezeit.* 4 vols. Leipzig, 1923-53

Köster, A. *Die deutsche Literatur der Aufklärungszeit.* Heidelberg, 1925

Pascal, Roy. *The German Sturm und Drang.* Manchester, 1953

Schneider, F. J. *Die deutsche Dichtung der Aufklärungszeit.* Stuttgart, 2nd ed., 1948

Strich, Fritz. *Goethe and World Literature.* London, 1949

Willoughby, L. A. *The Classical Age of German Literature.* Oxford, 1926

FROM ROMANTICISM TO NATURALISM

Benz, Richard. *Die deutsche Romantik. Geschichte einer geistigen Bewegung.* Leipzig, 4th ed., 1944

Haym, R. *Die romantische Schule.* 1870. 5th ed. by O. Walzel. Berlin, 1928

Huch, Ricarda. *Blütezeit der Romantik.* 3rd ed., 1908. *Ausbreitung und Verfall der Romantik.* Leipzig, 2nd ed., 1908. Together as *Die Romantik,* 1951

Kluckhohn, Paul. *Das Ideengut der deutschen Romantik.* Halle, 2nd ed., 1942

Kluckhohn, P. *Die deutsche Romantik.* Leipzig, 1924

Korff, H. A. *Geist der Goethezeit.* Vol. 3: *Frühromantik.* Vol. 4: *Hochromantik.* Leipzig, 1942-52

Lion, Ferdinand. *Romantik als deutsches Schicksal.* Stuttgart, 1947

Petersen, J. *Die Wesensbestimmung der deutschen Romantik.* Leipzig, 1926

Robertson, J. G. *The Genesis of Romantic Literary Theory.* London, 1923

Ruprecht, E. *Der Aufbruch der romantischen Bewegung.* Munich, 1948

Schultz, Franz. *Klassik und Romantik der Deutschen.* Stuttgart. Vol. 1, 1935. Vol. 2, 1952

Silz, W. *Early German Romanticism. Its Founders and Heinrich von Kleist.* Cambridge, Mass., 1939

Strich, Fritz. *Deutsche Klassik und Romantik oder Vollendung und Unendlichkeit. Ein Vergleich.* Munich, 3rd ed., 1928. Berne, 4th ed., 1949

Tymms, Ralph. *German Romantic Literature (1785-1830).* London, 1955

Walzel, O. *Deutsche Romantik. (Aus Natur und Geisteswelt.)* 2 vols. Leipzig, 1918

Willoughby, L. A. *The Romantic Movement in Germany.* Oxford, 1930

YOUNG GERMANY

Brandes, Georg. *Det unge Tyskland.* Copenhagen, 1890. English translation in *Main Currents in Nineteenth Century Literature,* Vol. 6, London, 1906

Butler, E. M. *The Saint-Simonian Religion in Germany: A Study of the Young German Movement.* Cambridge, 1926

Houben, H. H. *Jungdeutscher Sturm und Drang.* Leipzig, 1911

Petzet, Ch. *Die Blütezeit der deutschen politischen Lyrik,* 1840-50. Munich, 1903

Zäch, Alfred. *Der Realismus 1830-1885.* Berne, 1946

NATURALISM

Fischer, L. *Der Kampf um den Naturalismus.* Borna, 1930

Hanstein, H. von. *Das jüngste Deutschland.* 1900. Leipzig, 3rd ed., 1905

Heimatkunst

Bartels, A. *Heimatkunst*. Strassburg, 1916

Impressionism

Breysig, H. *Eindruckskunst und Ausdruckskunst*. Berlin, 1927

Hamann, R. *Der Impressionismus in Leben und Kunst*. Cologne, 1907. 2nd ed., Marburg, 1923

Expressionismus

Bahr, H. *Expressionismus*. Munich, 1918

Diebold, B. *Anarchie im Drama*. Frankfurt, 3rd ed., 1925

Edschmid, Kasimir. *Über den Expressionismus in der Literatur und die neue Dichtung*. Berlin, 1919

Martini, F. *Was war Expressionismus? Deutung und Auswahl seiner Lyrik*. Urach, 1948

Samuel, R., and Thomas, R. H. *Expressionism in German Life, Literature and the Theatre (1910-24)*. Cambridge, 1939

Schneider, F. J. *Der expressive Mensch und die deutsche Lyrik der Gegenwart*. Stuttgart, 1927

Utitz, E. *Die Überwindung des Expressionismus*. Stuttgart, 1927

Worringer, Wilhelm. *Nach-Expressionismus*. Leipzig, 1926

1880 to Today

Bartels, Adolf. *Die deutsche Literatur der Gegenwart*. Leipzig, 4th ed., 1901

Bithell, Jethro. *Modern German Literature 1880-1938*. London, 1939. 3rd ed., revised and enlarged, 1959

Kindermann, Heinz. *Das literarische Antlitz der Gegenwart*. Halle, 1930

Lange, Victor. *Modern German Literature 1870-1940*. New York, 1945

Mahrholz, W. *Deutsche Dichtung der Gegenwart*. Berlin, 1926

Meyer, R. M. *Die deutsche Literatur des XIXten und XXten Jahrhunderts*. 7th ed. Berlin, 1923

Mumbauer, J. *Die deutsche Dichtung der neuesten Zeit*. 2 vols. 1931-32

Naumann, Hans. *Die deutsche Dichtung der Gegenwart 1885-1933, vom Naturalismus bis zur Neuen Sachlichkeit*. Any edition before that of 1933, which is 'nazified'.

Soergel, Albert. *Dichtung und Dichter der Zeit*. Leipzig, 6th ed., 1922. *Neue Folge: Im Banne des Expressionismus*. 1925

Walzel, Oskar. *Deutsche Dichtung der Gegenwart*. Leipzig, 1925

Genres

DRAMA:

Arnold, R. F. *Das deutsche Drama*. Vienna, 1925

Arnold, R. F. *Das moderne Drama des XIX. Jahrhunderts*. Strassburg, 2nd ed., 1918

Bab, J. *Das Theater der Gegenwart*. Leipzig, 1928

Bruford, W. H. *Theatre, Drama, and Audience in Goethe's Germany*. London, 195

Busse, K. *Das Drama. (Aus Natur und Geisteswelt.)* 3 vols. Leipzig

Creizenach, W. *Geschichte des neueren Dramas*. Halle, 2nd ed., 1918-23

Eloesser, A. *Das bürgerliche Drama im 18. und 19. Jahrhundert*. Berlin, 1898

Freyhan, M. *Das Drama der Gegenwart*. Berlin, 1922

Holl, K. *Geschichte des deutschen Lustspiels*. Leipzig, 1923

Martersteig, M. *Das deutsche Theater im 19. Jahrhundert.* Leipzig, 2nd ed., 1924
Petsch, Robert. *Wesen und Formen des Dramas. Allgemeine Dramaturgie.* Halle, 1945
Rommell, W. *Die alt-Wiener Volkskomödie.* Wien, 1952
Stammler, W. *Deutsche Theatergeschichte.* Leipzig, 1925
Wiese, Benno von. *Die deutsche Tragödie von Lessing bis Hebbel.* 2 vols. Hamburg, 1948; 2nd ed., 1952

PROSE FICTION:

Geschichte des deutschen Romans von der Renaissance bis zu Goethes Tode. Series. *Deutsche Philologie im Aufriss.* Vol. 1, by Günther Weydt: *Vom 16. Jahrhundert bis zu Goethes Tode.* Vol. 2, by Rudolf Majut: *Vom Biedermeier bis zur Gegenwart.* Berlin and Bielefeld, 1955. 2nd ed., revised, 1959
Bennett, E. K. *A History of the German Novelle from Goethe to Thomas Mann.* Cambridge, 1934
Borcherdt, H. H. *Geschichte des Romans und der Novelle in Deutschland.* I. Teil *Vom frühen Mittelalter bis zu Wieland.* Leipzig, 1926
Böschenstein, H. *The German Novel 1939-44.* Toronto and London, 1949
Dresch, J. *Le roman social en Allemagne.* Paris, 1913
Hewett-Thayer, H. W. *The Modern German Novel.* Boston, 1924
Mielke, H., and Homann, H. J. *Der deutsche Roman des 19. und 20. Jahrhunderts.* Dresden, 5th ed., 1920
Petsch, Robert. *Wesen und Formen der Erzählkunst.* Halle, 2nd ed., 1942
Pongs, H. *Im Umbruch der Zeit. Das Romanschaffen der Gegenwart.* Göttingen, 1952
Rehm, Walther. *Geschichte des deutschen Romans.* 2 vols. Berlin and Leipzig, 1927
Scheidweiler, P. *Der Roman der deutschen Romantik.* Leipzig and Berlin, 1916
Spiero, Heinrich. *Geschichte des deutschen Romans.* Berlin, 1950

LYRIC POETRY:

Benn, Gottfried. *Probleme der Lyrik.* Wiesbaden, 1951
Closs, A. *Die neuere deutsche Lyrik vom Barock bis zur Gegenwart.* Series *Deutsche Philologie im Aufriss.* Berlin und Bielefeld, 1952 and 1955
Ermatinger, E. *Die deutsche Lyrik in ihrer geschichtlichen Entwicklung von Herde bis zur Gegenwart.* 3 vols. Leipzig and Berlin, 2nd ed., 1925
Kayser, W. *Geschichte der deutschen Ballade.* Berlin, 1936
Kommerell, Max. *Gedanken über Gedichte.* Frankfurt, 1948
Prawer, P. S. *German Lyric Poetry. A Critical Analysis of selected poems from Klopstock to Rilke.* London, 1952
Viëtor, Karl. *Geschichte der deutschen Ode.* Munich, 1923

ANTHOLOGIES:

Braun, Felix. *Der tausendjährige Rosenstrauch. Deutsche Gedichte aus tausend Jahren.* Vienna, 1949
Closs, A., and Mainland, F. W. *German Lyrics of the 17th Century.* London, 1947
Deutsche Gedichte. Eine Auswahl von den Merseburger Zaubersprüchen bis zu Dichtungen der Lebenden. In *Sammlung Dieterich.* Wiesbaden, 1949
Wehrli, Max. *Deutsche Barocklyrik.* In *Sammlung Klosterberg.* Basel, 1945

Bithell, Jethro. *An Anthology of German Poetry 1730-1830.* London, 1957
Bithell, Jethro. *An Anthology of German Poetry 1830-1880.* London, 1947
Bithell, Jethro. *An Anthology of German Poetry 1880-1940.* London, 1941. 6th ed., 1951
Forster, Leonhard. *The Penguin Book of German Verse.* London, 1957
Groll, Gunter. *De Profundis. Deutsche Lyrik in dieser Zeit. Eine Anthologie aus zwölf Jahren.* Munich, 1946
Pinthus, K. *Menschheitsdämmerung.* (Expressionistic verse.) Leipzig, 1919
Holthusen, Hans Egon, and Friedrich Kemp. *Ergriffenes Dasein. Deutsche Lyrik 1900-50.* Ebenhausen bei München, 1953

INDIVIDUAL WRITERS

LESSING:

Garland, H. B. *Lessing.* Cambridge, 1937
Kettner, G. *Lessings Dramen im Lichte ihrer und unserer Zeit.* Berlin, 1904
Oehlke, W. *Lessing und seine Zeit.* 2 vols. Munich, 1919
Schmidt, Erich. *Lessing: Geschichte seines Lebens und seiner Schriften.* 2 vols. Berlin, 4th ed., 1923
Wagner, A. M. *Lessing.* Berlin, 1931

HAMANN:

Nadler, Josef. *Johann Georg Hamann.* Salzburg, 1949
Unger, R. *Hamann und die Aufklärung.* Berlin, 1911. Reprint 1925

HERDER:

Bäte, L. *Johann Gottfried Herder. Der Weg – Das Werk – Die Zeit.* Stuttgart, 1949
Gillies, A. *Herder.* Oxford, 1945
Haym, R. *Herder.* 2 vols. Berlin, 1880-85
Kühnemann, E. *Herder.* Munich, 3rd ed., 1927
McEachran, F. *The Life and Philosophy of J. G. Herder.* Oxford, 1939

WIELAND:

Sengle, F. *Wieland. Sein Leben, sein Werk, seine Welt.* Stuttgart, 1949

GOETHE:

Bielschowsky, A. *Goethe: sein Leben und seine Werke.* Munich, 1895-1903; 42nd ed., 1922; revised edition by W. Linden, 1928
Butler, E. M. *The Fortunes of Faust.* Cambridge, 1952
Croce, B. *Goethe.* Bari, 1919. English translation, London, 1923
Fairley, Barker. *Goethe: as revealed in his poetry.* London, 1932
Fairley, Barker. *A Study of Goethe.* Oxford, 1947
Fairley, Barker. *Goethe's Faust. Six Essays.* Oxford, 1953
Fuchs, A. *Goethe: Un Homme face à la vie.* Paris, 1948
Hume Brown, H. *Life of Goethe.* 2 vols. London, 1920
Ibel, R. *Der junge Goethe 1765-1775.* Bremen, 1949
Lewes, G. H. *The Life and Works of Goethe, 1749-1832.* London 1855; in Everyman's Library, 1855
Meyer, R. M. *Goethe.* Berlin, 1894. 4th ed., 1913

Müller, Günther. *Kleine Goethebiographie.* Bonn, 1948
Rose, W. (editor). *Essays on Goethe.* London, 1949
Robertson, J. G. *Life and Work of Goethe.* London, 1932
Staiger, Emil. *Goethe 1749-1786.* Vol. I. Zürich, 1952
Viëtor, Karl. *Goethe. Dichtung, Wissenschaft, Weltbild.* Berne, 1949
Witkop, P. *Goethe.* Stuttgart, 1931
Zeitler, J. *Goethe-Handbuch.* 3 vols. Stuttgart, 1916-18

SCHILLER:

Buchwald. *Schiller.* 2 vols. Leipzig, 1937
Cysarz, H. *Schiller.* Halle, 1934
Garland, H. B. *Schiller.* London, 1949
Gerhard, Melitta. *Schiller.* Berne, 1950
Kühnemann, E. *Schiller und seine Welt.* Leipzig, 1934
Witte, W. *Schiller.* Oxford, 1949

GRILLPARZER:

Alker, Ernst. *Franz Grillparzer.* Marburg, 1930
Auernheimer, R. *Franz Grillparzer.* Vienna, 1948
Nadler, Josef. *Franz Grillparzer.* Vaduz, 1948
Nolte, F. O. *Grillparzer, Lessing and Goethe in the Perspective of European Literature.* Lancaster, Pa., 1938
Pollak, G. *Grillparzer and the Austrian Drama.* New York, 1907
Yates, Douglas. *Franz Grillparzer.* Vol. I. Oxford, 1946

HÖLDERLIN:

Bertaux, P. *Hölderlin.* Paris, 1935
Böckmann, Paul. *Hölderlin und seine Götter.* Munich, 1935
Boehm, W. *Hölderlins Leben.* 2 vols. Halle, 1928-30
Guardini, Romano. *Hölderlin: Weltbild und Frömmigkeit.* Leipzig, 1939
Heidegger, M. *Erläuterungen zu Hölderlins Dichtung.* Frankfurt, 1944; 2nd ed., 1951
Michel, W. *Das Leben Hölderlins.* Bremen, 2nd ed., 1948
Peacock, R. *Hölderlin.* London, 1938
Salzberger, L. S. *Hölderlin.* Cambridge, 1952
Stahl, E. L. *Hölderlin's Symbolism.* Oxford, 1945
Stansfield, Agnes. *Hölderlin.* Manchester, 1945

NOVALIS:

Beheim-Schwarzbach, Martin. *Novalis.* Stuttgart, 1939. 2nd ed., 1948
Hederer, Edgar. *Novalis.* Vienna, 1949

JEAN PAUL:

Kommerell, Max. *Jean Paul.* 1935. 2nd ed., 1939

ZACHARIAS WERNER:

Stuckert, Franz. *Das Drama Zacharias Werners.* Frankfurt, 1836

KLEIST:

Ayrault, R. *Heinrich von Kleist.* Paris, 1934
Blankenagel, J. C. *The Drama of Heinrich von Kleist.* London, 1931
Brahm, Otto. *Heinrich von Kleist.* 1844, 4th ed., 1911

Braig, F. *Heinrich von Kleist*. Munich, 1925
Kohrs, I. *Das Wesen des Tragischen im Drama Heinrichs von Kleist*. Marburg, 1951
March, Richard. *Heinrich von Kleist*. Cambridge, 1954
Martini, F. *Heinrich von Kleist und die geschichtliche Welt*. Berlin, 1940
Stahl, E. L. *The Dramas of Heinrich von Kleist*. Oxford, 1948

TIECK:

Minder, Robert. *Un poète romantique allemand: Ludwig Tieck*. Paris, 1936
Zeydel, E. H. *Ludwig Tieck, the German Romanticist*. Princeton, 1935

JOHANN ELIAS SCHLEGEL:

Wilkinson, Elizabeth M. *Johann Elias Schlegel, a Pioneer in Æsthetics*. Oxford, 1945

FRIEDRICH SCHLEGEL:

Mann, Otto. *Der junge Friedrich Schlegel*. Berlin, 1932

ARNIM:

Guignard, R. *Achim von Arnim*. Paris, 1936
Seidel, Ina. *Achim von Arnim*. Stuttgart, 1944

BRENTANO:

PFEIFFER-BELLI, W. *Clemens Brentano*. Freiburg *i*/B., 1947
Seidel, Ina. *Clemens Brentano*. Stuttgart, 1944

EICHENDORFF:

Brandenburg, H. *J. von Eichendorff, sein Leben und Werk*. Munich, 1922
Kunz, J. *Eichendorff. Höhepunkt und Krise der Spätromantik*. Oberursel, 1951

DROSTE-HÜLSHOFF:

Heselhaus, Clemens. *Annette von Droste-Hülshoff. Das Leben einer Dichterin*. Halle, 1943
Staiger, E. *Annette von Droste-Hülshoff*. Zurich, 1933

HEINE:

Atkins, H. G. *Heine*. London, 1929
Brod, Max. *Heinrich Heine*. Amsterdam, 1934. Revised ed. in English (translated by Joseph Witriol), London, 1956
Marcuse, L. *Heinrich Heine*. Hamburg, 1951
Mauclair, Camille. *La vie humiliée de Henri Heine*. Paris, 1930
Untermeyer, L. *Heinrich Heine: Paradox and Poet*. New York, 1937
Walter, H. *H. Heine*. London and Toronto, 1930
Wolff, H. J. *Heinrich Heine*. 2 vols. Munich, 1922

IMMERMANN:

Maync, Harry. *Karl Immermann. Der Mann und sein Werk im Rahmen der Zeit- und Literaturgeschichte*. Munich, 1921
Porterfield, A. W. *Immermann: A Study in German Realism*. New York, 1911

PLATEN:

Schlösser, R. *August Graf von Platen*. 2 vols. Munich, 1910-13

LENAU:

Bischoff, H. *Nikolaus Lenaus Lyrik*. 2 vols. Berlin, 1920-21
Reynaud, L. *Lenau et le lyrisme autrichien*. Paris, 1923

UHLAND:

Schneider, H. *Uhland. Leben, Dichtung, Forschung.* Berlin, 1920

MÖRIKE:

Goes, Albrecht. *Mörike.* Stuttgart, 1938
Mare, Margaret. *Eduard Mörike: The Man and the Poet.* London, 1957
Maync, H. *Eduard Mörike: sein Leben und Dichten.* Stuttgart, 4th ed., 1927. Revised ed., 1944
Wiese, Benno von. *Eduard Mörike.* Tübingen, 1950

E. T. A. HOFFMANN:

Bergengruen, Werner. *E. T. A. Hoffmann.* Stuttgart, 1948
Hewett-Thayer, H. W. *E. T. A. Hoffmann.* Princeton, 1948
Ricci, J. F. A. *E. T. A. Hoffmann.* Paris, 1947

GRABBE:

Schneider, F. J. *Christian Dietrich Grabbe. Persönlichkeit und Werk.* Munich, 1934

HEBBEL:

Meyer-Benfey, H. *Hebbels Dramen.* Göttingen, 1913
Purdie, E. *Friedrich Hebbel: A Study of his Life and Works.* Oxford, 1932
Rees, G. B. *Friedrich Hebbel as a dramatic artist.* London, 1930
Ziegler, K. *Mensch und Welt in der Tragödie Friedrich Hebbels.* Berlin, 1938

BÜCHNER:

Büttner, Ludwig. *Georg Büchner, Reaktionär und Pessimist.* Nuremberg, 1948
Knight, A. H. J. *Georg Büchner.* Oxford, 1951
Majut, Rudolf. *Lebensbühne und Marionette.* Germ. Studien, Vol. 100. Berlin, 1931
Majut, Rudolf. *Studien um Büchner: Untersuchungen zur Geschichte der problematischen Natur.* Germ. Studien, Vol. 121. Berlin, 1932
Mayer, Hans. *Georg Büchner und seine Zeit.* Wiesbaden, 1948
Oppel, Horst. *Die tragische Dichtung Georg Büchners.* Stuttgart, 1951
Viëtor, Karl. *Georg Büchner. Politik – Dichtung – Wissenschaft.* Berne, 1949

OTTO LUDWIG:

Mis, Léon. *Les œuvres dramatiques d'Otto Ludwig.* Lille, 1922-25
Raphael, G. *Otto Ludwig, ses théories et ses œuvres romanesques.* Paris, 1920

GOTTFRIED KELLER:

Baechtold, G. J. *Kellers Leben, Briefe und Tagebücher.* 3 vols. Stuttgart, 1915-16. 5th ed., enlarged by E. Ermatinger, Berlin, 1920
Böschenstein, H. *Gottfried Keller.* Berne, 1948
Faësi, R. *Gottfried Keller.* Berne, 1932
Maync, H. *Gottfried Keller. Sein Bildnis und seine Werke.* Frauenfeld, 1923
Stoessl, O. *Gottfried Keller.* Berlin, 1904. 2nd ed., 1921

C. F. MEYER:

Burkhard, A. *Conrad Ferdinand Meyer, the Style and the Man.* New York, 1932
Frey, A. *Conrad Ferdinand Meyer: sein Leben und seine Werke.* Stuttgart, 4th ed., 1925
Lerber, H. von. *Conrad Ferdinand Meyer.* Basel, 1949
Maync, H. *Conrad Ferdinand Meyer und sein Werk.* Munich, 6125

GOTTHELF:

Waidson, H. M. *Jeremias Gotthelf. An Introduction to the Swiss Novelist.* Oxford, 1953

PAUL HEYSE:

Petzet, E. *Paul Heyse, ein deutscher Lyriker.* Leipzig, 1914

RAABE:

Fehse, Wilhelm. *Wilhelm Raabe. Sein Leben und seine Werke.* Brunswick, 1937

STORM:

Heitmann, H. *Theodor Storm.* Stuttgart, 1943
Schütze, P., and Lange, E. *Theodor Storms Leben und Dichtungen.* Berlin, 4th ed., 1925
Stuckert, Franz. *Theodor Storm.* Tübingen, 1952

FONTANE:

Seidel, H. W. *Theodor Fontane.* Stuttgart, 1942
Wandrey, Konrad. *Theodor Fontane.* Munich, 1919

STIFTER:

Blackall, E. A. *Adalbert Stifter.* Cambridge, 1948
Hohoff, C. *Adalbert Stifter.* Düsseldorf, 1949
Lunding, Erik. *Adalbert Stifter.* Copenhagen, 1946
Michels, J. *Adalbert Stifter. Leben, Werk und Wirken.* Leipzig, 3rd ed., 1943

WAGNER:

Chamberlain, Houston Stewart. *Richard Wagner.* Munich, 7th ed., 1923
Lichtenberger, H. *Wagner poète et penseur.* Paris, 4th ed., 1907

NIETZSCHE:

Andler, C. *Friedrich Nietzsche: sa vie et sa pensée.* Paris, 1920-28
Bertram, Ernst. *Nietzsche. Versuch einer Mythologie.* Berlin, 1918, 9th ed., 1929
Jaspers, Karl. *Nietzsche.* Berlin, 1936
Knight, A. H. J. *Some aspects of the Life and Work of Nietzsche and particularly of his connection with Greek Literature and Thought.* Cambridge, 1933
Knight, G. Wilson, *Christ and Nietzsche.* London, 1948
Lavrin, Janko. *Nietzsche.* London, 1948

GERHART HAUPTMANN:

Bab, Julius. *Gerhart Hauptmann und seine besten Bühnenwerke.* Berlin, 1922
Behl, C. F. W., and Voigt, Felix A. *Gerhart Hauptmanns Leben. Chronik und Bild.* Berlin, 1942
Garten, Hugh F. *Gerhart Hauptmann.* Cambridge, 1954
Gregor, Joseph. *Gerhart Hauptmann. Das Werk und unsere Zeit.* Vienna, 1952
Schlenther, Paul. *Gerhart Hauptmann. Leben und Werke. Umgearbeitet und erweitert von Arthur Eloesser.* Berlin, 1922
Voigt, Felix A. *Antike und antikes Lebensgefühl im Werke Gerhart Hauptmanns.* Breslau, 1935

HUGO VON HOFMANNSTHAL:

Heuschele, Otto. *Hugo von Hofmannsthal. Dank und Gedächtnis.* Freiburg, 1949
Naef, Carl J. *Hugo von Hofmannsthals Wesen und Werk.* Zurich, 1938

STEFAN GEORGE:

Boehringer, Robert. *Mein Bild von Stefan George.* Düsseldorf, 1951
David, Claude. *Stefan George.* Lyons and Paris, 1952
Gundolf, Friedrich. *George.* Berlin, 1921
Jost, Dominik. *Stefan George und seine Elite.* Zurich, 1949
Morwitz, Ernst. *Die Dichtung Stefan Georges.* Berlin, 1934, and Godesberg, 1948
Salin, Edgar. *Um Stefan George.* Godesberg, 1948
Verwey, A. *Mein Verhältnis zu Stefan George.* Strassburg, 1936. (Translation of *Mijn verhouding tot Stefan George*)
Wolters, Friedrich. *Stefan George und die Blätter für die Kunst.* Berlin, 1930

RILKE:

Andreas-Salomé, Lou. *Rainer Maria Rilke.* Leipzig, 1928
Angelloz, J. F. *Rilke. Évolution spirituelle d'un poète.* Paris, 1952
Belmore, H. W. *Rilke's Craftsmanship.* Oxford, 1953
Buddeberg, Else. *Rainer Maria Rilke.* Stuttgart, 1955
Butler, E. M. *Rainer Maria Rilke.* Cambridge, 1941
Demetz, Peter. *René Rilkes Prager Jahre.* Düsseldorf, 1953
Günther, Werner. *Weltinnenraum. Die Dichtung Rainer Maria Rilkes.* Bielefeld, 1953
Holthusen, H. E. *Rilkes Sonette an Orpheus.* Munich, 1937
Holthusen, H. E. *Der späte Rilke.* Zurich, 1949
Holthusen, H. E. *Rilke.* Translated by J. P. Stern. In *Studies in Modern European Literature and Thought.* Cambridge, 1952
Kippenberg, Katharina. *Rainer Maria Rilkes Duineser Elegien und Sonette an Orpheus.* Wiesbaden, 1946
Mason, Eudoc. *Rilke's Apotheosis.* Oxford, 1938
Mason, Eudoc. *Lebenshaltung und Symbolik bei Rainer Maria Rilke.* Weimar, 1939
Olivero, F. *Rainer Maria Rilke. A Study in Poetry and Mysticism.* Cambridge, 1931
Ritzer, W. *Rainer Maria Rilke-Bibliographie.* Vienna, 1951
Rose, William, and Craig Houston, Gertrude. *Rainer Maria Rilke. Aspects of his Mind and Poetry.* London, 1938
Schröder, R. *Rainer Maria Rilke.* Zurich, 1952
Wydenbruck, Nora. *Rilke, Man and Poet. A biographical study.* London, 1949

THOMAS MANN:

Blume, Bernhard. *Thomas Mann und Goethe.* Berne, 1949
Cleugh, James. *Thomas Mann. A Study.* London, 1933
Eichner, H. *Thomas Mann. Eine Einführung in sein Werk.* Berne, 1953
Eloesser, A. *Thomas Mann, sein Leben und sein Werk.* Berlin, 1925
Hatfield, Henry. *Thomas Mann: an Introduction to his Fiction.* London, 1952
Heller, Erich. *The Ironic German.* London, 1958
Lesser, Jonas. *Thomas Mann in der Epoche seiner Vollendung.* Munich, 1952
Mayer, Hans. *Thomas Mann. Werk und Entwicklung.* Berlin, 1950

HERMANN HESSE:

Bode, H. *Hermann Hesse.* Frankfurt, 1948
Engel, O. *Hermann Hesse. Dichtung und Gedanke.* Stuttgart, 1947
Hafner, G. *Hermann Hesse, Werk und Leben.* Reinbek, 1947

RICARDA HUCH:

Bäumer, G. *Ricarda Huch*. Tübingen, 1949
Hoppe, Else. *Ricarda Huch. Weg – Persönlichkeit – Werk*. Stuttgart, 1951

THEODOR FONTANE:

Seidel, H. W. *Theodor Fontane*. Stuttgart, 1942
Wandrey, Konrad. *Theodor Fontane*. Munich, 1919

FRANZ KAFKA:

Beissner, F. *Der Erzähler Franz Kafka*. Stuttgart, 1952
Brod, Max. *Franz Kafkas Glauben und Lehre*. Munich, 1948
Neider, Charles. *Kafka. His Mind and Art*. London, 1949
Reiss, H. S. *Franz Kafka. Eine Betrachtung seines Werkes*. Heidelberg, 1952

HANS CAROSSA:

Haueis, Albert. *Hans Carossa*. Weimar, 1935
Hesse, Otto Ernst. *Hans Carossa*. Tübingen, 1929
Langen, August. *Hans Carrosa. Weltbild und Stil*. Berlin, 1955

ERNST JÜNGER:

Becher, H. *Ernst Jünger. Mensch und Werk*. Warendorf, 1949
Loose, Gerhard. *Ernst Jünger. Gestalt und Werk*. Frankfurt, 1957
Müller-Schwefe, E. *Ernst Jünger*. Wuppertal, 1951
Nebel, G. *Ernst Jünger*. Wuppertal, 1949
Paetel, H. *Ernst Jünger. Weg und Wirkung*. Stuttgart, 1948
Stern, J. P. *Ernst Jünger*. Cambridge, 1953

MONOGRAPHS ON RECENT WRITERS

Kindermann, Heinz. *Hermann Bahr*. Graz-Cologne, 1954
Bänziger, H. *Werner Bergengruen. Weg und Werk*. Thal, 1950
Klemm, Gunther. *Werner Bergengruen*. Wuppertal, 1949
Bab, Julius. *Richard Dehmel*. Leipzig, 1926
Freyhan, M. *Georg Kaisers Werk*. Berlin, 1925
Koenigsgarten, H. F. *Georg Kaiser*. Potsdam, 1928
Jappe, H. *Gertrud von le Fort*. Meran, 1950
Maync, H. *Detlev von Liliencron*. Berlin, 1920
Ihering, H. *Heinrich Mann*. Berlin, 1951
Schroeder, Walter. *Heinrich Mann*. Vienna, 1932
Liptzin, Solomon. *Arthur Schnitzler*. New York, 1932
Gottschalk, R. *Carl Spitteler*. Zurich, 1928
Boeschenstein, Hermann. *Hermann Stehr*. Breslau, 1935
Riemerscheid, Werner. *Georg Trakl*. Vienna, 1947
Bing, Siegmund. *Jakob Wassermann*. Berlin, 1929. *Erweiterte Ausgabe*, 1933
Blankenagel, J. C. *The Writings of Jakob Wassermann*. Boston, 1942
Kutscher, A. *F. Wedekind*. 3 vols. Munich, 1924
Koch, F. *Josef Weinheber*. Munich, 1942
Nadler, Josef. *Josef Weinheber*. Salzburg, 1952
Stuhrmann, L. *Josef Weinheber. Rausch und Mass*. Warendorf, 1951
Specht, R. *Franz Werfel*. Vienna, 1926
Puttkamer, A. von. *Franz Werfel*. Würzburg, 1952
Ebeling, Hans. *Ernst Wiechert*. Wiesbaden, 1947
Ollesch, H. *Ernst Wiechert*. Wuppertal, 1949

o

CHAPTER XI

GERMAN THOUGHT

I. STRUCTURE OF GERMAN PHILOSOPHIC THOUGHT

GENERAL

THE celebrated words of Fichte in the *Erste Einleitung in die Wissenschaftslehre*: 'The kind of philosophy a man chooses depends upon the kind of man he is', holds good, not only for individuals, but also for peoples. A people does not 'decide' for a given line of thinking any more than an individual 'chooses' his philosophy. It is born in them:

> *Und keine Zeit und keine Macht zerstückelt*
> *Geprägte Form, die lebend sich entwickelt.*

To use Goethe's word, this is their '*Daimon*'. But a people does not merely choose a philosophy as a whole: it chooses also, according to its national character, the particular viewpoints from which it will consider that whole. Such viewpoints are: the relationship of the mind with the outer world (Epistemology, *Erkenntnistheorie*); relationship with the origin and the meaning of Being (Metaphysics); relationship with Nature as the creative and created Force (Natural Philosophy); relationship with the reflection of life in Art (Æsthetics); relationship with acts of willing (Ethics); relationship with the community (Philosophy of the State). Formal Logic, Psychology, and Pedagogy, being practical and auxiliary sciences, are the least affected by national bias.

Of all these sections of philosophy, metaphysics has had the strongest attraction for German thought. Not that it has neglected the others – natural philosophy least of all; but it has often approached them in such a manner that they have been to some extent restricted, as it were, to becoming facets of the greater metaphysical crystal. This is especially true for Ethics, as treatment of this subject by Kant and even more by Fichte, Schelling, Hegel and Schopenhauer shows quite clearly. This does not mean that the practical aspect of Ethics, Moral Science, has been overlooked in German thought, but it is not one of its characteristic features. Characteristic is rather the apodictic way of the acceptance of moral truth: *Das Moralische versteht sich immer von selbst.* 'What is moral is no problem to be argued about: it is self-evident.' (F. Th. v. Vischer, in his philosophic novel *Auch Einer,* 1887.)

SECTION I. THE STATE

With this reservation made, ethics occupies in German thought just as important a place as in that of other peoples, except that in Germany it has been shifted in a peculiar way from the individual to the general community. In other words, the German philosophy of the State is basically an ethical philosophy; it sees the ethical individual life with its obligation to the sum of the ethical life of the State, with the object of attaining a form of society where both untrammelled economic security and untrammelled personal freedom shall be assured to the citizen. This ethical principle is not democratic, but socialist in the sense of a broadly free State socialism. If we disregard early ideas of this nature in Goethe's *Wilhelm Meisters Wanderjahre,* we see this line of thought running from Fichte's *Der geschlossene Handelsstaat* (1800) to Rathenau's *Von kommenden Dingen* (1918) and Spengler's *Preussentum und Sozialismus* (1919), three works of different character but all tending in the same direction. This basically ethical conception of the State in the minds of Germans has nothing to do with their alleged worship of the State as an idol. This pseudo-scientific myth – like most myths of its kind – arose in Germany itself and goes back in some measure to Schopenhauer's attacks on Hegel. John Stuart Mill in his classical essay *On Liberty* took as epigraph a passage, not from the English, but from the German philosophy of the State: 'Few persons, out of Germany, even comprehend the meaning of the doctrine which Wilhelm von Humboldt, so eminent both as a *savant* and as a politician, made the text of a treatise – that "the end of man, or that which is prescribed by the eternal or immutable dictates of reason, and not suggested by vague and transient desires, is the highest and most harmonious development of his powers to a complete and consistent whole."' (*The Sphere and Duties of Government,* from the German of Wilhelm von Humboldt, pp. 11-13: *Ideen zu einem Versuch, die Grenzen der Wirksamkeit eines Staates zu bestimmen.* Publ. in part 1792, complete in 1851.)

Hegel's conception of the State is the completion, not the contradiction of Humboldt's: '*Der Staat ist die Wirklichkeit der sittlichen Idee*' (*Grundlinien der Philosophie des Rechts,* 1880; *Werke,* ed. G. Lasson, Leipzig, 1905 ss. VI, 195). 'The State is the actuality of the ethical idea.' (*Hegel's Philosophy of Right,* transl. T. M. Knox, Oxford, 1942, p. 155, par. 257.) 'The State, in and by itself, is the ethical whole, the actualization of freedom; and it is an absolute end of reason that freedom should be actual' (l.c., VI, 349, note 152 to par. 258; Knox's transl. p. 279). Fichte goes even further: 'Freedom, in the actions of external life also, is the fostering soil for higher culture; a legislation which has the latter in view will give to the former the fullest scope possible, even at the risk that . . . governing may become somewhat more difficult and laborious.' (*Reden an die deutsche Nation*, 1807-8; 8th Lecture, Reclam ed. p. 119.) For, as a merely human institution, the State is nothing but a means to an ultimate end: morality. Its perfecting automatically makes the State unnecessary and brings it to an end. (*Posthumous Works*, Berlin 1834, II, 512.)

These quotations from Humboldt, Hegel and Fichte should serve as a grave warning against certain English books on the German (or 'Prussian') mentality, whose titles are better abandoned to oblivion. The passages may further emphasize in a signal manner the opinion expressed above, that in German philosophy even those sections which are not actually metaphysical themselves are often clothed in metaphysical thought. The following analysis is meant to explain the structure of this thought; it seeks to reduce the fundamental tendencies of German Metaphysics to the three ideas of 'Polarity', of 'Becoming' and of 'Intuition' (*Polarität, Werden*, and *Anschauung*).

Section 2. Polarity

The German conception of the universe is neither 'dualistic' nor 'monistic', but 'polar monistic'. That is to say, the fundamental forces which underlie the process of life and which keep it in action are 'contradictory' principles (not 'contrary' ones, as they are in Dualism, or 'identical' ones, as they are in Monism), which affect each other reciprocally, and which, in the intellectual sphere as in the physical, reveal themselves as a unity only in their dialectic correlation. If we wish to pursue the philosophic expression of this ontological process as far back as we are able to go, we must delve down into the pre-German, the common Teutonic stratum. We shall find that in contrast to the Monism of ancient Greek Hylozoism (a doctrine which regards matter as endowed with a living spirit), and to the Dualism of ancient Semitic Biblicism, the primitive Teutonic cosmogony as described in the Edda unmistakably shows a polar character. Out of heat and cold, friendliness and hostility, arises primeval life, Ymir. (*Snorra Edda*, Section *Gylfaginning*, 4.) In the Ginnungagap, the 'yawning abyss', one may recognize an earlier mythological form of what Jakob Böhme (p. 240) about 1600 called the *Ungrund*: 'an everlasting nothing, a silence without qualities or colours.' (*Sex Puncta Theosophica*, 1, 29.) In the *Ungrund*, where God is immanent, Nature brings herself to birth as a consequence of the division of His primordial will into two opposing principles. Arising out of this first immanently polar act follow all others, up to the self-division of the spirit into consciousness of self. Everything consists of a yet unseparated 'Yes' and 'No', from the primordial realm of God up to the third realm, the realm of phenomena, 'which was created out of the realm of darkness as well as the realm of light, for which reason it is both evil and good, cruel and kind'. (*Ibid.*, II, 37.)

The Ontogony of Böhme, the *'Philosophus Teutonicus'*, is taken up and developed further by Schelling (p. 421) in his book *Über das Wesen der menschlichen Freiheit* (1809). As early as 1798, in his essay *Von der Weltseele*, that is to say before he underwent the influence of Böhme, Schelling explained the basic process of all Being as polar. He held fast to this conception throughout all the phases of his philosophic development. In the essay which ushers in his later period, *Die Weltalter*, he is still writing: 'Antithesis eternally begets itself in order to be consumed by unity, and the antithesis is eternally consumed by the unity in order to revive itself ever anew.... This movement may also be conceived as a systole and diastole.' (1811 and onwards; first publ. posthumously in the *Works*, Stuttgart, 1856 ff., Division I, vol. VIII, pp. 230 and 231. English transl. by F. de Wolfe Bolman Jr., New York, 1942, pp. 117 and 118.) With this, we find ourselves immediately in contact with Goethe, who declared that in Schelling's insight he recognized his own:

> *Die endliche Ruhe wird nur verspürt,*
> *Sobald der Pol den Pol berührt.*
> *Drum danket Gott, ihr Söhne der Zeit,*
> *Dass er die Pole für ewig entzweit.*

The in and out movement of air in breathing is accordingly for Goethe a symbolically graphic illustration of what he recognized to be the basic rhythm of all life, the alternating processes of systole and diastole, contraction and expansion. At the same time, as a student of Spinoza (p. 435), he knows very well that in the Fount of all Being, to whom is given the name 'God', the divided poles fall together, as spring water returns again to its source. This *coincidentia oppositorum* is formulated in the language of mysticism by Spinoza's contemporary, Johannes Scheffler (Angelus Silesius, p. 241) as follows:

> *Im Eins ist alles eins; kehrt Zwei zurück hinein,*
> *So ist es wesentlich mit ihm ein ew'ges Ein.*

This is how Goethe, in *Zahme Xenien*, expresses the same thought:

> *Und alles Drängen, alles Ringen*
> *Ist ewige Ruh in Gott dem Herrn.*

Friedrich Hebbel (1813-63), a poet-thinker like Goethe, arrives as a

dramatist and a philosopher at the conception of complete contradiction
in all things: 'Dualism runs through all our views and thoughts, through
each single phase of our existence; it is our highest, last conception;
beyond it we have absolutely no basic idea. How life and death, health
and ill-health, time and eternity stand in contrast we can think and represent to ourselves, but not that which as a common, reconciling and
atoning force, lies behind these divided dualities.' (*Diary*, 2nd December
1840; transl. quoted from G. B. Rees, *Friedrich Hebbel as a Dramatic
Artist*, London, 1930, p. 11.) In Section 3 of our exposition we shall come
upon other thinkers in whose philosophy the principle of polarity occupies a central place. In order to avoid repetition they are being omitted
here, and it will suffice to mention that even for Romano Guardini
(1885–), the leading religious philosopher of Catholicism in Germany,
polarity is the basic phenomenon of life:

> Ob es sich nun um anatomisch-physiologische oder emotionale, intellektuelle
> oder gemeinschaftlich bezogene Erscheinungen handelt: Gegensätzlichkeit ist
> Erscheinungsweise, Bauform, Wirkstruktur des Lebens.
>
> (*Der Gegensatz*, 1925, p. 179)

This law of Polarity – Guardini prefers the designation 'enantiological
structure' – determines all spheres of intellectual, physical and social life.
As a religious conception it continues from ancient Germanic thought,
on through the post-medieval theosophies of the Protestant Böhme and
the Catholic Scheffler, through the unclerical humanism of Goethe and
Hebbel and the semi-clerical humanism of Schelling, as far as the clerical
humanism of the priest Guardini. This universal feeling is also at the root
of those formulations so frequent in German poetry of the alternating
interplay of joy and sorrow, which can be pointed out from the earliest
times:

> *als ie diu liebe leide ze allerjungiste git.*
>
> (*Nibelungenlied* A, 2315)
>
> (as enjoyment of love always gives pain in the end.)
>
> *swem nie von liebe leit geschach,*
> *dem geschach auch liep von liebe nie.*
>
> (Gottfried, *Tristan und Isolde*, 204 f.)
>
> (Whoso never felt pain from love, never felt delight from love.)

Or, in more generalized form:

> *alsus vert diu mennischheit*
> *hiute freude, morgen leit.*
>
> (Wolfram, *Parzival*, 103, 23 f.)
>
> (Thus there comes to all mankind
> Joy today, tomorrow pain.)

In the abstract language of Böhme:

> *Es ist keine Eigenschaft von der andern abgetrennt, sondern eine jede gibt die andere.*   (*Sex Puncta Theosophica*, IX 20.)

Schopenhauer's theory of the dialectic polarity between pain and tedium also belongs in this connection. (*Die Welt als Wille und Vorstellung*, I, par. 57.)

Finally, with this polar, antithetic character of the German attitude of mind to the world, there is also bound up another phenomenon, which scarcely appears in the literature of any other people. For there repeatedly occur at approximately the same date pairs of works (mostly novels) which express in a representative way the thought and feeling of their period, and yet in such a manner that the vision of the one springs from the intellect and that of the other from feelings. There prevails in the one a mood of objectivity and intellectualism, and in the other a mood of subjectivity and emotionalism, again a polar completion of the one view by the other, which may, for want of an exacter term, be classified in the commonly accepted categories of Classical and Romantic. Thus, around 1200, the transparent epics of Hartmann and the recondite *Parzival* of Wolfram complete each other as pictures of the Age of Chivalry. In the sixteenth century there appears alongside the sober didactic interpretation of human experience in the satirists and writers of stories the intoxicated rhapsody of life in Fischart's *Geschichtsklitterung* (1582). Goethe's *Wilhelm Meister* (1795-96) and its counterpart, Jean Paul's *Titan* (1800-3) stand, both in the description of their period and in its artistic presentation, in much the same relation as, say, *Erec* or *Iwein* to *Parzival*. (Wolfram and Jean Paul were both Bavarian Franconians.) In a similar way, Stifter's *Nachsommer* (1857) corresponds to Raabe's *Abu Telfan* (1867). Thomas Mann's *Der Zauberberg* (1924) and Albrecht Schaeffer's *Helianth* (1920) repeat in the 'twenties of the present century the complementary polarity of *Wilhelm Meister* and *Titan* even down to small details. They are representative masterpieces of the disparate streams of neo-classicism and neo-romanticism which have been flowing alongside each other since the turn of the century. The simultaneous appearance of both the western rationality of Stefan George and the eastern irrationality of Rilke illustrate another aspect of this bi-facial phenomenon. Sometimes such polarity comes to the surface in a single German writer, as in Gerhart Hauptmann for example, and it may even strike straight through one and the same work of his, as in *Und Pippa tanzt*. One can also observe this law of the 'creative tension' (*schöpferische Spannung* – Guardini) of a spiritual situation in other domains of the German creative mind. In philosophy Arthur Schopenhauer's doctrine of the all-powerful will and

Hegel's (p. 441) doctrine of the all-powerful spirit are historically contemporary with each other. In music, the end of the nineteenth century sees Wagner's Dionysian form of expression alongside the Apollonian form of Bruckner. But it is not only the neo-romantic period which overlaps with the neo-classical period; the first romantic period already overlaps with the first classical, especially if one considers the earlier representatives of the former such as Herder, Heinse and 'Maler' Müller. This apparent heterogeneity, which is in reality the polarity of a common idealistic basis, expresses the phenomenon in its widest and most general extent: it shows the two fundamental currents of the German mind in an opposition which has been very aptly termed by Fritz Strich the polarity of 'perfection' (classical) and 'infinity' (romantic). (*Vollendung und Unendlichkeit*.) In fact, however, romantic 'infinity' and classical 'perfection' are not an opposition of contraries, but polaric complements which often appear in one and the same person. They therefore belong closely together, because classical 'perfection' – as an ideal – is not conclusive 'completion', but a goal to be striven for and thus, just like romantic 'infinity', a *progressus ad infinitum*. The 'vertical' direction of Goethe-Faust's 'struggling endeavour' (*strebendes Bemühen*) and the 'horizontal' expanse of Humboldt's 'totality' (*Totalität*) and 'universality' (*Universalität*) have, in the last analysis, the same purpose. Accordingly, romantic 'infinity' and classical 'perfection' are both dynamic and therefore link up most closely with the second fundamental trend of German thought, that of *Werden* or 'Becoming'.

SECTION 3. BECOMING

The notion of 'Becoming' is not a specifically German one. Nor is it the notion of an evolutionary progress of history determined by a metaphysical law which makes it fall into successive periods, each of them the actualization of a spiritual or economic idea. From the historical philosophy of Joachim da Fiore[1] (1145-1202), containing mystical and theological elements, to the positivist 'Three-Stage Law' of Auguste Comte (1798-1857), the principle of a triadic development has been repeatedly laid down. Georg Friedrich Wilhelm Hegel also supposes such a cycle of triads, but with the German thinker it becomes the revelation of the general dynamic movement of the world-spirit (*Weltgeist*), which realizes itself 'in the consciousness of freedom'. From the viewpoint of world history the spirit progresses from the period of the Oriental, through the Greek into the Christian-German period. (*Vorlesungen über die Philosophie der Geschichte*, first in the *Works* of 1832 ff.,

[1] Or von Floris.

IX, 21-23.) From the viewpoint of an ontology of consciousness, cognition has also three stages: that of 'awareness of objects', of 'awareness of the self', and 'awareness of reason'; the latter develops again through the three stages of reason (*Vernunft* in the narrower sense), of the spirit, and of religion. (*Phänomenologie des Geistes*, 1807.) The spirit manifests itself as 'subjective spirit' (soul, consciousness, spirit as such), as 'objective' spirit (law, morality, ethical life), and as 'absolute spirit' (art, religion, philosophy.) Corresponding divisions into three are found in Hegel's *Wissenschaft der Logik* and in his lectures on *Naturphilosophie*.

There are also tripartite schemes, as mentioned already, outside Germany as well as in civilizations which are much older than that of Germany. One may find the germ of Hegel's trichotomies in Heraclitus, a relationship of which Hegel himself was well aware. But apart from the fact that the German spirit feels itself closely related to the Greek, the doctrine is developed by Hegel in a manner that must be regarded as peculiar to German thought. For the law set forth by Hegel concerning the three stages of the self-realization of the spirit as being the substratum of the process of life applies once more to the state of 'Becoming', the polar principle seen at work in all Being. At the same time Hegel subjects this principle not only to the idea of succession, but also to the idea of superimposition. The fundamental polarity, which underlies all the other polarities, is the tension between the infinite nature of the Idea and its finite actualization. What really sets and keeps the world going is the opposite character of this tension. It is at the root of all intellectual and physical life. Everything carries its opposite within itself, but when it changes into its own negation, this new stage, the 'antithesis', still contains the former positive stage, the 'thesis', and by this absorption produces a third stage, the 'synthesis'. This will, as a new 'thesis', again negative itself and initiate a corresponding process. In other words, the earlier stages are not annulled by the later ones, but live on in them in a modified form. As the new form is a higher one, this dialectic movement implies also a gradational polarity between the lower and the higher stages. The detailed facts of this process were given by Hegel in his *Enzyclopädie der philosophischen Wissenschaften*, first published in 1817. In Hegel, the principle of Becoming appears in its purest form. In other philosophies it is so closely interconnected with the principle of polarity – which is in itself a principle of movement – that one can hardly say which of the two ideas underlies the other as the fundamental principle. Nikolaus Cusanus or von Cues (1401-64), who, as uncompromisingly as Kierkegaard (pp. 357, 449) and Barth (pp. 413, 450), accepts the absolute transcendence and unknowableness of God, complements this *docta ignorantia* by the *principium coincidentiae oppositorum* in God. It is, however, only in the Creator that the opposites coincide; the created world is subject to the polar *principium contradictionis* as the fundamental law of all Becoming. This is recognized in a cognitive process whose three stages are the sensuous-imaginative, the rational-discursive and the intellectual-speculative, and whose opposition is resolved in the higher stage of the mystical-intuitive. The unceasing movement of all opposites towards their final oneness in God is seen in the image of a circle of infinite expanse, which brings the Finite back into the Infinite. Rudolf Odebrecht (*Nikolaus von Cues und der deutsche Geist*, Berlin, 1934) characterizes this process of perpetual emanating and remanating as *Kreispolarität* (circular polarity). Without overlooking the influence of antiquity exerted on Nikolaus through international scholasticism, Odebrecht states conclusively that this thought is in harmony with the conception advanced by Hegel (l.c., p. 47). Between the time of Nikolaus of Cues and Hegel there was a continuous series of philosophers representing the polar philosophy of Becoming, and the succession has remained unbroken up to the present time. Goethe's poem *Eins und Alles* (written in 1821, printed in 1823) can be looked upon as the *locus classicus* for this idea:

> *Und umzuschaffen das Geschaffne,*
> *Damit sich's nicht zum Starren waffne,*
> *Wirkt ewiges lebend'ges Tun.*
> *Und was nicht war, nun will es werden*
> *Zu reinen Sonnen, farb'gen Erden;*
> *In keinem Falle darf es ruhn.*

> *Es soll sich regen, schaffend handeln,*
> *Erst sich gestalten, dann verwandeln;*
> *Nur scheinbar steht's Momente still.*
> *Das Ew'ge regt sich fort in allen;*
> *Denn alles muss in Nichts zerfallen,*
> *Wenn es im Sein beharren will.*

Nature's great secret for the process of becoming of new forms is conceived by Goethe in a profound intuition. The same dynamic, but on the human level tragic, view of the world is expressed in sober prose by Hebbel. Man is, he says, 'the continuation of the act of creation, an eternally evolving, never completed creation, which prevents the completion, the petrifaction, and the stagnation of the world'. (*Diary*, 28th November 1838; transl. quoted from C. B. Rees, l.c., p. 12.) When Hebbel wrote these words he was not yet acquainted with Schopenhauer's philosophy; otherwise he might have referred to the following passage from *Die Welt als Wille und Vorstellung*: 'Permanent matter must constantly change its form, for under the guidance of causality mechanical, physical, chemical and organic phenomena, eagerly striving to appear, wrest matter away from each other, for each desires to reveal its own idea. This strife may be followed through the whole of Nature; indeed, Nature exists only through it . . . this strife itself is only the revelation of that variance with itself which is essential to the will.' (Vol. I, par. 27; Engl. transl. by R. B. Haldane and J. Kemp, 8th ed., London, n.y., I, 191 f.) It is true that the will, as the thing in itself (*das Ding an sich*), is unchangeable and, in this respect, static; but this integrating principle is for Schopenhauer too inextricably bound up with the eternal process of Becoming through polarity: 'that is, the sundering of a force into two qualitatively different and opposed activities striving after reunion.' (*Ibid.*; Engl. transl. I, 187.) Among the followers of Schopenhauer, but also of Schelling and Hegel, we find Eduard von Hartmann (1842-1906), who links the fundamental teaching of his two predecessors in a polar manner: 'Willing and ideating are always in indissoluble unity, both in the conscious and in the unconscious activity of the mind, and they form only the polarity of this unity.' (*Kategorienlehre*, 1896, II, p. 48.) In his Natural Philosophy Hartmann explains more exactly that this polarity found inherent in all Being is in a constant state of Becoming. 'If one regards the whole two-sided world of phenomena as the dynamic actuality of the absolute Idea of the Unconscious Spirit, then Nature and conscious intelligence, together with organic and inorganic Nature, are nothing but pieces cut out of this absolute "Idea", which stand to each other in the relationship of lower and higher stages, of which the lower are determined teleologically as means of attaining the higher.' (*System der Philosophie im Grundriss*, 1906-9, Vol. II, *Grundriss der Naturphilosophie*, p. 12.) From Eduard von Hartmann this line of thought leads on to the present day in Nicolai Hartmann (1882-1950), who clearly states that 'Becoming . . . is not contrary to Being, but is the general form of existence of the Real.' (*Möglichkeit und Wirklichkeit*, 1938, Chaps. 28-32; quoted from Hartmann's own presentation of his philosophy in the *Philosophen-Lexikon*, Berlin, 1949, Vol. I, p. 456.) How Hartmann sees the polar relationship of the lower to the higher spheres of Being cannot be explained here in any more detail. We can also do no more than mention Nicolai Hartmann's contemporary Theodor Litt (1880-) with the remark that he as well applies the dialectic of polar antithesis to his analysis of the cultural process of life.

If we look upon 'Becoming' as one of the fundamental trends of German thought, there must be something that corresponds to this philosophic abstraction in the very structure of the German soul. Its representative symbolic figure, Goethe's Faust, would alone amply corroborate this. *Faust* as an *Entwicklungsdrama* (drama of inner development) is only the counterpart to the well-known and typically German genre of the *Entwicklungsroman* (novel of inner development), which begins at the latest with *Parzival* and continues in almost unbroken succession through the centuries up to the present day. Without exaggeration it may be said that all great German novels are 'novels of development'. Looked at from this point of view, 'Romantic' poetry itself proves to be only a special case of the general law, even if its initiator, Friedrich von Schlegel, in the joy of discovery, saw it as something new and unique: 'The romantic way of poetry is still in the process of becoming; nay, it is its actual nature to be for ever only becoming, never to be perfected.' (116th *Fragment*; p. 29 of the original ed. of 1798, I, 2.)

To these general statements, many others could be added which specifically refer to man as subject to the law of Becoming. A few examples from different centuries may be quoted: Angelus Silesius (Johannes Scheffler) gives to the 33rd Epigram of the sixth book of his gnomic verses *Der cherubinische Wandersmann* (1675) the title *Man muss sich verwandeln*. Quite in Scheffler's sense, Schiller writes to Gottfried Körner in 1795 from Jena: *der Mensch ist nur, insofern er sich verändert.* (Schiller's Correspondence with Körner, Berlin, 1847, III, 240.) One of the most penetrating critics of the German character, Nietzsche, says in *Jenseits von Gut und Böse*, 1886, No. 244: 'The German himself *is* not, he *becomes*, he "develops". "Development" is therefore the specifically German discovery and stake in the great kingdom of philosophic formulae.' Nietzsche, however, forgets, in his bitter joy in his own ironical criticism, that he himself coined the phrase: 'Only he who changes remains akin to me', that his Superman, like Faust, is driven on by the idea of his heightened becoming, and that his doctrine of the 'eternal return' (*die ewige Wiederkunft*) finally meets that half-mystic metaphysics with which German philosophy begins: Nikolaus von Cues' infinite circle of all becoming.

Most closely connected with the three-stage polar dialectic of becoming is the German doctrine of the 'Third Reich'; fundamentally it is only one of its special forms. The fact that this formula of cultural philosophy was, against its true meaning, distorted by the National Socialists into a political application does not lessen its significance in German thought. The history of this idea has been treated in detail by Julius Petersen in his book *Die Sehnsucht nach dem 'Dritten Reich' in deutscher Sage und Dichtung* (1934), and we shall therefore refrain from examining again here the abundant material, but shall content ourselves with a few general remarks. The doctrine of the 'Third Reich' also corroborates the assertion made above, that it lies in the nature of German thinking to clothe with metaphysical radiance whatever it lays hold of, even in the realm of historical fact. It must be stated first of all that the idea of the 'Third Reich' certainly tallies to some extent with the three-period doctrine of non-German historical philosophers, but that it by no means coincides with it. Common to both is the division into three parts, the historical succession and the surpassing of two periods by a third. This scheme is found also in non-German trichotomies. Thus in France Saint-Simon, Turgot and Comte put forward three-stage-development theories in which the last period signifies the conclusion and crowning of the two previous ones. Turgot surmounts a period of mythological and one of metaphysical cognition with one of the exact sciences; according to Saint-Simon two 'critical' periods come after an 'organic' one, and Comte, who was presumably inspired by Turgot, makes a 'positivist' period follow upon 'theological' and 'metaphysical' periods. In England, Herbert Spencer divides the development of 'human opinion' into three phases: 'the unanimity of the ignorant, the disagreement of the enquiring, and the unanimity of the wise – it is manifest that the second is the parent of the third.' (*Education, Intellectual, Moral and Physical*, 1861.) In this connection it must not be forgotten that Spencer, who constructs his theory of evolution on polar-type processes (homogeneity-heterogeneity; integration-disintegration or dissipation; evolution-dissolution) is influenced by German scientific research, especially by Karl Ernst von Baer (1779-1851), and that Baer in turn springs from the school of Schelling and Lorenz Oken. Spencer has expressly acknowledged his indebtedness to the Germans (in *Progress, its Law and Cause*, 1857). These examples could obviously be multiplied: mention has already been made of Joachim da Fiore.

The German three-Reich-theory is fundamentally different from the purely historical three-period scheme, first of all by reason of its dialectic character, through which it puts itself in line with the German three-stage philosophy. The 'three kingdoms' not only arise out of each other in the course of history, but they also develop the Ideas of which they are the expression according to the scheme of Thesis-Antithesis-Synthesis. This, however, comes about in such a way that the triple dialectical interplay does not evolve (as, for example, in Hegel) through its own inherent destination towards an ultimate ideal state, but through the 'synthesis' of its 'thesis' and 'antithesis' arrives at a conclusion. Its teleological agent is limited, as it is confined to the realization of the entelechy already contained in the first stage, or at any rate not yet fully developed in the first two stages. The final stage is fulfilment, and this fulfilment is not seen dispassionately by the prophetic announcer as the objective result of a necessary course of events, but is awaited and longed for in a subjective way. The ardently desired result is strongly believed in; it is the realization of a secular eschatological hope, and has a quasi-religious character. This betrays its religious origin: the German word 'Reich' indicates not only the extent and unity of a country, but also the Kingdom of God. The line 'Thy Kingdom come' in the Lord's Prayer is in German *'Dein Reich komme'*. This Kingdom is the Third Kingdom of the Christian believer, coming after the two first kingdoms of paganism and Judaism. Accordingly the translation of the term *Drittes Reich* into English by 'Third Empire' is entirely wrong: it must be given as 'Third Kingdom'.

The idea of the Third Reich is thus a basically religious conception which was applied to the cultural life and to the state. In conformity with its origin it accords easily with the symbolism of the Trinity, and distinguishes the Kingdoms of the Father, the Son and the Holy Ghost as already in Joachim da Fiore's prophetic philosophy of history. Completely secularized and given a partially political application it does not appear before the beginning of the twentieth century: with Thomas Mann (*Friedrich und die grosse Koalition*, 1915), Arthur Moeller van den Bruck (*Das dritte Reich*, 1923) and Leopold Ziegler (*Das heilige Reich der Deutschen*, 1925), who, however, all start from a cultural point of view. On the other hand, Oswald Spengler (in *Der Untergang des Abendlandes*, 1918, Introduction, par. 7) dismissed the idea of the Third Reich as one of the scientifically inadequate speculations of history. At that time the concept and the words *Drittes Reich* had become so firmly established as part of the German language heritage that they appear repeatedly as the titles of books; in 1912, of Johannes Schlaf's novel (p. 290); in 1912, of Paul Friedrich's drama on Nietzsche; in 1921 in a drama of the same name by Hans Franck, and in 1925 in the third part of the Paracelsus novel of Guido Kolbenheyer. On Lothar Helbing's and Stefan George's *'Dritter Humanismus'*, see Bithell, *Modern German Literature 1888-1933*, London, 1939, p. 170.

SECTION 4. ANSCHAUUNG: INTUITION

The third pillar of German philosophic thought is the completely untranslatable term of *Anschauung*. The word used for this in English and French, 'intuition', is, in its epistemological sense, thoroughly inadequate; 'idea' and 'idée' (not in the Platonic sense but in that of the theory of knowledge) come nearer to the German word but do not exhaust its content because they do not render the element inherent in it of an irreducible elementary process. Kant differentiates between *reine Anschauung* (pure intuition) and *empirische Anschauung* (empirical intuition). Pure, i.e. *a priori*, intuition conditions all empirical intuitions by investing their 'materials' with the 'pure forms' of space and time, which, therefore, are the 'transcendental' (not 'transcendent') subjective elements of all sense experience. The further technical considerations of this philosophical term as used by Kant and others who developed his theories cannot be dealt with in any more detail here. For the purpose of this exposition it is a question only of the peculiar role which the development of this term plays in German thought. The German peculiarity, which here again reveals a close relationship with the Greek spirit, is the raising of *Anschauung* to the position of an absolute process, independent of and contrasted with discursive thinking; the latter is either regarded as a derived and hence secondary act of intelligence, or else it is anticipated in the *Anschauung* in a kind of instinctive short-cut. From this broad classification there result sub-divisions ranging upwards from *Schau* (vision) and *Schauen* (intuiting) to *intellectuale* or *intellektuelle Anschauung* (intellectual intuition).

The terms *Schau* and *Schauen* refer, like the English 'vision', which comes nearest to the German notion, not only to the appearance, but also to the essence of reality. A famous instance connected with this use of *Anschauung* by Goethe may illustrate the ambiguity of the term. Goethe regarded his perception of the *Urpflanze* (primal plant) as an 'experience' proceeding from *Anschauung*, but Schiller, to his annoyance, contradicted him and described it as an 'idea' (*Paralipomena zu den Annalen, Erste Bekanntschaft mit Schiller*, 1794, Jub. Ausg. xxx, 388 ff.). This criticism of Schiller's represents the 'western' interpretation, as against Goethe's German *Schau* or vision; soon afterwards, however, Schiller begins to understand Goethe's way of intuiting ideas and interprets it as follows: 'you proceeded from intuition to abstraction; now, you had to go back by re-transforming concepts into intuitions.' (Letter to Goethe, Jena, 23rd August 1794.) Goethe's thinking with the 'mind's eye' is too well known to need further discussion. It was for him a naturally inborn method of cognition, but he still felt it as a deep satisfaction to find himself in agreement with Spinoza's *cognitio intuitiva*.

A different question is whether Goethe's *Anschauung* and Spinoza's 'Third Stage of Cognition' can be brought to coincide. They overlap to some extent, but Spinoza's 'Third Cognition' – and in this he derives from neo-Platonism – is rather what German philosophy calls *intellectuale Anschauung*, thus precisely that somewhat mystical type of cognition which Goethe had not in mind and which Kant very definitely rejected. (*Critique of Pure Reason*, immediately before 'Conclusion of the Transcendental Aesthetic'; N. K. Smith's translation, London 1933, p. 90.) It is true that Kant in certain passages (*Critique of Judgment*, par. 77) very cautiously and by way of hypothesis faced up to the assumption of a kind of understanding 'which is, unlike our own, not discursive, but intuitive'. Goethe, in his essay *Anschauende Urteilskraft* (1820, Jub. Ausg. XXXIX, 33 f.) eagerly seized on this passage, saying that even if Kant presumably had in mind a 'divine', that is, a 'superhuman' understanding 'it might well be the same in the intellectual sphere: by intuiting ever-creative Nature we might make ourselves worthy to partake spiritually in her productions'. Goethe calls this, using Kant's words, an 'adventure of the reason' and, no less cautiously than Kant (in *Maximen und Reflexionen*, Jub. Ausg. IV, 231), he declares: '*Ordinary* intuition, a correct view of earthly things, is the heritage of common human intelligence. *Pure* intuition, both of the outer and inner world, is very rare.' The post-Kantian representatives of 'German Idealism' were less hesitant; they – Schelling in particular – built 'intellectual intuition' as a corner-stone into their systems.

By deciding in favour of 'intellectual intuition' they carry on a metaphysical speculation, flowing from neo-Platonic sources, which had already been taken up by the mystics of the thirteenth and fourteenth centuries, the fathers of German philosophy. Eckehart (*c.* 1260-1327), perhaps the pupil of the first great German scholastic, Albertus Magnus (*c.* 1200-80), proceeds from the very idea of the inadequacy of discursive cognition: '*Von wizzene sol man komen in ein unwizzen*' (From knowing shall one learn that one knows nothing), words which anticipate Nikolaus Cusanus'[1] idea of '*docta ignorantia*', as a pre-condition of all true cognition. He divides the process of cognition into three stages, that of the senses, that based on reason, and that transcending reason; his application of the trinitarian conception to an ontology of the cognizant spirit gives Eckehart room for an experience resulting from intellectual intuition: the *unio mystica* between the soul and the 'Godhead' (not the triune God) in the *einveltig grund* (the Undifferentiated) where the Created is not yet divided from the Creating.

The way from Eckehart to Böhme and through him to Schelling can be clearly discerned. Its next significant figure, however, is Nikolaus Cusanus. As we have already given particulars of his thought, we can dispense with a more detailed exposition and confine ourselves to the results as formulated by Odebrecht: 'Intellectual intuition is the only

[1] Nikolaus Cusanus had a good knowledge of Eckehart's writings.

way of overleaping the endless series of single rational thought-processes, and intellectual intuition alone can, by means of a synthesis, unreasoned and surpassing comprehension, link together these converging processes, seeing them as a whole' (l.c., 33 f).

Omitting intervening figures, we reach the age of Spinoza with Johannes Scheffler (Angelus Silesius, 1627-77). Scheffler adopted from Eckehart and other mystics the three stages of cognition, but greatly decreased the value of the first two. He is interested only in the third, that of intellectual intuition:

> *Mensch, wo Du deinen Geist schwingst über Ort und Zeit,*
> *So kannst Du jeden Blick sein in der Ewigkeit.*

This example from the *Cherubinischer Wandersmann* (1657, Bk. 1, 12) is representative of many variations of the same basic thought.

Gottfried Wilhelm von Leibniz (1646-1716) knew the principal work of his older contemporary Scheffler but rejected his quietistic mysticism. (*Considération sur la Doctrine d'un Esprit Universel*, 1702; in German in *Leibniz' Kleinere philosophische Schriften*, ed. R. Habs, Leipzig n.y. [1883], p. 228.) With him there begins in German philosophy a temporary opposition to the 'intellectual intuition' which reaches its climax in Kant. But Leibniz himself is cautious in his criticism. In connection with a discussion of the question of truth, he turns, without mentioning the name, against Malebranche's epistemological view that we behold all things in God (*nous voyons tout en Dieu*) and he advances his objections. But he adds: '*d'ailleurs une opinion ancienne, qui, raisonnablement comprise, ne doit pas être tout à fait rejetée.*' (*Meditationes de Cognitione, Veritate et Ideis*, 1684; Appendix to *La Monadologie*, ed. Lemaire, Paris, n.y., p. 47.) Accordingly, he allows as types of cognition *connaissance symbolique* and *connaissance intuitive*: '*et si elle (la connaissance) est tout à fait à la fois symbolique et intuitive, elle est parfaite en tout point.*' (Appendix to *La Monadologie*, p. 41.) In all cases Habs rightly translates 'intuition' as 'Anschauung'.

Still within the lifetime of Kant, and in opposition to him, the doctrine of intellectual intuition reaches its second high-water mark in German philosophic thinking. It is represented in its purest form by Friedrich Wilhelm Joseph von Schelling (1775-1824), who links his ideas first with Spinoza and then with Böhme, and not only fuses their ideas, but also remoulds them according to the requirements of his own system. In spite of this Schelling takes a critical view, at least in his earlier period, both of Spinoza's conception of 'intellectual intuition' and also of the notion as such. (*Philosophische Briefe über Dogmatismus und Kritizismus*, 1796; *Werke*, Stuttgart, 1856 ff., Div. 1, 316-26, 8th letter.) The doubts he expresses about Spinoza's method – whether rightly or wrongly is not the point here – partially anticipate his later criticism and his divergence from Fichte. The darkness of Schelling's conception is not illumined when he characterizes it in the ensuing period of his philosophy as the 'absolute identity' of the Ideal and of the Real, which again can be grasped only through *absolute Anschauung*: 'it is the sole possible direct cognition of the Absolute in which the Real and the Ideal attain to the neutral point through identification.' (*Philosophie und Religion*, 1804; *Works*, Div. I, VI, 24.) In this there come together potentiality and actuality, freedom and necessity. (*System der gesamten Philosophie*, 1804, posthumously, *Works*, Div. I, VI, 521 and 550.) 'As, however, reason is here the cognitive power, this *Anschauung* is an intuition of the reason, or, as otherwise termed, an intellectual intuition, and this alone shows us that its object can certainly not be a limited or finite one, not of course an object of the external senses, not even an object of the inner sense, but somewhat like the idea of *intellectuelle Anschauung* in Fichte.' (*Ibid.*, p. 153 f.)

The little word 'somewhat' (*etwa*) with which Schelling modifies the idea of *intellectuelle Anschauung* as conceived by Johann Gottlieb Fichte (1762-1814) already indicates his fundamental divergence from Fichte, who provided his original starting point. Fichte proceeds, according to Schelling, in the following way: 'If I imagine an external object, the thought and the thing are different, but if I imagine myself, the subject and the object are one, and in this unity there is intellectual intuition.' (*Ibid.*, 154.) Schelling could have been saved from this confusion of Fichte's psychological starting point with his own metaphysical mode of procedure by a glance at the beginning of Fichte's *Erste Einleitung in die Wissenschaftslehre* (1797, *Works*, Berlin, 1845 f., Vol. I, 422). Fichte, as a matter of fact, in his *Wissenschaftslehre* (first in two treatises in 1794, then repeatedly in various forms and publications) had moulded Kant's idea of the 'unity of consciousness' or 'the transcendental unity of apperception' into an original creative act. Kant had taught: 'The consciousness of myself in the representation "I" is not an intuition but a merely "intellectual" representation of the spontaneity of a thinking subject.' (*Critique of Pure Reason*, 2nd Bk. of the *Transcendental Analytic*, after the refutation of Idealism directed against Berkeley. N. K. Smith's translation, pp. 246-7.) In Fichte, Kant's 'intellectual representation' becomes 'intellectual intuition', though this notion was expressly rejected by Kant. To Fichte intellectual intuition is 'the immediate consciousness that I act and how I act; it is that through which I know anything, because I do it.' (*Grundlage der gesamten Wissenschaftslehre*, 1794; *Works*, I, 463.) Although Fichte believes himself here to be in complete harmony with Kant, he yet gives up in later works this favourite term of German philosophy in order to avoid confusion. In his book on '*The Vocation of Man*' (*Die Bestimmung des Menschen*, 1800) he uses only the term 'immediate consciousness' (*unmittelbares Bewusstsein*), and when he speaks in the same sense of 'free activity' (*freie Tätigkeit*), the emphasis has shifted more and more from the cognitive to the willing faculty: 'Self-acting reason is Will' (Part III, *Glaube*). None the less, the belief in the possibility of an intellectual intuition of the Absolute grows even stronger in Fichte's later development, though he does not use the term.

Fichte, in the seventh of his *Reden an die deutsche Nation* (1808), had already criticized the shadowy nature of the Absolute, defined by Schelling as the identity of the Ideal and the Real: 'finding a truly ultimate unity requires a train of reflection (not an intuition), carried through and brought to an end.' The same objection, that this absolute unity affirmed by Schelling could only be deduced by a process of thought, had already been raised by Hegel (1770-1831) in 1807, the year before the *Reden* were delivered. Hegel compares Schelling's Absolute with the 'Night... when, so they always tell us, the cows are all black.' (*Phänomenologie des Geistes*, Preface.) If, however, 'thought identifies itself with the being of the substance, and comprehends ... intuition as thought, it is still a question whether this intellectual intuition, relapsing into a state of undifferentiated dimness, does not present reality itself in an unreal manner.' (*Ibid.*, par. 21.) This criticism of Schelling and his school does not mean to say, however, that *intellectuale Anschauung*, as such, is for Hegel nonsense; he only rejects the idea that intellectual intuition can limit itself to the cognition of the 'pure essence' and neglect the 'form'. (*Ibid.*, par. 22.) In other words, Hegel will not have the concept of intellectual intuition applied to a vague and dark 'Absolute', but to the intuition of the intellect, to 'the eye of the concept of reason, which penetrates below the surface.' (*Vorlesungen über die Philosophie der Geschichte*; quoted here from *Auswahl aus Hegels Werken*, ed. Bülow, Leipzig, 1925, p. 153.)

Schopenhauer (1788-1860) pours the brimming vials of his scorn over the varying conceptions of intuition and self-intuition of the Absolute in the works of the hated '*Philosophaster-Trio*', Fichte, Schelling and Hegel: 'In German philosophy', he says, 'there now appears in place of clear terms and honest research "intellectual intuition" and "absolute thought"; the right method is now to impose on the reader, to bewilder him and mystify him and throw sand in his eyes by all kinds of artful tricks.' (*Preisschrift über die Freiheit des Willens*, 1841; IV, towards the end.) In contrast to the 'three famous sophists' Schopenhauer asserts of himself: 'I am always to be found at the standpoint of reflection, that is, rational deliberation and honest statement, never at that of *inspiration*, called intellectual intuition or absolute thought; though, if it received its proper name it would be called empty bombast and charlatanism.' (Preface to 2nd ed. of *Die Welt als Wille und Vorstellung*, 1844, Haldane and Kemp's translation, I, XXI; a similar sally previously in *Über die vierfache Wurzel des Satzes vom zureichenden Grunde*, 1831, Chap. IV, par. 20.) It is true that Schopenhauer never uses the term 'intellectual intuition'; but what he calls the 'self-cognition of the will', even if it is not the same thing, is yet cognate with Fichte's 'intellectual intuition of the absolute Ego', Schelling's 'intellectual intuition of the absolute identity of the Ideal and the Real' and Hegel's 'self-conception of the World-Spirit'. For, in each of these cases an 'intellectual' process is envisaged in which an Absolute becomes conscious of itself. In Schopenhauer's case the World-Will becomes conscious of itself through the Intellect as its 'presentation' (*Vorstellung*.) This is what Schopenhauer calls the 'self-cognition of the Will'. (*Selbsterkenntnis des Willens*.) The consummation of this 'self-cognition of the Will' is art; in music, the Will is even perceived in its immediate self-revelation. (*Die Welt als Wille und Vorstellung*, I, Bk. III, par. 52.) Here Schopenhauer stands nearer to Schelling than he would care to admit. For in Art, according to Schopenhauer, the objectification of the Will is immediately intuited; according to Schelling, the coincidence of the unconscious and the conscious streams of the Absolute manifests itself directly in Art. (*System des transzendentalen Idealismus*, 1800; *Works*, Pt. I, III, 627 f.)

The fact that the notions of *Anschauung* and *intellectuelle Anschauung* play an outstanding part in the thinker poets of the German Romantic movement, especially of the first generation, is the necessary outcome of their speculative and at the same time analytical attitude. Novalis (Friedrich Freiherr von Hardenberg, 1772-1801; see p. 260) denotes his philosophy as 'magical Idealism' and derives it from Fichte. (*Works*, ed. Minor, III, Nos. 58, 1165, 440, 930.) In Magical Idealism, intellectual intuition is an *Urhandlung* (fundamental process), made up of Feeling and Reflection in such a way that Feeling provides Reflection with the raw material for the intellectual intuition (l.c., III, 123). Hardenberg's introduction of Feeling into the concept is worthy of remark. Possibly the origin of his very complicated analysis concerning the relationship of feeling and intuiting is to be found in the system of his friend Friedrich Ernst Daniel Schleiermacher (1768-1834), who in the second of his discourses *Über die Religion* (1799) speaks of 'that mysterious moment that occurs in every sensuous perception, before intuition and feeling have even separated', qualities which 'are in origin one and undivided'. (For further details on this theory reference must be made to Rudolf Odebrecht's essay *Das Gefüge des religiösen Bewusstseins bei Fr. Schleiermacher, Blätter für deutsche Philosophie*, VIII, 1934, p. 284 ff.) But however independent Schleiermacher may be as an epistemologist in his interpretation of the relationship between feeling and intuition, as a metaphysician he clearly acknowledges agreement with Fichte (and Spinoza): 'Whenever I turn my gaze inward on myself I am at once in the Kingdom of Eternity. I look upon the working of the Spirit . . . which itself creates world and time.' (*Monologen*, 1800; 6th ed., Berlin, 1843, p. 16 and *passim*.) As Schleiermacher applies Fichte's philosophy to religion, so does his friend Friedrich von Schlegel (1772-1829) apply it to romantic poetry, the theory of which he develops in the important *Athenäum Fragment 116* (p. 28 f. of the original edition of 1798). An earlier *Fragment* reveals whence this doctrine comes: 'Intellectual intuition is the categorical imperative of this theory.' (*Ibid.*, p. 20.) Walzel designates Schlegel's *Lucinde* forthrightly as a 'novel of intellectual intuition'. (In *Deutsche Romantik*, Leipzig, 1923, vol. I, 63.) E. T. A. Hoffmann (1776-1822), again, develops his type of self-intuition with a tendency towards the occult, as was his way. (*Serapionsbrüder*, II, 3rd section, *Works*, ed. Ellinger, Berlin, etc., n.y., VI, 17; reference to Novalis and Schelling.) Within the limits of this survey we cannot go into his notion of the 'Serapiontic Intuition of Art' any more than we can go into the mystic doctrine of Zacharias Werner (1768-1823; see p. 265): 'By losing yourself you will learn to intuit.' (*Die Söhne des Tals*, Act V, Sc. 2.)

Heinrich Heine (1797-1856) is still under the spell of Romanticism when he emphasizes the connection between the German philosophy of *Anschauung* and the German experience of Nature: 'Only from a life steeped in intuition, from its "immediacy", sprang the German *Märchen*.' He values in this connection the *Anschauungsleben* of the child, that stage of our life when we have not yet learned 'to exchange laboriously the bright gold of intuitive insight for the paper money of book-definitions.' (*Die Harzreise*, 1826; *Works*, ed. Elster, III, 32.) But there is seen already in Heine, in connection with an attack on Victor Cousin, derision of the notion of intellectual intuition: 'Kant seems to have had a presentiment that one day a man will arise who will even understand his "Critique of pure Reason" merely by intuitive insight, without having learnt German discursively and analytically.' (*Die Romantische Schule*, 1833; l.c., V, 362.) And Heine is not the only one in whom the end of the Intuition philosophy of German Idealism announces itself. In the ranks of the Romantics themselves stands Tieck (p. 261), who mocks at them characteristically – that Romantic who by nature belongs rather to Rationalism. In his Novelle *Des Lebens Überfluss* (1839), he says, with respect to the staircase used for firewood by the lovers, and with a direct allusion to Kant: 'What is space? . . . A form of intuition. What is a staircase? A hypothetical notion.' But the landlord's disposition, Heinrich fears, 'is certainly too empirical and rationalistic for him to see that the true man and the deeper intuition do not stand in need of the ordinary transitional steps of that paltry prosaic approximation to a common conceptual scale . . . he will never be able to understand our immediate intuition.' 'Pure knowledge' likewise receives in this connection a satirical jibe. (*Works*, ed. Witkowski, Leipzig, n.y., III, 234.)

Tieck's satire is consonant with the times in which it is given expression; the strong reaction of the nineteenth century, with its trend towards realism, against any cognition of the Absolute reaches its peak in the radical denial of such cognition by Emil Du Bois-Raymond (1818-96). We might think now that the harsh *ignorabimus* of his world-famous lecture: *Über die Grenzen des Naturerkennens* (1872) would once and for all have put an end to all 'direct' and 'intellectual' intuitions in German philosophy. But these conceptions are too deeply rooted in German thought to be abandoned by the verdict of a physicist, and it is with them as with the French kings: '*Le roi est mort; vive le roi.*' In the second year of the new century Julius Hart (1855-1906; see p. 288) in *Die neue Welter-kenntnis* (Leipzig, 1902) proclaims once again this old cognition by 'intuitive knowledge'. 'And with this, the doctrine of *ignorabimus* is at once riddled with holes and revealed as a half-truth' (l.c., p. 103). With a not very apt reference to Kant and Schopenhauer, Hart declares: 'That intuition of the thing in itself reveals itself on closer inspection as nothing but pure intuition of living, creating and producing Nature itself.' (*Ibid.*, 322.) So far, this sounds like the statement of a positivist, but its connection with German Idealism and even Mysticism becomes at once completely clear on reading Hart's deduction in the following hymnic sentences: 'For the fact that we are enlightened and knowing, that we dwell in that lofty state of pure vision where the whole universe lies revealed before us, this alone means perfection and the highest joy of living. The whole universe descended into us and lies there in silence. Our Ego became the world and the world became our Ego. We, and we alone, are what exists. We are God' (l.c., p. 142). Hart's fitting the *principium coincidentiae oppositorum* into his system (*ibid.*, 133) leaves no doubt that the wheel has turned full circle. One may call Julius Hart unoriginal: Walther Rathenau (1867-1922) was certainly not. And yet one reads in his writings that there was 'a naïve error of all philosophy which had the presumption to penetrate all realms with the power of the intellect, of

Logic . . . without ever asking itself whether this intellectual power was an absolute one . . . or whether every realm of cognition did not rather demand adequate powers of the mind, whether tendencies did not manifest themselves in us of these powers in the faculties of intuition and of love inherent in the soul'. (*Von kommenden Dingen*, Berlin, 1918, p. 153.) The 'intuitive power of the visioning soul' (*ibid.*, 342) surpasses objective thinking: 'The criterion of objective thinking is intuition.' (*Zur Mechanik des Geistes*, Berlin, 1922, p. 57.) 'The soul, however, which does not think, but intuits, is incapable of error.' (*Ibid.*, 58.) Rathenau is a contemporary of Stefan George (1868-1933), in whose circle likewise the belief in an intuiting cognition is taken as the standard of universal experience. The philosophy of this circle was influenced by the Dionysian vision of Friedrich Nietzsche (1844-1900), in the mystical darkness of which the ecstatic thinker sought refuge from the over-glaring brightness of his intellect. (Ernst Bertram, *Nietzsche*, Berlin, 1922, Chap. *Eleusis*.) But even the professional philosophy of this period came back, along a road of the strictest logic, to an 'immediate experience of the essence of the world'. Edmund Husserl (1859-1938), in the course of the development of his phenomenological philosophy, arrived, on his way from the doctrine of Intentional Evidence of Franz Brentano (1838-1917), at a doctrine of the '*a priori* cognition of the essence'. (Cf. his own exposition of his philosophy in *Philosophen-Lexicon* I, 569 ff.) His school has branched out widely, in spite of the grave objections against modern intuitionism which were raised by Heinrich Maier (1867-1933) in his impressive work *Philosophie der Wirklichkeit*. (Vol. I *Wahrheit und Wirklichkeit*, Tübingen, 1926, p. 57 ff.) It is to be supposed that a philosophy of 'pure intuition' will never die out in Germany.

This concept, together with those of Polarity and Becoming, form the three main pillars of German philosophic thought. In Polarity, the unity of Being separates into two poles, and from their interchange of tension and release springs physical and spiritual life. In Becoming, the tension works as thesis and antithesis, and the release as synthesis; this lies at the root of historical life. In *Anschauung*, the tension between subject and object results in the release of a process which brings about cognitive life.

SECTION 5. RELIGION

This explains that in the sphere of religion German thought also shows itself, in express contrast to the dualistic thought of Jewish-Christian theology, to be fundamentally polar-monistic and even dynamically polar-monistic. The basic form of this metaphysical-religious idea is the belief in a cosmos pervaded by divine forces: '*Was wär' ein Gott, der nur*

von aussen stiesse!' ('What kind of a God would he be who stood outside
the universe, pushing it on!') (Goethe, *Prooemium.*) The designation of
this creed as 'Pantheism' is not correct and has always been rejected by
strict thinkers as a piece of popular thoughtlessness. For, as the monotheism of the Church postulates an opposition foreign to German thought
between God on the other side and the world on this side, between a
Creator and His creation, the introduction of a dualistic conception of
God into an idea monistic in itself is intellectually dishonest. To mention
only a few great names, Schelling and Schopenhauer have expressed
themselves particularly strongly against dogmatic pantheism, and so have
Leibniz and Kant in a more veiled manner. (See especially the first part
of Schelling's *Über das Wesen der menschlichen Freiheit* . . . , 1809, and his
earlier work of 1804 published posthumously, *System der gesamten Philosophie, Works* Div. I, vol. VI, p. 177; Schopenhauer in *Parerga und Paralipomena*, 1851, vol. II, par. 70.) Schopenhauer's scorn is even surpassed,
to mention two poet-philosophers, by Georg Büchner (in the so-called
Philosopher's scene of *Dantons Tod*, 1835) and by Lenau (in the '*Allgöttler*'
of his religio-philosophic epic *Savonarola*, 1836-7, Section *Weihnacht*).
Since the time of the Classics and with the exception of Klopstock, who
was to some extent still rooted in the Baroque period, there has not been
in German philosophy or poetry any really outstanding thinker who
has not rejected the monotheism of the Church. In the *Reimarus-
Fragmente* (1773-81) Lessing combated every revealed religion; in the
Abderiten (1774) Wieland unmistakably ridiculed the conduct of the
Church. Herder, the highest Church dignitary of Saxe-Weimar, professed a Spinoza-like religion in the *Gott-Gespräche* (1787), and the
'decidedly non-Christian' Goethe declared roundly, in his letter to
Johann Caspar Lavater (1741-1801), the Swiss theologian and religious
philosopher, concerning the latter's *Pontius Pilatus* (1785):

> Wer Wissenschaft und Kunst besitzt
> Hat auch Religion;
> Wer jene beiden nicht besitzt,
> Der habe Religion.
>
> (*Zahme Xenien*, IX)

Schiller expressed himself just as uncompromisingly as Goethe in his
Distichon *Mein Glaube* (1796):

> Welche Religion ich bekenne? Keine von allen,
> Die Du mir nennst. – Und warum keine? Aus Religion.

In the nineteenth century this anticlerical attitude comes to the fore in almost all great figures in the domain of the German mind. Even so highly conservative a political philosopher as Paul de Lagarde (1827-91) rejects all existing churches and demands that they give place to the 'national German religion'. This 'national German religion' would correspond to the nature of the German nation as willed by God, not however to the expression of this nature at one particular period when it might appear even in a diseased form. (*Deutsche Schriften*, 1878-81, originally in *Diagnose*, 1874, pp. 104 f.) At the root of this unwillingness to accept the dogmas of the Church lies a deep religious feeling. It can be followed in unbroken series through the neo-Spinozism of Wilhelm Wundt (1832-1920) up to the radical *Mythos-Atheos der Wissenschaften* of Leopold Ziegler (1881-) whose *Gestaltwandel der Götter* (1920) analyses theoretically what the Swiss poet-philosopher Carl Spitteler (1845-1924) had already presented symbolically in his epic *Olympischer Frühling* (1900-4). The last decisive blows against church religion were struck by David Friedrich Strauss (1808-74) in his unanswerable gospel criticism *Das Leben Jesu* (1835-6) and by Friedrich Nietzsche (1844-1900), especially in his later writings. No more than Goethe (cf. his last conversation with Ecker-mann) did these two, or the other writers mentioned above, make any attack on the ethical personality of Christ. Even Nietzsche's aversion concerns the gospels less than their treatment as dogma by the apostle Paul, a criticism in which Fichte and Schelling, among others, had already forestalled him. In this connection it is extremely significant that Nietzsche calls St. John's gospel 'the finest fruit' of Christianity. (*Der griechische Staat*, 1871; Works, *Taschenausgabe*, I, 211.) In making this statement he falls in with the predilection of German thinkers for St. John's gospel. Only some of the best-known among them can be mentioned here. Lessing states (in *Neue Hypothese über die Evangelien* . . . , 1777-8, par. 63): 'Only his (John's) gospel gave the Christian religion its true quality; it is only due to his gospel that the Christian religion has survived.' It is the beginning of this gospel and no other that Faust translates into 'his beloved German'. Schleiermacher regarded John as the most telling witness for the life and teachings of Christ (*Der Christliche Glaube* . . . , 1821-22, and elsewhere); Fichte expressly called himself a 'Johannine Christian' and asserted that his philosophy entirely agreed with that of the fourth gospel (*Die Anweisung zum seligen Leben*, 1806); Schelling saw in Johannine Christendom precisely a 'third Kingdom' and declared that after the first, the Petrine-Catholic, and the second, the Pauline-Protestant Church, will follow the third, the true Johannine Church of the future. (*Berliner Vorlesungen*, 1841-43.) Perhaps it is more than a chance that the very first religious-philosophical work known to us of all the Germanic literatures is the Gothic *Skeireins* (fifth century), which attempts an explanation of St. John's gospel. Quite isolated in the face of all this unreserved agreement with John's gospel there stands a discordant remark of Grillparzer, who speaks of the 'philosophico-mystical chatter of the disciple whom Christ loved best'. (*Works*, ed. Hock, Berlin, etc., n.y., XI, 48.) But it is just this contemptuous judgment of Grillparzer which explains the German preference for this particular gospel; it is its philosophico-mystical character, or, more exactly, its metaphysical character. For, as Wilhelm Wundt says so significantly for German thought: 'Philosophy and Metaphysics are in and of themselves identical concepts.' (*Völkerpsychologie*, vol. X, 200.) For Germans they certainly are. Hence their religion which, like all religions, has its roots in Metaphysics, can only be a philosophic one, as, on the other hand, their theology has a decidedly philosophic bent. Eckehart and his followers, Nikolaus Cusanus, Friedrich Schleiermacher, Albrecht Ritschl (1822-99), Karl Heim (1874-), Adolf von Harnack (1851-1930), Ernst Troeltsch (1865-1923), Karl Barth (1886-) and Catholic theologists such as Romano Guardini (1885-) are, all of them, philosophers. Thus German religious feeling can certainly be characterized, if not as humanistic Christianity, yet as a philosophic humanism, in which the humanistic ethos of the gospels and the metaphysical belief in an all-pervading cosmic soul have merged. The innumerable varieties of this basic form cannot be treated specifically here. They cannot be better explained than by two sentences from the first of Schleiermacher's discourses *Über die Religion*: 'Take the highest viewpoint of metaphysics and morality, and you will find that both have the same object as religion, namely, the universe and the relationship of mankind to the universe. Religion is susceptibility of, and taste for, the infinite.'

II. PERIODS OF GERMAN PHILOSOPHIC THOUGHT

SECTION 6. THE SITUATION IN EARLY, MIDDLE AND LATE MEDIEVAL TIMES

The situation of philosophy in Germany in the early Middle Ages, that is to say at the time of Charlemagne (768-814) and up to the eleventh century, cannot be separated from the situation of theology, as there existed no metaphysics independent of the ecclesiastical authority. The philosophic elements fused into theology were adopted from ancient philosophies, especially from Plato, Aristotle and the Stoics and from St. Augustine; their purest form, that is to say the one in which they are most independent of ecclesiastical dogma, is represented by Boethius (*c.* 480-525), a high official of Roman descent at the Gothic court, who drew up in the last years of his life a Stoic-Platonic theodicy. His *De Consolatione Philosophiae*, highly valued throughout the entire early medieval period, was translated into German and interpreted by the outstanding scholar and teacher of St. Gall, Notker Labeo (*c.* 952-1022). Notker stands in the tradition of the philosophically trained theologian Alcuin (735-804), the great Anglo-Saxon, who organized education in Charlemagne's empire, and of his rigidly dogmatic pupil Hrabanus Maurus (*c.* 784-865), who, as Abbot of Fulda and Archbishop of Mainz, commentated biblical and ecclesiastical writers. Among these scholars, Alcuin's successor at the Abbey school of Tours, Fredegisus (?-834), shows the beginnings of independent philosophic thought, as his treatise *De nihilo et tenebris* possibly contains German national thought and not solely ideas of Christian and ancient philosophy introduced from outside. For by denoting Nothing(ness) as a positive entity, perhaps as primal matter in contrast to the spirit, he raises a philosophic problem which introduced difficulties for the thinking of the Germans when they had to come to terms with the Semitic belief in a *creatio ex nihilo*, which was foreign to Germanic notions. For the androgynous and terrigenous Tuisto (Tacitus, *Germania*, 2) and the equally androgynous Ymir, the personification of primal matter (*Snorra Edda, Gylfaginning*, 4-6), are nature myths and symbols of polarity. Not before the dualist philosophy of the *Anno-Lied* (*c.* 1100) is the primeval state characterized by the spiritual entities of the 'Word' and of the 'Light' (Verses 19 ff.). In the fragment of a cosmogonic poem from the eighth century, the *Wessobrunner Gebet*, Nothing has still to be described by the negation of those phenomena whose non-existence was unimaginable to German thought: earth and heaven, tree and mountain, star and sun, moon and sea. If these conjectures are correct, we should have to look upon Fredegisus (ed. J. P. Migne, *Patrologia Latina*, vol. 105) as the first representative known to us of original German thought. His contemporary, Candidus von Fulda, author of the *Dicta Candidi de Imagine Dei*, already points more in the direction of scholastic philosophy. The most important pre-scholastic philosopher of the period was doubtless Johannes Scotus Eriugena (*c.* 810-880); as an Irishman and professor at the Universities of Paris and Oxford he belongs to international ecclesiastical philosophy and not to German philosophy, even if he was for a time in close contact with the Carolingian court circle of Charles the Bald. On the other hand, Gottschalk or Gotescalc (808-867), adversary of Scotus Eriugena and of Hrabanus, interpreted the doctrine of metaphysical determination in too narrowly theological a way to be numbered among philosophers proper.

What assures him an honourable place in the history of German thought is his inflexible adherence to his philosophico-theological persuasions, which moulded the life of this son of a Saxon Earl in so tragic a way. Up to 1000 then, one can scarcely speak of a clear situation of German thought, but only of thought in Germany as part of common Christian-European thought, decking out its dogma with the store of philosophic thought taken over from antiquity.

This applies also to some extent to the ensuing period of early and fully developed scholasticism, which lasts until about 1300. Its thought can, however, be claimed as philosophy in the true sense as, unlike the previous period, it does not embellish dogma with philosophy, but rather philosophy with dogma; but it still shows the interplay of a common European-Christian philosophy to which Germany contributed surprisingly little. The only German scholastic of importance is Count Albert von Bollstädt (Albertus Magnus, 1193?-1280), who can well be claimed as the greatest German polyhistor before Leibniz, but in whose philosophy scarcely any typically German features can be traced. The further development of German thought in this period is to be found more in poetry than in philosophy, and from this one obtains a good picture of the ethics of chivalry. The courtly epics, especially those of Wolfram von Eschenbach (c. 1170-c. 1220) mirror the ethical and religious attitude of the German soul at the height of the Middle Ages. The ethical ideal of *diu mâze* (= *Masshalten*) gains in inner freedom from its association with the æsthetic form of court life, and religious feeling is ennobled in a humanistic way; between the crude Judaism of the extermination of pagans in Konrad's *Rolandslied* (c. 1130) and the Christian tolerance towards the pagans in Wolfram's *Willehalm* (c. 1215) there lies a world of difference. Neither is the political and social behaviour of the Church any longer accepted uncritically, as Walther's attacks upon the Pope and the concurrence of contemporary writers show. The beginnings of this critical attitude already make themselves felt in Heinrich von Melk's (c. 1150) *Von des tôdes gehugede* (= *Remembrance of Death*) and *Priesterleben*.

The first golden age of German philosophy, the so-called 'German Mysticism', begins about 1300. This is linked particularly with the names of three Dominicans: Eckehart (c. 1260-1327), Johannes Tauler (c. 1300-61), and Heinrich Seuse or Suso (1300-66). The fact that in Eckehart the cognitive form of intellectual intuition, so much favoured by the Germans, was by now fully developed has already been shown in the first part of this exposition. It plays a smaller part in Tauler and practically none in the unsystematic Seuse. Deserving of notice is the fact that in the philosophic situation of this period German thought, after taking scarcely any part in early or fully developed Scholasticism, remained aloof also from late Scholasticism. Names such as those of Albert von Sachsen (c. 1316-90) and Gabriel Biel (1430-95) are almost forgotten. Both were Occamists; through Biel in particular the philosophy of the Englishman was passed on to Luther, William of Occam (1280-1349) being in contact with German scholars in the first half of the fourteenth century through his connection with the Emperor Louis the Bavarian. In contrast to logistic speculation on the essence of God and the discursive working out of gnoseological and ontological questions in Scholasticism, the so-called Mystics prefer the direct metaphysical experience of God and accordingly the intuitive method of cognition, which, however, must not on that account be regarded as unsystematic or inspired purely by feeling. This experience is in itself religious and needs no theological or philosophical support, although such support is not lacking, especially in Eckehart, who takes over much from the Italian Thomas Aquinas. (Thomas of Aquino; c. 1226-74.) In speaking of the Mysticism of Ecke-hart and his followers one must always bear in mind that it was not a Mysticism of enthusiasts, but of highly educated theologians who had gone through a thorough training by the Schoolmen, as was the case with their predecessors in the twelfth century, Bernard de Clairvaux and the Victorines. A clear line of thought can be seen stretching from the mystically visioned *deitas* in Eckehart's *Funken* (spark) to the God-Absolute of Schelling experienced by intellectual intuition; from Tauler's preaching of practical ethics rooted in metaphysics to the later Fichte, and also from Seuse's emotional cognition of the One-in-All to Johann Georg Hamann (1730-88) and Friedrich Heinrich Jacobi (1743-1809), who professed their direct knowledge by faith of the Transcendent. The course of German thought is thus shown clearly to have maintained its continuity throughout the centuries.

There is another characteristic feature common to both the thirteenth and the eighteenth centuries: in both cases a golden age of German poetry is crowned with a golden age of German philosophy. In the Medieval period the philosophy of 'German Mysticism' accompanies the last phase of the first *Blütezeit* in German literature and outlasts it, and in a similar way the philosophy of 'German Idealism' coincides with the second florescence in the eighteenth century. The period of 'German Idealism' about the turn of the eighteenth and nineteenth centuries is rounded off and concluded in the system of Hegel, which spans all departments of thought; and something similar occurs about the turn of the fourteenth and fifteenth centuries: Nikolaus von Cues (1401-64), absorbing previous systems in his work, embraces the whole realm of philosophy and stands in a corresponding position towards Eckehart, Tauler and Seuse, as Hegel does to Kant, Fichte and Schelling. Furthermore, just as beside Hegel's logistic world of reason there stands Schopenhauer's pantragic world of volition, so beside Nicolaus' positive explanation of universal laws there stand the desperate questions voiced by Johann von Tepl (c. 1350-c. 1414) as to the sense of a world which an inscrutable and pitiless will causes to roll on in unexplained alternations of life and death. The final prayer of the *Ackermann aus Böhmen* (between 1400 and 1413) expresses resignation to a force in which co-exist the 'Yes' and the 'No' and which works in paradoxical dialectic – the polar category of German thought:

> *aller heimlicher und niemands wissender sachen wahrhaftiger*
> *erkenner; ewiger freuden spender; irdischer wunnen storer.*
>
> (Chap. 34, towards the end; Spalding's
> edition, Oxford, 1950, p. 30.)

SECTION 7. THE SITUATION IN MEDIEVAL AND MODERN TIMES

As shown in the first part of this exposition, the philosophy of the dialectic 'Yes' and 'No' and their confluence in the *Ungrund* (the Ungrounded) of God, is erected into a system in the sixteenth century by Jakob Böhme (1575-1624). The philosophic situation of this century repeats that of the fourteenth in a form changed by the Reformation. In face of a theology burdened with philosophic problems, which both on the Protestant side and on the Catholic side is often the direct continuation of scholasticism, there stand the theosophic philosophies of Jakob Böhme, Agrippa von Nettesheim (1486-1535) and Paracelsus von Hohenheim (1493-1541). In some representatives of this group of mystics attitudes are already to be found which gain strength only in the next century: thus there is the latent pantheism of Valentin Weigel (1533-88), who also has some importance as an epistemologist (*Der güldene Griff*, 1616, published like all his works posthumously), and there is also the enlightened religious sentiment of the historical philosopher Sebastian Franck (1499-1542), writer of the *Cosmographia* (1534). Although a Protestant, he shares with the Catholic Erasmus of Rotterdam (1467-1536) the rejection of the narrow dogmatism of Luther and the other reformers. Erasmus, a Dutchman, belongs like Spinoza to the wider circle of German thought.

This linking of Christian-philosophic speculation with religious sentiment outside any church allegiance is in the seventeenth century stamped above all on Abraham von Franckenberg (1593-1652), who can be called without exaggeration, and not in this connection only, the Lessing of the Baroque period. He himself, as also his friend Daniel Czepko von

Reigersfeld (1605-60) and his widely differing pupil Johannes Scheffler (Angelus Silesius, 1624-77) carry on the ideas, which they knew well, not only of the older mystics but also of those of the sixteenth century. But in spite of his fanatical Catholicism it is particularly in Scheffler, through the historical relationship of his conception of an integrating principle to that of Spinoza, that the changed philosophical situation of the seventeenth century becomes clear. Scheffler's pantheistically conceived attitude to God reveals, behind the mysticism of his paradoxical diction, the experience of a completely changed relationship between transcendence and immanence. Like Spinoza, he tears down the absolute barrier between God and Man, between the temporal and the eternal. For Benedictus de Spinoza (1632-77), familiar with scholastic philosophy and also with Neoplatonic traditions, sets God equal with Infinite Substance or Nature, which appears to human knowledge in the two forms of Thought and Extension. His *Tractatus theologico-politicus* (1670), critically restricting belief in the Bible, precedes his *Ethica, ordine geometrico demonstrata* (1677, published after his death), which departs from all belief in the Bible. But neither Spinoza's metaphysics nor his philosophy of life, both of which a hundred years later exert such immeasurable influence on the German mind, have any effect on his younger contemporary, the Reichsfreiherr Gottfried Wilhelm von Leibniz (1646-1716). This philosopher, preparing the way for the epistemological transcendentalism of 'German Idealism', substitutes Spinoza's notion of a God-saturated Substance by that of a system of Monads, organically integrated as a result of 'pre-established harmony'. However, in spite of the introduction of a God-monad, Leibniz' philosophy does not result in a strict Dualism. (*La Monadologie*, 1714.) The fact that in his *Essai de Théodicée*, he tried to harmonize the idea of a beneficent God with the undeniable existence of pain and evil only shows that the ecclesiastical faith of his age is severely shaken and in need of artificial support. Likewise significant for the philosophical situation of the time is the fact that Leibniz, according to his own statement, finds it incompatible with the laws of mechanics to regard Substance as mere mass: he conceives it as the sum of centres of force which he designates as immaterial atoms or 'monads'. In Leibniz, as also in Spinoza, philosophy is no longer merely metaphysical speculation, but is already taking the direction of natural science. In Spinoza this changed attitude even gained expression in the outer form of his principal work: he develops his ideas in 'geometrical', that is to say, in mathematical and logical language. This penetration of natural scientific thought into philosophy, which had been preceded by the introduction of philosophic thought into the natural sciences, especially in the system of the Italian Galileo Galilei (1564-1642), forms the second outstanding feature of the intellectual situation in the seventeenth century. Franckenberg had already incorporated in his philosophy the new conception of the universe presented by the Pole Nicolaus Copernicus (1473-1543) and by the Italian Giordano Bruno (1548-1600), who had been influenced by Copernicus. On the other hand, Leibniz' theory of monads had already been forestalled in Bruno's philosophy. But in spite of the rejection by the Church of the new discoveries, which in Italy led to the trials of Galileo and Bruno, there is not yet in Germany any open antagonism between science and theology: neither Copernicus nor Johannes Kepler (1571-1630), the greatest German physicist and astronomer of the seventeenth century, doubted the authority of the Church and its fundamental doctrines. Nor is the leading German philosopher of this period, Leibniz, engaged in any conflict with the Church, and the influence of its most dangerous enemy, Spinoza, has not yet made itself felt. Even the 'Christian pessimism' which, in conjunction with a certain morbid delight in evil and cruelty, coloured German thought during and after the Thirty Years' War (Gryphius, Grimmelshausen, Moscherosch, Scheffler, etc.) is on the wane. The world, in spite of all inadequacies, appears harmonious and perfect. The optimism of the eighteenth century is in the air.

Like all optimistic philosophies failing to draw the strength of their conviction from opposition to pessimistic doctrines, the optimism of the eighteenth century did not produce any outstanding thinkers. Reichsfreiherr Christian von Wolff (1679-1754) was himself conscious of the eclectic character of his philosophy (letter of 27th January 1741 to Count Manteuffel), but he should not, as often happens, be regarded merely as a popularizer of Leibniz: as creator of a system based on faith in the ultimate explicability of the world, which attempts to reduce the diversity of interdependent phenomena to rationally interpretable principles in almost every walk of life, he is by no means insignificant. He is the initiator of modern German philosophic terminology, and he wrote almost all his numerous works in the German language, an innovation in which he had been preceded by the legal philosopher Christian Thomasius (1655-1728). Both proclaimed the gospel of enlightenment and toleration, without thereby abandoning their allegiance to the Church, Wolff speaking as a rationalistic dogmatist and Thomasius as a humanistic pietist. From humane conviction Thomasius, who had accepted the liberal ideas of John Locke (1632-1704), fought successfully against trials for witchcraft. His forerunners in this courageous undertaking, not lacking in danger in those days, should also be remembered in the history of

German thought: they were the physician Johann Weyer (1516-88), the Jesuits Adam Tanner (?-1632) and Friedrich von Spee (1591-1635), one of the foremost poets of his time, and the Pastor Balthasar Bekker (1634-98). In this growing desire for enlightenment and religious toleration, and not in its theoretical philosophy, lies the principal significance of German thought in the first half of the eighteenth century. Another point is closely linked with this: the world is perceived not only as bright and lucid, but also as well-ordered and beautiful. Its Creator, in whose existence the age still believes, is no longer seen as a tyrant who punishes and rewards, but as an artist. The first outstanding representative of this cosmic view is Anthony Ashley Cooper, third Earl of Shaftesbury (1671-1713), whose works appeared in collected form in the year of his death. Their spirit is spreading in Germany, but only reaches its full influence after the German translation by Hölty (p. 245) and Benzler (Leipzig, 1776-79), especially with Herder and Goethe. In this context it must not be overlooked how closely the outlook of Shaftesbury corresponds with that of Leibniz. As the existence of suffering and evil cannot be denied even by these optimistic philosophers, it is to be explained away in the so-called theodicies, or else an attempt is made to merge it organically as a necessary constituent of the progress of the world. The philosophic poet Albrecht von Haller (1708-77) already does this in his didactic poem *Vom Ursprung des Übels* (1734); following this in brighter tone there is the *Theodizee* of Johann Peter Uz (1720-96), first found in his collection of poems of 1755, where he expressly refers to Leibniz' treatise of 1710 with the same title. The latter work itself, however, is particularly significant of the close connection between optimism and the enlightened efforts to deliver Christianity from its confessional bonds; for Leibniz wrote *La Théodicée* at the request of Sophie Charlotte, Queen of Prussia, who was interested in philosophy, with a view to showing that doctrines common to the two Christian confessions make possible a fusion of Catholicism and Protestantism in favour of pure Christianity. With this unsuccessful endeavour to put an end to the fatal dissensions of the two Christian denominations there comes to its close in the first half of the eighteenth century the attempt to establish a national Church in Germany. The other problem which the German mind had been facing since the days of Charlemagne, that of bringing German thought to terms with the Pauline syncretism of Jewish-Hellenistic thought without any revolutionary break with the Church, remains equally unsolved.

This unsatisfactory development is one of the causes of by far the most important event in the second half of the eighteenth century, the acceptance of Spinozism as an element congenial to the German mind.

P

There appears the striking parallel event in the spiritual history of Germany that the doctrine of a Jew who has fallen away from his Church is overlaid with that of another Jew who had done likewise. Spinoza shares the fate of Schopenhauer and Kierkegaard: not until about half a century after the publication of his main work does his teaching attain full recognition. The isolated attempt of a certain Friedrich Wilhelm Stosch (1646-1704 or 1707) to smuggle Spinozism into German thought before 1700 by means of his anonymous and pseudo-polemical book *Concordia rationis et fidei* . . . (1692) had no success. Wider circles had their attention drawn to Spinoza when the Jewish philosopher Moses Mendelssohn (1729-86), well-known for his essay *Phaedon oder über die Unsterblichkeit der Seele* (1767), tried to vindicate his friend Lessing against the Christian philosopher Friedrich Heinrich Jacobi (1743-1819). But even before this controversy, which takes place in the years 1785-87, Spinoza's teaching has been taken up by the Classical writers, and it now penetrates into the Romantics as well. The significance it assumes for German philosophy and its new interpretations have been explained in more detail in the first part of this exposition. Spinozism is fused by Fichte, Schelling and, less intimately, by Hegel into the philosophy of the greatest thinker of the age, Immanuel Kant (1724-1804), who himself, however, derives not from Spinoza but, at least so far as his theory of knowledge is concerned, from Leibniz and the English empiricists. The basic ideas of his philosophy can be indicated only by the titles of his principle works: *Kritik der reinen Vernunft*, 1781. (Criticism of Knowledge not only of the phenomenal world, but also of the possibility of metaphysical knowledge and knowledge of God, the limited nature of all these cognitions being demonstrated.) *Kritik der praktischen Vernunft*, 1788. (The basic moral law of the 'categorical imperative' and the practical postulates of immortality, freedom of the will, and God.) *Kritik der Urteilskraft*, 1799. (First Part: the æsthetic faculties. Second Part: the teleological faculties.) *Grundlegung zur Metaphysik der Sitten*, 1785. (Ethics: the will, autonomous if guided by duty – true morality; in contrast to its obedience to rules imposed from without – mere legality.) *Die Religion innerhalb der Grenzen der blossen Vernunft*, 1793. (Philosophy of religion: the 'Son of God' as the incarnation of the ethical law founded on the moral disposition of the mind and not on deeds.) *Idee zu einer Geschichte in weltbürgerlicher Absicht*, 1784, and *Zum ewigen Frieden*, 1795. (Philosophy of History: lawful regulation of the relations between states and the abolition of war, not as an ideal of the future, but as a direct practical aim of policy.) *Metaphysische Anfangsgründe der Naturwissenschaft*, 1786, and *Opus postumum*, published in parts only between 1882 and 1920. (Metaphysics and science in conjunction with each other.) In this *Opus postumum* is to be sought the key to the philosophic situation towards the close of the eighteenth century. For it contains Kant's own reflections concerning the unperfected character of his system, which caused Fichte, his first 'improver', to bestow on Kant the designation of '*Dreiviertelkopf*' (three-quarter headed). This cutting expression occurs in a letter of the 28th September 1799 to the Kantist Karl Leonhard Reinhold (1758-1823), who, like Fichte, was engaged in seeking a common denominator for the subjectivity of knowledge and the objectivity of the known. In other words even Kant's contemporaries take exception to the fact that he has not closed the gap between 'transcendental' knowledge and its object, the 'thing-in-itself' (*das Ding an sich*). They are, furthermore, dissatisfied with the fact that Kant has driven metaphysics out through the front-door of 'pure reason', but let it in again through the back-door of 'practical reason'. In 1835 Heine is still mocking Kant in his *Zur Geschichte der Religion und Philosophie in Deutschland* (*Works*, ed. Elster IV, 259) by the allegation that the great philosopher had written the *Kritik der reinen Vernunft* purely to avoid taking away from his old servant Lampe his comforting belief in divine government of the world, that is to say, in a metaphysical Absolute. Behind the biting wit of this retrospective criticism lies the serious opinion of the philosophic world around the turn of the century. It is a philosophic situation typical of the German mind, which is naturally directed just as much to the metaphysical as to the systematic. Its dissatisfaction with Kant and the attempts this gave rise to on the part of Fichte, Schelling, Hegel and Schopenhauer to remodel Kant's philosophy, each according to his own ideas, into a self-contained whole, are outlined in the first part of this presentation.

There is in all probability a connection between the breaking-away of German thought in the eighteenth century from the orthodox teaching of the Church and the rise of a new science – Æsthetics, a development which has its parallels in England and France. In a perfect and harmonious world, which is (in the words of the English æstheticist Henry Home, 1696-1782) a phenomenon of 'intrinsic' not 'relative' beauty, the Beautiful must call forth in man theoretical considerations of its nature. Johann Christoph Gottsched (1700-66) bases his theory on Batteux and sees the nature of Art in a 'reasonable' imitation of reality; from him the line of thought passes to his pupil Johann Elias Schlegel (1719-49), for whom Art already means 'idealistically' selected similarity with the essential features of reality. Wolff's pupil Alexander Gottlieb Baumgarten (1714-62) separates æsthetics as a self-contained subject of study from the rest of philosophy; he explains the nature of the beautiful as a phenomenal perfection comprehended with knowledge directed by the feelings. Johann Georg Sulzer (1720-97) analyses this kind of feeling in his *Allgemeine Theorie der schönen Künste* (1771-74) from the standpoint of psychology, but does not detach it from moral experience. His theory is, to some extent, in conformity with that of Moses Mendelssohn, who, while not entirely separating 'sentiment' from 'morality', yet gives it high rank among the independent powers of the soul. His friend Gotthold Ephraim Lessing (1729-81) strikes out independently, in æsthetics as in other directions. *Laokoon* (1766) is chiefly concerned with the essential distinctions which exist between poetry and the pictorial and sculptural arts. The central theme of the *Hamburgische Dramaturgie* (1767-69) is to show the theory of drama as laid down by Aristotle and its misapplication by the French school. In this context Lessing holds up Shakespeare as the true heir of the Greeks and, therefore, as being more congenial to the German mind. After Bodmer (1740), J. E. Schlegel (1741) and Gottsched (1741 and 1742) Lessing's pioneer praise of Shakespeare (first in *Literaturbriefe*, 1759) was vitally important for the introduction of the English dramatist into Germany. (The first to mention him in Germany was D. G. Morhof in *Unterricht von der deutschen Sprache und Poesie*, 1682; the first translation of a Shakespearean play, *Julius Caesar*, was that by Graf von Borck, 1741.) The contribution to æsthetics made by Immanuel Kant has already been mentioned. Karl Philipp Moritz (1757-93), assured of an outstanding position in the history of German psychology owing to his novel *Anton Reiser* (1785-90) and his theoretical writings, even had a decisive influence on the verse rendering of Goethe's *Iphigenie* through one of his books on æsthetic subjects, the *Versuch einer deutschen Prosodie*, 1787. This is acknowledged by Goethe himself (*Italienische Reise*, 10th January 1787). Moritz and Friedrich von Schiller (1759-1805; *Über naïve und sentimentalische Dichtung*, 1795-6, etc.,) are the actual æstheticians of Classicism. Karl Wilhelm Ferdinand Solger (1780-1819), Schleiermacher, Schelling and Schopenhauer represent Romanticism. Concerning the æsthetics of the last two something was said in Part I; Solger's theory is in agreement with theirs on some points, but in the dialogues called *Erwin* (1815) he designates an imaginative process aroused by 'ironical' (i.e. self-reflective) emotion as the fountain-head of artistic experience. Schleiermacher's *Ästhetik* (first in the *Works* of 1842; expanded in the critical edition of R. Odebrecht, Berlin, 1931) is first and foremost a phenomenology of æsthetic consciousness, but it is not only that: by inclusion of the religious aspect a certain connection is established with Hegel's *Philosophie der Kunst*. (*Works*, 1835 ff., vol. x; *Enzyclopädie der philosophischen Wissenschaften*, 1817, pars. 556-563.) Hegel applies also to æsthetics his trichomatic system: he distinguishes not only three historical periods but also three different relationships between Idea and Material, and divides Art forms into the Symbolic, the Classical, and the Romantic. All these æstheticists, at least in questions of ancient Greek art and its national background, owe a debt to the classicist Johann Joachim Winckelmann (1717-68), whose idealized interpretation, *Gedanken über die Nachahmung der griechischen Werke in der Malerei und Bildhauerkunst* (1755), was only replaced towards the end of the century by Friedrich von Schlegel's less harmonious one (*Prosaische Jugendschriften*, ed. Jakob Minor, Vienna, 1882); his conception of Ancient Greece anticipates, to some extent, that of Nietzsche's *Die Geburt der Tragödie aus dem Geiste der Musik* (1872). The development of Æsthetics in the eighteenth century mirrors in its theories the actual development of German literature: its gradual disengagement from foreign influence.

The intellectual and spiritual situation of German thought around 1800 was described with deep insight by the political philosopher Adam von Müller (1779-1829) in his *Vorlesungen über die deutsche Wissenschaft und Literatur* (1806). He praises above all in the German philosophy of his time 'the fact that as a result of innumerable efforts which, though not perhaps well balanced, were certainly enormous, it tends towards that harmonization of the outer with the inner life which is significant of *Wilhelm Meisters Lehrjahre*.' (P. 81 of the reprint by Arthur Salz, Munich, 1920.) In this sentence Müller aptly sums up what had been attained: the reconciliation after painstaking work of the conflicting powers of reason and sentiment both in philosophy and in its application to the cultural life of the period.

After this peak of achievement the philosophical systems in the first half of the nineteenth century are less original, with the exception of Schopenhauer's work which, however, does not make its influence felt before the middle of the century. It is true that the majority of Hegel's writings (and the later part of Fichte's and Schelling's) were not published till between 1800 and 1830, but the thought of all three is rooted in the spiritual soil of the post-Kantian period of the eighteenth century. Hegel's philosophy certainly dominates in the first decades of the century, but it is already controverted by contemporary thinkers and is subsequently almost entirely neglected until, round the turn of the nineteenth and twentieth centuries, it is revived by the philosopher Adolf Lasson (1832-1917) and his equally eminent son Georg Lasson (1862-1932), the praiseworthy editor of a new edition. One section only of Hegel's thought, his philosophy of the State, becomes prevalent and even gains momentum, though in a transmuted form: the right wing of his school fuses it into

conservative ideas, the left wing into socialist doctrines, the main representatives of the latter being Karl Marx (1818-83; *Das Kapital*, 1867, 1885,
1893) and Friedrich Engels (1820-95). The third of the great Socialists of
this period, Ferdinand Lassalle (1825-64), also derives from Hegel, but
less as philosopher of State (*Staatsphilosoph*) than as metaphysician. (*Die
Philosophie Herakleitos des Dunklen von Ephesos*, 1858.) As a social reformer,
he does not follow the internationalism of Marx and Engels; he continues the national line of Fichte's *Der geschlossene Handelsstaat* (1800).
Not on the strength of his special ideas but by dint of their general trend
he is, like Bettina von Arnim (1785-1859; *Dies Buch gehört dem König*,
1843; *Gespräche mit Dämonen*, 1852) a forerunner of Spengler and Rathenau.

Apart from Hegel there is a second flowering of the 'German Idealism'
philosophy. Some of its representatives are also born in the eighteenth
century, but their works do not appear before 1800. A certain reaction
against the high flight of metaphysical speculation, especially against the
doctrines based on 'intellectual intuition', is a feature common to all of
them. The bent towards realism which is the main characteristic of the
nineteenth century is already evident in the oldest of them, Johann
Friedrich Herbart (1776-1841), who is equally independent as a metaphysician (*Allgemeine Metaphysik*, 1828-9) and as a psychological epistemologist (*Lehrbuch zur Psychologie*, *1816*). Both Johann Jakob Fries (1773-
1843) and Friedrich Eduard Beneke (1798-1854) reject the development
of Kant's philosophy in Fichte, Schelling, and Hegel and proceed – like
Schopenhauer, their contemporary – directly from Kant, but give his
theory of knowledge a turn to psychology. Gustav Theodor Fechner
(1801-87) and Hermann Lotze (1817-81) find themselves already in a
philosophical situation where they have to come to terms with the rising
power of the natural sciences, but in them also the tradition of 'German
Idealism' is still strong enough to prevent their building up a philosophy
based merely upon the interplay of mechanical forces; to Fechner the
integrating principle of the world is pan-psychic, to Lotze pan-spiritual.

The materialism they have avoided comes into full play in the contemporary 'monistic' school in which 'Force and Matter' (*Kraft und Stoff*)
have superseded the metaphysical Absolute. The book of the above title
(1855) by Ludwig Büchner (1824-99), the less radically conceived works
of Heinrich Czolbe (1819-73; e.g. *Die Grenzen und der Ursprung der
menschlichen Erkenntnis*, 1865) and the consequential materialism of Karl
Vogt (1817-95) and of Jakob Moleschott (1822-93) are, around the middle
of the century, characteristic of the decisive withdrawal from the intuitive
speculations of German Idealism. A movement which must be taken
much more seriously than this reaction against the spiritualism of the

preceding period is the idealistic materialism of their common ancestor, Ludwig Feuerbach (1804-72), whose philosophy, historically regarded, is not so much a break with German Idealism as its remoulding into an existential philosophic empiricism. For in his struggle against the Christian doctrine there lives on, in polemical form, the high cultural idealism of 'German Neo-Humanism' which runs continuously from Kant to Fries, Beneke, Lotze and Fechner. The true current of German thought passes through the negative metaphysics of Feuerbach and the critical metaphysics of this late group, and not through the 'Force and Matter' movement, which is nothing but an interlude of reaction, and it continues to Eduard von Hartmann (1842-1906), the last of the great German thinkers who during the nineteenth century worked out a self-contained metaphysical system. Hartmann fuses Schelling's Absolute (of the pre-conscious identity of the Ideal and the Real), Hegel's Absolute (of the World-Spirit attaining to knowledge of itself) and Schopenhauer's Absolute (the blindly-striving Will) into the Absolute of the 'Unconscious'. The question whether the cognition of the Absolute is accessible to knowledge of an intuitive sort he leaves open. As a matter of fact, he replaces intuition (in the *Kategorienlehre*, 1896) by the general function of 'speculative thought'.

A similar development, the gradual change from the Idealism of the previous period to the realistic methods of psychology and science, can be traced in Æsthetics. Friedrich Theodor von Vischer (1807-87) progressively grows out of the conceptions of his classical-romantic forerunners, especially Hegel, whose systematizing of the divisions of Art he first adopted in a different form. He more strongly emphasizes the psychological side; in his main work, *Ästhetik* (1846-57), he already anticipates the concept and the term *Einfühlen* (empathy) which plays so great a part around the turn of the nineteenth and twentieth centuries in the *Ästhetik* (1903-6) of Theodor Lipps (1851-1914). Moritz Carriere (1817-95) also derives from Hegel, both as philosopher and æstheticist, but in both respects he goes further back into the eighteenth century by again emphasizing the moral element in the nature of Art and attempting to overcome Hegel's pantheism in a religious sense similar to that of Johann Gottlieb's son Immanuel Hermann von Fichte (1796-1879), with whom he co-operated. Carriere's principal æsthetic work appeared in 1859. Two philosophers of whom mention was made above have also achieved important results as æstheticists. Rudolph Hermann Lotze makes the theory of the Beautiful part of that of value; he initiates a doctrine of Values which becomes of great importance in the further development of German thought. (*Über den Begriff der Schönheit*, 1845.)

Gustav Theodor Fechner already ranges Æsthetics among the 'experimental sciences'. His work *Zur experimentalen Ästhetik* did not appear until 1871.

This is significant; for the philosophical situation in the second half of the nineteenth century is distinguished by the fact that natural science now begins to exert a decisive influence on philosophic thought, after previously belonging rather to its borderline areas than to its central substance. The world-outlook of wide circles is determined by the popular scientific thought of the materialists mentioned above. The actual rejection of their notions does not take place before the turn of the century, but is already prepared by Julius Robert Mayer (1814-78) through his discovery of the law of conservation of energy and its transformation into heat (1842). As a consequence he also finds a new law of causation in which he considers once again Hume's central problem. A philosophical line of thought leads directly from Mayer to the physicist Wilhelm Ostwald (1853-1932), who spiritualizes the primitive ideas of the 'Force and Matter' monism by applying to them the philosophic conclusions drawn from Mayer's laws, and once more develops, in accordance with Schelling, a complete system of Nature philosophy. (*Die Energie und ihre Wandlungen*, 1888; *Die Überwindung des wissenschaftlichen Materialismus*, 1895; *Grundriss der Naturphilosophie*, 1908.) This doctrine he extends into a general cultural philosophy; his striking discoveries in the realm of colour theory concern the physicist as well as the æstheticist. The new philosophy of Neo-Positivism also springs from natural science: Ernst Mach (1838-1916) equates determinable reality with the sum-total of elements of perception apprehended in the consciousness. (*Beiträge zur Analyse der Empfindung*, 1886.) Richard Avenarius (1843-96) considers in his philosophy of 'Empiriocriticism' (*Kritik der reinen Erfahrung*, 1888-90) the inseparable nature of outer and inner experience, of the surrounding world and of the 'I' as the basic datum of all knowledge. The positivism of Eugen Dühring (1833-1921) strives on a scientific materialistic basis towards an individual-socialist order of society. (*Wirklichkeitsphilosophie*, 1895.) The Natural Philosophy of Ernst Haeckel (1834-1919), who is important as a naturalist but undistinguished as a philosopher, lies in the line of the *Kraft und Stoff* thinkers, but mixes its monism with pantheistic ideas resembling Goethe's. (*Die Welträtsel*, 1899.)

From the achievements of science in the closing period of the nineteenth century there springs a certain optimism, or rather an optimistic belief in the progress made towards a perfected humanity; but it is counterbalanced by a somewhat morbid attitude to life as the result of cultural surfeit. This is the final stage of a surge of pessimism which already appears before the mid-century in the psychic phenomenon of *Zerrissen-heit* (the Young-German form of splenetic world-weariness or *Welt-schmerz*) and attains its culminating point after 1850 under the growing influence of the philosophies of Schopenhauer and Richard Wagner (1813-83). The early work of Friedrich Nietzsche (1844-1900), *Die Geburt der Tragödie aus dem Geiste der Musik* (1872), is still in the wake of this tragic experience of life; but he soon outgrows this stage and the forced heroic optimism of his later doctrines becomes the decisive philosophic event of the century. Just as Kant towards the end of the eighteenth century demolished the valid conceptions of knowledge, so Nietzsche towards the end of the nineteenth undermines the valid conceptions of value. He sets against the democratic ideal of the greatest possible happiness of the greatest possible number that of the aristocratism of the 'superman', who holds himself responsible for the highest culture possible disregardful of his own happiness. This doctrine is preached above all in Nietzsche's prose-epic *Also sprach Zarathustra* (1883-4; 1891) with the prophetic passion of the really great poet. The working out of his *Der Wille zur Macht*, the work which in all probability would have become his most important and the clearest exposition of his system, was prevented by the onset of mental derangement. (Outline and partial completion 1884-88; published from posthumous papers in the 'Works'.) Nietzsche's voice is the voice of a new era which he foretells some half-century before it arrives. It is he who, along with his votary, the poet Stefan George (1868-1933), and with Stefan George's circle, determines the philosophic situation about 1900. The philosopher Alois Riehl (1844-1924) in his excellent book *Zur Einführung in die Philosophie der Gegenwart* (Halle, 1902; 6th ed. 1921) does not raise this point decisively enough. According to Riehl, the situation is characterized by a turning away from the great speculative systems of 'philosophic Idealism' and by a turning back to the rigour and clearness of Kant's 'critical' thought. This means for Riehl the examination of the consistency of the philosophic results of research, especially in Physics, by means of the fundamental laws of cognition as laid down by Kant. The title of his principal work is indicative of this: *Der philosophische Kritizismus und seine Bedeutung für die positivistische Wissenschaft*. (Vol. I, 1876, vol. II, 1, 1879, vol. II, 2, 1887.) In contrast to the 'Realism' of Riehl's interpretation of Kant, the 'Neo-Kantians' of the 'Marburg school' emphasize the subjective-idealistic element in Kant's Theory of Knowledge. Hermann Cohen (1842-1918) sees in it above all a process of knowing determined by the laws of mind, which as 'developing' thought produces the experience of scientific and cultural life. (*System der Philosophie*, vol. I, 1902, vol. II, 1904.) The

Kantism of Paul Natorp (1854-1924) is less mathematically and logistically
directed than that of Cohen and takes as its special objects Psychology,
Sociology and Pedagogy. (*Sozialpädogogik*, 1909.) Hence, around 1900,
thought deriving from Kant, both in Riehl and in the Marburg philosophers, tends to run, not towards a renewal of metaphysical speculation,
but rather towards philosophic control of all sciences, in order to guard
against their relapse into something purely practical and expedient. The
Kant-Gesellschaft, founded in 1905, devotes itself to the actual care of the
Kantian heritage. This society was conducted by Max Frischeisen-Köhler
(1878-1923), Arthur Liebert (1878-1946), and its founder Hans Vaihinger
(1852-1933), who had been publishing the *Kant-Studien* since 1897. The
fact that his own teaching, *Die Philosophie des Als-ob* (1911), was contemporary with ideas of Nietzsche is obvious: he stresses the 'fictitious',
i.e. the phenomenal, character of perceived reality, but shifts the centre
of gravity from the realm of 'Pure Reason' to that of 'Practical Reason',
that is, of ideas and beliefs. Vaihinger is, as he stated himself, also influenced both by Schopenhauer and by Friedrich Albert Lange (1828-75),
author of the admirable work *Die Geschichte des Materialismus* (1866).
Schopenhauer still has a powerful effect in other directions as well. As a
natural philosopher he is esteemed more highly than previously; upon
his work rests Neo-Vitalism, which is philosophically evolved in the
work *Die Philosophie des Organischen* (Leipzig, 1909) by Hans Driesch
(1869-1941). The break of Driesch with his teacher Haeckel is significant
for the changed situation of natural philosophy around 1900; when
Konrad Küster still offers in 1925 a *Schlüssel zur Lösung der Welträtsel*, the
effect of the book on the reader is that of a ghost from the past. (On the
importance of Küster for the intellectual life of Germany, see Albert
Soergel, *Dichtung und Dichter der Zeit*, Leipzig, 1928, p. 122 f.) To understand fully how obsolete the philosophy of this Haeckelian type of
monism already was round 1900, one must bear in mind that the philosophic results of the research into Physics by Heinrich Hertz (1857-94)
were already known in the 'nineties. (*Gesammelte Werke*, Leipzig, 1894-5.)
Alois Riehl emphasizes their great importance for philosophic thought
at the turn of the century, but mentions in the 6th edition (1921) of his
Zur Einführung in die Philosophie der Gegenwart only in a casual way the
name of Albert Einstein (1879-), although the first version of his theory
of Relativity had already been published in 1905. (*Zur Elektrodynamik
bewegter Körper*, in *Annalen der Physik*, XVII, 1905, pp. 891 ff.) On the
other hand, the authority of Kant is still so undisputed that even as late
as 1919 Ewald Sellin, in his book *Die erkenntnistheoretische Bedeutung der
Relativitätstheorie*, attempts to demonstrate that Kant's theory of knowl-

edge is entirely compatible with the new picture of the universe created by Einstein. Thus the intellectual situation in Germany about 1900 is fundamentally determined by Kant and the new science, but Schopenhauer, Wagner, Nietzsche and George have a wide-spread influence upon the life-philosophy of the period.

Of all these, the only influences still decisively effective by 1930 are those of science and of Nietzsche and George, although the work of Kant, Schopenhauer and Wagner still has a bearing on the thought of the time. Quietly extending beneath the surface is the value-philosophy of Franz Brentano (1838-1917). This was directed against Kant and his successors: in contrast to their cognitive theories it stresses the *a priori* character of self-evident truth both in knowledge and in morality. The influence of Brentano's school must not be underestimated; its chief members are Anton Marty (1847-1914), Carl Stumpf (1848-1936), Alexius von Meinong (1853-1920), Christian Freiherr von Ehrenfels (1859-1932), and, in the second generation, Oskar Kraus (1872-1942), Alfred Kastil (1874-1950), Richard Strohal (1888-), and Franziska Mayer-Hillebrand (1885-), who is now in charge of the Master's unpublished works. Brentano is also the starting point for Edmund Husserl (1859-1938: see Part I), from whose *Phänomenalismus* is again derived the work of Max Scheler (1874-1928). His Ethics (*Zur Phänomenologie und Theorie der Sympathiegefühle*, 1913), his religious philosophy (*Vom Ewigen im Menschen*, 1921) and his sociology (*Moralia*, 1923) are significant for their rejection of the positivism and criticism of the 1900 period. His works on the philosophy of the state are also important in connection with the intellectual situation about 1900. For in analogy with the political situation round 1800, a time between two European wars, the philosophy of the state again comes to the fore in 1930. Two works appear at approximately the same time, calling for the rehabilitation of national values: *Das Dritte Reich* (1923) by Artur Moeller van den Bruck (1876-1925), and *Das heilige Reich der Deutschen* (1925) by Leopold Ziegler (1881-). The works of Walther Rathenau (1867-1922), mentioned in Part I, have their parallel in the *Politische Schriften* of Oswald Spengler (1880-1936), which include among others the important *Preussentum und Sozialismus* (1919) and *Neubau des deutschen Reiches* (1924). The far-reaching agreement in thought between the 'conservative' Spengler and the 'democratic' Rathenau also offers an analogy with the situation between 1800 and 1810 in which appeared Fichte's socialist *Reden an die deutsche Nation* (1800) and A. v. Müller's conservative lectures *Über die deutsche Wissenschaft* (1807). The agreement between Spengler and Rathenau strengthens the contention expressed in Part I that the idea of the German state is to be realized not in the direction of democracy but in that of state socialism compatible with individual liberty. Spengler complements in this way on the practical side his theory of history laid down in *Untergang des Abendlandes*. (Part I, 1918, Part II, 1922.) Like Spengler's principal work, another 'structural' philosophy, the *Erfahrungswissenschaft der geistigen Erscheinungen*, which had already been worked out before and shortly after 1900 by Wilhelm Dilthey (1833-1911), became fully fruitful only after his death, e.g. in the work *Lebensformen* (1921) by his pupil Eduard Spranger (1882-). The æsthetics of Dilthey (e.g. *Das Erlebnis und die Dichtung*, 1905) has likewise had far-reaching effects. Standing independently at his side as æstheticists are two members of the older generation: Max Dessoir (1867-1947), after earlier specialized works, surveyed the position of æsthetics at the time in his *Ausblick auf eine Philosophie der Kunst* (Stuttgart, 1931); Johannes Volkelt (1886-1930) conceived a psychological theory of 'intuiting feeling' (*schauendes Erfühlen*) in which he seeks to embrace the various departments of æsthetics (*Ästhetik des Tragischen*, 1897; *System der Ästhetik*, 1905 and 1910; *Das ästhetische Bewusstsein*, 1920). Alfred Werner (1892-), the meritorious publisher of the monographs appearing as *Die philosophische Reihe* (1920-33), and of the periodical *Philosophische Studien*, 1949-51, is the pupil, not only of Dessoir, but also of both Johannes Rehmke (1848-1930), the very independent psychologist of the cognitive process, and of the sensitive and searching art-historian Heinrich von Wölfflin (1864-1945). The latter was the successor of the great Jakob Burckhardt (1818-97) in Basel. Partly in opposition to Volkelt and Dessoir and in substantial agreement with Husserl, Rudolf Odebrecht (1883-1945) began a highly important *Grundlegung einer ästhetischen Werttheorie* of which only the first volume, *Das ästhetische Werterlebnis*, has appeared (Berlin, 1927).

The years round 1930, like all transition periods, were already building up the fresh form that gives its stamp to the situation of German thought at the present day. *Die geistige Situation der Zeit*, in which Karl Jaspers (1883-) analyses the situation in 1931, would apply equally well to the year 1950. Martin Heidegger (1889-) had published his fundamental work *Sein und Zeit* by 1927, and the theological and philosophical *Römerbrief* of Karl Barth (1886-) appeared as early as 1918. Thus between about 1920 and 1930 a new philosophy—Existentialism – is in its beginnings. It gains vogue, particularly in Germany, Italy and France. Fritz Heinemann (1889-) claims to have been the first to characterize this movement by the name *Existenzphilosophie*: 'I understood by the term "*Existenzphilosophie*" a new approach, an attempt to overcome the one-sidedness of both rational and non-rational philosophy. Instead of setting out from the Cartesian *cogito* (meaning both consciousness and thought) it starts from the subject in its threefold relationship with man, with the universe and with God.' This statement of Heinemann refers to his book *Neue Wege der Philosophie: Geist, Leben, Existenz*, which appeared in 1929. Heinemann thus belongs to the founders of the German branch of this philosophy which ushers in the whole movement. We can here give consideration only to this branch, the fundamental ideal of which can be traced back to the Danish religious philosopher and psychologist Sören Kierkegaard (1813-55). At all events, the modern interpretation of the terms 'existence' (*Existenz*) and 'anxiety' (*Angst*) goes back to Kierkegaard.

Seen in the light of the time in which it sprang up, Existentialism is certainly – to use a term struck by Jaspers – the philosophy of a 'border-line situation' in the history of Europe. The outcome of the frightful events which have shaken Europe since 1914 has induced Jaspers to think out anew the whole problem of 'the origin and goal of history' (*Vom Ursprung und Ziel der Geschichte*, Berne, 1949). He is not in a position to offer any harmonizing *Total-Anschauung* in the manner of Hegel; he says: '*Geschichtsphilosophische Totalanschauung, wie wir (Jaspers) sie versuchen, soll die eigene Situation erleuchten im Ganzen der Geschichte*' (l.c., p. 109).

(The philosophical and historical comprehensive view we are attempting here is to throw light upon our own situation in the context of history as a whole.)

This situation, however, interests the existential philosopher, not as one among many stages in the course of events regarded pragmatically, but as the situation of a generation of individuals who have created it and who are responsible for their actions. In other words, man himself, his nature, and the meaning of his activities become the starting-point for consideration. At the same time concern with psychology withdraws to the background; discussion of this belongs to a bygone stage of Existentialism – that of Kierkegaard. The central question of this philosophy comes primarily from the Germans, and consequently it is in a metaphysical sense that it has been posed. This is done in the most radical form, going even beyond Kant's question as to whether Metaphysics was possible: Heidegger's lecture *Was ist Metaphysik?* (1929) investigates the pre-requisite conditions for the metaphysical attitude as such. One may say that the fundamental answer to this had already been given by Schopenhauer: at the root of Metaphysics is *das metaphysische Bedürfnis des Menschen* (the metaphysical impulse innate in man). One could also say it in Schelling's words: 'the first question of philosophy is . . . this: What is that which exists? What properties has it? What do I think of if

I think of that which exists?' (*Darstellung des Naturprozesses*, 1843-4; *Works*, Div. I, vol. x, p. 303.) But whereas Schelling's starting-point is the question of how the Absolute can devolve into finite Being, Heidegger derives the problem of Being from the metaphysical experiences of 'nothingness' (*Nichts*) and from 'anxiety' (*Angst*). In both cases, however, the approach, though beyond all Church religion, is yet undeniably a religious one, as it involves the meaning of Being and hence the meaning of man, who in this state of Being exists – *ex-sistit* – stands out. This rooting of all merely derived systems of Metaphysics – such as Kierkegaard held Hegel's to be – in the Metaphysics of the original question of every higher religion is actually the central concern of German existential philosophy. In its earlier forms, not only in Kierkegaard but also in Nietzsche, it remains partly involved with the subjective and the psychological, because both of these writers, as *Grenzmenschen* (borderline men), in the sense of Emil Lucka (*Grenzen der Seele*, 1914), produce their philosophy out of the sufferings of their individual lives; existential philosophy in Germany in its mature form has again developed objective and completely thought-out systems, the character of which in Barth's case is dogmatically religious, in Heidegger's areligious, and in Jaspers' semi-religious.

To compare their differences systematically would only mean repeating what has already been undertaken in countless books and essays. The following short statements must suffice. For Barth God is 'the eternal pure foundation of all that is' (*Römerbrief*, pp. 51 f. and *passim*), but He is not a metaphysical absolute in the sense given to Him by the post-Kantian philosophers. He apparently corresponds to Heidegger's *actus purus*, i.e. an entity transcending that transcendence which was experienced by the thinkers of 'German Idealism'. (For details see Max Müller, *Existenz-philosophie im geistigen Leben der Gegenwart*, Heidelberg, 1949, pp. 75-77; Müller's exposition is based on direct information.) Man, 'fallen' (Heidegger would say 'de-jected') from essence into (mere) existence through 'sin' (Heidegger would say 'guilt' in a metaphysical, not in a moral, sense) is separated from God by the boundary line of death (*Todeslinie*). Only for the 'elect' may it be possible to 'transcend' this relationship at the moment of being 'found' by God as a result of recognition of their existential situation; that is to say, for them to divine, out of the darkness and bewilderment of human existence, the light and security of Godly Being on the other side. We are not concerned here with the theological conclusions drawn by Barth, and wish only to emphasize the line linking him to Heidegger and Jaspers. Barth's 'death-line' to God is with Heidegger the boundary-line of death behind which there looms nothingness. Man is running forward (*läuft vor*) to this line, which is not a fixed one but one in process of becoming, towards which he 'flees' from the (likewise becoming) nothingness out of which he has sprung into 'existence'. Whereas, however, the *Mittelmensch* (commonplace man) – to use again Lucka's terminology – has no clear comprehension of his existential situation, the *Grenzmensch* (borderline man) is fully conscious of it, and, through being so, 'transcends' it, as Barth's 'elect' may be able to 'transcend' their fleeting existence. This death-line of Barth and Heidegger corresponds in Jaspers' philosophy to the death-line of 'shipwreck' (*Scheitern*) which is bound to be the final outcome of every *Grenzsituation* (borderline situation). With Barth as well as with Heidegger and Jaspers it is the metaphysical feeling of *Angst* (anxiety) which places us in the presence of the fundamental forlornness of our 'existence'. This 'anxiety', which has nothing to do with fear, is an emotional reaction in face of a menace inherent within the nature of Being as such. It is, however, at the same time the beginning of a turning towards *Gnade* (grace). In Barth it is a religious recognition of sinfulness based on the nature of 'fallen' Being itself, in Kierkegaard an ambivalent psychological situation between despair and hope. In Heidegger it is the beginning of redemption of 'true existence' (*Existenz*) from 'mere existence' (*Dasein*). Hence 'anxiety' is also the beginning of liberty, which leads, or rather which may lead, in the case of Barth to free acceptance of grace (much as it means to Kierkegaard the freedom of choice between grace and sin) and in the case of Heidegger to courageous awareness of our fate and philosophic acceptance of Existence in the face of death. To this undaunted attitude to life in Heidegger there corresponds in Jaspers that of *Trotz* (defiance) which, in full consciousness of the vanity and futility of all achievement, nevertheless acts as if 'foundering' (*Scheitern*) were not the ultimate end.

Owing to lack of space, we are unable to demonstrate here that this tragic-heroic attitude in Heidegger and especially in Jaspers is only the most recent form of a typically German attitude to life (accepted also by some French thinkers) which can be followed up in an unbroken series from the Edda down to Schopenhauer and Nietzsche. To classify it as sterile 'pessimism' is to display German thought in a completely false light. Another point in Existentialism which is typically German, and present in both Heidegger and Jaspers, is the close connection between Being and Becoming, which in Heidegger leads to important investigations into the nature of time and its relationship with Being. The linking of this Time-Being experience with that of death, which sometimes sounds like a philosophic accompaniment to the death-poetry of the Romantics and particularly of Novalis, must also be regarded as a

typically German feature of Existentialism. Particularly German is furthermore the idea of the polarity in all Being, emphasized above all by
Jaspers, which in his case does not finally reach dialectical adjustment as
it does in Hegel, but destines every existence to 'Scheitern' through its
unresolved tensional nature.

The basic problems of existential philosophy are modern in their setting,
but in their essence by no means so new to German thought as they appear
to the outside world. The questions of Heine's *Jüngling-Mann* (in *Die
Nordsee*, II, 7): '*Sagt mir, was bedeutet der Mensch? Woher ist er kommen?
Wo geht er hin?*' are answered in the sense of Heidegger and of his pupil
Sartre: '*Und ein Narr wartet auf Antwort.*' In comparison with Jaspers'
defiant affirmation of life, which urges man, regardless of the shipwreck
of his existence, to transcend his individual self and to widen it into the
Self of mankind, we have Goethe's Faust, who, after his early disillusion-
ment, can say:

> Und so mein Selbst zu ihrem Selbst erweitern,
> Und wie sie selbst, am End' auch ich zerscheitern.

The truly nihilistic philosopher of Existentialism in German thought is
neither Heidegger nor Jaspers, but the anarchic Max Stirner (1806-56),
who closes the introduction to his principal work, *Der Einzige und sein
Eigentum* (1845), with the following words: 'My concern is neither the
divine nor the human, but solely what is Mine, and it is nothing of a
general nature but is – unique, as I am unique. Nothing concerns me
more than myself!' (Reclam Ed. 14.) The German Existentialists,
however, in spite of knowing not only the isolation but also the tragic
solitariness of the 'I', proclaim activity within and for the community. It
is true they scorn the consolation of a fictitious 'Beyond' in religion and
Metaphysics. As precept they point to the example of man, for ever
suffering disillusionment and none the less for ever struggling upwards;
man, who, in his 'running forward into death', re-creates the Becoming
of 'mere existence' into 'true existence' by courageous acceptance of the
clearly realized polarity of life, its anguish and happiness:

> Der Erdenkreis ist mir genug bekannt,
> Nach drüben ist die Aussicht uns verrannt;
> Tor, wer dorthin die Augen blinzelnd richtet,
> Sich über Wolken seinesgleichen dichtet!
> Er stehe fest und sehe hier sich um;
> Dem Tüchtigen ist diese Welt nicht stumm.
> Was braucht er in die Ewigkeit zu schweifen!
> Was er erkennt, lässt sich ergreifen.

Er wandle so den Erdentag entlang;
Wenn Geister spuken, geh' er seinen Gang,
Im Weiterschreiten find' er Qual und Glück,
Er, unbefriedigt jeden Augenblick!

(*Faust* II, 11441-11452)

That is the final word of Goethe the Existential philosopher to the German mind.

BIBLIOGRAPHY TO CHAPTER XI

Titles of books and editions already given above are not (with one exception) mentioned again.

Ziegenfuss, Werner, and Jung, Gertrud. *Philosophen-Lexikon. Handwörterbuch der Philosophie nach Personen.* 2 vols. Berlin, 1949 and 1950

Kirchner, Friedrich. *Wörterbuch der philosophischen Grundbegriffe.* Neubearbeitung by Michaelis, Carl. *Philosophische Bibliothek,* vol. 67. Leipzig, 5th ed., 1907, repeated editions

Thormeyer, Paul. *Philosophisches Wörterbuch.* Leipzig, 4th ed., 1930

Überweg, Friedrich, and Heinze, Max. *Grundriss der Geschichte der Philosophie.* Berlin, 10th ed., 1909 seq., repeated editions. 5 vols. Basel, 1952

Deter, Christian Johann, and Frischeisen-Köhler, Max. *Abriss der Geschichte der Philosophie.* Berlin, 1923

Rogers, Arthur Kenyon. *A Student's History of Philosophy.* New York and London, 1920

Heine, Heinrich. *Geschichte der Religion und Philosophie in Deutschland.* Edited with comments and introduction by C. P. Magill. London, 1949

Wechssler, Eduard. *Esprit und Geist.* Leipzig, 1927

Majut, Hans. *Das Ewig-Griechische. Eine Seelenschau.* Augsburg, 1946

Clark, James M. *The Great German Mystics. Eckehart, Tauler and Suso.* Oxford, 1949

Cassirer, Ernst. *Freiheit und Form. Studien zur deutschen Geistesgeschichte.* Berlin, 1916

Strich, Fritz. *Klassik und Romantik oder Vollendung und Unendlichkeit.* Berne, 4th ed., 1949

Riehl, Alois. *Zur Einführung in die Philosophie der Gegenwart.* Leipzig and Berlin, 6th ed., 1921

Hübscher, Arthur. *Philosophie der Gegenwart.* Munich, 1949

Ruggiero, Guido de. *Existentialism.* Edited and introduced by Rayner Heppenstall. London, 1946

Mounier, Emmanuel. *Existential Philosophy, an Introduction.* Translated by Eric Blow. London, 1948

Wilkinson, Elizabeth. *Johann Elias Schlegel. A German Pioneer in Æsthetics.* Oxford, 1945

Meumann, E. *Einführung in die Ästhetik der Gegenwart.* Leipzig, 1908; 4th ed., 1930

Odebrecht, Rudolf. *Ästhetik der Gegenwart.* Berlin, 1932

Jodl, Friedrich. *Geschichte der Ethik in der neueren Philosophie.* 2 vols. Stuttgart, 3rd ed., 1923

Walzel, Oskar. *Deutsche Romantik.* 2 vols. Leipzig, 1918

CHAPTER XII

GERMAN MUSIC

THE recorded story of German music opens with the Minnesänger, who were the Teutonic counterpart of the Troubadours, and first became widely known in the reign of the Emperor Frederick Barbarossa (1152-90; see pp. 226 ff., 43, 45). It is continued by that of the Meistersinger (see pp. 229, 478), guilds whose members were not of noble birth as the Minnesänger had been, but mostly citizens who graduated through the five stages of Schüler, Schülerfreund, Sänger, Dichter, and Meister. They inherited a fine tradition, but interpreted it with a somewhat pedantic stiffness which led to a rapid decline in quality. Moreover, the invention of new melodies was discouraged by the practice of composing new poems to the old ones, some of which did duty constantly, and not always for congenial texts. Four of these tunes were known as *gekrönte Töne*, including one by Frauenlob (see p. 275), and another by Heinrich von Mugelin which has become very familiar through Wagner's use of it in his music-drama, 'Die Meistersinger'.

Contemporaneously with the Meistersinger, another element in German music began to assert itself, at first so humbly that none could have foreseen that from its ranks would emerge the most remarkable dynasty of musicians history has ever known. This was the so-called town-pipers. Originally wayfaring musicians, in the thirteenth century they had begun to band themselves in guilds, and thereby succeeded gradually in raising their social status. Such a guild was, for instance, the Brotherhood of St. Nicholas, established in Vienna in 1288. These guilds, which came to be known as town-pipers, may be looked upon as the ancestors of the town orchestras of later times. But of even greater interest is the fact that Hans Bach, the 'Spielmann', was apprenticed to Caspar Bach, town-piper of Gotha, and that other members of the Bach family followed the same calling. Johann Sebastian Bach was the Spielmann's great-grandson.

But we are anticipating. Whilst first Minnesänger, then Meistersinger and town-pipers were serving the popular taste in music, elsewhere the art itself was being revolutionized by the early polyphonists. But, though in Bach polyphonic art was to reach its culmination, Germany played but a small part in its early development. It is usual to ascribe to the Nether-lands the honour of bringing this new art to fruition, but we must not forget that JOANNES DE TINCTORIS (1446-*c.* 1511), himself a Fleming, gave England the credit for having invented it, and that the oldest known document is an English manuscript. Of German musicians at this time little was heard, and that little relates more to instruments than to com-position. It was for instance a German, Bernhard, organist to the Doge of Venice, who about 1470 so improved the pedals that, though they were certainly known before his time, he is generally regarded as their inventor. Another organist was CONRAD PAUMANN, the first German composer to earn a place in history. He was born at Nuremberg about 1410 and was blind, but became one of the most noted performers of his time. He died in 1473, and of his compositions only a few remain in existence. It is more usual to regard HEINRICH ISAAK (1450-1517) as the first of the Ger-man masters, as he was certainly the earliest to win renown as a composer. He was born about 1450 in Brabant, therefore a Fleming by birth, and he was probably a pupil of JACOB HOBRECHT (*c.* 1450-1505) or JOSQUIN DES PRÉS. He spent many years in the service of the Medici, but he afterwards became attached to the Court of the Emperor Maximilian, and since the Netherlands belonged to the Empire it was justifiable as well as convenient to regard him as German. The most distinguished of his contemporaries was HEINRICH FINCK, probably a native of Bamberg. Isaak died in 1517, Finck ten years later. Together they represent a distinct phase of German music, that preceding the Reformation.

It would be a fascinating intellectual exercise to probe the reasons why that great event, with the impetus it gave to congregational singing, should have had opposite effects upon the music of England and Germany. England was then enjoying a Golden Age in music. It is only in recent years that the extraordinary musical wealth of the Tudor period has been realized. After the Reformation the spate of great music ceased, and, save for the brief radiance of Purcell, musical England suffered an eclipse that was to endure for centuries. In Germany, which, as we have seen, had until then boasted little repute, the Lutheran chorale became the founda-tion of the art of Bach, and through him the root of all the glory that has accrued to that country's music. Though religious intolerance was common to most countries at the time, in Germany music did not suffer from it. John Taverner might be moved to express public repentance for having written his Masses for the Roman Church, but Martin Luther himself had the highest esteem for the motets of Isaak's pupil, LUDWIG SENFL (1490-*c.* 1555), who remained a Catholic to the end of his days. With the aid of his friend JOHANN WALTHER (1496-1570) Luther introduced the reformed chorale, and the new era opened. Of its earlier masters the most outstanding was JAKOB KALLWITZ (Sethus Calvisius), who was appointed in 1594 cantor at the Thomasschule and music director at the Thomaskirche in Leipzig, posts which Bach was to take up in 1723. Calvisius died at Leipzig in 1615.

The Lutheran chorale owed much to that other great source of German music, folk-song. It should, however, be noted that the traditional songs of the German people do not bear as deeply the impress of popular usage as, for instance, those of Somerset. Probably the reason lies in the characteristic German's predilection for accuracy. He learned his songs correctly, and there arose fewer of those 'variants' which are cherished by collectors of folk-songs. Many of the oldest songs to be found in German collections are of more or less known origin. Some of them are ascribed to Heinrich Isaak, who was a prolific song-maker. One of the earliest song-books was that of Heinrich Finck, who spent most of his life at the Polish court, but retired in his old age to Wittenberg. It is not improbable that his writings may have influenced Luther's taste in song. His grand-nephew, HERMANN FINCK (1527-58), was a learned musician and organist at Wittenberg. This period of German music may be said to end with the work of JOHANNES ECCARD (1553-1611), who was a pupil of ORLANDUS LASSUS or ORLANDO DI LASSO (1520-94; Franco-Belgian school). The tutorial influence of the Netherlands over German music was, however, to endure in a modified form a generation longer, when it was represented by three pupils of JAN PIETERSZOON SWEELINCK (1562-1621): SAMUEL SCHEIDT (1587-1654), HEINRICH SCHEIDEMANN (c. 1596-1663), and JAKOB SCHULTZ. The musical bearers of the last name, a common one in Germany, followed the custom of the day and called themselves Praetorius, which is its Latin equivalent. There were several of them, beside Jakob, the most famous being MICHAEL PRAETORIUS (1571-1621), a prolific writer whose 'Musae Sioniae' alone contains 1244 songs. Sweelinck, the creator of the organ fugue, which Bach was to carry to perfection, had some Italian learning, but his music retains the Northern characteristics.

Meanwhile the attention of German musicians turned more and more southwards, and Italian influence soon began to supplant that of the Netherlands. To some extent this was only an extension of the same tradition, for the Venetian school, to which many young German composers were attracted, was founded by ADRIAN WILLAERT, a native of either Bruges or Roulers. He was succeeded by GIOSEFE ZARLINO (1517-90) and the two GABRIELIS, uncle and nephew. The influence of the school is represented in German music chiefly by HANS LEO HASSLER (1564-1612) and HEINRICH SCHÜTZ, known as Sagittarius (1585-1672), pupils respectively of the elder and the younger Gabrieli. These were two masters whose fame spread over the Continent, and whose works are still performed, but they were the outstanding figures of a numerous company. Besides the Venetian group there were also some pupils of GIROLAMO FRESCOBALDI (1583-1643) of Ferrara, the great organist in Rome, among whom JOHANN JAKOB FROBERGER (1610-67) is the most important. And in South Germany there arose a little later another group which has affinities with French as well as Italian music, and in which the most distinguished names are those of Georg Muffat, descended from an English family which had emigrated in the sixteenth century, and Heinrich Biber, both of whom died in 1704. Yet it must not be supposed that the national trend found itself entirely swamped by this invasion of alien musical fashions, as was to happen later in England. Throughout this period the young German tradition maintained its vitality. In its earlier phase its outstanding representatives were JOHANN HERMANN SCHEIN (1586-1630), another of Bach's predecessors as Cantor of St. Thomas's, and MELCHIOR FRANCK (1573-1639), both prolific writers of church music. In the later phase there came into prominence a succession of great organists whom one may regard as the immediate precursors of Bach, who heard more than one of them in his youth. There was DIETRICH BUXTEHUDE (1637-1707), a Dane, organist at Lübeck; JOHANN ADAM REINKEN (1623-1722), a Dutchman, who succeeded Scheidemann at Hamburg; JOHANN PACHELBEL (1653-1706); JOHANN JOSEPH FUX (1660-1741) at Vienna; and Bach's immediate predecessor at Leipzig, JOHANN KUHNAU (1667-1722), the composer of 'Biblical' Sonatas. These are the outstanding names, but it was a period of great organists, through whom the sturdy German tradition founded by Martin Luther regained its ascendancy, at least so far as church music was concerned, and although the church no longer exercised such sway over music as it had done a century earlier, it was still the most powerful factor. Such was the musical situation in Germany when arose the first of the great classics who were destined to make her for generations, and even centuries, the predominant country in the world's music.

The great figure of JOHANN SEBASTIAN BACH (1685-1750) stands Janus-like at the crucial point of musical history, for in one direction he faces the polyphonic past, which he brought to fullest consummation, and in the other he faces a future in which he is destined to be regarded as the real founder of modern music. For Germany he inaugurated an era of genius. His German predecessors had been worthy men, some of them possessed of great talent, but measured by the standard of genius they would be classed as composers of the second or third rank. There was not one among them to be compared with PALESTRINA (1524-94) in Italy, or WILLIAM BYRD (1543-1623) in England. But from Bach to Wagner Germany was never without one or more musical geniuses of the foremost rank. It is to them that she owed her ascendancy in the musical world that reached its height in the nineteenth century.

Hereditary gifts are far from uncommon in musical history. The Couperins in France made music during two centuries, the Philidors during one, and in Italy, besides the two Gabrielis mentioned above, we have the famous instance of the two Scarlattis, father and son, each of whom belongs to the elect company of the great composers. In Germany five organists of the name of Valentin Hausmann followed in direct lineal succession. But the Bach dynasty stands alone. In the State Library, Berlin, is a manuscript of eighteen pages bearing the title 'Ursprung der musikalisch-Bachischen Familie'. Bach's first biographer, J. M. Forkel, borrowed it from Carl Philipp Emanuel, Bach's second son, who told him that it had been commenced by his father many years earlier. It has recently been published in facsimile under the editorship of Professor C. Sanford Terry. It gives particulars of fifty-three members of the Bach family, mentions many others, nearly all of them musicians, and the record is not complete. The founder of the family was Veit Bach, a miller by trade, whose only musical proclivity seems to have been a fondness for the lute, which he played even when the mill was working. It must have made a pretty blend, says Johann Sebastian, but at least he 'learned to keep time, and that apparently is how music began in our family'. His son, Johannes Bach, revealed so much musical talent that he was apprenticed at Gotha to Caspar Bach, probably his uncle, who was a town-piper. This is the Hans to whom we referred as the Spielmann (p. 454). Veit Bach died in 1619, Johannes in 1626. Of Caspar little is known, but from that time onwards the Bachs began to spread until they held almost a monopoly of all the musical posts to be had in Thuringia, whether as cantors, organists, or town musicians (for they soon ceased to be called town-pipers). Of Johann Sebastian's immediate precursors in the family, the most eminent as composers were Johann Christoph and Johann Michael, the two elder sons of Heinrich Bach and grandsons of the Spielmann. Both were organists, the elder at Eisenach, the younger at Gehren, where he was also town clerk.

Johann Sebastian was descended from another of the Spielmann's sons, his father being Johann Ambrosius Bach, town musician of Eisenach, where he was born 21st March 1685. His father taught him the violin, but died when the boy was only ten years old, whereupon he went to live with his uncle, Johann Christian of Ohrdruf (not to be confused with the above-mentioned Johann Christian of Eisenach), who taught him the clavichord. He studied at the Lyceum at Ohrdruf, and in 1700 was admitted chorister at St. Michael's, Lüneburg, where he made the most of his opportunities, working hard far into the night, listening to one of the finest organists of the day, Georg Böhm, who officiated at the neighbouring church of St. John's, and on more than one occasion taking a thirty-mile walk to hear the veteran Johann Adam Reinken at Hamburg. It is from this time that date Bach's earliest compositions. On 8th April 1703 he entered as violinist the private band of Duke Johann Ernst of Weimar, but already on 14th August of the same year he was installed as organist at Arnstadt. In October 1705 he obtained a month's leave, and set out on foot for distant Lübeck, in order to hear the greatest of his seniors, Dietrich Buxtehude. In those days it was customary for official posts to be continued in the same family. If there were no sons it was not unusual for the candidate for the succession to marry one of the occupant's daughters. Buxtehude himself had married the daughter of his predecessor at the Marienkirche, FRANZ TUNDER (1614-67). Just before Bach's visit he had received that of two young musicians from Hamburg, George Frederick Handel and Johann Mattheson, who were both employed at the opera there. But Buxtehude's daughter was a buxom wench, some twelve years older than Mattheson, who was Handel's senior, so that the young men counted the cost and fled. It is related that when Bach arrived in his turn a similar prospect was put before him, but, although he did not entertain it, his relations with Buxtehude were undisturbed, and he profited much by the intercourse. On 15th June 1707 he was appointed organist at Mühlhausen, where he remained about a year. Then he went to Weimar as Hof-Organist and Kammer-Musikus to the reigning duke, Wilhelm Ernst. This Weimar period lasted nine years, during the last three of which he was Konzertmeister. On 5th August 1717 Prince Leopold of Anhalt-Cöthen appointed him Kapellmeister, and 'Direktor unserer Kammer-Musik'. He did not leave Weimar without some difficulty. He was even placed under arrest for contumacy. The Cöthen period lasted six years. Then in 1723 he obtained, in succession to Johann Kuhnau, the post at Leipzig, which he held for twenty-seven years until his death on 28th July 1750. During the greater part of his career he paid visits to other towns, chiefly in the autumn, to play the organ or to meet other musicians. In the latter respect his visit to Halle in 1719 to meet Handel proved abortive, for the greatest of contemporary composers had just left for England. The most memorable of his journeys was that to Potsdam, where he arrived on Sunday 7th May 1747 at the invitation of

Frederick the Great, who welcomed him royally. It was for the Prussian
monarch that he wrote immediately afterwards the 'Musicalisches Opfer'.
He was twice married, first to his second cousin, Maria Barbara Bach, and
on her death to Anna Magdalena, daughter of Johann Caspar Wilcken,
Court trumpeter at Weissenfels. He had twenty children, seven by his
first, and thirteen by his second wife. Of them all only five sons and three
daughters survived him, most of the others having died in infancy or
childhood. Five of the sons followed their father's profession, and
achieved fame in varying degrees. Musically they contributed to inaugurate a new era. Two years after Bach's death his widow was in receipt
of charitable relief. If we have presented the bare facts of his life it is
because these form its material substance. It was a life of domestic piety
and industry with very few incidents of a spectacular or romantic character. His real life lay in his works, in which he accumulated so much
wisdom that the study of them is well-nigh inexhaustible. To his own
sons he appeared old-fashioned, because of the new currents that had
commenced to flow through the musical world. For a time his music
suffered eclipse, and many of his manuscripts were scattered, only to be
sought after and treasured a generation later.

Those currents originated in Italy and France. Bach was not unaware
of them, as may be seen by his Italian Concerto and French Overture, but
there was one aspect from which he held aloof: the opera. Founded at
Florence at the beginning of the seventeenth century, the opera had
rapidly spread throughout Italy, and thence to Paris. It also reached
Germany, but whereas in the French capital it became Gallicized under
JEAN-BAPTISTE LULLI (1633-87) and JEAN-PHILLIPE RAMEAU (1683-1764),
in Germany and Austria Italian performers were at first preferred, and
such attempts as Heinrich Schütz's (p. 457) 'Dafne' (1627) met with little
encouragement. Not until the reign of REINHARD KEISER (1673-1739) at
Hamburg can opera be said to have become indigenous in Germany. His
first work in this form was produced in 1701. Two years later there came
to play in his orchestra an eighteen-year-old violinist who was to make
history: GEORGE FREDERICK HANDEL (1685-1759).[1] But as the scene of the
history he made was almost entirely in this country it lies outside the scope
of this volume. Suffice it to say that he was born less than a month before
Bach, whom he survived by nearly nine years. Beyond all question he was
the greatest of the latter's contemporaries. Whilst, however, he was producing opera in England, his native land had to make the most of an
inferior, but for a time fashionable, composer, JOHANN ADOLF HASSE
(1699-1783), who wrote over a hundred operas and was the husband of

---

[1] German form: Georg Friedrich Händel.

the famous singer Faustina Bordoni. He began his career under Keiser, but its most flourishing period was passed at Dresden under the Elector Frederick Augustus II, who was also King of Poland, and whose court has provided material for many popular historical novels. Hasse's nearest rival was KARL HEINRICH GRAUN (1701-59), who became Frederick the Great's Kapellmeister. These men, whose music is remembered only by students, were far more conspicuous upon the musical horizon than Bach. Even in his own field GEORG PHILIPP TELEMANN (1681-1767), who wrote forty operas, but also a vast amount of instrumental music, and about 3000 works for the church, is said to have been better known at the time than the Leipzig Kantor. No doubt the superficial quality of such music as Hasse's or Telemann's made it easier to digest.

Soon, however, there was to arise a German operatic genius, the first since Handel, in RITTER CHRISTOPH WILLIBALD VON GLUCK (1714-87), a South German; but even he, when the time was ripe for the revolution he was to effect in the nature and form of opera, found it expedient to display its noblest results on a foreign stage. He had previously made journeys to London, whence he returned discomfited by Handel's gibe that he 'knew no more counterpoint than his, Handel's, cook', who, by the way, is stated to have been a very good musician; and to Paris, where he heard Rameau's operas, and made some friends who were to prove valuable later. He composed for Vienna and Prague a number of operas which are now forgotten, and then, in 1762, startled the world with *Orfeo ed Euridice*, the first-fruit of the new but as yet only partly developed train of thought he was pursuing. With the *Alcestis*, 1767, followed by *Paride ed Elena*, 1770, he launched the new style to which he had attained, and was dissatisfied with its reception at Vienna, where not even his popularity and the favour he enjoyed at Court were enough to sugar the pill of a shock to the conventional ideas of opera then prevailing. He thereupon took his wares to Paris, and it is there that his later masterpieces were produced, including the two *Iphigénies* and *Armide*, interspersed with revised versions of *Orphée* and *Alceste*. Meanwhile in Germany there was developing a new type of opera, the Singspiel, which is a Teutonic equivalent of the French *opéra comique*. Its real founder was JOHANN ADAM HILLER (1728-1804), whose models were Hasse and Graun. The form became popular, and there is no doubt that it exercised a great influence upon the development of opera itself. As in France, the description came to be affixed to works which today would be classed as grand opera. For instance Mozart calls his *The Magic Flute* a Singspiel.

What was happening during this time in other fields of music? The sons of Bach, as we have seen, turned from the ways of their titanic sire.

Burney has left it on record that in conversation Carl Philipp Emanuel Bach (1714-88) would describe canons as 'dry and despicable pieces of pedantry that anyone might write who would give his time to them', and that there were many more essential things than counterpoint. In this he was not being wantonly disrespectful, but merely yielding to the spirit of the times. As in Italy 150 years earlier, the current had set in a new direction. A new chapter of musical history was about to open, and, as usually happens, the signs were misread at the time. Because the new mode of writing had a certain grace and charm it was frequently associated with the *style galant*. Nor was the imputation always rejected, for it implied a measure of compliment. Who was to know at that time that C. P. E. Bach's sonatas were the seed from which was to grow the instrumental form which is Germany's most vital contribution to the *materia musica*? Most of the music, however attractive, was slight. Even his symphonies seem ill qualified to be the direct ancestors of the Immortal Nine, although the difference between father and son in orchestration alone must have been an unmistakable symptom of the great changes that were to take place.

This brief interlude formed a kind of prelude to the Viennese period, one of the most glorious in all musical history. That, too, began with deceptive attributes. The *style galant* appealed to elegant Vienna, and the rococo period, with its airs and graces, formed an environment in which music might be expected to behave as a courtier. But though it manifested these external qualities, even in the earlier phases of the period they were no indication of superficiality. Beneath the surface music – if one be permitted to speak of it as an organic entity – was in travail.

The first great composer of the new era was FRANZ JOSEPH HAYDN (1732-1809), universally acknowledged as the father of modern instrumental music. He was the second of the twelve children of a wheelwright at Rohrau in Lower Austria. Both the parents were musical and the family were in the habit of spending the evenings making music, the father's instrument being the harp. Sometimes the schoolmaster would take part, and he it was who took particular notice of Joseph's precocious talent. He was sent to school at Hainburg, where he was almost at once enlisted in the choir. There he attracted the attention of Georg Reutter, the precentor of St. Stephen's, Vienna, with the result that at eight years of age he became a scholar in the Kantorei attached to the cathedral. But Reutter was a harsh master, and the lad was not happy. Eventually, on the pretext of a boyish prank, but really because his voice had broken, he was turned into the street without a penny. This was in November 1749. He was homeless for a night, but found next day a refuge in the attic of

Spengler, a tenor singer who was at that time almost as poor as himself. He scraped a living by giving lessons and by playing the violin, sometimes in street serenades. Some months later he took a humble garret in the same house wherein lived Metastasio, the Italian dramatist, who was Court poet at Vienna and wrote thirty-four operatic libretti, some of which did duty more than once. Haydn was then working very hard, devoting every moment not engaged in earning his livelihood to the study of such works as Fux's *Gradus ad Parnassum* (counterpoint), and Mattheson's *Der vollkommene Kapellmeister*, and playing again and again the sonatas of C. P. E. Bach. Rumours of his industry reached Metastasio, who not only found the young musician employment, but introduced him to the Italian composer PORPORA (1686-1766), who engaged him as accompanist and treated him as a menial, but taught him a great deal. Meanwhile Felix Kurz, an actor whose pretty wife he had helped to serenade with a composition of his own, procured for him an order to compose a comic opera, *Der neue krumme Teufel*. About the same time he began to be known in society as accompanist, in which capacity he appeared at the private concerts of Prince von Hildburghausen. This led to his being taken up by Karl von Fürnberg, who engaged him to compose chamber music, and thus furnished the incentive to the first of the long series of string quartets by which Haydn is perhaps best known today. His first official appointment was as Kapellmeister to Count Morzin, a Bohemian nobleman, who entrusted him with an orchestra. This was the starting-point of another long series of works, the Symphonies. But his patron very soon encountered financial difficulties and his orchestra was disbanded, not, however, before the young conductor-composer had attracted the attention of Prince Paul Anton Esterhazy, who forthwith engaged him as his Kapellmeister. He remained actively in the service of that powerful family from 1761 to 1790. Prince Paul died in 1762, and was succeeded by Prince Nicolas Joseph, who, like Lorenzo de' Medici, became known as the Magnificent (der Prächtige). It was he who transformed an old hunting lodge at the southern end of the Neusiedler See into the splendid palace of Esterhazy, which a French visitor declared to be comparable only to Versailles. Here Haydn held musical sway until the Prince's death in 1790. Under his successors, first Prince Anton (son of Paul), and from 1794 Prince Nicolas (grandson of Nicolas Joseph), Haydn nominally retained his functions, with a pension and salary, but practically ceased to exercise them, and settled in Vienna. He paid two visits to England, in 1791-92 and 1794, and composed for the concerts directed in London by Johann Peter Salomon the two sets of symphonies which still bear the latter's name, and rank with his finest works in this form. His last important works were the oratorios, *The Creation* (1799), and *The Seasons* (1801). His death on 30th May 1809 is said to have been hastened by the terrors of the French bombardment. His output was enormous, and comprised almost every kind of composition as then practised. His impress upon symphonic form was such that long afterwards the shape of the first movement (Allegro) was conveniently known as Haydn-form. From 1795 onwards, when he was sixty-three years old, he seemed almost to start anew, producing, besides the oratorios named, several of his finest quartets, notably that (1797) containing the Emperor's hymn, which afterwards became the Austrian national anthem. His visits to England had doubtless contributed to influence his treatment of the oratorio, but his handling of the orchestra was at this time surprisingly vivid and modern. In this he was undoubtedly stimulated by the example of another composer who, because he was nearly twenty-four years Haydn's junior, is still sometimes assumed to be his follower, though Haydn outlived him by eighteen years, during which these great works were produced. This new influence in music was that of WOLFGANG AMADEUS MOZART (1756-91), perhaps the greatest natural genius the world has ever known.

LEOPOLD MOZART (1719-87), son of a bookbinder of Augsburg, became one of the Court musicians, and later vice-capellmeister, in the service of the Prince-Archbishop of Salzburg, and a composer of note. He had seven children, of whom only two survived the period of infancy: Maria Anna, born 29th August 1751, and JOHANN CHRYSOSTOM WOLFGANG AMADEUS (1756-91), born 27th January 1756. When the girl, 'Nannerl', reached seven years of age she became her father's pupil on the clavier, on which she rapidly became very proficient. Her little brother very soon displayed a lively interest in her lessons. From his fourth year he could retain in memory the music he heard her play, and even began to compose little pieces which his father wrote down for him. Astounded at such precocity, Leopold Mozart began his son's musical education in earnest, and by January 1762 was sufficiently convinced to take his two children to Munich, where their performance excited the admiration of the Court. On 19th September, in that same year, they set out for Vienna, breaking the journey to play to the Bishop of Linz, and to give concerts, with the result that their reputation had preceded them on their arrival in the Austrian capital, whence already on 16th October the proud father wrote to a friend at Salzburg a glowing account of the great people who were showing favour to the two gifted children. The Emperor called Wolfgang a *kleiner Hexenmeister*. The following year they journeyed to Paris, where appeared Wolfgang's first published compositions, and in 1764 to England, where they remained over a year. At eight years of age, according to his father, this marvellous boy knew all that one can require of a man of forty. In 1767 he wrote his first oratorio, and in 1768 his first opera. In the same year he was appointed Konzertmeister to the Prince-Archbishop of Salzburg. The latter died in 1772, and his successor was less inclined to favour the young musician, who resigned in 1777, when he made another journey to Paris, and was much impressed by the operas of Gluck, then being performed there. Some disappointments having intervened, he reconsidered his position and resumed his post at Salzburg until 1781, when he finally settled in Vienna. The following year he married Constance Weber. It is sad to contemplate that Mozart, who had been so idolized as a 'juvenile prodigy', was afterwards scarcely ever free from material worries, and often had to face real hardships. *The Marriage of Figaro*, which he produced in 1786, was received tepidly in Vienna, but rapturously in Prague, whereby that city earned the honour of being the first to know *Don Giovanni* in 1787. This roused unprecedented enthusiasm, as the result of which Mozart was appointed Court composer – at a very modest stipend – to the Emperor. It is related that King Friedrich Wilhelm of Prussia, who was fond of chamber music, and himself a moderately good 'cellist, offered him a far greater salary to remain at Potsdam, which he visited in 1789, and that the composer refused to break faith with the Emperor, but there are reasons to dismiss the whole story as apocryphal. Returning to Vienna he was once more beset with pecuniary difficulties. His last opera, *The Magic Flute*, was coldly received, and less than ten weeks later Mozart had passed away in his thirty-sixth year. A few months earlier he had received the visit of an anonymous stranger who commissioned from him a Requiem, paying half the stipulated price in advance. This was the composition upon which he was engaged when death overtook him. Afterwards it transpired that his visitor had been Leutgeb, steward to Count Walsegg, an amateur who desired fame as a composer, and thought Mozart would do him credit as a 'ghost'!

Though Haydn and Mozart embody in their works the spirit of the rococo period, it must not be thought that they monopolized the stage of musical history in the German-speaking countries. Composers of talent were numerous, and several of them attained to some eminence. But we have reached the age of the giants, whose stature makes their contemporaries appear of little account, though socially some of them may have been inconvenient rivals at the time. Nor must it be thought that all musical life was concentrated in Vienna. In this respect, as in others, the German is by instinct a particularist. Every little state, each small town, had its own musical community. It is in retrospect that we have come to call this the Viennese period. It is more than probable that such a claim would have been violently disputed at the time.

It was the achievement of Haydn and Mozart to establish on a firm basis the great classical forms of the sonata, the concerto, the symphony, and the string quartet, which were to endure for generations after them as a monument to the musical genius of the German race. For the greater part of a hundred years at least there was little actual deviation from those forms, but only elaboration, internal and external, the former consisting in a more profound study of the material, the result of which is shown in so-called 'development sections', the latter consisting in a fuller exploitation of the musician's armoury of means and resources. The first giant stride was taken by a composer, another Titan, who, as a lad of sixteen, improvised at the piano in the presence of Mozart, and was in the prime of life when Haydn died. This was LUDWIG VAN BEETHOVEN (1766-1827), of whom Mozart said on the occasion referred to, 'Look well after him, for he will one day set the world talking about him.' He came of a Flemish family, but both his father and grandfather were musicians in the service of the Elector of Cologne, within whose territory he was born, at Bonn, on 16th December 1770. His musical education was commenced in his fourth year by his father. In his eighth year he played at a concert. In 1781 he became a pupil of Neefe, the Court organist, and already the following year was deputizing for him during a temporary absence. In 1783, at little more than twelve years of age, he received his first official appointment in the Elector's service as 'Cembalist[1] im Orchester', and was promoted a year later to be second Court organist, on which occasion he appears for the first time on the electoral pay-roll. The only important events of his life at this time were a visit to Vienna in 1787, when Mozart heard him, and the making of several friendships destined to endure. Of these the most noteworthy were with the Breuning family and with Count Waldstein. In 1792 Haydn visited Bonn on his way home from London, and so warmly commended his compositions that the Elector, previously influenced by Count Waldstein, arranged for him to proceed to Vienna. His departure took place at the beginning of November, and he took with him an album of farewell messages from his many friends. Thus ended his Bonn period, six weeks before his twenty-second birthday. He had already composed numerous works, not all of which are extant. In later years he named as his first compositions a set of nine variations on a march by ERNST CHRISTOPH DRESSLER (1734-79) which dates from 1780, and three piano sonatas of 1781, which were published in 1783. Of the

---

[1] *Cembalo* is the Italian for harpsichord, the chief forerunner of the modern piano.

works which followed, which include songs, piano pieces, trios, quartets, a concerto, two cantatas, and a 'Ritter-Ballet', the most familiar is the Rondino for wind instruments, which is still a favourite in the concert-room.

Arrived at Vienna, he studied first with Haydn and JOHANN SCHENK (1753-1836), and, on the former's departure once more for England, with JOHANN GEORG ALBRECHTSBERGER (1736-1809) and IGNAZ SCHUPPANZIGH (1776-1830), respectively counterpoint and the violin. His apprenticeship may be said to have ended in 1795 when he made his first public appearance in Vienna with the piano concerto in C, at a concert for a musical charity which took place at the Burg Theatre on 29th March. From that moment his progress was uninterrupted. On the basis of a classification first put forward by a Russian musician, Wilhelm von Lenz, and afterwards universally adopted, it is customary to speak of three periods in his development as a composer. The first, during which he was still under the influence of Haydn and Mozart, extends to 1800. Its output comprises the first two symphonies, nine piano sonatas, including the *Pathétique*, and some chamber music ending with the first set of six string quartets. The second period covers his maturity until 1815, and comprises six symphonies, from the third ('Eroica') to the eighth, fourteen sonatas, including the *Pastorale*, *Waldstein*, and *Appassionata*, the opera *Fidelio*, the Mass in C, the 'Razoumowsky' quartets, violin concerto and later piano concertos. The third period, 1815-27, is the phase during which he was striving towards yet further conquests in the realm of sound, and produced the later piano sonatas, the great Mass in D, the ninth (choral) symphony, and the posthumous quartets. Though in his prime he excited the admiration of the whole musical world, these last works did not all meet with immediate appreciation, but in the light of subsequent musical history they make him appear as a prophet, laying the foundations on which the musical edifice of the future was to be reared. This is largely due to his use of the variation form in development. The variation of earlier days was mostly decorative. He led the way to a more intrinsic transformation of the musical idea, with analysis of its component elements and exploration of their possibilities. Long after his death this became the 'metamorphosis of themes' on which is based most of the romantic or 'programme' music of the nineteenth century, as well as the Leitmotiv system of Wagnerian music-drama.

Of the details of his life, the many devoted friendships he inspired, or his family troubles, this is not the place to write, but there is one affliction from which he suffered that cannot be left unmentioned. At thirty years of age he began to experience the symptoms of approaching deafness, a distressing noise in the ears. He consulted doctor after doctor without obtaining relief. He determined to grapple courageously with his fate, but the malady progressed unrelentingly, and in 1814 he was compelled to relinquish playing in public, though he continued for a time, on rare occasions, to conduct his works. At the first performance, given on 7th May 1824, of the Choral Symphony, he was so deaf that he did not hear the storm of applause which, in spite of an indifferent rendering, broke out on the conclusion of the work, and it was only when Caroline Unger, the solo soprano, turned him round to face the audience that he realized that it had been well received. His last illness began towards the end of 1826, turned to dropsy, and appears to have been unskilfully treated. Neither he nor his friends realized, however, that the end was near. Within a month of his death he was contemplating important works. He passed away on 26th March 1827.

Among the composers of the generation to which Beethoven belonged, only one attained such eminence as to be considered, for a time, his rival. This was JOHANN NEPOMUK HUMMEL (1778-1837), a native of Hungary, who excelled as a virtuoso of the piano, but whose compositions have not escaped the fate that overtakes the work of minor masters. Even LUDWIG SPOHR (1784-1856) is better remembered as a great violinist than as the composer of eleven operas, four oratorios, fifteen violin concertos, and a mass of chamber music. But in the years preceding and following that of Beethoven's death there died two of his younger contemporaries whose names endure. These were CARL MARIA VON WEBER (1786-1826) and FRANZ PETER SCHUBERT (1797-1828), whom it is customary to regard as the first musical protagonists of the Romantic Movement, though many of Beethoven's works, from the *Eroica* onwards, bear the unmistakable impress of the artistic and literary movement that was sweeping across Europe at that time. Weber was a pupil of Michael Haydn, younger brother of the 'father of modern music'. At fourteen years of age he produced an opera, *Das Waldmädchen*. After touring for some years he became conductor of the opera at Prague (1813) and Dresden (1817). His earlier dramatic works do not rise much above the level of the Singspiel, but with *Der Freischütz* (1820) he laid the foundation-stone of modern German romantic opera, which Wagner was later to transform into music-drama. It was followed by *Euryanthe* (1823) and *Oberon* (1826), which proved less successful. His output during his brief career was remarkably voluminous, but apart from his masterpiece only the overtures and a few piano works are performed with any frequency today. But if he had produced nothing more than *Der Freischütz* he must still be regarded as one of the outstanding figures in the story of German music.

In the esteem of posterity he is, however, overshadowed by a composer whose career was even shorter than his, but at least as productive. This was SCHUBERT, youngest of the fourteen children of a Viennese schoolmaster. He was born 31st January 1797, learned a little music from his father and from ANTONIO SALIERI (1750-1825), who taught at the 'Stadt-konvikt'[1] while he was a scholar there, but he was very largely self-taught, with Haydn, Mozart, and Beethoven for models. The earliest of his songs that was not destroyed is dated 30th March 1811. His first symphony dates from 1813, his first mass from 1814. In 1816 he abandoned his father's profession to devote himself exclusively to music, with the result that he lived precariously on the very edge of penury, receiving sometimes as little as a *gulden* for a piano piece or a song. He never succeeded in obtaining any of the salaried posts that were fairly numerous in Vienna at the time. Although he had been held in high esteem by his musical contemporaries, his larger works were still comparatively unknown when he died. Thus the most famous of his nine symphonies, the Eighth, better known as *The Unfinished*, was written in 1822, yet not performed till 1865 when the lost score was found at Graz; again, the score of his symphonic swan song, the Great C Major Symphony of 1828, was rediscovered by Schumann in Vienna in 1837 and first performed by Mendelssohn at Leipzig in that year, so that Schubert's fame as a symphonic writer may be described as posthumous.[2]

In his early symphonies Schubert followed in the footsteps of Haydn and Mozart, Beethoven's influence being felt to any marked extent only in the Fourth in C Minor, significantly called by its composer 'The Tragic'. It is not until the Eighth and Ninth that Schubert comes fully into his own as a symphonist. In *The Unfinished* we note a pervasive lyrical feeling truly Schubertian in its melancholy and pathos, while the C Major Symphony is characterized by an elemental force and a grandiose sweep of ideas which resulted in an extraordinary extension of the form – a feature referred to by Schumann as 'heavenly lengths'. Together with Beethoven's Ninth, Schubert's last symphony is the first example of that German tendency to the *kolossal* which was to reach its climax in the symphonic works of Bruckner and Mahler. Intense lyricism then, and through it expansion and loosening of the compact classical forms, were

[1] This was a Seminary founded by the Emperor Franz II in 1803 and run by the holy order of the Piarists. It was attached to the old University in the inner city (hence the name) and included among its scholars the choir-boys of the Imperial court chapel. The young Schubert stayed there from 1808 to 1813.

[2] Similarly, the incidental music to the play *Rosamunde* (1823) was unearthed in the Theater an der Wien in 1867 by two Englishmen, Arthur Sullivan and George Grove, the founder and first editor of the *Dictionary of Music and Musicians*.

Schubert's chief contribution to the development of nineteenth-century instrumental music.

Yet where Schubert fulfilled his most significant historic mission was as the creator of the Lied. He was the founder of that great line of German song writers represented by Schumann, Brahms, Hugo Wolf (1860-1903), Richard Strauss, and Mahler. In order to appreciate his revolutionary achievement in this medium it is necessary to cast a brief glance at the German song of the eighteenth century. There the musician was the poet's servant, his primary task being to throw the verses into greater relief by a discreet musical setting. The voice-part was unadventurous, the melodic line rather stiff and formal, or else it imitated the style of the German folk-song; and the piano-accompaniment in the main confined itself to a simple harmonic support. In other words, the music was not allowed to attain a significance of its own, as this would have been regarded as endangering the effect of the poem. To compare the Schubertian songs with those of his foremost predecessors such as JOHANN RUDOLF ZUMSTEEG (1760-1802), JOHANN FRIEDRICH REICHARDT (1752-1814) and KARL FRIEDRICH ZELTER (1758-1832; see p. 472) is to realize the fundamental change which Schubert brought about in the æsthetics of eighteenth-century verse settings. His approach was that of a musician in his own right. Far from being subservient to his poets he considered himself their equal endeavouring to *recreate* the mood and imagery of the verses in terms of voice and piano – to transmute verbal into musical poetry. Many of his great songs such as *Der Erlkönig, Gretchen am Spinnrad, Die Nonne, Gruppe aus dem Tartarus,* may be said to be miniature tone-poems. But Schubert would not have achieved all he did without two factors most favourable to the birth of the Lied. He came soon after the great flowering of German lyrical poetry which inspired his fertile, impressionable mind to music of an equally imaginative and evocative nature. Among Schubert's poets figure Goethe, Schiller, Hölderlin and Heine, not to mention a host of minor figures. The other favourable factor was the high level to which piano music had been raised by Beethoven. Beethoven had not only shown the wide range of which the piano was capable in the expression of profound intellectual and emotional experiences, but he had also enlarged its technical possibilities to the extent of making it the foremost solo instrument. Schubert applied these newly-found virtues to the piano accompaniment of his songs, and sometimes treated it in a manner foreshadowing the symphonic orchestra of the romantic music drama. In turn evocative and descriptive it reflects the general mood of the verses as well as the physical situation of a given poem, while the voice part, pliant and melodious, serves to enhance the verbal expression. Yet voice and piano are so closely integrated that in Schubert's more elaborate songs one without the other would be unthinkable.

This type became the model for all later German composers. Though none showed Schubert's emotional depth, his richness and range of creative imagination, some succeeded in adding to the Schubertian heritage. Thus Schumann enhanced the role of the piano in his two cycles *Dichterliebe* (Heine) and *Frauenliebe und Leben* (Chamisso), both of which are rounded off by a purely instrumental postlude; and Wolf enriched the piano part through chromatic harmony and the use of the Wagnerian *leitmotif*, at the same time paying minute attention in the voice part to the verbal inflexion of the verses. With Wolf the Lied achieves a degree of psychological truth and technical refinement unsurpassed since.

There is one aspect of Schubert's historical significance that is often overlooked: he was the last of the great composers to be unaware of the approaching schism that was to divide the world's music into 'classical' and 'popular'. Mozart would be engaged one day upon minuets for a Court ball, the next upon a symphony, and perhaps a week later upon a Mass. His serenades were played in the open air for entertainment, as popular music is today. Weber wrote the 'Favourite Waltzes' of the Empress Marie Louise on the occasion of her visit to Strassburg in 1812. In writing his Lieder, Schubert had no other thought than to make songs as well as he might. He could not know that after his death the lyric tradition would divide, one branch maintaining the standard of the Lied, whilst the other degenerated into the Salonlied, and then into debased types of which the once notorious English 'shop-ballad' is only one example. He was also, after his fashion, a 'waltz-king' in his own day; but no great composer after him has deigned to write music for the ballroom, his successors in that field being first JOSEF FRANZ KARL LANNER (1801-43) and then the Strauss dynasty (see Index). This cleavage, which has rent the musical world in twain, is perhaps the greatest misfortune that has ever befallen it, for it has led to the present estrangement, not to say mutual hostility, between the devotees of the higher forms of music and the untutored public that flocks to its lower forms for entertainment. It became a point of honour with good German musicians to dismiss contemptuously as *Kitsch* music that tickles the public ear, but Mozart did not consider it beneath him to write it.

With the passing, in three successive years, of Weber, Beethoven, and Schubert, it looked for a brief moment as if the era of German genius in music were at an end. Italian music flourished in the persons of Rossini, Donizetti, and Bellini, whose facile melodiousness swept across Europe, but in Germany the Singspiel appeared to be the only source that was not stilled. Here JOSEPH LINDPAINTERN (1791-1856) produced his twenty-eight operas in rivalry with KONRADIN KREUTZER (1780-1849), HEINRICH MARSCHNER (1795-1861), KARL REISSIGER (1798-1859), and ALBERT LORT-ZING (1803-51). The few contemporaries who attracted momentary attention in the field of the symphony are now completely forgotten.

But this lull in the progress of German music was more apparent than real. The succession in the direct line of genius was already assured. The illusion of an empty stage was due solely to the fact that the next actors upon it were hardly mature enough to make their entrance in state. The five years 1809 to 1813 had witnessed the birth of four men of genius, three of them German, the fourth a Hungarian with German associations, who were destined to revolutionize the music of the nineteenth century, and establish yet more firmly the German ascendancy over it. The first, not only by virtue of seniority, but because his precocious talent first made him famous, was FELIX MENDELSSOHN-BARTHOLDY (1809-47). Just as Weber and Schubert stood for the first phase of the Romantic Movement in German music, MENDELSSOHN and SCHUMANN (1810-56) are the outstanding representatives of its second phase, with LISZT (1811-86) and WAGNER (1813-83) to follow for its third phase.

Mendelssohn the composer was the grandson of Moses Mendelssohn the philosopher (p. 248), which caused his father, Abraham Mendelssohn, banker, sometimes ruefully to remark that he was known in his youth only as the son of the great Mendelssohn, and in later years only as the father of the great Mendelssohn. He was a wealthy man, and his son was never troubled with those material cares which beset the path of a musician possessed of ideas. According to some this may not have been an unmixed blessing, and his music might have had a sturdier character had it borne the impress of early struggles. But in reality its character was a reflection of that of the period in which he lived and worked (*Biedermeier*).[1] Of much greater advantage than material comfort was the fact that both his parents had to a remarkable degree the love of music that is characteristic of the Jews. They had, however, abandoned the faith of their fathers and become Lutheran Christians, in which religion their children were baptized. Young Felix learned the piano with his mother, afterwards with LUDWIG BERGER (1777-1839). He also studied the violin with KARL WILHELM HENNING (1784-1867), but in composition he was the pupil of Karl Friedrich Zelter (see p. 470), who is remembered for his intimate friendship with Goethe, whom the boy was privileged to visit several

---

[1] Karl Löwe (1796-1869) is also classed as a Biedermeier musician; his setting of many famous ballads (by Uhland, Freiligrath, Fontane) ring dramatically true.

times at Weimar. He was also acquainted with Weber and Spohr. At only ten years of age he composed a setting of the 19th Psalm which was performed at the Berlin Singakademie. By the time he was fifteen he had composed no less than twelve symphonies and a large quantity of other music, vocal and instrumental, including operas. Though several of these juvenile compositions were published and are included in his opus-list, the first two works which placed him among the masters were the String Octet (1825) and the overture to *A Midsummer Night's Dream* (1826), the latter the result of reading Shakespeare with his sister Fanny in the garden of the house to which the family had recently moved in the Leipziger Strasse, Berlin. This, in particular, is an astounding work for a lad of seventeen to have written, and if, as is sometimes said, he never really surpassed this stage, it was high enough to establish him for all time. To him also belongs the honour of having brought about the first performance since Bach's death of the St. Matthew Passion. This gave the impetus to the revival of interest in Bach's music, which had for many years been eclipsed by later modes of composition. In later years, when conducting the famous Gewandhaus Concerts at Leipzig, he was similarly instrumental in drawing attention to the larger works of Schubert. He paid several visits to England, where he became immensely popular. A tour in Scotland resulted in the *Hebrides* overture and the Scotch Symphony. His last great work was the oratorio *Elijah*, which is still an annual feature in the programme of countless choral societies. It was produced at the Birmingham Festival, 26th August 1846. The following summer his sister, Fanny Hensel, for whom he had a deep affection, died suddenly, and the shock, coming upon him after a period of overwork, hastened his death, which took place 4th November 1847, at the early age of thirty-eight. Apart from his larger works, which include four symphonies, three concertos (one for violin), and a considerable quantity of chamber music, his contribution to the literature of his instrument, the piano, not only gave pleasure to thousands in the form of *Songs without Words*, but also constituted a landmark in the development of the romantic style of pianoforte composition.

Still more true is this of Robert Schumann, who was born 8th June 1810 at Zwickau, another composer whose vocation was revealed early, for his first attempts were made at six years of age. He was, however, first destined to a legal career. In 1830 he relinquished the law and went to live in Leipzig with FRIEDRICH WIECK (1785-1873), with whom he studied the piano, and whose daughter he was eventually to marry, not without parental opposition. Four years later he founded the *Neue Zeitschrift für Musik*, which wielded under his direction great influence as the champion of all that needed and deserved one in the new music of the day. The greater part of his output consists of pianoforte music and Lieder, in both of which he set a very high standard. He also wrote, among other works, an opera, four symphonies, overtures, and much chamber music, among which the quintet for piano and strings ranks as his masterpiece. His Romanticism was of a more robust stamp than that of Mendelssohn, and had an even greater influence on the music of his time. He was also perhaps the most characteristically German figure in the music of the period, for Mendelssohn, apart from his racial antecedents, or perhaps because of them, was more international, and Liszt, whose star arose about the same time, was the complete cosmopolitan. This is conspicuously shown in the sentiment of Schumann's music, which is Teutonic through and through. In later years he developed symptoms of insanity, which led to his being placed, at his own wish, in the private asylum of Dr Richarz at Ednenich, near Bonn, where he died, 29th July 1856, at the age of forty-six. Two years earlier he had attempted suicide by throwing himself into the Rhine.

Whilst Mendelssohn and especially Schumann were developing this German aspect of the Romantic Movement, particularly in piano music, another great composer, but not a German, was revolutionizing the whole manner of writing for that instrument. This was FRÉDÉRIC-FRANÇOIS CHOPIN (1809-49), born in Poland, but half French by his parentage, and from his twenty-first year settled in Paris. He figures in this story only by virtue of his influence, the spreading of which to Germany is largely associated with the next great name on our list, that of Franz Liszt (p. 472), who was born 22nd October 1811 at Raiding, near Odenburg, in Hungary, studied the piano under KARL CZERNY (1791-1857), and theory under ANTONIO SALIERI (1750-1825), and made his first public appearance in Vienna, 1st December 1822, when he earned the admiration of Beethoven. The first part of his career was spent as a virtuoso of the piano, in which capacity he rose rapidly to the foremost rank. But his importance specifically to Germany lies in his associations with Weimar and with Wagner. In 1842 he undertook the direction of a certain annual number of concerts which necessitated his staying there three months of the year. In 1849 he became Court Kapellmeister, and took up his residence there for twelve years, and even after that, though he had made Rome his headquarters, he still continued to spend a proportion of his time in the little Thuringian city, which he made for the while the Mecca of the German musical world. His dream of making Weimar again an art centre such as it had been when Karl August was its Duke, and Goethe, Schiller, and Herder its leading lights, was never fully realized, but musicians came from all over the world to frequent the cénacle over which he held undisputed sway. At the opera he was responsible for the production of the earlier Wagner operas and a number of other important works by those who were regarded at the time as the coming men. In the concert room many composers, German and other, received from Liszt their first encouragement. It would scarcely be an exaggeration to say that Liszt's personal influence at Weimar was greater and more beneficial even than that he had previously as the greatest of all pianists. As a composer, apart from innumerable and somewhat unequal compositions and arrangements for his instrument, he is known chiefly as the inventor of the symphonic poem, an adaptation of sonata-form to the needs of programme music. The method was not entirely new, for Berlioz had attempted the same thing some years earlier, but with Liszt the idea took a definite shape. In this the so-called metamorphosis of themes was an integral factor. As we have seen (p. 467), it was a development of the Beethoven variation, with literary attributions which linked the changes of the theme with the vicissitudes befalling the character or characters in the poetic basis adopted for the work. The Berlioz-Liszt type of symphonic poem became the standard from their day to that of Strauss, and even of Schoenberg, whose *Pelléas und Mélisande* still adheres to it. The analogy of the principle with that of the Wagnerian music-drama is obvious. Since Liszt and Wagner had become friends by the time these principles were established, it is practically impossible to say whether one of them influenced the other or whether it was mere coincidence that they developed along converging lines. Perhaps Ernest Newman has put the case most fairly at the conclusion of *Richard Wagner as Man and Artist*, where he writes: 'The idea of the new form may have been Liszt's as much as Wagner's, or even more; but Liszt's music was not rich enough to do the full work of fertilization.' In reality the whole idea, whether of the generation of *cyclic* sonata form from a thematic cell, of the metamorphosis of themes, or of the Leitmotiv, can be traced back to those last works constituting, so to speak, Beethoven's testament which, though the contrary opinion prevailed at the time, Liszt and Wagner were interpreting more faithfully than composers in the direct line of succession such as Mendelssohn, Schumann, and Brahms.

But we are anticipating. We have now reached the fourth of those great figures who came into the world close upon each other's heels between 1809 and 1813. This was RICHARD WAGNER, born 22nd May 1813 at Leipzig, the most commanding musical genius of the century. His father was a police official, Karl Friedrich Wilhelm Wagner, who died when he was six months old. The following year his mother married

Ludwig Geyer, who was chiefly an actor, but also a painter and dramatist. The suggestion that Geyer may have been a Jew and Wagner's father has been put forward polemically, but on the flimsiest evidence, and, though there can be no certainty in the matter, is better disregarded. The family removed to Dresden, where Geyer died 30th September 1821. Whilst there, the boy Richard attended the Kreuzschule, where such talent as he displayed appears to have been dramatic rather than musical. In 1827 his mother returned to Leipzig, where he entered the Nikolai Gymnasium. It was here that his thoughts turned to music. He had a few lessons from Gottlieb Müller, but was mostly self-taught, with the aid of such books as JOHANN BERNARD LOGIER's (1777-1846) method of Thorough-Bass. He wrote a few works, one of which, an Overture in B flat, was performed at the Leipzig Theatre, but was received with laughter. Possibly this incident may have induced him to go to Theodor Weinlig, cantor of the Thomasschule, for a spell of concentrated study. Many compositions resulted, mostly conventional students' work, but furnishing evidence of skill and determination. During the two following years three Overtures were performed, two of them at the Gewandhaus Concerts. Moved by the study of Beethoven he also wrote a symphony in C which was performed at the Prague Conservatoire under Dionys Weber, and later at Leipzig. In all these works there is nothing that indicates more than promise. Wagner was not another Mendelssohn. His professional career may be said to have opened with conductorships at Würzburg (1833), Magdeburg (1834), Königsberg (1836), and Riga (1837-39). In 1834 he completed an opera, *Die Feen*, which was, however, not performed until after his death. In 1836, the year of his marriage to Wilhelmina (Minna) Planer, he completed another, *Das Liebesverbot*, which was produced at Magdeburg under his direction. It was at Riga that he commenced the composition of *Rienzi*, and was attracted to the subject of *The Flying Dutchman*. From Riga he travelled via England to Paris, where he stayed until 1842, experiencing great hardships. It was there that he first became acquainted with Liszt, who, though their first meeting was anything but auspicious, was destined to become his foremost champion in Germany. It was also there that he completed *Rienzi*, towards the end of 1840, and *The Flying Dutchman* in 1841. On his return to Dresden these were produced, respectively 20th October 1842 and 2nd January 1843, whereupon, in February, he was appointed Court Kapellmeister; *Tannhäuser*, completed in 1844, was produced 19th October 1845. The score of *Lohengrin* was finished in the spring of 1848, but before it could be produced, Wagner's indiscreet conduct during a period of political disturbance had led to his flight and banishment. He went first to Weimar, where he was aided by Liszt, thence to Zürich, where he settled for the time being, after a short journey to Paris. It was again Liszt who retrieved the situation by producing in his absence *Lohengrin* on the 26th August 1850 at Weimar, where he had already performed *Tannhäuser* on the 16th February 1849. Though the opera was to take many years to reach Berlin and Dresden, *Lohengrin* had the effect of turning the eyes of Germany to the exiled genius.

It should be noted that the basic ideas of Wagner's later operas were already germinating in his active brain. As early as 1845 he had in mind the subjects of *Die Meistersinger* and *Parsifal*. Three years later he had written the first version of the drama that was to become *Die Götterdämmerung*. In 1851 he wrote another drama, which became *Siegfried*, and the following year the poems of *Die Walküre* and *Rheingold*. Early in 1853 the whole text of the *Ring* was privately printed. Meanwhile, whilst these ideas were coming to fruition, he was writing no music. There is no record of composition between March 1848, when he completed *Lohengrin*, and October 1853, when he is known to have been engaged upon *Rheingold*. It suggests that the whole scheme of Wagnerian music-drama was evolved during this period. When the time was ripe for realizing the scheme, things moved rapidly. By the end of 1854 *Rheingold* and *Die Walküre* were composed, and the former scored. It was in that year that he conceived the idea of *Tristan und Isolde*, which was not to be developed until later. Apparently there is not one of the seven later music-dramas that was not already occupying his mind at the time, twenty-eight years before *Parsifal*, the last of them, was completed.

Of his private life, his relation with the Wesendoncks, his separation from his wife, it is scarcely necessary to write here. In 1855 he visited London to conduct eight concerts of the (now Royal) Philharmonic Society, and was roundly abused by those who still worshipped at the shrine of Mendelssohn. Other adventures in the concert-world took place in Paris and Brussels during the first three months of 1860. It was then that was planned the disastrous production of *Tannhäuser* in the 'Paris version' for which Wagner had rewritten the opening scene in the Venusberg. Only three performances were given, of which the first took place on 13th March 1861. Meanwhile he had been amnestied, except in Saxony, and was now able to return to Germany. The next three years were most unhappy. His constant efforts to arrange for the production of his works remained fruitless, and he was beset with financial worries which culminated in his having, in March 1864, to flee from his creditors. The old saying that the darkest hour comes before the dawn was never truer, for it was only six weeks later that King Ludwig II of Bavaria came to the rescue by inviting him to Munich, commissioning the completion of the *Ring*, and calling HANS VON BÜLOW (1830-94) to his capital to produce *Tristan*, which the Vienna Opera had previously relinquished after fifty-seven abortive rehearsals. The first performance took place 10th June 1865. The following year Wagner established himself at Triebschen, near Lucerne, which became his home until 1872, when he settled at Bayreuth. Two years earlier he had married Cosima, the daughter of Liszt, and divorced wife of von Bülow. He died 13th February 1883 at Venice. It only remains to add the date of production of his remaining music dramas: *Die Meistersinger*, Munich, 21st June 1868, under von Bülow; *Rheingold*, Munich, 22nd September 1869, under Wüllner; the completed *Ring*, Bayreuth, 13th-17th August 1876, under HANS RICHTER (1843-1916); and *Parsifal*, Bayreuth, 26th July 1882, under HERMANN LEVI (1839-1900). He paid one more visit to England in 1877, when he conducted in May eight concerts at the Albert Hall.

In the magnificent tonal edifice of Wagnerian music-drama the Romantic Movement reached its culmination, so far as music was concerned. Wagner had contrived a vast form and used it in the creation of a succession of masterpieces. Viewed from the angle of today it presents a certain appearance of finality. Many composers have striven to walk in his footsteps, if not to wear his mantle, but few have emerged from the attempt with any lasting credit to themselves. A generation after his death signs began to show themselves of the approach of another turning-point in musical evolution, similar to those of 1600 and 1750, but it was long before their meaning came to be read aright.

What was the essential aim of Wagner's operatic reforms? It was to correct the fundamental error which, according to him, traditional opera had committed, in that 'a means of expression (music) had been made the object, and that the object of expression (drama) had been made the means' (*Opera and Drama*, 1851). Wagner admitted that Gluck, and after Gluck, Méhul,[1] Cherubini[2] and Spontini[3] had done their best to express dramatic feeling in music, but essentially the drama was still a mere pretext for the music. Even Wagner's much admired Mozart 'embarked with the utmost indifference upon the composition of any text offered to him. All he did was to pour the fiery stream of his music into the operatic forms developing their musical possibilities to the utmost.' And as for Weber and Rossini,[4] theirs were operas dominated by pure melody, i.e. the musician in them took precedence over the dramatist.

Wagner envisaged a type of stage work in which all its constituents –

[1] Etienne-Nicolas Méhul (1763-1817).   [2] Salvador Cherubini (1760-1842).
[3] Gasparo Spontini (1774-1851).   [4] Gioacchino Rossini (1792-1868).

action, words, music, scenery and lighting effects – united to serve a single
master: the dramatic idea. He supported his theory of a *Gesamtkunstwerk*
by pointing to the ancient Greek drama with its combination of poetry,
action and music (such as there was), and argued that after the downfall
of the Athenian republic this union of the arts disappeared, each leading
an existence of its own; the attempts made during the Renaissance and
later to reunite the arts proved more or less abortive, yet the technique
and range of expression of the individual arts increased considerably.
According to Wagner, each separate branch of the arts had now reached
its limit of growth, and to allow it further growth would be bound to
make its results incomprehensible, fantastic and absurd. The time had
come when the individual arts were to be united again in a composite
work, the elements of which were to be fused organically and not to be
imagined as a more or less casual conglomeration of the individual arts –
'reading a romance by Goethe, in a picture gallery adorned with statues,
during a performance of a Beethoven symphony.' This single Art was
to be the *Musikdrama* – the modern equivalent of the Athenian drama.
And just as the Greek stage expressed the life and thought of ancient
Greece, so the music-drama had to deal with the vast issues and complexities of modern life. Wagner thus perceived what he called the *Kunstwerk
der Zukunft* as a microcosm, a reflection of the totality of the modern
world. And what of the kind of subjects suitable for it? This question
brings Wagner to a discussion of the modern drama, which, deriving
from the medieval romance and the Greek play, appeals, he says 'to our
intellect and not to our feeling'. Therefore 'the course to be followed by
the drama of the future will be a return from understanding to feeling' –
a postulate which embodies the central ideas of the German Romantic
Movement. In this new kind of drama the action must be such as to be
'completely justified in both character and scope by the feeling that
prompts it'. Already in 1844, seven years before the essay *Opera and Drama*
was contemplated, Wagner in a letter to Karl Gaillard declared that he
would never take a subject 'which might be used as well by an able play-
wright for spoken drama .... It is the province of the present-day
dramatist to give expression and spiritual meaning to material interests
of our time, but to the operatic composer falls the task of conjuring up
the holy spirit of poetry as it comes down to us in the sagas and legends
of past ages.' Mythology and legends are simple, concentrated, eternally
true, they appeal primarily to our emotions and, hence, are the given
subject for the musician. Just as the Greek dramatists chose stories from
their mythology, so the modern musical dramatist goes to the sagas and
legends of the Middle Ages for his subject-matter. They are the ideal

material from which poet and composer can form plots and characters and represent the vast world of human thought and passions. 'Here is the way', Wagner continues, 'to raise opera to a higher level, from the debasement into which it has fallen as the result of our expecting composers to take for their subjects commonplaces, intrigues, etc.,[1] – things which modern comedy and drama without music are far more successful in presenting.'

The crucial point, and one which is often overlooked in a consideration of Wagner's reforms, lies in the fact that he combined in his person dramatic poet and musician in as high a degree as was ever reached before or after. Wagner approached his task from a vantage point unique in the history of opera. Admittedly, CLAUDIO MONTEVERDI (1567-1643) and, later, Gluck sought to do justice to the dramatic requirements of opera, yet they needed the collaboration of another person, – the librettist, and thus were unable to achieve Wagner's close integration of drama and music. In Wagner, dramatic and musical conception not only went hand in hand, but the former was decisively influenced and moulded by the latter. Wagner's libretti, if considered as poetic drama – as he intended them to be so considered by publishing them in book-form in advance of the operas – are turgid, undramatic, slow-moving and tedious. Their intellectual and philosophical contents show confusion of thought, obscurities and inconsistencies; their *dramatis personae* are too remote and unreal for their tragic fate to rouse pity and terror. What the modern listener cares for is the wonderful transmutation of a vast and cumbersome complex of philosophical, mystical and religious thoughts into terms of poetic music for the stage. For all his theorizing on the supremacy of the dramatist over the musician it is in the last analysis Wagner's stupendous musical genius that gave his operatic reforms their artistic *raison d'être*.

In considering the musical aspect of these reforms we note in the first place Wagner's use of a symphonic orchestra. It was not for nothing that he never tired of claiming his musical descent from Beethoven rather than from such operatic composers as Gluck, Mozart and Weber. For in Beethoven's symphonies Wagner saw the expression of poetic and dramatic ideas; and since this was precisely his aim in the music-drama, he took the decisive step of applying Beethoven's symphonic technique to the medium of opera. The Beethovenian theme changes to the Wagnerian *leitmotif* and becomes the musical symbol for an idea or a character, capable of infinite transformations demanded by the psychological changes in the drama. Wagner's orchestra, with its continuous and ever-changing

[1] This was an attack largely directed at Giacomo Meyerbeer (1791-1864) and French Grand Opera.

web of motives, comments upon the action on the stage with such elo-
quence and power of suggestion that it may be said to contain the real,
the inner drama. In consequence the centre of musical interest held in
pre-Wagnerian opera by the singers and the stage, now shifts to the
symphonic orchestra, while the utterances of the Wagnerian characters
only serve to give us the precise ideas, the intellectual contents of the
emotions expressed by the orchestra. The set numbers of the older opera
such as the aria, the duet and the self-contained ensemble are discarded as
being incompatible with Wagner's principle of dramatic truth. Instead,
the singer is given a voice-part which fluctuates between arioso and
recitative and follows the inflexion of exalted speech; and free musical
declamation replaces the symmetric, formal song-melody of the traditional
opera. (From here it is but a short step to the *Sprechgesang* of the Schoenbergian School.)

Wagner's revolutionary reforms were epoch-making. The music-
drama became the established form of opera in the subsequent period
(Strauss, Debussy, Puccini) and is still the basis of most modern operas
(Schoenberg, Berg) though it is now strongly contested by the adherents
of the non-psychological *Musizieroper* (Stravinsky, Milhaud; see pp. 488,
494). Moreover, Wagner's chromatic harmony and, resulting from it, his
free handling of tonality were to lead to the break-up in modern music of
the major-minor system, while his orchestral style, multicoloured and immensely flexible, opened up a world of new sounds and thus laid the
foundations for the growth of musical Impressionism in Germany and
France. There was no musical nation in Europe that escaped Wagner's
impact.

In other branches of musical activity a curious situation developed
during Wagner's lifetime. There is no need to enumerate the countless
composers who were producing works now forgotten. Two contemporary names stand out with a prominence that not even Wagner could
completely overshadow. These are ANTON BRUCKNER (1824-96) and
JOHANNES BRAHMS (1833-97), who, apart from their individual achievements, were destined to find themselves in the uncomfortable position of
party figure-heads in the polemic to which Wagner's influence on symphonic music gave rise. Bruckner became the symbol of that influence,
Brahms that of classical purity in succession to Beethoven. But if Brahms
represented the Beethoven line of descent, Bruckner was no less representative of that from his countryman Schubert, with whom he has much
in common. He wrote nine symphonies, of which the last remained uncompleted. They are large, spacious works, deeply romantic in sentiment, with a pronounced tinge of Catholic mysticism, such as was to

find a more sophisticated yet far less convincing expression in the works of the religious sentimentalist César Franck. Bruckner's Catholicism was that of a mind naïvely devout, unquestioning and prone to ecstatic visions. He conceived the sole purpose and significance of his creative work to be the glorification of the divinity. With the Catholic saints his motto was *omnia ad maiorem Dei gloriam*, symbolized musically in the chorale themes of his symphonies and fervently proclaimed in their apotheotic finali. Linked with his deep-seated religious emotion was Bruckner's instinctive closeness to Nature, to the grandeur and lonely majesty of the Alps in whose neighbourhood this descendant of Upper Austrian peasant stock was born and reared. Bruckner's elemental nature feeling manifests itself in the tremendous sweep and ruggedness of his symphonic ideas no less than in the 'cosmic' climaxes of their development. A more idyllic pastoral atmosphere is conveyed in the scherzo movements in which the composer, following the time-honoured tradition of the Austrian symphonists (Haydn, Mozart and Schubert), resorts to *Ländler*-like tunes. Bruckner's deep admiration for Wagner, from whom he derived certain harmonic and orchestral features, earned him the hostility of those critics who remained unconverted to the new music, and it is they, rather than his own followers, who were responsible for the attempt to make Bruckner the Wagner of the concert room. In Central Europe he ranks as one of the great masters; and, although his music is said to travel badly, its intrinsic values are now being gradually recognized in other countries.

It is otherwise with BRAHMS, who, though essentially a Romantic, is regarded by many as the last of the great classics, to which view, of course, the alluring alliteration of the 'three B's' may perhaps have contributed by subconscious suggestion. He was born 7th May 1833 at Hamburg. As a young man of twenty he attracted the attention of Schumann, who, in his *Neue Zeitschrift für Musik* (vol. 39, nr. 18) bestowed a blessing upon him which has become historical. He was also championed by EDUARD HANSLICK (1825-1904) in opposition to Wagner, and had a lifelong friend in Joseph Joachim, the great violinist. After the death of Schumann he accepted an appointment at Detmold which enabled him to concentrate upon composition, but from 1862 he made his home in Vienna. Meanwhile his works had begun to make their appearance, and he found himself regarded as in the apostolic succession of the classics with such conviction that, when he produced his first symphony – which was not until his fifty-third year – it was hailed with indiscreet enthusiasm as the tenth, in allusion to Beethoven's nine. To some extent this may have reacted upon his own psychology; for the perfection to which he attained in his Lieder and smaller piano works suggests that the lyrical miniature was

his real vocation, and that the architectonics of the symphony and other
large structures were superimposed upon it by the subconscious desire to
live up to what was expected of him. His private life was, for a Romantic
composer, singularly uneventful, and his career is best followed in the
works by which he has enriched every form of music except opera. They
include four symphonies, three concertos (two for piano, and one for
violin), two overtures, a large quantity of chamber music for various
combinations, piano music, and a few choral works of which *A German
Requiem* is the most important. For some decades his admirers, by stressing
the intellectuality of his music, made of it a cult in which the vulgar were
scarcely expected to participate, but in recent years he has been gradually
popularized and today his works command large audiences except in the
Latin countries, where temperamental divergencies operate against them.
He died 3rd April 1897 at Vienna. With him the roll of great names in
the classical tradition comes to an end, unless we are disposed to accept
the claims of MAX REGER (1873-1916) to be so regarded. In his comparatively short career he wrote a vast quantity of music in all forms except
the dramatic, much of which is only now meeting with due appreciation.
It is not unlikely that future historians will come to regard him as a highly
interesting figure standing astride of two periods of musical evolution.
His meticulous treatment of his texture, in which sometimes each semi-
quaver will carry distinct implications, might be held to suggest the
Byzantine decadence of one period, whilst his intense preoccupation with
counterpoint heralds the reaction from harmonic luxuriance that was to
lead to the 'back to Bach' movement, which is a significant episode in the
later development of twentieth-century music in Germany.

But if there is a suggestion of Byzantinism in this obsession with
minutiae, its stigmata are more clearly discernible in the opposite extreme
of a passion for volume and dimensions. At this stage in the evolution of
German music we reach the period of the *kolossal*, which was clearly one
of decadence. It was only to be expected, for all æsthetic precedent shows
that a romantic movement, with its enlistment of outside aid, imports the
germs of disintegration. When the great tradition of Greek sculpture
abandoned its classic austerity in favour, first of romantic considerations,
and then of realism, it was a portent of its approaching end. The music of
the period that was passing had ceased to be self-reliant, and called in the
aid of extraneous, mainly literary, elements which were fated to hasten
its conclusion.

Let it not, however, be thought that decadence is without great artists.
The term itself belongs to art-chronology rather than art-criticism. It is
the fate, not the choice, of artists appearing at such a time to work in a

medium that is approaching exhaustion, and which prompts them to excesses in order to extract more juice from the squeezed orange. Of the composers of the *kolossal* phase, two stand head and shoulders above all others. These were GUSTAV MAHLER (1860-1911) and RICHARD STRAUSS (1864-1949).

Mahler is a complex personality difficult to place into any of the accepted artistic categories. He was a Jew who by his later conversion to Roman Catholicism attempted to escape from what he felt to be the narrowness and spiritual bias of his upbringing and background. It was a symbolic act, yet illusory in its effect, and only added to his inborn pessimism and conflict. He was a great conductor – perhaps the greatest of his time –; yet this, too, proved a source of conflict. For, unlike Richard Strauss, who took conducting in his stride, Mahler suffered from the tug-of-war between his extrovert activity as a conductor and the introversion demanded by his composing. As with Wagner, composing to him was not an end in itself but the vehicle to carry his *Weltanschauung* – a complex of ideas in which mysticism, pantheism, religion and Messianic visions entered into strange fellowship with notions from philosophy and metaphysics. In short, like so many artists and thinkers of the *fin de siècle*, he felt out of joint with himself and his time.

Hence Mahler's escape into the world of the mind, and hence the sadness, torment, conflict and despair which emanate from so much of his music. Like the true Romantic he was, he conceived of his works as autobiographies reflecting the currents and cross-currents of his intense emotional and spiritual life. TCHAIKOVSKY's (1840-93) approach in later years to symphonic writing was similar to Mahler's. Yet there the parallel ends. For Mahler's mind was of much stronger intellectual fibre, it commanded a far wider horizon and probed far more deeply into the dark recesses of a man's soul. Moreover, Mahler's intense subjectivity was coupled with the desire to identify his inner struggles with those of Man, i.e. to impart to the artistic projection of his Ego an objective quality. When, at the end of his Second Symphony, he introduces in Brucknerian fashion a chorale *Aufersteh'n, ja aufersteh'n* he is thinking, not of the individual soul, but of the Resurrection, of humanity at large; and when in the monumental Eighth he opens with the dramatic hymn *Veni creator spiritus*, he addresses the whole of mankind – an attitude in which we sense Beethoven's in the Ninth Symphony. Mahler's ideal audience is Everyman, and as Everyman he sees himself. Hence his conception of the symphony as the musical form in which to convey the totality of life. 'To me', he wrote in a letter, 'a symphony means the building-up of a world with every technical means available'; and in conversation with

JEAN SIBELIUS (1865-), whom he met at Helsinki in 1907, Mahler is reported as saying that 'a symphony must be like the whole world. It must embrace everything.'[1] Nothing less than a self-created microcosm would satisfy his Faustian yearnings, nothing less than the whole orbit of human thought and emotions must be the 'theme' of his symphonic disquisitions.

Therein lay at once Mahler's greatness and weakness: always aiming at the stars, but frequently only hitting the trees. 'I must keep on the heights, I cannot allow anything to irritate me or drag me down. It is hard enough to keep on that level all the time.' If that was Mahler's moral maxim, it also guided him in his creative work. Yet he worked against a handicap which seems to represent the crux of what might be termed the Mahlerian problem. His intellectual powers, his sheer will to create these symphonic 'worlds', often went beyond what he could do as a musician pure and simple. His creative faculty was often overpowered by the ambitious demands imposed upon it by his spiritual aspirations. Mahler the thinker and visionary was stronger than Mahler the musician. In the symphonies the musical thought *per se* often fails to carry conviction; the formal handling often conditioned by an inner programme forces the music to steer a course which is not always self-evident to the listener; Mahler is often long-winded and diffuse; and, lastly, the lyrical element, beautiful though it is, is allowed to expand and thus impairs the forward, dynamic character of the symphonic form.

Yet, on the other hand, there are immense riches. It is especially in the expression of certain emotional and mental states peculiar to Mahler that the music reaches a high degree of poignancy and lyrical beauty. In this context it is interesting to note that Mahler's symphonic lyricism shows a close link with his songs. In fact, in the first four of his symphonies he introduces themes from the songs which give a clue to the meaning of the music. But it is significant that beginning with the Fifth Symphony he refrains from such revealing self-quotations, and, moreover, turns in it and the following two works to pure instrumental writing.

In the First Symphony (1888) Mahler gives expression to an experience which first inspired his cycle *Lieder eines fahrenden Gesellen* (1884): the impact of a hostile world upon an idealistic youth. In the Second (1895) he poses the eternal and unanswerable question of the ultimate meaning of life, introducing the human voice in the song *Urlicht* and the chorus in the Resurrection chorale of the finale. In the Third (1896) Mahler confesses

[1] This totalitarian view is, presumably, one of the chief reasons why Mahler is so great a favourite with Soviet composers, on whose vast symphonic epics his influence is undeniable.

to a curiously naïve pantheism and includes a setting of Nietzsche's *Mitternachtslied* suggesting the essence of his programme. In the Fourth (1900) we are taken on a fantastic journey through the land of fairy-tale, a land without the sorrows and sufferings of our earthly life, and finally arrive in a children's paradise, to partake, in the company of saints and angels, of 'the heavenly joys' of which the soprano sings. The Fourth marks the close of a stage in Mahler's development. The thoughts and sentiments expressed here and in the previous three symphonies are essentially the same as those which inspired the series of his folk-song-like *Wunderhornlieder*, save that they appear more intense and articulate in their symphonic elaboration.

The next three symphonies (No. 5, 1902; No. 6, 1904; No. 7, 1905) are purely instrumental. Mahler had grown out of the naïve world of German folk-song poetry; and apocalyptic visions, the mystic romanticism of the Great Pan, a children's heaven, have no longer a place in his inner world. A pessimistic outlook asserts itself with increasing force. Personal experiences combine with his introvert cast of mind and the *Weltschmerz* of his age to make him turn to the problem of his own existence. Mahler draws more and more into himself and his thoughts assume a more abstract character. Hence the absence of words and song tunes in the three symphonies of his middle period. Yet behind them is the same impulse that led him to write the moving set of the *Kindertotenlieder* (1902). In the funeral march of the Fifth, the sinister hammer strokes of the Sixth, and the *Night Pieces* of the Seventh, Mahler expresses what has been described as 'the dark element' of his genius. It is already felt in his early works, but while there it manifests itself in isolated moments and is tempered by Mahler's youthful lyricism; in the later works it pervades practically every movement. Even the lovely *Adagietto* of the Fifth – a movement often played separately – is not without a gentle feeling of resignation.

With the Eighth Symphony (1907) Mahler attempted to halt this growing tendency to despair. He turns to words again – the Latin hymn *Veni creator spiritus* and passages from Goethe's *Faust*, Part II – to proclaim in monumental fashion the message of Christian love and charity. Yet for all its bold grandeur and majesty the feeling remains that the extravagant means employed in it (the work was dubbed 'Symphony of a Thousand') are not altogether commensurate with its intrinsic musical power.

It was the last time that Mahler reached out to embrace all mankind. With the subsequent *Das Lied von der Erde* (1908) and the Ninth Symphony (1909) he relinquished the conquest of 'whole worlds'. These two

works were written *sub specie mortis*, for in 1907 it was accidentally discovered that the composer was suffering from a chronic heart disease,
the knowledge of which filled his last four years with the constant fear
of death. There is little in the realm of symphonic music to reach the
pathos and heart-rending poignancy of the second and the last movements
of the *Song of the Earth* and the finale of the Ninth. In such music we
tread on new ground in the utterance of what is most personal and intimate in a man's unhappy mind. And it is here that Mahler seems the
prophet of much that characterizes our time. The sense of frustration,
futility and spiritual suffering which pervades his last composition is felt
by many artists of our age with similar persistence, though they express
it in different and starker terms. It is as if Mahler saw the writing on the
wall at a time when the foundation of European culture seemed still firm
and indestructible. This would appear to be no mere coincidence. For
Mahler came from that part of central Europe where the disruptive
changes that were later to throw the Continent into a cataclysm were felt
first. Like Schnitzler and Hofmannsthal, close contemporaries of his, he
vaguely sensed the ominous significance of those changes. Thus his late
works are intrinsically more contemporary than a great deal of what
passes as 'the music of our time'.

The other outstanding figure of that generation was Richard Strauss,
as extrovert an artist as Mahler was an introvert. Far less intellectual than
Mahler, and wholly unconcerned with *Weltanschauung* in his creative work,
he possessed a richer gift of invention; and, though much of his *œuvre*
lacks true distinction, it yet impresses by its verve, exuberance and
orchestral brilliance, and at its best it shows true genius. Strauss rose to
fame upon a succession of orchestral works in which he perfected the
form of the Lisztian Symphonic poem and brought the instrumental
achievements of Berlioz and Wagner to the pitch of dazzling virtuosity:
Macbeth (1887), *Don Juan* (1888), *Tod und Verklärung* (1889), *Till Eulenspiegel* (1895), *Also sprach Zarathustra* (1895), *Don Quixote* (1897), *Ein
Heldenleben* (1898), *Symphonia Domestica* (1903), and *Eine Alpensymphonie*
(1915). There was little that Strauss would not attempt to illustrate in
terms of the orchestra, from the bleating of sheep in *Don Quixote* to the
baby's crying in the *Symphonia Domestica*. Yet despite such realistic
touches, Strauss's tone-poems are romantic conceptions: musical studies
of poetic characters in action – music-dramas unstaged and wordless.
Mahler's symphonies too come close to the Wagnerian conception of
opera, yet while in them the 'drama' is abstract, with Strauss there is the
concrete image of great figures from world literature which is certainly
purer stuff for music than Mahler's philosophical disquisitions.

Strauss's technique was the same as Wagner's – a number of characteristic themes or *leitmotifs* are used, out of which the symphonic web is
woven and which, according to the literary programme, undergo various
metamorphoses. Yet Strauss's sense of form was nurtured on the classics:
his tone-poems are cast in the classical mould of sonata, rondo, or variation
with highly skilful and novel modification dictated by their subjects.

For Strauss, whose dramatic genius had shown such remarkable
manifestations in the tone-poems, it was but a step from symphonic music
to opera. In *Guntram* (1893) and *Feuersnot* (1901) he still presented himself
as Wagner's disciple, but with *Salome* (1905) and *Elektra* (1909) he became
a master in his own right. Realism being the order of the day in the
theatre Strauss's realism in these two works is directed toward a musical
representation of psychopathological states of mind. The action is concentrated into a single act in order to achieve the maximum of tension.
The orchestra, complex, highly discordant and seeking to produce *frissons*
by novel sounds, lays bare the perverted psyche of the characters and the
subconscious motives of their actions; the voice-parts alternate between
declamation, broken hysterical outcries and a broad luscious cantilena.
Yet in the next opera, *Der Rosenkavalier* (1911), Strauss, under the influence
of his librettist Hofmannsthal, left the sphere of morbid psychology and
excessive realism, and turned to a romantic comedy – and with it to the
genre of the older *Musizieroper*. True, the orchestra remains symphonic,
but with the difference that, while *Salome* and *Elektra* may be said to be
tone-poems with the voices superimposed on the orchestra, in *Rosenkavalier*
the singers are reinstated as the principal element. Moreover, although
the music is continuous, the set numbers of the pre-Wagnerian opera
emerge again. And instead of the intense chromaticism and discordant
harmonies of the two previous operas, Strauss now cultivates a euphonious
diatonic style imbuing his Italianate melody with a rich and expressive
lyricism. (This is one of the chief features accounting for the undiminished
popularity of this work.) In *Ariadne auf Naxos* (first produced in 1912 as
part of the incidental music to Molière's *Le Bourgeois Gentilhomme* and
made in 1916 into an independent one-act opera with a prologue) is a
brilliant essay in what was later to be known as the neo-classical style.
Ariadne may be defined as a pastiche on eighteenth-century *opera seria* and
buffa, the first represented by the mythological figures of Ariadne and
Bacchus, the second by characters from the *commedia dell'arte*. The interplay of these two contrasting sets of protagonists is mirrored in the music
with consummate skill and intimate refinement. Though largely a *jeu
d'esprit*, the opera is sheer delight and in the parts of Ariadne and Bacchus
reaches the inspired lyricism of *Rosenkavalier*. Strauss, it must be added,

was fortunate in having as librettist Hugo von Hofmannsthal (see p. 327), who provided him with a text of high literary quality and with situations which called for a musician of Strauss's talent and temperament. While their collaboration produced the best fruits in *Elektra*, *Rosenkavalier* and *Ariadne*, the subsequent *Die Frau ohne Schatten* (1919) and *Die ägyptische Helena* (1928) were far less successful. *Intermezzo* (1924), to the composer's own text, deserves mention for the reproduction in music of *Lustspielton*, i.e. a light, conversational treatment of the voices, with the lyrical element largely reserved to the orchestral interludes. The last decade or so of Strauss's life saw an Indian summer during which he poured out a whole string of operas and instrumental works, yet the classical beauty and purity of his very late style are unlikely to revise the verdict that it was the Strauss of the early romantic tone-poems, of the four operas from *Salome* to *Ariadne* and of a number of inspired songs (*Morgen, Traum durch die Dämmerung, Ständchen*, etc.,) who has secured a lasting eminence in the history of German music.

In HANS PFITZNER (1869-1949) Strauss encountered his most serious rival to the claim of being the most representative German opera composer of his generation. Pfitzner is little known outside central Europe, yet, like Bruckner and Mahler, he is there considered a great master. Describing himself as 'the last romantic', he advanced an æsthetic philosophy the central thesis of which was that Germany's last great period in music was the Romantic one and that in the twentieth century that country had outlived its musical hegemony (*Tonkünstlergefahr*, 1917; *Die neue Ästhetik der musikalischen Impotenz*, 1919). Pfitzner's music expresses a profound longing for the past and is pervaded by a melancholy and pessimism perhaps only to be expected of a composer who was as steeped in the writings of Schopenhauer as Pfitzner was. Characteristic of his attitude are two works both of which look back to the past. In the Romantic Cantata: *Von deutscher Seele* (1921), to poems by Eichendorff, Pfitzner seeks to convey the mystical yearnings of the German Romantic artist. In *Palestrina* (1915), an opera to his own text, he wrote a *Künstlerdrama* in which, freely adapting the life-story of the great sixteenth-century Italian church composer, he shows the spiritual loneliness of the artist amidst the worldliness and intrigues of his surroundings. Contrasting the *Meistersinger* (another 'artist's drama') with his own, Pfitzner declared Wagner's work as 'the apotheosis of the new, an affirmation of the future and life; in *Palestrina* on the other hand everything inclines to the past, there reigns in it compassion with death'. The opera makes its impact no less by the moral issue of the story than by its music, which is deeply felt and achieves a remarkable fusion of sixteenth-century vocal polyphony with Wagner's symphonic orchestra. *Palestrina* is perhaps the only work by which posterity will remember this epigone of Schumann and Wagner.

To Pfitzner's generation belongs ENGELBERT HUMPERDINCK (1854-1921), who rose to fame with *Hänsel und Gretel* (1893), the libretto of which is based on the old German fairy-tale. The great popularity of the work derives from Humperdinck's use of simple German folk-songs, which he skilfully treated in the manner of the Wagnerian *leitmotif*. In *Die Königskinder* (1897) he attempted to repeat the same formula, yet with less success. Other late Wagnerians were EUGEN D'ALBERT (1864-1932) and MAX VON SCHILLINGS (1868-1933). D'Albert, though Scottish-born, ranks as a German composer by virtue of his long residence in Germany. He was one of the finest pianists of his time and a prolific composer, notably of operas, in which Italian *verismo* is grafted on to the German music drama. His most successful work in this genre, one to be found in the repertoire of even the smallest German stage, is *Tiefland* (1903), after a story of Spanish origin, in which the dénouement is brought about by a brutal strangulation on the open scene. Like d'Albert, Schillings was influenced by the Italian brand of operatic realism and also by the Strauss of *Elektra*. In his best-known opera *Mona Lisa* (1915) Leonardo da Vinci's model is made the heroine of a cruel drama of jealousy, both her lover and her husband being suffocated in a cupboard. The suspense and dramatic fitness of the work recall Puccini's *Tosca*. The spirit of Goldoni and eighteenth-century *opera buffa* is revived in the works of the German-Italian ERMANNO WOLF-FERRARI (1876-1948), who produced delightful and neatly contrived comedies in *Die Vier Grobiane* (1906) and *Susannas Geheimnis* (1909). Similarly, FERRUCCIO BUSONI (1866-1924), the son of an Italian father and a German mother, sought to rescuscitate the old *commedia dell'arte* in a modern form in the theatrical capriccio *Arlecchino* (1917) and the comic opera *Turandot*[1] (1917), its libretto

[1] Gozzi's *fiabe drammatiche* (dramatic fables) attracted the attention of German writers from Lessing onwards; the proximity of the genre to the *Zauberoper* [which culminated in Mozart's *Die Zauberflöte* (1791), the libretto of which was influenced by Gozzi] and to the old *Stegreifkomödie*, in which improvisation by the actors is the rule, opened out avenues for inventiveness and stage effects. Gozzi's influence is also felt in the *Märchendrama* of Ferdinand Raimund (p. 266). The first successful adaptation was Schiller's *Turandot* (1801), rendered into iambic verse from a prose translation. The idea of the three riddles on which the action turns was taken by Gozzi from the *Arabian Nights*. It is curious that in each successive adaptation the riddles were changed; in Karl Gustav Vollmöller's cynical adaptation *Turandot* (1911) they have a lyrically veiled obscenity which passed unnoticed by all but a few when Sir George Alexander staged the play with Max Reinhardt's gorgeous setting and in J. Bithell's translation at St. James's Theatre in 1913. Busoni's opera, composed at Zurich in 1916, and performed there in 1917, and Vollmöller's farce are closely connected.

being freely adapted from Gozzi's play. With the Austrian FRANZ SCHREKER (1878-1934) German opera turned for a short period to French impressionism and symbolism. Schreker, who was his own librettist, showed a marked idiosyncrasy for subjects of a lurid and perverted eroticism (*Der Ferne Klang*, 1921; *Die Gezeichneten*, 1918; *Der Schatzgräber*, 1920). His so-called *Klangstil* – an orchestral style of remarkable lusciousness and iridescence – was, however, unable to conceal his mediocre melodic gift any more than the contrived 'theatre' of his libretti. Moreover, the general tendency of the period after the First World War was to move away from music of a romanticizing and psychological character towards simplicity of expression and economy of means, with the result that Schreker's operas soon went out of fashion. Another Austrian, ERICH WOLFGANG KORNGOLD (1897-1957), made a highly promising start in the two Straussian one-act operas *Der Ring des Polykrates* and *Violanta* (both 1916) and subsequently developed a harmonically complex and luxuriating style in *Die Tote Stadt* (1920) and *Das Wunder der Heliane* (1927), in which his erstwhile model Strauss rubs shoulders with Schreker and Puccini. Korngold's subsequent career in America shows a lamentable decline.

In the early years of the present century the musical situation in Germany was that composers striving, most of them vainly, to extricate themselves from the folds of Wagner's mantle, were driven to exaggeration of the expressive means. The orchestra, and the choral masses when added to it, were increased beyond all precedent. The 'pathetic' semitone, so richly expressive in *Tristan*, became more and more yearning in tone, – though, to do Strauss justice, he was the most diatonic of his German contemporaries – and works intended for the concert-room threatened to assume the dimensions of music dramas.

If Strauss and Mahler may be said to have consolidated Wagner's heritage, ARNOLD SCHOENBERG[1] (1874-1951), a younger man, broke away from it. After digesting the lessons learned from Wagner (String Sextet *Verklärte Nacht*, 1892; cantata *Gurrelieder*,[2] 1901-10, and tone-poem *Pelléas und Mélisande*, 1905) Schoenberg became aware that if he was to strike further in the expression of highly emotional 'contents' his Wagnerian language was no longer adequate. Tonal relationships based on the diatonic system with its major and minor keys, the traditional law of the resolution of dissonances and the functional organization of harmony he felt as fetters to be got rid of. He aimed at creating a language which, completely freed from such limitations, was to express in the most direct,

---

[1] Schoenberg changed the spelling of his name from the *Umlaut* when he settled in America.   [2] Danish songs of Jens Peter Jacobsen (p. 321).

subtle and pliable manner the complicated, intricate, abstract and extremely concentrated nature of his feelings and thoughts. Schoenberg took the first step in this direction in his Second String Quartet in F sharp minor (1907), two movements of which are written in what is called a free chromatic style. In developing it the composer broke away from all the classical laws of musical organization and replaced them by principles which derive from the purely expressive and colour qualities of music. He thus arrived at the expressionist style of his middle period, of which the melodrama *Pierrot Lunaire* (1912) is perhaps the most outstanding example – music of an extreme subjectivism making no endeavour to be understood by the *hoi polloi*. Seen in the light of Schoenberg's later development his expressionism marks a transitionary phase of a more or less experimental nature. Out of it grew his so-called twelve-note or atonal style – at once the most important and most controversial contribution to the evolution of modern music. It has opened new avenues of musical thought which are now being further explored by the younger generation of dodecaphonic (or twelve-note) composers of various countries. It has, moreover, added to the purely expressive quality of music; and works such as Schoenberg's Fourth String Quartet (1938), *Ode to Napoleon* (1942), *A Survivor from Warsaw* (1947), and the opera *Moses and Aaron* (1930-51) demonstrate the high degree of intense and concentrated expression of which dodecaphonic music is capable. While its structure and other technical aspects present an abstruse yet fascinating study to the intellect, it is on the plane of pure lyricism that Schoenberg created new and intrinsic values.

Schoenberg was the head of a school known as the Viennese atonalists, of whom ANTON VON WEBERN (1883-1943) and ALBAN BERG (1885-1935) were the most outstanding members. Of the two, Webern was the more consistent in the application of his master's technique and carried the concentration of expressionist forms still further. Thus his *Six Bagatelles for String Quartet* (1924) are musical aphorisms, each piece being of an average length of nine to ten bars. Tiny melodic fragments replace recognizable themes, and the texture of the music is completely dissolved into an invertebrate fluid mass of strange sounds. Webern's description of Schoenberg's expressionist style applies to his own music with heightened force: 'No motive is developed, at most a brief progression is immediately repeated. Once stated, the theme expresses all it has to say; it must be followed by something fresh.' In his later works Webern returned to a comparatively more coherent manner (Symphony for Small Orchestra, op. 21, 1928, and cantata *Das Augenlicht*, op. 26, 1935) without, however, lifting the veil from his enigmatic utterances. The

chief impression his music conveys to the uninitiated is that of an eschatological tension and, technically, of a complete and utter disintegration of
melody, harmony, and rhythm. Webern thus stands at the extreme end
of the blind alley into which musical expressionism was bound to lead. The
case of Berg was different. Starting as a Wagnerian in his Tristanesque
Piano Sonata op. 1 (1908) he maintained throughout his career his early
allegiance to an expansive, flexible and feminine lyricism. If Schoenberg
and Webern were on the whole more inventive than imaginative, in
Berg poetic imagination is felt throughout his *œuvre*. He first made use
of the dodecaphonic technique in the *Lyric Suite for String Quartet* (1925)
and continued to employ it since. Yet nowhere did he allow himself to
be ensnared by its complex rules, handling them with less rigidity than
either his master or his fellow pupil Webern. In the Violin Concerto
(1935) he consciously sought to fuse the twelve-note style with traditional
tonality by using a Carinthian folk-tune and a Bach chorale as part of his
thematic material. This poignant work dedicated 'to the memory of an
angel' was intended as a Requiem for Marion Gropius, a young friend of
Berg's who died in tragic circumstances at the age of seventeen. Berg's
dramatic masterpiece *Wozzeck*[1] (1920) is based on Georg Büchner's
Woyzeck (1879). Except for a short scene in twelve-note technique the
opera is written in the free chromatic style of Schoenberg's expressionist
period. Its integration of action, stage, words and music is so complete as
to represent a *ne plus ultra* of musico-dramatic union. Despite an almost
atomistic reflection in the music of the drama, close formal coherence is
achieved through a most skilful and suggestive use of the traditional forms
of instrumental music, the three acts of the opera being cast, respectively,
into a suite, a symphony, and variations. Büchner's drama, which
anticipates the expressionism of the 'twenties by almost a hundred years,
puts on the stage characters drawn with deliberate distortion and exaggeration: the psychopathic soldier Wozzeck, the neurotic Captain and
the crazy, sadistic Doctor, Wozzeck's pathetic mistress Marie being the
only protagonist with any semblance of normality. The nightmare effect
of the play is heightened by Berg's music to a degree only comparable
with that of Schoenberg's monodrama *Erwartung* (1909). While the basic
theme of *Wozzeck* was the demoralizing influence of society on the under-
privileged, in his next opera *Lulu* (practically completed in 1934) based
on Wedekind's *Erdgeist* and *Die Büchse der Pandora* (see p. 307), Berg
pursues the theme of perverted eroticism. Here again the fantastic

---

[1] The play (see p. 270) was first published as *Wozzick*, because Büchner's illegible
and time-faded handwriting was misread by Karl Emil Franzos, who was the first
to decipher it.

irreality of the drama is mirrored in the music with most suggestive force, and again musical coherence is achieved by the use of traditional forms such as arias, duets and ensembles; yet, unlike *Wozzeck*, Berg's last opera is wholly dodecaphonic.

Though their method of composing was revolutionary, in their æsthetics the Viennese atonalists upheld Wagner's fundamental axiom that 'music was the language of emotions'. In this they were violently opposed by the generation of German composers who grew to maturity in the period between the two world wars. The new movement was towards the restitution of the classical balance between form and content, a balance which the late romantics and the atonalists had increasingly tipped in favour of unimpeded self-expression. Already in the first decade of the twentieth century Busoni had preached a return to the simplicity and objectivity of the classical style (*Entwurf einer neuen Ästhetik der Tonkunst*, 1907), assigning to the criteria of form and craftsmanship a higher æsthetic value than that possessed by emotional significance. The stress on form as opposed to content led to a reaction against all music of a markedly subjective, emotional, psychological or philosophical character – in short, against works of an extra-musical, programmatic tendency. Hence the deliberate neglect of such typically romantic forms as the tone-poem and the music-drama and the cultivation of such more abstract, purely 'musical' forms as the sonata, suite and variation, and, on the stage, of the so-called *Musizieroper* of the eighteenth century. This new objective attitude led to a new style: neo-classicism. It was inaugurated by IGOR STRAVINSKY[1] (1882-) in his ballet *Pulcinella* (1920), for which he adapted material taken from the eighteenth-century Italian composer Pergolesi. One of the principal slogans of the new movement was 'back to Bach', Bach's works being thought to show music at its purest and most abstract. New Objectivity was, true enough, a potent antidote against the unrestrained emotionalism of the post-Wagnerian period. Yet its reverse side was the over-emphasis on technique and craftsmanship, with a concomitant neglect of expressive values which often resulted in works of a mechanical, jejune and dryly cerebral character. [An analogous movement started in France in the early 'twenties with ERIC SATIE's (1866-1925) *dépouillement* and was largely represented by a group of young composers known at the time as *Les Six* of whom DARIUS MILHAUD (1892-), FRANCIS POULENC (1899-) and ARTHUR HONEGGER (1892-) survived this rather arid period.]

At the head of the new movement stood PAUL HINDEMITH (1895-).

[1] Born near St. Petersburg; settled in Switzerland; later naturalized Frenchman; but since 1940 in U.S.A.

Like most German composers of his generation he began as a follower of the late Romantics, Brahms being his foremost model, while his marked bent for contrapuntal complexity derived from Reger. Yet it was not long before he embraced New Objectivity, pouring out work after work in which craftsmanship was an end in itself, expression being merely incidental or deliberately eschewed. Hindemith considered music to be no longer *art* in the nineteenth-century sense, but a *Handwerk*, a craft to be pursued with the utmost skill and intelligence – a conception originating in the great composer-craftsmen of the classical past. And just as up to the end of the eighteenth century composing largely signified writing music for practical needs – the church service, the ceremonial occasions and entertainments at Court, the *collegia musica* of the German univer-sities–so Hindemith and his German contemporaries wrote *Gebrauchsmusik*, functional or utility music, music conceived for such special purposes as the radio, the film and the school. Not only were works of this description wholly subservient to these uses, but they were also intended to bridge the chasm between the modern composer and the ordinary music lover – between 'the producer and the consumer of music', as Hindemith put it – a chasm which had begun to open soon after the death of Schubert and Weber. It was in order to bring modern music to the home and to tempt the amateur to play it, that Hindemith wrote, for example, the *Sing- und Spielmusiken für Liebhaber und Musikfreunde* (1928). The very title recalls the descriptions of eighteenth-century works of a similar purpose (*Sonaten für Kenner und Liebhaber* by C. Ph. E. Bach). In the preface Hindemith sets out his aims as follows: 'This music is written neither for the concert hall nor for the artist. It is to provide interesting and modern studies for those who wish, for their own pleasure, to sing and play, or to perform before a small circle of people who share this taste.' Similar ends served the so-called school operas such as his *Wir bauen eine Stadt* (1931) and Kurt Weill's (see below) *Der Jasager* (1930).

Throughout his career Hindemith has shown a strong preoccupation with musical didactics, which is another trait linking him with an ancient tradition. Thus his *Ludus Tonalis* (1946) may be described as a modern counterpart to Bach's *Well-Tempered Clavier*, consisting of a series of fugues and interludes which combine to illustrate modern piano technique as well as modern polyphony and tonality. The technical principles which underly not only this important composition but the whole of Hinde-mith's mature work were laid down by him in a comprehensive textbook *Unterweisung im Tonsatz* (1937), an exposition of the theory and practice of his own methods of composition and a most valuable contribution to the theoretical literature on twentieth-century music.

Hindemith is a composer of immense fertility, vitality, industry and resourcefulness. No less remarkable is his versatility. He has cultivated every medium, from songs, piano works and chamber music to symphonies, operas and oratorios, to say nothing of his many works for the film, the radio, and for electrical instruments. For many years he was viola player in a celebrated quartet, and often appeared as soloist in his own works such as *Der Schwanendreher* (1935), a kind of viola concerto, with material partly derived from German folk-song. Yet neo-classicism has remained the basis of his style, though during his *Flegeljahre* Hindemith was subject to influences from many quarters, including jazz and atonalism. He has now settled down to a style in which the principles of the classical forms combine with a marked tendency to subjective expression. This change, which began to show in the early 'thirties, produced the two masterpieces which Hindemith has not surpassed since: the opera *Mathis der Maler* (1938), to his own libretto, and a symphony of the same title based on material from the opera. Like Wagner's *Meistersinger* and Pfitzner's *Palestrina*, *Mathis* is an 'artist's drama', its central character being the great German painter Matthias Grünewald (*d.* 1528; see p. 517), Hindemith's symbol for the German artist of his own time. The story deals with the painter's life, which is set against the troubled background of the Peasant Wars in Southern Germany, his spiritual conflicts arising from his participation in the politics of his epoch, and his profound questioning of his artistic mission – all of which takes on a topical significance if interpreted, as it must be, as a reflection of Hindemith's own problems as man and artist while living in Nazi Germany. The conclusions he arrives at are summed up in the words spoken by one of the characters to Mathis: '*Wo nur für Kampf und Blut Platz ist, gedeiht nicht die Kunst. . . . Dem Volke entzogst du dich, als du zu ihm gingst, deiner Sendung entsagtest.*' *Mathis der Maler* is a challenge to the totalitarian dogma of the artist being a political animal, while its message is a warning that for an artist to serve any other master but his art is to forfeit his intellectual integrity and to discard his true mission. In its musical style the opera recalls the static character of an oratorio, containing long orchestral preludes, big choral scenes and extended slow-moving solo numbers and ensembles. It is more epic than dramatic. The technique of the Wagnerian *leitmotif* alternates with formal devices of the older opera, and much use is made of counterpoint, old German folk-songs, and of the Gregorian Chant, all of which lends the music an archaic atmosphere in tune with the ambience of the action. The symphony *Mathisder Maler* takes its inspiration from Grünewald's famous triptych on the Isenheim Altar, its respective three movements being entitled

Concert of Angels – The Temptation of St. Anthony – The Entombment.
Two of Hindemith's most notable contemporaries were KURT WEILL
(1900-50) and ERNST KŘENEK (1900-). Weill, a pupil of Busoni's, made his
name with operas of half-political, half-satirical tendencies, in which
bourgeois society was put in the pillory and declared responsible for the
social injustices of our time (*Aufstieg und Fall der Stadt Mahagonny*, 1927;
Die Bürgschaft, 1932). Significantly, the libretti of five of Weill's operas
were by the left-wing writer Bert Brecht (p. 353). Their close collaboration produced in *Die Dreigroschenoper* (1928) the most successful and, perhaps, the best-known of Weill's stage works. As model served John Gay's
The Beggar's Opera (1728), but the Englishman's harmless skit on Italian
opera and Handel was transformed by the two Germans into a mordant
satire of modern society and its public institutions. It is not an opera in
the accepted sense, but, like its English model, a *Singspiel*, consisting of
spoken dialogue which is interspersed with musical numbers (arias, duets
and parodistic chorales), the whole accompanied by a small orchestra.
Weill replaced the simple English folk-songs of Gay's original by jazz
tunes of a pungent rhythm and harmony, his argument being that jazz
was the folk-music of modern times. Until the advent of the Nazis *Die
Dreigroschenoper* enjoyed a most remarkable success in Germany, partly
because of its satire, partly because of its racy music.

Opera was also Křenek's chief medium, with which he experimented
in several directions: political satire (trilogy: *Der Diktator*, 1926; *Das
Geheime Königreich*, 1927; *Schwergewicht oder Die Ehre der Nation*, 1927);
sophisticated entertainment with jazz as the main ingredient (the farcical
detective thriller *Der Sprung über den Schatten*, 1923, and the sensational
Jonny spielt auf, 1926, in which a negro dance-band leader is the hero),
historic spectacle (*Karl V*, 1938, in twelve-note style); and classical tragedy
(*Das Leben des Orest*, 1930). Like Hindemith, Krenek allowed himself to
be influenced by the various 'isms' of the inter-war period; yet, unlike
Hindemith, he never succeeded in moulding his own individual manner
of speech. In turn neo-romantic, impressionist, expressionist, and neo-
classical, now flirting with simple major-minor diatonicism, now with
linear counterpoint and dodecaphony, Křenek's music reflects the spiritual
insecurity and lack of inner purpose characteristic of the German *Zeitgeist*
during the late 'twenties and early 'thirties. Křenek's intellect has always
been stronger than his creative instinct. A penetrating thinker, he contributed in *Über neue Musik* (1937) a remarkably lucid analysis of certain
technical and æsthetic problems of modern music; and his *Studies in
Counterpoint* (1940), written after his emigration to America in 1938, constitutes a valuable textbook on the Schoenbergian technique. Like

Křenek, ERNST TOCH (1897-), another Austrian who resided in Germany and settled in the United States in 1933, shows a tendency to chameleon-like changes of style.

German music from 1918 to 1933, though no longer occupying the leading position which it had enjoyed among Europe's musical nations since the last third of the eighteenth century, yet possessed vitality and adventurousness. This was to change almost overnight, with the rise to power of the National Socialists. Their racial theories led to the banning of all music by Jewish composers and, since the contribution to modern music by Jewish artists was considerable – Mahler, Ernest Bloch (1880-; an Americanized Swiss), Schoenberg, Weill, Milhaud –, modern music as a whole was declared as *Kulturbolschewismus*, i.e. decadent, alien to (*artfremd*) and destructive of the true German spirit. Even the works of such 'Aryan' composers as Hindemith could no longer be performed in public concerts, and eminent non-German musicians like Stravinsky and Bela Bartók (1881-1945; a Hungarian; died in New York) were placed on the black list. The result of this *Kulturpolitik* was to drive many of Germany's most noted artists into exile (largely to the United States), leaving the field to respectable mediocrities who were willing to conform to the tenets of *gleichgeschaltete Kunst* (seepp. 175, 177). The clock was put back to the nine-teenth century, and the cult of the German folk-song *per se* and as material for composition was strongly encouraged. (The parallel with music in Soviet Russia is noteworthy.) The overriding aim was to produce *arteigene Musik*, music stemming from Germany's 'blood and soil', an aim which condemned itself by the inferior results to which it led. The ostracism of all music of an advanced character hermetically shut off the German artist and his public from all knowledge of what was happening in the artistic and intellectual life of other countries. After the war German musicians confessed to an almost total ignorance of any modern foreign works written after 1933. This *lacuna* is now being filled apace, and it is significant that the average number of annual modern-music festivals given in Western Germany is said to be far higher than that of any other country. With the 'Iron Curtain' at present separating the Federal Republic from the German Democratic Republic – where music, like the other arts, appears to be harnessed to the same politically inspired æsthetics as prevail in Soviet Russia – it is difficult to form a picture of present-day German music as a whole. What appears certain, however, is the absence of a leading composer of international stature such as pre-war Germany possessed in Strauss and Hindemith. Whether this con-dition is the corollary of Hitler's disastrous cultural policies or the symp-tom of a more deeply lying cause: the exhaustion of the German musical genius, or of both – the question at present defies a clear-cut answer. Little is heard of post-war German music in England, and what is heard merely tends to confirm the fact that Hindemith, now in his sixtieth year, still remains the most outstanding German musician of today. His influence is considerable; but Stravinsky and the dodecaphonic Schoenberg have also found a number of eager disciples. Thus Stravinskyian neo-classicism allied to simple, folk-song-like music marks the style of CARL ORFF (1895-), whose scenic oratorio *Carmina Burana* (1937), set to a text partly in medieval Latin, partly in macaronic verse, enjoys great popularity. In the opera *Antigone* (1949) Orff closely follows Stravinsky in writing non-expressive, non-psychological and static drama. Like Hindemith, at one time, Orff aims at bringing modern music within the orbit of the ordinary listener by tunefulness and the avoidance of technical complexities. The Stravinskyian influence is also felt in WERNER EGK (1901-) and BORIS BLACHER (1903-), the latter experimenting also in the genre of satire (opera *Die Nachtschwalbe*, 1948). The dodecaphonists are to be found in the generation born between the two wars such as HANS ULRICH ENGELMANN (1921-) and HANS WERNER HENZLE (1926-).

Austria, in contrast to its German cousin, has been far less willing to embrace modern creeds. The heir to a great tradition, she has since the last third of the past century adopted a conservative, if not a reactionary, attitude. Bruckner, Wolf and Mahler had suffered from it; and, no less, Austria's progressive composers of the next generation. Some, like Schoenberg, Schreker, Toch and Křenek, sought a more congenial artistic climate in Germany, while others who remained in their native land, such as Berg and Webern, formed the centre of a very narrow circle of followers. (Significantly, it was Berlin, not Vienna, where *Wozzeck* was first produced in 1925, which was symptomatic of the historic fact that with the beginning of the twentieth century the centre of German music gradually shifted from the Austrian to the German capital.) 'Official' modern music in the Austria between the two wars was chiefly represented by two men: FRANZ SCHMIDT (1874-1949) and JOSEF MARX (1882-). Schmidt continued the Brucknerian tradition in his four considerable symphonies, while his two operas (*Notre Dame*, 1914 and *Fredegundis*, 1922) combine the technique of the romantic music-drama with harmonic and orchestral features from Strauss. Marx, on account of his rich harmonic style, counts as one of the few German impressionists (Romantic Piano Concerto, *Herbstsymphonie*). Outside Central Europe he is best known by his songs, in which he follows in the steps of Hugo Wolf.

In the picture presented by Austrian music since the end of the last war two chief tendencies may be observed. There are, on the one hand, the traditionalists – largely former pupils of Schmidt and Marx – whose fundamental leanings are towards a mildly modernized romanticism. On the other hand, there are those who aim at an intrinsically contemporary mode of expression but keep aloof from extremes, such as THEODOR BERGER (1915-), ANTON HEILLER (1916-), and GOTTFRIED VON EINEM (1918-). Einem's most outstanding work to date, the opera *Dantons Tod* (1947), after Büchner's play of that title (see p. 270), is noteworthy for the dramatic role assigned to the chorus and the ingenious assimilation of jazz with a symphonic orchestra. The chief Austrian heirs of Schoenberg are HANS ERICH APOSTEL (1901-) and HANNS JELINEK (1901-). The latter's *Zwölftonwerk*, op. 15, an extensive series of piano pieces, explores the structural possibilities of dodecaphony progressively from the simple to the most complex writing. Like Hindemith's *Ludus Tonalis*, it attempts to combine an educational purpose with artistic aims.

Within the orbit of German music falls also German-speaking Switzerland. Owing to its peculiar geographical position Switzerland as a whole had for many centuries been subject to the cultural influences from its great neighbours in the North-East, South, and West. It is, hence, not surprising that its musical history should have been more or less closely bound up with that of Central Europe, Italy, and France. Yet it is worth recalling that the Benedictine monasteries of St. Gall and Reichenau (see pp. 215, 507) played a decisive part in the very early development of polyphony, a part which is linked with the names of NOTKER BALBULUS (*c.* 840-912), TUTILO (*c.* 840-915) and BERNO (*d.* 1000). During the fifteenth century there flourished in Alemannic Switzerland the art of organ playing and organ building, and the fame of the Zurich composer LUDWIG SENFL (1490-*c.* 1555) reached as far as Scandinavia, where he was known as '*der jetzige Fürst der ganzen deutschen Musik*'. His motets and masses contain some of the finest examples of sixteenth-century church music. HANS GEORG NÄGELI (1773-1836) made his name as a composer, teacher, and writer on music, and to Beethoven students he is known as one of that master's publishers, with whom he kept up an interesting correspondence. Nägeli rendered great services to music in Switzerland by founding in 1811 the *Schweizer Bund*, a choral society with branches throughout the country. Yet it is not until the last third of the nineteenth century that we may begin to speak of typically German-Swiss composers. Following in the wake of the national movements in other small European countries German Switzerland began to produce musicians who, despite their strong allegiance to Wagner, Liszt, Brahms and, later, Reger, showed a certain ruggedness and severity in their music – attributes which, according to authorities on the subject, are to be found in the old Swiss folk-songs. The leader of this first generation of nationalist composers was HERMANN SUTER (1870-1926), whose link with the folk-music of his country is best shown in his choral works, while his oratorio *Le Laudi di Francesco d'Assisi* (1925) represents a synthesis of Gregorian plain song with Brahmsian technique. It has frequently been performed outside Switzerland. Brahmsian is also the music of FRITZ BRUN (1878-) while Wagner and Strauss are reflected in the works of WALTER COURVOISIER (1875-1931) and VOLKMAR ANDREAE (1879-), who is also known as an eminent conductor of Bruckner. Of the composers born between 1880 and 1900 OTHMAR SCHOECK (1886-1957) attracts most attention. His position in German Swiss music is that of a mediator between the late romanticism of Wolf and Reger (whose one-time pupil he was) and modern tendencies. It is largely as a song-writer and opera composer that Schoeck has made his most outstanding contributions. His strong lyrical vein is revealed in a prodigious output of songs, the choice of verses by Goethe, Eichendorff, Uhland, Hebbel, Keller, and Lenau underlining his close affinity with the great German song-writers, notably Wolf. In the operas it is less the action and the dramatic situation than the general theme of the subject which Schoeck seeks to convey. He thus stands nearer to Wagner than to Strauss, and Wagnerian is also the basic theme of his libretti: the conflict between man's evil demoniac powers and his better self (*Venus*, 1922; *Penthesilea*, 1927; *Vom Fischer un syner Fru*, 1930; *Massimilla Doni*, 1936; and *Das Schloss Dürande*, 1943). It is owing to the psychological problems posed in these operas that Schoeck's musical language here is more uncompromising and severer than in his songs. Schoeck remains the most notable figure in present-day Swiss German music and the acknowledged leader of the younger generation. To this belong ALBERT MOESCHINGER (1897-), PAUL MÜLLER (1898-), LUC BALMER (1898-), WILLY BURKHARD (1900-1957), CONRAD BECK (1901-), and HEINRICH SUTERMEISTER (1910-). With these the influences of Busoni (who lived in Zurich for some time during the First World War), of Honegger, and also of Hindemith are unmistakable. Yet a common denominator may be found in such 'Swiss' qualities as directness and austerity of expression, and a marked economy in the means employed. ROLF LIEBERMANN (1910-) pursues the path of dodecaphony in the opera *Leonore 40/45* (1952), the action of which takes place against the background of the recent war.

R

BIBLIOGRAPHY TO CHAPTER XII

GENERAL

Grove, G. *A Dictionary of Music and Musicians.* 5th ed., ed. Blom, London, 1954. (The 4th edition will also serve)
Oxford History of Music. London, 1905. (A new edition is to be published shortly.)
Moser, H. J. *Geschichte der Deutschen Musik.* Berlin, 1924
Young, Percy M. *A Critical Dictionary of Composers and Their Music.* London, 1954
The Music Masters. 4 vols., ed. Bacharach. London, 1954
Lambert, C. *Music Ho!* Pelican Books. London, 1948
Schuh, W. *Schweizer Musik der Gegenwart.* Zurich, 1948

GENRES

The Symphony. Ed. Hill. Pelican Books. London, 1949
The Concerto. Ed. Hill. Pelican Books. London, 1952
Cyclopaedic Survey of Chamber Music. Ed. Cobbett. London, 1929
Kobbé, G. *The Complete Opera Book.* Ed. Harewood. London, 1954
Bekker, P. *The Changing Opera.* London, 1935
Dent, E. J. *Opera.* Pelican Books. London, 1949
Owen, D. *Encyclopedia of the Opera.* London, 1956

INDIVIDUAL COMPOSERS

BACH:

Schweitzer, A. *J. S. Bach.* 2 vols. London, 1911
Spitta, Ph. *Johann Sebastian Bach.* 3 vols. London, 1899
Terry, C. S. *Bach – A Biography.* London, 1928
David, H. J. and Mendel, A. *The Bach Reader. A Life of Johann Sebastian Bach in Letters and Documents.* London, 1946
Mann, W. *Introduction to the Music of Bach.* London, 1950

BEETHOVEN:

Thayer, A. W. *The Life of Ludwig van Beethoven.* 3 vols. London, 1921
Bekker, P. *Beethoven.* London, 1925
Riezler, W. *Beethoven.* London, 1938
Scott, M. *Beethoven.* London, 1934. (*The Master Musicians* Series)
Tovey, D. F. *Beethoven.* London, 1945
Sullivan, J. W. N. *Beethoven.* Pelican Books. London, 1949

BERG:

Reich, W. *Alban Berg.* Vienna, 1937
Leibowitz, R. *Schoenberg and His School.* New York, 1949
Carner, M. *Alban Berg*, in *The Concerto.* Ed. Hill. Pelican Books. London, 1952
Redlich, H. F. *Alban Berg. The Man and his Music.* London, 1957

BRAHMS:

Kahlbeck, M. *Johannes Brahms.* 4 vols. Berlin, 1904-15
Specht, R. *Brahms.* London, 1930

Geiringer, K. *Johannes Brahms*. London, 1936
Latham, P. *Brahms*. London, 1948. (*The Master Musicians* Series)

BRUCKNER:

Kurth, E. *Bruckner*. Berlin, 1926
Engel, G. *The Life of Anton Bruckner*. New York, 1931
Newlin, D. *Bruckner, Mahler, Schoenberg*. New York, 1947
Capell, R. *Anton Bruckner*, in *The Symphony*. Ed. Hill. Pelican Books. London, 1949
Carner, M. *Of Men and Music*. 3rd ed. London, 1944

BUSONI:

Dent, E. J. *Ferruccio Busoni*. London, 1933
Busoni, F. *A New Æsthetic of Music*. New York, 1911

CORNELIUS:

Autobiographie. Leipzig, 1947

GLUCK:

Einstein, A. *Gluck*. London, 1936. (*The Master Musicians* Series)
Cooper, M. *Gluck*. London, 1935
Newman, E. *Gluck and the Opera*. London, 1895

HINDEMITH:

Strobel, H. *Paul Hindemith*. Berlin, 1931
Hindemith, P. *A Composer's World*. Harvard, 1952
Hindemith, P. *The Craft of Musical Composition*. New York, 1945

KŘENEK:

Mersmann, H. *Die Moderne Musik seit der Romantik*. Potsdam, 1931. (Handbuch der Musikwissenschaft, ed. Bücken)
Křenek, E. *Über Neue Musik*. Vienna, 1937
Křenek, E. *Music Here and Now*. New York, 1939
Křenek, E. *Studies in Counterpoint*. New York, 1940

LISZT:

Sitwell, S. *Liszt*. London, 1934
Searle, H. *The Music of Liszt*. London, 1954

MAHLER:

Specht, R. *Gustav Mahler*. Berlin, 1925
Walter, B. *Gustav Mahler*. London, 1936
Newlin, D. *Bruckner, Mahler, Schoenberg*. New York, 1947
Carner, M. *Of Men and Music*. 3rd ed. London, 1944
Sharp, G. *Gustav Mahler*, in *The Symphony*. Ed. Hill. Pelican Books. London, 1949
Mitchell, D. *Gustav Mahler. The Early Years*. London, 1958

MARSCHNER:

Münzer, G. *Heinrich Marschner*. Leipzig, 1901

MENDELSSOHN:

Radcliffe, Ph. *Mendelssohn*. London, 1954. (*The Master Musicians* Series)

MOZART:

Abert, H. *W. A. Mozart.* 2 vols. Leipzig, 1923-24
Einstein, A. *Mozart. His Character – His Work.* London, 1946
Blom, E. *Mozart.* London, 1945. (*The Master Musicians* Series)
Dent, E. J. *The Operas of Mozart.* 2nd ed. London, 1952
King, A. H. *Mozart in Retrospect.* London, 1955
The Letters of Mozart and his Family. 3 vols. Ed. Anderson. London, 1938

PFITZNER:

Abendroth, W. *Hans Pfitzner.* Munich, 1935

REGER:

Bagier, Guido. *Max Reger.* Stuttgart, 1923

SCHOENBERG:

Wellesz, E. *Arnold Schönberg.* London, 1925
Newlin, D. *Bruckner, Mahler, Schoenberg.* New York, 1947
Leibowitz, R. *Schoenberg and His School.* New York, 1949
Schönberg, A. *Harmonielehre.* 3 vols. Vienna, 1923
Schoenberg, A. *Style and Idea.* New York, 1950

SCHUBERT:

Deutsch, O. E. *Schubert. A Documentary Biography.* London, 1946
Einstein, A. *Schubert.* London, 1951
Hutchings, A. *Schubert.* London, 1945. (*The Master Musicians* Series)
Schubert. A Symposium. Ed. Abraham. London, 1946. (*Music of the Masters* Series)
Capell, R. *Schubert's Songs.* London, 1928
Brown, M. J. E. *Schubert. A Critical Biography.* London, 1958

SCHUMANN:

Niecks, F. *Robert Schumann.* London, 1925
Chissell, J. *Schumann.* London, 1948. (*The Master Musicians* Series)
Schumann. A Symposium. Ed. Abraham. London, 1953. (*Music of the Masters* Series)
Schumann, R. *On Music and Musicians.* London, 1947

STRAUSS, JOHANN:

Jacob, H. E. *Johann Strauss. A Century of Light Music.* London, 1940
Carner, M. *The Waltz.* London, 1948. (*The World of Music* Series)

STRAUSS, RICHARD:

Specht, R. *Richard Strauss und sein Werk.* Berlin, 1921
Newman, E. *Richard Strauss.* London, 1908
Armstrong, Th. *Strauss's Tone-Poems.* London, 1931. (*Musical Pilgrim* Series)
Blom, E. *The Rose Cavalier.* London, 1930. (*Musical Pilgrim* Series)
Erhardt, O. *Richard Strauss. Leben – Wirken – Schaffen.* Olten, 1953
Krause, E. *Richard Strauss. Gestalt und Werk.* Leipzig, 1954
Strauss, R. *Correspondence with Hugo von Hofmannsthal.* London, 1927
Strauss, R. *Briefwechsel mit Hugo von Hofmannsthal.* Compiled and edited by Franz and Alice Strauss. Zurich, 1952
Strauss, R. *Recollections and Reflections.* Ed. Schuh. London, 1953

WAGNER:

Newman, E. *A Study of Wagner*. London, 1899
Newman, E. *The Life of Richard Wagner*. 4 vols. London, 1933-47
Newman, E. *Wagner as Man and Artist*. 2nd ed. London, 1925
Jacobs, R. L. *Wagner*. London, 1935. (*The Master Musicians* Series)
Bekker, P. *Richard Wagner*. London, 1931
Wagner, R. *My Life*. London, 1911
Richard Wagner's Prose Works. Translated by W. Aston Ellis. 8 vols. London, 1892-99

WEBER:

Weber, M. M. *Carl Maria von Weber*. London, 1913
Saunders, W. *Weber*. London, 1940. (*The Master Musicians* Series)

WEBERN:

Leibowitz, R. *Schoenberg and his School*. New York, 1949

WOLF:

Newman, E. *Hugo Wolf*. London, 1907
Walker, F. *Hugo Wolf*. London, 1951

CHAPTER XIII

GERMAN PAINTING

WE frequently encounter, when reading criticisms of German art by non-German writers, a tendency to decry it as formless, or to deplore its insistence on illustrative rather than æsthetic elements. Such criticism is in reality based upon a comparison which requires the art of Central Europe to conform to certain æsthetic principles, the outcome of a *Weltanschauung* very different from the German. The pagan sensuousness of the Italians, the logical genius of the French enable these peoples to create an art of serene harmony, of exquisite lucidity. They find it easier to reconcile imaginative emotion and reality than the German, whose very consciousness of this conflict seems often the primary urge to artistic creation, manifesting itself in violent contrasts of unrestrained fancy and ruthless realism. A passion for psychological penetration may sometimes result in a lack of subtlety, but with its suggestion of superficial description the term 'illustration' ignores the greatest quality of German art – its extraordinary force of expression. Moreover, the accusation 'formlessness', with its insinuation of literal transcription, fails to recognize the German artist's power to compel the object to his will, according to no fixed standard of beauty but to the necessity of individual truth.

Yet to recognize in the art of Central Europe only a tendency towards boundless subjective expression is to ignore forces that constitute as important a part of its genius as this predilection towards the 'Gothic' and Romantic. For from time to time, in the conflict between spirit and matter, a sudden longing for clarification and harmony awakens in the German that 'yearning for the south' of which Georg Dehio with his great insight into the art of his country speaks. But northern classicism thus born is, through its very function of discipline and restraint, far removed from that of the Apolline south, and a true understanding of either can only be won through the realization of their divergent ideals.

When, with the foundation of the Holy Roman Empire, art was incorporated in the machinery of the State as a symbol of imperial and theocratic authority, Central Europe turned to the south. For neither the involved linearity characteristic of Germanic decorative art and the manuscripts

of the Irish monks in Britain and St. Gall, nor the Merovingian illuminations with their symbols of bird and fish were suited to the grandiose
dogmatic art dreamed of by Charlemagne. What these lacked – monumental representation of the human form – the Carolingians found in
late classic and Byzantine art, which provided them with a prototype both
for the painting of manuscripts and for fresco in church and palace. Of
the latter only inscriptions, 'tituli', remain. That the German monks who
copied the foreign designs aimed at classicism in any real sense, that they
were aware of the true significance of three-dimensional form in relation
to space, is scarcely credible, as indeed the rude and summary manner in
which these problems were treated proves. The name Carolingian
Renaissance, which is often applied to this period (750-918), can therefore
only be justified in as far as it denotes a decided attempt to create, like the
south, an art that concerns itself with the material world.

Under the Saxon and Ottonian kings (918-1024) illuminative art
continues as in the *Codex Egberti* on similar lines. But simultaneously the
expressive decorative line beloved of Germanic art reasserts itself against
the illusionistic form and impressionistic technique of the late classic.
Charged with an almost electric vitality it hastens over the page, causing
draperies to twist and coil or straighten to tongues of flame and rectangular
shapes rigid as metal (*Evangelist Markus München lat.* 4454). Three-
dimensional form is negated. But a sense for monumentality of design
gives the wild gesticulation and distortion of the figures an intensity
which often amounts to apocalyptic frenzy (*Evangelienbuch Otto III*).
Expression rather than representation is the key-note of this art, a tortured
subjectivity, a reaction against reality in favour of the transcendental.
The anthropomorphic interest of the south has here been subordinated
to an anaturalistic decorative ideal. Iconographically these anti-materialistic
tendencies are reflected in a frequent recurrence of the theme of the Last
Judgment (the *Weltuntergangsmotiv* beloved of German literature), not
only in manuscripts but on frescoes in the churches of this period.

Amongst the monastic schools of painting, TREVES, ECHTERNACH,
RATISBON, REICHENAU, the last was exceptionally productive in both
branches of this art. In the church of *St. Georg Oberzell* may be traced
the remains of a *Last Judgment* of about the year 1000, a supreme example
of the Ottonian style with its negation of three-dimensional form and the
division of the picture-plane into three parallel strips of brown, green,
and blue. A strict monumentality helps to create an atmosphere of suspense in the long file of apostles turned towards the enthroned Christ, the
terribilis vultus from whom the dread decree is about to fall. Then in a
wall-painting at *Burgfelden*, probably of the second half of the eleventh

century, we are confronted with the chaos of demolition, and again expressive power of line gives dramatic force to the onslaught of trump-blowing angel and pitch-forked devil.

This fresco falls under the period known as Romanesque, in which, with the development of building, painting was soon faced with a new problem – namely, its relation to the vault. In the *Klosterkirche Prüfening near Regensburg*, towards the middle of the twelfth century, the tectonic design of the vault is still ignored by the painter, though the arrangement of the hieratic figures on the walls shows a fine sensibility to the noble rhythm of the architecture. But in *Schwarzrheindorf* (1151-57) and in the chapter-house of *Brauweiler* church the painted scenes are divided to fit the caps, and colour is no longer applied in parallel strips but concentri-cally, the figures cutting the borders.

The majestic figures that loom isolated or in rows from the walls of twelfth-century German churches ornament also the glass-painting of this period. But in both cases a second style is met with in which descrip-tive scenes or single figures of comparatively small dimensions are enclosed within medallions, producing a rich jewel-like effect. Influences from France may be traced, but their origin might also be ascribed to a development from Ottonian illuminations of the school of Regensburg. A supreme example of the medallion style is to be found in the painted wooden ceiling of *St. Michael Hildesheim* (1186(?)-1200), in which the figures of Adam and Eve show an astounding comprehension of the human form. Simultaneously the totally anaturalistic treatment of the draperies with their writhing zigzag folds is characteristic of a mannerism of the time. The almost baroque intensification of these lightning lines with their negation of volume approaches the bizarre in the *Frankenberg Kirche, Goslar*. In a painting of the vault of *Sta. Maria zur Höhe, Soest* (1220-30) it becomes the direct expression of the transcendental. Defying the limitations of measurable space, it quickens the Byzantine monumentality where the angelic choir stand ranged around the Madonna with wings upspread like tongues of flame – *sub specie æternitatis*.

In the meantime a tendency towards a certain naturalism began to manifest itself, a love of description. Musicians and jongleurs enliven the feast of Herod, the heroes of the Old Testament appear wearing the armour and costumes of contemporary Knights (*Brauweiler*). In the *Hortus deliciarum*, pen-and-ink drawings which HERRAD, Abbess of Klos-terhohenburg (Alsace), prepared for the delight and edification of her nuns, scenes from everyday life intersperse a complex treatise of theology and science. Thinner draperies, following a softer flow of line, suggest vaguely the contours of the body (*Schwarzrheindorf*).

Crossing the threshold of the 'Gothic', period art awakens to a long-lost sensuousness. The purgatorial terror and apocalyptic vision of Ottonian and Romanesque times are exchanged for a dream of Paradise that finds its way earthward. Christ is no longer the dread majesty but the friend of the supplicator. The terrible countenance of the angels has grown tender that they may laugh and weep with the Madonna – herself no more the regal bearer of the sceptred prince, but the mother absorbed in her child. The artist has rediscovered the beauty of the earth, not, like the Greeks, as an end in itself, but as a mirror of the spirit of God. Under the influence of chivalry, man and woman seek to give their lives a new dignity by aspiring towards the ideal of *zuht* and *mâze* (the Aristotelian Μεσότης, the Ciceronian *temperantia modesta*). No Neo-classicism or Renaissance, perhaps, appears so Greek as the unconscious Hellenism of thirteenth-century sculpture, except that the Gothic dream of harmonious perfection was permeated by a dogmatic tendency that insists on the subjective and symbolic value of representation, regarding it as an incentive to spiritual contemplation and activity. In reality, the corporeal beauty of early Gothic sculpture is little more than an illusion, for the thirteenth century artist interested himself less in the anatomy of the body than in the draperies which rise and fall independently of movement in the limbs beneath. Nor are the painted figures confined to a real limit of space, but, moving against a formal background of gold or diaper work, cut the decorated border, oblivious of the boundaries of the finite.

Thus German art turns once more towards *'die Welt des schönen Scheins'*, curbing its passion for emotional expression, this time under the guidance of France – yet here, as in her literature, bending foreign influences to a need of her own. It is significant that in German thirteenth-century art idealism is permeated by an individuality, a dramatic sense that often causes French art, æsthetically more subtle, more sensitive though it be, to appear by comparison representative and conformable to type. As yet sculpture in its attendance upon architecture was the most expressive medium of medieval artistic thought, so that we must seek here rather than in painting characteristics peculiarly German. In the prophetic grandeur of the *Elizabeth of the Visitation* and in the immense spiritual control which renders more deeply significant the physical beauty of the Knight (Bamberg Cathedral) we become aware of qualities which almost foreshadow the art of Dürer. Painting during the thirteenth and early fourteenth centuries held a humbler place and remained, above all, essentially medieval and Gothic. In the form of fresco it enjoyed comparative importance in the churches of the Rhine, where interrelations with England have been traced. A particularly fine example of fourteenth-century wall-painting is found on the choir walls of the *Klosterkirche*, *Wienhausen*, near Celle, in the Province of Hanover, where figures in medallions are encompassed by a rich ornamentation of leafy tendrils. But fresco was forced to yield the power it had exercised on the Romanesque basilica, for, with the development of Gothic architecture, the walls were reduced to a minimum and the vast spaces between the skeleton of pier and tracery were spanned by painted glass. Sometimes, as in the *Three Kings Window* of Cologne Cathedral, slender Gothic figures rise against a diaper background crowned by fantastic architectural motifs, gleaming in golden-yellow and silver-grey. Later, vague attempts at perspective and modelling with half shadows make themselves evident. In its various branches, painting conforms to the idealistic manner described above. But when the artist's vision, rejecting abstraction for the illusion of physical beauty, turned earthward, the first seeds of medieval naturalism were unconsciously sown. Curiosity was gradually aroused for the manifold wonders of nature – a parallel to the conception of Thomas Aquinas, who tells us 'God rejoiceth in the beauty of all things'. The new interest manifests itself not only in an unlimited range of subject-matter, which includes countless illustrations to medieval romance and Minnelied, as for instance the illuminated Minnesinger manuscripts (*Manesse Codex* of Heidelberg) and Wolfram von Eschenbach's *Parzival* and *Willehalm* (Munich), or the great tapestries recounting the tale of *Tristan and Isôt* in *Wienhausen* near Celle (1300-25). Of far greater consequence than the increase in motifs are the first signs of a systematic observation of nature which seeks to clarify the chaos of appearances. As early as the fourteenth century a panel in the museum at Erfurt representing the *Birth of Christ* shows an attempt on the part of the artist to bring the architectural motif (still more or less a fantastic piece of decoration) into direct plastic relation with the figures. It is significant that the development of naturalism goes hand in hand with the emancipation of painting from its bondage to monumental decoration, the panels of the great altar (which gradually attains a great importance) affording an excellent background for actual pictures. Naturalistic tendencies received a great stimulus in influences brought by way of Avignon from Italy, where Giotto and the Sienese school had achieved triumphs in elucidating relations of volume and space. Thus Bohemia, under the patronage of Charles IV, who even invited Italian artists such as Tommaso da Modena to his court, became a prominent artistic centre of the fourteenth century. The majesty of the *Glatzer Madonna* (Berlin Kaiser Friedrich-Museum; fourteenth century) is no longer due to linear rhythm, but to a new

understanding of volume, whilst an increased interest in reality is seen in
The Birth of Christ (Hohenfurth Stiftsgalerie), an actual shed being introduced into a landscape. Influences from the school of Prague were
manifest in Bavaria and in the art of MEISTER BERTRAM of Hamburg. But
soon the attention of German artists was directed towards the west, to
Burgundy, where Italian form had been more thoroughly comprehended
and absorbed. The alien iconographical schemes adopted by Bohemia
were here dispensed with, whilst the structural truths underlying them
provided the Burgundians with the means of clothing religious scenes
naturalistcially according to their own environment.

Amongst the artists whom Philip the Bold entrusted with the decoration of the Carthusian Monastery at Dijon was a certain Hermann de
Coulogne, probably identical with HERMANN WYNRICH VON WESEL, to
whom must now be ascribed many of the works of the Cologne school
of the fourteenth century formerly attributed to MEISTER WILHELM. In
spite of its contact with Burgundy, this German school, which during
the earlier part of the century had favoured the delicately decorated and
brilliantly coloured English manner, continued to produce a style deeply
transfused with Gothic idealism. A lyric mood almost mystic in its
simple piety pervades these paintings, which later aroused such enthusiasm
among the nineteenth-century romanticists. Sometimes a tendency towards effeminacy is combined with power of expression, and *Die heilige
Veronika* (Munich, Pinakothek; early fifteenth century) shows an emotional depth that raises it to an outstanding place in German art. Burgundian influences are more marked in the works of the Westphalian
KONRAD VON SOEST. In his *Crucifixion* at Nieder-Wildungen (1404)
naturalism triumphs in the rendering of fashionable dress which enlivens
the picture with rich contrast. But the bodies with their lack of plasticity,
their spidery limbs, have a tapestry-like effect, and it is still the *linear*
rhythm that predominates.

In MEISTER FRANKE of Hamburg, probably synonymous with Heuselin
of Strassburg, we meet with an artist of true creative power. His strangely
naïve fancy and dramatic expression are very German. In *altar panels* in
the *Hamburger Kunsthalle* he was able, without the help of complex linear
perspective, to produce an effect of depth in space rarely known at this
time. The night hangs like a curtain spangled with stars where Mary
kneels whitely radiant amidst the lonely wooded landscape, but the mantle
with which the angels encircle her forms a cavern of living shadow.
Archaic streamers with inscriptions flutter through the air, yet they grow
small with the distance, and the face of God piercing the darkness is
dimmed by fleeting clouds.

In the middle-Rhine district a worldly chivalric art is reflected in the joyous picture of the *Paradiesgärtlein* (*c.* 1420). The Madonna sits amidst the flowers and trees of a fair pleasaunce surrounded by her saintly company, who, clad in sumptuous robes, make music and converse. It seems more than probable that, as with a great deal of medieval art, we are here faced with Eastern influences which recall, even iconographically, Persian art and, more remotely, a vision of the Mazdaian paradise.

Courtly ideals manifest themselves in frescoes that decorate many a castle chamber of the period, more especially in the Tyrol, where influences from the south mingle with others from north and west. Here in the castle of *Runkelstein*, near Bozen (Bolzano), the walls abound with scenes from the medieval romances of *Tristan and Îsôt*, and *Garel*. Courtiers join with ladies in the swinging rhythm of the dance beneath orchard trees; or in the *Adler Turm* at *Trient* the artist's vision roams over meadow, hill, and stream accompanying knight and lady, peasant and labourer as they pursue the tasks or pastimes meted out to the various seasons. Again one is reminded of Persian miniatures.

In Swabia LUKAS MOSER, enjoying the patronage of the art-loving lords who foregathered at the Council of Constance, became acquainted with the ideals of Burgundian art, and was thus enabled to play an important part in furthering the development of German fifteenth-century naturalism. In the *Tiefenbronner Altar* of 1431 several incidents are combined to form a continuous narrative, so producing the effect of a unified panorama, whilst delight in descriptive detail is rendered artistic by an appreciation of texture and atmosphere which manifests itself especially in a sensibility to the beauty of rippling expanses of water beneath the light.

During the fifteenth century the altar rises to a supreme position in German art. A great winged structure, its decoration was entrusted solely either to the hands of the painter or else employed also the art of the sculptor in wood which, enclosed in the middle shrine, becomes visible when the painted wings are opened on feast-days. And now painting really begins to vie with sculpture, permeating naturalism with a monumentality and a power of expression which hitherto only statuary had known. No longer tempered by the chivalric ideal of 'diu mâze' the art that thrived under the burghers of the fifteenth century was impelled by a real German lust for individuality to a violent and often brutal realism, whilst passion for subjectivity finds release in overwrought fantasy. These tendencies, rising to a climax towards the end of the century, contribute with similar traits shown in architecture to the development of a late Gothic style that triumphs over foreign influences as a supreme expression of German feeling.

Prominent amongst German-speaking painters of the early fifteenth century, KONRAD WITZ, of Basel (1390/1400-1446/47), inspired by the master of Flémalle, dedicates himself to solving the problems of plastic form. A distinct æsthetic vision, a fine sense of selection dominate his interest in actuality, so that his paintings show a unity lacking in much art of the period. Witz sees the world in terms of volume. In the *Heiligspiegelaltar* (Basel) his stocky figures – carved they seem out of blocks of wood – advance with plodding stride or stand gesticulating like automatons. Every trace of the swinging rhythm of early Gothic has departed. Divining almost instinctively the laws of gravity and corporeal structure which were to become a science with the Renaissance, he conceives space as cubically measurable, achieving this effect not only by intersections but by light and shade and the use of reflection and cast shadow. Delicate tones are incorporated in his strong, rich colouring. In the landscape background of his *Fischzug Petri* (1444, Geneva Museum) these qualities enable him to realize in nature a beauty more deep than the fleeting impression. Yet, for all his interest in physical truth, the German love of the anaturalistic expressive line remains. In the *St. Katharine and St. Magdalene* (Strassburg) the draperies are filled with an abstract momentum. Fold piles itself upon fold, but the flowing curves of earlier Gothic are frozen to jagged crystalline formations. Similar tendencies are found at this time in the art of Bavaria and Nuremburg, which remains for the most part crude and primitive and suffers from overcrowding, though some paintings, in particular those of HANS MULTSCHER and the MEISTER DES TUCHERALTARS often possess dramatic feeling.

A very different spirit pervades the paintings of STEPHAN LOCHNER (†1451), who, leaving the Lake of Constance for the Lower Rhine, gave the traditional idealism and effeminacy of Cologne painting a new monumentality. The lucidity of design, the broad rhythm of light and shade that blends the figures to a harmonious unity, creating an illusion of space, fill the *Adoration* in Cologne Cathedral and the *Presentation in the Temple* (1447, Darmstadt) with a serene harmony.

During the second half of the fifteenth century the interest of German artists, directed towards the schools of Rogier van der Weyden and Dierick Bouts, enjoys an interlude of comparative ease. The thick-set figures of Witz and his followers are replaced by slender graceful types robed in thinner draperies, their livelier movement filling the wide landscape with a variety of detail and contrast. Thus in the *St. George* (Lüneburg) of HINDRIK FUNHOF of Hamburg the tessellated hall is open to the country-side, which abounds with incidents of secondary interest, whilst legendary content is subordinated to contemporary anecdote. In

the *Crucifixion* (Munich, Pinakothek) of HANS PLEYDENWURFF (1420-72) of
Nuremberg the scene is expanded beyond the crowd foregathered at the
foot of the cross, and the white road by which these people must have come
winds its way amongst hills towards the turrets and timbered houses of
the little town. Or in the *Master of the Life of the Virgin Mary* an earnest
matter-of-fact feeling and a predilection for green reminiscent of Bouts
is allied to the delicate gleam of paint traditional in the Cologne school.

The last decades of the fifteenth century witness the division of German
painting into countless local schools. In some, the lust for expression,
lately suppressed by the happier Netherlandish naturalism, breaks forth
with redoubled violence, revelling in anguished and chaotic form. The
Bavarian and Franconian schools, particularly that of Dürer's master,
MICHAEL WOLGEMUT (1434-1519), tend towards what may be termed a
baroque Gothic. To what tangled complexity it may lead the *Crucifixion*
(Munich, Nationalmuseum) of JAN POLLACK bears witness, whilst the
power and dignity of an unknown Bavarian master's *Holy Trinity* (in
Blutenburg) proves the grand possibilities of this style.

Italy, too, was at this time experiencing her baroque naturalism, and
in the Tyrol the boundaries of north and south dissolve. The work of
MICHAEL PACHER († 1498) has much of the rock-hewn force of Mantegna.
But the figures are more attenuated, the angularity of the draperies that
throw up sharp edges of light reflects the style of the wood-carver, in
which art this master equally excelled. Since Witz no German painter
had so rejoiced in the glory of volume achieved by a scientific study of
linear perspective which recognizes in space a factor as important as the
human form. Theoretical knowledge helped Pacher to heighten the
dramatic significance of a scene. Space is used as an emotional medium.
In the *Cleansing of the Temple* (from the altar of St. Wolfgang in Tyrol)
the vast receding aisle seems indeed swept clean by the irate figure of
Christ. The dynamic force with which the angel in the *Baptism* (*ibid.*)
pierces the air was scarce seen again before the days of Tintoretto, whilst
the group of pitchers in the *Wedding Feast at Cana* (*ibid.*) seem to hold a
double miracle – suggesting almost twentieth-century cubism. And
neither before nor since has an artist penetrated the depths of animal
instinct as here in the *Adoration* (*ibid.*), where the light touching the
haunches of the ox, the muzzle, the horns makes one slowly aware of the
great beast which looms lost in dumb wonder from out the shadows of
the stable whilst angels circle on bright wings above.

MARX REICHLICH, another Tyrolese artist, concentrating his interest
upon light, uses a strange chiaroscuro as emotional element, whilst
RUELAND FRUEAUF of Salzburg and his son (who seems sometimes to

foreshadow the fairy-tale art of Schwind) incline to a quieter style practised in Swabia under HANS SCHÜCHLIN and BARTHOLOMÄUS ZEITBLOM. In strongest contrast to the violent passion of Bavarian late fifteenth-century art stands the gentle beauty of MARTIN SCHONGAUER's painting (1445-1491), which, inspired though it be by Rogier van der Weyden, became impregnated through the artist's personality with a spirit essentially German. In the exquisite *Maria im Rosenhag* (1473, Colmar) a supreme sense of form enables him to transfuse northern delight in detail with spiritual depth. A simple scene – Mary and the Child seated before a garden fence where birds perch amongst rose-briars and wild strawberries grow at the Madonna's feet. But the great swinging draperies with their impenetrable chasms of gloom rise sheer as rock, enclosing in their dark pyramid the bright surfaces of naked flesh, the melodious interchange of contrasted rhythm in the limbs, whilst above, two angels bearing a gigantic cross darken the sunlit air.

In his engravings Schongauer abandons himself to the decorative vagaries beloved of the late Gothic. But the very irrationality of design, the negation of organic construction, tends in the *Flight into Egypt* to render the playful work of the angels more convincing where the tree bends beneath their weightlessness. Those unaccustomed to German form may not realize perhaps that the design to which *Christ on the Mount of Olives* is subordinated has more than an ornamental value. The outline which, provided by the figure of Christ, may be traced again in the group combining the rock and the apostles, and once more in the silhouette of the tree, is based on no æsthetic norm of symmetry, but on an emotional motif born of the picture's spiritual content, the motif of supplication. In the *Carrying of the Cross* an ever-swelling rhythm manifests itself as a sequence of intricately studied detail and incident, even as the late Gothic church, abandoning itself to the dynamic energy of space, demands simultaneously the elaboration of each part. But no harmonious composition of well-proportioned figures could have rendered so convincing the tumultuous clamour and ruthless pressure of the mob, nor the weariness of the interminable climb up the hill. Those who have once realized the power of German art to translate emotion into immediate design will scarcely speak of formlessness and illustration. They will understand also why the graphic arts with their double possibility of detailed characterization and absolute expression rose to a supreme independence in Central Europe, whilst in Italy they remained as studies from nature and compositional schemes for the most part subservient to the monumental arts.

But Gothic art had run its course and betrays even in Schongauer a tendency to fall into decadence or effeminacy, and once again German art stood in dire need of that will to clearer vision and more objective thought which reasserts itself from time to time as a curb to subjective emotion. In the renaissance of the classic ideal in Italy it discovered a means of salvation, and simultaneously a new danger. That it did not share the doom of Netherlandish Romanism, and sink into slavish subjection to an alien form, is primarily due to the individuality of ALBRECHT DÜRER (1471-1528). Knowledge gained in two journeys to Italy urged him to no repudiation of national tradition but spurred on an inherent longing for a regeneration of German art. And indeed the name Reformation might lead to fewer misunderstandings of early sixteenth-century art in Central Europe than the designation Renaissance with its suggestion of Italian classic form. Even now the ideal of perfect beauty, of an æsthetic norm, proved less interesting to the German than the old quest of individual truth. Only a new comprehension of the laws of anatomical structure and monumental design enable him to express his aims with greater conviction than before. The acute thoroughness with which Dürer applied himself to the study of those problems which seemed so easily solved in Italy is characteristically northern. His own words, '*die Schönheit herausreissen aus der Natur*', betray an attitude towards nature different from that which seeks to build up ideally proportioned landscapes. Dürer's very knowledge of the structure and growth of tree and plant help him to render them overwhelmingly individual.

In the *St. Michael*, from the woodcut series of the Apocalypse, an understanding of movement gives the furious onslaught of the Archangel a dramatic vigour hitherto unknown. Yet Dürer, as his engraving and painting of *Adam and Eve* betray, was lured also to seek the norm of corporeal beauty. But characteristically his interest in the æsthetic problem is imbued with the semi-ethical aim of recovering that original beauty which man was forced to relinquish at his Fall. The idealistic Christ-like *Self-portrait* in Munich has a vertical tension, a realism in the nervous fingers utterly remote from the worldly self-assurance of Raphael's *gran'signori*. In the engraving *Knight, Death, and the Devil*, a formal problem that Donatello, Verrocchio, and Leonardo had loved, the relation of horse to rider in an equestrian group is permeated in Dürer's case with a symbolic meaning – the *miles Christianus* who rides on his way undaunted by the grim perils that beset his path. Or again in the woodcut *Christ's Farewell to His Mother*, a motif of antithesis – complex movement *versus* simple rest – is used as a direct emotional element. The figure of Jesus, whose calm resolution is expressed in strict finality of design and noble swing of draperies, affords a poignant contrast to the broken body of Mary, in whose robe the anaturalistic Gothic line writhes as though quickened by the anguish of her soul. The classic ideal of balance between vertical and horizontal plays a primary part in the design of the renowned engraving *Melancholia*. But simultaneously the sudden diagonal of the ladder, the menacing poise of the crystalline block, the ponderous pose of the woman herself change calm to an atmosphere of oppressiveness and paralysing gloom.

Expressive form is used by Dürer to render even the simplest intimate scene. Thus an almost classic design, in which lucidity of plastic form is intensified by brilliant light, creates an atmosphere of serenity where *St. Jerome* sits in his study surrounded by his beasts. Or the crisp lines of the woodcut fill many a scene from the *Life of the Virgin Mary* with the hum of household activity.

Not always are expression and form transfused to a perfect unity. Dürer's great improvements on the technique of the woodcut enabled him to produce an illusion of plasticity that lent itself to the creation of a more formal representative style, and we may sometimes regret the loss of unrestrained imaginative force that distinguished his earlier works. This tendency is especially evident in his paintings. But where monumentality is the direct means of intensifying emotion Dürer's work in this branch of art can stand side by side with that of the Italians. The *portraits* of his later years, which in their magnificently controlled form seem to reflect the iron character of the men who stood on the threshold of the Reformation, the *Rosenkranzmadonna*, with its atmosphere of mingled joy and gravity, the panels with the *Four Apostles* where the suppressed rage in the countenance of St. Paul seems echoed in tumultuous dissonances locked within the precipices of his mantle – all these are emblems of what this art, which sacrifices sensual beauty to expressive power, may achieve – the will of German classicism made manifest.

That passion for unrestrained imaginative emotion, which in Dürer's case is curbed by a tendency towards scientific objectivity and moral discipline, breaks forth as a flood of subjectivity in the painting of his contemporary MATTHIAS GRÜNEWALD (*c.* 1480-1528). Neither before nor since was the *Crucifixion* portrayed with so overwhelming a truth as on the tremendous panels of the *Isenheimer Altar* in Colmar. Yet reality as perceived by the eye or the laws of reason is utterly ignored. The scourged body that looms gigantic from the impenetrable darkness of night bears proportionally no relation to the remaining figures. Its size is symbol, is fulfilment of the prophecy proclaimed by the hand of the Baptist – '*Illum oportet crescere me autem minui*' – . The infinite linearity in the folds of the Magdalene's robe defies all possibility. But no plastic form could have rendered so convincing this utter abandonment to grief – a supreme contrast to the white rigidity of the other Mary who, in her agony, seems frozen to stone.

Grünewald beheld in the theme of the *Resurrection (ibid.)* not, like most Italians and even Dürer, an opportunity for anatomic corporeal representation, but a chance for dramatically supernatural expression – the annihilating force of the miracle. A broad treatment of paint, very different from Dürer's linear plasticity, adds to the passionate quality of his style, and the changing surfaces of brilliant colour follow the process of transubstantiation as the figure of Christ soaring upwards is dissolved in blinding light. For Grünewald light has more than a rational significance. As a magic element it can fill the earth with ecstatic vision. In the *Christmas (ibid.)* the angel's music seems light made audible – we can understand the conception of the nineteenth-century romanticists, '*ich höre das Licht*'. It is the substance of which the heavenly beings are born who, swept downward upon the fiery flood like leaves on the wind, bear the news to the amazed shepherds. Blue mountain, lake, and stream, the roses of that strange landscape are transfused with its glory, where the Madonna sits unaware of the miracle wrapt in contemplation of her Child.

In the background of this picture, and still more in that of *St. Paul and St. Anthony in the Desert (ibid.)*, we may study Grünewald's attitude towards nature – a strange pantheistic conception in which bird and beast, rock and plant, seem to lose their individual existence, and, intertwined to a pattern almost Chinese, merge in the infinite rhythm of being. Here, and in some small engraving or tinted sketch of Dürer's – *Christmas* or the *Madonna amongst many Animals* –, the landscape or architectural environment begins to assert its importance over the figures, a natural development of northern art which was never bound to the anthropomorphic conceptions of the south. But these, and yet more the romantic landscapes of ALBRECHT ALTDORFER (1480?-1538), WOLF HUBER (*c.* 1490-1553), and the SCHOOL OF THE DANUBE reflect a conception of nature far removed from the objective naturalism that had flourished beneath the influence of the Netherlands. The ruins and grottoes, the primeval trees trailing long strands of moss which form a background to incidents from the Old Testament or to legends of the saints provide the principal emotional element in the picture awakening a particular *Stimmung*. In Altdorfer's *Birth of the Virgin Mary* (Munich, Pinakothek) the vast spaces of vault and aisle with their intricate intersections and play of light and shadow defying the clear construction and perspective beloved of the Italian are the means of filling a quaint *genre*-scene with an atmosphere of heavenly festivity. Here the figurative motif of the circling garland of angels is still used to accentuate the dynamic quality of space, but in the

Birth of Christ (Vienna) the figures seem inwoven in the snow-bound darkness of the winter night by countless threads of light cast from the divine radiance above. The white war-horse that bears the black-mailed knight in his *St. George* (Munich) scarce treads the tangled undergrowth of the wood but hangs as though suspended before the impenetrable wall of foliage that rises sheer as a chasm to the edge of the picture frame – a forest perilous, opening as through a rift in the rock to the blue distance. No organic construction, no clear relation of volume and space is here, even the trunks of the trees have no plasticity, and the minute figures are but a point of light accentuating the oppressive density of the leaves. So Altdorfer foreshadows the nineteenth-century romanticists, beholding a landscape neither as a monumental composition nor as a foil to the actions of human beings, but as a fragment of the infinite in which man sees reflected his own mood. These tendencies, allied to a wild fantasy, find a perfect medium of expression in woodcut and chiaroscuro drawing in which curling white lines and dark shadows cover tinted paper with calligraphic swiftness subordinating figure and environment to a single rhythm. The same technique gives the figures of *witches* and *death* beloved of HANS BALDUNG GRIEN (1480?-1565) a terrible intensity. In his paintings strangely fantastic conceptions and mannerisms are rendered exquisite by a delicate Gothic ideal of beauty and a rare sensitiveness to colour and texture. Unforgettable are the white body of the woman, the pearl-grey snake against the mossy darkness of trees in the *Allegory of Wisdom* (1529, Munich, Pinakothek), or the blue velvet that gleams jewel-like from the darkness of the *Birth of Christ* (Frankfurt), a perfect foil to the bemused face and the long Gothic hands bathed in that extraordinary concentration of light. In the *High Altar of Freiburg Cathedral* (1513-1517) Baldung revels in the complexities of late Gothic design both in the composition of the paintings and in labyrinthine entanglement of decorative wood-carving. But passionate abandonment to movement was never rendered so expressive as in the master's woodcut of the *Ascension*, where the body of Christ, whirled by cherubs through the clouds, arouses a sense of immeasurable dynamic space.

Heavenly and profane elements intermingle with charming incongruity in the art of LUKAS CRANACH (1472-1553). But the naïve sensuality of the allegories in which he delights have little in common with the sublime detachment of the classic. These Venuses, Dianas, and Graces are porcelain-like figures with tripping feet and piquant gestures. These lemon groves and glades of laurel open on German meadows and pine-woods. Cranach lacks an understanding for monumental structure. Nature is for him an earthly *Paradise* (Kunsthistorisches Museum, Vienna), that holds a thousand infinitesimal wonders for the artist to discover. Master of gleaming surfaces, he models the figures of his maidens in tones of mother-of-pearl and bluish shadows, draping them with diaphanous veils. Watching animal life, he discovers the sleek beauty of fur and hide. He rejoices in the coolness of marble, the spring's crystal, the translucency of tranquil water, the gleaming pebble, the jewel-like flower. His woodcuts with their impetuous line strike a graver note, as also the portraits of those earnest pioneers of the Reformation who were his friends.

How inadequately the name renaissance fits German art of the sixteenth century may well be felt in reviewing the work of these painters. Each of them may betray at times a tendency to succumb to foreign influence, but classic form in the Italian sense is far more evident in the lesser artists of this period, in the last works of HANS HOLBEIN THE ELDER, in KULM-BACH, SCHÄUFELEIN, and BURGKMAIR, where, unassimilated, it at times produces a cold and barren atmosphere. But a continuous reassertion of old traditions, evident in the engravings and woodcuts of BEHAM, and especially in the passionate and graphic art of URS GRAF, and in the manneristic fantasies of NIKLAUS MANUEL DEUTSCH and HANS LEU, save German art from falling into dead formalism.

In HANS HOLBEIN THE YOUNGER (1497-1543) a will to simplification of form, born of an inner necessity, manifests itself in the astounding objectivity of such portraits as *Robert Cheseman* (The Hague), where the austerity of design is heightened by the severe background with its inscription in antiqua. So sure is his sense of form that his German love of characteristic detail results, as in the *Ambassadors Jean de Diuteville and Georges de Selva* (London National Gallery), in no loss of unity, whilst the warm glow of his colour renders hard construction sensuously palpable in the portrait of his *wife and children*. In the *Madonna with the Burgomaster Jakob Meyer* (Darmstadt) Holbein was able to build a formal composition with an ease Dürer had struggled in vain to achieve. The cartoons for the wall-paintings in the *Basler Rathaus* (1530) show a monumentality akin to Raphael's permeated by northern vigour. Yet in this objective mind lived also an urge for freer dramatic expression, and in his decorative designs for the *Haus zum Tanz* and the *Londoner Stahlhof* fancy runs riot in music, revel, and dance, whilst in the woodcut series of the *Totentanz* it abandons itself to the grim rhythm of death.

Thus during the first decades of the sixteenth century, German art alone was worthy, by its very independence, to stand beside the High Renaissance of Italy. In the succeeding period, Central Europe, like the other countries, fell beneath the sway of the so-called 'decadence'. Yet here again earlier German mannerism, visible in the last works of Cranach and Baldung Grien, has a *raffinement* very different from the lifeless schematism of much painting of the Italian Late Renaissance, and the artificial movements of these tightly modelled figures, whose enamel-like flesh gleams with ribbons and jewels, is subordinate to a linear rhythm that suggests the name Gothic rococo. Later German painting under TOBIAS STIMMER, CHRISTOPH SCHWARZ, JOHANN ROTTENHAMMER and others sinks to the level of an eclecticism common to the rest of Europe. But it is significant that where mannerism was understood not as mere formalism, but as a reaction against representation and the pagan sensuality of the Renaissance, Italian artists, Pontormo and even Tintoretto, turn to Germany to find in Dürer's rendering of Christ before Pontius Pilate motifs of psychological interest. Nor must it be forgotten that Germany had long before produced her El Greco in Matthias Grünewald.

The long years of comparative sterility that followed the German Renaissance were shadowed by the Thirty Years' War. And where the northern countries once more gave birth to a great era of painting, the field of activity had changed to the Netherlands. Yet a true understanding of the art of Rubens and Rembrandt is impossible unless we recognize therein the legacy of Dürer and Holbein, of Grünewald and Altdorfer, the Germanic spirit that, once more transfusing foreign ideals with its own feeling, produced a seventeenth-century art very different from that of the south. However, the immediate incentive, the development of Italian baroque, cannot be negated, and amongst the mediators between southern and northern art tribute must be paid to the German ADAM ELSHEIMER (1578-1610). Consorting in Rome with the circle of Annibale Carracci, he played an important part in the development of the ideal landscape of the seventeenth century in which the artist, breaking with the anthropomorphic conceptions of the Renaissance, seeks to attain unity between man and the cosmos. Central Europe had dreamed of some such idea long before; but, whereas Altdorfer abandons himself to a vague romantic dream of infinity, the baroque painter strives by a formal process of subordination to bring all parts into relation with the whole. Colour and light, freed from their dependence on the plastic object, become primary elements in design. A partiality for unbroken colour prevents Elsheimer from achieving altogether the baroque ideal, but his tree landscapes with their diagonal division of the picture-plane foreshadow Claude Lorraine; night-scenes such as the *Flight into Egypt* (Munich and Vienna), with their dimly lit figures merged in the vast expanse of nature, suggest the art of Rembrandt, whilst his compositions of interiors were adopted by Adriaen Brouwer and other exponents of Netherland *genre*.

Towards the end of the seventeenth and during the eighteenth centuries the art of Central Europe experienced a resurrection, not in painting, which under the historian of art JOACHIM SANDRART and others remained the slave of eclecticism, but in music and architecture. In the southern German territories, under the influence of the Counter Reformation, the tremendous dream of the baroque found its consummation in church and palace. In Central Europe alone, where the late Gothic had wrestled against finite plasticity, was the architect able to abandon himself utterly to the inebriation of space. Whilst in Rome the interior decorations of Andrea Pozzo and the virtuosi of false perspectives still betray vestiges of plastic isolation of form, those of the BROTHERS ASAM, their pupil MAT-THÄUS GÜNTHER, JOHANN ZICK and FRANZ ANTON MAULPERTSCH emulate rather the rococo of Tiepolo, who himself worked in Germany. Confronted by this worldly-mystic art, born of the spirit of St. Ignatius of Loyola and St. Teresa, of the ecstatic sublimation of the sensual, the senses reel, unable to distinguish between earth and heaven. Here every rational boundary is dissolved; architecture, sculpture, and painting flow to one inseparable harmony; and space is audible as music.

But moral conscience and inhibitions, added to the menace of the French Revolution, too soon assert themselves against the frivolities of the French rococo, whose influence permeated German art, while Neoclassicism, as it were an artistic parallel to the *Aufklärung*, preached the gospel of uplift. These new ideals are reflected particularly in the art of ANTON RAPHAEL MENGS (1728-79), whilst a simpler matter-of-fact conception characterizes the portraits of ANTON GRAFF (1736-1813) and the engravings of DANIEL CHODOWIECKI (1726-1801), a typical representative of the '*Zopfstil*', in which reminiscences of Watteau and the classic intermingle with great naïvety. Once more classicism manifests itself in its northern capacity as an influence of restraint. But now, united to no sensuous affirmation of the present but to a pessimistic longing for a world of beauty that has died, it results in the affectations of ANGELICA KAUFMANN (1741-1807) or the lifeless archæology of a JAKOB CARSTENS (1754-98) and a J. H. WILHELM TISCHBEIN (1751-1829), whom the patronage of Goethe raised to an unmerited fame. Here we see reflected Kant's theory of the supremacy of draughtmanship over colour and technique of painting, as also the ideals of the nineteenth-century public, who sought the criterion of a picture in the worth of its subject-matter. This surely is the only period where the criticism that German art is dependent on illustration is fully justified, for a gulf separates the spiritual expressiveness of the past from the literary aspirations of the nineteenth century, which were by no means limited to the region of Central Europe. In its retrospection, Neo-classicism shares a common basis with the Romanticism which developed as its counterpart, and in many cases the two styles are not easy to sunder. Thus the religious-nationalistic dream of the 'Nazarener' OVERBECK, SCHNORR v. CAROLSFELD, CORNELIUS, and those other members of the little company which gathered together in Rome with the aim of regenerating art by a pious discipline of life (a parallel to the original idea of the English Pre-Raphaelites) soon lost its specifically romantic character through a gradual subservience to Italian form. ALFRED RETHEL (1816-59), alone amongst historical painters, rising above the mediocrity of the Düsseldorf school, was able in the *Rathaus of Aachen* to transfuse Raphaelian form with a sternness characteristically German, whilst finding a yet freer scope for dramatic emotion in the woodcut series of the *Totentanz*, symbol of the revolution of 1848. Indeed where the painters ADRIAN LUDWIG RICHTER[1] (1803-44) and MORITZ VON SCHWIND (1804-71) allow their fancy free play in their intimate illustrations of folk-life, fairy-tale and legend, nineteenth-century Romanticism produced an art of true German sincerity, a perfect expression of the trim comfort and homely piety of the *Biedermeier* style of Schubert's time. For with Richter particularly, the figures are not 'arranged' to form monumental compositions, but tumble and rollick over the page, peep through a network of foliage or from under the eaves of a timbered cottage, recalling not only the woodcuts of Dürer's *Marienleben* but the playful, frolicking mood of Gothic and Nordic linear fantasies in general. In landscape also the German Romanticist, freeing himself from the tectonic schematic compositions of the Neo-classicists, was able to abandon himself once more to the magic of the infinite, the poetry of stream and forest, so that not seldom we are reminded of Altdorfer's art, except that in the nineteenth century the artist's sensuous vision inclined to be overruled by nostalgic yearnings for a golden past and an idyllic medieval world.

Some, however, more keenly sensitive to actual nature, realized that art demanded the use of vision no less than that of fancy. KARL SPITZWEG's (1808-85) humorous paintings of Philistine fads and foibles are rendered more artistic by an interest in the effect of light. Already before him KARL BLECHEN (1798-1840) seems in some of his landscapes to foreshadow the naturalism of the later nineteenth century, whilst in PHILIPP OTTO RUNGE (1778-1819) we find not only the various tendencies which later Romantic painters developed but a sensibility to atmospheric light and colour which make him appear almost a forerunner of the impressionists. He maintained for instance that an admixture of white dulls

[1] Richter, von Schwind, Spitzweg, Friedrich, Runge, Waldmüller, Anselm Feuerbach are the chief representatives in painting of Biedermeier.

the radiancy of the pigment. Yet Runge's attitude to painting remains fundamentally romantic or even mystic. His *Four Seasons* were intended as a fantastic musical poem. With the poet Tieck and the philosopher Jakob Böhme he dreamed of the unification of all the arts, the *Synästhesie*, in subordination to a higher Being, God-Nature.

His theory of colours and his 'colour-globe' brought him into contact with Schelling. Regarding colour as a mystery which we can only apprehend through flowers, he interpreted it as a symbolic manifestation of the Trinity, 'for Light itself lies beyond our realization'. In many ways Runge recalls the visionary painter Samuel Palmer, with whom he may indeed have had some direct or indirect contact, though the English artist's 'supernatural moonscapes' may suggest also an affinity with those of KASPAR DAVID FRIEDRICH (1774-1840). Whilst Palmer's creative anguish, however, found release in mystically exalted Virgilian idylls, Friedrich's spirit is weighed down by the realization of man's solitariness, his nothingness in face of infinity. Thus his figures, seen nearly always in back-view, rise as dark silhouettes against a waste of sky, watching a sail far out at sea at sunset, or stand lost in contemplation, gazing at the rising moon. Once more, as with Grünewald and the school of the Danube, these landscapes with their rocks and moss-clad conifers, half-shrouded by wraiths of mist, remind one of Asiatic art, though the European Romantic cannot attain the Oriental's detachment nor his self-annihilation before the mystery of the infinite. But there is, too, a strange rectangular simplicity and stillness about some of Friedrich's landscapes and interiors which seem to make them precursors of certain modern movements in German art.

The revolt against the poetic sentimental conception of painting which gave birth to the great movement of nineteenth-century naturalism was carried on in Germany by individuals rather than centres as in France, though Düsseldorf, under French and Belgian influences, specialized in *genre*. Something of the spirit of the Barbizon school is reflected consciously or unconsciously in most German landscape painting of the time, as for instance in that of the Austrian FERDINAND WALDMÜLLER (1793-1856), with his pictures of children playing in the sun-lit Vienna woods. Champion of dawning realism, ADOLF MENZEL (1815-1905), whose woodcuts illustrate Kugler's *History of Frederick the Great*, found inspiration not only in the glories of the past, but in actual impressions such as the *Potsdam Railway*. His early landscapes are reminiscent of Constable, whose paintings he studied at the Berlin exhibition of 1839, but, characteristically German, his linear accents are sharper in contrast to the atmosphere. Sometimes dramatic sense and colour, as in the *Théâtre*

Gymnase, suggest Delacroix. In the *Balkonzimmer* no trace is left of the sentimental conception of the romanticists (Schwind's young girl at the window greeting the morn); instead, we see a muslin curtain blown in the wind – the silhouette of a dark chair – light, air, and movement. *The Flute Concert of Frederick the Great* shows all interest in anecdote subordinated to the visual impression of transient motion and scintillating tremulous light. The realism of WILHELM LEIBL (1844-1900) provides a parallel to that of Courbet, but without the Frenchman's pathos. He moulds the figures of his peasants (*Drei Frauen in der Kirche, Das ungleiche Paar*) in a strict counterpoint of line and mass, light and colour, exaggerating the smooth strength of Holbein's objective form. But in his earliest portraits, perhaps the finest of nineteenth-century Germany, surface and a feeling for the atmospheric predominate. Under his influence WILHELM TRÜBNER (1851-1917), applying himself to the problem of *plein-air,* gave his landscapes fine construction and space through the bold use of strips of brilliant colour.

But the naturalistic cause was not allowed to attain victory unimpeded, and the middle of the nineteenth century rallied to the call of German idealism. Once again a number of artists, hoping to escape the pest of materialism, found their way to Rome. But their artistic conception was still bound to a realism that could not digest dogmatic poetic sentiment. Thus ANSELM FEUERBACH (1829-80), all too conscious of his lofty mission, struggled in vain to reconcile the momentary impression with a slowly evolved intellectual ideal, his would-be epic style degenerating into an ever bleaker pathos. The sensual vision of ARNOLD BÖCKLIN (1827-1901), intoxicated by nature, sought to personify elementary forces. In the play of the waves he sees Triton and mermaid at their watery sport. Meadow and wood are filled with the music of Pan's pipes. His idylls are the dreams of one who beholds the south with the eyes of the northerner, recognizing therein not static perfection but the mystery of the infinite. But Böcklin, like so many before or since, was unable to assimilate Italian form, and an ever-growing yearning for monumentality led to the domination of the figures over the landscape and a use of unbroken colour that destroy the very rhythm of nature he had sought to create. Thus also HANS THOMA (1839-1924) – with his strange admixture of realism and fairy-tale, his landscapes that are the purest embodiment of German *Volkstümlichkeit* – was wrecked on the same rock in his striving to translate into visible form the gigantic musical visions of Richard Wagner. One painter alone during this idealistic intermezzo came near a realization of his dreams, HANS VON MARÉES (1837-87), whose poetic art seems born, not of external literary influences, but of true creative vision, of imagination rather than fancy. He aspired to monumentality through an almost architectonic rendering of the nude that gives his figures the quality of the symbolic. His conception of form is, however, not built on structure alone but on the synthetical relation of volume and space, light, atmosphere, and colour, wherefore his art seems to reflect simultaneously the vision of Giorgione, Rembrandt, and the Greeks.

In the meantime the realists, absorbed in problems of *plein-air*, had embarked upon impressionism proper. Beholding the world almost scientifically in terms of atmosphere and light, its true devotees cared little for subject-matter or the relation of volume to space. Hence object and picture lose their tectonic structure, a fragment of nature disintegrated is reconstructed as a process of colour atoms, and the individuality of the artist manifests itself almost entirely in his technique. Supremely analytical, impressionism was developed to perfection by the logical genius of the French, whilst the Germans, in need of a more direct and subjective form of expression, were unable to fulfil the finest possibility of this passive art – its exquisite sensibility. As a result the average exponent of impressionism in Central Europe inclines to a certain literalism and technical carelessness, so that his art justifies by comparison the reputation of coarseness in feeling and design. Its greatest German adherents were by no means purists.

MAX LIEBERMANN's (1847-1935) early realism, which, in pictures such as the *Goose-pluckers* (1872, Berlin National Gallery) or *Brother and Sister* retains a certain monumentality in the design and pose of figures, gradually shows an increasing delight in the accidental and the transient impression. In the *Munich Beer Garden* (1883, Berlin), which suggests Manet and Renoir, a crowd of people are viewed collectively as a succession of tones and colour patches beneath the changing effect of light. But the comparative distinctness of single objects appears as a relic of that love for characterization which in his early works had sometimes almost amounted to caricature. Now, it is less an interest in the individual than a sociological tendency which insists on the theme *Grosstadtleben*, and so causes this and other paintings of the period to betray more than purely æsthetic feeling. Even later, linear tension and sharp delineation divide such works as the *Polo Players* (Hamburg) from the purest conception of impressionism with its complete disintegration of form. Still less compatible with the French ideal is the sentimentality of FRITZ VON UHDE (1848-1911), which vacillates between Tolstoyan ethics in sympathy with the workers and the oppressed, and the salon idealism of HANS MAKART (1840-84).

The art of LOVIS CORINTH (1858-1925) is not based on rationalism but on a baroque idealism akin to that of Rubens which, like the latter's final style, makes use of impressionistic technique. Dynamic form and an almost brutal sensuality of vision are far removed from the subtle nervosity of the French. Not always in his religious and mythological pictures are realism and imagination blent to a perfect unity, but the demonic power of such late portraits as *Bernt Grönvold*, the impassioned abandonment to nature in his last landscapes and flower-paintings with their broad surfaces of pure colour, prove Corinth's power to reawaken a fundamentally German conception of art.

A growing sensibility to the epidermis of things tended with many to a sensual suggestivity, an eroticism that ends in the decadent and the perverse. A would-be Satanism inspires FRANZ VON STUCK (1863-1928), whilst a predilection for the Salome theme discernible in literature and music of the period is found also in the paintings of various artists, including MAX SLEVOGT (1868-1932). However, impressionistic technique proved a means of salvation to the latter, enabling him to imbue fantastic etchings and drawings with a vitality that MAX KLINGER's (1859-1920), burdened by their intellectual content, had lacked.

Literary and illustrative tendencies, united to a reviving desire for a more linear or flat decorative treatment of the surface, were in the meantime giving birth to a German version of the style often designated as 'L'Art Nouveau', its greatest exponent being perhaps the Austrian painter GUSTAV KLIMT (1862-1918), who through his prodigious sense of colour raised his somewhat Beardsleyan vision to monumental proportions.

In the field of book-illustration, which proved perhaps the happiest medium for exponents of a decorative symbolist outlook, mention may be made of HEINRICH VOGELER (1894-1924), whose dreamy, Maeterlinckean visions have been recorded by Rainer Maria Rilke in his monograph on a group of artists who, from the year 1895 onward, gathered in a colony in the moorland village of *Worpswede* near Bremen. On the whole this group tend towards a freer naturalism, though the landscapes of OTTO MODERSOHN (1865-1943) reflect a poetic spirit, haunted by the elfish world of German fairy-tale, whilst his wife PAULA MODERSOHN-BECKER (1876-1907), whose passionate devotion to art found a moving record in her autobiography, possessed perhaps the most sensitive eye in the Worpswede school.

But a revolt against the relative passivity of pure impressionism had already manifested itself throughout Europe in attempts at firmer construction, bolder colour, and increased spiritual activity. In Switzerland the new ideals find a champion in FERDINAND HODLER (1853-1918), who dreams of a formal and moral regeneration of art. Here, plastic figures, whose anatomy is tortured like Signorelli's, whose hard modelling is reminiscent of Witz and Pacher, are subordinated to a decorative scheme, a symmetrical, chequer-board treatment of the surface. An expressive treatment of line in which old German traditions reassert themselves replaces the flaky illusionistic technique of impressionism. With his paradoxical theory of *parallelism*, which demands individual characterization within universal abstraction, freedom within rule, Hodler hoped to restore to fresco its lost monumentality. Thus: *Swiss on the Retreat after the Battle of Marignano* (Zurich Museum), and the *Revolt of the Students of Jena* (Jena University). A tendency towards symbolism, here apparent, is accentuated in the ensuing artistic development of Central Europe. It is significant that whilst in France and Italy post-impressionism recognized a goal in cubism and futurism, it adopts in the German-speaking countries more especially the extreme form of expressionism.

This new movement was heralded in by the Norwegian Edvard Munch, who had been living in Berlin for some years. His work (at first repudiated) found recognition in the *Sezession* of 1902, a society of anti-academic independents which had branches in Berlin, Munich and Vienna. Soon afterwards, three German architectural students at Dresden, ERNST LUDWIG KIRCHNER (1880-1938), ERICH HECKEL (1883-), KARL SCHMIDT-ROTLUFF (1884-), inspired by a passion for painting, founded a group 'Die Brücke' which, holding its first exhibition in Dresden in 1905, was joined by EMIL NOLDE (1867-) and MAX PECHSTEIN (1881-).

A similar movement, 'Die neue Künstlervereinigung', made its appearance in Munich in 1909, a Russian emigrant, WASSILY KANDINSKY (1866-1944) being one of the leaders. Other members included ALEXANDER KANOLDT (1881-1939), and ALFRED KUBIN (1877-), the latter a book-illustrator of demonic power, who together with Kandinsky later separated from the NKV and formed a third group named 'Der blaue Reiter', which was augmented first by FRANZ MARC (1882-1916) and AUGUST MACKE (1887-1914) and subsequently by PAUL KLEE (1879-1940).

All three groups, as was the case with the 'Expressionists' in general, were concerned in the creation of an antinaturalist art in which the painter, beholding nature only as a medium of subjective expression, seeks to bind arbitrarily selected objects to an abstract unity, thus reducing the representational element in design to a minimum. Whilst for the impressionist objects were passive to the natural influences of light and atmosphere, they become for the expressionist the active symbol of an idea.

Thus in painting a town the impressionist regards it as a fragment of infinity. Unconcerned by structural problems but interested in the ever-changing phenomena of the coloured surface, he is comparatively indifferent to individual subject-matter both as regards its form and its character. Hence he screens his houses with veils of foliage so as deliberately to destroy any effect of volume, delights to see their reflection broken in rippling expanses of water, and, bathing all in tremulous mist, finally negates the boundaries of town and nature. The expressionist, on the contrary, striving to penetrate the essence of things, sees the town concentrated to a knot of cubic and crystalline blocks (Alexander Kanoldt: *Subiaco* and *San Gimigniano*), or again, as a chaos of reeling edifices consuming space. His imaginative vision seeks, not the superficial appearance, but the underlying idea which is in truth a phantom of the brain, excited by the tumult and fever, the hysteria of the city (Conrad Felixmüller: *Stadtmensch*). So, too, in landscape the expressionist explores the primeval forces of nature, the dynamic energy of growth. Trees writhe in horrid spasm, ejected from a soil rent as in travail, the ears of the corn hang heavy with ripeness, we feel the generation of things (CHRISTIAN ROHLFS; 1849-1938). Or in mystic studies of animals he tries to submerge his will in that of the beast, seeking not the actual physical appearance but the mystery of instinct (Franz Marc: *The Bull*).

If one can indeed differentiate between the groups, one might say that in the case of the NKV artists one may notice, perhaps, a certain influence of French art and Cubism. To Nolde, on the other hand, whose autobiography constitutes perhaps one of the most poignant self-revelations, formal abstraction remained alien and cold. 'Paris', he wrote, 'had given me so little and yet I hoped for so much.' Seeking, like Pechstein, renewed springs of inspiration for the outworn intellectual art of Europe, he found fulfilment in a journey to the South Seas. But the burning richness of his colour serves a truly Nordic concept of art, and in his *Pietà* distortion for the sake of emotional expression recalls the exaggerations of medieval Pietàs and of Grünewald's 'Crucifixion'.

Marc too, even if he employs a rather more distinct 'pattern', seems to have set out in quest not so much of a formal as of a spiritual 'absolute'. The primal force which threw up the gigantic folds of the mountains curves no less the necks of the horses, spans the rainbow arch between heaven and earth. One is reminded of the poem 'Mensch' by the expressionist poet Kurt Heynicke. Wassily Kandinsky, indeed, upheld that 'the artist must have something to say, as his duty is not to control form but to match the form to the subject concerned'. The 'subject', however, is as far removed from representational standards as possible, 'inner' or emotional states being translated direct into line, form and colour rhythms according to a system of musical harmony and counterpoint, which he describes in a treatise, whilst his paintings bear such titles as 'Symphony in colour', etc.

Strange to relate, it was not only absolute painting but the 'distortions' of such artists as Nolde that National Socialist propaganda banned as 'decadent and Bolshevik', evidently unaware that non-representational art is far more akin to Germanic and Nordic tradition than the amalgam of realism and neo-classicism it sought to set up as model. Ironically, the Soviet itself is following in the same footsteps.

It is true that an utter emancipation from apparent 'reality' brings with it the danger of untrammelled subjectivity, and that the symbolism re-invoked by the expressionists, unlike medieval symbolism, is often com-prehensible only to the artist himself. But an enforced dogmatism cannot cure the neurosis of our century any more than could the expressionists' despairing attempt to find regeneration by affecting the simplicity of children or of Negro or Polynesian art.

That the German predicament was only part of the general bankruptcy of civilization and analytical thought is proved by the subsequent epidemic of 'Surrealism' in Europe as a whole, with its craving to wallow in horrors and to lay bare the unconscious processes of the mind. But it is perhaps significant that two of the greatest artists of irrational fantasy should have sprung from the roots of German expressionism. Thus with MAX ERNST (1891-) zoomorphic and anthropomorphic images move through a world in sequences as illogical as those of dream, though subordinate to an exquisite law of colour and texture, whilst the Swiss painter Paul Klee (p. 528) spins the thread of his cobweb fantasies across page or canvas, and through contrast of surface, lineal crescendo and diminuendo renders each encounter with the improbable inevitable as in the realm of fairy-tale. Paul Klee amongst all modern artists was indeed perhaps the happiest in reawakening the old Gothic-Nordic dynamism of line.

But what, we may ask, is the trend of German art today? The spiritual upheavals of two wars and the years between have caused such havoc that it is difficult to tell. Many are trying to recover the line of develop-ment arbitrarily cut short. Others have lost their roots in exile. Amongst the refugees, the Viennese painter OSKAR KOKOSCHKA (1886-) has con-tinued to show signs of maturing from the uncanny psychological penetration of his early portraits, in which he lays bare the pathological secrets of the soul hidden behind the mask of convention, through the darker passion of his second period (an analogy is afforded by the expres-sionist pathos of his plays) and thence to a new reverence for Nature. None the less, his nervous energy, wedded to remains of expressionist and impressionist technique, render his landscapes very different from the calm, objective and rectangular simplicity of a GEORG SCHRIMPF (1889-1938), or FRANZ LENK (1898-), whose art reminds us almost of the landscapes of Kaspar David Friedrich. Repudiating abstraction and the exotic, Kokoschka now maintains that as Europeans we must not lose face and turn back into the jungle, but resolutely combat chaos and decide in favour of organically developing Life and Humanity.

MAX BECKMANN (1884-1950), on the other hand, the exponent of new realism [represented also by OTTO DIX (1891-) and KARL HOFER (1878-)], was perhaps the most forceful of all German artists in rendering the horror and 'anxiety' of our mechanized, dehumanized age, though his power of vision prevented him from becoming an infuriated satirist as was the case with GEORG GROSS (1893-) or from falling into the naturalistic though sincere reform propaganda of KÄTHE KOLLWITZ (1867-1945).

Recent publications on the drawings of the sculptor ERNST BARLACH (1870-1938) with their intense yet formally powerful humanity show from what recent sources German art may still draw and yet remain essentially true to itself.

BIBLIOGRAPHY TO CHAPTER XIII

BOOKS OF GENERAL REFERENCE

'*Albertina*': beschreibender Katalog der Handzeichnnugen in der Graphischen Sammlung Albertina. 6 vols. Vienna, 1926-41

Burger, F., and Brinckmann, A. E. *Handbuch der Kunstwissenschaft.* 35 vols. Potsdam, 1913-30

Christoffel, U. *Die deutsche Kunst als Form und Ausdruck.* Augsburg, 1928

Clark, K. *Landscape into Art.* London, 1949

Closs, Hannah. *Art and Life.* Shakespeare Head Press. Oxford, 1936

Closs, Hannah. *Magie und Naturgefühl in der Malerei.* Bonn, 1936

Dehio, G. *Handbuch der deutschen Kunstdenkmäler.* 1914

Dehio, G. *Geschichte der deutschen Kunst.* 3 vols. Berlin, 1930-31

Graphische Gesellschaft (Facsimiles). 27 vols. Berlin, 1906-22

Hagen, O. *Deutsches Sehen. Gestaltungsfragen der deutschen Kunst.* Munich, 2nd ed., 1923

Mössel, E. *Vom Geheimnis der Form und der Urform des Seins.* Stuttgart, 1938

Muther, R. *Geschichte der Malerei.* 3 vols. Leipzig, 1922

Propyläen Kunstgeschichte. Berlin, 1925-39

Springer, A. *Handbuch der Kunstgeschichte.* Leipzig, 1923

Stange, A. *Deutsche Kunst um 1400.* Munich, 1923

Thieme-Becker. *Allgemeines Lexikon der bildenden Künstler.* 36 vols. Leipzig, 1907-50

Vollmer, H. *Kunstgeschichtliches Wörterbuch.* Leipzig, 1928

Wölfflin, H. *Kunstgeschichtliche Grundbegriffe.* Basel, 1948

Wölfflin, H. *Kleine Schriften.* Ed. by J. Gantner. Basel, 1946

From the Middle Ages to Dürer

Pächt, O. *Österreichische Tafelmalerei der Gotik*. Augsburg, 1929

Orienter, A. *Der seelische Ausdruck in der altdeutschen Malerei*. Munich, 1921

Worringer, W. *Formprobleme der Gotik*. Munich, 1922

Matejek, A. *Die böhmische Malerei des 14. Jahrhunderts*. Leipzig, 1921

Dorner, A. *Meister Bertram von Minden*. Berlin, 1937

Dvorák, M. *Naturalismus in der gotischen Skulptur und Malerei*. Munich, 1928

Wolff, F. *Michael Pacher*. Berlin, 1909

Hausenstein, W. *Tafelmalerei der deutschen Gotik*. Munich, 1922

Deusch, W. R. *Deutsche Malerei des 15. Jahrhunderts*. Berlin, 1939

Deusch, W. R., and Winkler, F. *Deutsche Malerei des 16. Jahrhunderts*. Berlin, 1935

Winkler, F. *Altdeutsche Tafelmalerei*. Munich, 1941

Ganz, P. *Holbein*. Phaidon Press. London, 1950

Schmid, H. A. *Hans Holbein der Jüngere*. Basel, 1945

Hagen, O. *Matthias Grünewald*. Munich, 1923

Niemeyer, W. *M. Grünewald. Der Maler des Isenheimer Altars*. Berlin, 1921

Burckhard, A. *Matthias Grünewald, personality and accomplishment*. Cambridge, Mass., 1936

Zülch, W. K. *Grünewald*. Berlin, 1938

Posse, H. *Lucas Cranachd.Ä.* Sammlung Schroll. Vienna, 1942

Friedländer, M. J. *Die Gemälde von Lucas Cranach*. Berlin, 1932

Wühr, H. *A. Altdorfer, W. Huber: Landschaften*. Die Silbernen Bücher. Berlin, 1938

Tietze, H. *Albrecht Altdorfer*. Deutsche Meister. Leipzig, 1923

Dvorák, M. *Schongauer und die niederländische Malerei*. Kunstgeschichte als Geistesgeschichte. Munich, 1928

Baum, J. *Martin Schongauer*. Sammlung Schroll. Wien, 1948

Friedländer, M. J. *Martin Schongauer*. Bibliothek der Kunstgeschichte. Leipzig, 1923

Glaser, C. *Die altdeutsche Malerei*. Munich, 1924

Curiel, H. *Hans Baldung Grien*. Munich, 1923

Mandach, C. von. *Niklaus Manuel Deutsch*. Urs Graf Verlag. Basel, n.d.

Dürer: Short Bibliography

A. With illustrations in loose portfolio, suitable for Exhibition:

    1. Dürer Society, London, 1898-1911. (Prints, Drawings, Pictures)

    2. Kürth, W. *Dürers sämtliche Holzschnitte*. (Woodcuts, complete.) Munich, 1927; also an English edition, 1927

B. Biographical:

    1. Conway, W. M. *Literary Remains of Albrecht Dürer*. Cambridge, 1889

    2. Waetzoldt, W. *Dürer and his Times*. English edition. Phaidon Press. London, 1950

C. Catalogues, etc.:

    1. *Engravings*
        Campbell Dodgson. *Albrecht Dürer*. London, Medici Society, 1926

    2. *Woodcuts*
        Kürth, W. See A. 2 above. (Woodcuts only)
        Campbell Dodgson. *Catalogue of Early German and Flemish Woodcuts in the British Museum*, vol. 1. London, 1903
        Barlow, T. D. *Dürer's Woodcuts*. King Penguin. 1949

GERMAN PAINTING 533

3. *Prints in General*
   Meder, J. *Dürer-Katalog.* Vienna, 1932. The most exhaustive modern catalogue of all Dürer's engravings and woodcuts
4. *Drawings*
   Winkler, F. *Die Zeichnungen Albrecht Dürers.* 4 vols. Berlin, 1936–39. The most complete catalogue of Dürer's drawings, all of them reproduced
   Schilling, E. *Drawings by Albrecht Dürer.* Holbein-Verlag, Basel. English edition, 1950
5. *Paintings, Engravings and Woodcuts*
   Klassiker der Kunst. Dürer. Ed. F. Winkler. 4th ed., Stuttgart, 1928

D. FURTHER DETAILS:

1. Blunt, A. *Artistic Theory in Italy 1450–1600.* Oxford, 1940
2. Dvořák, M. *Dürers Apokalypse.* Munich, 1928
3. Lange, K., and Fuhse, F. *Dürers schriftlicher Nachlass.* Halle a.S., 1893
4. Panofsky, E., and Saxl, F. *Dürers Kupferstich Melencolia I.* Leipzig and Berlin, 1923

FROM THE SEVENTEENTH CENTURY TO THE MODERN AGE

Drost, W. *Barockmalerei in den germanischen Ländern.* Handbuch der Kunstwissenschaft. Potsdam, 1926

Weizsäcker, H. *Die Zeichnungen Adam Elsheimers.* Frankfurt a.M., 1923

Hamann, R. *Die deutsche Malerei vom Rokoko bis zum Expressionismus.* Leipzig, 1930

Feulner, A. *Skulptur und Malerei des 18. Jahrhunderts in Deutschland.* Handbuch der Kunstwissenschaft. Potsdam, 1929

Deusch, W. R. *Malerei der deutschen Romantiker und ihrer Zeitgenossen.* Berlin, 1937

Brieger, L. *Die romantische Malerei.* Berlin, 1926

Folnesics, Josef. *Innenräume und Hausrat der Empire- und Biedermeierzeit in Österreich-Ungarn.* Vienna, 1902–3

Schmidt, Paul Ferdinand. *Biedermeiermalerei.* Munich, n.d. [1922]

Der stille Garten. (Collection of Biedermeier paintings.) Düsseldorf and Leipzig, n.y. [1908]

Hamann, Richard. *Die deutsche Malerei im 19. Jahrhundert.* Leipzig and Berlin, 1914

Boehn, Max von. *Carl Spitzweg.* Leipzig, 3rd ed., 1924

Waldmann, E. *Der Maler A. Menzel.* Sammlung Schroll. Vienna, 1942

Novotny, F. *Adalbert Stifter als Maler.* Sammlung Schroll. Vienna, 1941

Bie, R. *Deutsche Malerei der Gegenwart.* Weimar, 1930

Burger, F. *Einführung in die moderne Kunst.* Berlin-Neubabelsberg, 1917

Bahr, H. *Expressionismus.* Munich, 1916

Hamann, R. *Der Impressionismus in Leben und Kunst.* Berlin, 1923

Sydow, Eckhart von. *Die deutsche expressionistische Kultur und Malerei.* Berlin, 1920

Waldmann, E. *Impressionismus und Expressionismus.* Propyläenverlag, Berlin

Kandinsky, W., and Mark, F. *Der blaue Reiter.* Munich, 1912

Fechter, Paul. *Ernst Barlach. Zeichnungen.* Munich, 1935 and 1948

Modersohn-Becker, Paula. *Briefe und Tagebuchblätter.* Autobiography. Berlin, 1920

Fechter, Paul. *Der Expressionismus.* Munich, 1914

Nemitz, Fritz. *Deutsche Malerei der Gegenwart.* Munich, 1950

S

CHAPTER XIV

GERMAN ARCHITECTURE AND SCULPTURE

T HE first native architecture of Germany, as of other European countries, was based upon Roman tradition. But the portion of modern Germany which was occupied and civilized by the Romans was comparatively small, and was limited to the south-western corner of the present Republic. The Rhine formed the real frontier between the Roman Empire and the barbarians, though east of the Rhine lay the *Agri Decumates* (Tithe Lands), conquered in A.D. 83, and comprising the modern provinces of Württemberg, Baden, and northern Bavaria. This territory was separated from the wild German tribes by a Roman wall of great length, extending from the Rhine to the Danube. Hence the chief relics of Roman building are found in the towns on the west or left bank of the Rhine, including Cologne (Colonia Agrippinensis), Mainz (Mogontiacum), and especially Trier or Treves (Augusta Trevirorum). Bonn (Bonna) and Augsburg (Augusta Vindelicorum) retain their Latin names in a modified form, and in Cologne the familiar quadrangular plan of the Roman city may still be traced, with fragments of the fortifications. At Mainz and Cologne there were bridges and bridge-heads. Most of the old cities on the Rhine contain collections of Roman relics in their museums.

But it is at Treves that the most important remains of Roman architecture exist, for this was the chief town of Roman Germany, and during the fourth century it was frequently an imperial residence. In Treves are ruins of an important palace (illustrated by Dehio and Bezold, see Bibliography) and a large Basilica, probably built by Constantine in the fourth century and converted into a Protestant church about eighty years ago. This basilica consists of a plain rectangular hall of great size, with a semicircular apse at the north end raised above the general floor-level. The massive walls are of concrete faced with brick and are pierced with two tiers of large windows. The lofty roof is of timber and has the enormous span of over ninety feet. Beneath the floor was a heating system with a hypocaust.

Treves also possesses an amphitheatre, capable of accommodating 7000 or 8000 spectators, built on the slope of a vineyard-clad hill; the remains of another basilica, now incorporated in the Cathedral; ruins of Roman baths; and some vestiges of the original Roman bridge across the Moselle. But the most imposing of its surviving Roman relics is the huge Porta Nigra, famous even among the many great triumphal arches erected under the Empire. Originally it formed part of the city walls, and probably dates from the late third or early fourth century. Built of sandstone blocks without mortar, it has two archways for traffic, and is flanked on either side by towers. The central portion containing the gates is three storeys high, the towers four storeys externally and five internally. There are both inner and outer gates, the latter being closed by portcullises. The exterior of this huge building is embellished with sturdy stone columns of the Roman Doric Order, and all its windows have semicircular arched heads.

For four centuries from the date of the Porta Nigra we have little or no architecture to record in all the vast area of Germany. Treves, with its noble civic buildings, its orderly plan and its luxurious villas along the Moselle, was sacked several times by the Franks and lost its proud position as capital. But the influence of Roman architecture appears during the next building era which began during the reign of Charlemagne (768-814). The architecture of the period from the fall of the Roman Empire to the birth of the Gothic or Pointed style in the thirteenth century is commonly described as 'Romanesque', for the obvious reason that it was founded on Roman tradition. Germany, especially the Rhenish provinces and the Harz district, contains a large number of important Romanesque buildings. During the so-called 'Dark Ages' comparatively little building was carried on. But in the eighth century Christianity made great progress under the Frankish kings who now ruled western Germany. With their conquest of the Saxons in 804 and their subsequent conversion under Charlemagne the greater part of the country became Christian. From that time onwards we find that the slender current of belief surviving in the Rhenish strongholds of Roman Christianity developed rapidly in all the old cities, and soon led to the erection of a remarkable series of churches.

One of the first of these was the Dom or Cathedral of Aachen (Aix-la-Chapelle), built in 796-804 by Charlemagne, who, according to Eginhard, a contemporary writer, also repaired the churches throughout his dominions. He intended this building to serve as his mausoleum, and here he was buried in due course. When his tomb was opened in 1165, he was found seated on his throne in his imperial robes with a copy of the gospels upon his knee. The church is a domed polygon of sixteen sides, 105 feet in diameter externally. Round the central space, which is octagonal, runs a two-storied aisle, of which both storeys are vaulted. The construction of this somewhat complex building is sound and scientific, and it was richly decorated with materials brought from Theodoric's palace at Ravenna. Authorities vary as to the architect's nationality, one suggesting that he was of Italian birth,[1] another giving his name as 'Master Odo of Metz'.[2] The bronze doors and internal balustrades date from Charlemagne's time. With its domical form, its round arches, and its quasi-Corinthian columns, a Roman origin is obvious; but there is much disagreement among scholars as to whether it was actually copied from the somewhat similar church of St. Vitale at Ravenna, one of the chief centres of Byzantine architecture. The cathedral has undergone considerable alteration since it was built. A lofty and beautiful choir was added in late Gothic style (1414), and a fantastic conical roof over the dome in the seventeenth century.

Churches of similar type were erected at Essen and Ottmarsheim in Germany, and at Nymwegen in Holland; but the only other monument of Charlemagne's work which still stands in Germany is the quaint little chapel of the monastery at Lorsch, near Worms, probably dedicated in 774. Mention must also be made of the remarkable monastery at St. Gall in Switzerland, commenced in 829. A contemporary plan of the building remains, drawn in red and black ink on parchment, and is one of the earliest documents of the kind extant. It records for posterity the arrangements and internal economy of a great monastery of the Carlovingian period.

In spite of the architectural activity in Charlemagne's reign, during the latter part of the eighth century and the early years of the ninth, the next two hundred years produced very few buildings that still survive. The sole important exception is the abbey church of Gernrode, in the Harz Mountains, commenced in 960 or thereabouts and much altered a century or two later. Its most striking feature is the use of two apses, at the west end and at the east. The same remarkable treatment is to be found in the cathedrals of Worms, Mainz, and Treves; also in the abbey church at Laach; it may have existed at Speyer, and appears on the ancient plan of St. Gall (see above). Writers on architecture are perplexed as to the ritual that led to such an arrangement, which may have been occasioned by the need for two choirs (one for the monks, another for the townsfolk); or by a new rule of eastern orientation after the western apse had been built. But from an artistic point of view the practice is clearly unsatisfactory: the interest of the spectator is divided, instead of being led up to one 'focal point', and 'duality' is caused; while the fine effect that can be

1 Sir T. G. Jackson, *Romanesque Architecture*, vol. II, p. 3.
2 W. R. Lethaby, *Medieval Art*, p. 121.

obtained by means of a western portal, through which the altar is seen at the end of a long vista, is clearly impossible. The entrance to such a church has to be at the side, with a consequent loss of dignity.

The typical Romanesque cathedral in the Rhineland possesses, like the abbey of Gernrode, twin western spires with an apse between them, while others (e.g. Worms) have twin towers at the east end too. The plan of Gernrode is singularly irregular, for, though it is of the rectangular 'basilican' type, hardly any of its angles is, in fact, a true right angle. By a 'basilica' is meant an oblong building with side aisles and an apse or apses: a form derived from the Roman halls of justice which bore that name. It is thus distinct from the domical type of Aachen, and from the cruciform church with transepts which was usual in the later Middle Ages in Germany as in England and France. Most of the Romanesque churches in Germany are of this kind, but the cathedral of Spires (Speyer) has a transept.

Externally the church of Gernrode is decorated with arcading: that is, with rows of arches which serve no structural purpose. Round the top of the apse, beneath the eaves, is a band of small arcading, while the walls of the nave are ornamented with larger arches, pierced alternately with windows. This arcading is a characteristic feature of the so-called 'Lombard' style, practised in North Italy in the early Middle Ages, and perhaps carried back by Lombard architects from Italy to the banks of the Rhine. All the windows and doors have semicircular heads, and the windows are little more than narrow slits giving the minimum of light. The twin towers have conical tops, but at the abbey church of Corvey – built even earlier than Gernrode – the towers are finished with the typical Rhenish gabled spire, a feature seldom found outside the district, though in England there is an example at Sompting in Sussex. Another Lombard feature found at Gernrode is the alternate use of piers and columns to carry the arches of the nave; in the neighbouring church of Quedlinburg, almost contemporary, two columns are used between each pair of piers. The aisles at Gernrode are in two storeys and all the roofs are of timber, with flat ceilings. Vaulting, though so skilfully used at Aachen in Charlemagne's time, did not become common in Germany until a much later date.

During the two centuries 1000–1200 there was erected in Germany, mainly in the Rhenish provinces, a whole sequence of magnificent churches. Among these may be mentioned the cathedrals of Worms (1016–1181), Mainz or Mayence (1037–49), Spires or Speyer (1030 et seq.), Treves or Trier (1016–47), and Bonn; the abbey church of Laach (1093–1156); St. Godehard (1133) and St. Michael (1150–1241) at Hildesheim;

and in Cologne the churches of St. Mary in the Capitol (rebuilt 1047), St. Martin (1150-70), and the fine church of the Apostles. All these are pure Romanesque in design, unaffected by the introduction of pointed Gothic arches. The cathedral of Bamberg in Bavaria is the finest Romanesque church in South Germany.

The churches at Cologne just mentioned form an interesting group, for each of them has three apses: one in the usual position at the east end and the others at each end of a rather short transept. The Church of the Apostles has an octagonal cupola over the crossing of the transept, flanked on the east side by two slender octagonal turrets with curious gabled spires, and at the west end is a lofty square tower with a gabled spire, also flanked by two small turrets containing staircases. This profusion of towers is one of the most characteristic features of the Romanesque churches of Germany, invariably producing a striking and picturesque group. Treves, Spires, and Worms cathedrals, also Laach abbey, each have six towers of various forms and heights.

At Laach there is a remarkable western atrium, parvis or Paradise, from which one enters the church. It recalls the Byzantine example at Parenzo in Istria (fifth century).

Rose-windows and cornices, composed of miniature arcading beneath the eaves, are other notable details that mark the exteriors of most Rhenish churches of the period. Vaulting is used in all the churches mentioned except in the two at Hildesheim, where there are flat ceilings. The normal type of Rhenish Romanesque vaulting has one square bay in the nave for every two bays in the aisles, an exception being found at Laach where the vaulting bays are of equal width, showing an approach to the more skilful Gothic system. Thus in the typical German church of the period the vault becomes domical in shape because all the ribs are of semicircular form, and hence the diagonal ribs are higher than those of the four arches which support and enclose each bay. But it seems probable that many of the churches mentioned owe their vaults to the latter part of the twelfth century.

The alternate use of round columns and square piers in nave-arcades has already been mentioned, but a more common arrangement is a row of square piers with attached semi-cylindrical shafts. The somewhat dull and stark appearance of the interiors of most of these churches is due to the absence of a triforium. Although that feature is found at Gernrode (see above), most of the great Rhenish churches have a more or less blank wall between the top of the nave arcade and the bottom of the range of clerestory windows.

There is, indeed, little of decorative interest in the average German

Romanesque church interior. The few ornamented mouldings employed – such as the chevron, billet and dentil – resemble their Norman-English cousins, while the plain mouldings lack refinement of contour. When originally erected, these buildings doubtless depended for effect largely upon coloured decorations, now obliterated under many coats of whitewash. But there is one notable exception, St. Michael at Hildesheim. This church, as already mentioned, dates from the late twelfth century, and suffers more than most from the absence of a triforium, there being a wide stretch of blank wall between the nave arcade and the clerestory. But it contains a variety and amount of architectural ornament unrivalled among Romanesque churches in Germany. The richly sculptured capitals of the columns in the nave display an originality and gracefulness that is conspicuously absent in most German work of the period. The soffites of the arches above them, and the frieze under the aisle roof, are decorated with geometrical and flowing patterns in relief and coloured. The flat ceiling of the nave is painted with religious subjects in a great number of compartments (rectangular, circular, and quatrefoil), enriched with a floral pattern; and on the north wall is a frieze of angels modelled in stucco and painted.

The remarkable wealth of early sculptured art in Hildesheim is by no means confined to St. Michael's, and seems to owe its being to one man, Bishop Bernward (993-1022). This energetic prelate visited Rome in the year 1000, and on his return commenced the building of St. Michael's church for the Benedictine monastery which he had founded there five years earlier, finishing it in 1022 just before his death. This was quick work in the Middle Ages, considering the size and elaborate nature of the building; but modern scholarship no longer recognizes every bishop whose name is associated with such an enterprise as the architect of the building.[1] Of Bernward's church only the crypt and part of the superstructure remain, the rest of the work dating from a rebuilding after a fire in 1182.

The cathedral of Hildesheim, a church inferior in most respects to St. Michael's, contains still more important evidence of Bernward's artistic activity. The famous bronze doors at the west end are said to have been copied by Bernward from the cypress-wood doors of St. Sabina (fifth century) in Rome, and were made in 1015. Each door has eight panels, those on the left representing 'sins' from the Old Testament, while on the right are shown incidents in which Our Lord expiates those sins by His Atonement. But the subjects depicted on the doors of St. Sabina are

[1] See my book, *The Architect in History* (Oxford, 1927), pp. 53-129, for evidence on this point.

quite dissimilar: the arrangement of the panels is different, the execution is more skilful, and the wonderfully delicate border is not found at Hildesheim, where, however, two startling bronze knockers were introduced. There is also a remarkable Romanesque font in bronze at Hildesheim, boldly modelled, but of rather later date. Of Bernward's time is the immense bronze chandelier in the cathedral, over twenty feet in diameter, formerly decorated with figures of the Prophets, Evangelists, etc.; while elsewhere in the city are many objects of the same period in bronze, and gilt bronze, showing a very high level of craftsmanship. The curious bronze column erected by Bernward in one of the squares at Hildesheim, and decorated with a series of Bible stories which wind round it spirally after the fashion of Trajan's Column, shows the extent to which he was indebted to Rome. Electrotype reproductions of this column, of the doors from Hildesheim already mentioned, of another pair from Augsburg (1047-72), and of many other objects in bronze from Hildesheim are to be seen in the South Court of the Victoria and Albert Museum. Professor Lethaby is of opinion[1] that the famous 'Gloucester Candlestick', one of the treasures of the same museum, is in fact a work of that school; and he remarks on its similarity to an example preserved at Hildesheim. Much of the work in bronze at this period consisted of reliquaries, candlesticks, crucifixes, monstrances, and other small church furniture, but there are bronze effigies of Rudolph of Swabia (c. 1100) in the cathedral at Merseburg near Leipzig, and of Bishop Frederick (d. 1152) in Magdeburg Cathedral. There is also a fine Romanesque choir-screen in the Cathedral at Hildesheim, decorated with coloured and gilt reliefs in stucco, the figures being well modelled and the drapery skillfully treated.

Ivory carving was another branch of sculpture in which the Rhenish artists excelled; but most of these craftsmen were imported from Byzantium after the marriage of Otho II to the daughter of the Byzantine emperor in 972. A notable example of ivory work is the ambo or pulpit in the choir of Charlemagne's church at Aachen, presented by Henry II (d. 1024); but the ivory panels are of Alexandrian workmanship.

The transition from Romanesque to Gothic architecture in Germany is illustrated by the churches of St. Gereon (1200-27) and St. Cunibert (1205-48) at Cologne, the cathedral of Limburg, east of Coblenz (1213-42) and the Liebfrauenkirche at Treves (1227-43). At this period the German (or 'Holy Roman') Empire was of great extent, yet in spite of its vast importance, the German people borrowed the forms of Gothic architecture direct from France, a century after pointed arches and other Gothic features had made their first appearance at St. Denis. By this time England

[1] W. R. Lethaby, *Medieval Art* (London, 1904), p. 125.

had long cast aside her Norman architecture, and the graceful 'Early English' style of Salisbury was fully developed.

Nevertheless the new method of building was introduced reluctantly and slowly, as though the Germans still clung to their Rhenish Romanesque; and in Germany, as in Spain, the Gothic style always remained somewhat French in character, never becoming a national variant as it did in England and, to a much less extent, in Italy. So, in the four churches named above, round arches and other Romanesque features persist in spite of the appearance of new Gothic forms. The nave of St. Gereon at Cologne is an irregular decagon on plan, vaulted in domical form. Pointed arches are certainly used, but in all other respects the design is as Rhenish and as un-French as it could be. The same criticism applies to St. Cunibert at Cologne, and to the cathedral at Limburg, with its jumble of gabled spires, huddled on the steep bank of the river Lahn. The Liebfrauenkirche at Treves, with its graceful windows filled with geometrical tracery, appears at first sight a far more Gothic building, yet, even in this case, we find round arches as well as pointed, and a remarkable quasi-circular plan of unusual type.

But when we come to the slightly later church of St. Elizabeth at Marburg (1233-83), there is a great change. The building is entirely French in construction and design, save for two striking exceptions. It is a comparatively small church, just over 200 feet long and 70 feet wide internally, and the height to the crown of the vaulting is slightly under 70 feet. Now, whereas in France or England practically every vaulted church of this kind has side-aisles far lower than the central aisle or nave, at Marburg they are of the same height as the nave. The resultant internal effect is that of a large room divided by arches, a form known as the 'hall-church'. Moreover, instead of the usual French and English division of the walls into arcade, triforium, and clerestory, at Marburg there is no triforium and there are two ranges of windows of equal size, producing a monotonous appearance. This construction obviously precludes the employment of the flying buttresses so popular in France. A survival from Romanesque at Marburg is the use of apses at the end of the choir and each transept. In other respects (i.e. the arches and vaulting, the forms of doors and windows and mouldings, the twin spires at the west end, and the elaborate *flèche* over the crossing) the building conforms to the French type.

The church of the Cistercian abbey at Altenberg (1255-87), east of Coblenz, has no towers, but is a singularly complete and beautiful building on French lines, with low aisles, flying buttresses, and a fine *chevet* (apse) with radiating chapels.

Cologne Cathedral, certainly the largest Gothic church in Northern Europe, and by some critics regarded as one of the most magnificent, needs to be studied with great caution. It was commenced in 1248, on the site of a much older building, but its construction dragged on for centuries and was by no means completed in 1508, after which it remained unfinished and neglected for more than three hundred years. In the nineteenth century it was restored and completed at vast expense. But though the church was thus the work of a whole succession of architects from 1248 to 1880 – interrupted almost completely from 1508 to 1824 – it has nevertheless been built to the original design with very little variation. Indeed not only have the names of nearly all the 'masters' or architects concerned been preserved, but the common belief that medieval churches were built without plans is disproved by the fact that the great west front at Cologne was built in the nineteenth century from a drawing made in the fourteenth century and exhibited in the cathedral. Every visitor should see this drawing, which is ten feet high and a yard wide, beautifully finished and showing every detail of the architecture and ornament.

But when one comes to analyse this immense church dispassionately, ignoring mere bulk and mere elaboration, it suffers by comparison with the great French cathedrals, such as Beauvais and Amiens, from which it was so obviously and so unsympathetically copied. Thus Amiens is far wider than the typical English Gothic cathedral, but Cologne has double aisles and thus is far wider than Amiens (if one excludes the buttress-chapels, a later addition at Amiens). The internal height, 155 feet, is also decidedly greater. This proportion produces a feeling of shortness in the interior, much accentuated externally by the excessive height of the western towers. Now that the cathedral has been isolated by the demolition of the houses that formerly clung round its skirts in the usual continental fashion, these towers, beautiful in themselves, are seen to be too lofty for the cathedral. The cathedral is a Gothic church of the first magnitude as regards size, completeness, and craftsmanship; its shortcomings are apparent only to a coldly critical mind, and are subtle points of relative proportion, logical fitness in certain details, and perhaps excessive elaboration in some parts.

Freiburg Cathedral (1283-1330), although it has a Romanesque transept, is mainly coeval with Cologne, and in some respects is a more satisfactory design. It has a single tower at the west end, more happily proportioned to its length and height than the colossal twins at Cologne. But though there is a fine *chevet* at Freiburg, the whole exterior suffers from a break in the horizontal line of the main roof.

The cathedral of Ratisbon or Regensburg (1275-1534) has certain points in common with Cologne. The twin western towers are modern and the façade beneath them is of the fifteenth century. Internally the church is short, broad, and lofty. The two aisles terminate in apses, but externally this very German feature is hardly noticeable, and the principal *chevet* attracts all one's attention, with its flying buttresses, bold pinnacles, and cusped tracery in the windows.

Among German cathedrals (and in this connection we must think of Germany with its medieval boundaries), Strassburg comes next in importance to Cologne. The eastern part of the church is Romanesque, commenced in 1176. The nave, begun about 1250 and finished in 1290, is in a pure French style, and forms a most successful design. The height of the nave is not so overpowering as at Cologne. But the wonderful west front, which was begun by ERWIN VON STEINBACH in 1277 and completed by his descendants after his death, is an example of what Professor Lethaby[1] calls 'over-Gothic'. Fergusson[2] severely criticizes the architect's lack of artistic feeling and the defective proportion and mass of 'attenuated detail' which the façade displays. 'There is no building in either France or England', he concludes, 'where such great advantages have been thrown away in so reckless a manner and by so unintelligent a hand.' Long after Erwin's death, a single lofty spire was raised at one end of this façade. Whether he ever intended to have such a feature is doubtful; in any case it gives a curiously lop-sided appearance to the front, and seems to be always crying for its absent twin-brother.

The large cathedral at Ulm also aroused Fergusson's ire, but he conceded (in 1859) that the great west tower would be a noble structure if it could be completed, having been left less than half finished in the fifteenth century. Thanks to the existence of a fifteenth-century drawing for the ultimate completion, this work was actually done in 1877-90. The result is one of the loftiest and most graceful of all Gothic spires in Europe.

Another important example of German Gothic is St. Stephen's, Vienna (1300-1510). The west front of this cathedral is Romanesque, and has two polygonal towers of that period, but over the south transept is a magnificent late-Gothic spire, not so lofty as that at Ulm but even more beautiful. A corresponding spire over the north transept has never been finished. The nave of St. Stephen's is a 'hall-church' like that of Marburg, already described, and an enormous roof of steep pitch covers the whole of the nave and its aisles, its ridge being nearly 200 feet above the floor.

The Frauenkirche at Nuremberg (1354-61) and the Frauenkirche at

---

[1] W. R. Lethaby, *Medieval Art*, p. 275.
[2] J. Fergusson, *Handbook of Architecture* (1859), pp. 748-9.

Munich (1466-88) are both 'hall-churches' with lofty roofs and large traceried windows. The Munich example is built of brick and the exterior is not improved by the clumsy helmet-shaped roofs added to the tall towers at the beginning of the sixteenth century. The cathedral of Prague has a fine choir of the fourteenth century, and there is another beautiful choir in the Wiesenkirche at Soest (1314-1421).

Examples of the last phase of German Gothic, corresponding to French 'Flamboyant', are to be seen in the Liebfrauenkirche at Halle (1529-54), the church of St. Anna at Annaburg in Saxony (1499-1520), and the church of St. George at Dinkelsbühl in Bavaria (1444-99). All these buildings have very slender piers from which the vaulting springs without any intervening capitals, and all are 'hall-churches'.

In Northern Prussia it may almost be claimed, in spite of what has been said above, that a definitely native variety of Gothic was evolved. That region is destitute of building stone, and so developed a brick-building tradition. This development took place late in the Middle Ages, when the three chief cities – Hamburg, Lübeck, and Danzig – became prosperous through their connection with the Hansa League. Hamburg, unfortunately, lost all its best historical buildings in the terrible fire of 1842. In Lübeck is the Marienkirche (1250-1310), a fine but very severe building in brick with low aisles, flying buttresses, steep roofs, and two lofty western towers culminating in gabled spires. It is larger and more impressive than the cathedral, which, however, contains much interesting brickwork. The Marienkirche at Danzig (1343-1502) is a very different type of building, a 'hall-church', and its twin western towers lack spires. Like most late Gothic churches in Germany, it has windows of enormous height without transoms, the effect of which may or may not be successful according to circumstances. The transepts of this church terminate in gables of fantastic brickwork, impossible to describe without illustrations, and it is this original and striking use of brickwork, not always pleasing to English eyes, which forms the outstanding feature of North Prussian medieval buildings. We see it in many other churches: at Stralsund, Stettin, Prenzlau, Wismar, Thorn, Chorin, and Brandenburg, amongst others; in the Cistercian abbey at Pelplin and in the chapel of the Schloss at Marienburg. At Doberan is a fine Cistercian church of French Gothic type.

Nothing has yet been said of German secular architecture during the Middle Ages. The castles on the Rhine are supposed to be more attractive to foreign tourists than any German cathedrals or churches; but, in point of fact, very few of the early castles are of architectural importance, and few notable examples survive from the great days of the Hohenstaufen.

Among these may be mentioned the palace at Gelnhausen (1130-50), built by Frederick Barbarossa; the famous Wartburg, near Eisenach, associated with the life of Luther, and now restored so that it forms the most important example of medieval military architecture in Germany; the ruined castles of Münzenberg, near Nauheim, and of Reichenberg, near St. Goarshausen on the Rhine; several in Alsace; the Kaiserhaus at Goslar, in the Harz (c. 1050); and the castle of Dankwarderode (1175) at Brunswick. Of institutional buildings the chief example is the Schloss at Marienburg in East Prussia, founded about 1280 by the powerful knights of the Teutonic Order. All the buildings mentioned resemble contemporary churches in matters of architectural design and detail. Thus the remarkable brick town gates of Neubrandenburg follow the same fantastic lines as the Prussian brick churches already described.

Among European countries, Germany is singularly rich in medieval civic and domestic buildings. Of her old walled towns, Rothenburg in Bavaria is perhaps the best known to tourists, and with reason, for walls and towers are preserved there without the somewhat artificial impression that is produced by the restored fortress of Carcassonne, chief of all surviving medieval strongholds with the possible exception of Ragusa and Jerusalem. The best places in which German houses and town-halls of the later Middle Ages may be studied are Nuremberg, Rothenburg, Brunswick, Hildesheim, Goslar, and the other towns of the Harz; but such buildings are to be found in most of the old cities. For the most part they are of timber, with steep and enormous roofs in which the family washing is still hung to dry. To those who know where to look, Germany is a paradise for artists in search of picturesque street-scenes.

Sculpture in the Gothic period was chiefly confined to churches. But whereas Romanesque sculpture consisted for the most part of works in bronze or stucco, the use of stone for figure-sculpture became common by the beginning of the thirteenth century. Good early statues are found in the porches of the cathedrals of Paderborn and Münster, both in Westphalia. At Magdeburg is an equestrian figure (c. 1290) of the Emperor Otho I, one of the earliest medieval examples of this type of memorial; and there is much fine figure-sculpture in the cathedral porch. The tombs of Henry the Lion and his wife in the cathedral at Brunswick also date from the thirteenth century, but the best statuary of the period is in the cathedrals of Bamberg, Strassburg, and Cologne. At Bamberg the chief groups are on the 'Fürstentor', and represent the Last Judgment. On the S.E. or 'Marriage Porch' is another excellent group including figures of the Emperor Henry II and his wife, and near them is a small equestrian statue of Conrad III, admirably designed. The west front of Strassburg is notable for the generally high level of its decorative carving, especially foliage, and over the three doorways are groups of figure-sculpture. There are also notable statues of the middle thirteenth century over the south porch. At Cologne there are interesting polychrome statues of Christ and the Apostles on the piers of the cathedral choir, and a bronze effigy of Archbishop Conrad (*d.* 1261). Another important work, of about the same date, is the equestrian group in bronze of St. George and the Dragon in the market-place at Prague. Sculpture of the fourteenth century may be studied to advantage in Nuremberg, where the Frauen-kirche and the churches of St. Sebald and St. Lawrence contain many examples. At Augsburg there was a noted school of sculptors in wood. The cathedrals of Mainz, Frankfurt-on-Main, Naumburg, and Wechsel-burg also contain fine effigies. The art of portrait-sculpture reached a very high level in Germany in the fourteenth century, the native artists excelling in the carving of individual figures rather than carving of large groups.

Fifteenth-century sculpture went even farther in this direction, and was largely concerned with the elaborate decoration of wooden altars, rere-doses, choir-stalls, and other church furniture. South Germany was the centre of this activity, and families of wood-carvers grew up in Augsburg, Nuremberg, the Ammergau district, and elsewhere. JÖRG SYRLIN carved the fine choir-stalls of Ulm Cathedral between 1469 and 1474; his son carved the pulpit. VEIT STOSS carved the stalls, alter, and tabernacle of the Frauenkirche at Cracow between 1472 and 1494. ALBRECHT DÜRER, the painter (1471-1528), was also a wood-carver, and carried out the fine tabernacle in the chapel of the monastery at Landau. Most of the statues on altars and tabernacles were afterwards painted so that they should harmonize with pictures near them. Realistic sculpture in stone was also practised, examples being the 'Schreyer' monument (1492) on the exterior of St. Sebald's church at Nuremberg and the great tabernacle in Ulm Cathedral by ADAM KRAFFT (*c.* 1455-1507). At Nuremberg the family of VISCHER (p. 550) worked as sculptors in bronze during the fifteenth and sixteenth centuries.

The Renaissance in architecture reached Germany about half a century later than its first appearance in France, and is commonly said to have come from France, though that theory is not absolutely proved. In Italy this Renaissance of *Roman* architecture, for that is what the Renaissance really was in architecture, began when Filippo Brunelleschi, at the begin-ning of the fifteenth century, commenced his study of the Roman ruins with the avowed intention of utilizing Roman methods of construction in his great project of completing the unfinished dome of the cathedral of

Florence. By 1550 or so, when the first breath of the new movement began to ruffle the surface of German Gothic, the architectural Renaissance in Italy had already attained its full stature. The Italian campaigns of the French kings, Charles VIII, Louis XII, and Fran ois I, resulted in the importation of large numbers of Italian artists and small Italian works of art into France, so that before the middle of the sixteenth century the whole style of building in that country had been transformed. The position in Germany, on the other hand, was somewhat analogous to that in England. Renaissance ideas were adopted very slowly, and the only full-blown Italian designs found before 1620 or so are mere ornamental details or small works such as tombstones, executed for the most part by Italian craftsmen. England never adopted the Renaissance whole-heartedly until Inigo Jones introduced definitely Palladian canons of design in the Banqueting House at Whitehall, but from that time onwards Italian theories controlled English architecture. Now Germany never produced an Inigo Jones, and even when she finally abandoned her medieval tradition, late in the seventeenth century, the new architecture was a distinctly Baroque variant of the pure Palladian style. Most of her so-called Renaissance architecture from about 1550 to 1618, when the Thirty Years' War interrupted a great building era, was a hybrid of German-medieval and Italian elements; not unlike our own Elizabethan and Jacobean styles in its fanciful, picturesque, and exuberant character. The fashion which Germany thus adopted so reluctantly was alien to her genius, whereas in Italy, where Gothic had never attained a grip on the popular mind, it was welcomed with enthusiasm. The late Sir Thomas Jackson, a confirmed medievalist, regards the discovery in the fifteenth century of Vitruvius' famous treatise on architecture as an unmitigated calamity to the art of building: 'As they read the prescriptions for the several Orders, ... Vitruvius became the architects' Bible. Endless editions of this book have been published in various languages. It has been commented on till the comments have smothered the text. Its authority has been accepted as final and indisputable. The effect has been to bring the Art into bondage to formula, to enslave practice to theory, to extinguish originality, and to make architecture into a mechanical pursuit – in fact, instead of the architecture of freedom and imagination, to give us the architecture of the book.'[1]

Books of the Roman Orders of architecture began to appear in England and France about the middle of the sixteenth century, but the books which brought the glad tidings to Germany were mainly Flemish publications, such as the works of Vredeman de Vries (1563) and Wendel

[1] Sir T. G. Jackson, *Architecture* (London, 1925), pp. 247-8.

Dietterlin (1593). These volumes misrepresented or even caricatured the Roman Orders to some extent, partly because their authors had not troubled to verify their reconstructions on the spot. The freedom, or, as some would say, the licentiousness of these drawings, undoubtedly had its effect on German architecture of the seventeenth century.

One might expect that the powerful anti-clerical influence of Luther and the humanistic influence of the University of Heidelberg would have created a vogue for Italian Renaissance fashions in German architecture, but the strength of medieval tradition was too strong. Examples of the new style dated earlier than 1550 are very scarce and are chiefly minor details, such as the delicate decorations of the Residenz at Landshut in Bavaria (1536-43), the work of Italian craftsmen. At Spittal, near Villach in Austria, is the Palazzo Porcia (1530), with a courtyard in pure Venetian Renaissance style, but that is easily explained by the proximity of this building to Italy.

The number of examples of German Renaissance buildings between c. 1550 and the beginning of the Thirty Years' War (1618) is so great that they must be dealt with here briefly in groups according to their function, bearing in mind that at this period, even more than before, local character-istics are very evident. The building of churches in Germany, as in England, began to decline from the time of the Reformation. The division between Protestants and Catholics led to a redistribution of existing churches, the Protestants adapting to their form of worship such buildings as were allotted to them, and the Catholics erecting few new ones. In this process the Lutherans seem to have been singularly tolerant of such 'Popish' trappings as altars, statues, and decorations already existing in the churches, but they attached great importance to preaching, so that galleries were often added to accommodate increased congregations. Naturally the 'hall-church' type suited the purpose of the Protestants. But almost abreast of these changes came the Jesuits, who arrived in Vienna in 1551, and thence spread gradually through Austria into South Germany. They, too, had ideas about church-building, in some ways not unlike those of the Protestants, for they, too, favoured preaching and abhorred 'dim religious light'. But they introduced into Germany, where they could, the 'Jesuit' type of church which marks their progress all over Europe, and is often designed in the 'Baroque' manner to be described later in this chapter. German churches of this period include St. Michael's at Munich (1583-87), a Jesuit church with a façade of Italian type culmi-nating in a very German gable; the Hofkirche at Neuburg (c. 1608), a restrained Italian 'hall-church' anticipating the work of Wren a century later in England; and wildly extravagant designs like the Marienkirche at Wolfenbüttel (1608-22), a jumble of Italian and Gothic details, and the Protestant Stadtkirche at Bückeburg (c. 1612-16), which bears the significant legend '*Exemplum Religionis non Structurae*', and is perhaps best classified as a Baroque building.

The medieval castle had now given way to a less formidable dwelling, though many a *Schloss* of the Renaissance retains certain features recalling military needs. The standard example of German Renaissance architecture is the Schloss of Heidelberg, of which were added the Ottheinrichsbau in 1556-63, and the Friedrichsbau in 1601-7. The former addition suggests an architect borrowing Italian details from a copy-book, and assembling them without much intelligence, in such a way as to produce a thoroughly monotonous façade. The Friedrichsbau, on the other hand, displays a far more confident touch. Its bold gables, with their almost Baroque curves, are thoroughly German and relieve the Italian windows and pilasters beneath. Yet the Friedrichsbau is essentially a picturesque rather than a 'scholarly' design. The courtyard of the Schloss at Wolfenbüttel has a somewhat Italian appearance, that of the Bishop's Palace at Brixen (near to Italy) still more so. The great Schloss built at Aschaffenburg (1605-14) for the Archbishop of Mainz by a German architect is a fine, bold group with towers at each of its four angles and steep roofs above a many-windowed façade. A study of the plans of these *châteaux* shows their similarity to those of English country mansions designed by Thorpe and Smithson at the same time, with communicating rooms grouped round a central court and several staircases (e.g. Wilhelmsburg, near Schmalkalden, 1585-1609). At Schloss Hartenfels, near Torgau, are some remarkable staircases in towers (1549) on each side of a courtyard, recalling the famous example at Blois. Other interesting castles of the period are the Hamelschenburg near Hameln, the Schloss at Stuttgart (1553), Varenholz (1594-98), and Heiligenburg (1580), where the interior decorations resemble the work of the Italians at Fontainebleau.

Far more interesting than churches and *châteaux*, however, are the various civic buildings erected at this time when Germany was powerful and prosperous, and each of her semi-independent states and cities vied with its rivals in magnifying its importance. Among town-halls may be mentioned those of Molsheim in Alsace, Solothurn (1550), Posen (1550), Leipzig (1556), Wittenberg, Altenburg (1562-67), Schweinfurt (1570-72), Rothenburg (1572-90), Heilbronn (1577-82), Bremen (1612), Paderborn (c. 1614-16), and Augsburg (1615-20). The Rathaus at Molsheim is a perfect gem of transitional Gothic-Renaissance architecture; at the other end of the series is Elias Holl's Italian town-hall at Augsburg, but this is much less Italian than the surviving model of his first design. The porch

T

added to the Rathaus at Cologne in 1571 is a brave attempt to capture the spirit of Sansovino's Loggetta in Venice, but falls short of its object. In fact, the architects of the German Renaissance were most successful when they followed their own bent, used gables and dormers freely, and made no attempt to reproduce *in toto* alien buildings from the other side of the Alps.

The same applies to other municipal buildings, such as the Arsenals of Augsburg (1603-7) and Danzig (1605); the Pellerhaus at Nuremberg (1605); the Weigh-houses of Münster (1615) and Bremen; the Salt-house at Frankfurt-on-Main; the Kornhaus at Bremen (*c.* 1591); the Gewandhaus (Cloth-workers' Hall) at Brunswick (1590); and the town-gates of Danzig (1588-90) and Halberstadt (1552). Civic pride, too, led the citizens of many German towns to embellish their streets and squares with fountains. Finally, this period witnessed the erection of innumerable houses, mainly of timber with overhanging storeys, in all the old towns mentioned previously as centres of Gothic building, together with many others, including Osnabrück, Dinkelsbühl, and Celle.

Sculpture also flourished during the Renaissance, but by far the most important statues of the period were the great bronze statues executed by PETER VISCHER (1455-1529). His masterpiece is the monument to St. Sebald in the church of that name in his native city. This noble work, completed in 1519, occupied him and his five sons for thirteen years. Peter himself is represented among the numerous figures on the monument, where Renaissance forms mingle with Gothic. He also executed at least one or two of the twenty-eight magnificent bronze statues that surround the tomb of the Emperor Maximilian in the Hofkirche at Innsbruck, the figures of King Arthur and Theodoric being usually attributed to him. The Renaissance fountains mentioned above also include much fine bronze sculpture, those at Augsburg being especially noteworthy.

The word 'Baroque' (*Barocco* in Italian, *Barock* in German) is a nickname coined originally to describe something malformed or misshapen, hence bizarre or fantastic in form. Baroque architecture had its genesis among architects of the later Renaissance in Italy, who had gradually revolted against the strict canons of Vitruvius, in fact against the idea of 'the Architecture of the Book' as previously described in this chapter. Their new theories were eagerly adopted by the Jesuits, then in the full tide of Counter-Reformation activity, so that Jesuit buildings are nearly always Baroque. Hence the movement entered the German Empire mainly from Italy, through Austria and Bavaria, where Catholicism was always strong in the seventeenth and eighteenth centuries, and never penetrated far beyond the Catholic States of the south and west, where it was largely confined to churches, convents, and the great palaces of prelates or Catholic nobles.

There is a measure of truth in describing this architecture as bizarre and fantastic, for so it appears to eyes trained in the severe Roman rules of form and proportion. Much of its decoration is flamboyant and even vulgar, sculpture is used excessively and without regard to the limitations of material, and at its worst the style transgresses many sound canons of architectural decency and reticence. But, on the other hand, most Baroque buildings are interesting, and many are both picturesque and stately. The planning of Baroque churches, palaces, and country villas is always monumental, and the Baroque architects were the first since Roman days to give due consideration to the placing of their buildings in relation to surrounding architecture and landscape; indeed they were the founders of modern town-planning. Renaissance forms, i.e. revived Roman forms, were the basis of their designs. Thus columns and pilasters with the conventional entablatures, round arches, balustrades, acanthus foliage, and garlanded festoons of fruit, are employed, with statues clad in Roman togas and helmets. But all these hackneyed elements are used with a freedom which is refreshing to some people and shocking to others. Cornices are curved and twisted and interrupted, while sculpture casts aside all classical dignity and medieval stiffness to assume lively and even riotous poses which suggest that the cardinals and bishops of the seventeenth century had a vivid and sensual appreciation of the human form. These Baroque statues are indeed surprisingly, and sometimes disgracefully, alive. Saints in ecstasy are represented in so attractive a shape as to disturb all religious contemplation; even the Virgin in some cases seems to have been modelled from the naughty girl of the village, and is much too beautiful to be good. Yet in spite of all this, Baroque sculpture is usually as competent as it is realistic, and where it fails, it fails in disregarding the attribute of repose and dignity that all architectural statuary should possess.

Elsewhere I have treated this remarkable movement in Germany and Austria more exhaustively:[1] here it may be said that in those countries it may be studied to advantage. Vienna, Prague, Salzburg, and Würzburg abound in Baroque buildings of all kinds. Among churches, St. Michael's at Munich (1583-87), a Jesuit church already mentioned, is a very early example and is mainly Baroque in spite of the German gable above the façade. The following are typical of the developed style: the cathedral at Salzburg (begun in 1614) by an Italian architect; the Kollegienkirche

[1] M. S. Briggs, *Baroque Architecture* (London, 1913); also in German, *Barock-Architektur* (Berlin, 1914). Chapters X-XII deal with Austria and Germany.

at Salzburg (1696-1707) by FISCHER VON ERLACH; St. Peter's, St. Sebastian's and the Trinity church (1699), all at Salzburg; St. Nicholas' church (1673-1772), and the great block of Jesuit buildings known as the 'Klementinum' at Prague; the huge domed Karlskirche (1716-36) by Fischer von Erlach, and the University church (1627-31) in Vienna; the magnificent Benedictine abbey at Melk; the Theatine church at Munich (1661-75); the Stifthaug church at Würzburg (1670-91); St. Martin's at Bamberg (1686-1720); the Jesuit church at Mannheim (1733-56); the Egidienkirche at Nuremberg (1711-18); the Domkirche at Fulda (1704-12); the Frauenkirche at Dresden (1726-38); and the great monasteries of Wiblingen, Ottobeuren, and Banz; also St. Gall and Kloster Einsiedeln (1704-26) in Switzerland.

Baroque mansions include the Residenz of the Archbishop at Salzburg, with its unclerical stables, statues, and fountains; the Wallenstein, Czernin (1682), and Clam Gallas (1701-12) palaces in Prague; the Schwarzenberg (1706-25), Trautson (1711-14), and Kinsky (1709-13) palaces, and the Schloss Belvedere (1693-1724) in Vienna; several fine houses in Innsbruck and Bamberg; the Residenz in Würzburg (1720-44); the Zwinger palace in Dresden (1711-22); and parts of the Royal Palace in Berlin (1689-1713). The Hof-Bibliothek (1723-35), the Ministry of the Interior (1711-14), and the Reichskanzlei (c. 1728), among state buildings in Vienna, were all designed by Fischer von Erlach, the greatest Baroque architect outside Italy, unless we add Wren to that category.

The Baroque phase lasted to the third or fourth decade of the eighteenth century in Germany and Austria, as the dates given above show. It was then succeeded by a curious style known as the Rococo, derived by the grafting of dainty French details of the 'Louise Quinze' period on to a German Baroque stock. The chief example of the style is the palace of Sans Souci at Potsdam (1745-47), but French influence is even more apparent in such severe and dignified buildings as the Erbdrostenhof (1754-57) and Palace (1767-72) at Münster in Westphalia, and the Episcopal Palace (1728-41) at Strassburg, built by Cardinal de Rohan. Alsace had then become a part of France, and French architectural fashions dominated the western provinces of Germany.

The nineteenth century in England has been described as 'a period of architectural confusion'. The same stricture applies to Germany with equal force. The confusion began, as in England, with a 'Greek Revival', which had its chief seats in Munich and Berlin. The former city is adorned with numerous pseudo-Greek buildings by the architect LEOPOLD VON KLENZE (1784-1864), of which the Propylaea is perhaps the best-known example, and is as frankly Greek as the portico at Euston. The Pinakothek and the Glyptothek, with their significantly pedantic names, and the Walhalla are other buildings in Munich designed by Klenze. In Berlin, KARL FRIEDRICH VON SCHINKEL[1] (1781-1841), whose work was preceded by the Brandenburg Gate (1789) in the Greek style, designed the Royal Theatre, the Königswache, the Old Museum, and the Polytechnic School. These buildings are no doubt scholarly in composition, but utterly lifeless and utterly foreign to the German architectural tradition. Sculpture naturally followed the lead given by the architects, and, until the middle of the century, antique poses and classical costumes held the field.

The second half of the nineteenth century witnessed in Germany, as in England, a 'Battle of the Styles', that is, a conflict between 'revived Renaissance' architecture, and revived Gothic. Her victory in the Franco-Prussian War raised Germany to a position of great power and wealth, and building flourished as a natural result. Such designs as Raschdorff's cathedral (1894-1905) and Wallot's Reichstags-Gebäude (=Parliament Buildings, 1884-94), both in Berlin, are merely florid examples of the cosmopolitan Renaissance style of public building that pervaded all Europe, while the Lessing Theatre in Berlin exhibits a more favourable aspect of modern classic architecture. It is hardly necessary here to mention by name any more of these buildings, either neo-Roman or neo-Gothic, for they may be found in every large German city and they resemble, *mutatis mutandis*, English work of the period.

But early in the present century new tendencies had begun to filter into the Empire, curiously enough from England, where the doctrines of Ruskin, as developed by Morris, and applied on a small scale by comparatively obscure English architects, had led to a new view of architecture as 'right building', i.e. the right use of building materials and forms to meet modern needs. Instead of adopting the inevitable façade decorated with Roman Orders or Gothic tracery, as the chosen style required, German architects now turned their attention to such sordid essentials as plate-glass and steel-work, accepting these things frankly as gifts from heaven and modifying their canons of design to suit them. Beginning with small houses planned on the simple lines popularized in England by C. F. A. Voysey, C. R. Mackintosh, and their school in England, German architects next applied the principles of truthful design to business premises, shops, flats, and factories. Early examples are the stores of Tietz and Wertheim, in the chief cities, and several buildings by PETER BEHRENS, the leader of the new school. These included exhibition-pavilions at Oldenburg (1905) and Dresden (1906), a water-tower at Frankfurt a. M. (1912),

---

[1] Also important as a designer of Biedermeier furniture and of *Figurinen* (costumes for stage and fashions).

the huge A.E.G. factory at Berlin (1912), and the splendid and austere
administrative headquarters of the Mannesmannröhren-Werke at Düsseldorf (1913). The turbine-factory forming part of the A.E.G. works at
Berlin is a remarkable example of functional design. Later buildings by
Behrens included an enormous chemical-factory at Höchst a. M. (1920-24)
and a great by-products factory at Oberhausen (1921-25). Contemporary
with Behrens, and practising an equally original form of design, was
HANS POELZIG, whose chief works were a water-tower at Posen (1910), a
large chemical-factory at Luban (1912), two cinemas at Berlin, and an
imposing block of offices at Breslau (1912). Except the last example, of
which the façade has a large area of glass, and strong horizontal lines,
most of these buildings by Behrens and Poelzig, even when constructed
of steel or reinforced-concrete framing, are cased externally with brick
or stone. The same type of construction is used in FRITZ HÖGER's extraordinary Chilehaus at Hamburg (1923), a lofty office-building on a
cramped triangular site, with brickwork most imaginatively treated.
Other notable specimens of German architecture of this period are various
railway-stations, e.g. at Leipzig, Dortmund, Karlsruhe, and Köln-Deutz,
but especially at Stuttgart (1914-27, by PAUL BONATZ); and in memorials
erected after the First World War. Bonatz also built the Stadthalle at
Hanover (1910-14). Private houses, as already remarked, were strongly
influenced by English tradition at this period; and in their new housing
estate at Dahlhauser Heide (1907) the proprietors of Krupp's great works
followed the example of the new English garden-cities, substituting
picturesque grouping and semi-detached cottages for their previous
arrangement of tenement-blocks in straight rows.

Just before the first World War, a new tendency was apparent in the
trend of German architecture, mainly attributed to the teaching and
actual buildings of WALTER GROPIUS (b. 1883). He first came into prominence with his pavilion at the Cologne Exhibition in 1914, where he
used spiral staircases enclosed by glass, and a flat roof. In 1919 he was
appointed head of the Weimar School of Arts and Crafts and of the
Academy of Fine Art, which he soon amalgamated into a High School of
Design, 'Das Staatliche Bauhaus Weimar'. In 1925 this institution was
transferred to Dessau, and Gropius was given his chance in designing
entirely new premises, including residential accommodation for students.
These buildings represented an immense advance on anything hitherto
produced in Germany. Stark and uncompromising, they embodied all
the latest 'functional' ideas of reinforced-concrete construction, with a
lavish use of glass and a complete absence of architectural 'trimmings'.
Their influence, not only in Germany but all over Europe and in America,

was profound. The Bauhaus was not a school of architecture in the accepted sense, but rather a centre where individual designers of all kinds could obtain inspiration in design. Gropius soon created a large private practice, and resigned his post in 1928. The Bauhaus was closed in 1933 at the beginning of the Nazi régime, for reasons to be explained shortly.

Abreast of Gropius, another famous architect, ERICH MENDELSOHN (b. 1887), caused a sensation with his startling imaginative sketches for new buildings, published between 1914 and 1920. These were mostly for industrial buildings and involved a revolutionary use of steel and concrete. From 1912 to 1914 he had been employed in designing for the stage, a fact which explains some of his dramatic effects, but in 1920 he translated his ideas into facts by his amazing Einstein Tower at Potsdam. From that date onwards, till the Nazis assumed power in 1933, he continued to produce a succession of remarkable buildings including a hat-factory at Luckenwalde near Berlin (1923), the Schocken stores at Nuremberg (1925) and Stuttgart (1928), and the Universum Cinema at Berlin (1927). Another architect who acquired a large practice in Berlin was BRUNO TAUT (b. 1880), whose work consisted chiefly of housing-schemes. The design of Gropius, Mendelsohn and Bruno Taut differs from that of the architects previously mentioned in being 'international' or 'cosmopolitan' in character rather than distinctively German: most of it could be matched in France, Switzerland or Austria at the same period. It was essentially logical and functional in character, with nothing picturesque or romantic about it. Moreover, it was largely due to men who were either Jewish by birth or of liberal sympathies displeasing to Hitler, who became all-powerful in 1933. It is commonly stated that Hitler was merely an unsuccessful house-painter before he turned to politics, but that is only half the truth. His boyish ambition was to become an architect, and he would have realized that ambition had he not failed to pass the entrance-examination to the School of Architecture at Vienna owing to shortcomings in his general education, as a result of laziness at school and perhaps of parental indulgence. Frustrated at this early stage, he worked as a house-painter under sordid conditions, supplementing his scanty wages by selling drawings. Thwarted thus in youth, and possibly embittered also by his army service, he ultimately found a limitless outlet for his tastes when he became Dictator. From that moment he imposed those tastes relentlessly upon German architecture and sculpture, using his powers partly as a hobby and partly as a mission.

The result took two very different and contradictory forms. He was enamoured of classical architecture on the grand scale, perhaps influenced by the work of Schinkel in Berlin and of von Klenze in Munich, where so much of his life had been spent. At all events, he decided to adopt a modified form of Greek architecture for the vast programme of public buildings which he put in hand immediately. He soon got rid of Gropius, Mendelsohn and other apostles of the international style with their cosmopolitan modernism. They fled to England, to France, to Switzerland, to Palestine, and especially to the United States, where they found fame as well as fortune awaiting them. The majesty of the Third Reich was to be expressed in dignified stone buildings of classical form, and the type of some of those buildings seemed particularly appropriate for such treatment. The huge Sports Centre at Berlin, where the Olympic Games were held in 1937, was frankly inspired by the ruins of Olympia in Greece, and these were illustrated in German architectural magazines abreast of the new plans. ALBERT SPEER, a protégé of the Führer, became chief architect of the Reich. (In 1946, he figured prominently at the Nuremberg trials, for, during the Second World War, Hitler transferred him from architectural duties to the control of German war production.) The event which made his career was his success in the competition for the vast Congress Hall at Nuremberg, to hold 20,000 persons. In Nuremberg, too, he designed the magnificent stadium and the grand stands on the Zeppelin Field; in Berlin, the new Chancellery (Reichskanzlei) and the Sports Centre. Speer's work is commonly said to be uninspired, formal and correct; but it is by no means despicable, and certainly he had ideas of dignity and greatness that accorded well with his dictatorial patron's wishes. Hitler stated in 1938 that these tremendous schemes would compare with the Colosseum and the Parthenon, and that they would last a thousand years.

Under Speer's direction, the following architects worked on the buildings named: P. Ludwig Troost, War Memorial, Führerbau, and House of German Art, all at Munich; Ludwig and Franz Roff, Congress Hall at Nuremberg; Wilhelm Kreis, Military Headquarters in Berlin, Provincial Offices at Dresden; Hugo Röttcher and Theodor Dierksmeir, Tourist building in Berlin; Ernst Sagebiel, Aerodrome Buildings, Tempelhof, in Berlin; Werner March, Olympic Stadium, Berlin; H. H. Klaje, Military Academy, Berlin; Paul Baumgartner, Provincial Theatre at Saarbrücken. Abreast of all these imposing neo-classical buildings to impress the German *Herrenvolk* with a sense of their great destiny, Hitler deliberately encouraged the adoption of an entirely different style, to inculcate the idea of extreme Nordic nationalism, buildings which displayed old-German characteristics in an exaggerated degree. For youth-hostels and training-schools for leaders recourse was had to the picturesque tradition of the Black Forest and the Harz. Heavy carpentry, overhanging eaves, whitewashed walls, cheerful spots of coloured ornament, occasional carving, rustic furniture – everything was as un-classic as it could be. For housing schemes and even for most urban buildings, flat roofs and huge areas of glass gave place to the pitched roofs, gables and other pleasantries scorned by the Bauhaus group and the internationally-minded intelligentsia. It was, in fact, an elaborate Teutonic revival.

Then came the Second World War, and, towards its end, the destruction of many of the buildings, old and new, mentioned in this chapter. The energies of the nation have since been largely occupied in repairing war damage and replanning bombed cities. So far, it is not possible to say in which direction architectural fashion is moving: towards the cosmopolitan or 'advanced 'style so artificially and rudely interrupted in 1933, towards one of the two different styles favoured by Hitler, or towards a compromise. The last seems the most likely; for, though tall blocks of flat-topped tenements and offices appear in many of the projects for reconstructing the larger towns, even in those towns there is a tendency to restore the 'Altstadt' to something approaching its original form, and for small buildings the pitched roof is favoured, while picturesque and original details are freely used.

The story of German sculpture in the first half of the twentieth century closely resembles that of architecture, and for similar reasons. Up to 1933, though some capable sculpture had been produced, the country was not in the forefront. Some of the best artists, being of 'non-Aryan' birth or otherwise unacceptable to the new régime, fled abroad. A few of the others, including the leading figure, Georg Kolbe, managed to reconcile themselves to the new conditions. Generally speaking, Hitler encouraged a return to Greek tradition, featuring athletic and Nordic nude types in classical poses. Everywhere in his great new stadia and outside his new public buildings, muscular youths and maidens in stone or bronze were exhibited to stimulate a desire for physical fitness in German youth. Thus at the Sports Centre at Berlin were placed men with horses in stone by T. Wackerle; stone athletes by Arno Breker and Adolf Wamper; stone angels by Willy Meller; bronze figures of female athletes by Arno Breker, of a bull by Adolf Strübe, of eagles by Hilde Schlitter, of a resting athlete and a warrior by Georg Kolbe; and terra-cotta reliefs of men and horses by M. Laeuger and Arno Lehmann. Arno Breker also executed fountains and other statuary elsewhere in Berlin. Additional sculpture worth mention includes Kolbe's 'The Couple' at Hanover, representing a slim Nordic youth and girl; Fritz Klimsch's lovely seated figure of a girl at the Olympic Stadium; Ernst Seger's 'Leaping Figure' at the bathing-beach on the Wannsee near Berlin; Eberhard Encke's extremely classical

Discus Thrower'; Ernst Barlach's (p. 354) fine wooden statue of 'A Fugitive'; Hermann Pagel's powerful group of 'The Exiles'; and Gerhard Marck's charming bronze figure of 'Seraphita'.

BIBLIOGRAPHY TO CHAPTER XIV

ROMAN:

Krüger, E. *Die Trierer Römerbauten.* Trier, 1909

Schmidt, C. W. *Baudenkmäler der römischen Periode in Trier.* Trier, 1845

MEDIEVAL AND GENERAL:

Bergner, H. *Kirchliche Kunstaltertümer in Deutschland.* Leipzig, 1905

Boisserée, S. *Denkmäler der Baukunst am Nieder-Rhein.* Munich, 1844

Bumpus, T. F. *Cathedrals of the Rhine and North Germany.* London, 1906

Clasen, K. H. *Die gotische Baukunst.* Potsdam, 1930

Dehio, G. *Handbuch der deutschen Kunstdenkmäler.* 5 vols. Berlin, 1905-12

Dehio, G., and Bezold, G. von. *Die kirchliche Baukunst des Abendlandes.* Stuttgart, 1890

Dohme, R. *Geschichte der deutschen Baukunst.* Berlin, 1887

Foerster, E. J. *Denkmäler deutscher Baukunst, Bildnerei und Malerei.* Leipzig, 1855

Göbel, H. *Das süddeutsche Bürgerhaus.* Dresden, 1908

Hartel, A. *Architektonische Details und Ornamente der kirchlichen Baukunst.* 2 vols. Berlin, 1891

Haupt, A. von. *Die Baukunst der Germanen von der Völkerwanderung bis zu Karl dem Grossen.* Leipzig, 1909

Lachner, C. *Geschichte der Holzbaukunst in Deutschland.* Leipzig, 1887

List, C. *Bildhauer-Arbeiten in Österreich-Ungarn.* Vienna, 1901

Lübke, W. *Ecclesiastical Art in Germany.* Edinburgh, 1873

Lübke, W. *Geschichte der deutschen Kunst.* Stuttgart, 1890

Möller, G. *Denkmäler der deutschen Baukunst.* Leipzig, 1852

Otte, H. *Geschichte der romanischen Baukunst in Deutschland.* Leipzig, 1874

Pinder, W. *Deutsche Dome des Mittelalters.* Düsseldorf, 1910

Sauerlandt, M. *Deutsche Plastik des Mittelalters.* Düsseldorf, n.d.

Schaefer, C., and Stiehl, O. *Die Kirchbauten des Mittelalters in Deutschland.* 1901

Stiehl, O. *Das deutsche Rathaus im Mittelalter.* Leipzig, 1905

Stiehl, O. *Backsteinbauten in Norddeutschland und Dänemark.* Stuttgart, 1923

Whewell, W. *Architectural Notes on German Churches.* Cambridge, 1842

RENAISSANCE AND BAROQUE:

Bezold, G. von. *Die Baukunst der Renaissance in Deutschland.* Leipzig, 1908

Braun, J. *Die Kirchenbauten der deutschen Jesuiten.* 2 vols. Freiburg i. B., 1908-11

Dehio, G. *Die Kunst des 17. und 18. Jahrhundert.* Leipzig, 1900

Fritsch, K. E. O. *Denkmäler deutscher Renaissance.* Berlin, 1912

Gurlitt, C. *Geschichte des Barockstils; Deutschland, etc.*, vol. iii. Stuttgart, 1887-89

Gurlitt, C. *Das Barock- und Rokoko-Ornament Deutschlands.* Berlin, 1889

Hager, W. *Die Bauten des deutschen Barocks.* Leipzig, 1940

Haupt, A. von. *Baukunst der Renaissance in Frankreich und Deutschland.* Berlin, 1923

Haupt, A. von. *Backsteinbauten der Renaissance in Norddeutschland.* Frankfurt a. M., 1899

Hegemann, H. W. *Deutsches Rokoko.* Königstein, 1942

Herz, R. *Berliner Barock.* Berlin, 1928

Hoffmann, J. *Baukunst und dekorative Skulptur der Renaissance in Deutschland.* Stuttgart, 1909

Horst, C. *Die Architektur der deutschen Renaissance.* Berlin, 1928

Kick und Pfeiffer. *Barock, Rokoko und Louis XVI in Schwaben und der Schweiz.* Stuttgart, 1897

Lambert und Stahl. *Residenzen und Gärten des 18. Jahrhunderts.* Leipzig, 1909

Lübke, W., and Haupt, A. von. *Geschichte der Renaissance in Deutschland.* 2 vols. Stuttgart, 1927

Lübke-Semrau. *Die Kunst der Barockzeit und des Rokoko.* Stuttgart, 1905

Muther, R. *Die Renaissance im Norden und die Barockzeit.* Berlin, 1912

Niemann, G. *Palast-Bauten des Barockstils in Wien.* 2 vols. Vienna, 1881

Ohmann, F. *Architektur und Kunstgewerbe der Barockzeit, des Rokoko und Empires.* Vienna, 1908

Ortwein, A., and others. *Deutsche Renaissance in Österreich.* Leipzig, 1884-87

Pevsner, N. *Leipziger Barock.* Dresden, 1928

Pinder, W. *Deutscher Barock.* Düsseldorf, 1912

Pinder, W. *Die deutsche Plastik.* Potsdam, 1929

Popp, H. *Die Architektur der Barock- und Rokokozeit in Deutschland und der Schweiz.* Stuttgart, 1913

Schmerber, H. *Das deutsche Schloss- und Bürgerhaus im 17. und 18. Jahrhundert.* Strassburg, 1902

Schmoll and Stähelin. *Barockbauten in Deutschland.* Leipzig, 1874

Springer, A. *Der Rokokostil.* Bonn, 1886

Stange, A. *Die deutsche Baukunst der Renaissance.* Munich, 1926

Tietze-Conrat, E. *Österreichische Barockplastik.* Vienna, 1920

Wackernagel, M. *Baukunst des 17. und 18. Jahrhundert in den germanischen Ländern.* Berlin, 1915

MODERN:

Anon. *Erich Mendelsohn: Skizzen, Entwürfe, Bauten.* Berlin, 1930

Anon. *Erich Mendelsohn: Structures and Sketches.* London, n.d.

Aumonier, W. *Modern Architectural Sculpture.* London, 1930

Cremers, P. J. *Peter Behrens.* Essen, 1928

Giedion, S. *Gropius.* Paris, 1931; *Walter Gropius.* London, 1954

Gropius, W. *The New Architecture and the Bauhaus.* London, 1935

Hajos, E. M., and Zahn, L. *Berlin Architektur der Nachkriegszeit.* Berlin, 1928

Hegemann, W. *Werner March.* Berlin, 1930

Heilmeyer, A. *Die moderne Plastik in Deutschland.* Bielefeld, 1903

Hoeber, F. *Peter Behrens.* Munich, 1913

Platz, G. A. *Die Baukunst der neuesten Zeit.* Berlin, 1927

Pommern, H. V. *K. F. von Schinkel: Lebenswerk.* Berlin, 1942

Rave, P. O. *K. F. von Schinkel. Lebenswerk.* Berlin, 1948

Rittich, W. *Architektur und Bauplastik der Gegenwart.* Berlin, 1938

Speer, A. *Neue deutscher Baukunst.* Berlin, 1943

Tamms, F. *Paul Bonatz.* Stuttgart, 1937

Taut, Bruno. *Modern Architecture.* London, 1929

Whittick, A. *Erich Mendelsohn.* London, 1940

Whittick, A. *European Architecture in the 20th Century* (Vols. I-II). London, 1950

Yerbury, F. R. *Modern European Buildings.* London, 1928

INDEX